LSAT® LOGIC GAMES PREP 2023

Published by Kaplan North America, LLC dba Kaplan Publishing
1515 West Cypress Creek Road
Fort Lauderdale, Florida 33309

ISBN: 978-1-5062-8723-2
10 9 8 7 6 5 4 3 2 1

Kaplan Publishing print books are available at special quantity discounts to use for sales promotions, employee premiums, or educational purposes. For more information or to purchase books, please call the Simon & Schuster special sales department at 866-506-1949.

TABLE OF CONTENTS

PART TWO: GAME TYPES UNLOCKED

Your Kaplan Resources—Getting Started

HOW TO USE THIS BOOK

Three Keys: Practice, Personalization, and Expertise

Some LSAT prep materials are written to demonstrate the author's mastery of the test, but *Logic Games Prep* is designed to build **your** mastery and raise **your** score. Empirical evidence makes it clear that the majority of test takers consider the Logic Games section to be the most difficult section on the test. However, it is equally clear that, on average, Kaplan students make their biggest improvements in this section. The three keys to their success are practice, personalization, and expertise, and those keys distinguish *Logic Games Prep* from any other title.

Practice. No matter who you are—no matter your starting point or ultimate goal—practice is the foundation for LSAT mastery. In *Logic Games Prep*, you'll find **over 30 real logic games** from officially released LSAT PrepTests (more than in any other Logic Games–specific title available). Each is accompanied by Kaplan's exclusive **"worked example" explanations** that break down each game's setup and all of its questions, step by step. In addition, this book contains **hundreds of exercises** that target all of the skills and strategies you'll learn. In the book's online resources, there are video lessons (the **LSAT Channel Spotlight** features) that highlight special topics and exclusive strategies from some of Kaplan's most highly rated LSAT instructors. Also online, you'll find the LSAT Logic Games Training Camp which contains sets of skill-building exercises to help you get sharp and stay sharp with everything you'll learn. In short, everything you need for Logic Games mastery is right here.

Personalization. LSAT logic games are consistent, but LSAT test takers vary. Your strengths, weaknesses, learning style, study time, and motivations are not exactly like anyone else's. *Logic Games Prep* was created with that in mind. Every lesson in this book ends with an **assessment** that will help you **evaluate your own personal performance**, and each assessment is accompanied by **recommendations tailored to your results**. When you knock a particular skill or game type out of the park, the recommendations give you next steps and suggestions for advanced practice. When you run into an area that requires more work, the recommendations guide you to further practice with the fundamentals.

Expertise. In these pages, you'll encounter the knowledge and experience of more than a dozen Kaplan LSAT experts—not only **teachers**, but also **instructional designers** and even **psychometricians**, who analyze the test's design, scoring, and validity. Collectively, this team of top scorers has trained tens of thousands of LSAT test takers, helping them to achieve their goal scores and gain acceptance to the nation's top law schools. They know the LSAT. They know LSAT test takers. Most importantly, **they are now your team**.

The skills tested on the LSAT—including those tested in the Logic Games section—are strongly correlated to your performance in law school. Indeed, they are skills you will use throughout your legal career. This book gives you everything you need to master the Logic Games section, and thus, to get a head start on the reasoning skills you'll use as an attorney. **Welcome to the start of your legal education**.

Take a few minutes to learn how *Logic Games Prep* is designed, how you can get the most out of each chapter, and how you can design a study schedule that fits your life as you learn to unlock LSAT logic games.

This Book's Organization

For you to master LSAT logic games, you'll need to learn the skills involved, practice them, and assess your performance on each one. This book is designed to allow you to take all three of those steps with each of the skills that form the foundation for success on logic games. To make the process as efficient and effective as possible, the book is divided into four sections.

Getting Started

This is where you are right now. Here, you'll learn how to use the book (and its associated online features) to maximize your performance. You'll see how the lessons in this book have been designed by Kaplan's Learning Science and Instructional Design teams to maximize efficacy and retention for every learner. This includes information about how to assess your own performance and personalized recommendations for further practice on each skill. Also included here are three model study schedules, tailored to different lengths of preparation.

Next, you'll find information about how to log into your online Study Plan, what's available there, and how and when to use it. *Logic Games Prep* is more than just a book. The LSAT Channel Spotlight features also give you the opportunity to learn from some of our finest instructors, and the explanations and analyses available for PrepTests 71 and 73 (two official LSAT tests available free in LawHub with an LSAC LSAT Prep subscription) demonstrate the power of self-assessment on your practice.

The final portion of the Getting Started material introduces you to the LSAT, and then specifically to the Logic Games section. You'll learn about the test's structure and format, the core skills that it tests, how it's scored, and how law schools use those scores to evaluate applicants. After this, there is a short introduction to the Logic Games section, which includes an LSAT Channel Spotlight lesson on the secrets that Kaplan's expert instructors tell their students who are just beginning their Logic Games preparation. You'll learn more about The LSAT Channel Spotlight lessons in the section of this introduction focused on your online resources.

Part I: Logic Games Method and Strategy

The foundation of success on logic games is the five-step Kaplan Logic Games Method. By mastering the Logic Games Method, you'll learn to handle logic games effectively within the short amount of time provided on the LSAT (four logic games in 35 minutes).

KAPLAN LOGIC GAMES METHOD

- **Step 1: Overview**—Ask four key questions to assess the game's entities and action(s).
- **Step 2: Sketch**—Create a simple framework in which to record the game's rules and deductions.
- **Step 3: Rules**—Analyze and draw the game's explicit rules.
- **Step 4: Deductions**—Combine the game's rules and restrictions to reveal what must, can, and cannot be true within the game.
- **Step 5: Questions**—Approach each question strategically to maximize the number of correct answers in the shortest amount of time.

This part of the book has four chapters. Chapter 1 introduces the Logic Games Method and demonstrates how LSAT experts use it to handle full logic games. Chapter 2 goes deeper into Steps 1 and 2, and gives you the opportunity to practice and assess your performance on these Steps. Chapter 3 breaks down Steps 3 and 4, again with ample practice and self-evaluation. Chapter 4 introduces the question types found in the Logic Games section, provides strategies for answering each type, and then allows you to practice and assess with full, officially released LSAT logic games.

There are two more LSAT Channel Spotlight lessons in this part of the book. One, at the end of Chapter 3, focuses on Limited Options, a powerful type of deduction LSAT experts use to simplify and speed up their performance on certain games. The other, at the end of Chapter 4, examines how LSAT experts use previous work to unlock certain LSAT questions quickly and accurately.

Part II: Game Types

In the second part of the book, you'll learn to apply the Logic Games Method to specific game types. This part of the book has seven chapters:

- Chapter 5: Basic Strict Sequencing Games
- Chapter 6: Complex Strict Sequencing Games
- Chapter 7: Loose Sequencing Games
- Chapter 8: Formal Logic and Selection Games
- Chapter 9: Matching and Distribution Games
- Chapter 10: Hybrid Games
- Chapter 11: Rare Games

In each of Chapters 5–11, you'll learn how to identify the game type and how the testmaker introduces variations within the tasks. Then, you'll have the opportunity to practice applying each step of the Logic Games Method to the game type in question. When you're ready, you'll assess your mastery of the game type with full officially released LSAT games. Each chapter ends with recommendations for additional practice on games at three skill levels: Foundations, Mid-Level, and Advanced. Chapter 6 ends with an LSAT Channel Spotlight feature on Circular Sequencing, a rare but challenging variation on this common game type. Chapter 10 ends with an LSAT Channel Spotlight feature on the Dinosaur game, a Hybrid game that some consider the hardest game ever to appear on an officially released LSAT test.

Chapter 8—the chapter covering Selection games—also includes a section with lessons covering everything you need to know to master Formal Logic as it is tested in the LSAT Logic Games section. Formal Logic is tested more comprehensively in the LSAT's Logical Reasoning section, so this section may improve your performance on the LSAT beyond the Logic Games section, as well. The Formal Logic section features an LSAT Channel Spotlight feature on two conditional statements that hold the key to unlocking many Selection games. Even if you're a Formal Logic whiz, this Spotlight will be worth your time.

Chapter 11—on the two rarest game types: Process and Mapping—is shorter than the other chapters in this part of the book. Although you are unlikely to encounter one of these games, understanding their defining features and having practice with officially released examples of each type will give you confidence that there is nothing you could see on test day that you aren't familiar with. The LSAT Channel Spotlight in this chapter covers a Process game from December 2016, the first game of these rare types to show up on a released LSAT in more than a decade.

Appendices

At the end of the book, you'll find helpful information collected into a handful of short appendices:

- Appendix I: Logic Games—Timing and Section Management—A short essay filled with tips and strategies LSAT experts use to finish the section faster and to maximize their scores.
- Appendix II: The Countdown to Test Day—Advice about how best to study and practice during the week (and on the day) before your official exam.
- Appendix III: Logic Games Index—A list of every logic game on every officially released LSAC PrepTest, including section, question numbers, and game type.
- Appendix IV: Logic Games Strategies—A quick reference digest covering the Logic Games Method, game types, model sketches, and rules.
- Appendix V: Formal Logic Statements and Translations—A quick reference digest covering conditional statements, contrapositives, and cause-effect relationships.

You'll want to read Appendices I and II after you've done the bulk of your work in this book. Appendix I is especially helpful if you plan to take full-length LSAT tests or complete Logic Games sections as practice in your run-up to test day.

The remaining Appendices are there for your reference. Familiarizing yourself with Appendix IV, in particular, may be the best way for you to put your finger on a particular definition or sketch pattern when you need it.

This Book's Instructional Design

"Instructional Design" is a fancy way of talking about how this book helps you learn, practice, and retain skills. In each chapter of this book, you will find one or more lessons, each focused on a specific Learning Objective, or on two or three related objectives. To get the most out of this book, it is helpful for you to become familiar with each piece of a lesson.

Learning Objective

Each Learning Objective is a measurable performance goal that contributes to your mastery of the LSAT Logic Games section. Here's one from Chapter 3:

LEARNING OBJECTIVES

In this section of Chapter 3, you'll learn to

- Analyze and draw logic games rules effectively.

Pay attention to the Learning Objective that forms the basis for the lesson you're in. Logic games are complex, and it is easy to become distracted by an interesting feature of a sample game or question on which you are working. This can lead you off on tangents that take your focus away from the goal of the lesson. Each lesson culminates with a quiz or a series of exercises that allow you to evaluate your performance on the lesson's learning objective. Keep your focus on the "need to know," and don't get caught up in the "nice to know."

Prepare

Accompanying the Learning Objective is the Prepare portion of the lesson. Here, you'll learn the terms, definitions, and concepts you need to know for the lesson. These are often illustrated with relevant examples. Study the Prepare section carefully so that you will be ready to put the strategies and tactics outlined there into practice.

Practice

This portion of the lesson gives you the opportunity to apply what you've learned in context. Practice exercises will range from the analysis and drawing of individual rules all the way up to practice on full games. In the practice sections, work at your own pace, and make your best effort to apply the lesson's skills to the examples at hand. When you have completed a Practice exercise, compare your work to the analysis of Kaplan LSAT experts, always found at the end of the Practice section. Don't merely check to see that you got the correct answer. Read the experts' analyses thoroughly to see their thought processes and to make sure your analysis was as effective and efficient as possible.

Throughout this book—especially in the Practice and Perform portions of lessons—you'll see the analyses of Kaplan LSAT experts depicted in a format called a "worked example," and it provides you with a chance to think along with a Logic Games superstar as he or she approaches all or part of a logic game. Expert analysis is always laid out with the expert's thinking adjacent to the official test question. Where the LSAT is demonstrating more than one step of the Logic Games Method, you'll see the steps in bold to help you train yourself to take the most effective route through the game setup or question.

Here are a few things to be aware of whenever you study expert analyses:

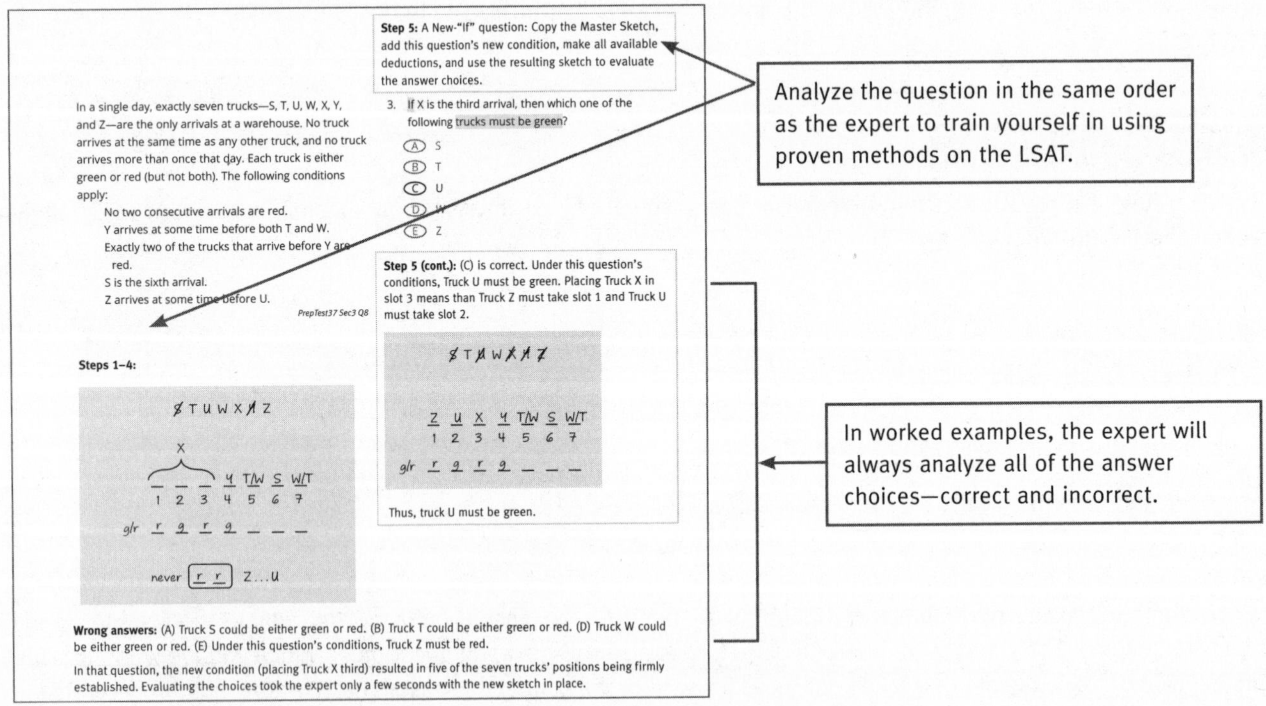

Throughout the book, you'll have practice exercises in which you'll have the chance to analyze a game's setup, rules, or question stems. Use the spaces provided to record your own analysis. In the answers and explanations, we'll always provide expert analysis so that you can compare your thinking to that of an LSAT expert.

Practice 1

Directions: Analyze and draw each of the following Strict Sequencing game rules.

Rule	My Analysis
1. There are exactly three appointments between D's appointment and C's appointment.	
2. There is, at most, one spot between H's spot and J's spot.	
3. If L is the second car, then M is the first car.	
4. J and K both have lower-numbered positions than H, or H has a lower-numbered position than both J and K.	
5. D is in position 4.	
6. C is immediately after D but before E.	
7. S is after both T and V.	
8. P finishes later than Q, but earlier than R.	

The format of our expert analyses is the result of work by leading academics in learning science. Merely answering LSAT questions and checking to see whether you got the right answer is fine, but studies indicate that studying expert thinking alongside actual test material produces better results and is a more effective (and faster) way to master LSAT skills. As you complete the questions, don't just check to see if you got them right or wrong. Use each question as an opportunity to better understand the patterns of the test, as well as your own strengths and weaknesses.

When you complete full games (as in the Full Game Practice and Perform sections for Chapters 4-11), the worked examples containing the expert analyses will be found in your online resources. These are in PDF files that you can review on your computer, or download and print out, as you prefer.

In other cases—particularly when you are practicing rules and deductions—the exercises are laid out to provide more space for you to record your answers.

Practice 2

Directions: Take a couple of minutes to review the game setup, summarize your Overview analysis, and recreate the initial sketch. Then, one at a time, analyze the rules, answer the questions about each one, and draw the rule either inside or underneath the sketch framework.

A novelty-item sales representative is tasked with arranging on a shelf six new products—an art kit, a bandanna, a charm bracelet, a disco ball, a pair of earrings, and a fleece pullover—bearing the logo of a popular band. Strict company guidelines dictate that in arranging the items from left to right, one at a time, the sales representative must conform to the following restrictions:

The art kit must be in one of the two middle spaces.
The charm bracelet must be in a space next to one of the end spaces.
The fleece pullover must be two spaces to the left of the disco ball.
The art kit must never be placed immediately to the left of the fleece pullover.
The earrings must be somewhere to the left of the bandanna.

1. [Step 1] Summarize your Overview analysis:

2. [Step 2] Create an initial Sketch:

3. [Step 3] Analyze and draw the Rules:
    - For each rule, answer the following questions and draw the rule in the appropriate box.
        - What does the rule restrict, and what does it leave open?
        - What are the rule's negative implications, if any?
        - Can the rule be depicted inside the sketch framework?

Rule 1:	Rule 4:
Rule 2:	Rule 5:
Rule 3:	

For these exercises, you'll find the expert analysis in italics.

Practice 2

A novelty-item sales representative is tasked with arranging on a shelf six new products—an art kit, a bandanna, a charm bracelet, a disco ball, a pair of earrings, and a fleece pullover—bearing the logo of a popular band. Strict company guidelines dictate that in arranging the items from left to right, one at a time, the sales representative must conform to the following restrictions:

The art kit must be in one of the two middle spaces.
The charm bracelet must be in a space next to one of the end spaces.
The fleece pullover must be two spaces to the left of the disco ball.
The art kit must never be placed immediately to the left of the fleece pullover.
The earrings must be somewhere to the left of the bandanna.

1. [Step 1] Summarize your Overview analysis: *A Strict Sequencing game in which a sales rep is placing six items in order from left to right, one per position, along a shelf.*

2. [Step 2] Create an initial Sketch:

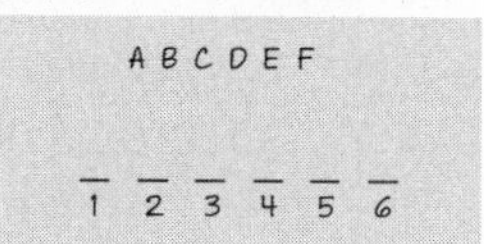

3. [Step 3] Analyze and draw the Rules:
   - Rule 1:
     - Can the rule be depicted inside the sketch framework? *Yes.*
     - Draw the rule:

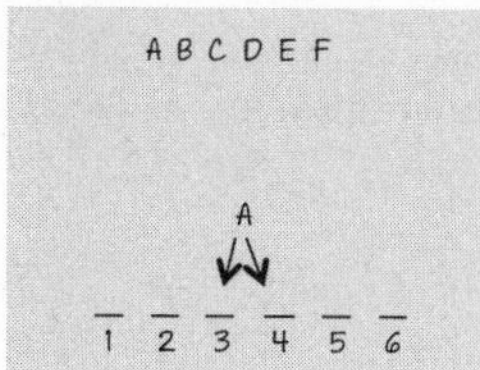

   - Rule 2:
     - What does the rule restrict, and what does it leave open? *This rule restricts C to one of two positions (slot 2 or slot 5).*
     - What are the rule's negative implications, if any? *Simply that C will not be in slots 1, 3, 4, or 6.*
     - Can the rule be depicted inside the sketch framework? *Yes.*
     - Draw the rule:

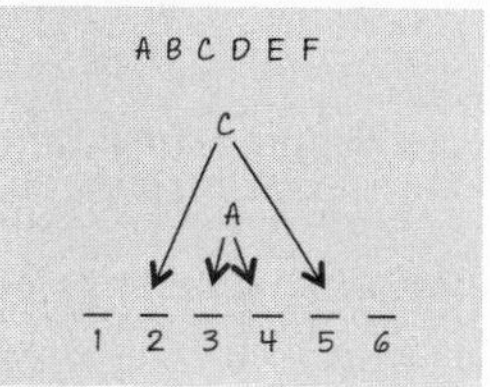

Perform

In the Perform portion of each lesson, you will put your new skills to the test. Perform exercises look and feel just like those you do in the Practice portion of each lesson, but they come with timing guidelines. Your goal here is not perfection, but valid self-assessment. Do your best under the timing guidelines, and then, when you're done, compare your work to that of a Kaplan LSAT expert. Thorough review is a great learning opportunity, not just to find out what you got right and wrong, but to see how top scorers applied the Logic Games Method and its associated strategies and tactics to maximum effect.

For Chapters 4-11, the answers and explanations for complete game Perform quizzes are found in your online resources. Review them on your computer, or download and print them, as you prefer, but make sure to review them thoroughly.

Assess

Most Perform exercises are followed by specific criteria that you can use to evaluate your performance. For Perform exercises with full LSAT logic games, the assessment criteria will be the number of logic games questions you answered correctly. For Perform exercises that lack a numerical value (such as number correct), the assessment will outline how you should compare your performance to that of an LSAT expert to get a clear perspective on your skill level. Assessments are accompanied by recommended next steps for each level of mastery.

For the assessments accompanying the game-type chapters in Part II, the recommended additional practice refers to games from officially released LSAT tests. Here's the recommended additional practice from Chapter 5:

Recommended Additional Practice: Basic Strict Sequencing

All of the following games will provide good practice on basic Strict Sequencing games. They are grouped by difficulty as determined from empirical student practice results. All PrepTests included are available on LawHub with an LSAC LSAT Prep Plus subscription.

Foundations

PrepTest 70, Section 3, Game 1: Benefit Concert

PrepTest 67, Section 3, Game 2: Literary Theory Lectures

PrepTest 63, Section 2, Game 2: Skydiving Team

PrepTest 62, Section 3, Game 4: Testifying Witnesses

PrepTest 57, Section 1, Game 1: Student Activities

Mid-Level

PrepTest 66, Section 3, Game 2: Shopping Center Businesses

PrepTest 64, Section 2, Game 1: Employee Parking

PrepTest 62, Section 3, Game 1: Motel Service Appointments

PrepTest 56, Section 1, Game 1: Saxophone Auditions

PrepTest 54, Section 3, Game 3: Cake Layers

Advanced

PrepTest 71, Section 2, Game 4: Paintings in a Museum

PrepTest 69, Section 2, Game 1: Manuscript Ages

PrepTest 63, Section 2, Game 3: Vehicle Service

PrepTest 59, Section 1, Game 2: Museum Photographs

PrepTest 59, Section 1, Game 4: Organization's Annual Meetings

Complete explanations and analysis for all of the more-than-70 official LSAT tests on LawHub that come with an LSAC LSAT Prep Plus subscription are available in Kaplan's LSAT Link and Link+ tools. Visit **www.kaptest.com/lsat/courses/lsat-self-study** to learn more or to purchase LSAT Link or Link+.

Recommended additional practice is drawn from officially released LSAT PrepTests, all of which are contained in LSAC's LawHub, the digital practice tool available through LSAC's LSAT Prep Plus platform. For the record, released PrepTests in paper-and-pencil format remain available for purchase from LSAC (both individually and in bundles of 10), but the content is identical to those same PrepTests on LawHub.

To create a LawHub account, visit **www.lsac.org/lawhub**. LSAC offers a free version, called LSAT Prep, that has a small handful of released tests, including PrepTests 71 and 73. Explanations for both of these tests are included in your online resources for this book. LSAC also offers a paid subscription, called LSAT Prep Plus, with more than 70 released tests. These include all the tests corresponding to the additional recommended questions in this book. Learn more details in the part of this Getting Started section called How to Use Your Online Resources.

For complete explanations and analysis of every test and question available on LawHub through LSAC's LSAT Prep Plus subscription, you'll want to link your LSAC account to Kaplan's LSAT Link or Link+ (a premium version with hundreds of curated Mastery Practice assignments). You'll see more details about LSAT Link and Link+ in a few pages, under the heading Next-Level Self-Prep. Visit **www.kaptest.com/lsat/courses/lsat-self-study** to learn more and to purchase LSAT Link and Link+.

Reflect

At the very end of each lesson, you'll see a series of short thought exercises that will keep what you've learned fresh in your mind. Some students find it helpful to write out their answers to make their reflection more concrete. In any case, review the Reflect questions and keep them in mind until you come back to the book for your next lesson.

HOW TO USE YOUR ONLINE RESOURCES

Logic Games Prep comes with a wealth of online resources. They provide additional instruction, practice, and feedback that will aid your logic games preparation and improve your LSAT score. In this section, you'll learn how to access these resources, what they include, and how to use them.

Log In to Your Online Study Plan

The online Study Plan gives you access to even more Logic Games content and instruction, including The LSAT Channel Spotlight videos.

Register for your Online Center using these simple steps:

1. Go to https://kaptest.com/moreonline and find the appropriate book listed. Click the "Register" button next to it.
2. Enter the password as directed and click on "Next."
3. The Online Center will appear in your shopping cart free of charge. Click "Proceed to checkout" and complete your registration.
4. Once registered, click on the "personalized Student Homepage" link to access your online materials.

Please have your book with you because you will need information from the book to access your account.

Access to the Online Center is limited to the original owner of this book and is nontransferable. Kaplan is not responsible for providing access to the Online Center for customers who purchase or borrow used copies of this book. Access to the Online Center expires one year after you register.

Take a minute to log in now. Get familiar with the contents and organization of the online Study Plan. That way, you'll be ready to use the resources as they come up in your work with this book.

What's In the Online Study Plan

Here's what you have in your online resources:

- **Video: Getting Started**—Hear from Kaplan's lead instructional designer about how to make the most of your prep with *Logic Games Prep*.
- **LSAT Channel episode: Screen Time: Prepping for the Digital LSAT**—Get acquainted with strategies for the LSAT digital interface.
- **Full-game Perform Quiz explanations**—In Chapters 4-11, your self-evaluation will be done on complete officially released LSAT games. There is an answer key in the book that you can use to quickly score your results, but the complete worked examples with in-depth expert analysis are found in your online resources. They are PDF files, so you can review them on your computer, or download and print them, as you prefer.
- **LSAT Channel Spotlight videos**—Each LSAT Channel Spotlight feature in Logic Games Prep is accompanied by a video lesson from one or more of Kaplan's top LSAT instructors. The videos present full answers and explanations for logic games found in LSAT Channel Spotlight features in the book. After the title of each video in this list, you'll see the location of the corresponding Spotlight feature in the book:
    - *Secrets of Logic Games Preparation* (Getting Started)
    - *Limited Options* (Chapter 3)
    - *Using Previous Work* (Chapter 4)
    - *Circular Sequencing* (Chapter 6)
    - *Minimum Increasers and Maximum Decreasers* (Chapter 8)

    - *The Dinosaur Game* (Chapter 10)
    - *The Return of Process* (Chapter 11)
- **The LSAT Logic Games Training Camp**—This is a place for you to hone the skills you're learning in this book. It is made up of sets of fast-paced online drills to give you "reps" on deductions and strategies central to Logic Games mastery. There are Training Camp drills for each of Chapters 2-10, and they are broken up into Foundations, Mid-Level, and Advanced sets to fit your individual strengths and opportunities. Training Camp drills can be done at any time, as a warmup, a refresher, or just to keep you sharp.
- **"Fundamentals" quizzes**—For Chapters 2–4, one or more of the Assessments may recommend that you practice and review an additional quiz on the foundations of each lesson topic.
- **PrepTest Analysis and Explanations**—The best full-length LSAT test practice experience is available through the testmaker, LSAC, on its LawHub platform, where you can take released tests in the official digital interface, with the same tools and timing you'll see on test day. Register for LawHub at **www.lsac.org/lawhub**. LSAC offers a free version of its practice tool, called LSAT Prep, with a small number of released exams, including PrepTests 71 and 73. Because Kaplan recommends that every self-prep student use at least those two free practice tests, you'll find complete explanations for every question on those tests in your online companion to this book.

  For self-prep students who choose to upgrade to LSAC's paid option (called LSAT Prep Plus), with more than 70 released tests to take in the digital interface, Kaplan offers LSAT Link, our exclusive scoring and analytics tool. When you link your LSAC LSAT Prep Plus subscription to Kaplan, your answers from tests taken in LawHub will automatically export to Link, where you'll get in-depth analysis and explanations for all 70+ PrepTests. With the premium version, LSAT Link+, you'll also have access to 240 uniquely curated Mastery quizzes to target each LSAT question type at different levels of difficulty (including more than 2,000 officially released LSAT questions not available on LSAC's LawHub). Find out more about LSAT Link and Link+ in the part of this Getting Started chapter called Next-Level Self-Prep or by visiting **www.kaptest.com/lsat/courses/lsat-self-study**.
- **Additional Free LSAT Resources**—This section contains links to additional free LSAT study and practice resources created by Kaplan. Click in to see our latest free trials and assets.

When to Use Your Online Resources

Your online resources are always available. You should watch the "Getting Started" video as soon as possible, along with this section of the book. At the end of this section, you'll find The LSAT Channel Spotlight feature "Secrets of Logic Games Prep," so watch its corresponding video as well. You'll meet The LSAT Channel faculty that deliver the other Spotlight lessons and get valuable tips that these top scorers give their students at the beginning of class. We include one full LSAT Channel episode—Screen Time: Prepping for the Digital LSAT. Learning the fundamentals about the Logic Games section does not require this episode, but you'll want to view this episode to make sure you're ready to put your skills into practice on the interface you'll see on test day.

Other LSAT Channel Spotlight videos correspond to the Spotlight features in the book, so watch them after reading those special sections. As previously mentioned, whenever a Spotlight feature contains a practice logic game, the teacher will give complete answers and explanations in the video, along with unique instruction containing special tips and strategies for attacking the Logic Games section on test day.

You will want to review the Full-Game Perform explanations thoroughly after every Perform quiz in Chapters 4 through 11. Studying the expert analyses will not only allow you to understand the right and wrong answers, it will provide a model of efficiency and strategy for you to emulate on test day.

The Logic Games Training Camp drills, on the other hand, can be used at any time. They provide quick, skills-based practice that sharpens and refines your approach to the Logic Games section. Since they are entirely online, you can even do them when you are on the go or outside of your routine, scheduled study time.

The "Fundamentals" quizzes accompany the Perform exercises and Assessments in Chapters 2–4. If your Assessment recommends any of these quizzes, you should definitely take and review them accordingly. The quizzes provide excellent additional practice for the topics covered in these chapters, so you should feel free to try them out any time you want additional practice.

You'll use the explanations for PrepTests 71 and 73 after you complete them as full LSAT practice tests.

NEXT-LEVEL SELF-PREP

Integrate Your Prep With LSAC Digital Practice and Khan Academy LSAT

While this book contains expert strategies and tactics for each section and question on the LSAT along with ample practice, you may plan to take advantage of other prep resources available to the self-prepper. Two such assets, one created by and one endorsed by the testmaker, are particularly popular: 1) LSAC's LSAT Prep Plus, a low-cost subscription to officially released practice tests, and 2) Khan Academy LSAT, a set of free written and video lessons with practice exercises. Kaplan wants to help you use all available resources as effectively and efficiently as possible. To that end, here are a few tips for using Kaplan's LSAT Prep Plus book in conjunction with LSAC digital practice and Khan Academy instruction. You'll find more information about all of the Kaplan tools and programs designed for the self-prep student at **www.kaptest.com/lsat/courses/lsat-self-study**.

LSAC Digital Practice / LawHub

The LSAT is unique among standardized tests because LSAC (the Law School Admissions Council), the organization that makes and administers the LSAT, makes so many of their previously released tests available to the public. Most standardized testing organizations release few, if any, of their official tests. The LSAC calls their released LSATs "PrepTests," and, with an LSAC Prep Plus subscription (visit **www.lsac.org/lawhub** to purchase), you have access to more than 70 PrepTests in LawHub, a web-based library that allows you to practice in the official digital testing environment. That's a terrific collection of practice materials for students prepping for the LSAT, but it is also more than 160 hours of testing, and doing test after test on repeat is not the best use of your time. Here are a few pointers for getting the most out of LawHub.

Take a "diagnostic" test. Take one full-length test right at the start of your prep to get a baseline for your LSAT score and a first look at your strengths and weaknesses (at least by section) on the test. Don't put too much weight on your initial score. Instead, use your results to guide and focus your reading and study toward maximum efficiency. PrepTest 71 is a good choice. It's relatively recent, and it's one of the released LSATs included in LSAC's free version of LawHub (called LSAT Prep), so you can use it right away, even if you haven't yet upgraded to the full LawHub library (called LSAT Prep Plus).

Plan out your test usage. While a full LSAT Prep Plus subscription includes more than 70 LSATs, it can be frustrating to start a test and discover you've already seen some of its games, passages, or questions. That's why it's a good idea to set aside a few recent tests for your full-length and timed-section practice. For most preppers, one full-length test per week is a good average. If your study schedule is wide open, you may be able to take two full-length tests during some weeks. Remember, however, that learning and improvement come from reviewing your tests to analyze your results and performance, so budget time for that as well as the roughly two-and-a-half hours you'll need to take a full-length LSAT.

Of the tests available through LawHub, this book uses questions from PrepTests 23, 25, 29, 33, 35, 37, 41, 43, 45, 57, and 80. It is more difficult to avoid duplication when you're using Khan Academy LSAT prep because it uses at least some questions from 39 different released LSATs in its lessons, tests, and practice sets. Kaplan's LSAT Link, our analysis and explanations companion to LawHub, contains a chart showing test usage—including Khan Academy prep—to help you avoid "spoiling" PrepTests. The premium version, Link+, also curates quizzes with more than 2,000 officially released LSAT practice questions that do not overlap with the tests included in LawHub. There's more to say about LSAT Link in the next tip too.

Review your tests and self-assess. While LawHub serves as an almost inexhaustible library of practice tests, it does not provide any explanations or analysis of your results. As you work through this book, you'll learn to identify the different question, game, and passage types used by the LSAT. Keeping track of your performance by question type is essential to identifying the patterns that allow you to personalize your prep and master the test. Doing this on your own is time-consuming, and there's a learning curve just for quickly and accurately identifying each game type and question type. It is also hard to self-assess accurately if you don't have complete explanations so that you distinguish questions you misunderstood from those on which you just "goofed" or ran out of time.

Here again, Kaplan's LSAT Link serves as the essential tool for the self-prep student. When you link your LSAC Prep Plus/LawHub account to Kaplan, your answers for all completed PrepTests export to Link, Kaplan's analysis-and-explanation hub. Your tests are automatically scored and your results analyzed by section, game, and question type. You can review your performance test by test or cumulatively, and results for each question link directly to complete explanations written by Kaplan LSAT experts. To learn more or to purchase LSAT Link and Link+ (the premium version with 240 curated Mastery Practice quizzes), please visit **www.kaptest.com/lsat/courses/lsat-self-study**.

Khan Academy LSAT Prep

In 2018, LSAC partnered with Khan Academy to offer free LSAT prep tools available to everyone. Khan Academy LSAT offers brief videos, written assignments, and practice quizzes containing a number of officially released questions from the same PrepTests that LSAC has posted on LawHub. Unfortunately, there is no direct link between Khan Academy LSAT and LSAC's LawHub. There is a post in one of Khan Academy's FAQs that indicates the PrepTests used by Khan Academy (**www.khanacademy.org/test-prep/lsat/lsat-lessons/about-official-lsat-prep/a/list-of-lsat-practice-tests-available-on-khan-academy**), but there is no indication of which specific questions are used. Khan Academy's full-length tests appear in a digital interface different from the official one used on LawHub, and the sections of the test may be in a different order on Khan's site, so use caution if you take a PrepTest on LawHub and try to transfer your answers to Khan Academy by hand.

On the whole, the Khan Academy notes and videos present a nice introduction to the various LSAT questions, and while they were not made in coordination with any Kaplan book or course, you should not be concerned that Khan's instruction will be in conflict with the methods and strategies you learn in this book. Here's a tip for getting the most out of Khan's videos as you work through Kaplan's *LSAT Logic Games Prep*.

Learn the Differences in Terminology

Khan Academy-To-Kaplan Nomenclature Chart

From the testmaker (LSAC) to Khan Academy to Kaplan and other test-prep providers, everybody seems to have slightly different naming conventions for the sections and questions on the LSAT. Because Kaplan encourages you to make use of free Khan Academy prep alongside Kaplan books and resources, here's a handy chart to show you the correspondence between our categories and terminology.

Khan Academy Name(s)	Kaplan Name(s)
Logic Games Game Types	
Ordering	Strict Sequencing
	Loose Sequencing
Grouping	Selection
	Distribution
	Matching
Mixed Setup	Hybrid
N/A	Mapping
N/A	Process
Logic Games Question Types	
Given Info: Basic	Acceptability
	Partial Acceptability
Given Info: Could	Could Be True *or* Could Be False
Given Info: Must	Must Be True *or* Must Be False
New Info: Could	New-"If"/Could Be True *or* New-"If"/Could Be False
New Info: Must/Cannot	New-"If"/Must Be True *or* New-"If"/Must Be False
Equivalent Rule	Rule Change
	Rule Substitution
Min-Max	Minimum-Maximum
	Earliest-Latest
	How Many?
Completely Determine	Completely Determine

Khan Academy Name(s)	Kaplan Name(s)
Logical Reasoning Question Types	
Identify the conclusion	Main Point
Identify an entailment	Inference
Infer what is most strongly supported	
Identify or infer an issue in dispute	Point at Issue
Identify the technique	Method of Argument
Identify the role	Role of a Statement
Identify the principle	Principle
Match the structure	Parallel Reasoning
Match principles	Parallel Principle
Identify a flaw	Flaw
Match flaws	Parallel Flaw
Necessary Assumption	Assumption (Necessary Assumption)
Sufficient Assumption	Assumption (Sufficient Assumption)
Strengthen	Strengthen
Weaken	Weaken
Identify what is most/least helpful to know	[Kaplan treats these as a subtype of Strengthen/Weaken questions]
Explain	Paradox
Resolve a conflict	

Khan Academy Name(s)	Kaplan Name(s)
Reading Comprehension Passage Types (subject matter)	
Humanities	Humanities
Law	Law
Science	Natural Science
Social Science	Social Science
Reading Comprehension Passage Structures	
N/A	Theory/Perspective
N/A	Event/Phenomenon
N/A	Biography
N/A	Debate
Comparative Reading	Comparative Reading

Khan Academy Name(s)	Kaplan Name(s)
Reading Comprehension Question Types	
Main point	Global
Recognition	Detail
Clarifying meaning	[Kaplan treats these as a subtype of Inference Qs.]
Purpose of reference	Logic Function
Organizing information	[Khan's category includes Q-types Kaplan would put under Global, Logic Function, or Inference.]
Inferences about views	Inference
Inferences about information	
Inferences about attitudes	
Applying to new contexts	Logic Reasoning: Principle
Discovering principles and analogies	Logic Reasoning: Parallel
	Logic Reasoning: Principle
Additional evidence	Logic Reasoning: Strengthen/Weaken
Primary purpose	Global

GO DEEPER IN YOUR AREAS OF GREATEST OPPORTUNITY FOR SCORE IMPROVEMENT

The LSAT Channel

Effective LSAT prep cannot be one-size-fits-all. Even two test takers with an identical score will have distinct strengths and weaknesses. As you learn yours from taking and reviewing practice tests and learning strategies and tactics from programs such as Khan Academy LSAT Prep (or, indeed, from this book), you'll discover areas in which you need more work on the fundamentals and others where you're ready to challenge yourself with harder and harder questions. Enter the LSAT Channel, Kaplan's nightly live instruction platform for lessons on almost every conceivable concept and skill rewarded by the exam.

For years, students in Kaplan's comprehensive courses have enjoyed the LSAT Channel with more than 100 distinct hour-long episodes taught by some of the highest-rated instructors in the Kaplan faculty. Now, the LSAT Channel is available to self-prep students as well. You can attend live lessons where you can ask questions and interact with the instructor and online TAs. If you can't attend a live lesson, every episode is available in an archive of recordings available to stream on demand. You can search the upcoming schedule and the archive by subject matter, by difficulty level (Foundations, For Everyone, and Advanced lessons are available), and even by instructor (so that you can find more teaching from your newly discovered favorites).

With the LSAT Channel, you can personalize your instruction with the same specificity and nuance that LSAT Link+ provides for your test analyses and practice. Find out more about the LSAT Channel here: **www.kaptest.com/lsat/courses/lsat-self-study**.

The Hardest Real LSAT Questions

Diligent work with Kaplan's LSAT Prep Plus and the supplemental tools and programs just outlined will raise your LSAT score, but what do you work on when you've already established a strong score and you're ready to push into the stratosphere? That's exactly the practice, analysis, and strategy Kaplan's LSAT Hardest Questions program provides.

Informed by the empirical results of tens of thousands of LSAT test-takers, Kaplan experts have selected the 100 most challenging Logical Reasoning questions along with the 20 hardest logic games and 20 hardest Reading Comprehension passages of all time. With Kaplan's LSAT Hardest Questions, you'll try these head-scratchers on your own and then watch video analysis by elite instructors from Kaplan's LSAT faculty. They'll break down what makes each question, game, or passage so challenging; reveal patterns found in the hardest LSAT items; and provide strategies you can use to crack the toughest questions with increased confidence and speed.

These are the kinds of questions that distinguish scores among the top percentile test takers. This means that LSAT Hardest Questions won't be for everyone, but if you're ready for the challenge, you can find more information at **www.kaptest.com/lsat/courses/lsat-self-study**.

Looking for Even More?

At Kaplan, we're thrilled you've chosen us to help you on your journey to law school. Beyond this book, there's a wealth of additional resources that we invite you to check out to aid you with your LSAT preparation and your law school application.

- *LSAT Prep Plus*—Kaplan's book LSAT Prep Plus is a comprehensive guide to the LSAT exam with expert methods and strategies for every section and question type. It contains hundreds of officially released LSAC questions, along with the drills, exercises, and practice sets on all of the skills you'll need for LSAT mastery.
- Comprehensive LSAT Courses—Of course, we'd be remiss if we did not mention the world's most popular LSAT preparation courses. Visit our website to learn about our comprehensive prep options. Choose from Live Online, Self-Paced, and Private Tutoring options, depending on your needs and learning style. View course options and upcoming class schedules at **www.kaptest.com/lsat/lsat-courses**.

You have a lot to do. Before you dive into your LSAT logic games prep, take a look at how Kaplan's expert faculty suggests you organize your study schedule.

MODEL STUDY SCHEDULES

Logic Games Prep is written so that you can, time permitting, start at page 1 and work straight through to the end. Indeed, to the LSAT experts who worked on this book, that would be ideal: take it all in, and absorb everything you can. To do that, you'll need to start your logic games preparation about a month and half (or more) before your official test day. Because not every student can start that early (or may not have as much time during the week), the following condensed schedules focus on the material that will likely be the most important to your LSAT score—the fundamental concepts and the most common game types on recent tests.

The following models should be used as a starting point as you design your own study schedule. They are based on the rough assumption that you can dedicate around 10–12 hours per week to logic games preparation. If you have more time, you may be able to finish these plans faster, of course. Be sure to consider other factors—school, work, other LSAT prep, and so on—as you plan your personal roadmap to Logic Games mastery. Note that the weeks count down to test day.

Comprehensive (6 weeks or more)

By getting an early start on your Logic Games prep, you will likely have the opportunity to complete the work in this book and additional practice from other sources.

Week 6
Logic Games Prep

Getting Started
LSAT Channel Spotlight: Secrets of Logic Games Preparation
Chapter 1: The Logic Games Method
Chapter 2: Logic Game Types and Sketches
Chapter 3: Logic Games Rules and Deductions (up through "How to Interpret and Sketch Rules")
Chapter 8: Formal Logic and Selection Games Unlocked (complete "Formal Logic in LSAT Logic Games")

Online Study Plan

Video: *Getting Started*
LSAT Channel Spotlight Video: *Secrets of Logic Games Preparation*
[If recommended] Quiz: "Game Types and Sketches Fundamentals"
[If recommended] Quiz: "Identifying and Sketching Rules Fundamentals"
[Optional] LSAT Channel lesson: Fundamentals of Formal Logic (found in the LSAT Course Preview)

Additional Practice

Take one timed, full-length PrepTest on LSAC's LawHub. If you have Kaplan's LSAT Link, review your results and, if you have Link+, complete your top recommendations for Logic Games Mastery Practice.

Week 5
Logic Games Prep

Chapter 3: Rules and Deductions (starting with "How to Combine Rules to Make Deductions")
LSAT Channel Spotlight: Limited Options
Chapter 4: Logic Games Questions
LSAT Channel Spotlight: Using Previous Work

Chapter 5: Basic Strict Sequencing Games Unlocked

Online Study Plan

LSAT Channel Spotlight Video: *Limited Options*
LSAT Channel Spotlight Video: *Using Previous Work*
[If recommended] Quiz: "Deductions Fundamentals"
[If recommended] Quiz: "Question Types Fundamentals"

Additional Practice

See "Recommended Additional Practice" for Chapter 5. If you have Kaplan's LSAT Link+, complete your top recommendations for Logic Games Mastery Practice.

Week 4
Logic Games Prep

Chapter 6: Complex Strict Sequencing Games Unlocked
[Optional] LSAT Channel Spotlight: Circular Sequencing
Chapter 7: Loose Sequencing Games Unlocked

Online Study Plan

LSAT Channel episode: Screen Time: Prepping for the Digital LSAT
[Optional] LSAT Channel Spotlight video: *Circular Sequencing*

Additional Practice

See "Recommended Additional Practice" for Chapter 6.
See "Recommended Additional Practice" for Chapter 7.
If you have Kaplan's LSAT Link+, complete your top recommendations for Logic Games Mastery Practice.

Week 3
Logic Games Prep

Chapter 8: Formal Logic and Selection Games Unlocked (If you have already done "Formal Logic in LSAT Logic Games," complete all of the sections on Selection Games)
LSAT Channel Spotlight: Minimum Increasers and Maximum Decreasers
Chapter 9: Matching and Distribution Games Unlocked (up through "Matching Games—Full Games with Questions")

Online Study Plan

LSAT Channel Spotlight video: *Minimum Increasers and Maximum Decreasers*

Additional Practice

See "Recommended Additional Practice" for Chapter 8.
See "Recommended Additional Practice" for Chapter 9 (Matching Games).
If you have Kaplan's LSAT Link+, complete your top recommendations for Logic Games Mastery Practice.

Week 2
Logic Games Prep

Chapter 9: Matching and Distribution Games Unlocked (complete the sections on Distribution Games)
Chapter 10: Hybrid Games Unlocked
LSAT Channel Spotlight: The Dinosaur Game

Online Study Plan

LSAT Channel Spotlight video: *The Dinosaur Game*

Additional Practice

See "Recommended Additional Practice" for Chapter 9 (Distribution Games).
See "Recommended Additional Practice" for Chapter 10.
If you have Kaplan's LSAT Link+, complete your top recommendations for Logic Games Mastery Practice.

Week 1
Logic Games Prep

Review Chapters 1-4
Appendix I: Logic Games—Timing and Section Management
Appendix II: The Countdown to Test Day
[Optional] Chapter 11: Rare Games Unlocked—Process and Matching
[Optional] LSAT Channel Spotlight: The Return of Process

Online Study Plan

[Optional] LSAT Channel Spotlight Video: *The Return of Process*

Additional Practice

Take one timed, full-length PrepTest on LSAC's LawHub. If you have Kaplan's LSAT Link, review your results and, if you have Link+, complete your top recommendations for Logic Games Mastery Practice.

Test Day
Take the LSAT and crush the Logic Games section.

Efficient (4 to 5 weeks)

With about a month until your test day, you may be able to complete the entire book, but your time is limited. This schedule will help you be judicious about where to focus your efforts. Work through the chapters and sections in this model schedule first. Then, if you find that you have more time than expected, complete the remaining chapters of the book.

Week 4
Logic Games Prep

Getting Started
LSAT Channel Spotlight: Secrets of Logic Games Preparation
Chapter 1: The Logic Games Method

Chapter 2: Logic Game Types and Sketches
Chapter 3: Logic Games Rules and Deductions
LSAT Channel Spotlight: Limited Options

Online Study Plan

Video: *Getting Started*
LSAT Channel Spotlight Video: *Secrets of Logic Games Preparation*
LSAT Channel Spotlight Video: *Limited Options*
[If recommended] Quiz: "Game Types and Sketches Fundamentals"
[If recommended] Quiz: "Identifying and Sketching Rules Fundamentals"
[If recommended] Quiz: "Deductions Fundamentals"

Additional Practice

Take one timed, full-length PrepTest on LSAC's LawHub. If you have Kaplan's LSAT Link, review your results and, if you have Link+, complete your top recommendations for Logic Games Mastery Practice.

Week 3
Logic Games Prep

Chapter 4: Logic Games Questions
LSAT Channel Spotlight: Using Previous Work
Chapter 5: Basic Strict Sequencing Games Unlocked
Chapter 7: Loose Sequencing Games Unlocked

Online Study Plan

LSAT Channel Spotlight Video: *Using Previous Work*
[If recommended] Quiz: "Question Types Fundamentals"

Additional Practice

See "Recommended Additional Practice" for Chapter 5.
See "Recommended Additional Practice" for Chapter 7.
If you have Kaplan's LSAT Link+, complete your top recommendations for Logic Games Mastery Practice.

Week 2
Logic Games Prep

Chapter 6: Complex Strict Sequencing Games Unlocked
Chapter 9: Matching and Distribution Games Unlocked (read the chapter introduction and "Real-Life Distribution," and then complete the sections on Distribution games)

Online Study Plan

LSAT Channel episode: Screen Time: Prepping for the Digital LSAT

Additional Practice

See "Recommended Additional Practice" for Chapter 6.
See "Recommended Additional Practice" for Chapter 9 (Distribution Games).

If you have Kaplan's LSAT Link+, complete your top recommendations for Logic Games Mastery Practice.

Week 1
Logic Games Prep

[Optional] LSAT Channel Spotlight: Minimum Increasers and Maximum Decreasers (Chapter 8)
Chapter 10: Hybrid Games Unlocked
[Optional] LSAT Channel Spotlight: The Dinosaur Game
Appendix I: Logic Games—Timing and Section Management
Appendix II: The Countdown to Test Day

Online Study Plan

[Optional] LSAT Channel Spotlight video: *Minimum Increasers and Maximum Decreasers*

Additional Practice

See "Recommended Additional Practice" for Chapter 10.
Take one timed, full-length PrepTest on LSAC's LawHub. If you have Kaplan's LSAT Link, review your results and, if you have Link+, complete your top recommendations for Logic Games Mastery Practice.

Test Day
Take the LSAT and crush the Logic Games section.

Last-Minute (2 to 3 weeks)

With just two weeks until test day, you will need to make some hard choices. The material outlined in this schedule provides the fundamentals of the Logic Games Method and its associated strategies, and focuses your practice on the game types you are most likely to encounter on test day.

Week 2
Logic Games Prep

Getting Started
LSAT Channel Spotlight: Secrets of Logic Games Preparation
Chapter 1: The Logic Games Method
Chapter 2: Logic Game Types and Sketches*
Chapter 3: Logic Games Rules and Deductions*
[Optional] LSAT Channel Spotlight: Limited Options
Chapter 4: Logic Games Questions*
*You may need to cut out some or all Practice exercises to complete these chapters.

Online Study Plan

Video: *Getting Started*
LSAT Channel Spotlight Video: *Secrets of Logic Games Preparation*
[Optional] LSAT Channel Spotlight Video: *Limited Options*
[If recommended] Quiz: "Game Types and Sketches Fundamentals"
[If recommended] Quiz: "Identifying and Sketching Rules Fundamentals"
[If recommended] Quiz: "Deductions Fundamentals"

Additional Practice

If time permits more work during this week, you should move on to Chapter 5: Basic Strict Sequencing Games Unlocked. Strict Sequencing is, by far, the most common game type on the LSAT.

Week 1

Logic Games Prep

Chapter 5: Basic Strict Sequencing Games Unlocked
Chapter 7: Loose Sequencing Games Unlocked
Chapter 9: Matching and Distribution Games Unlocked (read the chapter introduction and "Real-Life Distribution," and then complete the sections on Distribution games)
Appendix I: Logic Games—Timing and Section Management
Appendix II: The Countdown to Test Day

Online Study Plan

LSAT Channel episode: Screen Time: Prepping for the Digital LSAT

Additional Practice

Take one timed, full-length PrepTest on LSAC's LawHub. If you have Kaplan's LSAT Link, review your results and, if you have Link+, complete your top recommendations for Logic Games Mastery Practice. Otherwise, complete as much additional Practice as possible from the following chapters:
See "Recommended Additional Practice" for Chapter 5.
See "Recommended Additional Practice" for Chapter 7.
See "Recommended Additional Practice" for Chapter 9 (Distribution Games).

The model Last-Minute schedule cuts out a lot of material, but focuses on what you are most likely to see on test day, and on the areas in which you can make the greatest impact on your score in a short amount of time.

Note: You can use the LSAT Logic Games Training Camp exercises at any time. They are fast-paced drills designed to hone your skills, and they are done online. Use them to supplement your more intensive study sessions when you're away from your desk, or when you want a quick workout or warmup.

LSAT REASONING AND STRATEGY

Why the LSAT?

You're reading this book because you want to be a law student. Well, your legal education starts now.

Every year, Kaplan surveys the admissions officers from law schools all around the country, and every year, the majority of them tell us that the LSAT is the most important factor in your law school application—more important than GPA, the personal statement, letters of recommendation, and other application requirements. Admissions officers routinely cite poor LSAT scores as the biggest "application killer," and they tell us it is the part of the application that they check first. You may already know how important the LSAT is, but what you may not know is why. The LSAT tests skills relevant to law school and to the practice of law. Moreover, the LSAT is the one factor common to all applications. It levels the playing field for candidates regardless of academic background. The LSAT doesn't care what you majored in or where you went to school.

The LSAT is probably unlike any other test you've taken in your academic career. Most tests you've encountered in high school and college have been content-based—that is, they required you to recall a certain body of facts, formulas, theorems, or other acquired knowledge. But the LSAT is a skills-based test. It doesn't ask you to repeat memorized facts or to apply learned formulas to specific problems. You will be rewarded for familiarity with patterns that make the LSAT predictable, and ultimately all you'll be asked to do on the LSAT is think—thoroughly, quickly, and strategically. There's no required content to study! Sound too good to be true? Well, before you get the idea that you can skate into the most important test of your life without preparing, consider the skills that you'll need to build. Admissions officers care about your score because the LSAT tests the skills you'll use on a daily basis in law school. It's the best predictor law schools have of the likelihood of your success at their institution.

That begins to explain why law schools value the LSAT so highly. But, even so, why would this test include logic games as a way of evaluating potential law students?

Why Logic Games?

One question that LSAT instructors hear over and over from students is "What in the world do logic games have to do with law school?" It's a good question. The answer is "Quite a bit, actually." Seeing why that's the case, however, requires us to step back and take a broader look at both law school and the LSAT.

In law school, you'll hear professors tell you that it is their job—the school's job—to teach you "how to think like a lawyer." That's a clever way of saying that, in law school, you learn and practice and refine the *skills* that attorneys use every day. These include logical reasoning skills such as the ability to assess the validity of arguments, to strengthen and weaken those arguments with relevant information, and to determine what can and cannot be deduced from a set of facts. Likewise, law school—and the practice of law—requires adept reading comprehension to sort quickly and accurately through dense, lengthy statutes, cases, contracts, and reports. So far, so good, but what does any of that have to do with logic games?

On the surface, logic games are little puzzles about obviously fictional people, places, and things. Sometimes, the scenarios you're given (Mixtapes? Movie studios? Toy dinosaurs???) seem almost whimsical. Even the colloquial name—logic *games*—implies that they're supposed to be fun, and, separated from the pressure and anxiety of the exam, you have to admit that they are fun (at least kind of). All of that masks the fact that logic games test a crucial set of law school skills.

When you look at an officially released LSAT test, notice that the testmaker (LSAC) refers to the Logic Games section as Analytical Reasoning. Already, that sounds more important than playing a "game," but a closer look at the kinds of analysis you do in Analytical Reasoning really tells the story. Logic games always reward the correct application of a set of rules to a situation or pattern, and usually to hypothetical variations on the pattern. Subject matter aside, the notorious Dinosaur Game (discussed in detail following Chapter 10 of this book) is a perfect example. In that game, you are told that, to create a window display, a toy store has to select from several kinds of toy dinosaurs, each in a number of colors. There are six rules about the kinds and colors that the store must choose. Then, the test asks you six questions about what must, can, or cannot be true about the window display. Here are three of them:

13. If the tyrannosaur is not included in the display, then the display must contain each of the following EXCEPT:

14. Which one of the following is a pair of toys that could be included in the display together?

16. If both the iguanadon and the ultrasaur are included in the display, then the display must contain which one of the following?

PrepTest57 Sec1 Qs 13, 14, and 16

In law school, you will be asked to read hundreds of legal cases, statutes, and administrative guidelines. When you come to class, your professors will question you to make sure you accurately distilled the rules of law contained in those cases and documents. (That's the reading comprehension part.) Then, they will grill and test you on the application of those rules to various real and fictional scenarios. In the process of doing that, the professors will present you with "hypotheticals." That is, they will add or change facts in the case and ask you which of the rules are still applicable or how the outcome might be different under the changed circumstances. The analytical reasoning skills you'll need for this are quite similar to those you will use to solve logic games. In this section, the LSAT strips away the lengthy passages and gives you the rules directly, so that they can focus on your ability to analyze and apply rules to given patterns. Law schools use your LSAT score to determine how prepared you are for the rigors of legal education, and your ability to quickly and accurately apply complex rule sets to various situations is central to their assessment.

So why would the testmaker use something as trivial (and downright bizarre) as a window display of toy dinosaurs to test this all-important law-school skill? One reason is you, the "collective you" of all law-school applicants. You come from a variety of academic and professional backgrounds, from English to Engineering to Criminal Justice. Law schools want that diversity of backgrounds and expertise in every incoming class. Thus, they want the law-school admissions test to be neutral in terms of subject matter. It is not in their interest to favor chemists or philosophers or anyone else by having the test focus on areas of expertise or knowledge. Another reason is probably just for fun. You've got three years of the emoluments clause and the parol evidence rule ahead of you. Enjoy playing with the plastic dinosaurs while you can.

So, that helps explain why the LSAT includes the Logic Games section, which is the focus of this book. Before making Logic Games your full-time job, however, take a few minutes to consider the context of the full LSAT test.

Four Core Skills—What the LSAT Tests

Now you may be thinking, "What does the Logic Games section have to do with torts? How can Logical Reasoning predict my success in Civil Procedure?" In this book, you are going to be taught a series of Learning Objectives, which are bundled around four key skills—key because they're what the LSAT rewards, key because they're what law school demands. We'll call them the Core Skills:

Reading Strategically

Reading for structure and staying ahead of the author (anticipating) is what Strategic Reading is all about. Both your law professors and the LSAT want you to cut through the jargon and explain what the case or passage says. Reading strategically helps you zero in on exactly what opinions are present and how that knowledge will be rewarded in the question set.

Analyzing Arguments

The essence of Logical Reasoning and the essence of lawyering is Analyzing Arguments. To analyze an argument in the LSAT sense, you must distinguish the argument's conclusion from its evidence. Then, determine what the person making the argument is taking for granted. The assumptions the author makes are what allow you to strengthen or challenge arguments on the LSAT. Likewise, in a courtroom, attorneys will need to understand, analyze, evaluate, manipulate, and draw conclusions from the arguments of their opponent, their own clients, and the judge.

Understanding Formal Logic

Conditional, or If/Then statements, are incredibly important in rules of law. "If/Thens" tell you what must, can, or can't be true in a given situation or when a particular rule is or isn't applicable. The very first chapter of this book will train you to seek out the Formal Logic embedded in LSAT questions and logic games and to manage its implications flawlessly. For a lot of students, this is the most intimidating of the Core Skills, but facing up to it is incredibly valuable. It brings a rigor to your reasoning that will allow you to answer questions—on the LSAT and in law school—with confidence and precision.

Making Deductions

Making Deductions is rewarded in every section of the test, but it is key in Logic Games. In that section, you're given a set of conditions and rules and then asked to apply them to various hypothetical cases: "If J goes on Wednesday, then which one of the following must be true?" or "If the van has more miles than the sedan, and the sedan has more miles than the motorcycle, then which one of the following could be false?" That's just what law school exams demand. In law school, the rules and restrictions come from the dozens (potentially hundreds) of cases and statutes you will read during a semester. Just as you'll learn to do with Logic Games rules, judges synthesize rules in order to determine the outcome of a case.

Structure of the LSAT

The LSAT consists of four multiple-choice sections: one scored Logical Reasoning section, one scored Logic Games section, one scored Reading Comprehension section, and one unscored "experimental" section that will look exactly like one of the other multiple-choice sections. These four multiple-choice sections can appear in any order on test day. A short break will come between the second and third sections of the test. There is also an unscored, 35-minute LSAT Writing essay that you will complete online at any time up to one year after your official test date.

Section →	Number of Questions →	Minutes
Logical Reasoning	24–26	35
Reading Comprehension	26–28	35
Logic Games	22–24	35
"Experimental"	22–28	35
LSAT Writing	One essay	35

These are the four sections you'll see on test day; they may occur in any order.

Familiarize yourself with the structure of each section.

Logical Reasoning

The Logical Reasoning section consists of 24–26 questions based on short passages, which we'll call *stimuli*, of around two to five sentences each. Each stimulus may be a short argument or a series of statements of fact or opinion. Each stimulus will have one corresponding question that tests your ability to do such things as spot the structure of arguments, identify assumptions and flaws, strengthen or weaken arguments, or find inferences.

Reading Comprehension

This section consists of three passages, typically made up of two to five paragraphs—about 500 words apiece—and one set of paired passages, together about the same length as each of the three single passages. Each passage is accompanied by anywhere from five to eight questions. The Reading Comprehension section has had 27 questions on every LSAT released since 2007 but historically has had anywhere from 26 to 28 questions. Reading Comprehension on the LSAT is an exercise in reading for structure and for multiple points of view. You'll learn to trace the outline of the passage as you read and to distinguish the author's viewpoint from the viewpoints of others mentioned in the passage, as well as to stay a step ahead of where the author is going by reading predictively.

Logic Games (Analytical Reasoning)

The LSAT's Analytical Reasoning section, known popularly and in this book as Logic Games, consists of four game scenarios along with accompanying rules. Each game is accompanied by 5–7 questions. The Logic Games section has had 23 questions on every LSAT released since 2007 but historically has had from 22 to 24 questions. With only 23 questions, it has the fewest of any scored section. Logic Games may nevertheless be the section you fear the most—many students do—but also the one on which you make your biggest improvements. Many students quickly take to the puzzle aspect of this section. Logic Games tests your ability to interpret, combine, and apply rules and to deduce what can and cannot happen as a result. While the games may look daunting at first, they can be mastered with a systematic technique and proper use of scratchwork.

Experimental

The experimental section is an additional, unscored section of Logical Reasoning, Reading Comprehension, or Logic Games. You will not know what type of experimental section you will get, and it can show up anywhere, including after the break. You'll have to bring your A-game for the entire test, as there is no reliable way to determine which section is experimental while you're taking the test. In case you're wondering, the LSAC includes an experimental section on the LSAT as a way to test questions for future administrations of the exam.

Exception: a research section testing brand-new question formats. There is one case you could encounter on test day in which your experience with the unscored section of the LSAT will be different than that described in the preceding paragraph. Here's why it's happening and what to expect. Beginning in June 2022, the LSAC began testing questions for a brand-new (and as yet undefined) section type that will replace the Logic Games section in the future. Because these questions will be obviously different than the standard sections of the LSAT, test takers to whom these questions are being administered will be told by their online proctor after Section 3 of their test that they have completed their three scored sections (those students having seen one each of Logical Reasoning, Reading Comprehension, and Logic Games, of course, at that point in their test). These students will then be told that in Section 4, they will see a research section testing novel question formats. LSAC asks that these students please do their best on the new items and then complete a short survey to provide data on their reactions to the questions and the techniques used to solve them.

Remember that no matter which type of unscored section you encounter on test day (standard experimental or new question research), your three scored sections will be identical to those seen by all test takers in your administration. Don't try to guess which format you have during the exam; doing so is distracting and unproductive. Do your best on each section you see. If you have a traditional experimental section, you won't know during your test which section is experimental. If you happen to be in the cohort receiving the brand-new items, you'll find out after Section 3.

LSAT Writing

Within one year after your official LSAT, you are required to complete a 35-minute LSAT Writing sample online on your own computer. Your task is to write a short essay in which you choose between two courses of action and justify your choice based on facts presented in the prompt's fictional scenario. While unscored, your LSAT Writing essay is submitted to all law schools to which you apply and admissions officers use it as part of their evaluation process.

LSAT Scored Sections

Logic Games

One section with four games and 22–24 questions

Logic Games questions reward you for sequencing, matching, distributing, or selecting entities on the basis of rules that combine to limit the acceptable arrangements.

Logical Reasoning

One section with 24–26 questions

Logical Reasoning questions reward you for analyzing arguments to strengthen or weaken them or to identify their assumptions and flaws. Other LR questions require you to draw valid inferences from a set of facts.

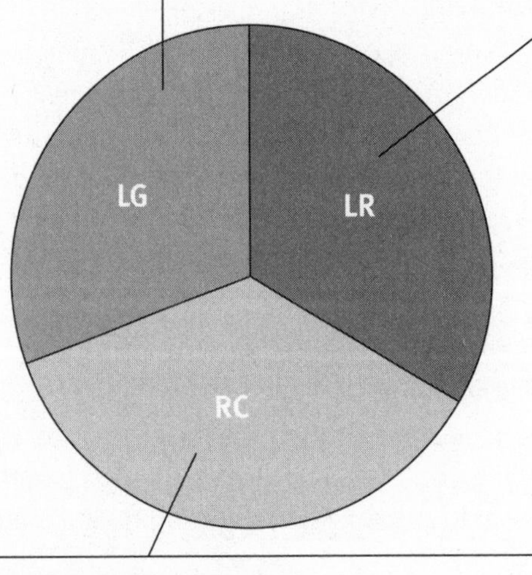

Reading Comprehension

One section with four passages and 26–28 questions

Reading Comp questions reward you for identifying the author's purpose and main idea, drawing valid inferences from the passage, and determining how and why the author uses certain details.

The Digital LSAT Interface

The official LSAT is administered digitally (taken on your personal device), and getting practice with the interface and tools of the digital test is essential to your preparation. The most direct way to get familiar with the digital interface is to use the LSAC's familiarization tool on its website: **www.lsac.org/lsat-prep-get-familiar**. That page has video tutorials and full practice tests in a web-based version of the official testing interface. There is also a very helpful FAQ about the digital test and its implications for registration, scoring, accommodated testing, and so on: **www.lsac.org/lsat/taking-lsat/about-digital-lsat**.

Make the most of those LSAC resources. In the meantime, what follows is a quick introduction to the digital interface with some helpful strategy notes from Kaplan's expert instructors who have used it and have some best practices to pass on to test takers.

Here's a screenshot of a generic question, taken from the Digital LSAT interface. We've labeled the buttons to show you what each of them does.

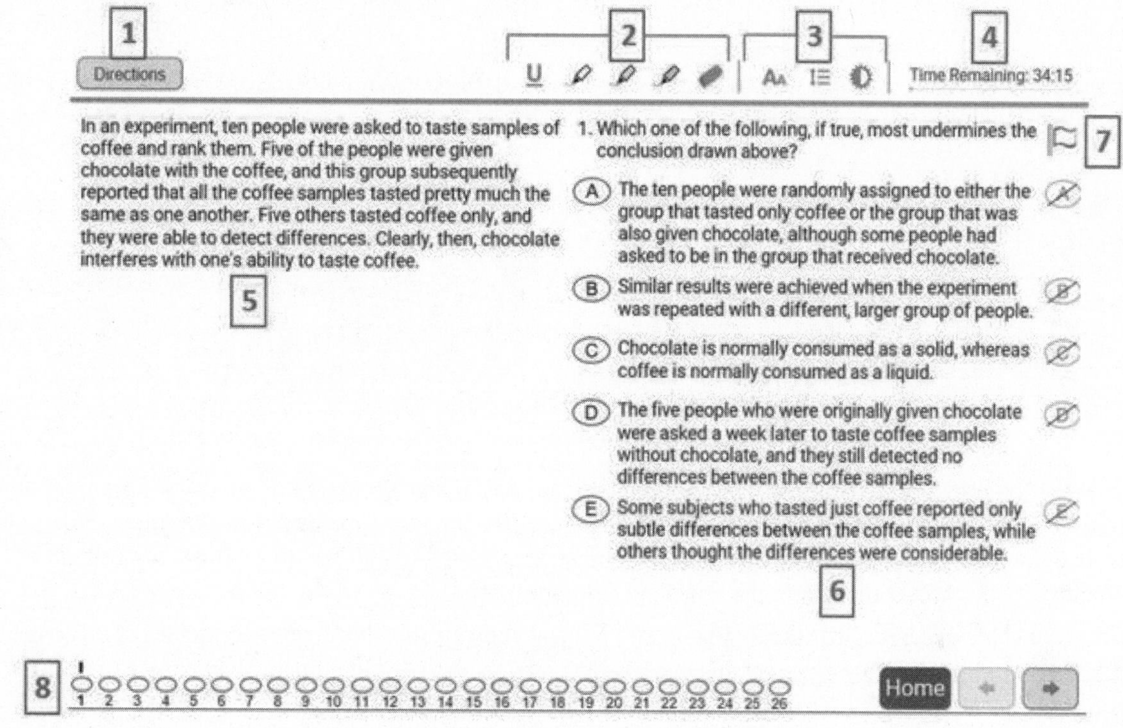

Digital LSAT screen layout LSAC.org

Here's what we've labeled along with a few strategy notes that apply to all three scored sections of the test.

1. The "Directions" button will take you back to the Directions slide at the start of the test section. When you're on the Directions page, this button changes to say "Questions." If you click the button while you're on the Directions page, it will take you back to the last question at which you were looking.
2. These icons activate the underlining and highlighting tools (there are three highlighter colors), and an eraser tool to remove underlines or highlights you've made.

PRACTICE TIP

As you use the LSAC practice tests in the official interface, practice using your device. Do you prefer a mouse or touchpad? Or do you prefer to use your touchscreen or stylus? Make those decisions before test day.

3. These three tools allow you to adjust font size (four options), line spacing (three options), and brightness (a slider).

> **PRACTICE TIP**
>
> Practice using these tools until you're familiar and comfortable with them. That way, you'll know from the get-go how you want to adjust the view for each section of the test.

4. This is the section timer. It will start at 35:00 and count down to 00:00. For the first 30 minutes of the section, you can hide the timer by clicking on the numbers.

> **PRACTICE TIP**
>
> Some test takers like to see the timer. Others get anxious having the clock in their peripheral vision. There is no right or wrong way to use the timer. Try it out in practice to see what works best for you.

5. This is where the question's stimulus or prompt will be. For Logical Reasoning, that means the argument or paragraph on which the question is based; for Logic Games, it means the game's setup and rules; and, for Reading Comprehension, it means the passage. For passages and paragraphs too long to fit on the screen, there will be a scroll bar that controls just the text in the left-hand column.
6. This column will always have the question stem and answer choices. Clicking a circle to the left of an answer choice selects that choice as the correct answer. Clicking a circle to the right of an answer choice will grey down that choice. Note: You must click a choice from the left-hand circles; greying down four answer choices does not automatically select the correct answer. This may look or sound confusing at first, but it's quite intuitive after just a few minutes of practice.

> **DIGITAL LSAT STRATEGY**
>
> Among the high-scoring LSAT experts we surveyed about their use of the digital interface, no feature gained as universally high praise as the "grey down" bubbles. Top scorers on the LSAT develop tremendous acumen and confidence that allows them to eliminate incorrect choices after one read-through. They all appreciated the added clarity of being able to visually eliminate the choice with one click.

6a. On questions in which the right-hand column text will not fit onscreen, you'll see upward arrows to the right of the answer choices. These allow you to collapse answer choices until the text no longer requires a scroll bar. Collapsing answers you've confidently eliminated will help you avoid rereading and confusion.

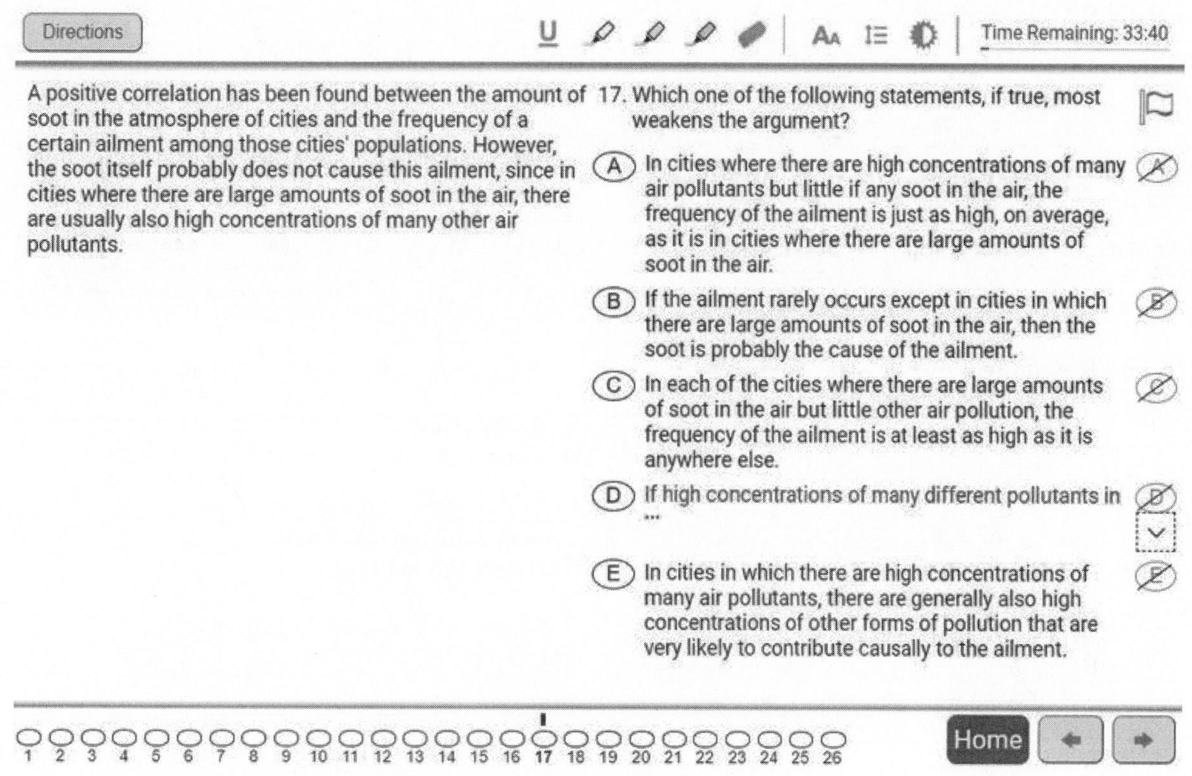

Collapsible answer choices LSAC.org

7. This flag allows you to mark questions. Our LSAT experts use it in two situations. Some flagged questions that they skipped or left unanswered. All of the experts, however, used the flag for questions to which they wanted to return, time permitting. In some cases, these were questions for which they had picked an answer, but had low confidence in their choice and wanted to give it one more look. In other cases, these were questions on which the expert had eliminated (greyed down) two or three of the answers and wanted to come back for a final decision on the remaining choices.

DIGITAL LSAT STRATEGY

Strategic skipping and guessing are important tactics for effective time management on the LSAT. Test experts know that all questions carry equal weight in calculating their final score, so they avoid wasting too much time on any single question. The flag tool on the digital test is a huge improvement over any technique available for keeping track of skipped questions in the paper test booklet.

8. The horizontal bar at the bottom of the screen is for navigation. We call it the "bubble bar," and it indicates questions for which you've selected a correct answer, questions you've left blank, and any question you've flagged, answered or not. The current on-screen question is indicated by a small vertical bar above the bubble. Clicking on a bubble in the navigation bar will automatically advance you to that question. The forward and back buttons in the far bottom right will move you one question forward or back.

How the LSAT is scored

Here's how the LSAT is scored. Your performance is assessed on three scales: raw score (# correct), scaled score, and percentile.

Percentile *(Scaled score)*	10th *(139)*	20th *(143)*	30th *(146)*	40th *(149)*	50th *(151)*	60th *(154)*	70th *(156)*	80th *(160)*	90th *(164)*	95th *(167)*	99th *(172)*
# Correct	28	33	36	40	43	47	51	56	61	64	69

Estimated conversions-actual tests will vary slightly

LSAT Score Breakdown

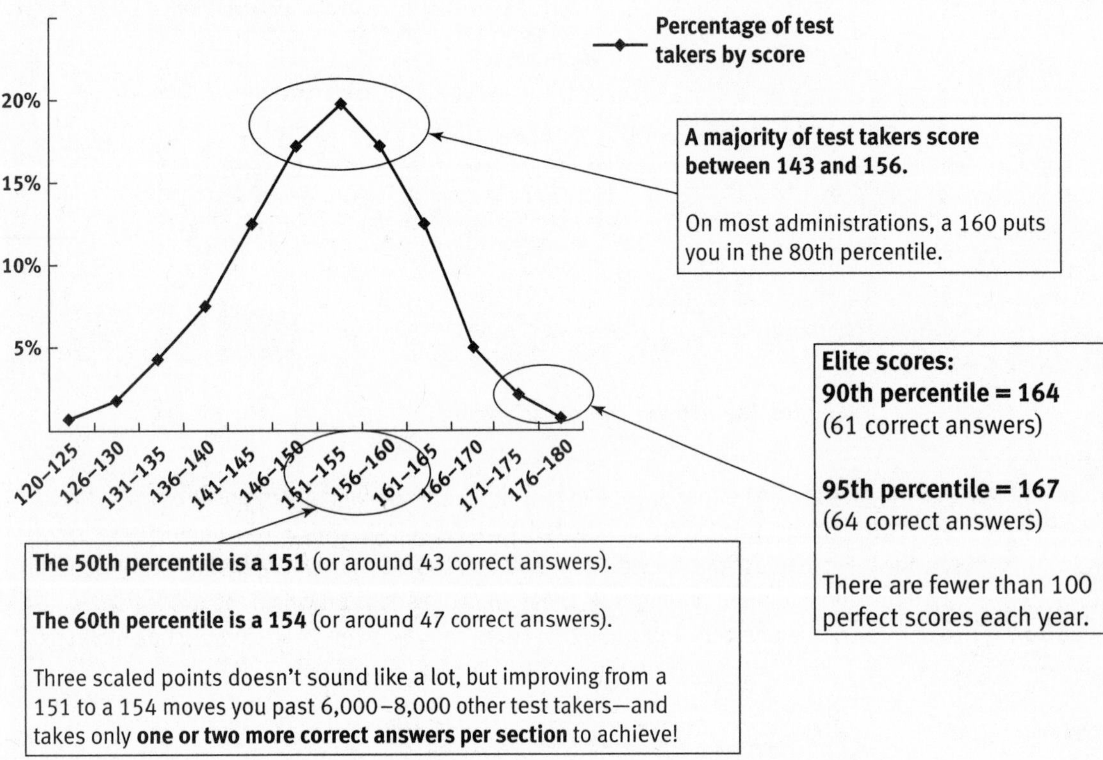

Raw score is simply the number of questions answered correctly.

Scaled score, the familiar 120–180 number, is a conversion of the raw score. Here, a raw score of 51—that is, 51 correct answers—converts to a scaled score of 156. A raw score of 43—meaning 43 correct answers—converts to a scaled score of 151. On a different test, a raw score of 43 might convert to a 150 or a 152. To account for differences in overall difficulty, each test has a slightly different raw score-to-scaled score conversion table.

Percentile score indicates how a test taker performed relative to other test takers over a three-year period. The conversion from scaled score to percentile score remains relatively stable, with only minor variations over the years. Test after test, a 151 scaled score is approximately a 50th percentile score.

The way in which the LSAT is scored has three important implications for your performance:

- First, the number of *right* answers determines your score. There is no guessing penalty. Never leave a question blank on the LSAT.
- Second, every question is worth the same, regardless of how hard it is. Learn to spot difficult questions and leave them for the end of each section. Find the easy questions and rack up points. If you're going to run out of time or need to guess, you want to do so on the tough stuff.
- Third, every additional correct answer can leapfrog you ahead of hundreds—or even thousands—of other test takers, your competition. How's that for inspiration?

What's a Good LSAT Score?

What you consider a good LSAT score depends on your own expectations and goals, but here are a few interesting statistics.

If you got about half of all of the scored questions right (a raw score of 37–38), you'd earn a scaled score of roughly 147, putting you in about the 30th percentile—not a great performance. However, as you saw above, a little improvement goes a long way. Getting only one additional question right every 10 minutes (throughout the scored sections) would give you a raw score of around 47, pushing you up to 154, which is about the 60th percentile—a huge improvement.

So, you don't have to be perfect to do well. On a typical LSAT, you can still get around 18–19 questions wrong and still end up in the 160s—or about 14 wrong and get a 164, a 90th percentile score. Even a perfect score of 180 often allows you to miss a question or two.

Here is a chart detailing some top law schools and the scores of their admitted students.

Rank*	School	25th–75th %ile LSAT* (Scaled)	25th–75th %ile UGPA*	25th–75th %ile LSAT** (Raw)
1	Yale University	170–175	3.79–3.97	67–71
6	New York University	166–171	3.65–3.89	63–68
10	Duke University	167–170	3.59–3.84	64–67
12	University of California–Berkeley	163–169	3.65–3.89	59–66
14	University of Texas–Austin	162–168	3.41–3.84	58–65
19	University of Southern California	162–166	3.56–3.85	58–63
26	Boston College	161–163	3.32–3.65	57–59
30	University of Wisconsin–Madison	156–163	3.30–3.72	50–59
41	University of Florida	156–161	3.33–3.77	50–57
51	Tulane University	155–160	3.22–3.62	48–56
65	Northeastern University	154–163	3.30–3.69	47–59
72	University of Cincinnati	153–158	3.24–3.76	45–53
86	University of Oregon	154–159	3.20–3.64	47–54

* *U.S. News & World Report*, 2018 Law School Rankings
** *Estimated score conversion*

Registration for and Administration of the LSAT

Historically the LSAT was administered by the Law School Admission Council (LSAC) four times each year. However, the LSAC has recently made changes to offer the LSAT more frequently.

LSAT FACTS

As of the time that this book went to press, LSAC offers nine adminstrations of the LSAT each testing year (June–May):

- June
- July
- September
- October
- November
- January
- February
- March
- April

Check **www.lsac.org/lsat/lsat-dates-deadlines-score-release-dates** for complete, accurate, and up-to-date test administration information.

For each administration, test takers are given multiple days and time slots from which to schedule their individual test. Dates and times may be different for tests administered outside the United States, Canada, and the Caribbean.

How do I register for the LSAT? Register for the LSAT online at www.lsac.org. Check the LSAC website for details on the procedures, deadlines, and fee schedules.

When should I register? Register as soon as you have chosen your test date. Registration is typically due about five weeks before Test Day. As of 2018, there is no longer a "Late Registration" period.

Can I change my test date or location? You can change your test dates (subject to an additional "change" fee) via the LSAC website. Timely changes of test date are not reported to schools; "no-shows," however, are reported.

What is the CAS? Upon signing up for the LSAT, you also need to register with the Credential Assembly Service (CAS) as part of the application process required by every ABA-approved law school. CAS receives your undergraduate transcripts and distributes a summary of your undergraduate performance, along with your letters of recommendation, evaluations, and LSAT score report to each of the law schools to which you apply. www.lsac.org lists the fees and sign-up details for CAS.

When are law schools' application deadlines? All law schools provide their application deadlines on their websites. Most schools require that the LSAT be taken no later than the spring for admission the following fall; a few schools may have winter deadlines, while others will accept a later LSAT score. Because most schools use a "rolling admissions" process, taking the test earlier is preferable; also, taking the test earlier gives the test taker a chance to repeat the LSAT prior to most application deadlines.

Can I repeat the LSAT? As of the September 2019 LSAT, test takers are limited to three administrations within any testing year (June–May), five administrations within any period of five testing years, and seven administrations in their lifetime. If you cancel your score after taking the test, that test administration still counts toward your total allowed administrations. Any test taker who achieves a score of 180 may not take another LSAT in her lifetime (but why would anyone want to?).

How do law schools view multiple LSAT scores? What is Score Preview? This varies from school to school. Very few schools now average multiple scores as was the policy in the past, but most consider *all scores from a five-year period* when evaluating applications. On your first-ever LSAT administration, you may (for a fee) select the Score Preview option, allowing you to cancel your score within five days of receiving your score with no reporting to law schools. All subsequent scores and cancellations will show on your report.

Accommodations

If you have a disability, you may be able to receive testing accommodations for the LSAT. Accommodations are granted for physical, learning, and cognitive impairments severe enough to qualify as a disability relevant to test taking. A wide variety of accommodations are available. You must be registered for a test date before you can request accommodations, however, so register early. Your application for accommodations will require you to submit a full evaluation by a qualified professional who specializes in your particular disability as well as score reports from previous standardized admissions tests (SAT, GRE, etc.), any records of accommodations you received for those tests, and any records of accommodations you received from your undergraduate institution(s). All of these things can take time to prepare and must be submitted several weeks before your test date, so start your process as early as possible. If for any reason you move test dates, you will be required to resubmit your application, so be sure to hold on to copies of your records just in case.

Be aware that qualifying for accommodations on the LSAT is generally harder than it is for undergraduate accommodations, though recent policy changes by the LSAC now treat prior accommodations on other standardized admissions tests as sufficient evidence to grant you similar accommodations for the LSAT. Keep in mind that LSAC grants accommodations only when documentation clearly demonstrates disability in an area directly related to test taking. If you are denied accommodations and feel the denial was in error, you can submit an appeal with additional documentation provided that there is enough time for the LSAC to process the appeal before Test Day.

If you are granted accommodations from LSAC, your score will not be flagged as accommodated on your official score report. Law schools are now unable to distinguish an accommodated score from a score received under standard testing conditions. Given that the greatest difficulty many test takers face on Test Day is the timing demands of the LSAT, you should seek out accommodations as soon as possible if you feel you are qualified for them.

If you believe you have a disability that requires testing accommodations, start by reviewing the accommodations page on the LSAC website to get the most updated information on deadlines and required forms. Remember that this process is subject to change by LSAC at any time, so it is crucial that you get the most recent information directly from LSAC. Full information about accommodated testing is available at **www.lsac.org/lsat/lsac-policy-accommodations-test-takers-disabilities**.

LSAT Study Skills

Imagine you want to get more physically fit, so you get yourself a gym membership. Will the gym membership be sufficient for you to accomplish your goals? Of course not. You actually have to use the gym. And, once you get started, you'll need to use proper technique to maximize your results. If you're not sure how to get started, if you're overwhelmed by all the machines you find, or if you try to take shortcuts and don't put in the appropriate time and effort, you may not see the results you were hoping for.

You see where this is going. Kaplan is your gym. We're your mental workout. You've already committed to using our materials. But just as showing up at the gym is not enough for you to improve physically, picking up this book is not enough to raise your score either. You need to work out. You've been provided with a suite of assets, both print and online. But it's up to you to use them. And here's the best part: The work of dozens of Kaplan teachers, researchers, and testing experts has gone into creating not only the expert analysis in this book but also the Smart Reports® analytics, online material, and study plans that accompany it.

The LSAT is entirely a skills-based test. It is coachable. It is practicable. And there are lots of ways to practice. Some methods are great; others not so much. Expect us to show you the best ways to practice. Expect us to show you the patterns of the test and how to tackle every question type. Expect us to show you how to manage every section.

Still, to reach your full potential on the LSAT, you're going to need to work hard. We will show you precisely what you need to do, but ultimately it's up to you to do it.

LSAT Strategy and the Three Levels of Practice

On test day, you'll be asked to deal with stringent testing policies and procedures, all while answering approximately 100 multiple-choice questions (of which 75 typically count toward your score). It's grueling and intense. And, depending on how the tech-check process and test administration go, the entire procedure may end up lasting close to three hours.

For those sections that count toward your score, taking control means increasing your speed only to the extent you can do so without sacrificing accuracy. Your goal is not to attempt as many questions as possible; your goal is to get as many questions correct as possible.

For many people, the single biggest challenge of the LSAT is time. If you had unlimited time to take this test, you'd likely perform quite well. But you don't. You have a strict 35 minutes to complete each section, and many students are not able to tackle every question in the time allotted. For you, this means three things:

- It's important that you learn not only how to answer the questions effectively but also how to answer them efficiently.
- It's important to approach each section strategically, knowing which questions to attack first and which questions to save for last.
- It's important that you prepare for the rigors of approximately three hours of testing. You'll want to maintain maximum focus from the first section through the last.

Achieving these goals won't happen overnight. Obviously you need to put in the work to get better. Specifically, though, you need to work on your foundational skills first, then improve on moving through the test more quickly and efficiently. To achieve your goals, use these three levels of practice: Mastery, Timing, and Endurance.

Mastery is about learning the patterns of the exam and how to identify them in new questions. You'll gain command of new efficient, effective techniques that you will repeatedly practice on specific drills as well as on individual question types. You'll study the answers and explanations to learn how the testmaker builds questions and answer choices. You'll identify why right answers are right and why wrong answers are wrong. What traps do you consistently fall into? How do you avoid them? That's precisely what Mastery practice is for.

Once you've learned the skills individually, it's time to try full-length section practice, or ***Timing***. Taking the LSAT can seem like a marathon, but it's really a series of sprints—four 35-minute tests. Section management—how to recognize and apply the patterns you've learned efficiently to maximize the number of questions you get correct—is what Timing practice teaches you to do.

And finally, there's ***Endurance***. Can you maintain your ability to identify and apply these patterns efficiently throughout the whole exam? Some students discover that they are great at focusing for two sections but struggle through the last section or two of the test. Taking practice tests will help you build your stamina. But a word of warning: the single biggest trap students fall into as they prepare for the LSAT is taking test after test after test.

Think about it like learning a musical instrument. If you're trying to learn the piano, do you schedule a piano recital every other day? No, of course not. It's the piano *practice* that allows you to improve. While full-length tests are important, they should be spaced out and taken only when you're sure you've made some improvement through your Mastery and Timing practice.

By approaching your preparation this way—starting with Mastery, layering in Timing, and then adding in Endurance—you'll be fully and properly prepared by Test Day.

Keeping Time on the LSAT

One of the most common concerns heard about the LSAT is "If I only had more time, I would be able to get through all the Games/Reading Comp passages/Logical Reasoning questions." Though it may seem unfortunate that you only have 35 minutes for each section, keep in mind that this timing constraint is deliberate. You are not alone in thinking that it's difficult to get through the sections in the given time. But the timing constraint isn't necessarily a hindrance to success; precisely *because* concerns about timing are so universal, you can get a big leg up on your competition by understanding how to maximize your performance in those 35 minutes.

Initially, your goal when working on Mastery questions is to understand and use Kaplan Methods while becoming more familiar with question types and gaining greater competency. Once a degree of mastery has been attained, it is time to turn your attention to completing a section within the 35-minute time period.

On test day, you have an on-screen timer that counts down from 35 minutes in each section. You can hide the timer until five minutes remain in the section. At that point, a pop-up appears with your 5-minute warning and you won't be able to proceed until you dismiss it. From that point on, you cannot hide the on-screen timer. When you practice with LSAC materials using their digital interface, the on-screen timer will work in the same way as it does on Test Day.

Some students may still find it convenient to do some of their timed practice using paper LSAC PrepTests and sections. That's great. All the questions and sections on the paper tests continue to provide excellent, test-like material. There is one caveat: When using paper tests, you will need to time yourself using a watch or timer.

LSAT Attitude

In the succeeding chapters, we will arm you with the tools you need—both content and strategy—to do well on the LSAT. But you must wield this LSAT arsenal with the right spirit. This involves taking a certain stance toward the entire test.

Those who approach the LSAT as an obstacle and rail against the necessity of taking it don't fare as well as those who see the LSAT as an opportunity. Think about it: this is your chance to show law schools your proficiency in the Core Skills. A great LSAT score will distinguish your application from those of your competition.

- Look at the LSAT as a challenge but try not to obsess over it; you certainly don't want to psych yourself out of the game.
- Remember that the LSAT is important, but this one test will not single-handedly determine the outcome of your life.
- Try to have fun with the test. Learning how to unlock the test's patterns and to approach its content in the way the testmaker rewards can be very satisfying, and the skills you'll acquire will benefit you in law school and your career.

Confidence

Confidence in your ability leads to quick, sure answers and a sense of well-being that translates into more points. Confidence feeds on itself; unfortunately, so does self-doubt. If you lack confidence you end up reading sentences and answer choices two, three, or four times, until you confuse yourself and get off track. This leads to timing difficulties that perpetuate a downward spiral of anxiety, rushing, and poor performance.

If you subscribe to the proper LSAT mindset, however, you'll gear all of your practice toward taking control of the test. When you've achieved that goal—armed with the principles, techniques, strategies, and methods Kaplan has to offer—you'll be ready to face the LSAT with confidence.

Stamina

The LSAT is a grueling experience, and some test takers simply run out of gas before it's over. To avoid this, take full-length practice tests in the weeks before the test. That way, four sections will seem like a breeze (well, maybe not a breeze, but at least not a hurricane). On the other hand, don't just rush from one practice test right into another. Learn what you can from your review of each test, then work on your weaknesses and build your strengths before tackling another full-length test. You should plan on spending just as much time to review your practice tests as you did to take them.

Managing Stress

Take Control. Research shows that if you don't have a sense of control over what's happening in your life, you can easily end up feeling helpless and hopeless. Try to identify the sources of the stress you feel. Which of these can you do something about?

Set Realistic Goals. Facing your problem areas gives you some distinct advantages. What do you want to accomplish in the time remaining? Make a list of realistic goals. You can't help but feel more confident when you know you're actively improving your chances of earning a higher test score.

Acknowledge Your Strengths. Make a list of your strengths that will help you do well on the test. Many students are experts at listing which aspects of the test they struggle with. But a student who also has knowledge of her ever-expanding list of strengths will have more confidence and a better perspective on what to target to improve.

Get Exercise and Eat Well. Whether it is jogging, biking, yoga, or a pickup basketball game, physical exercise stimulates your mind and body and improves your ability to think and concentrate. Likewise, good nutrition helps you focus and think clearly. A surprising number of students fall out of good habits in these areas, ironically because they're spending so much time preparing for the test.

Keep Breathing. Conscious attention to breathing is an excellent way to manage stress. Most of the people who get into trouble during tests take shallow breaths. They breathe using only their upper chests and shoulder muscles and may even hold their breath for long periods of time. Breathe deeply in a slow, relaxed manner.

Stretch. If you find yourself getting spaced out or burned out as you're studying for or taking the test, stop for a brief moment and stretch. Stretching will help to refresh you and refocus your thoughts.

Imagine Yourself Succeeding. If you are continually filled with self-doubt about the test, it will be difficult to overcome those feelings and perform well on the test. Although preparing for the test can take many weeks or months of extensive practice, you must be able to visualize that you will gain confidence and take control of the test. Confidence gained through preparation will lead to better performance. Do not wait for it to occur the other way around.

The LSAT Mindset

You may have heard something about a popular concept known as "Growth Mindset." It has a great deal of applicability to any challenge that seems daunting—and the LSAT can certainly seem daunting.

The idea, coined by noted researcher Dr. Carol Dweck and promoted by many others, is that how you feel about the likelihood of success has a lot to do with whether success will in fact take place. Specifically, if you believe that success (in whatever endeavor) is based on factors over which you have no control—like I.Q., or schooling, or social class, or luck—you're said to have a *fixed mindset.* People with a fixed mindset about an activity tend to get discouraged more quickly and give up sooner, when early bad results just confirm the notion that "I can't do this."

On the other hand, those with a *growth mindset* firmly believe that it's effort, training, and learning that always make the big difference. And in study after study, those with a growth mindset tend to keep working hard, even in the face of setbacks. They "hang in there" past the pain points, and eventually see breakthroughs. Talent, they believe (and Dr. Dweck confirms), can be acquired, *if* your attitudes allow talent to grow.

Can you think of instances in your life when you said "I can't do this" and were proven right? And other times when you firmly believed in your success, and success came to pass? Dr. Dweck is the first to point out that all of us hold a mix of fixed and growth attitudes, a fact that would be foolish to deny. What we have to do—and this gets us back to the LSAT—is stay very, very watchful of our fixed-mindset thoughts and deeds, so we can move closer to a growth mindset in what we think and do.

Here are some tactics that can help foster a growth mindset in your logic games work:

- Never say, "I can't do these questions/games/passages." It's okay to say, "I can't do questions/games/passages *yet.*"
- Always seek out feedback on your work. If the question or section went well, how could it have gone better? If you crashed and burned, where did you go wrong, and is there another approach you could've taken? (Kaplan's answer explanations are a fantastic, 24/7 source of feedback and insights, and they're full of positive messaging, too.)
- The basic questions and games lay the groundwork for the tougher ones, so don't pooh-pooh your success on lower-difficulty material. "Work hard on the fundamentals," Dr. Dweck advises, echoing famous basketball coach John Wooden. Incidentally, Dr. Dweck warns against the idea of "the mistake-free game" promoted by coach Bobby Knight. Your goal, she says, shouldn't be mistake-free performance, but "full preparation and full effort."
- Never credit "your smarts" (whatever *that* means!) with creating the right sketch, interpreting a rule correctly, or getting a question right. And of course "I'm not smart enough" isn't the reason you had a setback. Your *effort* earns you success, and more (or different) *effort* will overcome today's setbacks and lead to learning and improvement over time. Always give yourself an A for Effort.

Shifting to a growth mindset isn't easy, and Carol Dweck herself reminds us that "the path to a growth mindset is a journey, not a proclamation." Instead of announcing, to others or to yourself, that you're going to "Go Growth," just start practicing—and reacting to practice—with these ideas in mind. You may be amazed at how your point of view, and your performance, start to change.

In The LSAT Channel Spotlight feature that follows, you'll learn some of the secrets for successful preparation that Kaplan's top faculty members impart to their students. In the video that accompanies the Spotlight you'll see and hear from these outstanding coaches and mentors.

The LSAT Channel Spotlight

Secrets of Logic Games Preparation

by The LSAT Channel Faculty

Watch the video lesson for this Spotlight in your online Study Plan.

Students who come to *The LSAT Channel* get to hear from some of Kaplan's most experienced and highly rated LSAT faculty. When it comes to logic games, the message they hear most clearly is: Kaplan knows logic games—inside out, forward and backward—and we've got the method and strategies that will (with practice) help you get them, too. Each of these coaches and mentors has his or her own special insights. In the video that accompanies this Spotlight, you'll meet The LSAT Channel faculty, and hear what each of them tells students at the beginning of their logic games prep. Here are a few of the themes they hit upon:

You Do Logic Games All the Time

If you've ever ranked the *Star Wars* movies from best to worst, chosen teams for a pick-up basketball game, or separated clothes into laundry and dry cleaning, you've done a logic game. While it may be true that you've never before had to answer questions quite like these *on a test*, you engage in logic games tasks every day. Logic games present you with small, real-world puzzles that may, at first, seem abstract or technical, but are really quite practical. And, you *can* do them.

There Is Always Enough Information to Answer Every Question

There are two criteria for a good game—not just for logic games, but even games we play with friends or against the computer—they need to be challenging, and they need to be fair. If we're honest, challenging games are more fun. We quickly lose interest in puzzles that are too easy to solve, or in games we always win. Logic games are challenging, but always fair. Before a game appears on an official LSAT, it has been tested on thousands of test takers to make sure it has all of the information needed to answer every question. You'll find the confidence that you can extract that information every time.

Patience Can Make You Faster

The Logic Games section gives you 35 minutes for four games. That means you have approximately 8½ minutes for each game and its accompanying questions. The time pressure *is* real, but the best response to that pressure is counterintuitive. To increase your efficiency on logic games, you need patience. LSAT experts know that creating a thorough, accurate setup and sketch depicting all of the game's rules and deductions will allow them to get through the questions much more quickly. For some games, the setup may be so complete that you can answer the questions in a matter of a few seconds apiece.

Logic Games "Feel" Harder than They Really Are

Fact-based, data-driven analysis is at the heart of Kaplan's approach to LSAT preparation. When it comes to logic games, the data reveals a big lesson: Test takers' perception of logic games is out of line with their performance. For many years now, Kaplan has surveyed LSAT test takers after every exam, and, no surprise, they consistently rate Logic Games as the hardest section on the test.

Percent of Test Takers Who Said Each Section Was the Hardest, 2014–18

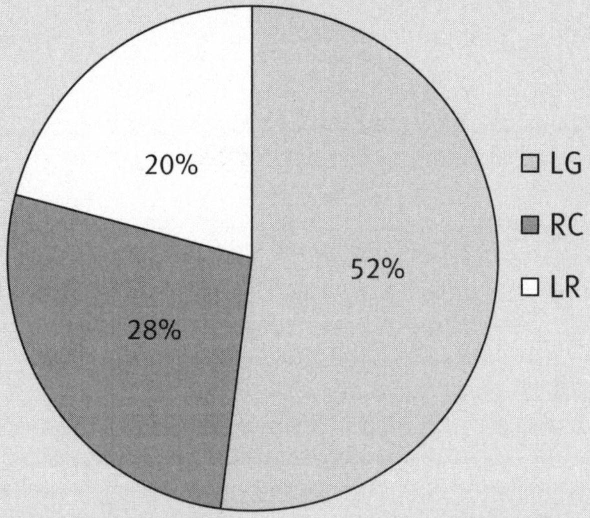

At Kaplan, we also record the actual results that students receive when they take official LSAC tests for practice. The students' performance tells a different story. On most LSATs, the Logic Games section is not noticeably harder than the other sections, and on many tests, it's actually the easiest section overall.

Percent Incorrect by Section, 2014–18

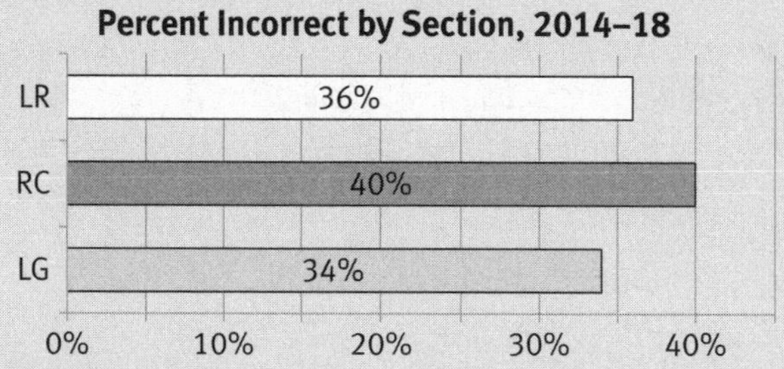

Experienced LSAT instructors know that students often make their biggest improvements in the Logic Games section. The bottom line: Don't let logic games' reputation intimidate you. Don't listen to the chatter. You, like thousands of successful students before you, can learn to master this section of the LSAT.

Small Improvements Produce Big Results

You saw this demonstrated earlier, in the section about LSAT scoring. There are only 101 questions on the typical LSAT test, and given that the LSAT is scored on a curve, adding just five more correct answers to your score can move you past 10 percent of test takers. Depending on your starting score, 10 additional correct answers could move your score past a quarter of all law school applicants. That means the improvements you make in just the Logic Games section can have an enormous impact on your law school application.

The LSAT Channel

Kaplan launched *The LSAT Channel* in 2015 to bring nightly live instruction from our most highly rated LSAT teachers to every student enrolled in a comprehensive LSAT prep course. Since then, students all over the country (and the world) have had access to over 100 unique hours of instruction for every testing cycle. The *LSAT Channel* faculty is constantly creating new lessons on special topics to provide their strategic insights to ambitious test takers.

Now, The *LSAT Channel* instructors have developed several Spotlight lessons exclusively for *Logic Games Prep*. Whenever you see one of these Spotlight features in the book, you'll not only get the expertise provided on the page, but also have a chance to practice the strategies explained there, and to learn directly from the instructors through the videos in your online Study Plan.

Take a few minutes to meet the faculty, here and in the accompanying video. They'll motivate you and set you on the path to logic games success. Ready to get started?

JEFF BOUDREAU

"I love teaching logic games because once you understand them, they're actually fun, and if studying for the LSAT can be enjoyable, getting the score you want is a whole lot easier."

DESCRIBES TEACHING STYLE AS: Excited, fun-loving, caring

BOBBY GAUTAM

"Doing games is relaxing and addicting. Teaching them is arguably even more fun because once students see the moves and patterns, the games virtually teach themselves, and engagement is high."

DESCRIBES TEACHING STYLE AS: Clear, compassionate, lively, humorous, passionate

HANNAH GIST

"Logic Games are based on patterns: the same things show up over and over. This means you can memorize the common tricks to stay one step ahead of the LSAT. The payoff from practicing and teaching Logic Games is huge!"

DESCRIBES TEACHING STYLE AS: Patient, energetic, encouraging, accessible, proficient

GENE SUHIR

"I love teaching logic games because I love seeing students have a 'lightbulb' moment when they realize that one or two key deductions unlock the whole game for them! And then students can really bust through those questions and collect the rewards over and over again when they spot those patterns!"

DESCRIBES TEACHING STYLE AS: Energetic, passionate, entertaining, coherent

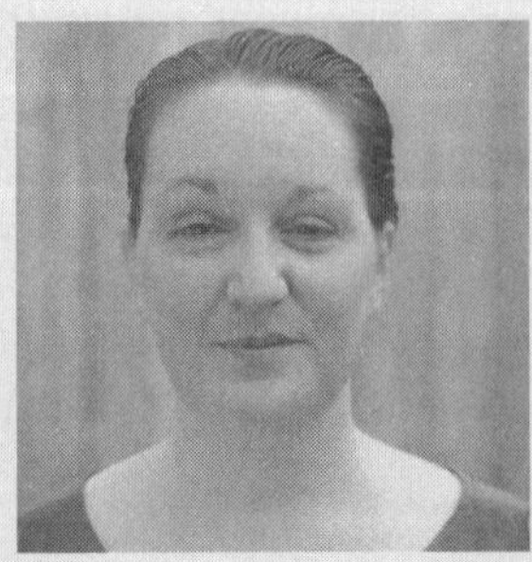

MELANIE TRIEBEL

"Logic games are fun; after all, they're games! The key to learning to love them is understanding how predictable they are. The test has us play similar games over and over. Just like any other game, the more times you play, the more you become a master."

DESCRIBES TEACHING STYLE AS: Enthusiastic, simplified, geeky, detailed

PART ONE

Logic Games Method and Strategy

CHAPTER 1

The Logic Games Method

In the Logic Games section of the LSAT, your goal—as it is throughout the test—is to answer the questions correctly. That statement may seem absurdly obvious, but it is also easy to overlook. As you work through this book, you'll encounter a variety of game types, numerous patterns and sketches that reflect them, rules for formal logic, and detailed strategies for handling everything you'll encounter in this section of the test. Don't lose sight of the real goal: getting the questions right.

With that in mind, take a look at a typical LSAT Logic Games question.

---

4. If exactly three of the trucks are green, then which one of the following trucks must be green?

   (A) S

   (B) T

   (C) U

   (D) W

   (E) Z

PrepTest37 Sec3 Q9

Here's another absurdly obvious statement: You cannot answer this question, at least not without more information. All Logic Games questions ask you about what must, can, or cannot be true given a particular situation and the rules and restrictions surrounding it. Here, you lack the context—what's all this about trucks and colors?—to make sense of the situation.

Pulling this question out from the rest of the game highlights a key point of this chapter: The background information and rules, and sketches you'll make to take control of them, are all there to provide the context that allows you to answer the questions. Indeed, when you've learned to effectively interpret and set up logic games, you'll discover that answering at least some of the questions is a snap, and you'll gain the confidence of knowing that you always have the information you need to find the correct answer to every question.

Now, take a look at that question within the context of the full game. Notice that the question is the fourth one in the game's question set. To the LSAT expert, the questions are simply applications of the situation, rules, and restrictions described in the opening scenario. The rest of this chapter will show you the method that experts use to turn that information into a sketch or diagram that they apply to answer all of the questions confidently and efficiently.

Analysis: This paragraph sets out the task. It defines the players or entities for which you must account, tells you what to do with them—in this case, to put the entities in order and to assign them certain attributes (colors)—and provides rules and limitations on how the entities can be arranged. This "setup" always contains all of the information you need to answer every question.

Questions 1–6

In a single day, exactly seven trucks—S, T, U, W, X, Y, and Z—are the only arrivals at a warehouse. No truck arrives at the same time as any other truck, and no truck arrives more than once that day. Each truck is either green or red (but not both). The following conditions apply:

No two consecutive arrivals are red.

Y arrives at some time before both T and W.

Exactly two of the trucks that arrive before Y are red.

S is the sixth arrival.

Z arrives at some time before U.

4. If exactly three of the trucks are green, then which one of the following trucks must be green?

(A) S
(B) T
(C) U
(D) W
(E) Z

PrepTest37 Sec3 Qs 6–11

Analysis: All of the questions reward an understanding of what is and is not possible given the game's action and restrictions. In one way or another, they all ask you to distinguish what must be true from what could be false or what must be false from what could be true. This game's fourth question presents a hypothetical variation within the game and asks for what must be true under those conditions.

The analyses on this page reflect what the LSAT expert sees at a glance. Over the remainder of this chapter, you'll learn the 5-step method that the expert uses to translate the game's information into correct answers.

Here are the remaining questions accompanying the logic game setup on the preceding page. Try all of the questions on your own before continuing through the rest of this chapter.

1. Which one of the following could be the order, from first to last, in which the trucks arrive?

(A) X, Z, U, Y, W, S, T
(B) X, Y, Z, U, W, S, T
(C) Z, W, U, T, Y, S, X
(D) Z, U, T, Y, W, S, X
(E) U, Z, Y, T, S, W, X

2. For which one of the following pairs of trucks is it the case that they CANNOT both be red?

(A) S and X
(B) T and S
(C) U and W
(D) W and T
(E) X and Z

3. If X is the third arrival, then which one of the following trucks must be green?

(A) S
(B) T
(C) U
(D) W
(E) Z

5. For exactly how many of the seven trucks can one determine exactly how many trucks arrived before it?

(A) one
(B) two
(C) three
(D) four
(E) five

6. Which one of the following pairs of trucks CANNOT arrive consecutively at the warehouse?

(A) U and Y
(B) X and Y
(C) Y and T
(D) Y and W
(E) Y and Z

LEARNING OBJECTIVES

In this chapter, you'll learn to

- List the steps of the Kaplan Logic Games Method and articulate the purpose of each step.

Prepare

The method you'll learn in this chapter provides an effective approach to all logic games you will encounter on the LSAT. Learning and practicing the method will make you efficient with your time as you manage all of the game's information, and confident as you apply that information to correctly answer the questions.

THE KAPLAN LOGIC GAMES METHOD

Step 1: Overview
Step 2: Sketch
Step 3: Rules
Step 4: Deductions
Step 5: Questions

In Chapters 2 through 4, we'll go into more detail about these steps and the skills associated with each of them. For now, your task is simply to learn them, and to learn what each step accomplishes as an LSAT expert uses them to tackle a logic game.

First, we'll walk you through an expert's step-by-step application of the Logic Games Method to the game you just saw. Then, you'll practice on another game. After that, you'll assess your mastery of the steps in the method.

Step 1: Overview

Before you can accomplish anything in a logic game, you need to understand your assignment, your *task*, if you will. The LSAT describes game scenarios as small, well defined, real-world jobs. In the next few chapters, for example, you will be asked to arrange some dresses in a closet with numbered hangers, divide a group of boaters into two boats, and match models of cars to the standard features they offer. In any case, you should always take a few seconds to make sure you understand the task. Doing so allows you to make a useful, accurate sketch in which to record the specific details and to account for all of the game's moving parts.

To make the overview process as efficient as possible, LSAT experts ask four questions—the SEAL questions—while conducting the Overview step.

STEP 1: OVERVIEW—THE SEAL QUESTIONS

Situation—What is the real-world scenario being described? What is the deliverable information—an ordered list, a calendar, a chart showing what's matched up?

Entities—Who or what are the "moving parts," the people or things I'm trying to sequence, select, distribute, or match up?

Action—What is the specific action—sequencing, selection, distribution, matching (or a combination of those)—that I'm performing on the entities?

Limitations—Does the game state parameters (e.g., "select four of seven" or "sequence the entities one per day") that restrict how I will set up or sketch the game?

Here's how an LSAT expert might answer the SEAL questions in the Truck Arrivals game.

LSAT Question		Analysis
In a single day, exactly seven trucks—S, T, U, W, X, Y, and Z—are the only arrivals at a warehouse. No truck arrives at the same time as any other truck, and no truck arrives more than once that day. Each truck is either green or red (but not both). The following conditions apply: *PrepTest37 Sec3 Qs 6–11*	→	**Step 1: Overview** What is the game's **situation**? Trucks are arriving in a particular order, and each truck is either red or green. What **entities** are involved in this game? The trucks—S, T, U, W, X, Y, and Z. What is/are this game's **action**(s)? Sequencing (the order in which the trucks arrive) and Matching (the color of each truck). Are there any **limitations** on this game's entities or action? The trucks arrive one at a time, and each is only one color.

With practice, you'll be able to complete an Overview in a few seconds. Indeed, the expert's internal monologue probably sounds more like this.

LSAT Question		Analysis
In a single day, exactly seven trucks—S, T, U, W, X, Y, and Z—are the only arrivals at a warehouse. No truck arrives at the same time as any other truck, and no truck arrives more than once that day. Each truck is either green or red (but not both). The following conditions apply: *PrepTest37 Sec3 Qs 6–11*	→	This is a Sequencing/Matching Hybrid. Seven trucks arrive one at a time, and each is either green or red.

The LSAT expert then translates that simple description into a powerful tool: the game's sketch.

Step 2: Sketch

The actual picture of the game that you draw on your scratch paper—your Sketch—is the result of the clear mental picture you develop in the Overview. Logic games are nearly impossible if you try to keep all of the information in your head. A strong sketch is simple, easy to read, and often based on something familiar: If a game's action involves scheduling, for example, your sketch may mimic a calendar, or if the game involves putting people or items into different groups, your sketch might be a table.

STEP 2: SKETCH

Create a sketch that depicts the game's action(s) and limitations.

Aim for a sketch that is easy to read, quick to replicate, and able to account for what is certain and uncertain based on the game's rules.

For the Truck Arrivals game, the LSAT expert would prepare something like this.

In a single day, exactly seven trucks—S, T, U, W, X, Y, and Z—are the only arrivals at a warehouse. No truck arrives at the same time as any other truck, and no truck arrives more than once that day. Each truck is either green or red (but not both). The following conditions apply:

PrepTest37 Sec3 Qs 6–11

Step 1:
This is a Sequencing/Matching Hybrid. Seven trucks arrive one at a time, and each is either green or red.

Step 2: Sketch

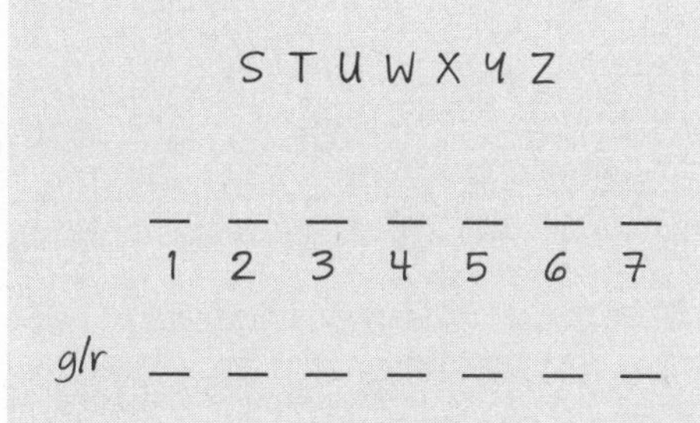

You'll learn to think of this as a standard sketch pattern for Sequencing-Matching Hybrid games. Here, the top line of dashes allows you to keep track of information about the order in which the trucks arrive while the bottom line is where you can record each truck's color. You'll soon see that certain game actions produce similar sketches time after time, resulting in some time-saving patterns. Don't become complacent about sketching, however. A useful sketch must reflect the game's task, and sometimes you'll need to render unique twists on standard sketch patterns.

Step 3: Rules

Once you have the basic framework of your sketch, you're ready to record the game's rules. The rules are always listed under the game's opening paragraph, and they're indented so that they're easy to distinguish from the background scenario.

STEP 3: RULES

- Whenever possible, add information directly into your Sketch framework.
- If you cannot build the rule directly into the Sketch framework, make a shorthand graphical representation of it below or beside the framework.
- Write out the rules in a way that matches the style and conventions of the Sketch framework.
- Consider both the positive and negative implications of the rule.
- Write similar rules consistently, the same way from game to game.

Here's the LSAT expert's depiction of the rules in the Truck Arrivals game. Take a moment to review them and match up each new diagram to its corresponding rule.

In a single day, exactly seven trucks—S, T, U, W, X, Y, and Z—are the only arrivals at a warehouse. No truck arrives at the same time as any other truck, and no truck arrives more than once that day. Each truck is either green or red (but not both). The following conditions apply:

No two consecutive arrivals are red.
Y arrives at some time before both T and W.
Exactly two of the trucks that arrive before Y are red.
S is the sixth arrival.
Z arrives at some time before U.

PrepTest37 Sec3 Qs 6–11

Steps 1–3

S T U W X Y Z

					S	
1	2	3	4	5	6	7

g/r _ _ _ _ _ _ _

never [r r]

Y ... T
Y ... W

r ... r ... Y

Z ... U

You'll learn much more about depicting rules in Chapter 3. For now, a few of the things that the LSAT expert has done are worth noting. 1) Rule 4 is built directly into the sketch; Truck S will never move. 2) The note "Never" followed by the box around the two Rs indicates Rule 1: Red trucks never arrive consecutively. 3) Rules 2 and 3 both involve Truck Y, so the expert has depicted them in relationship to one another.

LOGIC GAMES STRATEGY

Never make assumptions in logic games. Any restrictions must be explicitly stated, or deduced from the stated rules.

In the Truck Arrivals game, you are told that red trucks never arrive consecutively. That does not mean that green trucks cannot arrive consecutively. Some test takers want to assume that each arrival is a different color than the one before it, but you would need more information to reach that conclusion.

Having the rules depicted as a part of the overall sketch is a big step toward answering a game's questions efficiently and effectively, but it is the next step that can make the biggest difference.

Step 4: Deductions

This is the step that most untrained test takers overlook. Even those who instinctively understand the value of making a sketch and depicting the rules often fail to take the time to determine what must be true or must be false beyond what the game's rules explicitly state.

An LSAT expert, however, knows that in most games, it is possible to combine rules (or to combine rules with the game's overall limitations) in ways that reveal greater certainty within the game. As you practice, you'll start to make valuable deductions even as you are working through the rules. For now, though, be systematic and rigorous in this step to train yourself to get all of a game's potential deductions.

The vast majority of deductions come from one of five patterns, easily remembered with the mnemonic BLEND. Use this as a checklist, not a series of steps. You don't need to look for Blocks of Entities first, necessarily, but you don't want to miss any blocks that may produce additional information.

STEP 4: DEDUCTIONS

Blocks of Entities—two or more players that are always grouped together

Limited Options—rules or restrictions that limit the overall setup to one or the other of two acceptable arrangements

Established Entities—a player locked into a specific space or group

Number Restrictions—rules or limitations that provide guidance about the number of entities assigned to a group or space

Duplications—entities that appear in two or more rules and allow the rules to be combined

To make deductions as efficiently as possible, an LSAT expert begins by taking note of the entities that are most restricted or constrained by the rules. Note that Truck S is an Established Entity stuck in space 6. Which other entity is most constrained by the rules in the Truck Arrivals game? Examining the sketch, an LSAT expert immediately identifies Truck Y as an important entity in this game. Truck Y is a perfect example of a Duplication (the fifth item in the BLEND checklist).

LSAT Question

In a single day, exactly seven trucks—S, T, U, W, X, Y, and Z—are the only arrivals at a warehouse. No truck arrives at the same time as any other truck, and no truck arrives more than once that day. Each truck is either green or red (but not both). The following conditions apply:

> No two consecutive arrivals are red.
>
> Y arrives at some time before both T and W.
>
> Exactly two of the trucks that arrive before Y are red.
>
> S is the sixth arrival.
>
> Z arrives at some time before U.

PrepTest37 Sec3 Qs 6–11

Steps 1–3:

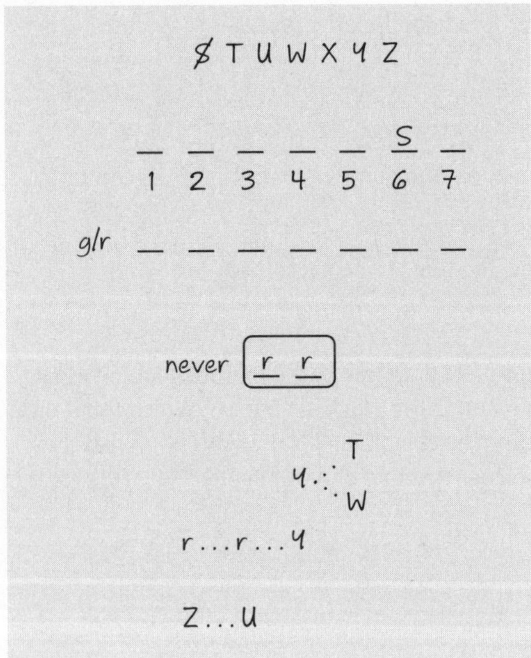

Deductions

Step 4: Truck Y appears in both Rule 2 and Rule 3, and as a result, it is constrained by two red trucks that must come before it and Trucks T and W that must come after it. Because of Rule 1, the two red trucks that come before Truck Y must be separated by at least one green truck: r-g-r . . . Y. Thus, the earliest slot in which Truck Y can appear is slot 4. Likewise, because Truck Y must be followed by Trucks T and W, and because Rule 4 places Truck S in slot 6, the latest Truck Y can appear is also slot 4.

S T U W X Y Z

_ _ _ Y T/W S W/T
1 2 3 4 5 6 7

g/r r g r _ _ _ _

Because of Rule 1, the truck arriving in slot 4 (you now know that this is Truck Y) must be green.

S T U W X Y Z

_ _ _ Y T/W S W/T
1 2 3 4 5 6 7

g/r r g r g _ _ _

The only undecided arrivals are in slots 1, 2, and 3. Those must be Trucks Z and U, in that order (Rule 5) and Truck X (the unrestricted, or *floater*, entity in this game). In other words, slots 1–3 could be X-Z-U, Z-X-U, or Z-U-X.

S T U W X Y Z

X

_ _ _ Y T/W S W/T
1 2 3 4 5 6 7

g/r r g r g _ _ _

never r r Z...U

We'll refer to the final sketch, with all of the deductions in place, as the Master Sketch. With the Master Sketch as a point of reference, the LSAT expert can now expect to make relatively short work of the questions.

Step 5: Questions

The first four steps of the Logic Games Method—conducting the Overview, making a useful Sketch, depicting the Rules, and making the available Deductions—are necessary, but not sufficient to success in the Logic Games section. LSAT experts know that the ultimate goal is to answer the question not just correctly, but also quickly. Remember that you have about 8 ½ minutes per game on test day. To get through all of the questions in that amount of time, you'll have to leverage the Master Sketch to save time. Don't be surprised if you spend three or four minutes setting up the game and making the deductions. You'll find that you can answer the questions much more quickly and confidently with all of that work clearly laid out on the page.

STEP 5: QUESTIONS

Be able to characterize both correct and incorrect answers.

Know the different question types and how to approach each one.

Don't hesitate to draw a new sketch for New-"If" questions.

Use deductions and previous work to eliminate answers quickly.

Here's how an LSAT expert would manage each of the questions in the Truck Arrivals game.

Partial Acceptability Question

The majority of logic games open with an Acceptability question. The correct answer is the one that breaks none of the rules. All four of the wrong answers violate at least one of the game's rules or limitations. The expert's strategy is simple, and remarkably efficient: Apply the rules, one by one, to the answer choices, and eliminate answer choices that violate the rule.

In a single day, exactly seven trucks—S, T, U, W, X, Y, and Z—are the only arrivals at a warehouse. No truck arrives at the same time as any other truck, and no truck arrives more than once that day. Each truck is either green or red (but not both). The following conditions apply:

No two consecutive arrivals are red.

Y arrives at some time before both T and W.

Exactly two of the trucks that arrive before Y are red.

S is the sixth arrival.

Z arrives at some time before U.

PrepTest37 Sec3 Q6

Steps 1–4:

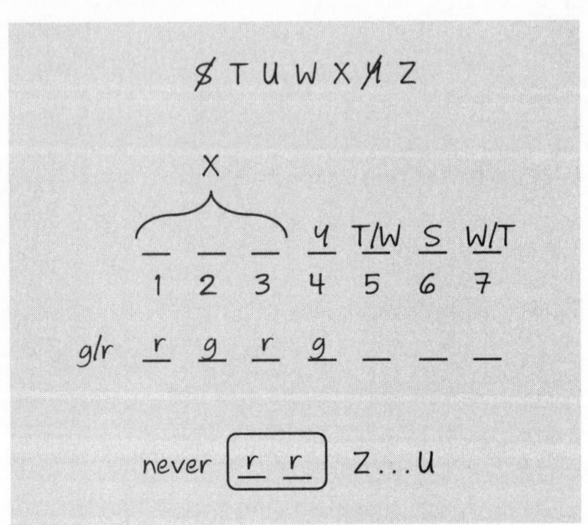

Step 5: An Acceptability question: Each wrong answer will violate one or more rules so use the rules to eliminate incorrect choices.

1. Which one of the following could be the order, from first to last, in which the trucks arrive?

   (A) X, Z, U, Y, W, S, T

   (B) X, Y, Z, U, W, S, T

   (C) Z, W, U, T, Y, S, X

   (D) Z, U, T, Y, W, S, X

   (E) U, Z, Y, T, S, W, X

Step 5 (cont.): (A) is correct. This choice abides by all of the rules. The answer choices show only the trucks, not their colors, so Rule 1 is of no help in this question. Rule 2 knocks out two answer choices: (C) and (D), in which either W or T appears earlier than Y. Strike those two choices. Rule 3 knocks out choice (B), where Y is placed too early to have two red trucks precede it in the sequence. Rule 4 eliminates choice (E), where S is fifth, not sixth in order.

Wrong answers: (B) Violates Rule 3 by placing Truck Y too early in the sequence. (C) Violates Rule 2 by placing Trucks W and T earlier in the sequence than Truck Y. (D) Violates Rule 2 by placing Truck T earlier in the sequence than Truck Y. (E) Violates Rule 4 by placing S fifth instead of sixth in the sequence.

By approaching Acceptability questions this way—using the rules to eliminate answer choices that violate them—LSAT experts usually answer them in a matter of seconds. Trying to tackle these questions the other way around—testing each answer choice against the rules—is inefficient. You may wind up going back and forth between the rules several times before finding out which rule it violates, or finding out that it happens to be the answer that does not violate any of the rules.

Must Be False Question

Sometimes, the testmaker will ask you straight out, "Which one of the following must be false?" A question like this—which asks for an impossible situation within the game's context—is just a variation on that. To tackle these questions, the LSAT expert simply consults the Master Sketch containing all of the rules and deductions.

In a single day, exactly seven trucks—S, T, U, W, X, Y, and Z—are the only arrivals at a warehouse. No truck arrives at the same time as any other truck, and no truck arrives more than once that day. Each truck is either green or red (but not both). The following conditions apply:

No two consecutive arrivals are red.
Y arrives at some time before both T and W.
Exactly two of the trucks that arrive before Y are red.
S is the sixth arrival.
Z arrives at some time before U.

PrepTest37 Sec3 Q7

Steps 1–4:

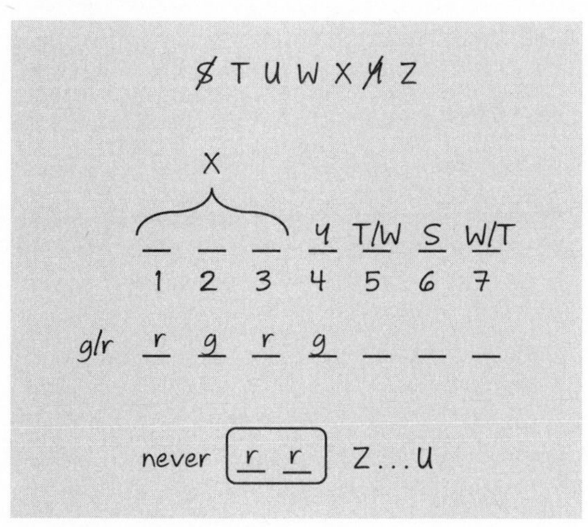

Step 5: A Must-Be-False question: Consult the Master Sketch to evaluate the answer choices.

2. For which one of the following pairs of trucks is it the case that they CANNOT both be red?

(A) S and X
(B) T and S
(C) U and W
(D) W and T
(E) X and Z

Step 5 (cont.): The trucks in the correct answer cannot both be red. The trucks in the wrong answers *could* both be red.
(B) is correct; T and S will be in consecutive slots (whether T is fifth or seventh). Rule 1 prevents consecutive trucks from both being red. T and S *cannot* both be red.

Wrong answers: (A) S could be red if the trucks in slots 5 and 7 are green, and X could be in slot 1 or 3. Both could be red. (C) W could be red in either the fifth or seventh slot, as long as slot 6 is green, and U could be in slot 3. Both could be red. (D) Slots 5 and 7 could both be red, as long as slot 6 is green. Both could be red. (E) Z could be in slot 1 and X could be in slot 3. Both could be red.

Notice how the expert characterized both the correct *and* the incorrect answer choices before evaluating the answer choices. It may be easier for you to spot answers in which both trucks can be red. Knowing that this characterizes a wrong answer makes working through the choices much faster.

LOGIC GAMES STRATEGY

Once you are certain of the correct answer, you do not need to evaluate the remaining choices.

If an LSAT expert evaluated the answer choices for Question 2 in order, starting with (A), she could move on to the next question after testing (B). She would not have to check (C), (D), or (E) provided that she is certain of the criteria for the correct answer.

Every question has one demonstrably correct answer and four demonstrably incorrect answers. Early on in your practice, it's probably worth the time to check every answer choice to develop your evaluative skills. As you gain familiarity and confidence, you will be able to take advantage of time-saving tips like this one.

New-"If"/Must Be True Question

This next question is a New-"If" question. The LSAT expert knows to redraw the Master Sketch, adding the question's new stipulation ("X is the third arrival"), and making any additional deductions triggered by the new information. The correct answer here will name a truck that must be green under this question's new stipulation.

Step 5: A New-"If" question: Copy the Master Sketch, add the new condition, make all available deductions, and use the resulting sketch to evaluate the answer choices.

In a single day, exactly seven trucks—S, T, U, W, X, Y, and Z—are the only arrivals at a warehouse. No truck arrives at the same time as any other truck, and no truck arrives more than once that day. Each truck is either green or red (but not both). The following conditions apply:

No two consecutive arrivals are red.

Y arrives at some time before both T and W.

Exactly two of the trucks that arrive before Y are red.

S is the sixth arrival.

Z arrives at some time before U.

PrepTest37 Sec3 Q8

3. If X is the third arrival, then which one of the following trucks must be green?

(A) S
(B) T
(C) U
(D) W
(E) Z

Steps 1–4:

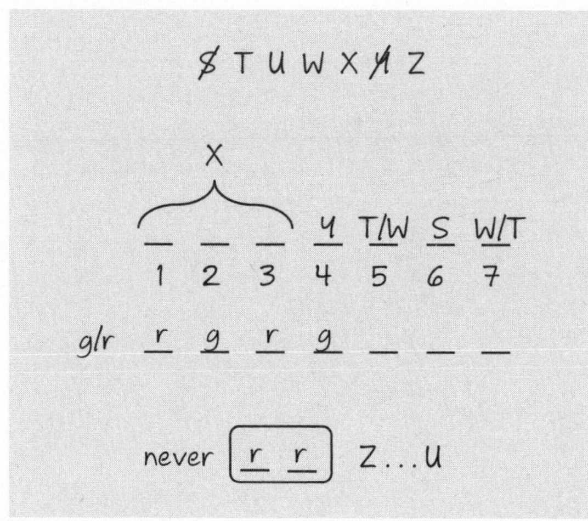

Step 5 (cont.): (C) is correct; Under this question's conditions, Truck U must be green. Placing Truck X in slot 3 means than Truck Z must take slot 1 and Truck U must take slot 2.

S T U W X Y Z
Z U X Y T/W S W/T
1 2 3 4 5 6 7
g/r r g r g

Thus, truck U must be green.

Wrong answers: (A) Truck S could be either green or red. (B) Truck T could be either green or red. (D) Truck W could be either green or red. (E) Under this question's conditions, Truck Z must be red.

LOGIC GAMES STRATEGY

Leave the Master Sketch alone. For New-"If" questions, copy the Master Sketch, label this copy with the question number, and add the question's new information there.

It may be tempting to save time by adding a New-"If" question's new condition into the Master Sketch and making any additional deductions there, but you will likely need the Master Sketch again to answer further Must Be True/Must Be False type questions, or you may have additional New-"If" questions with different conditions (indeed, the next question in this game is just that). Either way, trying to erase the work you've done for one question in order to restore the Master Sketch leads to confusion and mistakes.

New-"If"/Must Be True Question

This question is very similar to question 3, but the conditions have changed. Once again, the LSAT expert quickly copies the Master Sketch and adds this question's new information to the copy, making the additional deductions there.

Step 5: A New-"If" question: Copy the Master Sketch, add the new condition, make all available deductions, and use the resulting sketch to evaluate the answer choices.

In a single day, exactly seven trucks—S, T, U, W, X, Y, and Z—are the only arrivals at a warehouse. No truck arrives at the same time as any other truck, and no truck arrives more than once that day. Each truck is either green or red (but not both). The following conditions apply:

No two consecutive arrivals are red.

Y arrives at some time before both T and W.

Exactly two of the trucks that arrive before Y are red.

S is the sixth arrival.

Z arrives at some time before U.

PrepTest37 Sec3 Q9

4. If exactly three of the trucks are green, then which one of the following trucks must be green?

(A) S

(B) T

(C) U

(D) W

(E) Z

Steps 1–4:

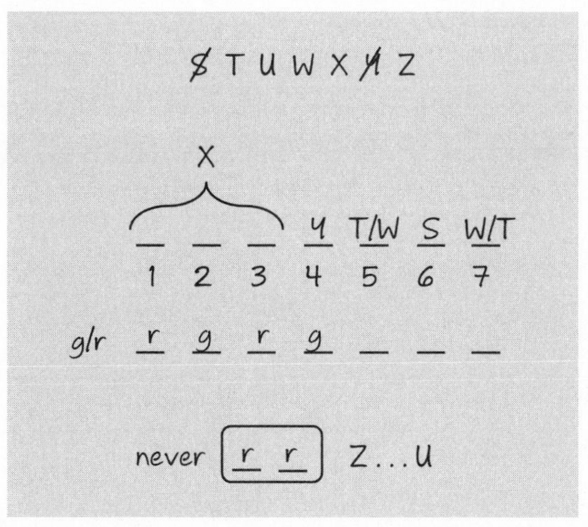

Step 5 (cont.): (A) is correct; Under this question's conditions, Truck S must be green. The trucks in slots 2 and 4 are always green. If there is to be just one more green truck, it will have to take slot 6 to prevent having any red trucks arrive consecutively (Rule 1).

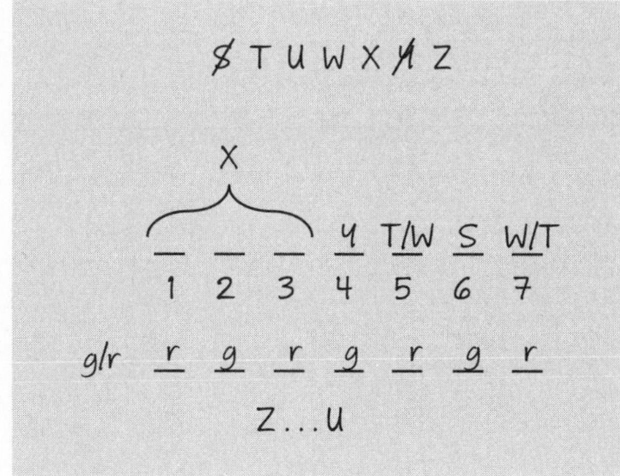

Thus, Truck S must be green.

Wrong answers: (B) Under this question's conditions, Truck T must be red, whether it is fifth or seventh. (C) Truck U could be either green or red. (D) Under this question's conditions, Truck W must be red, whether it is fifth or seventh. (E) Truck Z could be either green or red.

"How Many" Question

This question type is pretty rare. It asks for the number of entities—the number of trucks in this case—that are placed with certainty once and for all. There is no New-"If" condition, so an LSAT expert recognizes that this question can be answered directly from the Master Sketch.

In a single day, exactly seven trucks—S, T, U, W, X, Y, and Z—are the only arrivals at a warehouse. No truck arrives at the same time as any other truck, and no truck arrives more than once that day. Each truck is either green or red (but not both). The following conditions apply:

No two consecutive arrivals are red.

Y arrives at some time before both T and W.

Exactly two of the trucks that arrive before Y are red.

S is the sixth arrival.

Z arrives at some time before U.

PrepTest37 Sec3 Q10

Steps 1–4:

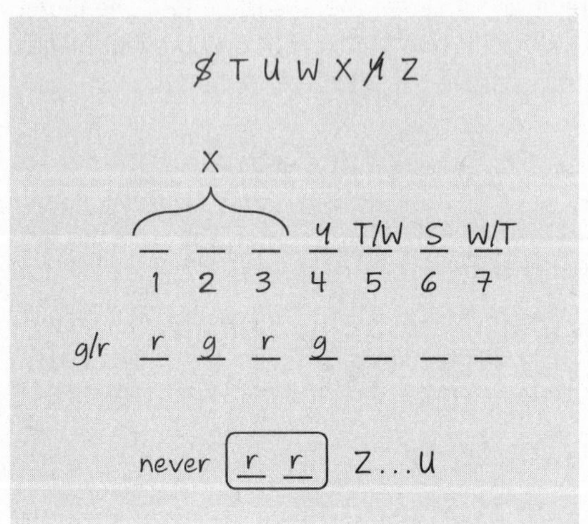

Step 5: A "How Many" question:

5. For exactly how many of the seven trucks can one determine exactly how many trucks arrived before it?

(A) one
(B) two
(C) three
(D) four
(E) five

Step 5 (cont.): (B) is correct; The placements of Trucks S and Y are completely determined. Rule 4 established the placement of Truck S. Combining Rule 2 with Rules 1 and 4 established that Truck Y must take slot 4. Those are the only two trucks whose placement is determined once and for all.

"How Many" questions, like this one, fall under the category of Numerical Questions. Related questions may ask for the minimum or maximum number of entities that may be selected or placed in a certain grouping, or the earliest or latest that an entity can appear within a sequence. In every case, you will be able to determine the correct answer and every wrong answer will simply be too low or too high. You'll learn about all of the question types in Chapter 5. For the time being, recognizing that this question does not contain a New-"If" condition and can, therefore, be answered directly from the deductions in the Master Sketch, is all that you need to know.

Must Be False Question

This one is quite similar to the second question in this game's set.

> **Step 5:** A Must-Be-False question: Use the Master Sketch to evaluate the answer choices.

In a single day, exactly seven trucks—S, T, U, W, X, Y, and Z—are the only arrivals at a warehouse. No truck arrives at the same time as any other truck, and no truck arrives more than once that day. Each truck is either green or red (but not both). The following conditions apply:

No two consecutive arrivals are red.

Y arrives at some time before both T and W.

Exactly two of the trucks that arrive before Y are red.

S is the sixth arrival.

Z arrives at some time before U.

PrepTest37 Sec3 Q11

6. Which one of the following pairs of trucks CANNOT arrive consecutively at the warehouse?

(A) U and Y

(B) X and Y

(C) Y and T

(D) Y and W

(E) Y and Z

> **Step 5 (cont.):** Eliminate any choice in which the pair of trucks *could* arrive consecutively. The correct answer cites a pair of trucks that *cannot* arrive consecutively. (E) is correct; Truck Y is always in slot 4. Truck Z can be only in slots 1 or 2. These trucks can never be consecutive.

Steps 1–4:

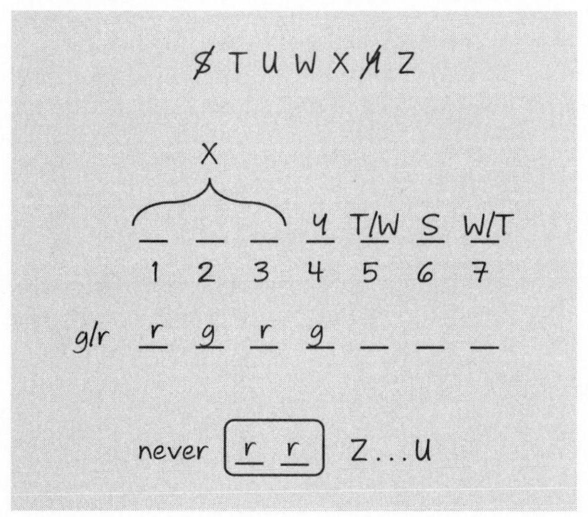

Wrong answers: (A) Truck Y is always in slot 4. Truck U could be in slot 3. (B) Truck Y is always in slot 4. Truck X could be in slot 3. (C) Truck Y is always in slot 4. Truck T could be in slot 5. (D) Truck Y is always in slot 4. Truck W could be in slot 5.

That's a look at the Logic Games Method in action. Once the LSAT expert analyzed the setup and made all of the deductions, answering the questions was fairly straightforward. Now, not all games have as many deductions as this one did, but it is always important that you know everything about the game—about what must, can, and cannot be true of the entities—that you can.

In the next portion of this chapter, you can practice the steps of the Logic Games Method on a new setup. Don't worry if you make mistakes at this point; you have lots of practice ahead of you. Concentrate on the steps of the Method, and on the purpose of each step.

Practice

Directions: Perform steps 1–4 of the Logic Games Method on the following game setup and rules, and answer the accompanying questions. Create any required sketches on a separate piece of scratch paper. When you're finished, compare your work to the expert analysis on the following pages.

A little league baseball team manager has to schedule his rotation of six starting pitchers—Atwood, Blevins, Chen, Dante, Engle, and Fuentes—for the first six games of the season. Each pitcher will start exactly once. The manager has decided to strictly adhere to the advice of his pitching coach as follows:

Chen, the team's strongest pitcher, will start the first game.
Atwood will start the game immediately after the game Dante starts due to the two pitchers' contrasting styles.
Fuentes will start a later game than the game Atwood starts.
Engle will not start the game immediately after the game Chen starts.

Step 1

1. What is Step 1 of the Logic Games Method, and what is its purpose?

2. What are the four questions you ask in Step 1?

3. What is your Step 1 analysis of this particular game?

Step 2

4. What is Step 2 of the Logic Games Method, and what is its purpose?

5. What is your Step 2 analysis of this particular game?

Step 3

6. What is Step 3 of the Logic Games Method, and what is its purpose?

7. What is your Step 3 analysis of this particular game?
   - Rule 1:
   - Rule 2:
   - Rule 3:
   - Rule 4:

Step 4

8. What is Step 4 of the Logic Games Method, and what is its purpose?

9. What are five patterns you always look for during Step 4?

10. What is your Step 4 analysis of this particular game?

    - Which entities appear in two rules? What can you learn from combining those rules?
    - In which slots would Dante NOT be allowed?
    - In which slots would Atwood NOT be allowed?
    - In which slots would Fuentes NOT be allowed?
    - Which entities COULD be in slot 2?
    - Is there a *floater*, in other words, an entity that is unrestricted by any rule or limitation? If so, which one(s)?

Step 5

11. What is Step 5 of the Logic Games Method, and what is its purpose?

12. What strategy should you use for the following question?

    "Which one of the following could be the order, from first to last, of the little league team's starting rotation?"

    - Which rule does the sequence C, E, B, D, A, F violate?

13. What strategy should you use for the following question?

    "Which one of the following is a pitcher who could pitch in the team's second game?"

    - Which pitchers could be the correct answer to that question?

14. What strategy should you use for the following question?

    "If Atwood pitches third in the team's rotation, then which one of the following could be true?"

    - What would the characteristic of the four wrong answers be to that question?
    - Would the statement "Fuentes pitches fourth" be a correct or incorrect answer to that question?
    - Would the statement "Blevins pitches second" be a correct or incorrect answer to that question?

15. [Bonus, high difficulty question] Placing Engle in which slot would completely determine the team's pitching rotation?

Explanations

The LSAT expert's answers are given in italics. Compare your answers to the expert's, and if you missed anything, revisit the game's setup to see where you went off track.

> A little league baseball team manager has to schedule his rotation of six starting pitchers—Atwood, Blevins, Chen, Dante, Engle, and Fuentes—for the first six games of the season. Each pitcher will start exactly once. The manager has decided to strictly adhere to the advice of his pitching coach as follows:
>
> Chen, the team's strongest pitcher, will start the first game.
>
> Atwood will start the game immediately after the game Dante starts due to the two pitchers' contrasting styles.
>
> Fuentes will start a later game than the game Atwood starts.
>
> Engle will not start the game immediately after the game Chen starts.

Step 1

1. What is Step 1 of the Logic Games Method, and what is its purpose? *Step 1 is Overview—in other words, reviewing the game's opening paragraph to understand the game's task and its moving parts.*
2. What are the four questions you ask in Step 1? *The SEAL questions: What is the SITUATION? Who or what are the ENTITIES? What is the game's ACTION? What LIMITATIONS are given in the game's opening paragraph?*
3. What is your Step 1 analysis of this particular game? *The SITUATION is creating a baseball team's six-person starting rotation, so the task is just to write out the list in an acceptable order. The ENTITIES are the pitchers—A, B, C, D, E, and F. The game's ACTION is basic Strict Sequencing*, with the intuitive LIMITATION of one pitcher per spot in the rotation.*

   *You will learn the names of all the standard game types in Chapter 2.

Step 2

4. What is Step 2 of the Logic Games Method, and what is its purpose? *Step 2 is Sketch, and its purpose is to write out a simple, easily repeatable framework in which to record the details of the game's rules and restrictions.*
5. What is your Step 2 analysis of this particular game? *Here, the sketch will just consist of a shorthand list of the pitchers and six numbered slots. The slots could be arranged horizontally or vertically, whichever seems most natural.*

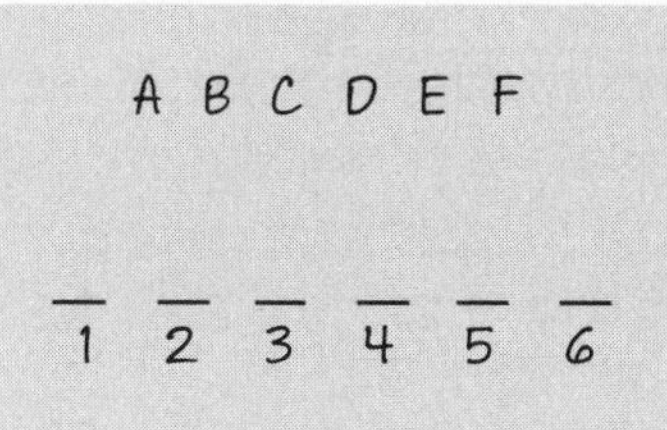

Step 3

6. What is Step 3 of the Logic Games Method, and what is its purpose? *Step 3 is Rules, and its purpose is to analyze each of the rules (considering both their positive and negative restrictions) and to record them in a way that aligns with the sketch framework.*
7. What is your Step 3 analysis of this particular game?
   - Rule 1:

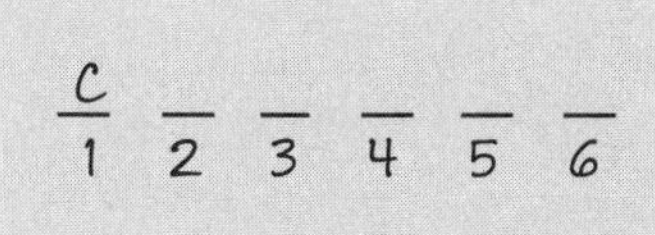

   - Rule 2:

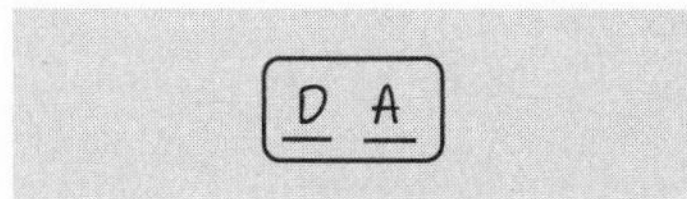

   - Rule 3:

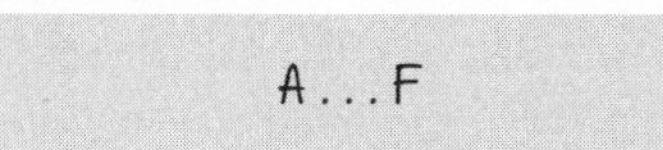

   - Rule 4:

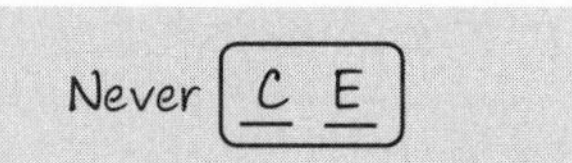

Here's the sketch at the end of Step 3.

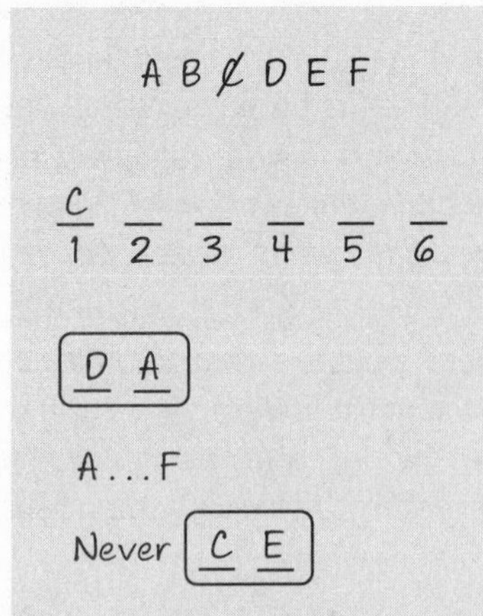

Step 4

8. What is Step 4 of the Logic Games Method, and what is its purpose? *Step 4 is Deductions, and its purpose is to combine rules to determine what must be true or must be false in the game.*
9. What are five patterns you always look for during Step 4? *BLEND: Blocks of Entities, Limited Options, Established Entities, Number Restrictions, and Duplications*
10. What is your Step 4 analysis of this particular game?
    - Which entities appear in two rules? What can you learn from combining those rules? *Atwood appears in Rules 2 and 3. Chen appears in Rules 1 and 4. Rules 2 and 3 can be combined to deduce that the string DA . . . F will always appear in that order. Rules 1 and 4 combine to deduce that Engle will never be the second pitcher in the rotation.*

A B ¢ D E F

C
1 2 3 4 5 6
~E (under 2)

D A . . . F

- In which slots would Dante NOT be allowed? *Because Dante has to pitch before Atwood and Fuentes, Dante can never pitch fifth or sixth.*
- In which slots would Atwood NOT be allowed? *Because Atwood must pitch after Dante and before Fuentes, and because Chen is always the first pitcher, Atwood cannot pitch second or sixth.*
- In which slots would Fuentes NOT be allowed? *Because Fuentes must pitch after Dante and after Atwood, and because Chen always pitches first, Fuentes cannot pitch second or third.*

A B ¢ D E F

C
1 2 3 4 5 6
2: ~E ~A ~F; 3: ~F; 5: ~D; 6: ~D ~A

D A . . . F

- Which entities COULD be in slot 2? *Because Chen is already assigned to slot 1, and because Engle (Rule 4) and Atwood and Fuentes (Rules 2 and 3) are all prevented from pitching second, the only pitchers who could pitch second are Blevins and Dante.*
- Is there a *floater*, in other words, an entity that is unrestricted by any rule or limitation? If so, which one(s)? *There are no rules or restrictions on Blevins. Aside from slot 1 (which is always Chen's spot), Blevins can pitch in any position.*

This is the game's Master Sketch.

A B ¢ D E F

C B/D
1 2 3 4 5 6
2: ~E ~A ~F; 3: ~F; 5: ~D; 6: ~D ~A

D A . . . F

Step 5

11. What is Step 5 of the Logic Games Method, and what is its purpose? *Step 5 is Questions, and its purpose is to answer the questions as quickly and confidently as possible by using the appropriate strategy for each question type.*

12. What strategy should you use for the following question?

    "Which one of the following could be the order, from first to last, of the little league team's starting rotation?" *This is an Acceptability question. The fastest, surest way to answer it is to apply each rule to the answer choices and eliminate any answers that violate the rule.*

    - Which rule does the sequence C, E, B, D, A, F violate? *That violates Rule 4, which prevents Engle from pitching immediately after Chen.*

13. What strategy should you use for the following question?

    "Which one of the following is a pitcher who could pitch in the team's second game?" *This is a Could Be True question; just test the answer choices against the Master Sketch to see which one is possible. The four wrong answers will all name pitchers who CANNOT pitch second.*

    - Which pitcher(s) could be in the correct answer to that question? *The correct answer must be either Blevins or Dante, the only two pitchers who can take the second spot in the rotation.*

14. What strategy should you use for the following question?

    "If Atwood pitches third in the team's rotation, then which one of the following could be true?" *This is a New-"If" question. The best way to approach it is to make a copy of the Master Sketch, label it with the question number, add in the new conditional information, and make any additional deductions available as a result. For the record, if Atwood pitches third, then Dante pitches second. Blevins, Engle, and Fuentes would take slots 4, 5, and 6, but they could be in any order.*

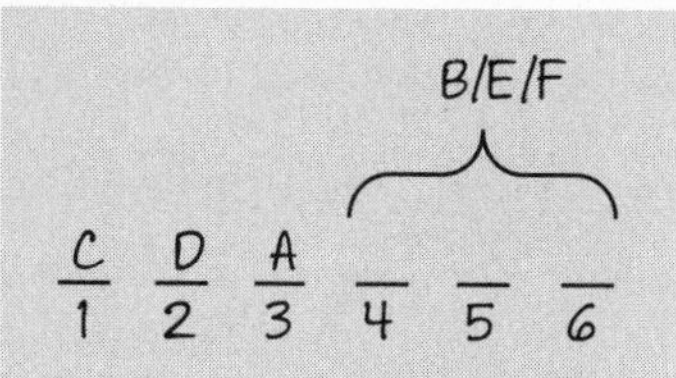

    - What would the characteristic of the four wrong answers be in that question? *The four wrong answers Must Be False.*
    - Would the statement "Fuentes pitches fourth" be a correct or incorrect answer in that question? *That statement could be true, so this would be a correct answer.*
    - Would the statement "Blevins pitches second" be a correct or incorrect answer in that question? *That statement must be false—Dante pitches second in this question—so this would be an incorrect answer.*

15. [Bonus, high difficulty question] Placing Engle in which slot would completely determine the team's pitching rotation? *Giving Engle the third spot in the rotation would determine every pitchers' position. With Engle third, Blevins must pitch second. The remaining pitchers—Atwood, Dante, and Fuentes—must pitch in order determined by Rules 2 and 3, that is, they must go DA ... F. With only slots 4, 5, and 6 open to them, the rotation is entirely determined.*

C	B	E	D	A	F
1	2	3	4	5	6

Test out Engle in slots 4, 5, and 6 if you like. None of those placements will completely determine the rotation.

On the following pages, you'll find the Perform quiz (your self-assessment) for Chapter 1. After you complete it, compare your answers to those in the Answer Key. Because Chapter 1 provides the foundation for everything you'll be doing, you want to make sure you know the Logic Games Method by heart before moving on to the chapters that break down the steps of the Method and apply them to all of the various game types.

Perform

Fill in the following blanks, listing the steps and strategies associated with the Logic Games Method.

Kaplan Logic Games Method

Step 1: ______________

→ 4 questions to ask before Step 2

-
-
-
-

Step 2: ______________

Step 3: ______________

Step 4: ______________

→ 6 things to look for before Step 5

-
-
-
-
-
- Note any unused entities known as ______________

Step 5: ______________

Logic Games Questions

What is the strategy for Acceptability questions?

____

What is the strategy for Must Be/Could Be questions?

____

What is the strategy for New-"If" questions?

____

Explanations follow on the next page. ▶ ▶ ▶

Explanations

Kaplan Logic Games Method

Step 1: ***Overview***

→ 4 questions to ask before Step 2
- Situation
- Entities
- Action
- Limitations

Step 2: ***Sketch***

Step 3: ***Rules***

Step 4: ***Deductions***

→ 6 things to look for before Step 5
- ***Blocks of Entities***
- ***Limited Options***
- ***Established Entities***
- ***Numbers***
- ***Duplication***
- Note any unused entities known as ***Floaters***

Step 5: ***Questions***

Logic Games Questions

What is the strategy for Acceptability questions?

Go rule by rule to eliminate each answer choice that violates a rule.

What is the strategy for Must Be/Could Be questions?

Consult the Master Sketch to see if the question can be answered immediately. If not, use sketches from New-"If"s, as well as the Acceptability question correct answer, to eliminate answers. The sketch from a New-"If" could also help pick a Could Be True answer. If multiple answer choices still remain use trial and error.

What is the strategy for New-"If" questions?

Draw a new sketch that incorporates the new information.

Types of Questions By Percentage, 2014–2018

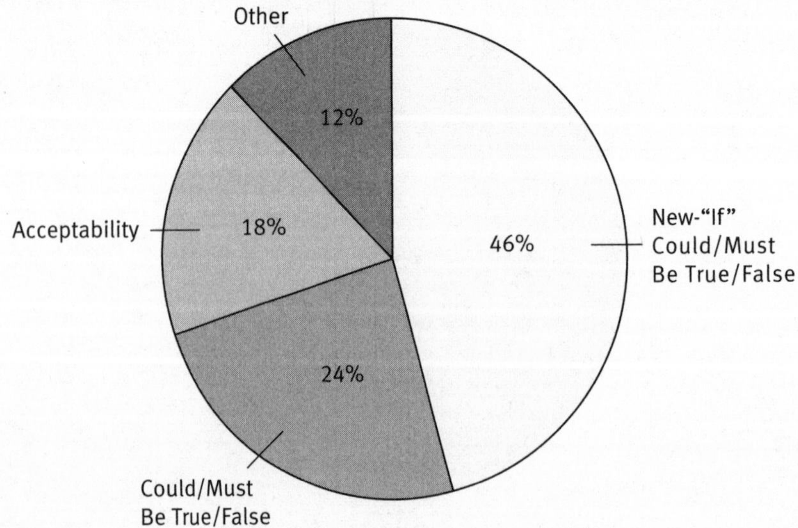

**PrepTests 72–86; released 2014–2018*

Assess

The self-assessment criteria for this chapter's Perform quiz is necessarily more strict than those in later chapters. To get the most out of all the study and practice available in this book, you *must* know the steps of the Logic Games Method by heart.

If you were able to list out the steps accurately: congratulations. You're ready for the valuable strategies and tactics you'll learn for each step.

If there were any steps you misidentified or forgot: Study the Logic Games Method once more before moving on to the following chapters, in which you'll drill down into each step in detail.

If you missed any of the question strategies, you'll have the opportunity to practice those thoroughly in Chapter 4. For now, the most important thing to remember is that you will use the sketch and deductions you make to answer the questions, so your work with Steps 1–4 is essential to success in the Logic Games section of the LSAT. The work you'll do in the next two chapters will introduce you to the basic logic game types seen on the test, and will give you the tools and strategies to analyze and sketch the setups, rules, and deductions you will encounter most often.

Reflect

Now that you've seen the Logic Games Method, take a few minutes to reflect on the following questions:

- What is the purpose of Step 1, and why does an expert always take that step?
- What is the purpose of Step 2, and why does an expert always take that step?
- What is the purpose of Step 3, and why does an expert always take that step?
- What is the purpose of Step 4, and why does an expert always take that step?
- What is the purpose of Step 5, and why does an expert always take that step?
- Did any part of the Logic Games Method surprise you?
- Are there specific steps in the Logic Games Method that excite you?
- Were any of the steps confusing? How will you get additional practice with those steps?
- How will you approach Logic Games differently the next time you practice them?
- What techniques did you see applied to the game in this chapter that you can immediately put to use the next time you practice Logic Games?

As you practice Logic Games further, review the explanations thoroughly. The explanations will cover each step in the Logic Games Method and help make clear how every game can be done most efficiently and effectively.

CHAPTER 2

Logic Game Types and Sketches

In this chapter, you get to drill down into Steps 1 and 2 of the Logic Games Method. You'll learn the most common game types and begin collecting a library of the most common sketch patterns.

Game types are based on the action or task you're expected to complete. For example, the Truck Arrivals game in Chapter 1 was a Sequencing/Matching Hybrid game because you were asked to determine the order in which the trucks arrived at the warehouse, and you had to match a color (green or red) to each truck. Even though that game had two actions, the sketch allowed you to depict the task clearly, and the rules and deductions left very little ambiguity about the final arrangement.

There are four basic actions in logic games: Sequencing, Selection, Distribution, and Matching. As you learn to identify the game types, it is helpful to associate them with real-world situations. The truth is that you handle these kinds of tasks all the time. When you rank the *Star Wars* movies from best to worst, or when you decide the order in which your friends will take turns bowling, you're doing a Sequencing game. When you choose who to invite or not invite to dinner, you're engaged in Selection. Any time you choose teams for a pick-up basketball game, you're completing a Distribution task. Keep it simple, and look for the real-world model to the task described in the game.

Associating logic game tasks with real-world situations will help you make clear, useful sketches, too. If you're deciding on a class schedule, you probably use a calendar so that you can make sure no day is too busy or that nothing overlaps. So, in a game that asks you to account for appointments on a person's work calendar, it would be natural for you to jot five spaces horizontally, and label them *M-Tu-W-Th-F*. The examples you will encounter in this chapter will provide a great starting point for how to sketch the games you'll see on test day, but always read the game setup carefully to have your sketch reflect the situation, entities, action, and limitations described.

HOW TO IDENTIFY AND SKETCH THE GAME TYPES

Prepare

In this chapter, you'll practice Steps 1 and 2 of the Logic Games Method together. That's because the sketch (Step 2) is the direct result of your Overview analysis (Step 1). Said another way, the best test of your work in Step 1 is the accuracy of your work in Step 2.

LEARNING OBJECTIVES

In this chapter, you'll learn to

- Identify the actions and limitations that characterize common LSAT logic game types
- Create clear, useful sketches for each logic game type

At the end of this chapter, you will test your ability to recognize six types of logic games based on their actions, and to create accurate sketches for each type.

Refresh (Activate Prior Knowledge)

To get the ball rolling, review the Step 1 and Step 2 analysis that the LSAT expert applied to the game you saw in Chapter 1.

In a single day, exactly seven trucks—S, T, U, W, X, Y, and Z—are the only arrivals at a warehouse. No truck arrives at the same time as any other truck, and no truck arrives more than once that day. Each truck is either green or red (but not both). The following conditions apply:

PrepTest37 Sec3 Qs 6–11

Step 1: First, the expert conducted an overview of the game's opening paragraph by asking the SEAL questions.

- What is the game's **situation**? Trucks are arriving in a particular order, and each truck is either red or green.
- What **entities** are involved in this game? The trucks—S, T, U, W, X, Y, and Z
- What is/are this game's **action**(s)? Sequencing (the order in which the trucks arrive) and Matching (the color of each truck)
- Are there any **limitations** on this game's entities or action? The trucks arrive one at a time, and each is only one color.

Step 2: Based on the Step 1 analysis, the expert created a sketch that depicts the game's action(s) and limitations. The sketch should be easy to read, quick to replicate, and able to account for what is certain and uncertain based on the game's rules. This was the result:

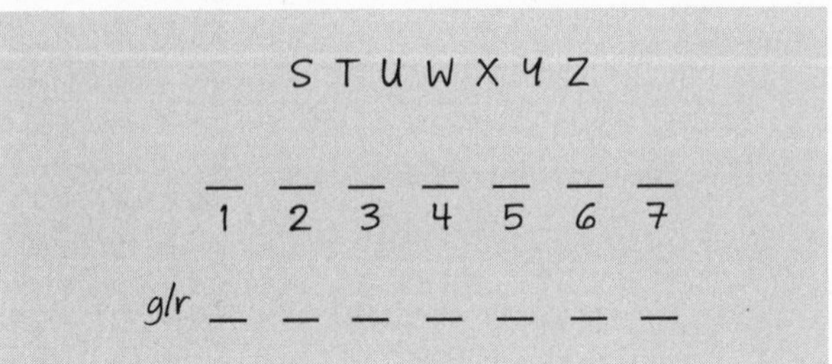

Now, compare that analysis to another expert's work on a game you haven't seen before. See how well you can anticipate the expert's analysis here. Take a minute to consider the setup:

On one afternoon, Patterson meets individually with each of exactly five clients—Reilly, Sanchez, Tang, Upton, and Yansky—and also goes to the gym by herself for a workout. Patterson's workout and her five meetings each start at either 1:00, 2:00, 3:00, 4:00, 5:00, or 6:00. The following conditions must apply:

PrepTest45 Sec3 Qs 1–6

Step 1: First, the expert conducts an overview of the game's opening paragraph by asking the SEAL questions.

- What is the game's **situation**? A woman scheduling five meetings and a workout for the afternoon.
- What **entities** are involved in this game? five clients—R, S, T, U, and Y—and the workout—W
- What is/are this game's **action**(s)? Sequencing
- Are there any **limitations** on this game's entities or action? She meets each client once, one at a time, and the meetings and the workout happen on the hour, from 1:00 through 6:00.

Step 2: Here, the Step 1 analysis shows a game with one action—Sequencing. The sketch should reflect the calendar-like description of the setup.

R S T U W Y

_ _ _ _ _ _
1 2 3 4 5 6

As it turns out, this game is a Strict Sequencing game, the most common game type on the LSAT.

In this chapter, you'll learn to analyze various game types you could encounter on test day. The game types are defined by their action or actions. The pie chart that follows the definitions shows you how often each game type has appeared on released LSAT exams administered over the most recent five-year period for which accurate data is available.

GAME TYPE ACTIONS

- Strict Sequencing: Ordering or ranking entities with respect to defined positions
- Loose Sequencing: Ordering or ranking entities with respect to each other
- Selection: Choosing a smaller group of entities from a larger group
- Matching: Matching two kinds of entities to each other, or matching attributes to a list of entities
- Distribution: Separating entities into two or more smaller groups
- Hybrid: Performing a task that involves two or more of the actions described above; e.g., Sequencing/Matching, Distribution/Sequencing, or Selection/Distribution

Type of Games By Percentage, 2014–2018

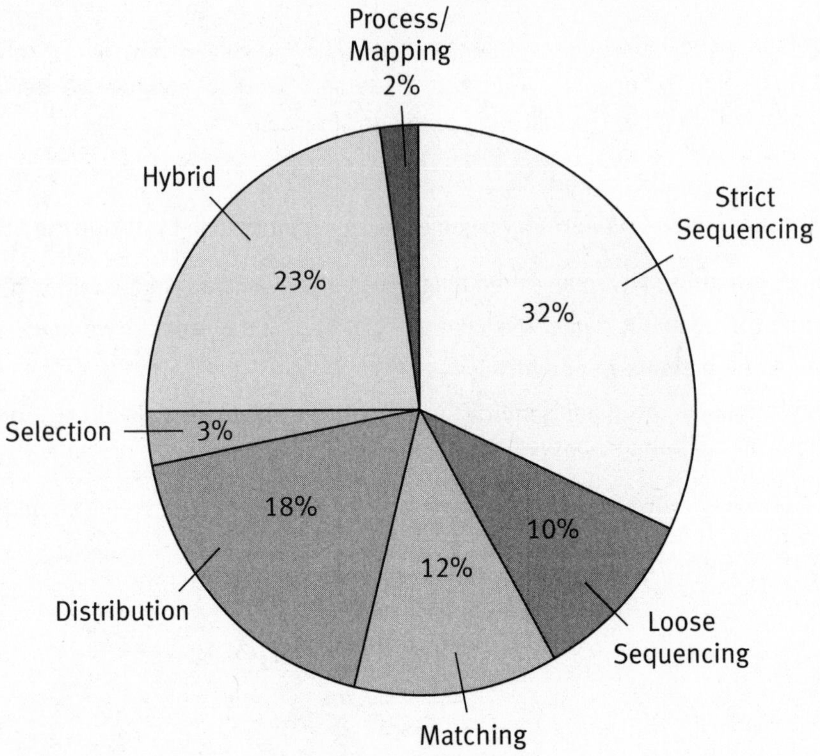

Process/ Mapping 2%
Strict Sequencing 32%
Loose Sequencing 10%
Matching 12%
Distribution 18%
Selection 3%
Hybrid 23%

**PrepTests 72–86; released 2014–2018*

Logic Game Types Illustrated

Take a closer look at the game actions we defined in the previous Logic Games Strategy box. For each, you'll see a model game setup and a suggested sketch.

> **LOGIC GAMES STRATEGY**
>
> As you practice logic games, develop and maintain a library of common sketch frameworks for each game type. There are a limited number of game actions that correspond to sketch templates that will be useful again and again.

Strict Sequencing Games

Sequencing games are, by far, the most common games on recent LSATs. The testmaker uses several variations on Sequencing, as you'll see here, and in even more detail in Chapters 5, 6, and 7.

LOGIC GAMES STRATEGY

Sequencing games ask you to put things in order:

- Chronologically (either using units of time—years, weeks, days, or hours—or simply using the notions of "earlier" and "later")
- Spatially (either horizontally or vertically, and with specific positions—for example, runners in lanes 1 through 6—or by using notions such as "higher and lower" or "east and west")
- By rank or result (such as first place through seventh place, or "best to worst")
- By size or amount (such as "most to least expensive")

More than 80 percent of Sequencing games are Strict Sequencing games, meaning that the positions are numbered (1, 2, 3...) or named (Monday, Tuesday, Wednesday...) and that the rules refer to specific positions or to a precise number of positions between entities (e.g., "B sits in the sixth chair," "C and D are in adjacent lanes," or "E speaks later than F and exactly one speech is given in between them"). Strict Sequencing games may include rules that provide a relative relationship between entities ("P speaks later than Q speaks"), but will always provide one or more rules related to the *strict* positions. Basic Strict Sequencing games are covered in detail in Chapter 5.

Here's a model Strict Sequencing setup and its initial sketch:

Six figurines—A, B, C, D, E, and F—are arranged in a line from left to right on a shelf, with each figurine in a different spot. The following conditions apply:

→

Step 1:
Situation: Arranging figurines in a single line along a shelf

Entities: Six figurines—A, B, C, D, E, and F

Action: Sequencing

Limitations: One figurine per position

Step 2:

A B C D E F

__ __ __ __ __ __
1 2 3 4 5 6

Because Strict Sequencing games are so common, you will see a number of variations on this game type. For example, the testmaker could ask you to sequence five entities two times in different orders. Another variation might involve a difference between the number of entities and positions. If the game tasks you with sequencing seven appointments over five days, you would know that at least one or two of the days have multiple appointments. On the other hand, if the game asked you to sequence five events over the course of seven years, you would know that at least two of the years saw none of the events occur. These "complex" Strict Sequencing games are covered in detail in Chapter 6.

LOGIC GAMES STRATEGY

Never *assume* anything in a logic game. Rather, pay close attention to the limitations in the game's setup.

If a Strict Sequencing game lists seven people to schedule for appointments over seven days, your instinct will be that one person is scheduled per day. But, for that limitation to apply, the setup or rules must state "one appointment per day."

Here's a "double sequencing" twist on Strict Sequencing and its suggested sketch.

In a blind taste test, two professional food critics—Peters and Quimby—will each sample five breakfast cereals—Berry Bombs, Cocoa Clusters, Fruity Flakes, Marshmallow Mouthfuls, and NutriNuggets—one at a time. To ensure fairness, each critic will test the cereals in a different order, in accordance with the following restrictions:

→

Step 1:

Situation: Two critics testing the same five cereals, but in a different order

Entities: The cereals—B, C, F, M, and N

Action: Double Sequencing, five items are sequenced two times

Limitations: "one at a time" and a "different order" for each critic

Step 2:

```
        B  C  F  M  N

P:  __  __  __  __  __

Q:  __  __  __  __  __
     1   2   3   4   5
```

The sketch for that "complex" Strict Sequencing game isn't all that different from one for a standard Strict Sequencing setup. It simply provides two lines of slots, one for each food critic, in accordance with the action and limitations described in the paragraph.

Loose Sequencing Games

While not nearly as common as Strict Sequencing, Loose Sequencing games have accounted for about 10 percent of all games on released LSATs over the past five years.

The opening setup of a Loose Sequencing game may not appear any different than that of a Strict Sequencing game. It is the *rules* that distinguish Loose Sequencing. In Loose Sequencing, none of the rules refer to specific positions, and none of the rules separate entities by a specific number of positions. In Loose Sequencing, all of the rules relate entities relative to one another (e.g., "B is ranked higher than C" or "H is opened later than L").

The reason that it is important to distinguish Loose Sequencing from Strict Sequencing is because Loose Sequencing is best managed with a different kind of sketch. Because Loose Sequencing rules relate the entities to one another, you can create a kind of "branching tree" that will show the relationships among the entities as they are restricted by the rules. Loose Sequencing games are covered in detail in Chapter 7.

Here's a model Loose Sequencing game and its accompanying *branching tree* sketch:

Seven magazines—G, H, J, K, L, M, and N—are ranked from most honest to least honest by an organization concerned with journalistic integrity. Each magazine receives a different rank, and no other magazines are ranked. The following conditions apply:

Both H and L are ranked higher than M.

J is ranked lower than G.

N is ranked lower than M.

K is ranked lower than N.

M is ranked higher than J.

→

Step 1:

Situation: A "most to least" ranking of magazines

Entities: The magazines—G, H, J, K, L, M, and N

Action: Sequencing, specifically Loose Sequencing, because all of the rules give relative relationships among the entities

Limitations: No ties

Step 2:

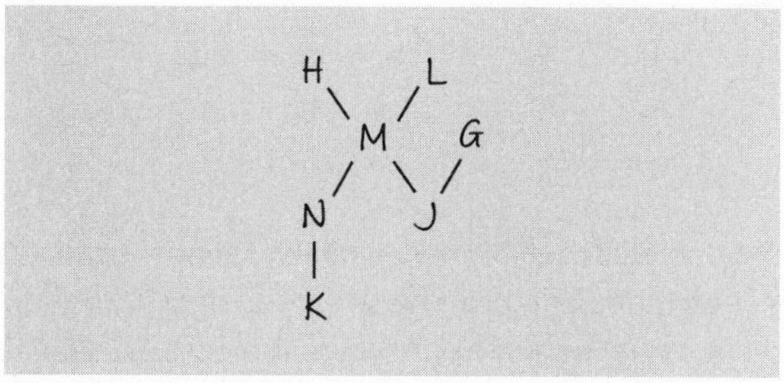

```
H     L
 \   /
   M     G
  / \   /
 N    J
 |
 K
```

By the way, it is common in Loose Sequencing for the rules to account for every entity, such that they all appear in the sketch's "tree" as they do in this example.

NOTE: For the Practice and Perform quizzes in this chapter, we won't include the rules. Thus, for some of the Sequencing setups you see, it may be unclear whether you would ultimately use a Strict or Loose Sequencing sketch. That's fine. Make a note of the ambiguity and jot down what the Strict Sequencing sketch would look like.

Selection Games

In recent years, Selection games have been quite rare, accounting for less than five percent of the games on released LSATs. Unlike Sequencing games, Selection games do not appear on every test.

LOGIC GAMES STRATEGY

Selection games ask you to choose some items and reject others from a list of items. Selection games may:

- Stipulate the number to be chosen (e.g., "the manager will interview exactly four of the seven applicants"),
- Limit the number to be chosen ("Mark will invite at most five of the seven marketers to the company retreat"), or
- Leave the number to be chosen ambiguous (e.g., "From among seven dishes on the catering menu... Carol will decide which to serve at the reception").

On Selection games that do not provide a specific number of entities to choose from the initial list, most LSAT experts forego making a sketch. Instead, they simply write out the initial list of entities, circle those that are chosen, and cross out those that are rejected. This is the most efficient approach for New-"If" questions (e.g., "If A is selected, then which one of the following must be true") because re-writing the list of entities takes almost no time at all. Here's an example:

A child is selecting stickers to put on her notebook. She can choose from six stickers, one each representing an apple, a banana, a cat, a dog, an egg, and a fan. The following conditions apply:

→

Step 1:

Situation: A child choosing stickers for her notebook

Entities: The stickers—A, B, C, D, E, and F

Action: Selection

Limitations: None (no minimum or maximum given)

Step 2

(A) B C Ø E F

In Selection games that provide no limitations, expect to see questions that ask you about the minimum or maximum number of entities that can be selected (e.g., "Which one of the following is the maximum number of stickers the child could put on her notebook?"). When the game's setup limits or establishes the number of items you will select, they cannot ask that kind of question, of course.

For Selection games in which the number of entities to be selected is precisely established, many LSAT experts choose to use an "In/Out" sketch. These sketches are slightly more complicated, but they clearly represent the number of items that need to be selected or rejected to complete an acceptable solution to the game. Here's an example of this variation on Selection games:

From a list of eight songs—O, P, Q, R, S, T, U, and V—Mary will choose five songs to sing at an event. The following conditions apply:

Step 1:

Situation: A singer choosing five of eight songs to perform at an event

Entities: The songs—O, P, Q, R, S, T, U, and V

Action: Selection

Limitations: Choose exactly five

→ **Step 2**

O P Q R S T U V

in | out

_ _ _ _ _ | _ _ _

1 2 3 4 5 | 6 7 8

Over the years, roughly half of Selection games have specified a number of entities for you to choose. More recently, there has been a roughly equal three-way split among Selection games that stipulate an exact number, those that limit the number (e.g., "pick at least four"), and those that leave the number open.

Selection games will be covered in detail in Chapter 8.

Distribution and Matching Games

Distribution and Matching games are similar, so much so that even LSAT experts will sometimes argue about the category to which a particular game should belong. Giving a game the "right" name is less important than accurately analyzing its setup and drawing a useful sketch. The most important distinction between Distribution and Matching games is the number of times entities may be used.

> **LOGIC GAMES STRATEGY**
>
> To distinguish between Distribution and Matching games consider the entities.
>
> In Distribution, entities are divided into two or more groups or teams, and each entity is placed into *exactly one* of the groups. In Matching, entities may be assigned *one or more* attributes, tasks, or items.

In a standard Distribution game, you are given a list of entities and asked to divide them into two or more subgroups. Each entity is an individual person or item, and can be placed into only one group at a time. Think of dividing up 10 people into two five-person basketball teams. Each player goes to one team or the other, not both.

Here's a standard Distribution set up and sketch:

Becky is adding six new baseball cards—one each for players named Morgan, Nettles, Oliver, Palmer, Quisenberry, and Rodriguez—to her card collection. She will place each of the cards into one of two binders, labeled Binder 1 and Binder 2. The following conditions apply:

Step 1:

Situation: A collector adding cards to one of two binders

Entities: Six cards—M, N, O, P, Q, and R

Action: Distribution

Limitations: Each card goes into one binder, but there are no restrictions on how many cards she may add to each binder.

Step 2:

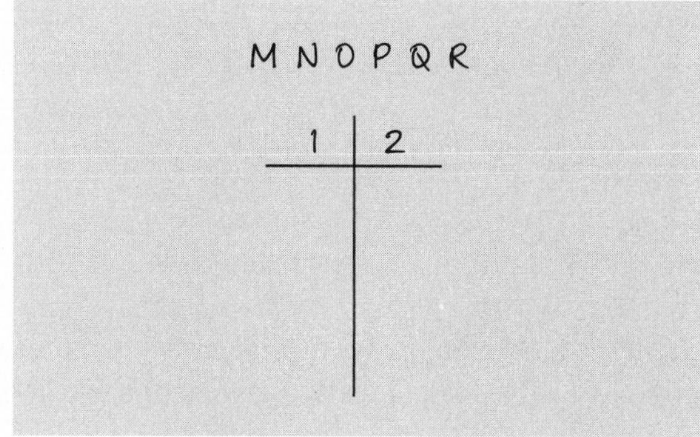

In the typical Matching game, you are provided with a list of people, places, or things, and then with another list of attributes, features, or items that you will assign to the first group. The big difference from Distribution is that, in a Matching game, the attributes, features, or items may be assigned to *one or more* of the "anchor" entities in the first list. Think of five basketball players. One or more may be wearing a wristband. One or more may have a knee brace. One or more may be wearing a particular brand of shoes.

Here's an example of a Matching game setup and sketch:

A restaurateur is opening five new locations—one each in the towns Gascon, Henderson, Junction City, Klondike, and Loredo. Each new location will feature one or more of his chef's famous desserts—apple tart, cheesecake, plum pudding, and strudel. The following conditions apply:

Step 1:
Situation: A restaurateur deciding which desserts to offer at five restaurant locations

Entities: The restaurants—G, H, J, K, and L—and the desserts—a, c, p, and s*

Action: Matching

Limitations: At least one dessert per location, but no limitation on how many restaurants may feature each dessert

Step 2:**

→

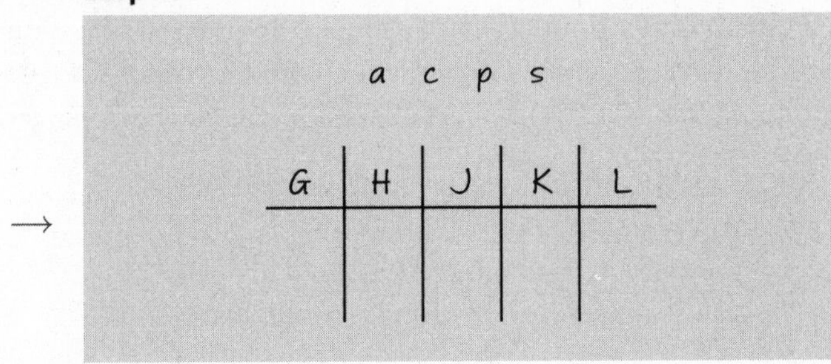

or

	G	H	J	K	L
a					
c					
p					
s					

*Note that the LSAT expert uses capital letters to represent the restaurants, and lower case letters to represent the desserts. Being able to distinguish between the two lists of entities in Matching games is always helpful.

**Note that you are given two options for the sketch that should accompany this Matching game. There is no evidence to suggest that one is better than the other, and for LSAT experts, the choice between a list and a grid is simply a matter of taste. Practice setting up Matching games both ways so that you can see which sketch template works best for you.

Distribution and Matching games are covered in detail in Chapter 9.

Hybrid Games

Hybrid games are those that combine two (or, very rarely, three) of the standard logic game actions (Sequencing, Selection, Distribution, and Matching). Hybrid games are not always harder than single-action games, but they always reward careful attention in the Overview phase. Once you identify that there are two actions within the game, consider how the actions affect one another so that you can represent them effectively in your sketch. Usually, one action is primary and the other secondary. If a Hybrid combines Selection and Sequencing, for example, you will need to know who is selected before you can determine their order.

LOGIC GAMES STRATEGY

The most common Hybrid games on recent tests have been:

- Sequencing/Matching (put a number of entities in order, and assign an attribute—such as a color or job—to each entity or position)
- Distribution/Sequencing (divide a larger group into smaller groups—usually just two—and then put the members of each subgroup in order)
- Selection/Sequencing (choose a smaller group from a larger one, and then put the members of the smaller group in order)
- Selection/Distribution (choose a smaller group from a larger one, and then subdivide the selected entities into subgroups)

Although Hybrid games always contain at least two actions, they usually feature simple versions of those actions. For example, in a Sequencing/Matching Hybrid game, you may have to put six runners into six lanes, one per lane, and then assign each runner a jersey color, say blue, green, or red. You are unlikely to see any twists, such as double sequencing or uneven numbers, in the Sequencing action of a Hybrid game. Likewise, if Matching is one of the actions, you will likely need to match just one attribute to each entity.

Take a look at some model setups and sketches for the Hybrid games discussed in the Logic Games Strategy box.

Sequencing/Matching Hybrid Games

In Sequencing/Matching Hybrids, you are asked to arrange several entities in order, and then match an attribute (it is almost always just one attribute) to each entity or position in the sequence. Here's an example:

Each of seven records—S, T, U, V, W, X, and Y—is placed on a shelf in one of seven spots, with spot 1 on the far left of the shelf and spot 7 on the far right. No spot contains more than one record, and each record contains music from a single genre: country, hip-hop, or jazz. The following conditions apply:

Step 1:

Situation: Lining up records on a shelf and identifying the genre of each record

Entities: Seven records—S, T, U, V, W, X, and Y—and three genres—c, h, and j

Action: Sequencing/Matching Hybrid

→ Limitations: Records sequenced one per position, and each record has exactly one genre

Step 2:

```
—  —  —  —  —  —  —   STUVWXYZ

—  —  —  —  —  —  —   c h j
1  2  3  4  5  6  7
```

Distribution/Sequencing Hybrid Games

Distribution/Sequencing Hybrids task you with divvying up a set of entities into teams or groups (almost always two), and then sequencing the entities within each team. Here's a typical Distribution/Sequencing Hybrid game setup:

Eastern State University's Dance team has been asked to join the school's marching band for a parade. The dance team has eight dancers—Benton, Carlson, Davis, Esai, Farrell, Gabrielson, Hutchins, and Joro. The eight dancers will be split into two dance lines—Line A and Line B—and the dancers in each line will be assigned positions—1 through 4—in which to march. The dancers' arrangement will obey the following restrictions:

→

Step 1:
Situation: A dance team lining up for a parade

Entities: Eight dancers—B, C, D, E, F, G, H, and J

Action: Distribution/Sequencing Hybrid

Limitations: Each team has four dancers, sequenced one per position

Step 2:

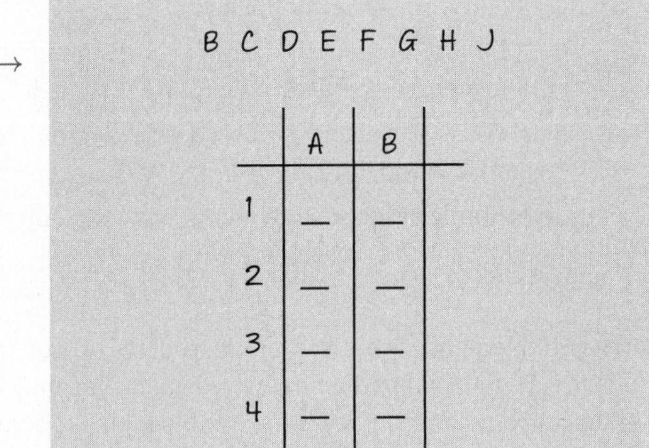

Selection/Sequencing Hybrid Games

In Selection/Sequencing Hybrid games, your job is to select a handful of members out of the initial entity list, and then to put the selected entities in order. Selection/Sequencing Hybrid games often look something like this:

From among seven witnesses to an industrial accident—Cirillo, Emegwale, Garrison, Hunt, Legrande, Petarski, and Taylor—a plaintiff's attorney will select four to be deposed at his office. Each of the four witnesses selected will be deposed on a single day from Monday through Thursday of the upcoming week. The attorney will consider the following restrictions:

→

Step 1:
Situation: An attorney scheduling depositions

Entities: Seven witnesses—C, E, G, H, L, P, and T

Action: Selection/Sequencing Hybrid

Limitations: Choose exactly four of seven, one deposition per day, M–Th

Step 2:

C E G H L P T

M Tu W Th | out

Selection/Distribution Hybrid Games

In Selection/Distribution Hybrids, the task is to select a handful of members out of the initial entity list, and then to divide them into two (or, rarely, three) groups. Here's a model Selection/Distribution Hybrid game setup:

Next week, the seven members of Woodbury's town council—Allen, Bennett, Chen, Dillard, Emery, Flippo, and Guilini—will meet to determine the composition of two subcommittees, one on parks and one on schools. Each subcommittee will have three members, and no council member may serve on more than one subcommittee. The following restrictions apply:

Step 1:

Situation: A town council creating two subcommittees

Entities: Seven council members—A, B, C, D, E, F, and G

Action: Selection/Distribution Hybrid

Limitations: Choose six out of seven, and divide those chosen into two three-person subcommittees

Step 2:

→

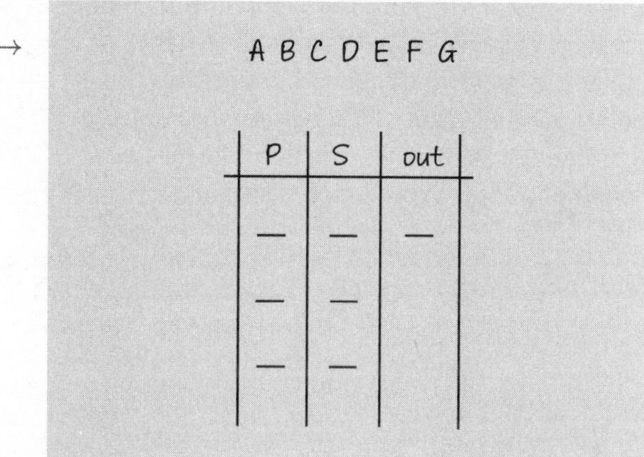

The testmaker could combine any of the standard game actions to create a Hybrid game, but the four Hybrids just illustrated are, by far, the most common. The other combinations are rare enough that they don't warrant too much of your study and practice time. For good measure, you will see a rare Selection/Matching Hybrid game in the Special Feature called "The Dinosaur Game" after Chapter 10.

Hybrid Games are covered in detail in Chapter 10.

Rare Game Types: Process and Mapping Games

There are two extremely rare game types that the test has featured in the past: Process games and Mapping games. Indeed, they are so rare that you should focus on learning all of the standard actions and common Hybrids before diving into them.

Process games were fairly common in LSATs administered in the early 1990s, but then disappeared from the test for more than two decades. PrepTest 80 (December 2016) surprisingly featured a Process game, the first to appear on a released test in more than 20 years. At this point, there is no way to know if this game signals a return to Process by the testmaker, or if it was just a one off. You can study that game in the Special Feature titled "2016: The Return of Process" in the middle of Chapter 11.

The LSAT has featured only five mapping games among the more than 80 officially released tests. Four of those appeared in 1992 and 1995. There was one more on PrepTest40 (June 2003). Since that time, the testmaker appears to have abandoned Mapping as a game type, and there has been nothing to indicate that a new Mapping game is imminent.

Chapter 11 covers what you need to know about these rare game types.

Practice

Now, practice your skills at identifying game types and creating sketches. This section contains two Practice Sets, each with eight model logic game setups. Practice Set 1 contains relatively simple setups, while in Practice Set 2, some of the setups are a little more complex. After each set, you can see analysis and sketches of LSAT experts, and get advice about how to compare your work to theirs.

Practice Set 1

Directions: Take no more than 16 minutes to perform Steps 1 and 2 of the Logic Games Method on the following eight model setups. For each, conduct the Overview by answering the SEAL questions, and then create a simple, accurate initial Sketch.

Logic Game setup		My Analysis
1. The judge at a dog show is determining the final rankings of seven dogs—an affenpinscher, a bulldog, a collie, a dachshund, a mastiff, a pointer, and a Westie. The dogs are ranked from first through seventh with no ties. The following conditions apply to the judge's decisions:	→	**Step 1:** Situation: Entities: Action: Limitations: **Step 2:**
2. A natural history museum curator is deciding which of the following animal models—a Camelops, a Dire Wolf, a Glyptodon, an Irish Elk, a Mastodon, a Sabre-tooth Cat, and a Wooly Mammoth—to feature in a diorama on extinct Ice Age mammals. The curator's decisions must accord with the following considerations:	→	**Step 1:** Situation: Entities: Action: Limitations: **Step 2:**

Logic Game setup		My Analysis
3. The manager of a snack concessions business must assign six employees—Johnson, Lemond, Mtumbe, Norton, Oliver, and Pate—to various positions at a parade. Four of the employees will be assigned to specific kiosks numbered 1 through 4 along the parade route. The other two employees will "float," walking up and down the parade route to sell snacks to the crowd. The employees' assignments must conform to the following constraints:	→	**Step 1:** Situation: Entities: Action: Limitations: **Step 2:**
4. A student is getting ready to move home from her dormitory at the end of the Spring semester. From among nine items of clothing—four sweaters, one each of the colors blue, green, red, and yellow, and five blouses, one each in the colors blue, green, red, white, and yellow—she will choose four items to take home, four items to donate to charity, and one item to wear. The following conditions apply:	→	**Step 1:** Situation: Entities: Action: Limitations: **Step 2:**
5. Five friends—Emily, Gabriela, Lawrence, Maren, and Thomasina—are creating costumes for their town's upcoming Renaissance Faire. As part of their costumes, each friend will carry between one and three of the following props: an axe, a crossbow, a dagger, a pike, and a shield. The friends select the props for their costumes according to the following conditions:	→	**Step 1:** Situation: Entities: Action: Limitations: **Step 2:**

Logic Game setup		My Analysis
6. A software company is developing four new apps codenamed Projects A, B, C, and D. Four of the company's employees—Grayson, Hiller, Lutowski, and Mihn—will each work on between one and three projects, and on no other projects. The assignment of employees to projects is subject to the following restrictions:	→	**Step 1:** Situation: Entities: Action: Limitations: **Step 2:**
7. A quality control manager will sample six soda pop flavors—cola, ginger ale, lemon-lime, orange, raspberry, and tamarind—to ensure that each one meets the company's standards for flavor and quality. She will sample each flavor one time according to the following conditions:	→	**Step 1:** Situation: Entities: Action: Limitations: **Step 2:**
8. This year, the theme of North Grove Elementary School's fall pageant is ecology. For a song about coral reefs, six students—Jiro, Kandace, Maurice, Rutger, Sudeepa, and Teri—will stand in six positions from stage left to stage right, one student for each position. Each of the students will be dressed in one of three costumes—anemone, clownfish, or dugong. The assignments of position and costume accord with the following conditions:	→	**Step 1:** Situation: Entities: Action: Limitations: **Step 2:**

Explanations

Compare your work to that of the LSAT experts. Pay close attention to each game's action and sketch. If you missed any of the games' actions, go back to the description and illustration of that game type to clear up any confusion. Don't worry if the language you use to answer the SEAL questions is different than that of the experts as long as your analysis is accurate. When comparing sketches, look for cases in which the expert's analysis was clearer, simpler, or easier to recreate than yours was.

Logic Game setup	My Analysis
1. The judge at a dog show is determining the final rankings of seven dogs—an affenpinscher, a bulldog, a collie, a dachshund, a mastiff, a pointer, and a Westie. The dogs are ranked from first through seventh with no ties. The following conditions apply to the judge's decisions: →	**Step 1:** Situation: A judge determining the final standings at a dog show Entities: Seven dogs—A, B, C, D, M, P, and W Action: Sequencing. If the rules refer to specific positions, this will be Strict Sequencing. If the rules give only relative positions among the dogs, this will be Loose Sequencing. Limitations: No ties, one dog per position **Step 2:** This is the Strict Sequencing sketch: A B C D M P W _ _ _ _ _ _ _ 1 2 3 4 5 6 7 If the game turns out to be Loose Sequencing, the sketch will be a "tree" showing the dogs' relative positions to one another.
2. A natural history museum curator is deciding which of the following animal models—a Camelops, a Dire Wolf, a Glyptodon, an Irish Elk, a Mastodon, a Sabre-tooth Cat, and a Wooly Mammoth—to feature in a diorama on extinct Ice Age mammals. The curator's decisions must accord with the following considerations: →	**Step 1:** Situation: A museum curator choosing models for a diorama Entities: Seven models—C, D, G, I, M, S, and W Action: Selection Limitations: None **Step 2:** C D G I M S W

Logic Game setup	My Analysis
3. The manager of a snack concessions business must assign six employees—Johnson, Lemond, Mtumbe, Norton, Oliver, and Pate—to various positions at a parade. Four of the employees will be assigned to specific kiosks numbered 1 through 4 along the parade route. The other two employees will "float," walking up and down the parade route to sell snacks to the crowd. The employees' assignments must conform to the following constraints: →	**Step 1:** Situation: A concessions manager assigning employees for specific and general positions at a parade Entities: Six employees—J, L, M, N, O, and P Action: Selection/Sequencing Hybrid Limitations: Four of the six selected for specific assignments, one per position **Step 2:** 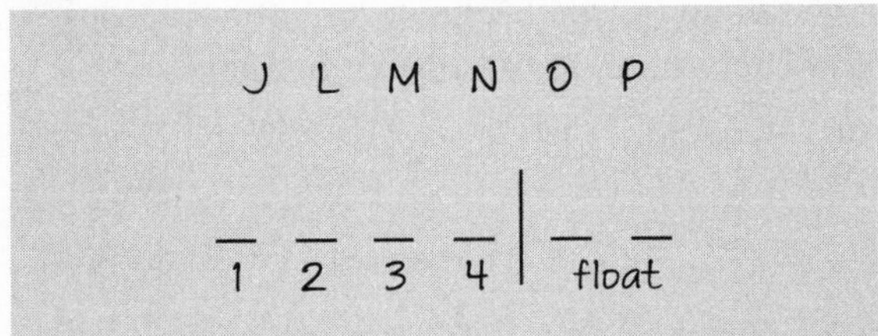
4. A student is getting ready to move home from her dormitory at the end of the Spring semester. From among nine items of clothing—four sweaters, one each of the colors blue, green, red, and yellow, and five blouses, one each in the colors blue, green, red, white, and yellow—she will choose four items to take home, four items to donate to charity, and one item to wear. The following conditions apply: →	**Step 1:** Situation: A student separating clothes to pack, donate, and wear Entities: Nine clothing items—B_S, G_S, R_S, Y_S, B_B, G_B, R_B, W_B, and Y_B Action: Distribution Limitations: Take home four, donate four, wear one **Step 2:** 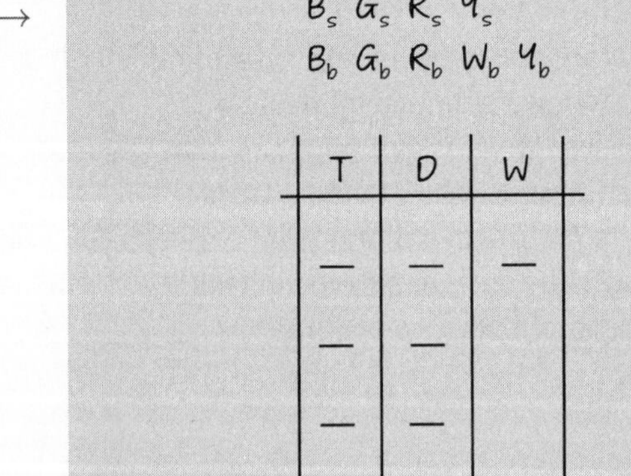

Logic Game setup	My Analysis
5. Five friends—Emily, Gabriela, Lawrence, Maren, and Thomasina—are creating costumes for their town's upcoming Renaissance Faire. As part of their costumes, each friend will carry between one and three of the following props: an axe, a crossbow, a dagger, a pike, and a shield. The friends select the props for their costumes according to the following conditions: →	**Step 1:** Situation: Friends selecting items for costumes Entities: Five friends—E, G, L, M, and T—and five props—a, c, d, p, and s Action: Matching Limitations: Each friend chooses between one and three props. **Step 2:** 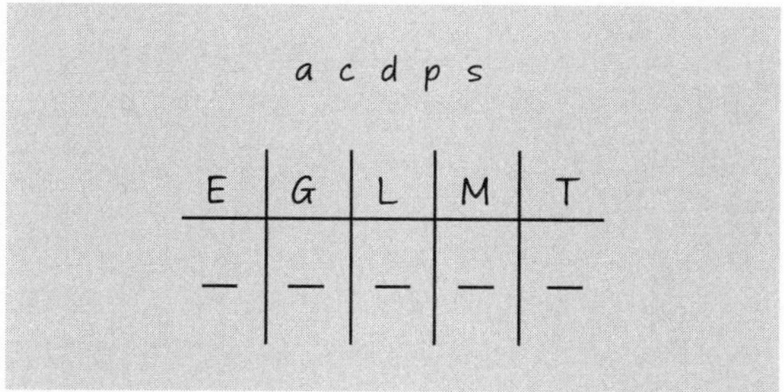
6. A software company is developing four new apps codenamed Projects A, B, C, and D. Four of the company's employees—Grayson, Hiller, Lutowski, and Mihn—will each work on between one and three projects, and on no other projects. The assignment of employees to projects is subject to the following restrictions: 	**Step 1:** Situation: Software company assigning employees to projects Entities: Four projects—a, b, c, and d—and four employees—G, H, L, and M Action: Matching Limitations: Each employee is assigned to between one and three of the projects. **Step 2:** 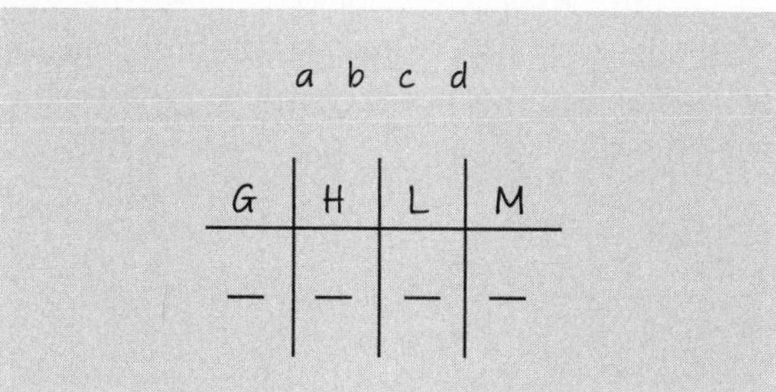

Logic Game setup	My Analysis
7. A quality control manager will sample six soda pop flavors—cola, ginger ale, lemon-lime, orange, raspberry, and tamarind—to ensure that each one meets the company's standards for flavor and quality. She will sample each flavor one time according to the following conditions:	**Step 1:** Situation: A manager sampling six different flavors of soda Entities: Six flavors—C, G, L, O, R, and T Action: Sequencing. If the rules refer to specific positions, this will be Strict Sequencing. If the rules give only relative positions among the soda flavors, this will be Loose Sequencing. Limitations: Each flavor sampled one time → **Step 2:** This is the Strict Sequencing sketch: C G L O R T _ _ _ _ _ _ 1 2 3 4 5 6 If the game turns out to be Loose Sequencing, the sketch will be a "tree" showing the sodas' relative positions to one another.
8. This year, the theme of North Grove Elementary School's fall pageant is ecology. For a song about coral reefs, six students—Jiro, Kandace, Maurice, Rutger, Sudeepa, and Teri—will stand in six positions from stage left to stage right, one student for each position. Each of the students will be dressed in one of three costumes—anemone, clownfish, or dugong. The assignments of position and costume accord with the following conditions:	**Step 1:** Situation: Students taking positions on stage for an ecology pageant Entities: Six students—J, K, M, R, S, and T—and three costumes—a, c, and d Action: Sequencing/Matching Hybrid → Limitations: One student per position, and one costume per student **Step 2:** _ _ _ _ _ _ J K M R S T _ _ _ _ _ _ a c d 1 2 3 4 5 6

When you're ready, practice Steps 1 and 2 of the Logic Games Method on Practice Set 2, in which you'll see somewhat more complex setups.

Practice Set 2

Directions: Take no more than 16 minutes to perform Steps 1 and 2 of the Logic Games Method on the following eight model setups. For each, conduct the Overview by answering the SEAL questions, and then create a simple, accurate initial Sketch.

Logic Game setup		My Analysis
9. At a switching yard, seven freight cars—T, U, V, W, X, Y, and Z—are assigned to seven positions—numbered 1 (closest to the front of the train) through 7 (closest to the back of the train). Each freight car carries one type of product—dry goods, foodstuffs, or machinery. The order of the cars and the cargo each carries are subject to the following restrictions:	→	**Step 1:** Situation: Entities: Action: Limitations: **Step 2:**
10. Officials are determining the order in which six gymnasts—Quinn, Roland, and Sung from Bradley School; Tucker and Umali from Carlton Academy; and Winters from Dearborn Prep—will compete in the floor exercises portion of a gymnastics competition. Gymnasts from the same school may not compete consecutively. The officials must adhere to the following criteria:	→	**Step 1:** Situation: Entities: Action: Limitations: **Step 2:**

Logic Game setup		My Analysis
11. The environmental agency of Country X is assembling a scientific research team to assess conditions in a remote mountainous region of the country. The team will consist of four of the following eight candidates: botanists Able and Barker; cartographers Dennis, Elwood, and Fuqua; and zoologists Montrose, Norwood, and Olague. Selection of the research team will be determined by the following restrictions:	→	**Step 1:** Situation: Entities: Action: Limitations: **Step 2:**
12. During the upcoming week, Professor Howser must schedule exactly two appointments with each of four graduate students—Aaliyah, Clark, Jennifer, and Marcus—and hold open office hours exactly two times. Professor Howser has two appointment times, one in the morning and one in the afternoon, each day, Monday through Friday. The professor's schedule for the upcoming week will conform to the following constraints:	→	**Step 1:** Situation: Entities: Action: Limitations: **Step 2:**
13. A homeowner is arranging six houseplants—an aloe, a cactus, a dracaena, an ivy, a lily, and a spider plant—by placing each on the left, center, or right of one of two shelves—an upper shelf and a lower shelf. The placement of the plants corresponds to the following considerations:	→	**Step 1:** Situation: Entities: Action: Limitations: **Step 2:**

Logic Game setup		My Analysis
14. El Dorado Middle School's Chess Club has eight students—8th Graders Cole, Morimoto, Peters, and Stein, and 7th Graders Dillard, Francis, Nowak, and Orban. The club will enter two four-person teams—called Team 1 and Team 2—into an upcoming tournament. Each club member is assigned to exactly one team. One player on each team is designated as that team's captain. The teams must adhere to the following restrictions:	→	**Step 1:** Situation: Entities: Action: Limitations: **Step 2:**
15. Three dancers—Kathryn, Martha, and Twyla—will each wear costumes consisting of a dress, a shawl, and a hat. Each piece of clothing is a single color—floral white, pale green, or sky blue. The following restrictions apply to the dancers' choice of colors:	→	**Step 1:** Situation: Entities: Action: Limitations: **Step 2:**
16. Eight players—A, B, C, D, E, F, G, and H—and one dealer are seated around a poker table. Each player is assigned to one of eight seats, numbered 1 through 8 clockwise from the dealer's left. The assignment of players to seats will conform to the following conditions:	→	**Step 1:** Situation: Entities: Action: Limitations: **Step 2:**

Explanations

Compare your work to that of the LSAT experts. Pay close attention to each game's action and sketch. If you missed any of the games' actions, go back to the description and illustration of that game type to clear up any confusion. Don't worry if the language you use to answer the SEAL questions is different than that of the experts as long as your analysis is accurate. When comparing sketches, look for cases in which the expert's analysis was clearer, simpler, or easier to recreate than yours was.

Logic Game setup		Analysis
9. At a switching yard, seven freight cars—T, U, V, W, X, Y, and Z—are assigned to seven positions—numbered 1 (closest to the front of the train) through 7 (closest to the back of the train). Each freight car carries one type of product—dry goods, foodstuffs, or machinery. The order of the cars and the cargo each carries are subject to the following restrictions:	→	**Step 1:** Situation: Putting freight cars in order for a train, and determining the cargo of each car Entities: Seven train cars—T, U, V, W, X, Y, and Z—and three types of cargo—d, f, and m Action: Sequencing/Matching Hybrid Limitations: One car per position, and one type of cargo per car **Step 2:** 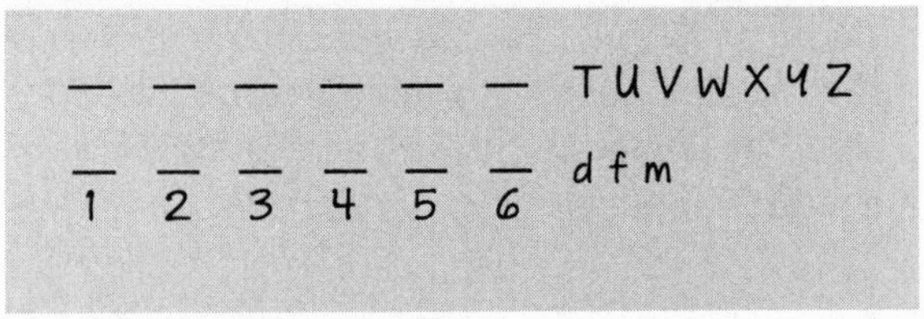 _ _ _ _ _ _ TUVWXYZ _ _ _ _ _ _ dfm 1 2 3 4 5 6
10. Officials are determining the order in which six gymnasts—Quinn, Roland, and Sung from Bradley School; Tucker and Umali from Carlton Academy; and Winters from Dearborn Prep—will compete in the floor exercises portion of a gymnastics competition. Gymnasts from the same school may not compete consecutively. The officials must adhere to the following criteria:	→	**Step 1:** Situation: Determining the order in which six gymnasts will perform floor exercises Entities: Three students from Bradley—Q, R, and S—two from Carlton—T and U—and one from Dearborn—W Action: Strict Sequencing (The limitation on students from the same school would be unlikely in a Loose Sequencing game.) Limitations: One student per position; never consecutive positions for students from the same school **Step 2:** 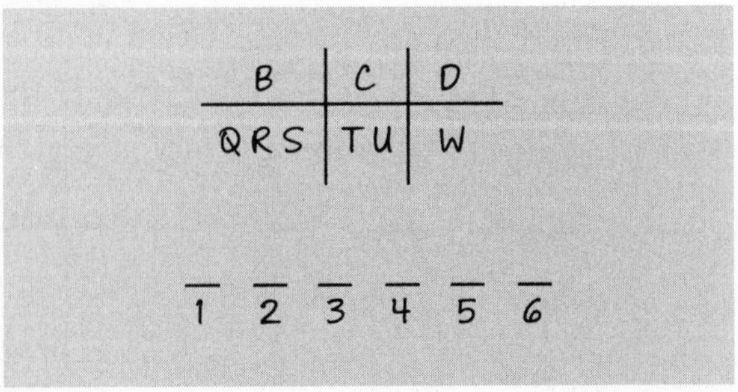 B | C | D QRS | TU | W _ _ _ _ _ _ 1 2 3 4 5 6

Logic Game setup	Analysis
11. The environmental agency of Country X is assembling a scientific research team to assess conditions in a remote mountainous region of the country. The team will consist of four of the following eight candidates: botanists Able and Barker; cartographers Dennis, Elwood, and Fuqua; and zoologists Montrose, Norwood, and Olague. Selection of the research team will be determined by the following restrictions:	**Step 1:** Situation: Choosing scientists for a research team Entities: Two botanists—A and B—three cartographers—D, E, and F—and three zoologists—M, N, and O Action: Selection Limitations: Choose four of the eight scientists  **Step 2:** 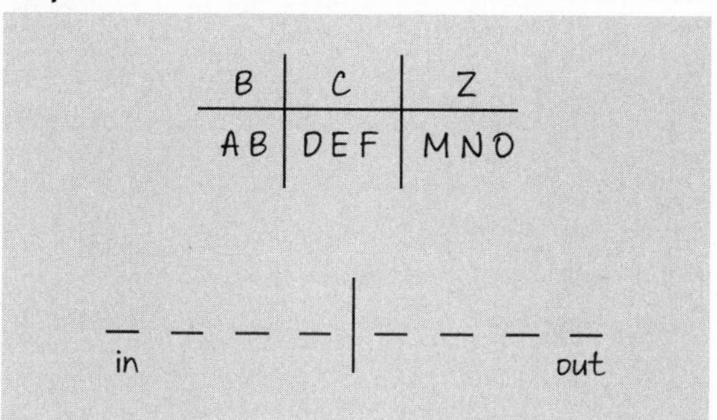
12. During the upcoming week, Professor Howser must schedule exactly two appointments with each of four graduate students—Aaliyah, Clark, Jennifer, and Marcus—and hold open office hours exactly two times. Professor Howser has two appointment times, one in the morning and one in the afternoon, each day, Monday through Friday. The professor's schedule for the upcoming week will conform to the following constraints:	**Step 1:** Situation: A professor schedules office hours and meetings with graduate students Entities: Four students—A, C, J, and M—and two office hours spots Action: Strict Sequencing (Double) Limitations: Two appointments with each student **Step 2:** → 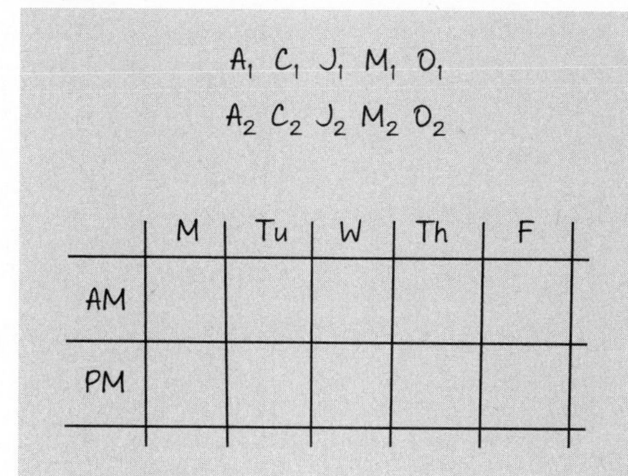

Logic Game setup	Analysis
13. A homeowner is arranging six houseplants—an aloe, a cactus, a dracaena, an ivy, a lily, and a spider plant—by placing each on the left, center, or right of one of two shelves—an upper shelf and a lower shelf. The placement of the plants corresponds to the following considerations: →	**Step 1:** Situation: A homeowner arranging houseplants on shelves Entities: Six houseplants—A, C, D, I, L, and S Action: Distribution/Sequencing Hybrid Limitations: Three plants per shelf, one plant per position **Step 2:** 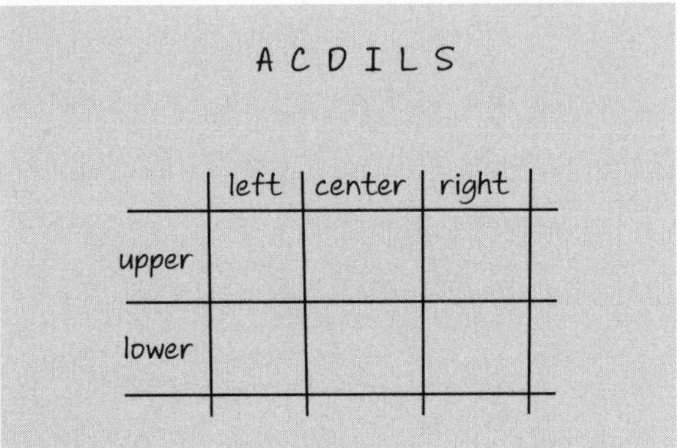
14. El Dorado Middle School's Chess Club has eight students—8th Graders Cole, Morimoto, Peters, and Stein, and 7th Graders Dillard, Francis, Nowak, and Orban. The club will enter two four-person teams—called Team 1 and Team 2—into an upcoming tournament. Each club member is assigned to exactly one team. One player on each team is designated as that team's captain. The teams must adhere to the following restrictions: →	**Step 1:** Situation: Dividing students into teams, and designating team captains Entities: Four seventh graders—D, F, N, and O—and four eighth graders—C, M, P, and S Action: Distribution Limitations: Four students per team, one captain per team **Step 2:** 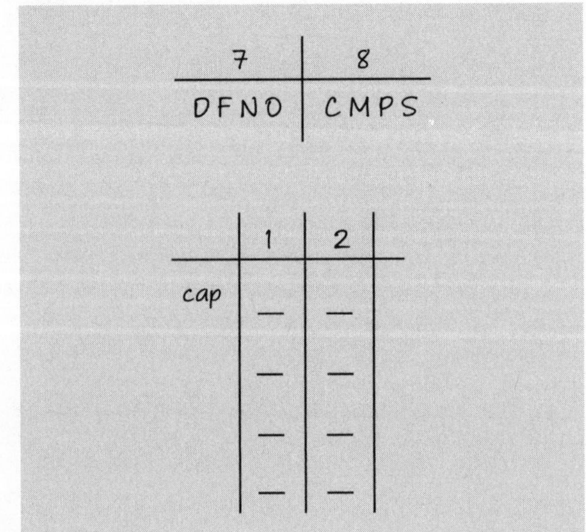

Logic Game setup	Analysis
15. Three dancers—Kathryn, Martha, and Twyla—will each wear costumes consisting of a dress, a shawl, and a hat. Each piece of clothing is a single color—floral white, pale green, or sky blue. The following restrictions apply to the dancers' choice of colors: →	**Step 1:** Situation: Assigning costume pieces with different colors to three dancers Entities: Three dancers—K, M, and T—and three costume pieces—D, S, and H—each in one of three colors—fw, pg, and sb Action: Matching Limitations: One color per costume piece for each dancer **Step 2:** 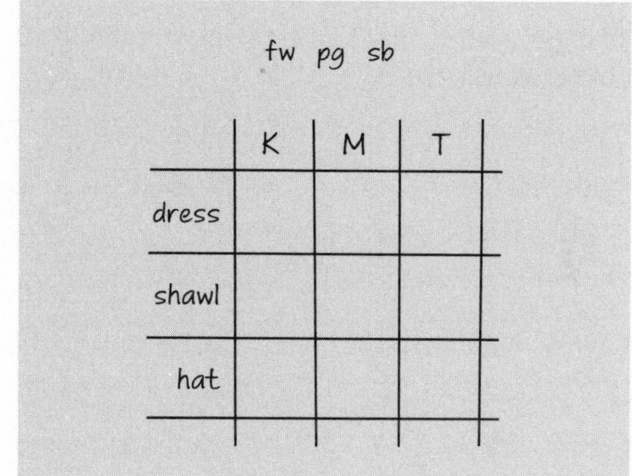
16. Eight players—A, B, C, D, E, F, G, and H—and one dealer are seated around a poker table. Each player is assigned to one of eight seats, numbered 1 through 8 clockwise from the dealer's left. The assignment of players to seats will conform to the following conditions: →	**Step 1:** Situation: Arranging card players around a table Entities: Eight players—A, B, C, D, E, F, G, and H Action: Sequencing (Circular) Limitations: One player per seat **Step 2:** 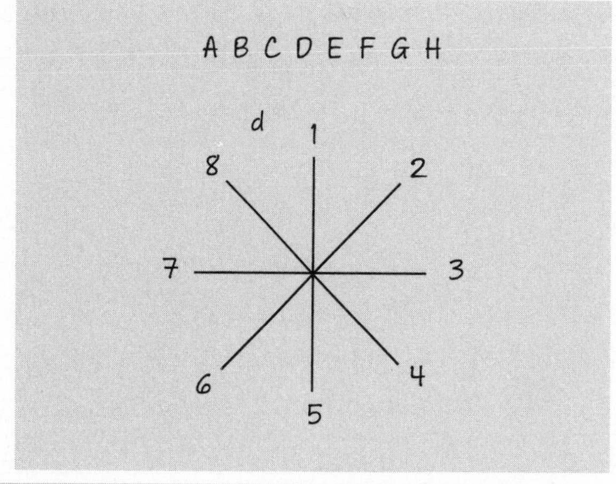

After comparing your work on the Practice Sets with that of the experts, do any review and study you feel is warranted to correct any mistakes you may have made. When you're ready, turn to the self-assessment in the Perform quiz.

Perform

Use the following quiz to assess your mastery of Steps 1 and 2 of the Logic Games Method.

Directions: Take no more than 22 minutes to perform Steps 1 and 2 of the Logic Games Method on the following eleven model setups. For each, conduct the Overview by answering the SEAL questions, and then create a simple, accurate initial Sketch.

Logic Game setup		My Analysis
1. A florist is delivering seven bouquets—A, B, C, D, E, F, and G—to seven different clients. Each client will receive exactly one of the bouquets. The order of the deliveries, from earliest to latest, conforms to the following rules:	→	**Step 1:** Situation: Entities: Action: Limitations: **Step 2:**
2. The manager of a department store is deciding which five pieces of furniture to display in a store window. There are seven pieces for the manager to choose from—a bookcase, a chair, a desk, a lamp, a mirror, a nightstand, and a table. The manager will make her selection based on the following rules:	→	**Step 1:** Situation: Entities: Action: Limitations: **Step 2:**

Logic Game setup		My Analysis
3. A coin collector is preparing to sell some of his coins. He has five coins—A, B, C, D, and E—that he will place in a display box. Each coin will occupy one of five spots, numbered one through five and arranged from left to right. Each of the coins will be assigned a different value, the cheapest coin being priced at $10 and the most expensive coin at $30. The other coins are priced at $5 increments between those values. The following conditions apply:	→	**Step 1:** Situation: Entities: Action: Limitations: **Step 2:**
4. A grocer is determining the location in which to place a number of new food items. Each one of the following products—avocado juice, banana yogurt, cashew bars, kale bread, pistachio butter, quinoa flour, and yellow rice—will be placed in exactly one of the following aisles: 1, 2, or 3. The grocer makes her decisions based on the following rules:	→	**Step 1:** Situation: Entities: Action: Limitations: **Step 2:**
5. A pharmaceutical company is planning on releasing a series of six new medications tentatively named N, P, Q, R, S, and T. Each medication will be released at a different time, and each medication will be marketed to exactly one of the following demographics: people who suffer from insomnia, people who suffer from migraines, or people who suffer from ulcers. The following conditions apply:	→	**Step 1:** Situation: Entities: Action: Limitations: **Step 2:**

Logic Game setup		My Analysis
6. In order to learn more about the new students in her class, a teacher attempts to determine which extracurricular activities these students are involved in. Each of her new students—J, K, L, M, and N—participate in at least one and at most three of the following activities: archery team, basketball, chess club, foreign language club, and glee club. The students' activities correspond to the following conditions:	→	**Step 1:** Situation: Entities: Action: Limitations: **Step 2:**
7. An arborist is determining the order in which to plant a series of trees. He will plant one tree of each of the following varieties—elm, gingko, maple, oak, sycamore, tulip, and willow—along the top of a ridge. Each tree will be separated from the next tree by ten feet, and each tree will be numbered 1 through 7, moving from east to west, according to the following stipulations:	→	**Step 1:** Situation: Entities: Action: Limitations: **Step 2:**
8. Pamela is throwing a surprise party for her friend Sam. In considering which of the following friends—F, G, H, J, K, L, and M—to invite to the party, Pamela adheres to the following conditions:	→	**Step 1:** Situation: Entities: Action: Limitations: **Step 2:**

Logic Game setup		My Analysis
9. A dental student is learning how to identify different teeth. Teeth always fit this pattern, moving from the front of the mouth to the back: central incisor, lateral incisor, canine, first premolar, second premolar, and first molar. She has six teeth labeled A, B, C, D, E, and F. Each tooth is a different type, and each fits one of the labels described above. As she attempts to match each tooth to its proper place in the mouth, she must adhere to the following conditions:	→	**Step 1:** Situation: Entities: Action: Limitations: **Step 2:**
10. At an architectural firm, each of seven employees—A, B, C, D, E, F, and G—will be assigned to either Project X or Project Y, but not both. Each team has at least two team members. After the completion of each team's project, the team members will be evaluated and ranked according to their performance among members of the group. No team member shares the rank of any other team member. The following conditions apply:	→	**Step 1:** Situation: Entities: Action: Limitations: **Step 2:**
11. During an observational experiment, a scientist notices a chimpanzee select exactly four of six possible objects—a book, a rubber duck, a marble, a ping pong paddle, a shoe, and a toy train—and then place each of the selected items on a different shelf. The shelves are numbered from 1 (the lowest) to 4 (the highest). The scientist makes the following observations:	→	**Step 1:** Situation: Entities: Action: Limitations: **Step 2:**

Explanations

Compare your analysis and sketches to those of LSAT experts. Keep track of any case in which you misidentified the Action in the model setup, and any case in which you drew a sketch framework that does not match the game type.

Logic Game setup		My Analysis
1. A florist is delivering seven bouquets—A, B, C, D, E, F, and G—to seven different clients. Each client will receive exactly one of the bouquets. The order of the deliveries, from earliest to latest, conforms to the following rules:	→	**Step 1:** Situation: A florist is deciding the order of seven deliveries. Entities: The seven bouquets—A, B, C, D, E, F, and G Action: Sequencing. If the rules mention specific positions or separate entities by a specific number of spaces, this will be Strict Sequencing. If the rules mention only the relative positions of the entities, this will be Loose Sequencing. Limitations: Because each of the deliveries will be to one client, no client gets multiple bouquets or zero bouquets. **Step 2:** If the game is Strict Sequencing, this is the opening sketch A B C D E F G (earliest) _ _ _ _ _ _ _ (latest) 1 2 3 4 5 6 7 If the game is Loose Sequencing, the sketch will be a "tree" as established by the rules.
2. The manager of a department store is deciding which five pieces of furniture to display in a store window. There are seven pieces for the manager to choose from—a bookcase, a chair, a desk, a lamp, a mirror, a nightstand, and a table. The manager will make her selection based on the following rules:	→	**Step 1:** Situation: A store manager is deciding which pieces of furniture she wants to put on display. Entities: Seven pieces of furniture—B, C, D, L, M, N, and T Action: Selection. Pick five of the seven pieces of furniture. Limitations: Exactly five of the seven pieces will be selected. **Step 2:** Because there is a pre-determined number of pieces of furniture to choose, use an in-out sketch: B C D L M N T in | out _ _ _ _ _ | _ _

Logic Game setup	My Analysis
3. A coin collector is preparing to sell some of his coins. He has five coins—A, B, C, D, and E—that he will place in a display box. Each coin will occupy one of five spots, numbered one through five and arranged from left to right. Each of the coins will be assigned a different value, the cheapest coin being priced at \$10 and the most expensive coin at \$30. The other coins are priced at \$5 increments between those values. The following conditions apply: →	**Step 1:** Situation: A coin collector is arranging coins in a display box, and each coin has a different monetary value. Entities: The five coins—A, B, C, D, and E—and the five values—\$10, \$15, \$20, \$25, and \$30 Action: Sequencing/Matching Hybrid. Put the coins in order, and determine the value of each coin. Limitations: Each coin will be used, and each spot will have a coin. **Step 2:** Some rules might match a dollar value to a coin, but ultimately each coin will occupy a single spot, and so will each dollar value. Set up a sketch that has two layers, one for the coins and one for the values. — — — — — A B C D E — — — — — 10, 15, 20, 25, 30 1 2 3 4 5
4. A grocer is determining the location in which to place a number of new food items. Each one of the following products—avocado juice, banana yogurt, cashew bars, kale bread, pistachio butter, quinoa flour, and yellow rice—will be placed in exactly one of the following aisles: 1, 2, or 3. The grocer makes her decisions based on the following rules: →	**Step 1:** Situation: A grocer is trying to figure out where to place new food items. Entities: The food items—A, B, C, K, P, Q, and Y Action: Distribution. Sort the seven food items into the three aisles. Limitations: Each food item will be placed into exactly one of the three aisles. **Step 2:** Because each item is going to be placed into exactly one aisle, this is a Distribution game. Set up a table: 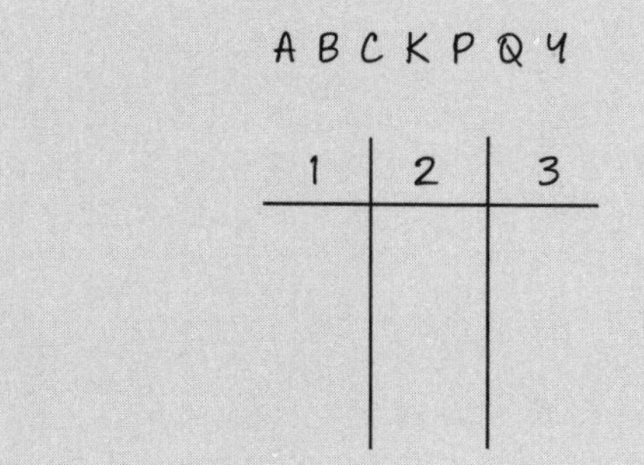

Logic Game setup	My Analysis
5. A pharmaceutical company is planning on releasing a series of six new medications tentatively named N, P, Q, R, S, and T. Each medication will be released at a different time, and each medication will be marketed to exactly one of the following demographics: people who suffer from insomnia, people who suffer from migraines, or people who suffer from ulcers. The following conditions apply: →	**Step 1:** Situation: A drug company is scheduling a roll out of new medications. Entities: The six new drugs—N, P, Q, R, S, and T—and the people to whom the drugs will be marketed—i, m, and u Action: Sequencing/Matching Hybrid. In addition to determining the order of the release of the drugs, also determine each drug's type. Limitations: Every drug gets its own release date, and every drug is marketed to only one group. There are no limitations yet on how many drugs are of each type. **Step 2:** — — — — — — NPQRST — — — — — — imu 1 2 3 4 5 6
6. In order to learn more about the new students in her class, a teacher attempts to determine which extracurricular activities these students are involved in. Each of her new students—J, K, L, M, and N—participate in at least one and at most three of the following activities: archery team, basketball, chess club, foreign language club, and glee club. The students' activities correspond to the following conditions: →	**Step 1:** Situation: A teacher is figuring out which activities her students are involved in. Entities: The five students—J, K, L, M, and N—and the five distinct activities—a, b, c, f, and g Action: Matching. Determine which activities each student participates in. Limitations: Each student will participate in a minimum of one and a maximum of three of the listed activities. There is no limit on how many students can participate in each activity—for example, it's possible that none of the students participate in glee club, but it's also possible that they all do. **Step 2:** Set up a table with the students affixed at the top of the sketch. a b c f g J | K | L | M | N — | — | — | — | —

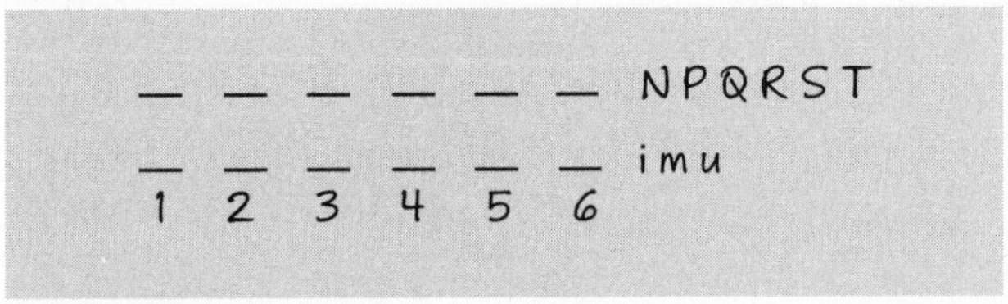

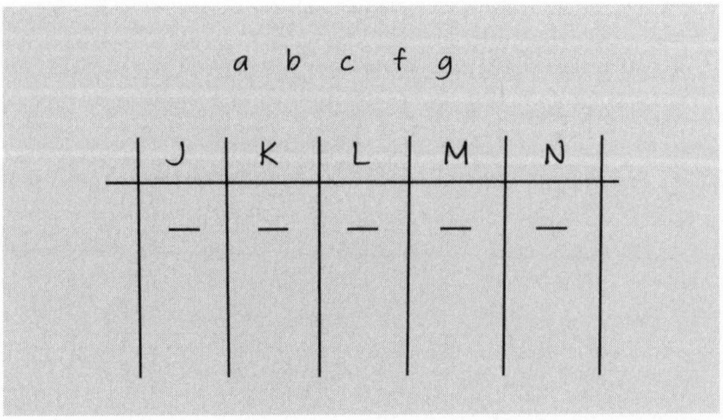

Logic Game setup	My Analysis
7. An arborist is determining the order in which to plant a series of trees. He will plant one tree of each of the following varieties—elm, gingko, maple, oak, sycamore, tulip, and willow—along the top of a ridge. Each tree will be separated from the next tree by ten feet, and each tree will be numbered 1 through 7, moving from east to west, according to the following stipulations: →	**Step 1:** Situation: An arborist is arranging trees in a line. Entities: The seven tree varieties—E, G, M, O, S, T, and W Action: Sequencing. If the rules mention specific positions or separate entities by a specific number of spaces, this will be Strict Sequencing. If the rules mention only the relative positions of the entities, this will be Loose Sequencing. Limitations: Each tree gets its own spot, and the arrangement is horizontal—east to west. **Step 2:** If the game is Strict Sequencing, this is the opening sketch (keep in mind you will need to correctly label the sketch east and west): E G M O S T W west _ _ _ _ _ _ _ east 7 6 5 4 3 2 1
8. Pamela is throwing a surprise party for her friend Sam. In considering which of the following friends—F, G, H, J, K, L, and M—to invite to the party, Pamela adheres to the following conditions: →	**Step 1:** Situation: A person is making a list of friends to invite to a party. Entities: Seven friends—F, G, H, J, K, L, and M Action: Selection. Pamela is deciding which friends to invite to the party. Limitations: None so far. Pamela could decide to invite none or all of the friends. **Step 2:** In an open-ended Selection game like this, your sketch is simply the roster of entities. You can then circle or cross out entities as they are selected or rejected in specific questions. FGHJKLM

Logic Game setup	My Analysis

9. A dental student is learning how to identify different teeth. Teeth always fit this pattern, moving from the front of the mouth to the back: central incisor, lateral incisor, canine, first premolar, second premolar, and first molar. She has six teeth labeled A, B, C, D, E, and F. Each tooth is a different type, and each fits one of the labels described above. As she attempts to match each tooth to its proper place in the mouth, she must adhere to the following conditions:

→

Step 1:
Situation: A dental student matching teeth to a fixed pattern.

Entities: The teeth—A, B, C, D, E, and F—and the different positions—CI, LI, CAN, P1, P2, M1.

Action: Sequencing. The student must arrange the teeth according to a fixed layout.

Limitations: Six spots for the teeth, and six different teeth. Each tooth will fit into one of the six spots.

Step 2:
Set up a Strict Sequencing sketch, and clearly label the pattern of teeth.

A B C D E F

front __ __ __ __ __ __ back
CI LI CAN P1 P2 M1

10. At an architectural firm, each of seven employees—A, B, C, D, E, F, and G—will be assigned to either Project X or Project Y, but not both. Each team has at least two team members. After the completion of each team's project, the team members will be evaluated and ranked according to their performance among members of the group. No team member shares the rank of any other team member. The following conditions apply:

→

Step 1:
Situation: Determining the projects to which different employees will be assigned, and the rank each employee achieves.

Entities: The employees—A, B, C, D, E, F, and G

Action: Sequencing/Distribution Hybrid.

Limitations: Each employee will be placed in exactly one group, and each employee receives a separate rank.

Step 2:
In a Distribution/Sequencing game, anchor your sketch around the Distribution action.

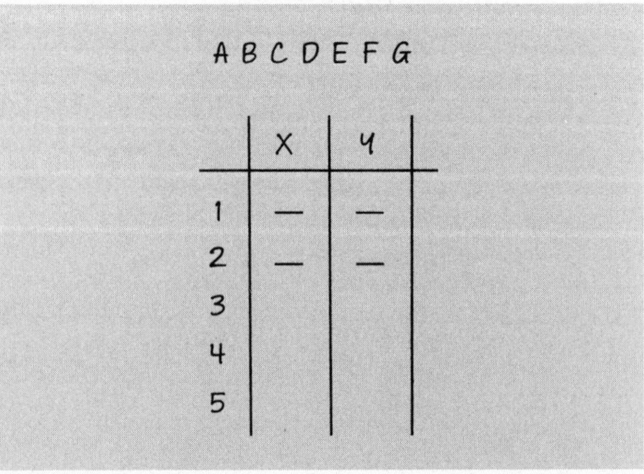

Logic Game setup	My Analysis
11. During an observational experiment, a scientist notices a chimpanzee select exactly four of six possible objects—a book, a rubber duck, a marble, a ping pong paddle, a shoe, and a toy train—and then place each item on a different shelf. The shelves are numbered from 1 (the lowest) to 4 (the highest). The scientist makes the following observations: →	**Step 1:** Situation: In a research facility, a scientist watches a chimpanzee perform certain actions. Entities: The six objects—B, D, M, P, S, and T Action: Selection/Sequencing Hybrid. Determine the four items that are selected, and put them in order from lowest to highest. Limitations: Exactly four of the six items are selected. **Step 2:** A vertical sketch matches the physical arrangement of the shelves. In addition to the four shelves, find a way to account for the two objects that are not selected. B D M P S T 4 __ | __ 3 __ | __ 2 __ | out 1 __ |

Assess

If your analysis was accurate and your sketch was appropriate in:

9–11 of the model sketches: Congratulations! You're well on your way to mastering Steps 1 and 2 of the Logic Games Method. Move on to Chapter 3 to study and practice Steps 3 (Rules) and 4 (Deductions).

6–8 of the model sketches: Good work! You have a solid foundation for Steps 1 and 2 of the Logic Games Method, but still have room to improve your skills in identifying and sketching game types. Make a note of the game types you misidentified, and study the description and illustration of those game types once more before moving on to Chapter 3. Keep the list to help you remember the game types to which you will want to give extra attention in Chapters 5–10.

1–5 of the model sketches: Keep at it. On test day, you'll need to make quick, accurate assessments of each game type you encounter, and you'll want to have a "library" of standard sketches committed to memory. First, study the Prepare portion of this chapter again to make sure you understand any of the game types you misidentified in the Perform quiz. Then, take and review the quiz titled "Game Types and Sketches Fundamentals" found in your online center. As you move forward, pay attention to the Step 1 and Step 2 analysis of each game you encounter, even in cases where the book is focusing on later steps of the Logic Games Method.

To stay sharp, practice the drills in the Logic Games Training Camp for this chapter in your Online Study Plan. Training Camp drills are divided into Fundamentals, Mid-Level, and Advanced sets.

Reflect

Think back over the work you did in this chapter.

Did you consistently conduct an Overview by answering the SEAL questions for each game setup?
How does mentally picturing a game's Situation help you understand the game's task and turn it into a useful sketch framework?
What do the entities tell you about a game's action? What may be different when the setup includes two or more *types* of entities? What may be different when the entities are subdivided in the setup?
What are four basic logic game actions? What are the most common Hybrid combinations of those actions?
What kinds of limitations does the testmaker impose upon a game in the game's setup? Were there any cases in which you took limitations for granted even though the limitations were not explicit?

In the coming days, take note of real-life jobs and tasks that mimic the standard game actions:

Sequencing: making schedules, or ranking or prioritizing items
Selection: choosing what to serve or who to invite to something
Distribution: creating teams, or separating things into different boxes or drawers
Matching: assigning items or tasks to different people, or matching attributes to different items

Try to envision how the testmaker would turn such tasks into logic games. What kinds of limitations would the test impose? What kinds of rules and restrictions might apply?

CHAPTER 3

Logic Games Rules and Deductions

THE ROLE OF RULES AND DEDUCTIONS IN LOGIC GAMES

Most LSAT experts would agree that the skills you'll learn in this chapter are the most important tools you can add to your logic games repertoire. Here, you'll learn to analyze and draw a game's rules and then—and this is what sets real Logic Games masters apart from the crowd—to combine the game's rules and limitations to determine everything that can be deduced about what must, can, and cannot be true about the arrangement of entities. Gaining mastery of the skills in this chapter is your ticket to handling the questions quickly and accurately on a consistent basis.

To this point, you've seen how LSAT experts conduct the Overview and Sketch steps of the Logic Games Method. They analyze the Situation, Entities, Action, and overall Limitations to form a clear mental picture of their task. Then, they translate that mental picture into a diagram that will hold all of the relevant restrictions. In Chapter 2, you focused on clearly analyzing a game's big picture. Now, you'll see the rules of the games as well, and you'll use the next two steps of the Logic Games Method to produce a comprehensive Master Sketch for each game. Here, you'll have plenty of opportunities to practice analyzing and sketching rules and then combining them to make all available deductions.

When LSAT experts draw out a game's rules, they depict them clearly, in a way that matches and fits into the framework of their sketch and accounts for what the rule does and does not mean. In the first part of this chapter, you'll see how LSAT experts are able to do that within each of the common game types using the typical sketches introduced in Chapter 2.

In the second part of this chapter, you'll learn how experts then combine the rules to determine what must, can, and cannot be true of the entities in the game. LSAT experts use a checklist of five common patterns to ensure that they spot all of the game's deductions and are able to tackle the game's questions with confidence, knowing that they have maximized the available information. At the end of the chapter, you'll see a Special Feature on one of those patterns—Limited Options—that can, in some games, double the power of your Master Sketch.

HOW TO INTERPRET AND SKETCH RULES

LEARNING OBJECTIVES

In this section of Chapter 3, you'll learn to:

- Analyze and depict Logic Games rules effectively
  Before jotting down a rule, LSAT experts make sure that they understand the rule thoroughly. They are careful not to read more into a rule than what it says while, at the same time, accounting for all of the restrictions that the rule imposes within the game.

Prepare

LSAT experts know that rules are their best friends. With no rules, a Strict Sequencing game that asks you to arrange seven entities into seven slots, one per slot, has 5,040 acceptable arrangements. Add just one rule—"P is placed sixth"—and you reduce the number of acceptable arrangements to just 720. Depending on the additional rules, it's not uncommon for such a game on the LSAT to have fewer than 20 possible solutions. In short, it is the rules that make games manageable.

In this section of the chapter, you'll see the strategies and tactics that LSAT experts use to analyze and depict Logic Games rules in the most helpful way. First, you'll learn the most common rule patterns. Then, you'll look at sets of rules within the context of game setups. You'll have the opportunity to practice analyzing and drawing the rules associated with game setups. Finally, you'll assess your skill level with four more model and official game setups.

LOGIC GAMES STRATEGY

When analyzing and drawing a rule, always ask:

- Who/what does the rule restrict?
- Who/what does the rule leave undetermined?
- Is the rule stated in affirmative or negative terms?
- If stated affirmatively, can I learn something concrete from its negative implications (or vice versa)?
- Can I place the rule directly into the sketch framework?
- If not, how can I best draw the rule to account for what it does and does not restrict?

Common Rule Patterns

Rules, of course, are specific to the logic game setups they accompany. They restrict the entities within the given framework. But, just as there are a handful of game actions that occur again and again, so are there standard types of rules. Take a look at the affirmative and negative implications of the most common rules that appear in logic games.

Established Entities Rules

Established entities are committed to a particular position or placement throughout the game. *Affirmative* rules creating established entities are clear and concrete, and should be written directly into the sketch framework. For example, in a Sequencing game, you might see:

Lana is the fourth presenter.

L
1 2 3 4 5 6

Similarly, you might see the following in a Distribution game:

Quincy is assigned to Team 2.

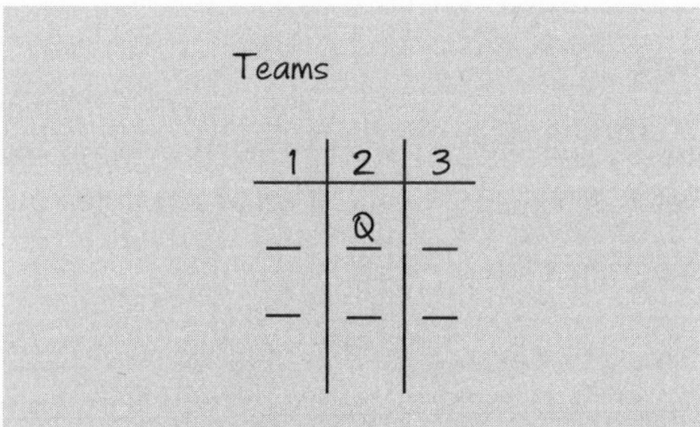

The *negative* implications of these rules are equally straightforward: The established entity does *not* go anywhere else. Because an established entity's placement is so clear, there is no reason to record the negative implications in the sketch.

There are two similar types of rules worth mentioning here.

Rules that limit an entity's placement

The most common rules of this type *affirmatively* restrict an entity to one of two positions. Like pure established entity rules, these rules can usually be depicted within the sketch framework. The Sequencing game example would state something such as:

Tom presents either first or sixth.

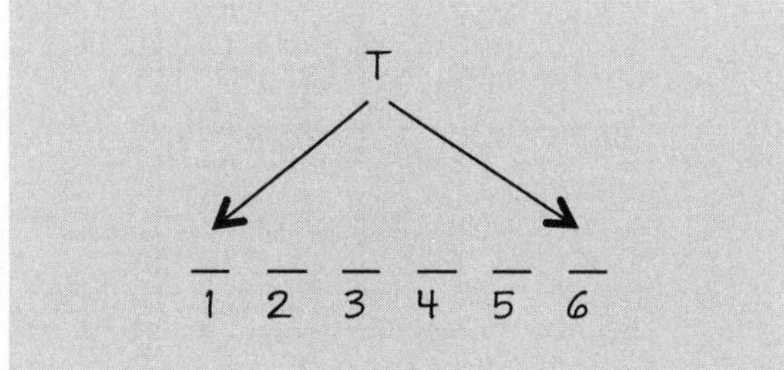

In a Distribution game, such a rule would look something like this:

Percy is assigned to either Team 2 or Team 3.

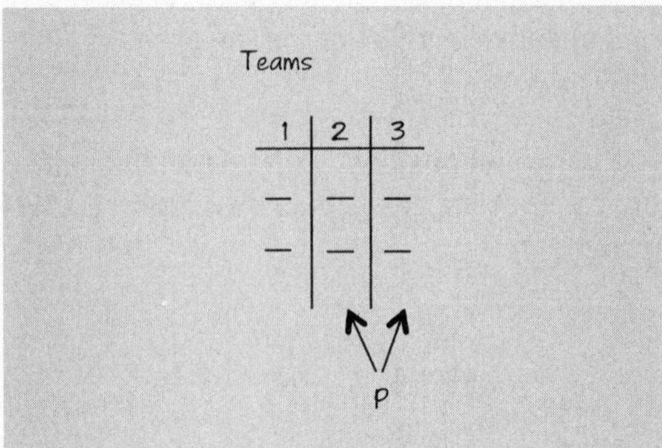

Here, again, the negative implications are clear: The entity restricted by the rule *cannot* appear in any other position.

Note: If the entity that is restricted to one of two positions directly impacts additional entities and determines or restricts their placements, you may choose to draw out two sketches so that you can depict the resulting deductions. These so-called Limited Options sketches are discussed along with other deductions in the second half of this chapter, and in the Special Feature at the end of this chapter.

Rules forbidding a particular placement

The terminology may be a little confusing here because these are rules that *affirmatively* forbid an entity from taking a particular slot or placement. While these rules are far less restrictive than those establishing an entity's placement, they are just as easy to add to the sketch. A typical Sequencing game example would be:

Frank does not give the second presentation.

1 2 3 4 5 6
~F

The *negative* implication of that rule is that Frank *can* present in any other position. If you tried to indicate all of the places Frank could go, your sketch would get far too cluttered and confusing.

If you see a rule forbidding placement in a Matching game, you might depict it within a grid. Imagine a game with four employees—A, B, C, and D—assigned one or more of four tasks—w, x, y, or z.

Employee A does not perform Task *y*.

	A	B	C	D
w				
x				
y	X			
z				

Ordering Rules

These rules are the bread and butter of Sequencing games or of Hybrid games that include a Sequencing task. They *affirmatively* restrict two or more entities relative to one another. The simplest examples say something such as:

George presents before Dawn presents.

```
__ __ __ __ __ __
1  2  3  4  5  6

      G...D
```

That rule cannot effectively be drawn into the sketch framework because it leaves open too many possible placements for the two entities. It is best to depict it beneath or beside the sketch using ellipses to indicate that the distance between the two entities is not determined. You can, however, add its *negative* implications to the sketch. Since George must present before Dawn presents, Dawn cannot present first, and George cannot present last.

```
__ __ __ __ __ __
1  2  3  4  5  6
~D             ~G
      G...D
```

If an ordering rule includes three entities, it is even more restrictive. Consider the following, and note how the expert drew out both the affirmative and negative aspects of the rule:

Michael presents at an earlier time than Oscar, but at a later time than Stephanie.

```
__ __ __ __ __ __
1  2  3  4  5  6
~O ~O       ~S ~S
~M             ~M

      S...M...O
```

Another common example might be worded like this:

David and Hiromi both present after Candace presents.

```
__ __ __ __ __ __
1  2  3  4  5  6
~D          ~C ~C
~H

          ..D
       C:
          ..H
```

Note that while David and Hiromi both follow Candace in that rule, you learn nothing about David and Hiromi relative to one another. Be sure not to read more into a rule than what it explicitly states.

By the way, some LSAT experts always add the negative implications to the sketch, while others are comfortable with just jotting down the affirmative rule underneath. Go with what works best for you, but be certain that you understand a rule's negative implications even if you don't write them out.

Distance Rules

This category of rules is associated specifically with Strict Sequencing games and Hybrid games with a Strict Sequencing component. They *affirmatively* tell you how close to one another two entities are placed (but they may not tell you anything about the entities' relative order). Here are some examples from a game that determines the lanes in which sprinters will run:

A and B run in consecutively numbered lanes.

1 2 3 4 5 6

A B or B A

The lanes in which J and K run are separated by exactly one lane.

1 2 3 4 5 6

K/J _ J/K

The lanes in which X and Y run are separated by at least one lane.

1 2 3 4 5 6

X/Y _ ... Y/X

Notice that none of those rules tell you anything about the order in which the runners are sequenced, only about how far from one another they are. LSAT experts are careful not to add restrictions that are not explicitly stated in the rules. Because the rules say nothing about the order of the entities, there is little to learn from the *negative* implications of these rules beyond the obvious statement that the entities cannot be closer or farther apart than what the rule states.

If, however, a rule indicates both distance *and* order, you can add the negative implications to the sketch. For example:

E runs in a lane numbered exactly two higher than the lane in which L runs.

1 2 3 4 5 6
~E ~E ~L ~L

L _ E

Blocks of Entities Rules

Blocks of Entities are created whenever a rule *affirmatively* states that two entities must "travel together." In Strict Sequencing games, this occurs whenever two entities must be placed consecutively or when two entities are separated by an exact number of spaces. Some LSAT experts will draw a box around Blocks of Entities rules to remind themselves that the block will take up a certain number of slots.

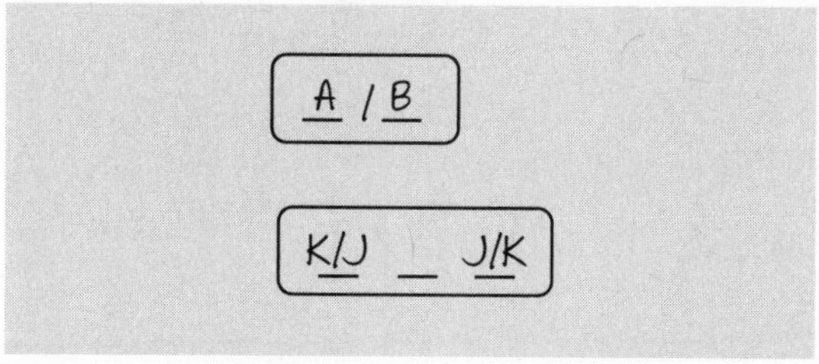

A / B

K/J _ J/K

Rules creating blocks of entities are also quite common in Distribution games. The wording is usually straightforward.

> Oliver plays on the same team as Priscilla.

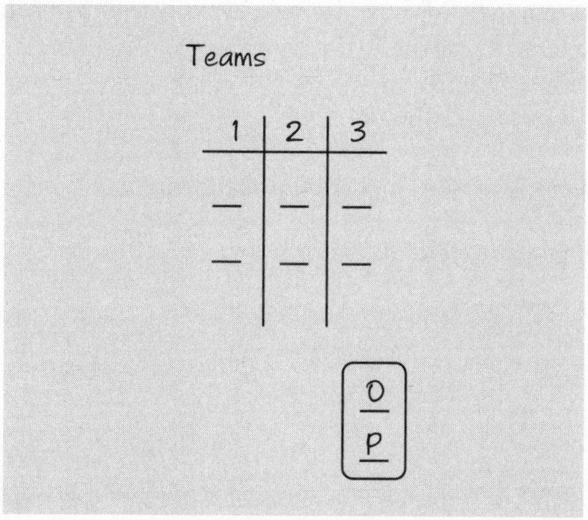

Teams

1	2	3
—	—	—
—	—	—

O
P

Notice how the LSAT expert depicted that rule in a way that matches the sketch framework.

Blocks of entities become very important in the deductions step of the Logic Games Method. There, you can see how other rules intervene to limit the acceptable placement of the block. On their own, they don't carry many *negative* implications beyond requiring that the two entities in the block stay together.

It is worth noting that you will occasionally see rules that force entities to stay apart. You can think of them as "anti-blocks."

> T and U do not run in consecutively numbered lanes.

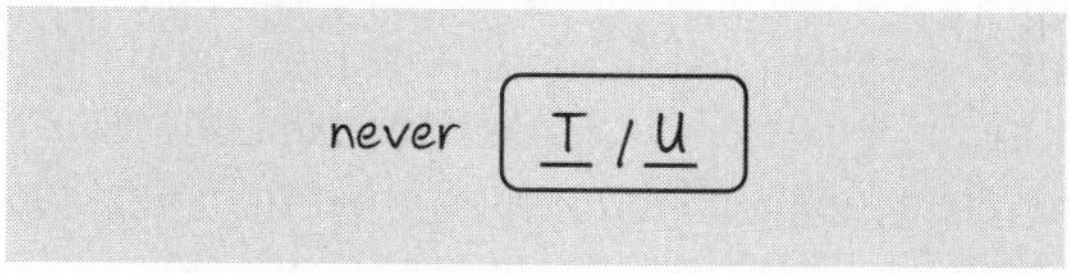

never T / U

> Barbara and Colin do not play on the same team.

never B
C

On a tactical note, if the rule about Barbara and Colin appeared in a Distribution game with exactly two teams—let's call them Team Red and Team Blue—you could record this rule inside the sketch framework.

Teams

Red	Blue
B/C	C/B
—	—
—	—

Conditional (Formal Logic) Rules

You can recognize conditional rules from their "if-then" format, although they may be worded in a number of ways. The rule "If X is selected, then Y is selected" is exactly the same as "X is selected only if Y is selected" or even "X is not selected unless Y is selected." That's because the rule's "If" clause is sufficient to trigger its "then" clause, and its "then" clause is necessary for its "If" clause.

Most LSAT experts choose to jot down these rules in a standard shorthand.

If Carla is selected, then David is also selected.

If C → D

Clearly, that rule applies whenever Carla is selected (her selection is sufficient to ensure his). The rule is also triggered when David is *not* selected (his selection is necessary for hers). LSAT experts will routinely jot down the contrapositive of any conditional Formal Logic rule by reversing and negating the entities in the rule. For the rule about Carla and David, that would look like this:

If ~D → ~C

Think of the tildes (~) as meaning "not."

While you will occasionally run across a conditional rule in other types of games, these rules are at the core of Selection games. So close is this association that you'll find a large portion of Chapter 8—the chapter on Selection games—devoted to everything you need to know to use Formal Logic in LSAT logic games. You can study that section at any time, but conditional rules are rare enough in game types other than Selection that you are probably safe waiting until you study that chapter before taking the deep dive into Formal Logic. (As an aside, Formal Logic is much more common in the Logical Reasoning section of the LSAT than it is in the Logic Games section, so learning how to interpret conditional statements may improve your overall LSAT score even beyond the work you are doing in this book.)

Number Rules

These rules are most consistently associated with Matching and Distribution games. They sometimes *affirmatively* specify the number of entities that can be assigned to a group, as in this Distribution game:

Exactly three of the students are assigned to Team Red.

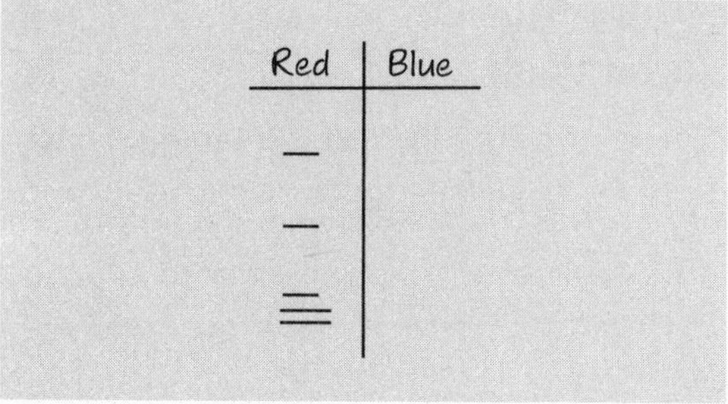

Or, they might restrict the number of entities or attributes assigned to two groups or individuals relatively, as in this Matching game (the axes of the grid represent employees A, B, C, and D, and tasks w, x, y, and z):

Employee B is assigned more of the tasks than Employee D is assigned.

B > D

	A	B	C	D
w				
x				
y				
z				

Number rules become very important in Step 4 of the Logic Games Method because they may trigger several deductions. Take the rule about the two employees. If other rules or restrictions make it clear that Employee D performs two of the tasks, you now know that Employee B must perform three or four of the tasks. On the other hand, if it turned out that Employee B performs two of the tasks, you would now know that Employee D can perform only one task, at most.

Rules In Context

Knowing the types of rules you will encounter is helpful, but it is only within a game's full context or setup that you can fully appreciate the rules' impact on the entities. Start your work here by reviewing a game you've already seen.

Refresh (Activate Prior Knowledge)

Here are the setup and rules from the Truck Arrivals game that you saw in Chapter 1.

In a single day, exactly seven trucks—S, T, U, W, X, Y, and Z—are the only arrivals at a warehouse. No truck arrives at the same time as any other truck, and no truck arrives more than once that day. Each truck is either green or red (but not both). The following conditions apply:

No two consecutive arrivals are red.
Y arrives at some time before both T and W.
Exactly two of the trucks that arrive before Y are red.
S is the sixth arrival.
Z arrives at some time before U.

PrepTest37 Sec3 Qs 6–11

Steps 1 and 2: You will recall that this is a Sequencing/Matching Hybrid game. Your tasks are to account for the order in which the trucks arrive and to assign each truck a color.

S T U W X Y Z

_ _ _ _ _ _ _
1 2 3 4 5 6 7

g/r _ _ _ _ _ _ _

Step 3: Now, review how the LSAT expert analyzed and drew each rule with the common rule patterns in mind.

No two consecutive arrivals are red.

This is a negative rule about the distance between two entities (referred to previously as an "anti-block"). Since it doesn't provide enough information to draw anything into the sketch, depict it underneath the framework.

_ _ _ _ _ _ _
1 2 3 4 5 6 7

g/r _ _ _ _ _ _ _

never [r r]

Y arrives at some time before both T and W.

This is an ordering rule involving three entities. It tells you that Y precedes T and W, but does not give any information about the relative order of T and W. Note that you now know that Y cannot arrive sixth or seventh, and that neither T nor W can arrive first. The rule cannot be drawn into the framework, so write it underneath in a way that orients it to the sketch layout.

1 2 3 4 5 6 7

g/r

never r r

Y ... T / W

Exactly two of the trucks that arrive before Y are red.

This is another relative ordering rule that tells you that two of the trucks arriving before Y are red. You now know that Y cannot arrive first or second (and, if you remember Rule 1, which prevents consecutive red arrivals, you know that Y cannot arrive third, either). You cannot write this rule directly into the sketch, but because Y has already been mentioned in Rule 2, you can combine your sketch for Rule 1 with your sketch for Rule 2. If that doesn't occur to you, it's okay, because you will combine them during Step 4 as you make deductions.

1 2 3 4 5 6 7

g/r

never r r

r...r...Y ... T / W

S is the sixth arrival.

This rule establishes the position of S once and for all. Build this one directly into the sketch framework.

S (6)

1 2 3 4 5 6 7

g/r

never r r

r...r...Y ... T / W

Z arrives at some time before U.

This is one more relative ordering rule: Z arrives before U arrives. You now know that Z cannot arrive seventh, and that U cannot arrive first. Jot down the rule in shorthand underneath the sketch.

S
— — — — — — —
1 2 3 4 5 6 7

g/r — — — — — — —

never [r r]

r...r...Y... T / W

Z...U

Because you've seen that game before, you may already be looking ahead to the deductions you can make by combining the rules. That's great. On test day, you will roll right from the Rules step into the Deductions. In fact, you'll have the chance to revisit the deductions in the Truck Arrivals game in the next section of this chapter, which covers Step 4.

First, though, take a look at an expert's analysis of the rules step in another game—Patterson's Meetings. You saw this game's setup, but not its rules, in Chapter 2. Take a minute or two to review the setup, and then try to anticipate how the expert will analyze and draw each rule.

On one afternoon, Patterson meets individually with each of exactly five clients—Reilly, Sanchez, Tang, Upton, and Yansky—and also goes to the gym by herself for a workout. Patterson's workout and her five meetings each start at either 1:00, 2:00, 3:00, 4:00, 5:00, or 6:00. The following conditions must apply:

Patterson meets with Sanchez at some time before her workout.
Patterson meets with Tang at some time after her workout.
Patterson meets with Yansky either immediately before or immediately after her workout.
Patterson meets with Upton at some time before she meets with Reilly.

PrepTest45 Sec3 Qs 1–6

Steps 1 and 2: You will recall that this is a Strict Sequencing game. The task is to account for the order in which Patterson conducts her five meetings and her workout.

R S T U W Y

— — — — — —
1 2 3 4 5 6

Step 3: Now, take a look how the LSAT expert analyzed and drew each rule with the common rule patterns in mind. Take note of cases in which you accurately anticipated the way in which the expert would draw out the rules, and anywhere your anticipated analysis differs from the expert's.

Patterson meets with Sanchez at some time before her workout.

This is an ordering rule. You know that the Sanchez meeting precedes the workout, but you don't know by how many hours it precedes the workout. Since the rule doesn't provide enough information to draw anything into the sketch, depict it underneath the framework.

```
__ __ __ __ __ __
1  2  3  4  5  6

   S...W
```

Patterson meets with Tang at some time after her workout.

This is another ordering rule. It tells you that the workout precedes the meeting with Tang, but not by how much. The rule cannot be drawn into the framework, so it, too, will go underneath the framework. If you noticed that the workout was also mentioned in Rule 1, you can combine the rules in your drawing. If you didn't notice that immediately, you will combine Rules 1 and 2 during the Deductions step.

```
__ __ __ __ __ __
1  2  3  4  5  6

   S...W...T
```

Patterson meets with Yansky either immediately before or immediately after her workout.

This is a distance rule—the Yansky meeting and the workout are consecutive—but it does not tell you about the order of the two meetings. Like Rules 1 and 2, this rule mentions the workout. Again, if you noticed that, you can combine this rule with the first two, or you can depict it separately and make that combination in the Deductions step.

```
__ __ __ __ __ __
1  2  3  4  5  6

   S...[W/Y]...T
```

Patterson meets with Upton at some time before she meets with Reilly.

Here, you have one more ordering rule. The Upton meeting precedes the Reilly meeting, but there is no information about the distance between the two meetings. Depict the rule underneath the framework.

```
__ __ __ __ __ __
1  2  3  4  5  6

   S...[W/Y]...T
   U...R
```

You'll return to Patterson's Meetings in the second part of this chapter to make all of the deductions that follow from these rules.

Before turning to practice and assessment in the Rules step, take a look at an expert's analysis of one more logic game's setup and rules. This one is more complex than Patterson's Meetings, and you haven't seen it before at all. Once again, take a minute or two to review the game's setup and rules, and try to anticipate the expert's work.

Exactly six people–Lulu, Nam, Ofelia, Pachai, Santiago, and Tyrone–are the only contestants in a chess tournament. The tournament consists of four games, played one after the other. Exactly two people play in each game, and each person plays in at least one game. The following conditions must apply:

Tyrone does not play in the first or third game.

Lulu plays in the last game.

Nam plays in only one game and it is not against Pachai.

Santiago plays in exactly two games, one just before and one just after the only game that Ofelia plays in.

PrepTest45 Sec3 Qs 7–12

Steps 1 and 2: The Situation is a chess tournament with six players and four games, and the task is to schedule the players in each game. The Entities are the players—L, N, O, P, S, and T. The Action here is Strict Sequencing, but the Limitations introduce added complexity. Each game has exactly two players, so with four games to play, there are eight slots to fill. Because there are only six players, however, at least one player must appear in more than one game. Here is the initial sketch:

```
L N O P S T

1  2  3  4

__ __ __ __
__ __ __ __
```

Step 3: Now, take a look how the LSAT expert analyzed and drew each rule with the common rule patterns in mind. Take note of cases in which you accurately anticipated the way in which the expert would draw out the rules, and anywhere your anticipated analysis differs from the expert's.

Tyrone does not play in the first or third game.

This rule prevents Tyrone from playing in two of the games, Games 1 and 3. It does not tell you whether he plays in one or both of the remaining games.

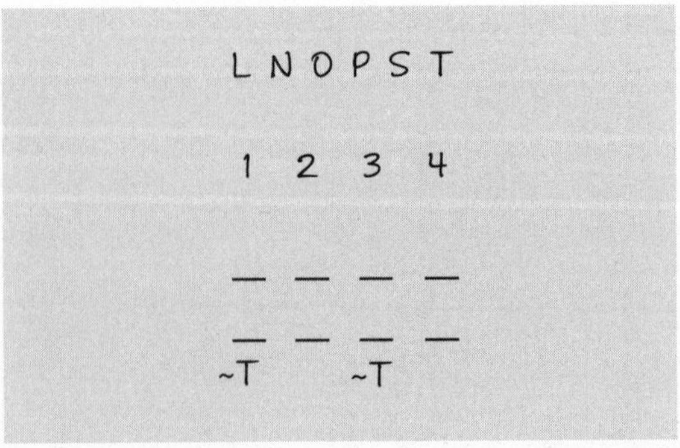

```
L N O P S T

1  2  3  4

__ __ __ __
__ __ __ __
~T    ~T
```

Lulu plays in the last game.

This rule creates a "quasi-Established Entity." While Lulu will definitely play in Game 4, remember that, in this game, an entity may be scheduled more than once. Draw L in Game 4 within the sketch framework, but don't forget that, without further restrictions, Lulu may play again.

```
LNOPST

1 2 3 4

_ _ _ L

_ _ _ _
~T  ~T
```

Nam plays in only one game and it is not against Pachai.

This rule contains a number restriction—Nam plays only one game—and creates an "anti-block"—Nam and Pachai are never in the same game. Note the number restriction above N in the roster of entities, and note the rule that prevents the N-P pairing next to or underneath the sketch framework.

```
 1
LNOPST
                    N
1 2 3 4      never  -
                    P
_ _ _ L

_ _ _ _
~T  ~T
```

Santiago plays in exactly two games, one just before and one just after the only game that Ofelia plays in.

Here is a rule that contains two number restrictions—Santiago plays in two games, and Ofelia plays in one—and creates a block of three consecutive spaces: S-O-S. Note the number restrictions above the roster of entities, and represent the block next to or underneath the framework.

```
 1 1  2
LNOPST
                    N
             never  -
                    P
1 2 3 4

_ _ _ L           S O S

_ _ _ _
~T  ~T
```

With that sketch, you will be ready to make all of the deductions in the Chess Tournament game (and, by the way, there are a lot to make in that one). Before moving on to Step 4, however, take time to practice analyzing and drawing the rules in context. You'll have three new model setups, and then a new official LSAC game setup. Because you haven't seen these game setups before, you'll need to start with Steps 1 and 2 to identify the games' actions and produce their initial sketches. Then, do your best to analyze and sketch the games' rules as the LSAT experts did in the preceding games in this chapter.

Practice

Directions: Read and analyze the game setup and record your analysis as indicated. In this practice section, work at your own pace, and answer every question thoroughly. Explanations for all four practice game setups follow the practice section.

Practice 1

A geologist is organizing a display of seven gemstones—amethyst, beryl, diamond, emerald, fluorite, garnet, and jade. The gemstones will be arranged in a single row in a glass display case, labeled 1 through 7 consecutively from left to right, with one stone occupying each position. The arrangement of the gemstones must conform to the following conditions:

The diamond must occupy a higher-numbered position than the amethyst, but a lower-numbered position than the garnet.
The emerald and the fluorite must occupy consecutively numbered positions.
The beryl must occupy a higher-numbered position than the emerald.
The diamond must occupy position number 3.

1. [Step 1] Summarize your Overview analysis:

2. [Step 2] Create an initial Sketch:

3. [Step 3] Analyze and draw the Rules:
   - For each rule, answer the following questions and then draw the rule in the appropriate box.
     - What does the rule restrict, and what does it leave open?
     - What are the rule's negative implications, if any?
     - Can the rule be depicted inside the sketch framework?

Rule 1:	Rule 2:
Rule 3:	Rule 4:

Practice 2

A chocolatier is putting together boxes of truffles for fundraisers at three local schools—X, Y, and Z. Each school will get a box with at least one of the five available flavors—hazelnut, maple walnut, peanut butter, raspberry, and white chocolate. Each flavor will be included in at least one of the boxes, subject to the following conditions:

The box for school X will include hazelnut truffles.
Maple walnut truffles will be used in more boxes than white chocolate truffles.
Peanut butter truffles will be used in exactly one box, and no other flavor will be included in that box.

1. [Step 1] Summarize your Overview analysis:

2. [Step 2] Create an initial Sketch:

3. [Step 3] Analyze and draw the Rules:
   - For each rule, answer the following questions and then draw the rule in the appropriate box.
     - What does the rule restrict, and what does it leave open?
     - What are the rule's negative implications, if any?
     - Can the rule be depicted inside the sketch framework?

Rule 1:	Rule 2:
Rule 3:	

Practice 3

An accountant is scheduling meetings with six clients—Able, Baker, Charlie, Delphine, Erica, and Frankie—over a four-day period, from Monday through Thursday. On each day, two appointments are available, one in the morning and one in the afternoon. In addition, two staff meetings will be scheduled over the same period. Each client and staff meeting must be assigned a different appointment time. The schedule is governed by the following conditions:

The staff meetings are not scheduled in the afternoon.
Charlie's and Frankie's meetings are scheduled for the same day.
Delphine's meeting is scheduled for some time prior to Frankie's meeting.
Baker's meeting is scheduled in the morning.
The accountant will meet with Erica and Baker on different days.

1. [Step 1] Summarize your Overview analysis:

2. [Step 2] Create an initial Sketch:

3. [Step 3] Analyze and draw the Rules:
   - For each rule, answer the following questions and then draw the rule in the appropriate box.
     - What does the rule restrict, and what does it leave open?
     - What are the rule's negative implications, if any?
     - Can the rule be depicted inside the sketch framework?

Rule 1:	Rule 2:
Rule 3:	Rule 4:
Rule 5:	

Practice 4

A showroom contains exactly six new cars—T, V, W, X, Y, and Z—each equipped with at least one of the following three options: power windows, leather interior, and sunroof. No car has any other options. The following conditions must apply:

V has power windows and a sunroof.
W has power windows and a leather interior.
W and Y have no options in common.
X has more options than W.
V and Z have exactly one option in common.
T has fewer options than Z.

PrepTest35 Sec3 Qs 6–12

1. [Step 1] Summarize your Overview analysis:

2. [Step 2] Create an initial Sketch:

3. [Step 3] Analyze and draw the Rules:
   - For each rule, answer the following questions and then draw the rule in the appropriate box.
     - What does the rule restrict, and what does it leave open?
     - What are the rule's negative implications, if any?
     - Can the rule be depicted inside the sketch framework?

Rule 1:	Rule 2:
Rule 3:	Rule 4:
Rule 5:	Rule 6:

Explanations

Compare your work to that of an LSAT expert. Pay close attention to how the expert analyzed each rule and then depicted it within or beneath the game's initial sketch.

Practice 1

A geologist is organizing a display of seven gemstones—amethyst, beryl, diamond, emerald, fluorite, garnet, and jade. The gemstones will be arranged in a single row in a glass display case, labeled 1 through 7 consecutively from left to right, with one stone occupying each position. The arrangement of the gemstones must conform to the following conditions:

The diamond must occupy a higher-numbered position than the amethyst, but a lower-numbered position than the garnet.
The emerald and the fluorite must occupy consecutively numbered positions.
The beryl must occupy a higher-numbered position than the emerald.
The diamond must occupy position number 3.

1. [Step 1] Summarize your Overview analysis: *A geologist is arranging seven stones in positions numbered 1 through 7, one stone per position. This is a Strict Sequencing game as indicated by rules 2 and 4.*

2. [Step 2] Create an initial Sketch: *This calls for a standard Strict Sequencing sketch framework.*

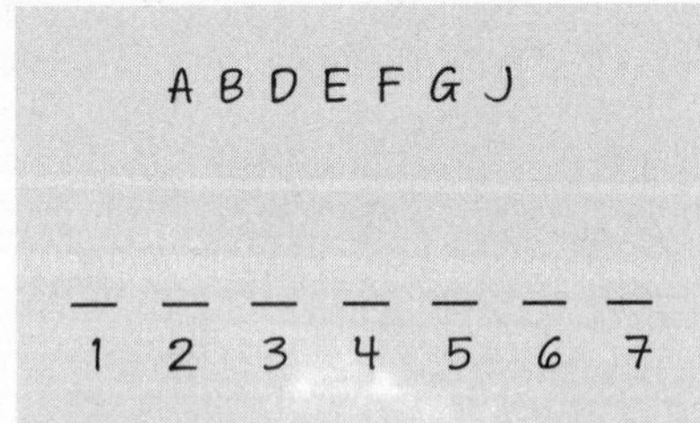

3. [Step 3] Analyze and draw the Rules:
   - Rule 1:
     - What does the rule restrict, and what does it leave open? *This rule gives the relative relationship among three of the stones: A-D-G. The rule does not say how close or how far the three entities are from one another.*
     - What are the rule's negative implications, if any? *Amethyst cannot occupy positions 6 or 7. Diamond cannot occupy positions 1 or 7. Garnet cannot occupy positions 1 or 2.*
     - Can the rule be depicted inside the sketch framework? *No.*
     - Draw the rule:

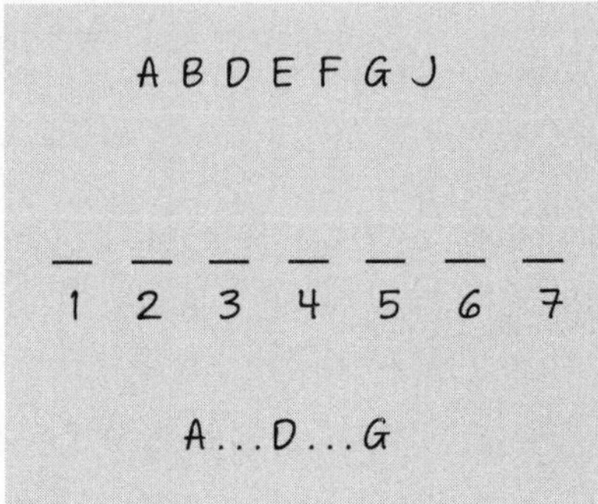

   - Rule 2:
     - What does the rule restrict, and what does it leave open? *This rule creates a block of entities by dictating that the emerald and the fluorite are placed consecutively. The rule does not dictate the order in which the two are placed.*
     - What are the rule's negative implications, if any? *None, apart from the fact that the entities may not be split up.*
     - Can the rule be depicted inside the sketch framework? *No.*
     - Draw the rule:

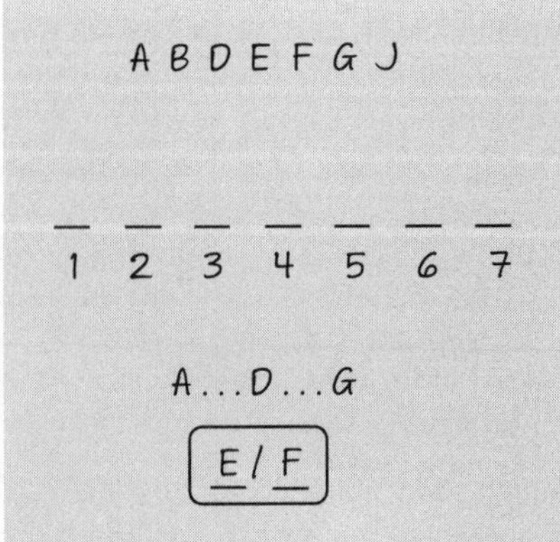

- Rule 3:
  - What does the rule restrict, and what does it leave open? *This rule gives the relative order of the emerald and the beryl, but does not say how close or far away the two entities must be.*
  - What are the rule's negative implications, if any? *The emerald cannot occupy position 7, and the beryl cannot occupy position 1.*
  - Can the rule be depicted inside the sketch framework? *No. Because you already know that emerald and fluorite are a block, you may make the deduction that beryl comes after the block and simply append this rule to Rule 2. If you don't do that now, you will when making the deductions in Step 4.*
  - Draw the rule:

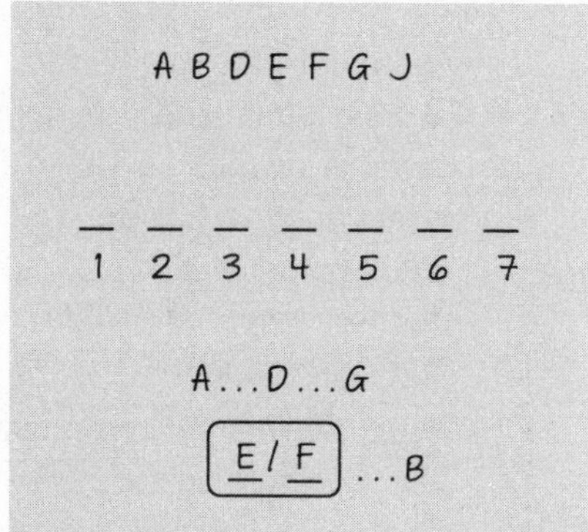

- Rule 4:
  - What does the rule restrict, and what does it leave open? *This rule establishes the diamond's position once and for all. It leaves nothing open.*
  - What are the rule's negative implications, if any? *No other entity can occupy position 3.*
  - Can the rule be depicted inside the sketch framework? *Yes.*
  - Draw the rule:

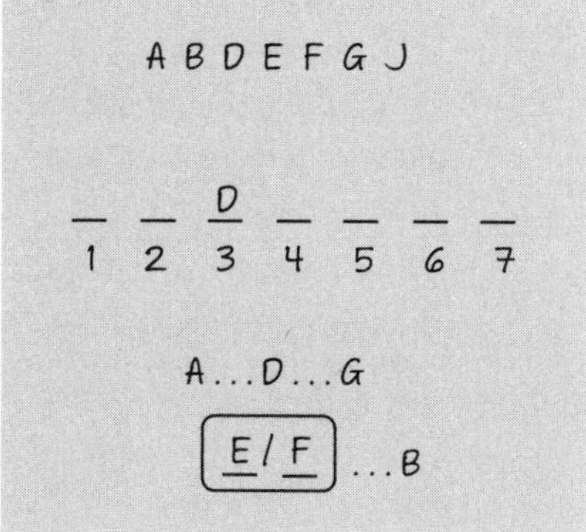

Practice 2

A chocolatier is putting together boxes of truffles for fundraisers at three local schools—X, Y, and Z. Each school will get a box with at least one of the five available flavors—hazelnut, maple walnut, peanut butter, raspberry, and white chocolate. Each flavor will be included in at least one of the boxes, subject to the following conditions:

> The box for school X will include hazelnut truffles.
>
> Maple walnut truffles will be used in more boxes than white chocolate truffles.
>
> Peanut butter truffles will be used in exactly one box, and no other flavor will be included in that box.

1. [Step 1] Summarize your Overview analysis: *The situation finds a chocolate shop putting together three different boxes, each with truffles of five different flavors. Flavors can appear in more than one of the boxes, so this is a Matching game. The key limitation is that each flavor must appear at least once among the three boxes.*

2. [Step 2] Create an initial Sketch: *This is a standard Matching game, so the initial sketch may be a list*

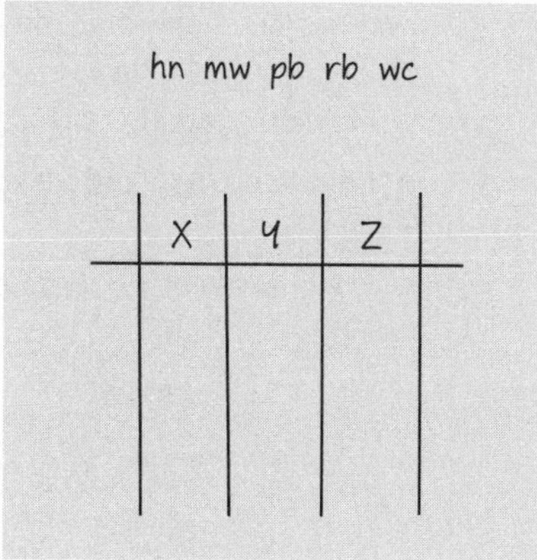

or a grid.

	X	Y	Z
hn			
mw			
pb			
rb			
wc			

3. [Step 3] Analyze and draw the Rules:
   - Rule 1:
     - What does the rule restrict, and what does it leave open? *This rule establishes one placement for hazelnut, in the box for School X. Note that hazelnut may appear in more than one box, and that School X may have other flavors in its box.*
     - What are the rule's negative implications, if any? *Nothing yet.* (Note: If this were a Distribution game, in which each flavor could appear only one time, you would know hazelnut's only placement. Since this is a Matching game, however, the flavor may show up in another box as well.)
     - Can the rule be depicted inside the sketch framework? *Yes.*
     - Draw the rule: *Here's Rule 1 in the list-style sketch.*

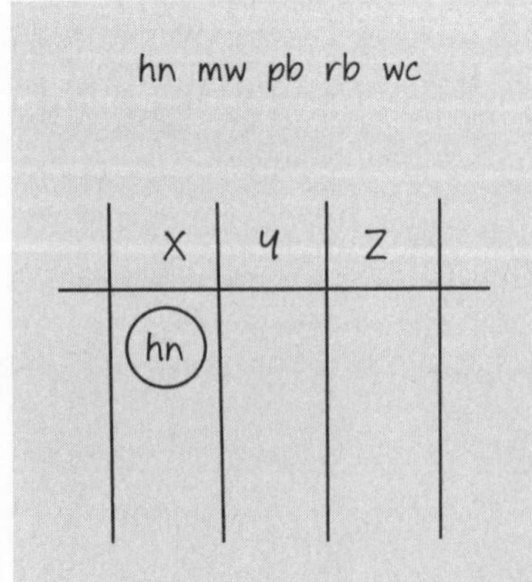

And here it is in the grid-style sketch.

	X	Y	Z
hn	✓		
mw			
pb			
rb			
wc			

   - Rule 2:
     - What does the rule restrict, and what does it leave open? *This rule provides relative number restriction: Maple walnut will be used more times than white chocolate. We don't yet know if maple walnut is used two or three times, or if white chocolate is used one or two times.*
     - What are the rule's negative implications, if any? *Maple walnut cannot be used only once, and white chocolate cannot be used more than twice.*
     - Can the rule be depicted inside the sketch framework? *No.*
     - Draw the rule: *Underneath either the list-style or the grid-style sketch, add this:*

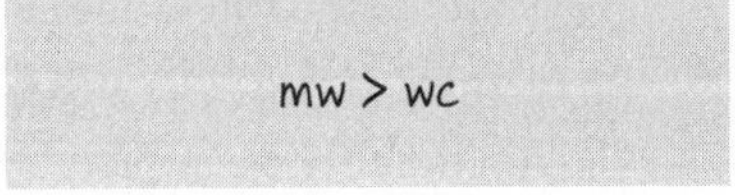

   - Rule 3:
     - What does the rule restrict, and what does it leave open? *This rule provides two restrictions on the peanut butter flavor: Peanut butter can appear in only one box, and it must be the only flavor in that box.*
     - What are the rule's negative implications, if any? *No other flavor can appear in a box with peanut butter.*

- Can the rule be depicted inside the sketch framework? *You could anticipate the deduction that because hazelnut is already in School X's box, peanut butter cannot be in that box, and indicate that peanut butter must be in either School Y's or School Z's box.* (Note: You will explore the full implications of this deduction when you come back to this game in Step 4.)
- Draw the rule: *This is the final sketch (including Rule 3) in the list-style sketch.*

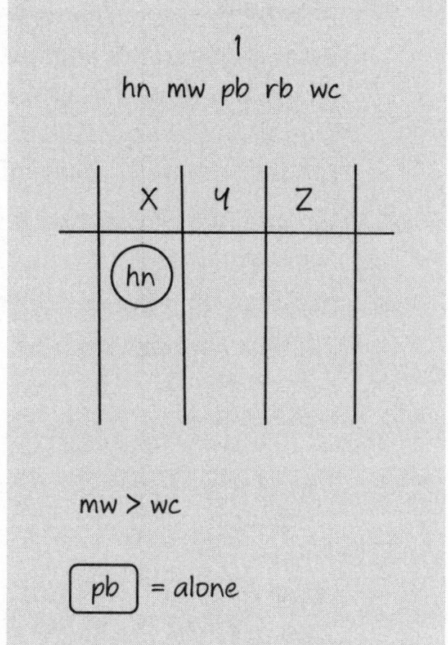

And here it is in the grid-style sketch.

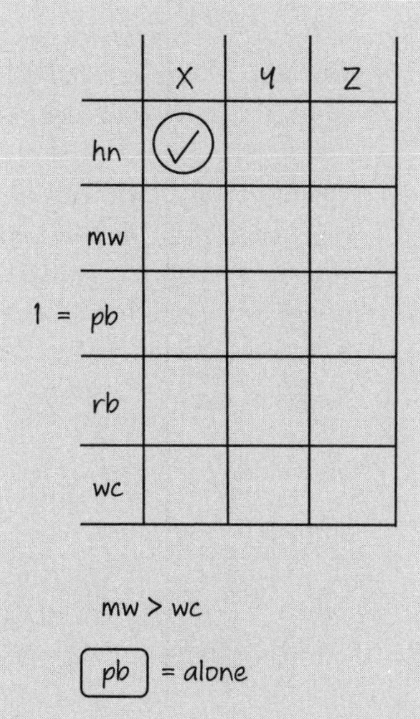

Practice 3

An accountant is scheduling meetings with six clients—Able, Baker, Charlie, Delphine, Erica, and Frankie—over a four-day period, from Monday through Thursday. On each day, two appointments are available, one in the morning and one in the afternoon. In addition, two staff meetings will be scheduled over the same period. Each client and staff meeting must be assigned a different appointment time. The schedule is governed by the following conditions:

> The staff meetings are not scheduled in the afternoon.
> Charlie's and Frankie's meetings are scheduled for the same day.
> Delphine's meeting is scheduled for some time prior to Frankie's meeting.
> Baker's meeting is scheduled in the morning.
> The accountant will meet with Erica and Baker on different days.

1. [Step 1] Summarize your Overview analysis: *In this situation, the task is to create a four-day—Monday through Thursday—schedule for an accountant's office. Each day has two appointment slots—AM and PM. Over the four days in question, the accountant schedules six client meetings and two staff meetings (the eight entities). This is a complex Strict Sequencing game. The explicit limitation in the setup is intuitive: Each of the eight meetings is scheduled for a different one of the eight appointment slots.*

2. [Step 2] Create an initial Sketch: *The sketch must account for the two appointment slots each day.*

A B C D E F S_1 S_2

M Tu W Th

AM __ __ __ __

PM __ __ __ __

3. [Step 3] Analyze and draw the Rules:
   - Rule 1:
     - What does the rule restrict, and what does it leave open? *This rule prevents either of the two staff meetings from being scheduled in the afternoon. It does not, however, tell us the days on which the staff meetings are scheduled.*
     - What are the rule's negative implications, if any? *Because the rule is negative, its "negative implication" is affirmative: The staff meetings are scheduled for the morning.*
     - Can the rule be depicted inside the sketch framework? *Because specific days are not stipulated, the rule cannot go inside the framework. It can, however, sit right next to the AM and PM lines of the sketch.*
     - Draw the rule:

M Tu W Th

AM __ __ __ __ S_1 S_2

PM __ __ __ __ $\not{S}_1$ $\not{S}_2$

   - Rule 2:
     - What does the rule restrict, and what does it leave open? *This rule creates a block of entities: C and F are scheduled on the same day. The rule does not tell you which of the two entities takes the morning or the afternoon.*
     - What are the rule's negative implications, if any? *None, apart from the fact that no other entities are on the same day as either C or F.*
     - Can the rule be depicted inside the sketch framework? *No.*
     - Draw the rule: *Note the rule underneath the sketch framework.*

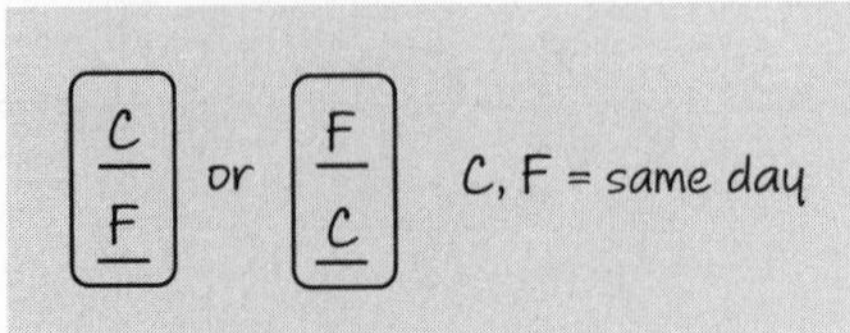

   - Rule 3:
     - What does the rule restrict, and what does it leave open? *This rule gives the relative order of D and F, but does not tell us how close or far apart their appointments are.* (Note: Be careful not to assume, without further information, that D and F must be on different days. D's appointment could be in the morning and F's appointment in the afternoon of the same day and still abide by this rule's parameters.)
     - What are the rule's negative implications, if any? *D's appointment cannot be Thursday afternoon, and F's appointment cannot be Monday morning.*
     - Can the rule be depicted inside the sketch framework? *No.*
     - Draw the rule: *Note the rule underneath the sketch framework.*

D . . . F

   - Rule 4:
     - What does the rule restrict, and what does it leave open? *This rule limits B's appointment to one of the morning slots, but does not say anything about the day on which B is scheduled.*
     - What are the rule's negative implications, if any? *B's appointment cannot be in the afternoon.*
     - Can the rule be depicted inside the sketch framework? *Because specific days are not stipulated, the rule cannot go inside the framework. It can, however, sit right next to the AM and PM lines of the sketch.*
     - Draw the rule:

M Tu W Th

AM __ __ __ __ S_1 S_2 B

PM __ __ __ __ $\not{S}_1$ $\not{S}_2$ $\not{B}$

- Rule 5:
  - What does the rule restrict, and what does it leave open? *This rule creates an "anti-block" by stipulating that B and E will never be on the same day. It says nothing about the two entities' relative order. B might have an appointment before or after E's appointment.*
  - What are the rule's negative implications, if any? *This is a negative rule, so its "negative implication" is affirmative: B and E have appointments on different days.*
  - Can the rule be depicted inside the sketch framework? *No*
  - Draw the rule: *Note the rule underneath the sketch framework.*

never [E/B] or [B/E]   E, B = different days

Here is the game's sketch including all of the rules.

A B C D E F S_1 S_2

M Tu W Th

AM __ __ __ __ S_1 S_2 B

PM __ __ __ __   ~~S_1~~ ~~S_2~~ ~~B~~

[C/F] or [F/C]   D . . . F

never [E/B] or [B/E]

Practice 4

A showroom contains exactly six new cars—T, V, W, X, Y, and Z—each equipped with at least one of the following three options: power windows, leather interior, and sunroof. No car has any other options. The following conditions must apply:

V has power windows and a sunroof.
W has power windows and a leather interior.
W and Y have no options in common.
X has more options than W.
V and Z have exactly one option in common.
T has fewer options than Z.

PrepTest35 Sec3 Qs 6–12

1. [Step 1] Summarize your Overview analysis: *The situation here involves determining which of three features (the entities) correspond to each of six cars in a showroom. The features may appear on more than one car, so this is a Matching game. The key limitations are that each car has at least one of the features, and there are no other features.*

2. [Step 2] Create an initial Sketch: *As a Matching game, this can be sketched using a list*

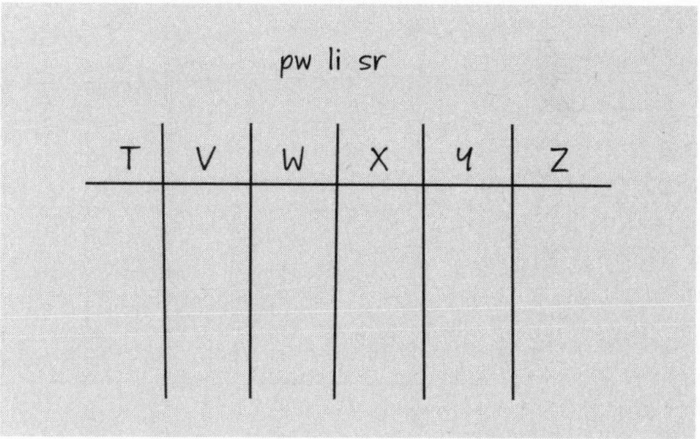

or as a grid.

	T	V	W	X	Y	Z
pw						
li						
sr						

3. [Step 3] Analyze and draw the Rules:
   - Rule 1:
     - What does the rule restrict, and what does it leave open? *This rule affirmatively assigns two features—power windows and a sunroof—to Car V. It does not say that these are Car V's only features.*
     - What are the rule's negative implications, if any? *None, for now.*
     - Can the rule be depicted inside the sketch framework? *Yes.*
     - Draw the rule: *Record the feature assignments in Car V's list*

pw li sr

T	V	W	X	Y	Z
	pw				
	sr				

or inside the grid.

	T	V	W	X	Y	Z
pw		✓				
li						
sr		✓				

   - Rule 2:
     - What does the rule restrict, and what does it leave open? *This is the same kind of rule as Rule 1, but it assigns two features—power window and leather interior—to car W. Again, without additional rules, you don't know that these are Car W's only features.*
     - What are the rule's negative implications, if any? *None, for now.*
     - Can the rule be depicted inside the sketch framework? *Yes.*
     - Draw the rule: *Record the assignments in Car W's list*

pw li sr

T	V	W	X	Y	Z
	pw	pw			
	sr	li			

or inside of the grid.

	T	V	W	X	Y	Z
pw		✓	✓			
li			✓			
sr		✓				

   - Rule 3:
     - What does the rule restrict, and what does it leave open? *This is a negative assertion: Cars W and Y have no features in common.*
     - What are the rule's negative implications, if any? *You could phrase this affirmatively: The features for Car W are totally different than those for Car Y.*
     - Can the rule be depicted inside the sketch framework? *If you anticipate the deductions that (as a result of Rule 2) Car Y will have a sunroof and no other features, and that Car W will not have a sunroof, you could record those inside the sketch. If not, you will get to those when you return to the game for Step 4 of the Logic Games Method.*
     - Draw the rule: *For now, record the restriction underneath the sketch.*

W ≠ Y Nothing in common

- Rule 4:
  - What does the rule restrict, and what does it leave open? This rule provides a relative number restriction: *Car X has more features than Car W.*
  - What are the rule's negative implications, if any? *You should be able to phrase the inverse of this rule: Car W has fewer features than Car X.*
  - Can the rule be depicted inside the sketch framework? *If you anticipate the deductions that (as a result of Rule 2) Car X will have all three features, and that Car W will not have a sunroof, you could record those inside the sketch. If not, you will get to those when you return to the game for Step 4 of the Logic Games Method.*
  - Draw the rule: *For now, record the restriction underneath the sketch.*

X > W

- Rule 5:
  - What does the rule restrict, and what does it leave open? *This rule provides an affirmative assertion: Cars V and Z have exactly one feature in common. It does, however, not say anything about what that feature is.*
  - What are the rule's negative implications, if any? *You may anticipate the deduction that (as a result of Rule 1) Car Z will not have both power windows and a sunroof. If it did, that would violate Rule 5 because Cars V and Z would have two features (not exactly one) in common.*
  - Can the rule be depicted inside the sketch framework? *No.*
  - Draw the rule: *For now, record the rule underneath the sketch.*

V = Z exactly 1 in common

- Rule 6:
  - What does the rule restrict, and what does it leave open? *This rule provides another relative number restriction: Car T has fewer features than Car Z.*
  - What are the rule's negative implications, if any? *The inverse phrasing for this rule is that Car Z has more features than Car T.*
  - Can the rule be depicted inside the sketch framework? *You can record the fact that Car Z will have either two or three features while Car T will have either one or two. The deductions will refine the number restrictions even further.*
  - Draw the rule: *For now, record the rule underneath the sketch.*

T<Z

In a list-style sketch, here is a depiction of all of the rules.

pw li sr

T	V	W	X	Y	Z
	pw	pw			
	sr	li			

X > W   W ≠ Y Nothing in common

T<Z   V = Z exactly 1 in common

In a grid-style sketch, the sketch with all of the rules would look like this.

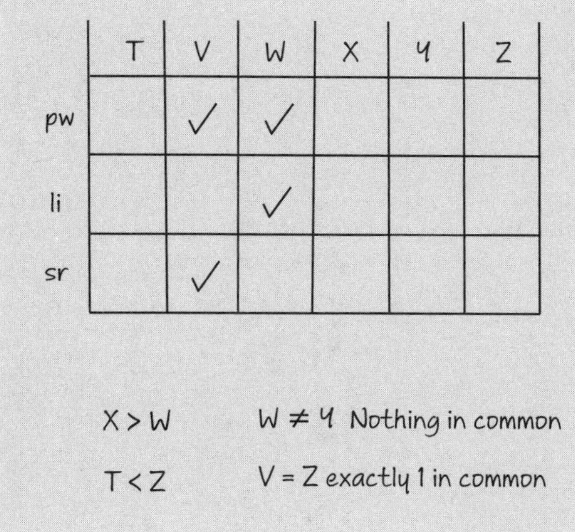

Now that you have practiced analyzing and depicting the rules on several games, assess your skill level with the following Perform exercise. In format, the Perform section will be identical to the Practice exercise you just completed. You will have four logic game setups accompanied by their rules, and you will analyze them in the same way.

Perform

Directions: Take no more than four minutes to read and analyze the game setup and record your analysis as indicated. Explanations for each practice game setup follow the practice section.

Perform 1

A filmmaker is planning to create a short film with exactly five scenes. The scenes will all be shot in one day and will be filmed in order, with each scene completed before filming begins on the next. Each scene will feature at least one of four actors—Jenkins, Kwan, Lozano, and Millstone—and no others. Each actor will appear in exactly two of the scenes. The schedule must conform to the following conditions:

No actor's second scene will be filmed at the same time as another actor's second scene.
Exactly one actor will appear in the third scene of the film.
Millstone's first scene will be filmed before Lozano's first scene.
Any scene in which Lozano is filmed will feature at least one other actor.

1. [Step 1] Summarize your Overview analysis:

2. [Step 2] Create an initial Sketch:

3. [Step 3] Analyze and draw the Rules:
    - For each rule, answer the following questions and then draw the rule in the appropriate box.
        - What does the rule restrict, and what does it leave open?
        - What are the rule's negative implications, if any?
        - Can the rule be depicted inside the sketch framework?

Rule 1:	Rule 2:
Rule 3:	Rule 4:

Perform 2

Eight students—Bonham, Cullen, Dao, Farina, Gerber, Holt, Karlsson, and Logan—are assigned to do research on three court cases—R, S, and T. Each student will research exactly one case in accordance with the following:

Bonham is assigned to research case R.
Farina and Logan are not assigned to research the same case.
Karlsson is assigned to research a case with exactly two other students.
Gerber and Holt are assigned to research a case together, with no other student assigned to research that case.

1. [Step 1] Summarize your Overview analysis:

2. [Step 2] Create an initial Sketch:

3. [Step 3] Analyze and draw the Rules:
   - For each rule, answer the following questions and then draw the rule in the appropriate box.
     - What does the rule restrict, and what does it leave open?
     - What are the rule's negative implications, if any?
     - Can the rule be depicted inside the sketch framework?

Rule 1:	Rule 2:
Rule 3:	Rule 4:

Perform 3

Every Sunday, a zookeeper gives presentations on each of five snakes—an eastern indigo snake, a king snake, a milk snake, a python, and a rat snake. The presentations are held at 1:00, 2:00, 3:00, 4:00, and 5:00. Exactly one snake is exhibited at each presentation. Visitors are invited to hold some, but not all, of the snakes. Visitors are allowed to observe, but not to hold, the others. The schedule of presentations must conform to the following conditions:

Visitors are invited to hold the king snake and at least one other snake.
Visitors are allowed to observe, but not to hold, the last snake presented.
The milk snake is presented before the king snake.
The python is presented before any snake that visitors are invited to hold.

1. [Step 1] Summarize your Overview analysis:

2. [Step 2] Create an initial Sketch:

3. [Step 3] Analyze and draw the Rules:
   - For each rule, answer the following questions and then draw the rule in the appropriate box.
     - What does the rule restrict, and what does it leave open?
     - What are the rule's negative implications, if any?
     - Can the rule be depicted inside the sketch framework?

Rule 1:	Rule 2:
Rule 3:	Rule 4:

Perform 4

A closet contains exactly six hangers—1, 2, 3, 4, 5, and 6—hanging, in that order, from left to right. It also contains exactly six dresses—one gauze, one linen, one polyester, one rayon, one silk, and one wool—a different dress on each of the hangers, in an order satisfying the following conditions:

The gauze dress is on a lower-numbered hanger than the polyester dress.
The rayon dress is on hanger 1 or hanger 6.
Either the wool dress or the silk dress is on hanger 3.
The linen dress hangs immediately to the right of the silk dress.

PrepTest41 Sec2 Qs 1–7

1. [Step 1] Summarize your Overview analysis:

2. [Step 2] Create an initial Sketch:

3. [Step 3] Analyze and draw the Rules:
   - For each rule, answer the following questions and then draw the rule in the appropriate box.
     - What does the rule restrict, and what does it leave open?
     - What are the rule's negative implications, if any?
     - Can the rule be depicted inside the sketch framework?

Rule 1:	Rule 2:
Rule 3:	Rule 4:

Explanations

Compare your work to that of an LSAT expert. Pay close attention to how the expert depicted the rules within or beneath the game's initial sketch.

Perform 1

A filmmaker is planning to create a short film with exactly five scenes. The scenes will all be shot in one day and will be filmed in order, with each scene completed before filming begins on the next. Each scene will feature at least one of four actors—Jenkins, Kwan, Lozano, and Millstone—and no others. Each actor will appear in exactly two of the scenes. The schedule must conform to the following conditions:

No actor's second scene will be filmed at the same time as another actor's second scene.
Exactly one actor will appear in the third scene of the film.
Millstone's first scene will be filmed before Lozano's first scene.
Any scene in which Lozano is filmed will feature at least one other actor.

1. [Step 1] Summarize your Overview analysis: *A filmmaker is filming five scenes. Because they are filmed "in order," this is a Sequencing game. The actors will be assigned in order. Each scene features at least one actor, and each actor will be assigned twice, for a total of eight assignments. With more assignments than scenes, some scenes must feature multiple actors.*

2. [Step 2] Create an initial Sketch: *Set up a horizontal sequence of five scenes, with one slot in each scene. The entities should be listed by initial, with two of each initial. Because order is important, use a subscript 1 and 2 to differentiate each actor's first and second scene.*

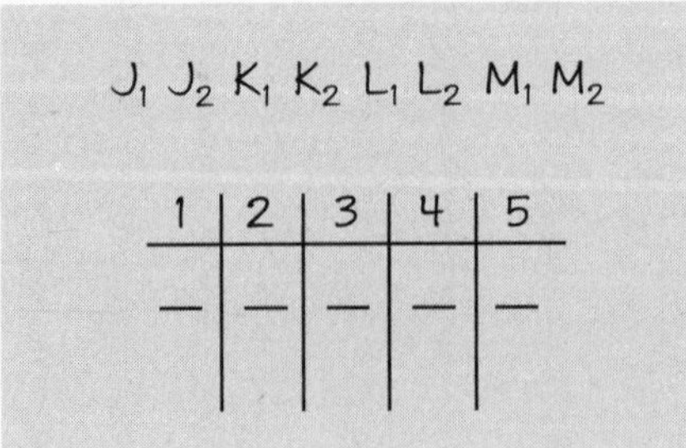

3. [Step 3] Analyze and draw the Rules:
   - Rule 1:
     - What does the rule restrict, and what does it leave open? *This is a negative assertion. No two actors will film their second scenes together.*
     - What are the rule's negative implications, if any? *Essentially, this means every actor's second scene will be a different scene.*
     - Can the rule be depicted inside the sketch framework? *As presented, no. Some clever test takers may realize that an actor's second scene cannot be scene 1, so the four actors' second scenes will appear in scenes 2 through 5. In that case, a 2 can be established in each slot under those scenes.*
     - Draw the rule:

   - Rule 2:
     - What does the rule restrict, and what does it leave open? *This is a number rule, establishing a single actor in scene 3. However, it could be any of the actors.*
     - What are the rule's negative implications, if any? *There cannot be two or more actors in scene 3.*
     - Can the rule be depicted inside the sketch framework? *Yes. Use a double-line to indicate that no more slots will be added to that column.*
     - Draw the rule:

1	2	3	4	5
—	—	=	—	—

- Rule 3:
  - What does the rule restrict, and what does it leave open? *This rule indicates order (Millstone's first scene must be before Lozano's first scene) but not "distance" (you don't know how many spaces earlier Millstone's first scene must be).*
  - What are the rule's negative implications, if any? *Millstone's first scene cannot be scene 4 or 5, and Lozano's first scene cannot be scene 1.*
  - Can the rule be depicted inside the sketch framework? *No.*
  - Draw the rule:

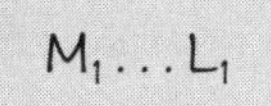

- Rule 4:
  - What does the rule restrict, and what does it leave open? *This rule invokes numbers to create an open-ended block. Any scene with Lozano will have at least a second actor, but could have more. It does not indicate which scenes they are, nor who will be in the scene with Lozano.*
  - What are the rule's negative implications, if any? *Lozano cannot be in a scene alone.*
  - Can the rule be depicted inside the sketch framework? *No.*
  - Draw the rule:

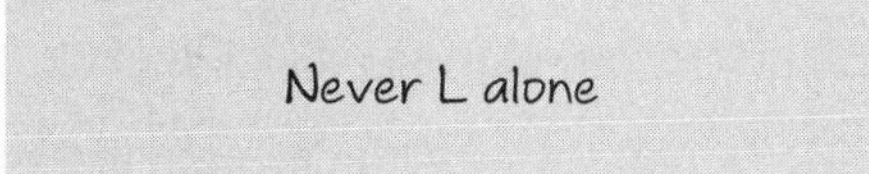

Perform 2

Eight students—Bonham, Cullen, Dao, Farina, Gerber, Holt, Karlsson, and Logan—are assigned to do research on three court cases—R, S, and T. Each student will research exactly one case in accordance with the following:

Bonham is assigned to research case R.

Farina and Logan are not assigned to research the same case.

Karlsson is assigned to research a case with exactly two other students.

Gerber and Holt are assigned to research a case together, with no other student assigned to research that case.

1. [Step 1] Summarize your Overview analysis: *Eight students are being assigned to research three court cases. Each student is assigned to exactly one case, making this a Distribution game. There's no limit to the number of students on any given case.*

2. [Step 2] Create an initial Sketch:

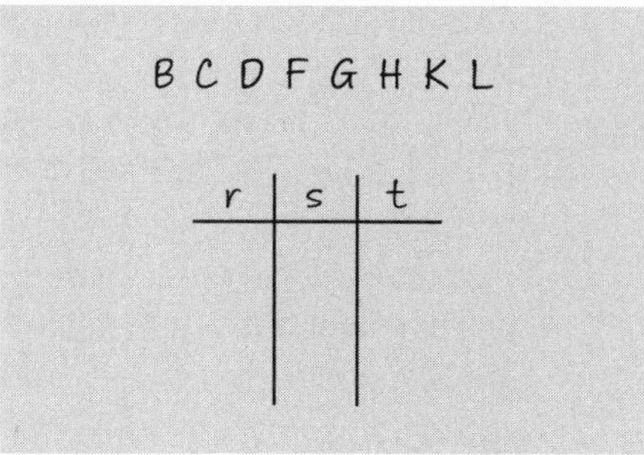

3. [Step 3] Analyze and draw the Rules:
   - Rule 1:
     - What does the rule restrict, and what does it leave open? *This rule establishes Bonham to case R. Other students can be assigned to case R, but Bonham is done.*
     - What are the rule's negative implications, if any? *Bonham is not assigned to case S or T.*
     - Can the rule be depicted inside the sketch framework? *Yes.*
     - Draw the rule:

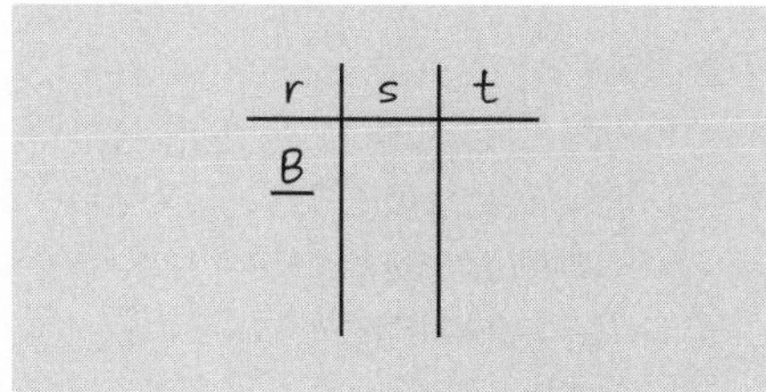

   - Rule 2:
     - What does the rule restrict, and what does it leave open? *This rule creates an anti-block. Farina and Logan cannot be together, but they could each still be assigned to any case.*
     - What are the rule's negative implications, if any? *The positive spin is that Farina and Logan will appear on different cases.*

  - Can the rule be depicted inside the sketch framework? *No.*
  - Draw the rule:

- Rule 3:
  - What does the rule restrict, and what does it leave open? *This rule sets a numeric restriction, creating an open-ended block. One case will have exactly three students, one of whom will be Karlsson. It could be any of the three cases, and there's no restriction on the other two students.*
  - What are the rule's negative implications, if any? *Karlsson cannot be alone, with just one other student, or with three or more other students.*
  - Can the rule be depicted inside the sketch framework? *No.*
  - Draw the rule:

- Rule 4:
  - What does the rule restrict, and what does it leave open? *This rule creates a block of Gerber and Holt, and nobody else. It does not indicate which case this will be.*
  - What are the rule's negative implications, if any? *Neither Gerber nor Holt can be assigned with anybody else.*
  - Can the rule be depicted inside the sketch framework? *No.*
  - Draw the rule:

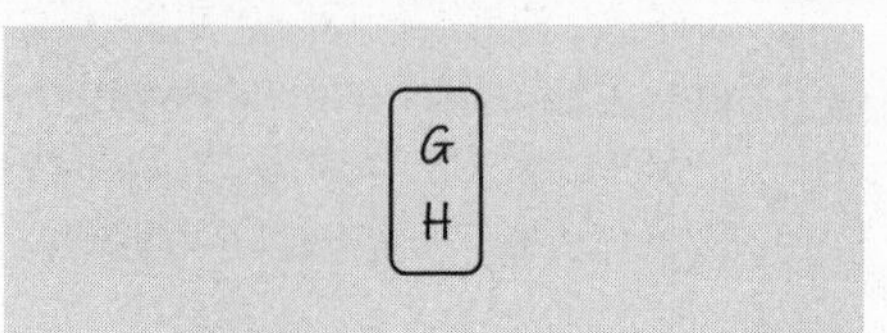

Perform 3

Every Sunday, a zookeeper gives presentations on each of five snakes—an eastern indigo snake, a king snake, a milk snake, a python, and a rat snake. The presentations are held at 1:00, 2:00, 3:00, 4:00, and 5:00. Exactly one snake is exhibited at each presentation. Visitors are invited to hold some, but not all, of the snakes. Visitors are allowed to observe, but not to hold, the others. The schedule of presentations must conform to the following conditions:

> Visitors are invited to hold the king snake and at least one other snake.
> Visitors are allowed to observe, but not to hold, the last snake presented.
> The milk snake is presented before the king snake.
> The python is presented before any snake that visitors are invited to hold.

1. [Step 1] Summarize your Overview analysis: *Five snakes are being presented at a zoo. Determine the order in which they are presented, and determine which ones can be held and which ones can solely be observed. This is a classic Sequencing/Matching hybrid. Each snake appears once, with one slot for each, so the sequencing is standard one-to-one. At least one snake can be held, but at least one snake will be observed only. The exact numbers are not defined.*

2. [Step 2] Create an initial Sketch:

```
 1  2  3  4  5
__ __ __ __ __  EKMPR
__ __ __ __ __  h o
```

3. [Step 3] Analyze and draw the Rules:
   - Rule 1:
     - What does the rule restrict, and what does it leave open? *This rule presents two pieces of information: a number requirement (at least two snakes can be held) and an established match (the king snake can be held). The second snake is still unknown, and there could still be other snakes that are held. Also, there's no indication when these presentations occur in the sequence.*
     - What are the rule's negative implications, if any? *None.*
     - Can the rule be depicted inside the sketch framework? *No.*
     - Draw the rule:

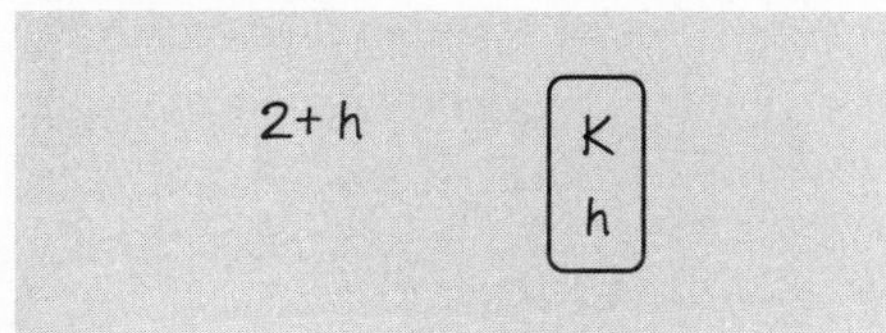

   - Rule 2:
     - What does the rule restrict, and what does it leave open? *The last snake (5:00) is not held, just observed. It's still not mentioned which snake it is.*
     - What are the rule's negative implications, if any? *None.*
     - Can the rule be depicted inside the sketch framework? *Yes.*
     - Draw the rule:

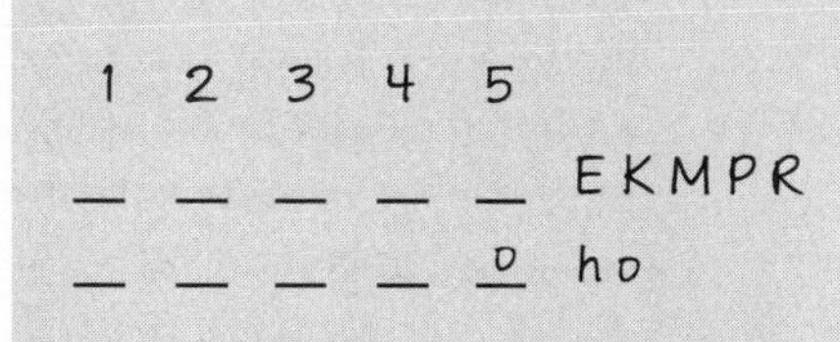

   - Rule 3:
     - What does the rule restrict, and what does it leave open? *This rule presents ordering: the milk snake before the king snake. It's not mentioned how far apart they are.*
     - What are the rule's negative implications, if any? *Because the milk snake comes earlier, it cannot be last. And because the king snake comes later, it cannot be first.*
     - Can the rule be depicted inside the sketch framework? *No.*
     - Draw the rule:

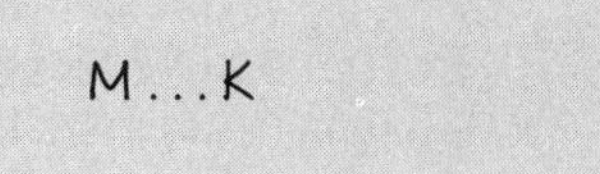

   - Rule 4:
     - What does the rule restrict, and what does it leave open? *This rule presents more ordering: The python is presented before any snake that is held. It's not mentioned how much before, so the python can appear any number of spaces before the first held snake.*
     - What are the rule's negative implications, if any? *Because the python comes earlier, it cannot be last. And because snakes that are held come later, the first snake cannot be held. This also implies that the python itself cannot be held, so it must be observed only.*
     - Can the rule be depicted inside the sketch framework? *No.*
     - Draw the rule:

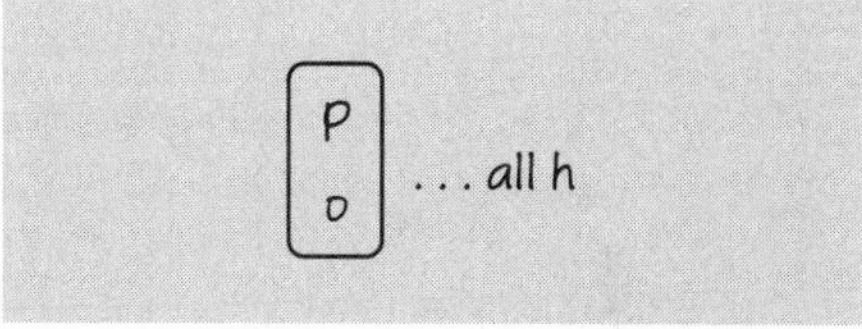

Perform 4

A closet contains exactly six hangers—1, 2, 3, 4, 5, and 6—hanging, in that order, from left to right. It also contains exactly six dresses—one gauze, one linen, one polyester, one rayon, one silk, and one wool–a different dress on each of the hangers, in an order satisfying the following conditions:

The gauze dress is on a lower-numbered hanger than the polyester dress.
The rayon dress is on hanger 1 or hanger 6.
Either the wool dress or the silk dress is on hanger 3.
The linen dress hangs immediately to the right of the silk dress.

PrepTest41 Sec2 Qs 1–7

1. [Step 1] Summarize your Overview analysis: *There are dresses hanging on numbered hangers in a closet. As the hangers are "in order," this is a Sequencing game. Each dress is on a different hanger. With six dresses and six hangers, this is standard one-to-one sequencing.*
2. [Step 2] Create an initial Sketch:

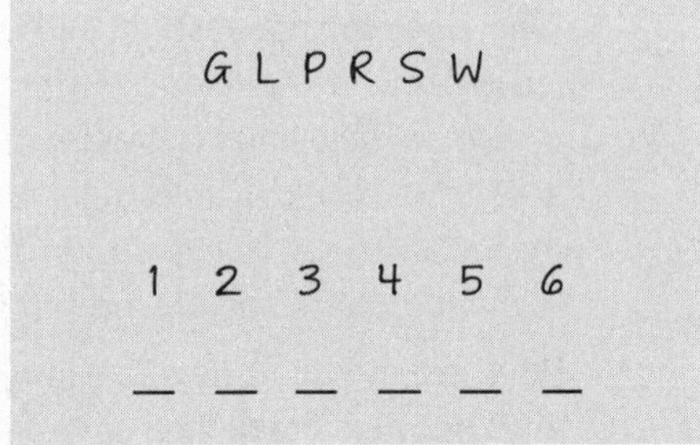

3. [Step 3] Analyze and draw the Rules:
   - Rule 1:
     - What does the rule restrict, and what does it leave open? *This rule indicates ordering. Gauze will appear before polyester. There can be any number of spaces in between, or they could be next to one another.*
     - What are the rule's negative implications, if any? *Because gauze comes earlier, it cannot be on hanger 6. And because polyester comes later, it cannot be on hanger 1.*
     - Can the rule be depicted inside the sketch framework? *No.*
     - Draw the rule:

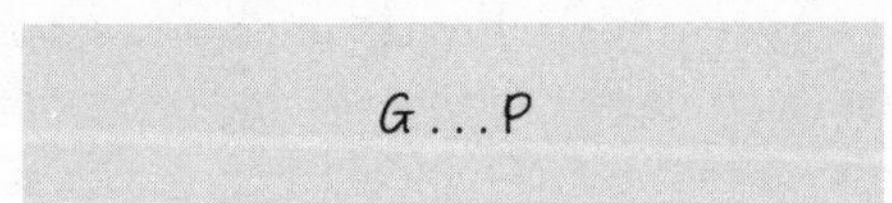

   - Rule 2:
     - What does the rule restrict, and what does it leave open? *This rule limits the rayon dress to two hangers: 1 or 6. Any other dress can occupy the other slot.*
     - What are the rule's negative implications, if any? *The rayon dress cannot be on any hanger from 2 through 5.*
     - Can the rule be depicted inside the sketch framework? *Yes, or it can be simply notated to the side.*
     - Draw the rule:

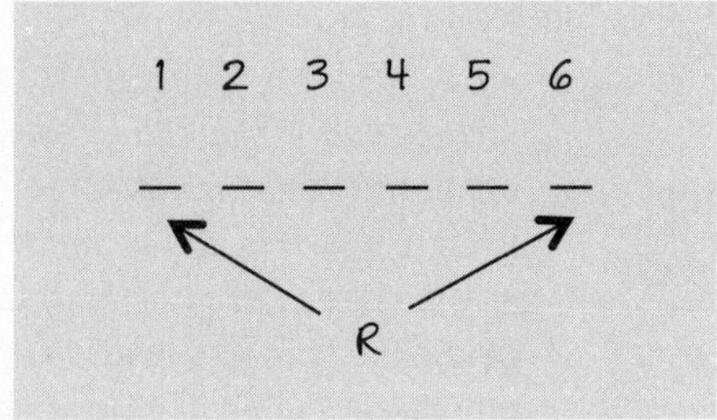

   - Rule 3:
     - What does the rule restrict, and what does it leave open? *This establishes one of two entities on hanger 3: the silk dress or the wool dress. The other dress can still hang anywhere else.*
     - What are the rule's negative implications, if any? *No other dress can hang on hanger 3.*
     - Can the rule be depicted inside the sketch framework? *Yes.*
     - Draw the rule:

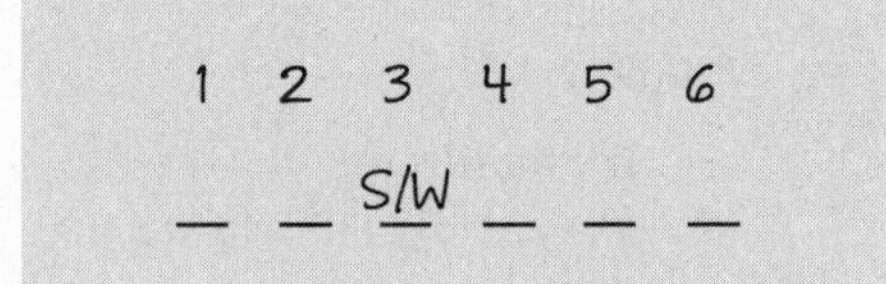

   - Rule 4:
     - What does the rule restrict, and what does it leave open? *This rule creates a block of silk immediately before linen. There's no restriction on where this block can appear in the sequencing.*
     - What are the rule's negative implications, if any? *Because the silk dress comes earlier, it cannot be on hanger 6. And because the linen dress comes later, it cannot be on hanger 1.*
     - Can the rule be depicted inside the sketch framework? *No.*
     - Draw the rule:

Assess

Assess your performance according to the following criteria:

Game Types and Initial Sketches

At this point, you should be able to identify the action(s) of the standard game types. If you got all four of them correct here, well done. If there were any games you misidentified, return to Chapter 2 to review the definitions and illustrations of Logic Games actions and types.

Your initial sketches do not need to be exact replicas of those the LSAT experts drew. Superficial or stylistic differences are irrelevant. Assess your sketch frameworks by noting three considerations:

1) Did your framework fit the game's action (i.e., was it appropriate for the game type)? If "Yes," you are in great shape. If, for any of the setups, you chose a format that did not match the game type appropriately, return to Chapter 2 and review the model sketches there.

2) Was it accurate (with the correct number and orientation of positions)? If "Yes," well done. If there were any errors in your sketch frameworks, consider whether they were "sloppy" errors (e.g., the game had six positions, but you put seven), or whether you fundamentally misunderstood a description or limitation within the game's setup. Disciplining yourself to read with precision and accuracy is a key overarching skill for LSAT success.

3) Was it as simple as possible given the game's setup? This assessment is somewhat more subjective. On test day, accuracy is far more important than "elegance." LSAT experts, however, know that they will likely need to copy the Master Sketch one or more times when answering the questions (you may remember this from the New-"If" questions in Chapter 1), and thus, they strive to make their sketch frameworks as simple as possible. If there were cases in which your sketches were unnecessarily complicated, learn how to simplify them from the expert examples.

Rules

Assuming your analyses of the game types and your initial sketches were accurate, evaluate your performance on the rules as follows.

If you correctly analyzed and drew **more than 75%** of the rules in this Perform exercise correctly: Great job. Review any rules that you misunderstood or drew incorrectly to determine if there are any patterns. For example, did you miss rules associated with a particular game type or rules that describe certain types of restrictions, such as relative position or blocks of entities?

If you correctly analyzed and drew **51% to 75%** of the rules: Review the descriptions and illustrations of the rule types in the Prepare section of this chapter. Additionally, note the game types in which you mischaracterized any rules. In Chapters 5, 8, 9, and 10, you will have the opportunity to again study and practice the rule patterns associated with the standard game types. Make a note to yourself to study those sections carefully.

If you correctly analyzed and drew **50% or less** of the rules: You have some work to do. From this point forward, the book will assume that you can analyze and sketch rules with a fair degree of confidence and accuracy. First, review the Prepare section of this chapter. Then, try the quiz titled "Analyzing and Sketching Rules Fundamentals" found in your online center. Once you have completed that, you should feel far more confident with Step 3 of the Logic Games Method.

To stay sharp, practice the drills in the Logic Games Training Camp for this chapter in your Online Study Plan. Training Camp drills are divided into Fundamentals, Mid-Level, and Advanced sets.

Reflect

Think back over the work you did in this section of Chapter 3.

- Are you beginning to recognize the standard game types as they are described in the games' setups?
- Can you associate certain types of rules with particular game types (e.g., relative order rules occur in Sequencing games)?
- Do you recognize rules that can be depicted within a game's sketch framework, and distinguish them from those that must be written underneath or beside the sketch?
- Are you becoming more confident that you can draw out a rule in a way that matches the sketch?
- When you look at the way you've drawn out a rule, does it clearly reflect the way in which that rule did *and did not* restrict the entities?

In the coming days and weeks, take note of real-life considerations that mimic Logic Games rules. They pop up in all sorts of unexpected places. Some examples might be:

- You go out with a group of friends and you make sure that two of them sit next to each other: Tom and Becky will sit in adjacent positions.
- You have two coworkers who don't get along, so no one wants them assigned to the same project: Ellie and Mitchell will not both be assigned to work on the Taylor account.
- Even something as simple as the food you order could be described in logic games terms: If I order a muffin, then I will definitely get coffee.

Logic games mimic real world tasks, although they often seem to impose arbitrary and abstract rules upon them. In real life, you usually know the reason behind the rule, which makes your decisions more concrete. Noting when day-to-day tasks impose restrictions similar to those found on the test can help to demystify the logic games experience and makes you feel more immersed in the kinds of reasoning and analysis you'll do on test day.

HOW TO COMBINE RULES TO MAKE DEDUCTIONS

LEARNING OBJECTIVES

In this section of Chapter 3, you'll learn to

- Combine rules and restrictions to make valid deductions in logic games.

Prepare

Now that you've learned to analyze and draw the rules, you're ready for Step 4 of the Logic Games Method—Deductions. In this section, you'll learn to catalog the restrictions and rules limiting the possible arrangements within a game and to combine them to establish what must, can, and cannot be true in all cases. More than any of the other steps, this is the one that separates the LSAT expert from other test takers. Making all of the available deductions within a game will put you in control of the questions to a degree others cannot match.

Although making deductions stands as a distinct step within the Logic Games Method, you've actually had a bit of a head start on the thinking and analysis you'll do here. Considering the negative implications of rules can help you add information to a game's sketch. For example, a rule such as "Jonathan is scheduled for an earlier day of the week than Edith is scheduled" allows you to conclude that Edith will not take the first day of the schedule and Jonathan will not take the last day. Deductions of this sort make explicit the implications of a rule. A similar example stems from a rule such as "Hwang and Munoz will not be drafted by the same team." In a Distribution game with exactly two teams, you could deduce that each team drafts at least one player, either Hwang or Munoz.

The work you'll do in this section takes making deductions a step further. Here, instead of making the implications of a single rule explicit, you'll learn to combine two or more rules and bring the implications of that combination to light. To see a simple example, imagine that a Sequencing game with six positions has the following rules:

> Barney may not occupy the first position.
> Judith will be assigned a higher-numbered position than Barney's position.

From Rule 1 alone, you can exclude Barney from Position 1. From the second rule alone, you know Judith may not take Position 1 and Barney may not take Position 6.

```
__  __  __  __  __  __
1   2   3   4   5   6
~B                  ~B
~J

B...J
```

By combining these two rules, you can deduce that the earliest position Judith may occupy is Position 3, and thus, exclude her from Position 2 as well.

```
__  __  __  __  __  __
1   2   3   4   5   6
~B  ~J              ~B
~J

B...J
```

Deductions such as this may not seem earth-shattering, but knowing with certainty (and noting in your Master Sketch) that an entity cannot occupy a particular position will help you answer one or more of the questions. The testmaker may reward you directly with a correct answer that mirrors the deduction or indirectly by including wrong answers suggesting that an arrangement you've determined is impossible is actually acceptable.

When they first approach Step 4, the Deductions step, some students feel that something mysterious or almost magical is happening as so much of the game takes shape. The LSAT expert, however, knows that nothing could be further from the truth. The step of making deductions is thoroughly practical and methodical. You work from what is most certain and concrete in the game and check for anything else that information allows you to determine. Moreover, the LSAT expert knows that deductions stem from combinations of five types of rules, easily memorized with the BLEND checklist you first saw in Chapter 1.

To master Step 4 of the Logic Games Method, you'll need to hone your ability to do three things.

LOGIC GAMES STRATEGY

To make the deductions in a logic game efficiently and effectively, follow these steps:

1. Identify the most restricted entities and positions within the game.
2. Use the BLEND checklist to make all available deductions.
3. Identify *floaters* (unrestricted entities) after making all available deductions.

Before practicing this step on logic games setups, take a closer look at the process of making deductions.

Making Deductions Effectively and Efficiently

Spot the Most Restricted Entities and Positions

As you read earlier in this chapter, rules and restrictions are your greatest allies in solving logic games. Without the rules, there are hundreds (or, in some games, thousands) of possible arrangements. After you add in the rules, however, there will be only a handful of acceptable solutions, and the game will be much more manageable. In the Deductions step of the Logic Games Method, you are making those limitations explicit, and adding them to the sketch, your visual description of the game.

Established entities—those whose position is set once and for all—are obviously the most restricted entities within a game. They can't move. Always check to see if other entities are related by rule to the established entity, as their position will be affected as well. Take, for example, a distribution game with two rowing teams that includes the following rules:

> Brenda rows in boat 2.
>
> Sabrina and Brenda do not row in the same boat.

Given that Brenda's position is established, Rule 2 allows you to confidently place Sabrina in Boat 1.

Boat 1	Boat 2
S	B
__	__
__	__
__	__

In some games, there are no established entities, or the established entities are not directly related to other entities. In that case, seek out the entities or positions that have the greatest amount of restriction placed upon them by the rules. Truck Y in the Truck Arrivals game provides a great example.

Refresh (Activate Prior Knowledge)

In a single day, exactly seven trucks—S, T, U, W, X, Y, and Z—are the only arrivals at a warehouse. No truck arrives at the same time as any other truck, and no truck arrives more than once that day. Each truck is either green or red (but not both). The following conditions apply:

> No two consecutive arrivals are red.
>
> Y arrives at some time before both T and W.
>
> Exactly two of the trucks that arrive before Y are red.
>
> S is the sixth arrival.
>
> Z arrives at some time before U.

PrepTest37 Sec3 Qs 6–11

S T U W X Y Z

1	2	3	4	5	6	7
__	__	__	__	__	S	__

g/r __ __ __ __ __ __ __

never r r

Y ... T
Y ... W

r ... r ... Y

Z ... U

Here, Rule 4 establishes the position of Truck S (it arrives sixth), but no other rules relate another entity to Truck S or to the sixth slot. Thus, to make effective deductions, you'll want to move on to the next most restricted entity. Truck Y should pop out because it is mentioned in two rules (Rules 2 and 3). Truck Y is restricted by two trucks (Trucks T and W) that must *follow* it, and by two positions (both occupied by red trucks) that must *precede* it. That alone would tell you that Truck Y is restricted to the third, fourth or fifth positions.

r...r...y.:·T
·W

Now, however, the established entity—Truck S in the sixth slot—comes into play. Since both Truck T and Truck W must follow Truck Y, the fifth slot is denied to Truck Y, as well, limiting Truck Y to only the third or fourth positions. But, there is yet another restriction that limits Truck Y. Rule 1 stipulates that red trucks may not arrive consecutively. If the first three trucks that arrive are red, green, and red respectively, Truck Y must arrive fourth.

S T U W X Y Z

X

_ _ _ Y T/W S W/T
1 2 3 4 5 6 7

g/r r g r g _ _ _

Making those deductions solves a huge chunk of the game. Two of the trucks' arrival positions are established. Two more trucks are limited to a pair of positions. The colors of the first four arrivals are established as well. Concentrating on the most restricted entities made it possible to spot those deductions effectively and efficiently.

The Truck Arrivals game also illustrates the value of the BLEND checklist. Rules 2 and 3, in particular, exemplify the D in BLEND, Duplications. When two rules share a common entity, they can be combined to reveal additional restrictions within the game. The next portion of this chapter zeroes in on BLEND to show you how to find all of a game's deductions.

Use the BLEND Checklist to Make All Available Deductions

Not every game has deductions as strong as those in the Truck Arrivals game, but nearly every game has some additional information for you to uncover. The best way to ensure that you're spotting all of this extra help is by using the BLEND checklist, which catalogs the five patterns most likely to result in valid deductions in logic games.

STEP 4: DEDUCTIONS

BLEND

- **B**locks of Entities—two or more players that are always grouped together
- **L**imited Options—rules or restrictions that limit the overall setup to one or the other of two acceptable arrangements
- **E**stablished Entities—a player locked into a specific space or group
- **N**umber Restrictions—rules or limitations that provide guidance about the number of entities assigned to a group or space
- **D**uplications—entities that appear in two or more rules and allow the rules to be combined

Remember that BLEND is not a series of steps, and not all games contain all five types of rules and restrictions. As you note down a game's limitations and rules, learn to ask which of the five BLEND elements they represent. That way, you'll head into Step 4 anticipating the deductions you're most likely to make.

Blocks of Entities

Blocks of entities—two entities that must be placed together—are very common in Sequencing games. In these games, the strongest blocks are created by rules requiring entities to occupy consecutive positions in a particular order. For example:

Gregory must occupy the position immediately after Dawn's position.

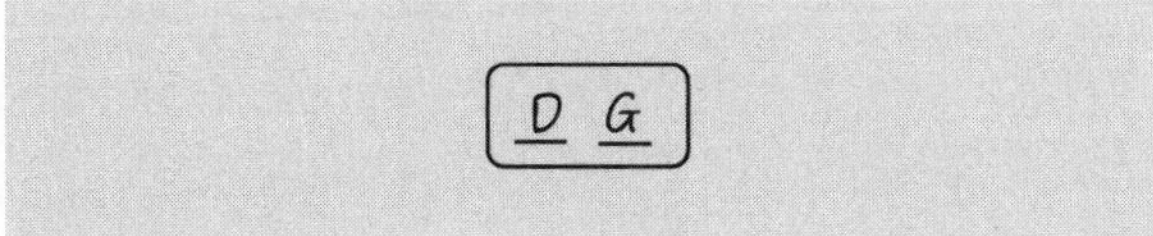

To place that block within the game's framework, you'll have to find two consecutive open positions that are acceptable for both D and G. Blocks of entities may interact with established entities or with other blocks to produce deductions. Adding a little context for this rule helps to illustrate this. Picture a six-position Strict Sequencing game with the following rules.

Gregory must occupy the position immediately after Dawn's position.
Tom occupies the third position.
Farrah's position is earlier than Tom's.

Because the position of T is fixed, and because F must occupy one of the two slots that precede T's position, the D-G block can occupy only the fourth and fifth or the fifth and sixth positions.

Other Sequencing rules can produce blocks that are slightly less restrictive. Take a rule requiring the entities to occupy consecutive spaces in either order. You'll still need two consecutive open spaces for this block, but the entities within the block can swap positions.

Charles and Hillary occupy consecutive positions.

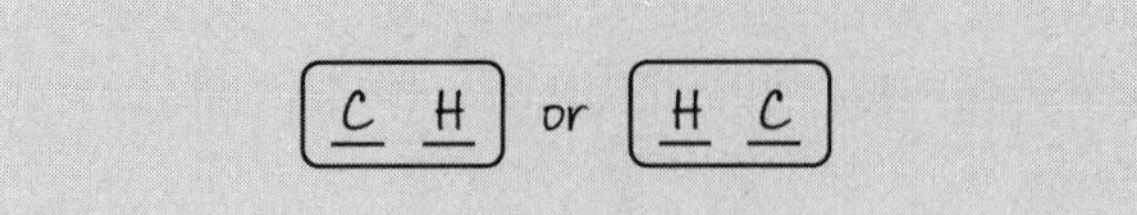

A rule that gives the relative order of two entities, but does not limit how close or how far apart they must be, creates a "loose block." These are far less restrictive, but still worth considering as you make deductions.

Rupa occupies a position later than Quincy's.

Q...R

Blocks can also lead to powerful deductions in a Distribution game. Consider the following model game setup.

The intelligence minister of a small nation will place seven spies—code named M, N, Q, R, S, T, and U—as follows: one will be assigned to the embassy in Ankara; three are assigned to the embassy in Budapest; and three are assigned to the embassy in Cairo. Each spy receives exactly one placement in accordance with the following restrictions:

Q and S are assigned to the same embassy.

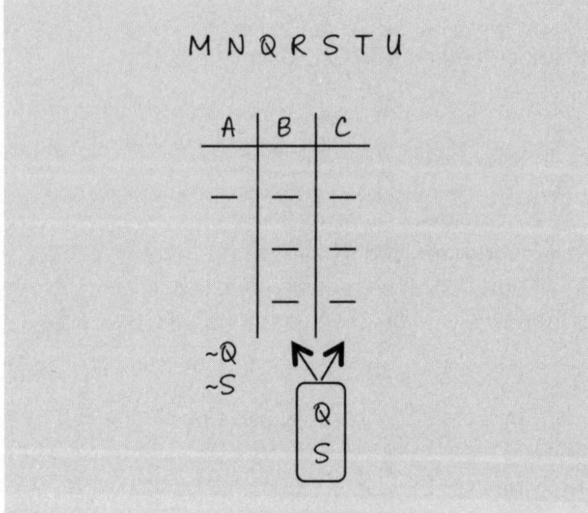

In Distribution games, blocks of entities most often lead to deductions when they interact with number restrictions. In this case, the number restrictions outlined in the game's setup allow the Q-S block only two acceptable assignments. Depending on what the game's additional rules contain, you may be able to limit the Q-S block to a specific group, or you may find out that it is valuable to create sketches for both of the possible placements of the block. When you create two parallel sketches, you are making the deduction called Limited Options.

Limited Options

Limited Options can be one of the most powerful deductions that you can make. Discovering that a game breaks down into just two (or, very rarely, three) distinct patterns can make handling the questions a snap. But, it takes practice to recognize when this deduction is available. There is a Special Feature on Limited Options at the end of this chapter that breaks down the types of rules that can lead to Limited Options. It is accompanied by a video in which an LSAT Channel expert illustrates Limited Options on a logic game you haven't tried before.

To spot the opportunity to use Limited Options in a game, look for a rule or a combination of rules that creates two distinct patterns, each of which then triggers additional deductions. To illustrate this definition, add a couple more rules to the model game setup about the spies in three cities.

> The intelligence minister of a small nation will place seven spies—code-named M, N, Q, R, S, T, and U—as follows: one will be assigned to the embassy in Ankara; three are assigned to the embassy in Budapest; and three are assigned to the embassy in Cairo. Each spy receives exactly one placement in accordance with the following restrictions:
>
> Q and S are assigned to the same embassy.
> Neither M nor U is assigned to the embassy in Ankara.
> S and U are not assigned to the same embassy.
> T is assigned to the embassy in Cairo.

MNQRSTU

A	B	C
—	—	—
	—	—
	—	—

~Q
~S

Q S (block, arrows to B and C)

Here, Rule 1 combined with the number restrictions outlined in the game's setup led to the deduction that the Q-S block can be placed only in Budapest or Cairo. Because the placement of S triggers a further restriction in Rule 3, it is worth creating dual Limited Options sketches to explore what happens in each of two acceptable patterns. Then, add Rule 3 to each of the two options.

M N ~~Q~~ R ~~S~~ T U

Opt. 1

A	B	C
—	Q	—
	S	—
	—	—

~Q ~U
~S

Opt. 2

A	B	C
—	—	Q
	—	S
	—	—

~Q ~U
~S

Now, add Rules 2 and 4 to each option's sketch.

M N ~~Q~~ R ~~S~~ ~~T~~ U

Opt. 1

A	B	C
__	Q	T
	S	__
	__	__

~Q ~S ~M ~U (A); ~U (B)

Opt. 2

A	B	C
__	__	Q
	__	S
	__	T

~Q ~S ~M ~U (A); ~U (C)

The two options make it possible to learn more about Spy U. In Option I, Spy U must be assigned to Cairo. In Option II, Spy U will go to Budapest. Note, too, that in either option, only Spy N or Spy R is available for placement in Ankara.

M N ~~Q~~ R ~~S~~ ~~T~~ ~~U~~

Opt. 1

A	B	C
N/R	Q	T
	S	U
	__	__

~Q ~S ~M ~U (A); ~U (B)

Opt. 2

A	B	C
N/R	U	Q
	__	S
	__	T

~Q ~S ~M ~U (A); ~U (C)

Finally, because there is no room left for placements in Cairo in Option II, you can now place Spy M firmly in Budapest. Thus, in Option II, the third spy placed in Budapest will be either Spy N or Spy R, whichever does not go to Ankara.

M N Q R S T U

Opt. 1

A	B	C
N/R	Q	T
	S	U
	—	—
~Q ~S ~M ~U	~U	

Opt. 2

A	B	C
N/R	U	Q
	M	S
	N/R	T
~Q ~S ~M ~U		~U

In logic games that break down into Limited Options, it is quite common for one of the two options to result in a more complete Master Sketch. Here, Option II is nearly "solved," with only the placements for Spies N and R undetermined. In Option I, on the other hand, three spies—M, N, and R—can still swap positions.

Refresh (Activate Prior Knowledge)

Another game you've worked with already—the one about the Chess Tournament—breaks down into Limited Options. Take a moment to review the setup and rules of that game, and try to anticipate how an LSAT expert will proceed through the Deductions step.

Exactly six people—Lulu, Nam, Ofelia, Pachai, Santiago, and Tyrone—are the only contestants in a chess tournament. The tournament consists of four games, played one after the other. Exactly two people play in each game, and each person plays in at least one game. The following conditions must apply:

Tyrone does not play in the first or third game.

Lulu plays in the last game.

Nam plays in only one game and it is not against Pachai.

Santiago plays in exactly two games, one just before and one just after the only game that Ofelia plays in.

PrepTest45 Sec3 Qs 7–12

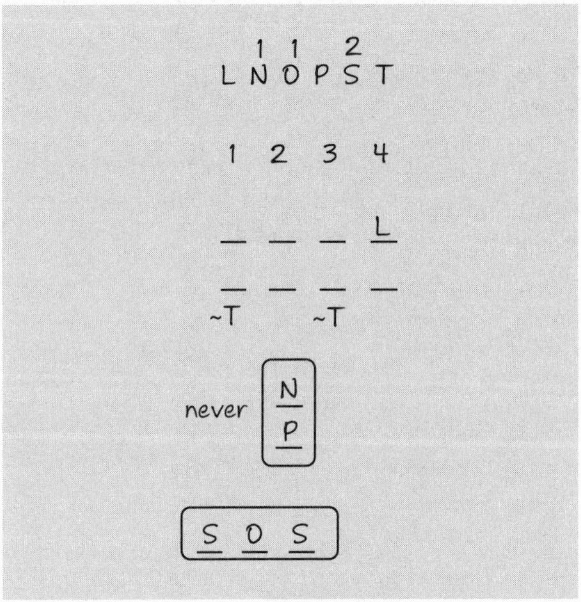

---

1 1 2
L N O P S T

1 2 3 4

_ _ _ L

_ _ _ _
~T ~T

never N/P

S O S

What is the most restrictive rule in this game? Rule 2 establishes one placement for Lulu, but remember, in this game's setup, Lulu might play twice. Rule 4, however, creates a block of three entities (S-O-S) that will have to fit into a schedule of just four games. For the LSAT expert, that leads to Limited Options: The S-O-S block will fit only in games 1–3 or games 2–4.

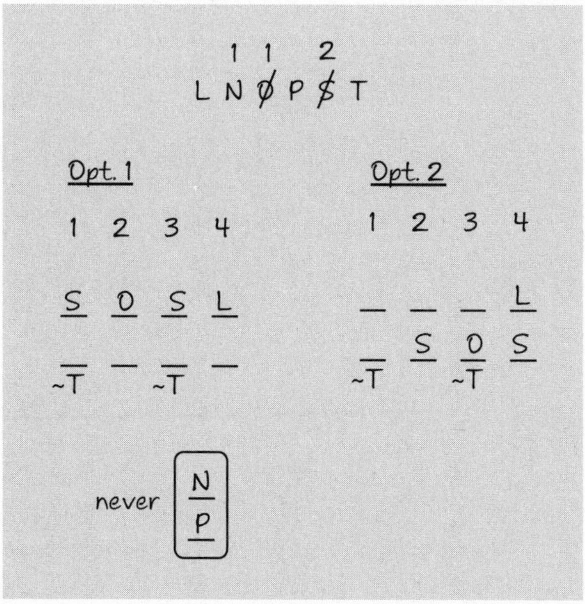

Each of those options accounts for all of the possible placements for Santiago and Ofelia. Thus, in both options, there are four open slots. In Option I, you know that Tyrone will play in game 2, game 4, or both, but you can't go much further than that. In Option II, however, Tyrone's only available game is game 2. What else can you determine in Option II?

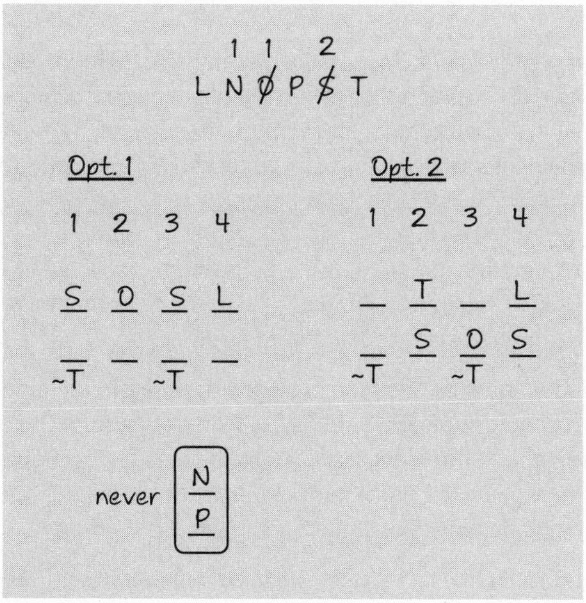

Consider the role of Rule 3 in Option II. Nam and Pachai cannot play against each other. Thus, one of them will play in game 1 and one of them in game 3. Regardless of which one plays in game 1, the opponent in that game must be Lulu, the only player eligible to take Option II's final slot.

1 1 2
L N Ø P $ T

Opt. 1
1 2 3 4
S O S L
~T ~T

Opt. 2
1 2 3 4
P/N T N/P L
L S O S
~T ~T

never N/P

Typically, just one of the games in an LSAT Logic Games section will break down into Limited Options (sometimes, none of them do, and rarely, two), so don't try to force every game into dual sketches. Learn to spot the patterns that divide a game into two patterns leading to additional deductions. When you do, the Limited Options deduction can help you answer the game's questions more quickly and confidently.

Established Entities

Established entities are those that are, by rule, placed in one permanent position. While that alone is helpful, deductions follow from established entities when they affect the placement of other entities. Always check to see if the established entity is mentioned in any other rule, and whether its placement prevents a block of entities from taking certain positions (in Sequencing games) or being placed on certain teams (in Distribution games).

Number Restrictions

Number restrictions are most prominent (and most helpful) in Distribution and Matching games. That's because the size of the groups into which you're divvying up the entities (Distribution) or the number of attributes, items, or tasks you're trying to assign (Matching) determines much of the game's outcome.

In Distribution games, you may find number restrictions in a game's setup. In the model game about the spies, for example, the numbers in each group were explicit: "one [spy] will be assigned to the embassy in Ankara; three are assigned to the embassy in Budapest; and three are assigned to the embassy in Cairo." In those cases, look for the impact that the number restrictions have on the placement of blocks of entities. It is routine for the testmaker to set up Distribution games in a way that limits blocks of entities to only one or two groups.

If a Distribution game's setup paragraph does not state or limit the number of entities that will be assigned to each group, look for a rule that does. Consider this model setup:

> A group of seven friends—Adam, Benji, Carole, Deng, Esther, Felicia, and Graham—is attending a soccer game. Each friend will wear a shirt in exactly one of the home team's colors—red and yellow. The friends' decisions about which color to wear must accord with the following considerations:
>
> More of the friends will wear red shirts than wear yellow shirts.

A B C D E F G

4-7	0-3
R	Y

From that comparative number restriction, you can conclude that the maximum number of yellow-shirted friends is three. Any more than that, and yellow shirts would outnumber red. There is still a lot of leeway, however. In fact, from that rule alone, you don't know that anyone wears a yellow shirt.

In a typical Distribution game, you will get a little more assistance from the rules, even if the rules do not explicitly mention the number of entities per team. For example:

> A group of seven friends—Adam, Benji, Carole, Deng, Esther, Felicia, and Graham—is attending a soccer game. Each friend will wear a shirt in exactly one of the home team's colors—red and yellow. The friends' decisions about which color to wear must accord with the following considerations:
>
> More of the friends will wear red shirts than wear yellow shirts.
> Graham wears a yellow shirt.
> Deng and Esther wear shirts of different colors.

A B C D E F G

4-7	0-3
R	Y
D/E	G
__	E/D
__	

Adding the established entity—Graham—to the yellow-shirt column, and depicting the "anti-block" pair—Deng and Esther—within the sketch framework, has a dramatic impact on the game's numbers. With at least two of the friends wearing yellow shirts, you now have only two options: two yellow shirts and five red shirts or three yellow shirts and four red shirts. Depending on the game's subsequent rules, you might choose to depict this with the following Limited Options sketches. In fact, in the case in which there are only two yellow shirts, you can virtually complete the sketch.

A B C D E F G

Opt. 1

4-7 R	0-3 4
D/E	G
—	E/D
—	—
—	

Opt. 2

4-7 R	0-3 4
D/E	G
A	E/D
B	
C	
F	

In Matching games, the initial setup might limit the number of attributes you can match to each of the recipients (the people, places, or things to which you are matching), but it will almost never determine the exact number for each recipient. Additional number restrictions are often found in the rules. Here's an example:

> In preparation for a lecture, each of four archaeologists—Rand, Singer, Tulsi, and Wang—will study at least one and at most three of the following artifacts recovered from a prehistoric dwelling—an arrow point, a bowl, a diadem, and an effigy. In determining who will study each item, the archaeologists conform to the following considerations:
>
> Rand will study more of the items than Singer.
> Wang studies the diadem.
> Rand does not study any item that Wang studies.

R > S

1-3 ea. arch

	2-3 R	1-2 S	T	W
a				
b				
d	X			✓
e				

In this example, the opening setup limits the archaeologists to between one and three of the items, i.e., everyone studies something, but no one studies everything. The first rule further limits the numbers for Rand and Singer. If Singer studies just one item, then Rand may study either two or three. If Singer studies two of the items, then Rand will definitely study three. Rules 2 and 3 combine to prevent Rand from studying the diadem, so if Singer studies two of the items, Rand will study the arrow point, the bowl, and the effigy.

Number restrictions are relatively rare in Sequencing games. For the most part, Sequencing games have an equal number of entities and positions, and they tell you straight out that there are no ties among the entities. In those games, the numbers are already as simple as they can be (six entities, six slots, one-per-slot), and there is no way to further restrict the game's framework. In a complex Strict Sequencing game in which you have to schedule, say, seven appointments over five days, you might get a rule that sets or limits the number of entities per day (e.g., "Exactly one appointment will be scheduled for Wednesday," or "Tuesday is a day on which two of the appointments are scheduled"), but for the most part, Sequencing games lack this item from the BLEND checklist.

In Selection games, your task is to choose some of the entities and reject others. Roughly half of all Selection games purposely do not tell you the number of entities to select because that is what they ask about.

> What is the maximum number of employees who could be chosen to attend the company retreat?
> If Joanna is chosen to attend the company retreat, how many other employees must be chosen to attend the retreat?

In games of that type, the game setup stipulates merely that "some" or "at least one" of the entities is selected. You will use the game's conditional rules (e.g., "If Joanna is chosen to attend the retreat, then Matt is also chosen, but Kim is not") to determine the minimum or maximum number selected, or the numbers selected in various circumstances.

The other "half" of Selection games, however, tell you in the setup precisely how many entities to select. Number restrictions can come into play with Selection games of this type if the entities are subdivided into different categories. Here's an example:

> From among eight city employees—two city council members: Addams and Bernard; three police officers: Klaus, Lemark, and McCaffrey; and three teachers: Ritchie, Sanchez, and Xavier—the mayor will name exactly five to represent the city as a delegation to the city's sister municipality in another country. The mayor's selections conform to the following restrictions:
>
> > Exactly two police officers will be named to the delegation.
> > Ritchie and Sanchez cannot both be named to the delegation.

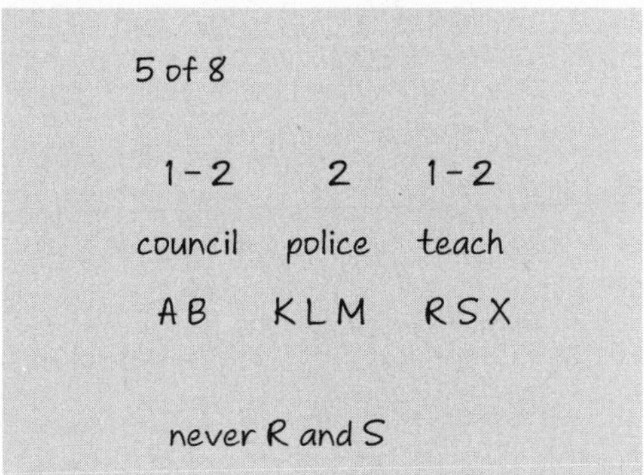

Here, the first rule states an explicit number restriction: Exactly two police officers are selected. Because Ritchie and Sanchez are both teachers, the second rule implicitly limits the number of teachers who may be selected to a maximum of two. As a result, you know that at least one city council member will join the delegation (notice that nothing in the game's setup required that).

If you run across a game of this type, it is always valuable to determine how the numbers selected from among the subgroups of entities break down. In this game, the mayor could choose either one city council member, two police officers, and two teachers, or the mayor could choose two city council members, two police officers, and one teacher. Because the numbers break down into exactly two acceptable patterns, a Limited Options sketch may be helpful.

5 of 8

1–2 2 1–2
council police teach
AB KLM RSX

never R and S

Opt I _ | _ _ | _ _
Opt II _ _ | _ _ | _

With dual Limited Options sketches in place, two things are clear, even from the partial set of rules presented here: In Opt I, Xavier will be selected, along with one of the other teachers (who cannot both be selected), and in Opt II, both Council members must be selected.

5 of 8

1–2 2 1–2
council police teach
AB KLM RSX

never R and S

Opt I _ | _ _ | R/S X
Opt II A B | _ _ | _

Duplications

Duplications may be the last item in the BLEND checklist, but they are probably the most common type of deductions. Duplications occur anytime an entity is mentioned in two rules. This "duplicator" entity allows the rules to be combined, and doing so almost always reveals additional restrictions within the game.

In Sequencing games, a rule creating a "loose" block of entities very often shares an entity with another rule that creates a block (or "loose" block) of entities. For example:

R's position is later than M's position.
T's position is earlier than M's position.

T...M...R

In Strict Sequencing games, these "strings" of relative ordering relationships may sometimes include as many as four or five of the entities, but three is the most common.

In a typical Loose Sequencing game, all of the rules combine to create a "tree" of relative relationships. Here's an example:

> A film festival advisory committee must determine the order in which to present awards in each of six categories—comedy, documentary, foreign, historical, independent, and nature—on the festival's closing night. Exactly one award will be presented for each film category, and no awards are presented at the same time. The committee will adhere to the following guidelines to determine the order of the presentations:
>
> The award for foreign film is always presented at some time before the award for comedy.
> The award for comedy is always presented at some time after the award for documentaries.
> The award for foreign film is always presented at some time after the awards for historical and nature films.
> The award for independent films is always presented before the award for historical films.

```
I— H\
     F\
   N/   C
      D/
```

You will revisit this model game setup in Chapter 7, which focuses specifically on Loose Sequencing. For now, take notice of the following: 1) every rule stipulates the relative order between two or among three entities, 2) every rule shares a "duplicator" entity with at least one other rule, and 3) by the end of the rules, all six entities have been accounted for in the Master Sketch. Those criteria make this an example of the archetypal Loose Sequencing game.

Duplications also play a huge role in Selection games. Because virtually all of the rules in Selection games are conditional, the result of one rule may trigger another rule. Here's a typical example:

> If A is selected, then C is selected.
> If C is selected, then E is not selected.

```
If A → C → ~E
```

By combining those two rules, you can deduce that anytime A is selected, E will be rejected. It's not hard to spot a connection like that one—in which the result of one rule is the explicit trigger of another—but there can be more to creating these "strings" of conditions. Inherent in every conditional (Formal Logic) rule is a parallel rule known as the contrapositive. If you are familiar with that much of Formal Logic, you could also deduce from the rules above that anytime E is selected, both C and A will be rejected. If you aren't familiar with Formal Logic, make sure to study the section of Chapter 8 that covers this topic in detail. Learning this small slice of Formal Logic tested in LSAT Logic Games will also help you master the Logical Reasoning section of the test.

In Distribution and Matching, Duplications can occur in a variety of settings. Any two rules that share a common entity can be combined. The Matching game setup describing the archaeologists provided a couple of examples.

> In preparation for a lecture, each of four archaeologists—Rand, Singer, Tulsi, and Wang—will study at least one and at most three of the following artifacts recovered from a prehistoric dwelling—an arrow point, a bowl, a diadem, and an effigy. In determining who will study each item, the archaeologists conform to the following considerations:
>
> Rand will study more of the items than Singer.
> Wang studies the diadem.
> Rand does not study any item that Wang studies.

R>S

1-3 ea. arch

	2-3 R	1-2 S	T	W
a				
b				
d	X			✓
e				

Here, Rules 2 and 3 share Wang, and by combining them, you can conclude that Rand does not study the diadem. Moreover, because Rules 1 and 3 both mention Rand, you are able to conclude that Rand will study at least two, and maybe all three of the arrow point, the bowl, and the effigy.

You have ample opportunity to practice making deductions in all of the common game types featured on the LSAT. In each of Chapters 5–10, you'll find a section that outlines the types of deductions most often found in the game type covered in detail in the chapter along with model setups and rules on which to hone your skills. At the end of each of those chapters, there are full games in which you will, of course, need to use all five steps of the Logic Games Method (Deductions included) to answer the questions.

Refresh (Activate Prior Knowledge)

Before moving on, take time to review an LSAT expert's Step 4 analyses for one more game you've worked with before, the one on Patterson's meetings. Take a couple of minutes to refresh your memory of the game's setup and rules; then, try to anticipate the deductions that the expert will make.

On one afternoon, Patterson meets individually with each of exactly five clients—Reilly, Sanchez, Tang, Upton, and Yansky—and also goes to the gym by herself for a workout. Patterson's workout and her five meetings each start at either 1:00, 2:00, 3:00, 4:00, 5:00, or 6:00. The following conditions must apply:

Patterson meets with Sanchez at some time before her workout.
Patterson meets with Tang at some time after her workout.
Patterson meets with Yansky either immediately before or immediately after her workout.
Patterson meets with Upton at some time before she meets with Reilly.

PrepTest45 Sec3 Qs 1–6

R S T U Y W

_ _ _ _ _ _
1 2 3 4 5 6

S...W
W...T
[W Y] or [Y W]
U...R

First, the LSAT expert looks for the most restricted entity in the game. It is the workout, which is mentioned in Rules 1, 2, and 3, making it a kind of "super duplicator," if you will. Combining all three rules produces the following string:

S...[W/Y]...T

The expert then uses that string to make explicit the negative implications of those three combined rules. Because Sanchez is, at a minimum, followed by the workout, Yansky, and Tang, the meeting with Sanchez may not be at 4:00, 5:00, or 6:00. Conversely, because Tang is, at a minimum, preceded by Sanchez, the workout, and Yansky, the meeting with Tang cannot be at 1:00, 2:00, or 3:00. Because the workout and Yansky are bookended by Sanchez and Tang, neither the workout nor the meeting with Yansky can be at 1:00 or at 6:00.

R S T U Y W

_ _ _ _ _ _
1 2 3 4 5 6
~T ~T ~T ~S ~S ~S
~W ~W
~Y ~Y

S...[W/Y]...T

Finally, the expert can record the negative implications of Rule 4: the meeting with Reilly cannot be at 1:00, and the meeting with Upton cannot be at 6:00. Given all of the restrictions on the first and final slots in the game, the expert can deduce that Patterson meets with either Sanchez or Upton at 1:00, and with either Reilly or Tang at 6:00.

R S T U Y W

S/U _ _ _ _ T/R
1 2 3 4 5 6
~T ~T ~T ~S ~S ~S
~W ~W
~Y ~Y
~R ~U

S...[W/Y]...T
U...R

Even though this game had no established entities, by focusing on the most restricted entity and using the Duplications found among the rules, the expert was able to make several deductions that will prove valuable in answering the game's questions.

Note the Floaters

After you've used the BLEND checklist, always take a moment to account for all of the entities in the game: Which are now established in a single position? Which ones are limited to only some of the possible positions? And which ones are "floaters," still unconstrained by any rule or restriction? In your initial roster of the entities, mark the floaters in some way. Many LSAT veterans will use a little star, asterisk, or question mark above a floater. Likewise, they may choose to cross out the established entities in the roster, knowing that they will not need to account for those entities going forward. By the end of Step 4 in the Truck Arrivals game, the positions of Trucks S and Y are established, but Truck X remains a floater.

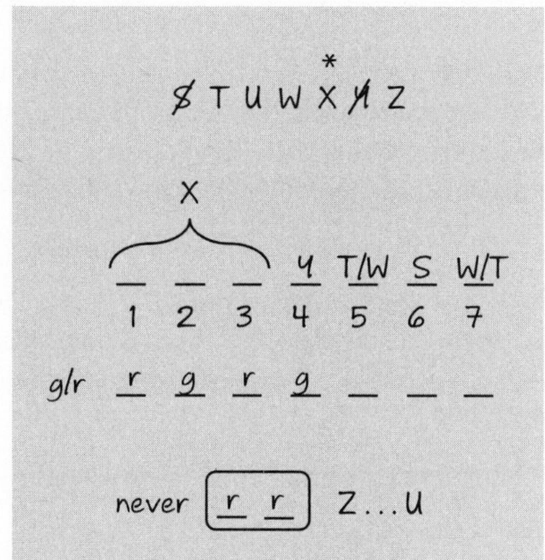

How to Know When You've Made All of the Game's Deductions

An irony of learning to make deductions is that it's sometimes hard to stop. That is to say that, on some games, you may find yourself looking for additional deductions that just aren't there. All LSAT instructors have heard students say, "I got behind on time because I kept thinking that there must be more to figure out, and then I didn't have enough time to answer the questions."

So, how do you know when to move on to the questions? There are two ways to answer this question, and they amount to the same thing. The first way to think about this is: When you have exhausted the BLEND checklist and have made all of the deductions available from it, you're ready for the questions. The other way to express this idea is to say: When deduction gives way to speculation, you've made all of the available deductions. Deductions are the certain results of rules and restrictions. Speculations are guesses about what *might* happen if something were true.

There will always be some ambiguity left in the game. If there weren't, there would be no "game," no puzzle left to solve. As you practice with the setups that follow, stay aware of your own thought process. Are you combining rules to determine ineluctable results, or are you merely trying out arrangements to see if they work? When you find yourself doing the latter, get back to the BLEND checklist. As you continue to practice, your confidence that you can make the available deductions will grow, as will your ability to discern when you have all of the useful information recorded and it is time to move on to the questions.

Practice

Directions: In each game setup, first reacquaint yourself with the setup and rules. Then, combine the rules and restrictions to make all available deductions, recording your analyses as indicated. Finally, test your deductions by answering the questions that accompany each game. You can find expert analysis and explanations at the end of the Practice section.

Practice 1

A geologist is organizing a display of seven gemstones—amethyst, beryl, diamond, emerald, fluorite, garnet, and jade. The gemstones will be arranged in a single row in a glass display case, labeled 1 through 7 consecutively from left to right, with one stone occupying each position. The arrangement of the gemstones must conform to the following conditions:

The diamond must occupy a higher-numbered position than the amethyst, but a lower-numbered position than the garnet.

The emerald and the fluorite must occupy consecutively numbered positions.

The beryl must occupy a higher-numbered position than the emerald.

The diamond must occupy position number 3.

Here is the sketch for this game after Step 3: Rules.

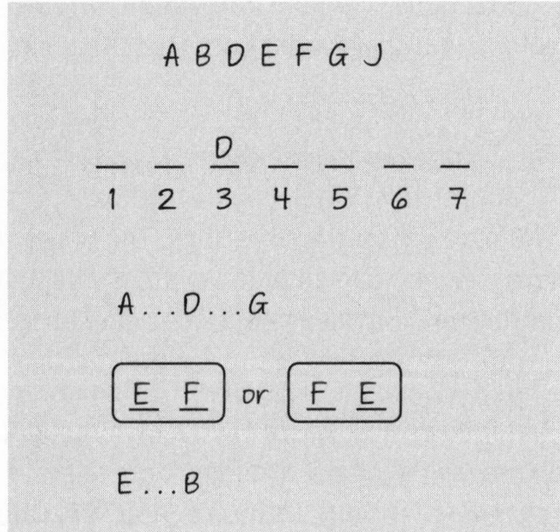

1. Which entities or positions are the most restricted in this game? Why?
2. Which elements from the BLEND checklist can you identify in this game? Are there
   - Blocks of entities? If so, what are they?
   - Limited Options? If so, which rule(s) trigger them?
   - Established Entities? If so, which ones?
   - Number Restrictions? If so, describe them.
   - Duplications? If so, which rules share an entity?
3. Combine the rules and restrictions to create a Master Sketch depicting all of the deductions available in this game:
4. Evaluate your sketch by answering the following questions:
   - Which positions are available for the amethyst?
   - Provide a complete and accurate list of the entities that could be assigned to position 4.
   - Which entities *must* appear in positions numbered lower than the garnet's position?
   - In which position(s) could jade appear?

Practice 2

A chocolatier is putting together boxes of truffles for fundraisers at three local schools—X, Y, and Z. Each school will get a box with at least one of the five available flavors—hazelnut, maple walnut, peanut butter, raspberry, and white chocolate. Each flavor will be included in at least one of the boxes, subject to the following conditions:

> The box for school X will include hazelnut truffles.
> Maple walnut truffles will be used in more boxes than white chocolate truffles.
> Peanut butter truffles will be used in exactly one box, and no other flavor will be included in that box.

Here is the sketch for this game after Step 3: Rules.

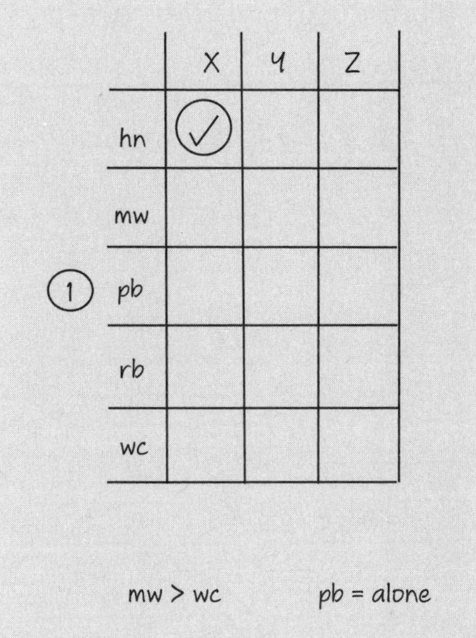

1. Which entities or positions are the most restricted in this game? Why?
2. Which elements from the BLEND checklist can you identify in this game? Are there
    - Blocks of entities? If so, what are they?
    - Limited Options? If so, which rule(s) trigger them?
    - Established Entities? If so, which ones?
    - Number Restrictions? If so, describe them.
    - Duplications? If so, which rules share an entity?
3. Combine the rules and restrictions to create a Master Sketch depicting all of the deductions available in this game:
4. Evaluate your sketch by answering the following questions:
    - Would the following be an acceptable arrangement of flavors? School X: hazelnut, raspberry, white chocolate; School Y: peanut butter; School Z: hazelnut, maple walnut.
    - What is the maximum number of boxes that could contain white chocolate truffles?
    - Which school's box must contain maple walnut truffles?
    - If School Y's box contains hazelnut truffles, which flavor(s) cannot be used in School Y's box?

Practice 3

An accountant is scheduling meetings with six clients—Able, Baker, Charlie, Delphine, Erica, and Frankie—over a four-day period, from Monday through Thursday. On each day, two appointments are available, one in the morning and one in the afternoon. In addition, two staff meetings will be scheduled over the same period. Each client and staff meeting must be assigned a different appointment time. The schedule is governed by the following conditions:

The staff meetings are not scheduled in the afternoon.
Charlie's and Frankie's meetings are scheduled for the same day.
Delphine's meeting is scheduled for some time prior to Frankie's meeting.
Baker's meeting is scheduled in the morning.
The accountant will meet with Erica and Baker on different days.

Here is the sketch for this game after Step 3: Rules.

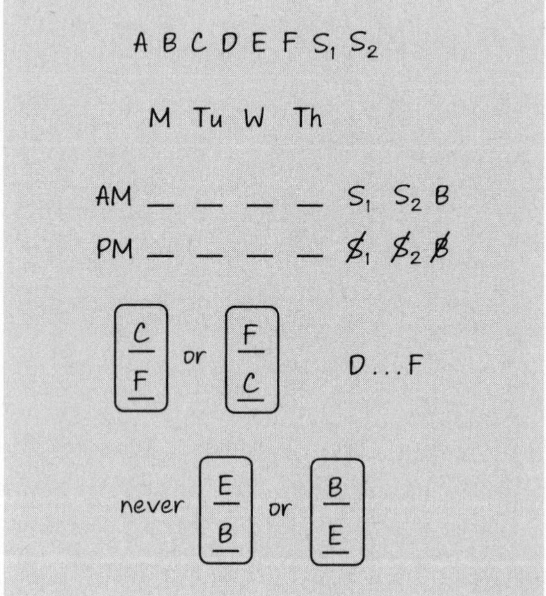

1. Which entities or positions are the most restricted in this game? Why?
2. Which elements from the BLEND checklist can you identify in this game? Are there
   - Blocks of entities? If so, what are they?
   - Limited Options? If so, which rule(s) trigger them?
   - Established Entities? If so, which ones?
   - Number Restrictions? If so, describe them.
   - Duplications? If so, which rules share an entity?
3. Combine the rules and restrictions to create a Master Sketch depicting all of the deductions available in this game:
4. Evaluate your sketch by answering the following questions:
   - Write out a complete and accurate list of meetings that cannot be scheduled for Monday.
   - Write out a complete and accurate list of meetings that must be scheduled for a morning (regardless of day).
   - Write out a complete and accurate list of meetings that must be scheduled for an afternoon (regardless of day).
   - If Baker's meeting is scheduled for Tuesday morning, who are the clients whose meetings could be scheduled on Tuesday afternoon?

Practice 4

A showroom contains exactly six new cars—T, V, W, X, Y, and Z—each equipped with at least one of the following three options: power windows, leather interior, and sunroof. No car has any other options. The following conditions must apply:

V has power windows and a sunroof.
W has power windows and a leather interior.
W and Y have no options in common.
X has more options than W.
V and Z have exactly one option in common.
T has fewer options than Z.

PrepTest35 Sec3 Qs 6–12

Here is the sketch for this game after Step 3: Rules.

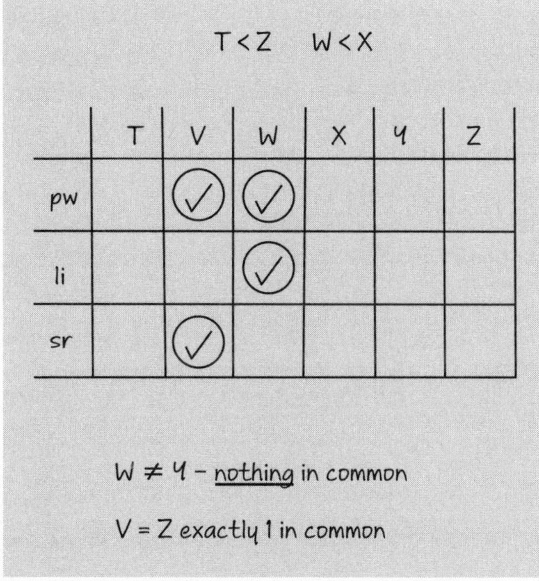

1. Which entities or positions are the most restricted in this game? Why?
2. Which elements from the BLEND checklist can you identify in this game? Are there
   - Blocks of entities? If so, what are they?
   - Limited Options? If so, which rule(s) trigger them?
   - Established Entities? If so, which ones?
   - Number Restrictions? If so, describe them.
   - Duplications? If so, which rules share an entity?
3. Combine the rules and restrictions to create a Master Sketch depicting all of the deductions available in this game:
4. Evaluate your sketch by answering the following questions:
   - Is any car permitted to have all three options? If so, which one(s)?
   - How many of the cars will have exactly one of the options? Which ones are they?
   - Which cars may not have a leather interior?
   - What is the maximum number of cars that could have a sunroof?

Explanations

Compare your work to that of an LSAT expert. Pay close attention to how the LSAT experts combined the rules and restrictions to make deductions, and how they depicted those deductions within the sketch frameworks.

Practice 1

A geologist is organizing a display of seven gemstones—amethyst, beryl, diamond, emerald, fluorite, garnet, and jade. The gemstones will be arranged in a single row in a glass display case, labeled 1 through 7 consecutively from left to right, with one stone occupying each position. The arrangement of the gemstones must conform to the following conditions:

The diamond must occupy a higher-numbered position than the amethyst, but a lower-numbered position than the garnet.
The emerald and the fluorite must occupy consecutively numbered positions.
The beryl must occupy a higher-numbered position than the emerald.
The diamond must occupy position number 3.

Here is the sketch for this game after Step 3: Rules.

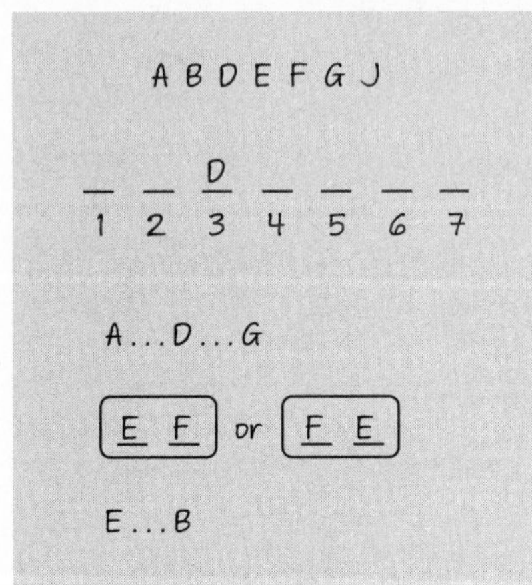

1. Which entities or positions are the most restricted in this game? Why? *The diamond is established in position 3 (Rule 4), locking the amethyst into either of positions 1 or 2 (Rule 1).*
2. Which elements from the BLEND checklist can you identify in this game? Are there
   - Blocks of entities? If so, what are they? *Rule 1 creates a "loose" block of A . . . D . . . G. Rule 2 stipulates that E and F must be consecutive, in either order. Rule 3 creates a "loose" block of E . . . B.*
   - Limited Options? If so, which rule(s) trigger them? *N/A*
   - Established Entities? If so, which ones? *The diamond, in position 3 (Rule 4).*
   - Number Restrictions? If so, describe them. *N/A*
   - Duplications? If so, which rules share an entity? *Rules 1 and 4 share D. Rules 2 and 3 share E.*
3. Combine the rules and restrictions to create a Master Sketch depicting all of the deductions available in this game: *Because D is established in position 3 (Rule 4), and also part of a three-entity string (A . . . D . . . G, Rule 1), A is restricted to either position 1 or position 2, while G must take one of positions 4–7.*

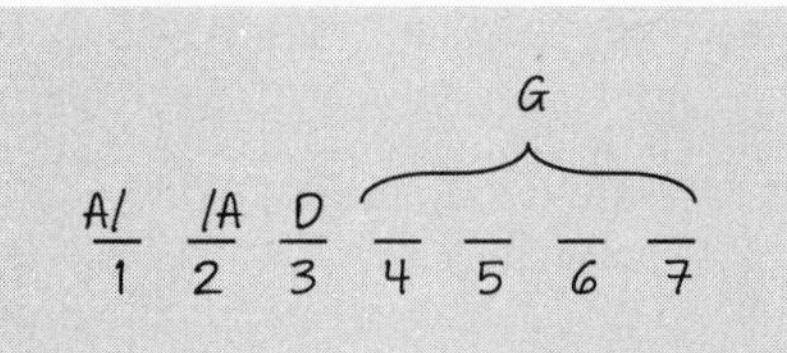

Combine Rules 2 and 3 to create a string of E/F . . . B.

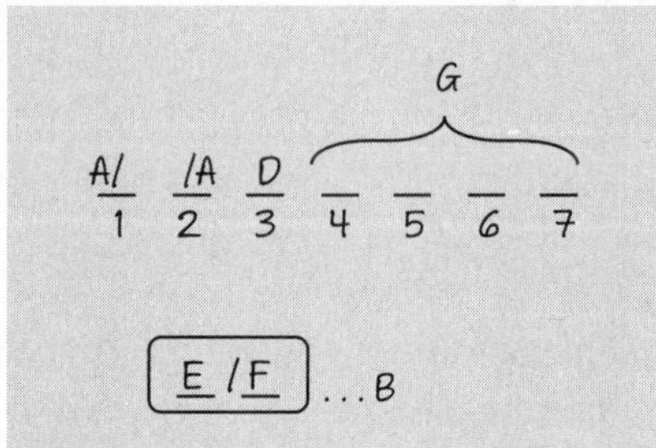

Because E and F are a block of entities that requires two consecutive positions, neither E nor F may go in positions 1 or 2. Thus, J, the only remaining unrestricted entity, must take whichever of positions 1 or 2 not taken by A.

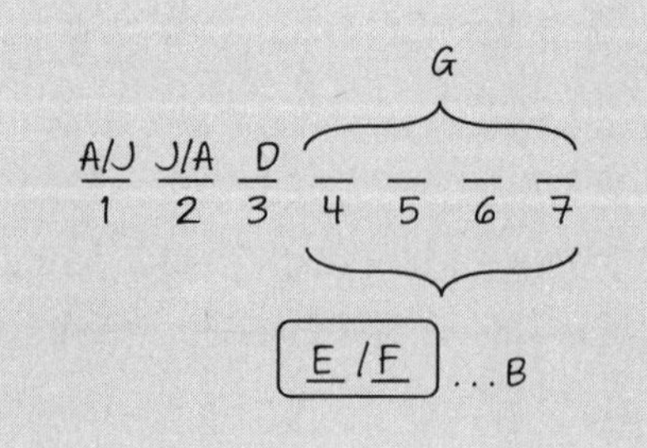

There are no floaters.

4. Evaluate your sketch by answering the following questions:
    - Which positions are available for the amethyst? *Positions 1 or 2.*
    - Provide a complete and accurate list of the entities that could be assigned to position 4? *Emerald, fluorite, garnet.*
    - Which entities *must* appear in positions numbered lower than the garnet's position? *Amethyst, jade, diamond. Note: Emerald, fluorite, and beryl could appear in positions numbered lower than the garnet's positions, but they do not have to.*
    - In which position(s) could jade appear? *Positions 1 or 2.*

Practice 2

A chocolatier is putting together boxes of truffles for fundraisers at three local schools—X, Y, and Z. Each school will get a box with at least one of the five available flavors—hazelnut, maple walnut, peanut butter, raspberry, and white chocolate. Each flavor will be included in at least one of the boxes, subject to the following conditions:

The box for school X will include hazelnut truffles.
Maple walnut truffles will be used in more boxes than white chocolate truffles.
Peanut butter truffles will be used in exactly one box, and no other flavor will be included in that box.

Here is the sketch for this game after Step 3: Rules.

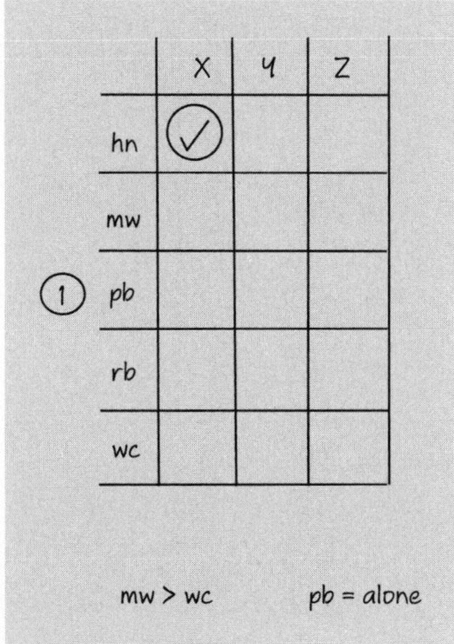

1. Which entities or positions are the most restricted in this game? Why? *The most restricted flavor is peanut butter, which cannot be mixed with any other flavors. Hazelnut flavor is established in School X's box, but it may appear in another box as well.*
2. Which elements from the BLEND checklist can you identify in this game? Are there
    - Blocks of entities? If so, what are they? *N/A*
    - Limited Options? If so, which rule(s) trigger them? *The three rules combine to produce a Limited Options scenario involving peanut butter and maple walnut, but it takes a couple of steps to reach this deduction. See the explanation for question 3.*
    - Established Entities? If so, which ones? *Hazelnut is "quasi-established": It must be used in School X's box, but because this is a Matching game, it may be used in another box, too.*
    - Number Restrictions? If so, describe them. *1) Peanut butter flavor can appear in exactly one box. 2) Maple walnut flavor is used in more boxes than white chocolate.*
    - Duplications? If so, which rules share an entity? *N/A*
3. Combine the rules and restrictions to create a Master Sketch depicting all of the deductions available in this game: *Hazelnut will be used in School X's box (Rule 1), and peanut butter cannot be mixed with any other flavor, so peanut butter cannot be used in School X's box.*

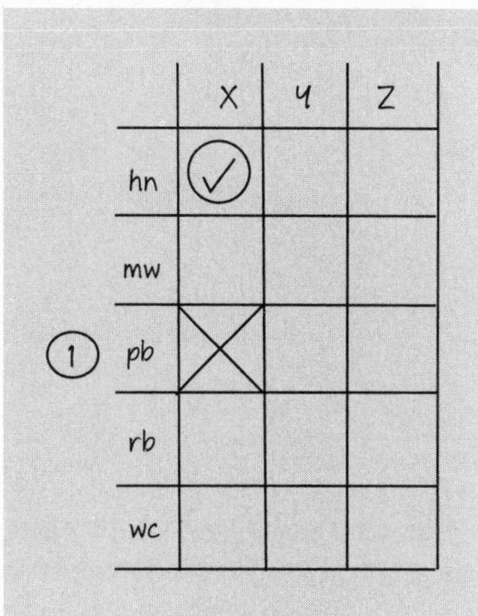

Since peanut butter must be used in exactly one box, it will go <u>*alone*</u> *into either School Y's or School Z's box, and cannot be used in any other box. This creates a Limited Options scenario calling for dual sketches.*

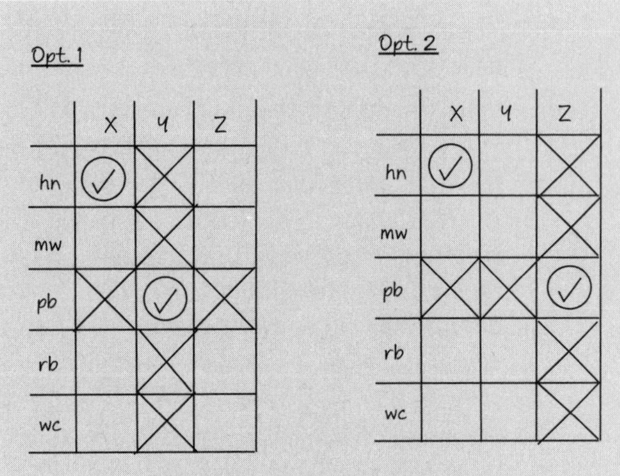

Maple walnut must be used in more boxes than white chocolate (Rule 2). The Limited Options make clear that, in either scenario, maple walnut will be used in two boxes and white chocolate in one box. Maple walnut will always be used in School X's box, and again in either School Y's or School Z's, whichever does not *contain peanut butter. Fill in the placements for maple walnut, and mark white chocolate with a "1" as a reminder that it may not be used twice.*

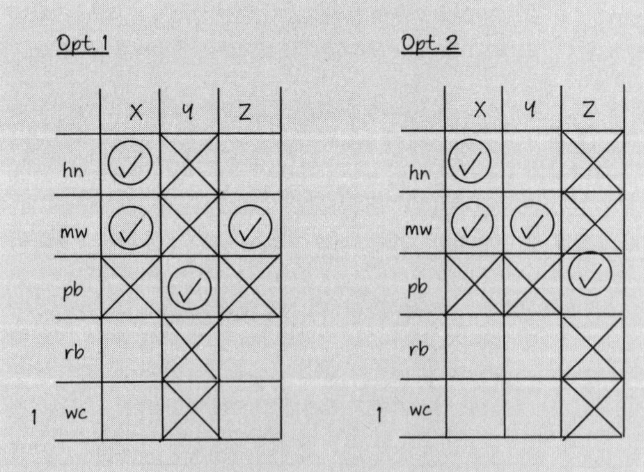

Raspberry flavor is a floater. It may appear in one or two boxes, but not in all three because of the rule requiring peanut butter to be alone (Rule 1).

4. Evaluate your sketch by answering the following questions:
   - Would the following be an acceptable arrangement of flavors? School X: hazelnut, raspberry, white chocolate; School Y: peanut butter; School Z: hazelnut, maple walnut. *No, Rule 2 requires that maple walnut be used in more boxes than white chocolate is used.*
   - What is the maximum number of boxes that could contain white chocolate truffles? *One.*
   - Which school's box must contain maple walnut truffles? *School X.*
   - If School Y's box contains hazelnut truffles, which flavor(s) cannot be used in School Y's box? *Peanut butter.*

Practice 3

An accountant is scheduling meetings with six clients—Able, Baker, Charlie, Delphine, Erica, and Frankie—over a four-day period, from Monday through Thursday. On each day, two appointments are available, one in the morning and one in the afternoon. In addition, two staff meetings will be scheduled over the same period. Each client and staff meeting must be assigned a different appointment time. The schedule is governed by the following conditions:

The staff meetings are not scheduled in the afternoon.
Charlie's and Frankie's meetings are scheduled for the same day.
Delphine's meeting is scheduled for some time prior to Frankie's meeting.
Baker's meeting is scheduled in the morning.
The accountant will meet with Erica and Baker on different days.

Here is the sketch for this game after Step 3: Rules.

```
A B C D E F S1 S2

M  Tu  W  Th

AM __ __ __ __  S1 S2 B
PM __ __ __ __  ~~S1~~ ~~S2~~ ~~B~~

[C/F] or [F/C]    D...F

never [E/B] or [B/E]
```

1. Which entities or positions are the most restricted in this game? Why? *Frankie, who must follow Delphine and share a day with Charlie.*
2. Which elements from the BLEND checklist can you identify in this game? Are there
   - Blocks of entities? If so, what are they? *Charlie and Frankie must have their meetings on the same day (Rule 2). Delphine and Frankie are a "loose" block: D . . . F (Rule 3).*
   - Limited Options? If so, which rule(s) trigger them? *N/A*
   - Established Entities? If so, which ones? *N/A*
   - Number Restrictions? If so, describe them. *N/A*
   - Duplications? If so, which rules share an entity? *Rules 2 and 3 share Frankie and can be combined.*
3. Combine the rules and restrictions to create a Master Sketch depicting all of the deductions available in this game: *This game has no established entities and only one duplication. Combine Rules 2 and 3 (if you didn't do so when writing out the rules).*

```
D... [C/F] or [F/C]
```

Note the negative implications of the D . . . C/F deduction: C/F cannot take Monday, and D will not have a meeting on Thursday.

```
A B C D E F S1 S2

M  Tu  W  Th

AM __ __ __ __  S1 S2 B
PM __ __ __ __  ~~S1~~ ~~S2~~ ~~B~~
   ~C       ~D
   ~F

D... [C/F] or [F/C]

never [E/B] or [B/E]
```

Now, note that either C or F will take one morning slot and one afternoon slot. Because B's meeting and the two staff meetings are also in the morning, the meetings with A, D, and E will all be in the afternoon.

```
A B C D E F S1 S2

M  Tu  W  Th

AM __ __ __ __  S1 S2 B C/F
PM __ __ __ __  ~~S1~~ ~~S2~~ ~~B~~ F/C A, D, E
   ~C       ~D
   ~F

D... [C/F] or [F/C]

never [E/B] or [B/E]
```

That's as far as the deductions go. You know the four meetings that will be scheduled in the morning slots, and the four for the afternoon slots, but you don't know the specific day on which any meeting will be scheduled.

4. Evaluate your sketch by answering the following questions:
   - Write out a complete and accurate list of meetings that cannot be scheduled for Monday. *Charlie, Frankie.*
   - Write out a complete and accurate list of meetings that must be scheduled for a morning (regardless of day). *Baker and both staff meetings.*
   - Write out a complete and accurate list of meetings that must be scheduled for an afternoon (regardless of day). *Able, Delphine, Erica.*
   - If Baker's meeting is scheduled for Tuesday morning, who are the clients whose meetings could be scheduled on Tuesday afternoon? *Able and Delphine; Charlie and Frankie must be on the same day (Rule 2), and Erica's meeting cannot be on the same day as Baker's (Rule 4).*

Practice 4

A showroom contains exactly six new cars—T, V, W, X, Y, and Z—each equipped with at least one of the following three options: power windows, leather interior, and sunroof. No car has any other option. The following conditions must apply:

V has power windows and a sunroof.
W has power windows and a leather interior.
W and Y have no options in common.
X has more options than W.
V and Z have exactly one option in common.
T has fewer options than Z.

PrepTest35 Sec3 Qs 6–12

Here is the sketch for this game after Step 3: Rules.

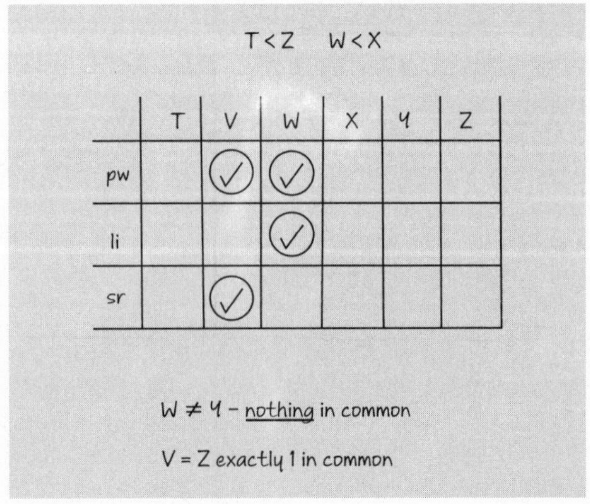

1. Which entities or positions are the most restricted in this game? Why? *Car W is at the center of three rules (Rules 2, 3, and 4) which assign it two features and limit it in relationship to two other cars (X and Y).*
2. Which elements from the BLEND checklist can you identify in this game? Are there
   - Blocks of entities? If so, what are they? *N/A*
   - Limited Options? If so, which rule(s) trigger them? *N/A*
   - Established Entities? If so, which ones? *Rule 1 gives Car V two features, and Rule 2 gives Car W two features. Because this is a Matching game, however, the features may be given to other cars as well.*
   - Number Restrictions? If so, describe them. *1) Rule 4 stipulates that Car X has more features than Car W. 2) Rule 6 requires that Car Z have more features than Car T.*
   - Duplications? If so, which rules share an entity? *There are three: 1) Car W is shared by Rules 2, 3, and 4; 2) Car V is shared by Rules 1 and 5; and 3) Car Z is shared by Rules 5 and 6.*
3. Combine the rules and restrictions to create a Master Sketch depicting all of the deductions available in this game: *Begin with Car W, which already has power windows and a leather interior (Rule 2). Combine that with Rule 3. If W and Y have nothing in common, then Car Y must have a sunroof, and cannot have either of the other features. By the same token, Car W may not have a sunroof.*

	T	V	W	X	Y	Z
pw		✓	✓		✗	
li			✓		✗	
sr		✓	✗		✓	

Then, combine Rule 2 with Rule 4. For Car X to have more features than Car W, Car X must have all three features.

	T	V	W	X	Y	Z
pw		✓	✓	✓	✗	
li			✓	✓	✗	
sr		✓	✗	✓	✓	

At this point, Cars W, X, and Y are completely determined. Consider the rules that restrict Cars T, V, and Z. You know Car V already has power windows and a sunroof (Rule 1). Rule 5 requires that V and Z have exactly one feature in common, so Car Z will have either power windows or a sunroof, but <u>*not*</u> *both.*

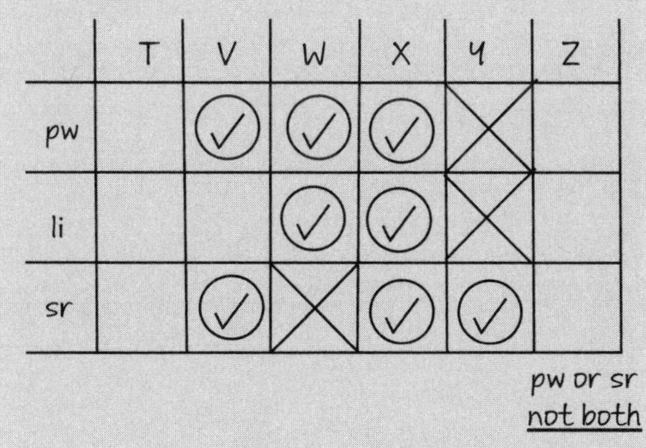

Rule 6 now allows for additional deductions about Cars T, V, and Z. For Car Z to have more features than Car T, Car Z must have either two or three features. It cannot have three, or it would break Rule 5, so it must have two features. One of Car Z's features must be a leather interior (remember, its other feature will be the one feature it has in common with Car V, either power windows or a sunroof, but not both). Since Car Z will have a leather interior, Car V will not (again, so that the two cars do not violate Rule 5). Finally, because Car Z has two features, Car T must have just one. Car T's one feature could be any of the three features available in the game.

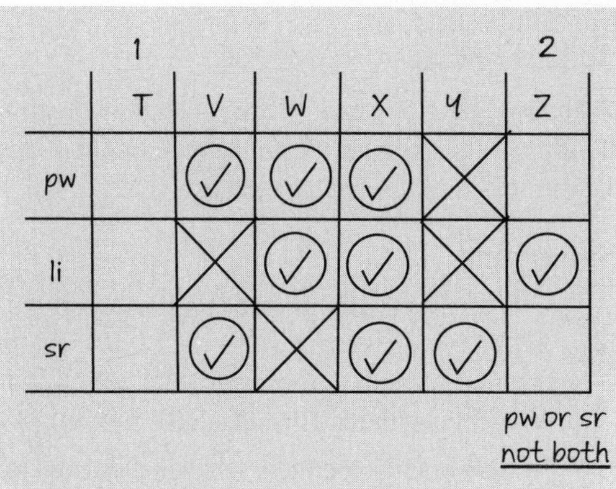

That game had an extraordinary number of deductions. In four of the six cars that anchor the game, the feature sets are completely determined. That's unusually high, but by following through on the BLEND checklist and making all of those deductions, you're in a position to answer the questions much more quickly and confidently than you would be without the deductions in place.

4. Evaluate your sketch by answering the following questions:
   - Are any of the cars permitted to have all three options? If so, which one(s)? *Car X is the only car that may have all three options. In fact, it is required to have all three.*
   - Which cars, if any, will have exactly one of the options? *Cars T and Y will have exactly one of the options.*
   - Which cars may not have a leather interior? *Cars V and Y may not have leather interiors.*
   - What is the maximum number of cars that could have a sunroof? *Five cars —T, V, X, Y, and Z—could have sunroofs.*

Perform

Directions: Take one minute to refresh your memory of each game's setup and rules. Then, take no more than five minutes to catalog the rules and combine them to make all available deductions. Test your deductions by answering the questions at the end of each exercise.

Perform 1

A filmmaker is planning to create a short film with exactly five scenes. The scenes will all be shot in one day and will be filmed in order, with each scene completed before filming begins on the next. Each scene will feature at least one of four actors—Jenkins, Kwan, Lozano, and Millstone—and no others. Each actor will appear in exactly two of the scenes. The schedule must conform to the following conditions:

No actor's second scene will be filmed at the same time as another actor's second scene.
Exactly one actor will appear in the third scene of the film.
Millstone's first scene will be filmed before Lozano's first scene.
Any scene in which Lozano is filmed will feature at least one other actor.

Here is the sketch for this game after Step 3: Rules.

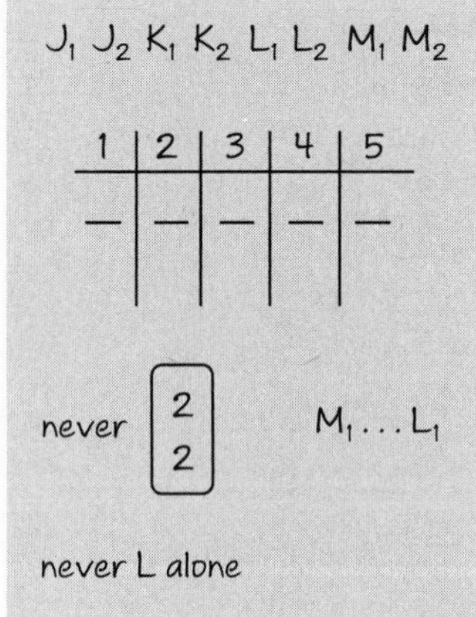

1. Which entities or positions are the most restricted in this game? Why?
2. Which elements from the BLEND checklist can you identify in this game? Are there
   - Blocks of entities? If so, what are they?
   - Limited Options? If so, which rule(s) trigger them?
   - Established Entities? If so, which ones?
   - Number Restrictions? If so, describe them.
   - Duplications? If so, which rules share an entity?
3. Combine the rules and restrictions to create a Master Sketch depicting all of the deductions available in this game:
4. Evaluate your sketch by answering the following questions:
   - Which scenes could be Millstone's second scene?
   - Which scenes could be Kwan's first scene?
   - What is the maximum number of actors that can appear in any scene?
   - If Jenkins appeared in scene 3, who could appear in scene 5?

Perform 2

Eight students—Bonham, Cullen, Dao, Farina, Gerber, Holt, Karlsson, and Logan—are assigned to do research on three court cases—R, S and T. Each student will research exactly one case in accordance with the following:

Bonham is assigned to research case R.
Farina and Logan are not assigned to research the same case.
Karlsson is assigned to research a case with exactly two other students.
Gerber and Holt are assigned to research a case together, with no other student assigned to research that case.

Here is the sketch for this game after Step 3: Rules.

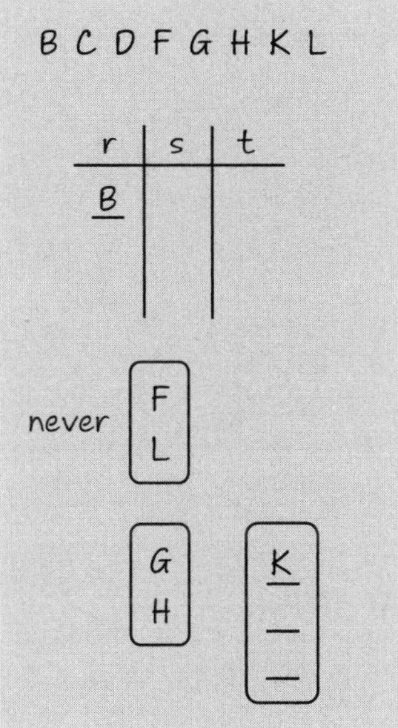

1. Which entities or positions are the most restricted in this game? Why?
2. Which elements from the BLEND checklist can you identify in this game? Are there
   - Blocks of entities? If so, what are they?
   - Limited Options? If so, which rule(s) trigger them?
   - Established Entities? If so, which ones?
   - Number Restrictions? If so, describe them.
   - Duplications? If so, which rules share an entity?
3. Combine the rules and restrictions to create a Master Sketch depicting all of the deductions available in this game:
4. Evaluate your sketch by answering the following questions:
   - Who are all of the students that CANNOT be assigned to case R?
   - Which students could be assigned to any of the three cases?
   - What is the minimum number of students for any case?
   - If Cullen and Dao are together, who could be the third person assigned to that case?

Perform 3

Every Sunday, a zookeeper gives presentations on each of five snakes—an eastern indigo snake, a king snake, a milk snake, a python, and a rat snake. The presentations are held at 1:00, 2:00, 3:00, 4:00, and 5:00. Exactly one snake is exhibited at each presentation. Visitors are invited to hold some, but not all, of the snakes. Visitors are allowed to observe, but not to hold, the others. The schedule of presentations must conform to the following conditions:

Visitors are invited to hold the king snake and at least one other snake.
Visitors are allowed to observe, but not to hold, the last snake presented.
The milk snake is presented before the king snake.
The python is presented before any snake that visitors are invited to hold.

Here is the sketch for this game after Step 3: Rules.

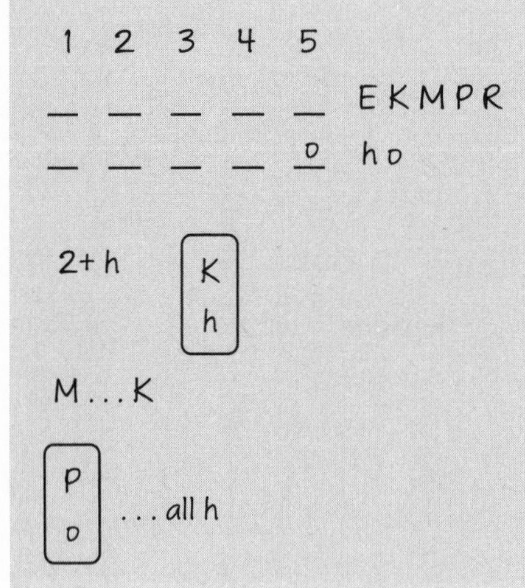

1. Which entities or positions are the most restricted in this game? Why?
2. Which elements from the BLEND checklist can you identify in this game? Are there
   - Blocks of entities? If so, what are they?
   - Limited Options? If so, which rule(s) trigger them?
   - Established Entities? If so, which ones?
   - Number Restrictions? If so, describe them.
   - Duplications? If so, which rules share an entity?
3. Combine the rules and restrictions to create a Master Sketch depicting all of the deductions available in this game:
4. Evaluate your sketch by answering the following questions:
   - What is the earliest time a snake could be held?
   - What is the maximum number of snakes that could be held?
   - Which snakes could be presented at 4:00?
   - What snake would be presented at 5:00 if the eastern indigo snake could be held?

Perform 4

A closet contains exactly six hangers—1, 2, 3, 4, 5, and 6—hanging, in that order, from left to right. It also contains exactly six dresses—one gauze, one linen, one polyester, one rayon, one silk, and one wool—a different dress on each of the hangers, in an order satisfying the following conditions:

The gauze dress is on a lower-numbered hanger than the polyester dress.
The rayon dress is on hanger 1 or hanger 6.
Either the wool dress or the silk dress is on hanger 3.
The linen dress hangs immediately to the right of the silk dress.

PrepTest41 Sec2 Qs 1–7

Here is the sketch for this game after Step 3: Rules.

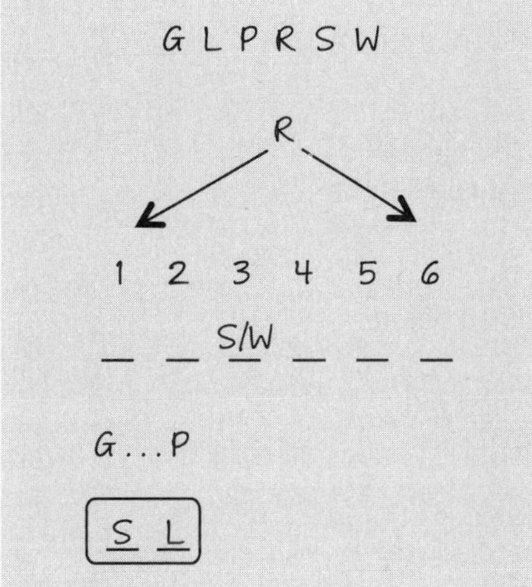

1. Which entities or positions are the most restricted in this game? Why?
2. Which elements from the BLEND checklist can you identify in this game? Are there
   - Blocks of entities? If so, what are they?
   - Limited Options? If so, which rule(s) trigger them?
   - Established Entities? If so, which ones?
   - Number Restrictions? If so, describe them.
   - Duplications? If so, which rules share an entity?
3. Combine the rules and restrictions to create a Master Sketch depicting all of the deductions available in this game:
4. Evaluate your sketch by answering the following questions:
   - Which dress (or dresses) could be on any of the six hangers?
   - Which dresses could be on hanger 6?
   - Which dresses could be immediately to the left of the rayon dress?
   - How many dresses can you determine if the silk dress is on hanger 1?

Explanations

Compare your work to that of an LSAT expert. Pay close attention to how the LSAT experts combined the rules and restrictions to make deductions, and how they depicted those deductions within the sketch frameworks.

Perform 1

A filmmaker is planning to create a short film with exactly five scenes. The scenes will all be shot in one day and will be filmed in order, with each scene completed before filming begins on the next. Each scene will feature at least one of four actors—Jenkins, Kwan, Lozano, and Millstone—and no others. Each actor will appear in exactly two of the scenes. The schedule must conform to the following conditions:

> No actor's second scene will be filmed at the same time as another actor's second scene.
> Exactly one actor will appear in the third scene of the film.
> Millstone's first scene will be filmed before Lozano's first scene.
> Any scene in which Lozano is filmed will feature at least one other actor.

Here is the sketch for this game after Step 3: Rules.

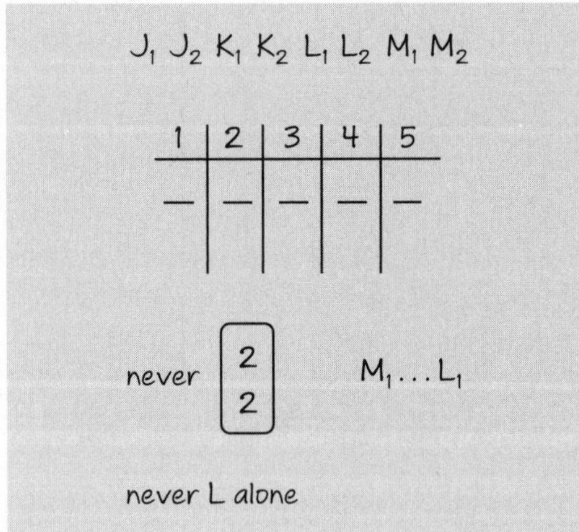

1. Which entities or positions are the most restricted in this game? Why? *The most restricted actor is Lozano, who has to wait until Millstone appears first, and also cannot appear alone.*

2. Which elements from the BLEND checklist can you identify in this game? Are there
   - Blocks of entities? If so, what are they? *Nothing concrete, but Lozano will always be part of a block with somebody, and that will be important.*
   - Limited Options? If so, which rule(s) trigger them? *N/A*
   - Established Entities? If so, which ones? *N/A*
   - Number Restrictions? If so, describe them. *By Rule 1, the four actors will all have different scenes for their second scene. That means four separate scenes will feature an actor's second scene. Rule 2 limits scene 3 to one actor, and Rule 4 requires any scene with Lozano to feature at least two actors.*
   - Duplications? If so, which rules share an entity? *Lozano is mentioned in Rules 3 and 4.*

3. Combine the rules and restrictions to create a Master Sketch depicting all of the deductions available in this game:

   Numbers are most important here, so start there. Logically, all actors' first scenes precede their second scenes, so scene 1 cannot be any actor's second scene, and scene 5 cannot be any actor's first scene. By Rule 1, four different scenes feature an actor's second scene. They must be scenes 2 through 5, one actor in each.

1	2	3	4	5
—	—2	—2	—2	—2

Scene 3 is now finished, with a single actor's second scene. Scene 5 cannot feature an actor's first scene, and can only have one actor's second scene. So, scene 5 is now closed off.

1	2	3	4	5
—	$\_\_{2}$	$\_\_{2}$	$\_\_{2}$	$\_\_{2}$

Lozano cannot be alone, so Lozano cannot be in scene 3 or scene 5. Also, Lozano cannot be in scene 1 because Millstone's first appearance has to be before Lozano's. So, Lozano must appear in scenes 2 and 4. Scene 2 will be Lozano's first scene, and must be shared with somebody else's second scene, at least. Scene 4 will be Lozano's second scene, and must be shared with someone else's first scene.

1	2	3	4	5
—	L_1	$\_\_{2}$	$\_\_{1}$	$\_\_{2}$
	$\_\_{2}$		L_2	

Millstone's first scene must precede Lozano's, so Millstone's first scene must be scene 1.

1	2	3	4	5
M_1	L_1	$\_\_{2}$	$\_\_{1}$	$\_\_{2}$
	$\_\_{2}$		L_2	

Scene 4 has to include someone's first scene. Lozano's and Millstone's are established elsewhere, so it must be either Jenkins's or Kwan's. That actor's second scene will be the one in scene 5. Thus, scene 4 cannot be the first scene for both Jenkins and Kwan, so it will just be one of them. That closes off scene 4.

1	2	3	4	5
M_1	L_1	$\_\_{2}$	J/K_1	J/K_2
	$\_\_{2}$		L_2	

There are now seven slots in the sketch, and there need to be eight (two for each actor). With scenes 3, 4, and 5 closed off, the final slot can be added to either scene 1 or scene 2.

4. Evaluate your sketch by answering the following questions:
   - Which scenes could be Millstone's second scene? *Scene 2 or 3. Scene 4 is Lozano's second scene, and scene 5 has to be the second scene for the actor's whose first scene is scene 4.*
   - Which scenes could be Kwan's first scene? *Scene 1, 2 or 4; Scene 3 can only have someone's second scene.*
   - What is the maximum number of actors that can appear in any scene? *Three; the one slot that is left to add could be added to scene 2, allowing scene 2 to have Lozano's first scene, Millstone's second scene, and one other actor's first scene (either Jenkins or Kwan).*
   - If Jenkins appeared in scene 3, who could appear in scene 5? *It would have to be Kwan, who would be the only person left whose first scene could be scene 4.*

Perform 2

Eight students - Bonham, Cullen, Dao, Farina, Gerber, Holt, Karlsson, and Logan—are assigned to do research on three court cases—R, S and T. Each student will research exactly one case in accordance with the following:

Bonham is assigned to research case R.
Farina and Logan are not assigned to research the same case.
Karlsson is assigned to research a case with exactly two other students.
Gerber and Holt are assigned to research a case together, with no other student assigned to research that case.

Here is the sketch for this game after Step 3: Rules.

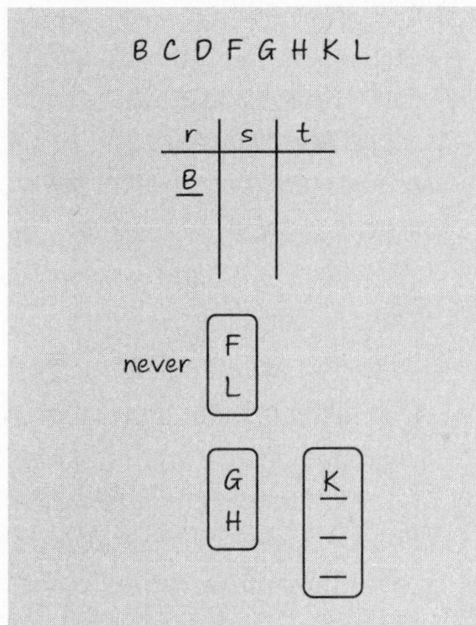

1. Which entities or positions are the most restricted in this game? Why? *Gerber and Holt must be in a group all by themselves, and case R is already occupied partially by someone else.*
2. Which elements from the BLEND checklist can you identify in this game? Are there
   - Blocks of entities? If so, what are they? *Gerber and Holt have to be together.*
   - Limited Options? If so, which rule(s) trigger them? *N/A*
   - Established Entities? If so, which ones? *Bonham is already established on case R.*
   - Number Restrictions? If so, describe them. *Rules 3 and 4 set numbers for two cases: one will have three students (including Karlsson) and another will have two (Gerber and Holt).*
   - Duplications? If so, which rules share an entity? *N/A*
3. Combine the rules and restrictions to create a Master Sketch depicting all of the deductions available in this game:

   The block of Gerber and Holt cannot be placed on case R because Bonham is already there. Thus, Gerber and Holt can only be assigned to case S or T.

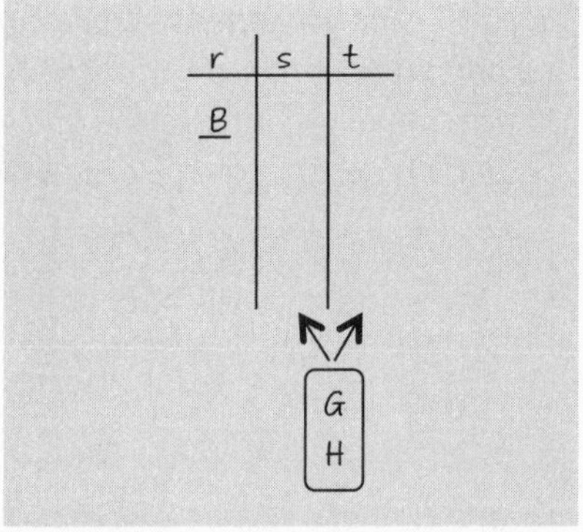

By Rule 3, one case will have exactly three students (including Karlsson). By Rule 4, a second case will have exactly two students (Gerber and Holt). With eight students in total, the third case will have the remaining three students.

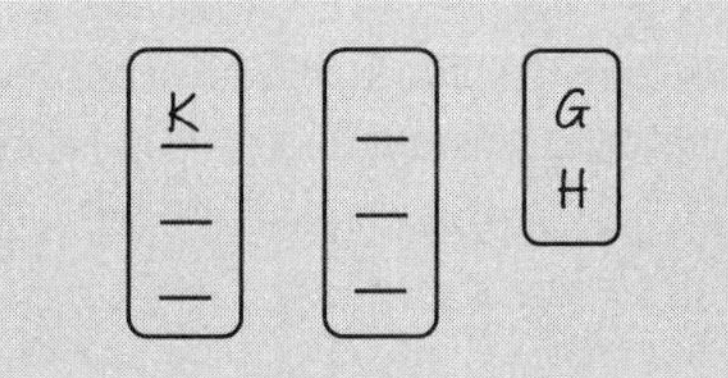

The case with two students is filled. That leaves the two cases with three students. One has Karlsson. Farina and Logan cannot be together, so one will be with Karlsson, and the other will be on the other case.

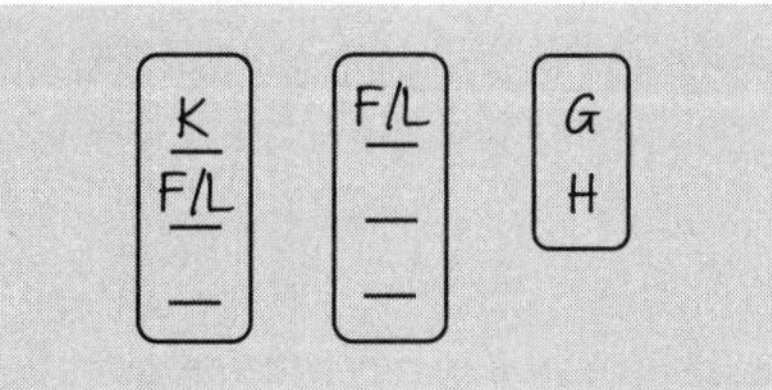

Case R cannot be the case with two students, so it will have three students. It could be the one with Karlsson or the one without Karlsson. Either way, though, it will also include Farina or Logan.

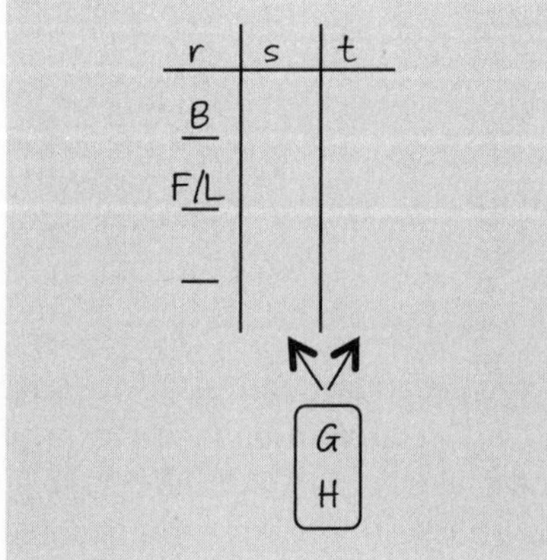

4. Evaluate your sketch by answering the following questions:
   - Who are all of the students that CANNOT be assigned to case R? *Gerber and Holt, who must be by themselves and thus cannot be with Bonham.*
   - Which students could be assigned to any of the three cases? *Cullen, Dao, Farina, Karlsson, and Logan.*
   - What is the minimum number of students for any case? *Two—the case with Gerber and Holt; the other cases have three students each.*
   - If Cullen and Dao are together, who could be the third person assigned to that case? *Farina or Logan; if it were anyone else, a second case would have Gerber and Holt, and Farina and Logan would be assigned together to the remaining case, violating Rule 2.*

Perform 3

Every Sunday, a zookeeper gives presentations on each of five snakes—an eastern indigo snake, a king snake, a milk snake, a python, and a rat snake. The presentations are held at 1:00, 2:00, 3:00, 4:00, and 5:00. Exactly one snake is exhibited at each presentation. Visitors are invited to hold some, but not all, of the snakes. Visitors are allowed to observe, but not to hold, the others. The schedule of presentations must conform to the following conditions:

> Visitors are invited to hold the king snake and at least one other snake.
>
> Visitors are allowed to observe, but not to hold, the last snake presented.
>
> The milk snake is presented before the king snake.
>
> The python is presented before any snake that visitors are invited to hold.

Here is the sketch for this game after Step 3: Rules.

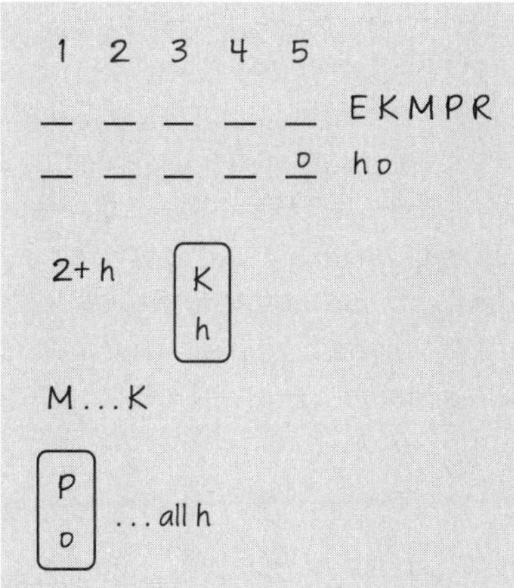

1. Which entities or positions are the most restricted in this game? Why? *The king snake is most restricted because it must be held and it must come after the milk snake, as well as the python. The python is also heavily restricted because it has to be presented before every snake that's held. The 5:00 position is also very restricted because it must have a snake that is only observed, and there are multiple snakes that must appear earlier.*
2. Which elements from the BLEND checklist can you identify in this game? Are there
   - Blocks of entities? If so, what are they? *The king snake matches to "held" and the python matches to "observed."*
   - Limited Options? If so, which rule(s) trigger them? *N/A*
   - Established Entities? If so, which ones? *Rule 2 establishes the 5:00 snake as observed only.*
   - Number Restrictions? If so, describe them. *Rule 1 sets a minimum of 2 snakes held, the king snake and at least one other.*
   - Duplications? If so, which rules share an entity? *Rules 1 and 3 both mention the king snake.*

3. Combine the rules and restrictions to create a Master Sketch depicting all of the deductions available in this game:

   The king snake is most significant. It must be held, so it cannot be presented at 5:00. And because it's held, it has to be presented later than the python, so it cannot be at 1:00. It also has to be presented later than the milk snake, so it cannot be at 2:00. That means it will be presented at 3:00 or 4:00.

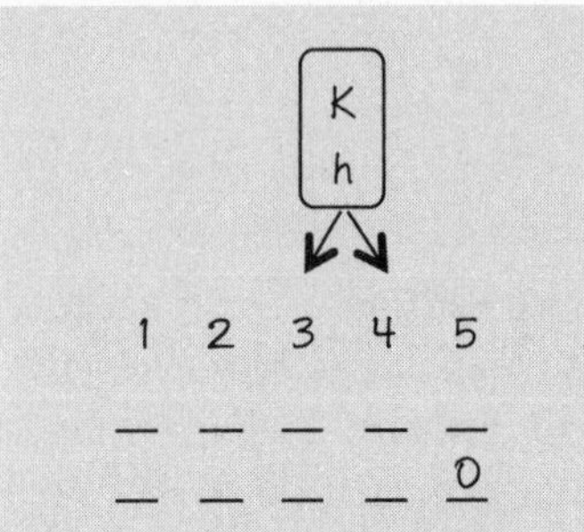

   The latest the king snake can appear is 4:00, and the python and the milk snake must both be earlier. So neither one can be presented at 4:00 or 5:00. That leaves just the eastern indigo or the rat snake for the 5:00 presentation.

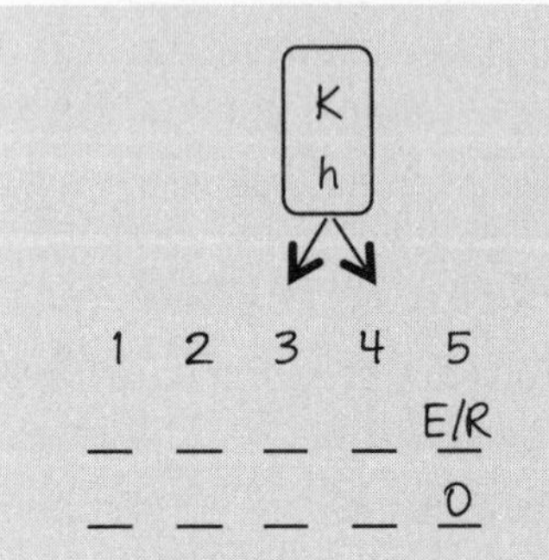

   The python has to appear before all snakes that are held. That means the python itself cannot be held, so the python will just be observed. That also means the snake at 1:00 cannot be held, so it must be just observed.

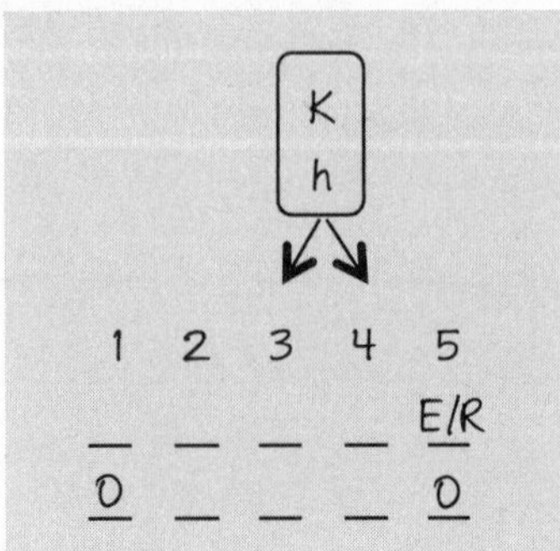

   At least two snakes are held, and the python must appear before them both. Also the 5:00 snake is just observed. The python must appear before that snake, too, so the python could only be presented at 1:00 or 2:00.

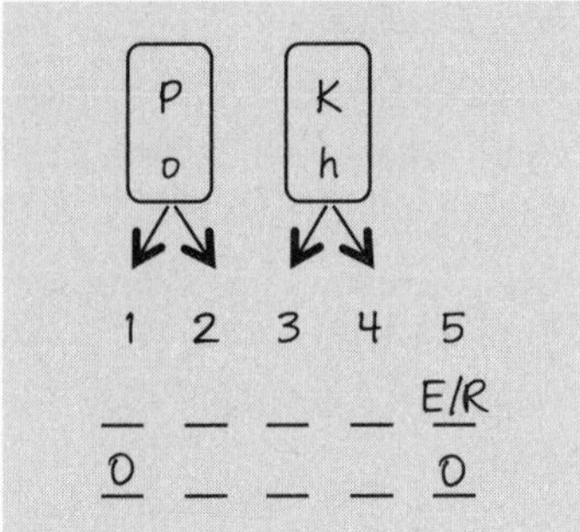

4. Evaluate your sketch by answering the following questions:
   - What is the earliest time a snake could be held? *It would be 2:00, allowing the python to be displayed at 1:00.*
   - What is the maximum number of snakes that could be held? *Three; the 5:00 is not held, and the 1:00 cannot be held because of the python. But, if the python was at 1:00, the three snakes at 2:00, 3:00, and 4:00 could all be held.*
   - Which snakes could be presented at 4:00? *The eastern indigo, the king snake, or the rat snake.*
   - What snake would be presented at 5:00 if the eastern indigo snake could be held? *The rat snake. The 5:00 snake is observed only. The other snakes are either held or have to be presented earlier.*

Perform 4

A closet contains exactly six hangers—1, 2, 3, 4, 5, and 6—hanging, in that order, from left to right. It also contains exactly six dresses—one gauze, one linen, one polyester, one rayon, one silk, and one wool—a different dress on each of the hangers, in an order satisfying the following conditions:

The gauze dress is on a lower-numbered hanger than the polyester dress.
The rayon dress is on hanger 1 or hanger 6.
Either the wool dress or the silk dress is on hanger 3.
The linen dress hangs immediately to the right of the silk dress.

PrepTest41 Sec2 Qs 1–7

Here is the sketch for this game after Step 3: Rules.

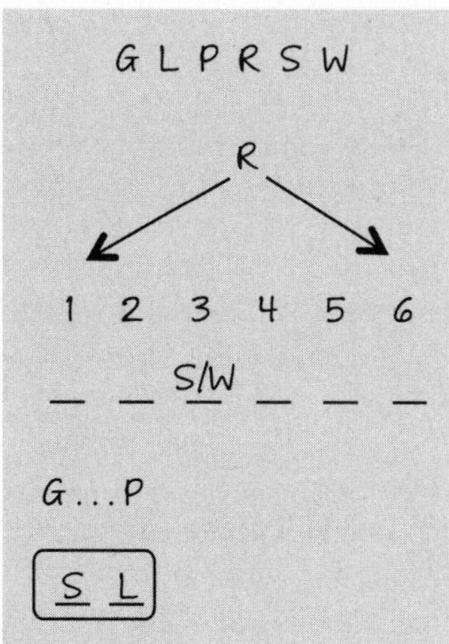

1. Which entities or positions are the most restricted in this game? Why? *Rayon, which is limited to two positions. And hanger 3 is similarly limited to just two dresses.*
2. Which elements from the BLEND checklist can you identify in this game? Are there
    - Blocks of entities? If so, what are they? *Yes, the silk and the linen dresses are consecutive, in that order.*
    - Limited Options? If so, which rule(s) trigger them? *No; Rules 2 and 3 each provide only two options, but neither one provides enough substantial deductions to warrant two sketches.*
    - Established Entities? If so, which ones? *Rule 3 establishes the silk or wool on hanger 3.*
    - Number Restrictions? If so, describe them. *N/A*
    - Duplications? If so, which rules share an entity? *The silk dress is mentioned in both rules 3 and 4.*
3. Combine the rules and restrictions to create a Master Sketch depicting all of the deductions available in this game:

    There's very little to find here. The fact that the gauze dress has to be lower than the polyester dress means that the gauze dress cannot be on hanger 6 and the polyester dress cannot be on hanger 1.

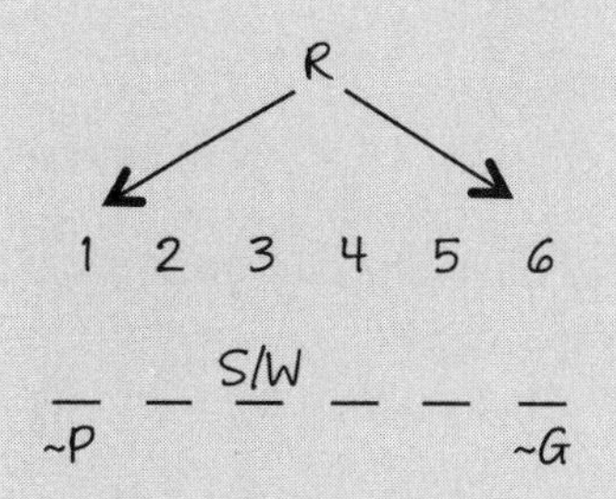

Similarly, because the silk dress has to be lower than the linen dress, the silk dress cannot be on hanger 6 and the linen dress cannot be on hanger 1. Further, the one place this block cannot go is hangers 2 and 3, because the linen dress cannot be on hanger 3. So, the silk dress cannot be on hanger 2.

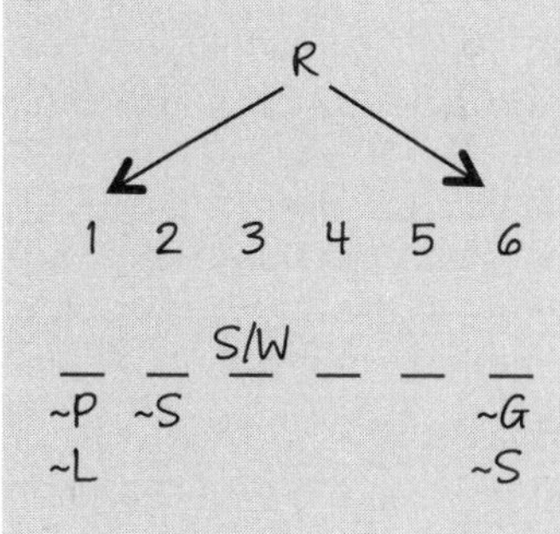

4. Evaluate your sketch by answering the following questions:
    - Which dress (or dresses) could be on any of the six hangers? *None. The sketch shows restrictions for five dresses, and the wool dress cannot take hanger 4. That's because when wool is not on hanger 3, silk is, and in that case, linen must take hanger 4.*
    - Which dresses could be on hanger 6? *Linen, polyester, rayon, or wool.*
    - Which dresses could be immediately to the left of the rayon dress? *This would require the rayon dress to be on hanger 6. In that case, hanger 5 cannot be the gauze dress (Rule 2) or the silk dress (Rule 4). So, it could only be the polyester, the linen, or the wool dress.*
    - How many dresses can you determine if the silk dress is on hanger 1? *All six; this would put the linen on hanger 2, the wool on hanger 3, and the rayon on hanger 6. The gauze and polyester would then be on hangers 4 and 5, in that order.*

Assess

Assess your performance according to the following criteria. If you were able to make

All or most of the deductions in 3 to 4 of the logic games: Congratulations! That is outstanding work at this point in the book. Move on to Chapter 4 and dive into Step 5 of the Logic Games Method covering the strategies LSAT experts use to answer logic games questions quickly and accurately.

All of the deductions in at least 2 of the games, or at least some of the deductions in 3 to 4 of the games: Review your work to determine the game types and deductions types on which you will need more work. Review the deduction types as they are described in the Prepare portion of this subchapter, and make a note to study the Deductions step in the appropriate game type chapter (Chapters 5–8).

All of the deductions in only 1 of the games, or only some of the deductions in 2 to 3 of the games: First, review this subchapter thoroughly. Second, take the "Deductions Fundamentals" quiz found in your online center. Third, make sure to review the expert analysis for Step 4 of the Logic Games Method on all games you study or practice in the remainder of this book.

To stay sharp, practice the drills in the Logic Games Training Camp for this chapter in your Online Study Plan. Training Camp drills are divided into Fundamentals, Mid-Level, and Advanced sets.

Reflect

Think back over the work you did in this portion of Chapter 3.

- Are you now able to identify the most restricted entities and/or positions within a game's framework?
- Can you identify each of the five common deductions in the BLEND checklist?
- Are you able to more quickly and accurately note into your Master Sketch the additional information revealed by deductions?
- Do you now look for and spot unrestricted floaters among the entities?
- Are you better able to assess when you have made all of a game's deductions and know that you are ready to move on to the questions?

In the coming days and weeks leading up to test day, take note of real-world situations in which you make deductions.

- Are you able to state day-to-day rules affirmatively and negatively, (e.g., "disabled parking only" means that cars without a disability tag are forbidden)?
- Are you able to identify the constraints or rules that lead to valid deductions?
- Can you distinguish authentic deductions (the necessary result of two or more "rules") from mere preferences or assumptions?

The LSAT Channel Spotlight

Limited Options

By Gene Suhir

Watch the video lesson for this Spotlight in your online Study Plan.

Limited Options, the situation in which an entire logic game breaks down into two (or, rarely, three) acceptable patterns, is often the most helpful deduction you can make. Unfortunately, Limited Options can also be one of the hardest deductions for test takers to spot. Here are a few rules of thumb that will help you exploit this powerful deduction tool.

Think of Limited Options as the testmaker's way of saying "either ... or." Indeed, at times, the rule giving rise to Limited Options is just that literal, e.g., "George must be interviewed fourth or sixth." With Limited Options, you draw two sketches of the game, one for each of the acceptable patterns. Once you've created the dual sketches and have filled in the additional deductions that arise within each one, you're usually left with only a handful of acceptable arrangements. You'll be close to seeing all of the ways that the game can be completed.

Limited Options stem from one of three conditions. It's worth remembering what they are.

A "Key Player"

This describes a situation in which a particular entity can take exactly two positions or placements, either of which gives rise to additional restrictions among the remaining entities. Take a look:

Six students—Becca, Charles, David, Edwina, George, and Hiromi—will be interviewed one at a time by a reporter for the school newspaper. The interviews will be conducted consecutively, first through sixth, according to the following restrictions.

George must be interviewed fourth or sixth.

Hiromi's interview will be conducted immediately before or immediately after George's interview.

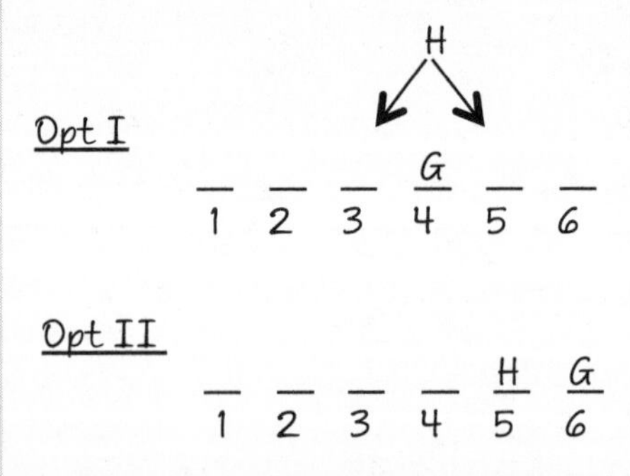

Since George is restricted to exactly two interview slots, and since his placement explicitly affects Hiromi's placement, George is a "Key Player," and dual Limited Options sketches are called for. Additional rules in this game should be built into both sketches whenever possible.

Number Restrictions

Number restrictions can occur in any type of game, but they are especially helpful in Distribution and Matching games. When the groups you are creating must fall into one of two number patterns, it is almost always worth it to create dual Limited Options sketches. Here's an example.

Five citizens—P, Q, X, Y, and Z—will vote in Country Y's upcoming parliamentary elections. Each citizen will vote for exactly one of three parties—the Conservative Party, the Economic Party, or the Reform Party. Each party receives a vote from at least one of the citizens. Votes are subject to the following criteria:

> Either two or three of the five citizens votes for the Economic Party.
>
> Q and Z both vote for the same party.

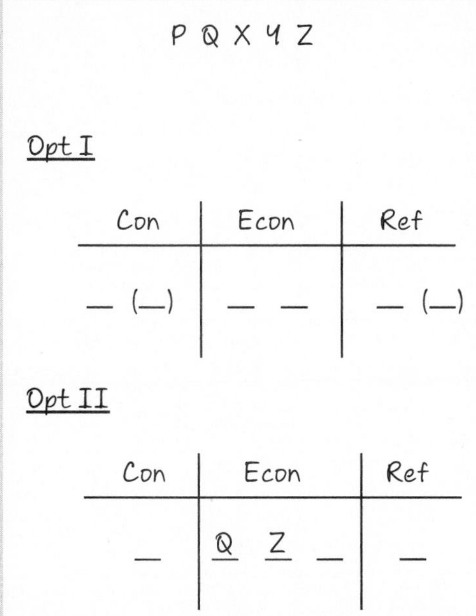

In this game, Option II, in which three citizens vote for the Economic Party, gives you an additional deduction: Q and Z, who must vote the same way, will definitely vote Economic because there is insufficient room for two votes in either of the other parties. Without additional rules, you can't make that same deduction in Option I because either Conservative or Reform could receive two votes (as represented by the slots in parentheses) in this option. Other rules in this game may allow you to make additional deductions in one or both options.

Blocks of Entities

In the previous example, the voting block of Q and Z could be placed concretely in one of the numbers-based options. In other games, however, it may be a block of entities that creates the Limited Option situation. Consider this Strict Sequencing example.

Six first-year students at a military academy—A, B, C, D, E, and G—will be assigned to six bunks, numbered 1 through 6, in the first-year student dormitory. Each first-year student is assigned to exactly one bunk.

> A is assigned to a bunk numbered two higher than the bunk to which G is assigned.
>
> D is assigned to bunk 4.

A B C D E G

	1	2	3	4	5	6
Opt I	G	_	A	D	_	_
Opt II	_	_	G	D	A	_

Because D is an Established Entity, assigned once and for all to bunk 4, the block created by the G_A rule can be placed in exactly two places. Once you've created the dual sketches, you should incorporate this game's other rules into both sketches.

Limited Options can, in some cases, take you from dozens of possible arrangements down to just a handful, maybe as few as five or six. Indeed, it's not uncommon for one of the two options to be filled in entirely by the time you're done making all of the game's deductions.

In this Spotlight video, an LSAT Channel coach will take you through the game on the following pages. You'll see the awesome power of Limited Options in action.

Questions 1–6

On a Tuesday, an accountant has exactly seven bills—numbered 1 through 7—to pay by Thursday of the same week. The accountant will pay each bill only once according to the following rules:

Either three or four of the seven bills must be paid on Wednesday, the rest on Thursday.

Bill 1 cannot be paid on the same day as bill 5.

Bill 2 must be paid on Thursday.

Bill 4 must be paid on the same day as bill 7.

If bill 6 is paid on Wednesday, bill 7 must be paid on Thursday.

1. If exactly four bills are paid on Wednesday, then those four bills could be

(A) 1, 3, 4, and 6

(B) 1, 3, 5, and 6

(C) 2, 4, 5, and 7

(D) 3, 4, 5, and 7

(E) 3, 4, 6, and 7

2. Which one of the following is a complete and accurate list of the bills any one of which could be among the bills paid on Wednesday?

   (A) 3, 5, and 6
   (B) 1, 3, 4, 6, and 7
   (C) 1, 3, 4, 5, 6, and 7
   (D) 2, 3, 4, 5, 6, and 7
   (E) 1, 2, 3, 4, 5, 6, and 7

3. If bill 2 and bill 6 are paid on different days from each other, which one of the following must be true?

   (A) Exactly three bills are paid on Wednesday.
   (B) Exactly three bills are paid on Thursday.
   (C) Bill 1 is paid on the same day as bill 4.
   (D) Bill 2 is paid on the same day as bill 3.
   (E) Bill 5 is paid on the same day as bill 7.

4. If bill 6 is paid on Wednesday, which one of the following bills must also be paid on Wednesday?

   (A) 1
   (B) 3
   (C) 4
   (D) 5
   (E) 7

5. If bill 4 is paid on Thursday, which one of the following is a pair of bills that could also be paid on Thursday?

   (A) 1 and 5
   (B) 1 and 7
   (C) 3 and 5
   (D) 3 and 6
   (E) 6 and 7

6. Which one of the following statements must be true?

   (A) If bill 2 is paid on Thursday, bill 3 is paid on Wednesday.
   (B) If bill 4 is paid on Thursday, bill 1 is paid on Wednesday.
   (C) If bill 4 is paid on Thursday, bill 3 is paid on Wednesday.
   (D) If bill 6 is paid on Thursday, bill 3 is also paid on Thursday.
   (E) If bill 6 is paid on Thursday, bill 4 is also paid on Thursday.

PrepTest29 Sec3 Qs 1–6

Complete answers and explanations are provided in The LSAT Channel Spotlight video "Limited Options" in your online Study Plan.

CHAPTER 4

Logic Games Questions

This is where all of your work on Logic Games pays off. All that you've learned so far—how to conduct an Overview, build a Sketch, populate it with the Rules, and combine the rules to make Deductions—has prepared you for the skills you'll learn and practice here. If you've taken the preceding chapters seriously—if you've really conquered Steps 1 through 4 of the Logic Games Method—you may be surprised by how quickly and confidently you are able to answer Logic Games questions. Indeed, that's the reason that LSAT experts spend 3–4 minutes before tackling a game's questions doing the setup and critical-thinking steps that you've been practicing up to this point.

Nonetheless, there are still a few skills to learn to handle the Logic Games question sets efficiently and to avoid needless and costly mistakes. One of the biggest components of mastery in this chapter involves identifying, quickly and accurately, what each question is calling for. Many test takers lose points in the Logic Games section because, after having done strong analyses, they simply answer the wrong question. They might, for example, choose an answer that clearly must be true even though the question stem calls for the choice that could be false. Or, they pick out a scenario that could be true when the question credits only the choice that must be true. In the section of this chapter dedicated to Must Be/Could Be questions, you will learn to assess levels of certainty and truth values, a skill that will pay off when you practice New-"If" questions as well. Make sure to study these concepts carefully.

Other mistakes that poorly trained test takers make with Logic Games questions lead to wasted time and effort even when they don't lead to wrong answers. Students who try to test every choice by drawing innumerable diagrams lose time that an LSAT expert, confident in the deductions he has made in the Master Sketch, is able to preserve. Others, who are in too much of a hurry to draw even one new sketch (to account for a new condition in a New-"If" question stem, let's say), become so confused trying to hold dozens of arrangements in their heads that they can't quickly or confidently eliminate wrong answers.

In this chapter, you'll learn how best to handle every Logic Games question. We'll break the questions into a handful of question types and show you effective strategies for each one.

HOW TO ANSWER LOGIC GAMES QUESTIONS STRATEGICALLY

LEARNING OBJECTIVES

In this chapter, you'll learn to

- Identify the Logic Games question types,
- Characterize the correct and incorrect answer choices in each question type, and
- Apply the appropriate strategy to each question type.

Prepare

To answer a Logic Games question correctly, you will need to recognize the question type and be able to characterize the one correct and four incorrect answer choices. To then answer the question quickly and confidently, you'll need to apply the appropriate strategy. In the first part of this chapter, you'll learn all of the question types that appear in the Logic Games section of the LSAT, and the strategies and tactics associated with each one. The Prepare portion of the chapter is thus fairly lengthy. Whenever there is a question type that you saw in Chapter 1, you'll revisit it here to help activate your prior knowledge and make the strategies come to life.

To practice and assess your skill level in Logic Games questions you will, naturally, need full games. You can't answer the questions (at least not effectively) without the work you've done in the Overview, Sketch, Rules, and Deductions steps of the Logic Games Method. Therefore, in the Practice and Perform portions of this chapter, you will have the opportunity to answer all of the questions from the officially released games you've been setting up and analyzing in the previous chapters. You'll have additional opportunities to practice answering Logic Games questions in all of the game-type chapters that follow (Chapters 5–11).

LOGIC GAMES STRATEGY

Question Types appearing in the Logic Games section include:

- Acceptability Questions
- Must Be/Could Be Questions
- New-“If” Questions
- Other Question Types:
  - Complete and Accurate List Questions
  - Completely Determine Questions
  - Numerical Questions
    - Minimum/Maximum
    - Earliest/Latest
    - “How Many”
  - Rule Alteration Questions
    - Rule Change
    - Rule Substitution
  - Supply the “If” Questions

The first three items in that list—Acceptability, Must Be/Could Be, and New-“If” questions—are, by far, the most frequent question types in the Logic Games section, and you'll spend the bulk of your practice time on them. The remaining question types are fairly infrequent, and on some tests, some of them may not appear at all. While it is important that you are able to recognize them and to understand what they are asking for, you do not need to dedicate as much study and practice to them. If one of these question types comes up in a game you're studying, and you don't remember how LSAT experts approach it efficiently, come back to this chapter to refresh your memory.

Types of Questions By Percentage, 2014–18

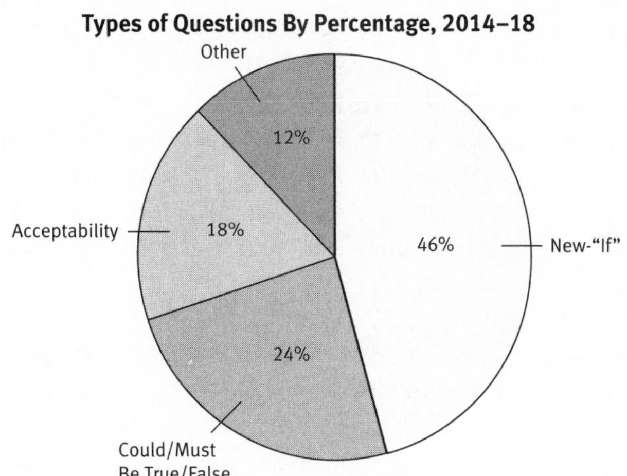

**PrepTests 72–86; released 2014–2018*

Logic Games Question Types

Now, take a look at the various question types in more detail.

Acceptability Questions

Most LSAT logic games feature one Acceptability question, and usually, it is the first question in the set. On rare occasions, you'll find a game with no Acceptability question, and very rarely, a game with two. You'll learn to look forward to Acceptability questions because they can be answered correctly in a matter of seconds once you learn to use the suggested strategy.

Identifying Acceptability Questions

Acceptability questions ask for an arrangement or selection of the entities in the game that does not violate any of the game's rules or restrictions. You can recognize Acceptability questions from question stems like these:

> Which one of the following is an acceptable schedule of all of the dentist's appointments for the day?

> Which one of the following could be an accurate account of the doctors who work at each of the town's three clinics?

> Which one of the following could be a complete and accurate list of employees chosen to attend the company retreat?

Note: From time to time, you will see Partial Acceptability questions that ask for an acceptable arrangement of part of the game's full setup. The question stems for Partial Acceptability might look like this:

> Which one of the following is an acceptable schedule of the dentist's first three appointments for the day?

> Which one of the following could be an accurate account of the doctors who work in Clinics A and B?

Don't let Partial Acceptability question stems throw you. The characteristics of the right and wrong answers, and the strategy you will use to answer these questions, are exactly the same as those in regular Acceptability questions. Just make sure you are concentrating on the parts of the game's setup designated by the question stem.

Characterizing the Answer Choices in Acceptability Questions

It is almost tautological to say that the correct answer to an Acceptability question is "acceptable." A more helpful characterization of the correct answer choice here is that it is the one answer choice that does *not* violate any of the game's rules or restrictions. The reason that definition is more helpful is that it allows you to easily comprehend the four wrong answers; they are the answers that *do* violate one or more of the game's rules or restrictions.

Answering Acceptability Questions Strategically

By characterizing the one correct and four incorrect answer choices as you've just seen, you avail yourself of one of the Logic Games section's biggest time saving strategies: Answer Acceptability questions by testing the rules one by one against the answer choices. Start with Rule 1. Grey down any and all answer choices that break this rule. Indeed, strike through the entire answer choice; once you know an answer violates one rule, there is no need to check it against any of the others. Move on to Rule 2, and repeat the process on only those answer choices that did not violate Rule 1. Continue this process with the remaining rules until only one choice remains. That's the correct answer, the one that violates none of the rules. Circle it, and move on to the next question.

Untrained test takers will often instinctively try to answer Acceptability questions "backward," by checking each answer choice to see if it violates any of the rules. This is terribly time consuming because, when you check answer choice (A), you don't know if it violates Rule 1, Rule 2, Rule 3, or Rule 4, or if it is the correct answer and does not violate any of the rules. The same applies to choices (B), (C), (D), and (E). You could wind up checking each answer choice against multiple rules before settling on the correct answer.

Refresh (Activate Prior Knowledge)

Take another look at the Acceptability question from the Truck Arrivals game that you first saw in Chapter 1. This time, it will be broken down so that you can see the LSAT expert's analysis rule-by-rule, as described in the strategy. Take a moment to refresh your memory of the game, and then try applying the strategy to the question. After you've given it a shot, follow along as the expert tests the rules against the answer choices.

In a single day, exactly seven trucks—S, T, U, W, X, Y, and Z—are the only arrivals at a warehouse. No truck arrives at the same time as any other truck, and no truck arrives more than once that day. Each truck is either green or red (but not both). The following conditions apply:

No two consecutive arrivals are red.
Y arrives at some time before both T and W.
Exactly two of the trucks that arrive before Y are red.
S is the sixth arrival.
Z arrives at some time before U.

PrepTest37 Sec3 Q6

Steps 1–4:

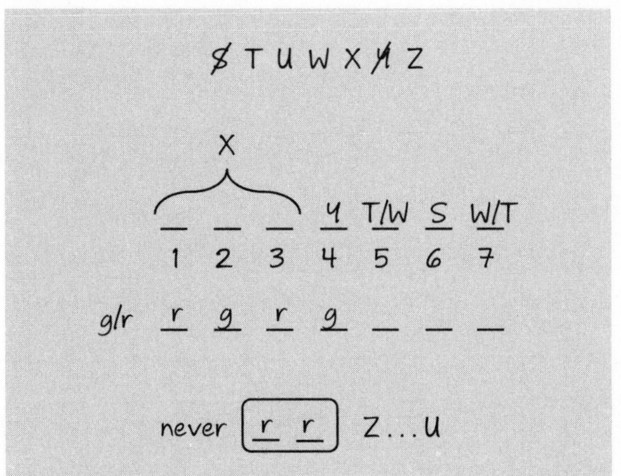

Step 5: An Acceptability question: Test the rules, one by one, against the answer choices.

1. Which one of the following could be the order, from first to last, in which the trucks arrive?

(A) X, Z, U, Y, W, S, T
(B) X, Y, Z, U, W, S, T
(C) Z, W, U, T, Y, S, X
(D) Z, U, T, Y, W, S, X
(E) U, Z, Y, T, S, W, X

Step 5 (cont.):

Test Rule 1:

In a single day, exactly seven trucks—S, T, U, W, X, Y, and Z—are the only arrivals at a warehouse. No truck arrives at the same time as any other truck, and no truck arrives more than once that day. Each truck is either green or red (but not both). The following conditions apply:

No two consecutive arrivals are red.
Y arrives at some time before both T and W.
Exactly two of the trucks that arrive before Y are red.
S is the sixth arrival.
Z arrives at some time before U.

PrepTest37 Sec3 Q6

Steps 1–4:

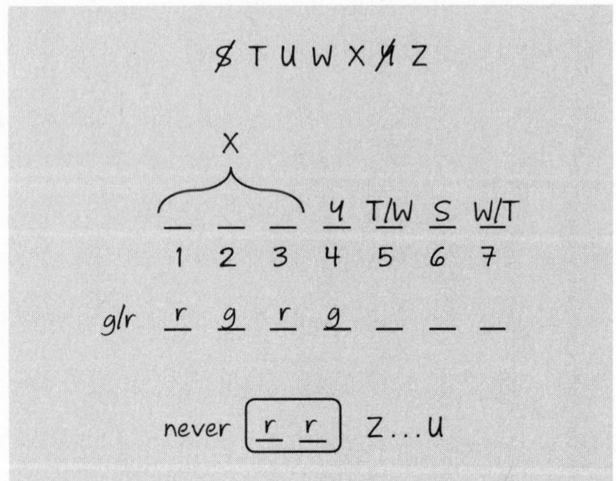

Step 5: An Acceptability question: Test the rules, one by one, against the answer choices.

1. Which one of the following could be the order, from first to last, in which the trucks arrive?

   (A) X, Z, U, Y, W, S, T
   (B) X, Y, Z, U, W, S, T
   (C) Z, W, U, T, Y, S, X
   (D) Z, U, T, Y, W, S, X
   (E) U, Z, Y, T, S, W, X

Step 5 (cont.): The answer choices show only the trucks, not their colors, so Rule 1 is of no help here.

Technically, this is a Partial Acceptability question, since this question asks only about the order of the trucks' arrivals (Sequencing) while the full game also calls for you to assign each truck a color (Matching). Remember that the same strategy still applies. It happens from time to time, as it did here, that a rule doesn't eliminate any of the answer choices in an Acceptability or Partial Acceptability question. An LSAT expert just moves on to test Rule 2:

In a single day, exactly seven trucks—S, T, U, W, X, Y, and Z—are the only arrivals at a warehouse. No truck arrives at the same time as any other truck, and no truck arrives more than once that day. Each truck is either green or red (but not both). The following conditions apply:

> No two consecutive arrivals are red.
> Y arrives at some time before both T and W.
> Exactly two of the trucks that arrive before Y are red.
> S is the sixth arrival.
> Z arrives at some time before U.

PrepTest37 Sec3 Q6

Step 5: An Acceptability question: Test the rules, one by one, against the answer choices.

1. Which one of the following could be the order, from first to last, in which the trucks arrive?

   (A) X, Z, U, Y, W, S, T
   (B) X, Y, Z, U, W, S, T
   (C) Z, W, U, T, Y, S, X
   (D) Z, U, T, Y, W, S, X
   (E) U, Z, Y, T, S, W, X

Step 5 (cont.): The answer choices show only the trucks, not their colors, so Rule 1 is of no help in this question. Rule 2 knocks out two answer choices: (C) and (D), in which either W or T appears earlier than Y. Grey down those two choices.

Steps 1–4:

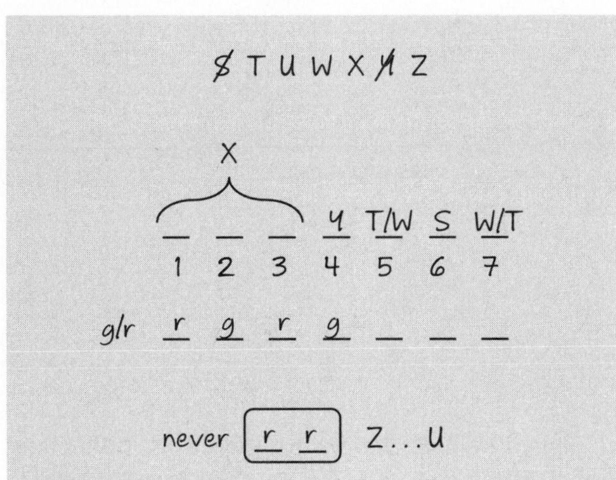

Wrong answers: (C) Violates Rule 2 by placing Trucks W and T earlier in the sequence than Truck Y. (D) Violates Rule 2 by placing Truck T earlier in the sequence than Truck Y.

Now, that's progress. Keep going, and test Rule 3:

In a single day, exactly seven trucks—S, T, U, W, X, Y, and Z—are the only arrivals at a warehouse. No truck arrives at the same time as any other truck, and no truck arrives more than once that day. Each truck is either green or red (but not both). The following conditions apply:

No two consecutive arrivals are red.

Y arrives at some time before both T and W.

Exactly two of the trucks that arrive before Y are red.

S is the sixth arrival.

Z arrives at some time before U.

PrepTest37 Sec3 Q6

Steps 1–4:

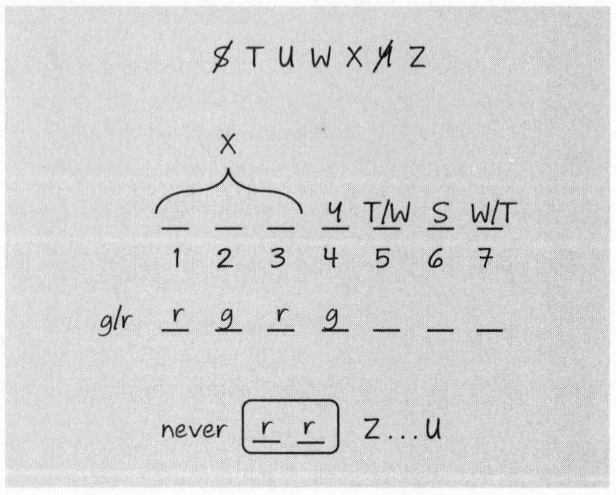

Step 5: An Acceptability question: Test the rules, one by one, against the answer choices.

1. Which one of the following could be the order, from first to last, in which the trucks arrive?

(A) X, Z, U, Y, W, S, T
(B) X, Y, Z, U, W, S, T
(C) Z, W, U, T, Y, S, X
(D) Z, U, T, Y, W, S, X
(E) U, Z, Y, T, S, W, X

Step 5 (cont.): The answer choices show only the trucks, not their colors, so Rule 1 is of no help in this question. Rule 2 knocks out two answer choices: (C) and (D), in which either W or T appears earlier than Y. Rule 3 knocks out choice (B), where Y is placed too early to have two red trucks precede it in the sequence.

Wrong answers: (B) Violates Rule 3 by placing Y in a position that cannot be preceded by two red trucks. (C) Violates Rule 2 by placing Trucks W and T earlier in the sequence than Truck Y. (D) Violates Rule 2 by placing Truck T earlier in the sequence than Truck Y.

Now, you need to eliminate only one more answer choice, and you'll have the correct answer spotted. Test Rule 4:

Step 5: An Acceptability question: Test the rules, one by one, against the answer choices.

In a single day, exactly seven trucks—S, T, U, W, X, Y, and Z—are the only arrivals at a warehouse. No truck arrives at the same time as any other truck, and no truck arrives more than once that day. Each truck is either green or red (but not both). The following conditions apply:

No two consecutive arrivals are red.

Y arrives at some time before both T and W.

Exactly two of the trucks that arrive before Y are red.

S is the sixth arrival.

Z arrives at some time before U.

PrepTest37 Sec3 Q6

Steps 1–4:

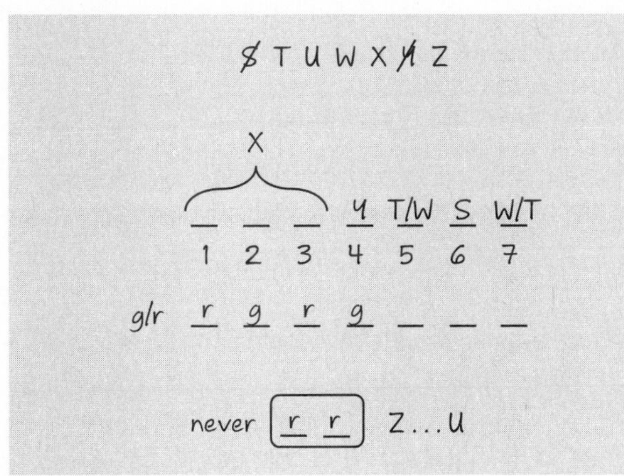

1. Which one of the following could be the order, from first to last, in which the trucks arrive?

(A) X, Z, U, Y, W, S, T
(B) X, Y, Z, U, W, S, T
(C) Z, W, U, T, Y, S, X
(D) Z, U, T, Y, W, S, X
(E) U, Z, Y, T, S, W, X

Step 5 (cont.): (A) is correct; This answer choice does not violate any of the rules. The answer choices show only the trucks, not their colors, so Rule 1 is of no help in this question. Rule 2 knocks out two answer choices: (C) and (D), in which either W or T appears earlier than Y. Rule 3 knocks out choice (B), in which Y is placed too early to have two red trucks precede it in the sequence. Rule 4 knocks out choice (E), in which S is fifth, not sixth.

Wrong answers: (B) Violates Rule 3 by placing Truck Y in a position that cannot be preceded by two red trucks. (C) Violates Rule 2 by placing Trucks W and T earlier in the sequence than Truck Y. (D) Violates Rule 2 by placing Truck T earlier in the sequence than Truck Y. (E) Violates Rule 4 by placing Truck S fifth, not sixth.

By greying down the wrong answer choices as soon as it is clear that they violate even one of the rules, the LSAT expert makes short work of any Acceptability question. Practice this strategy whenever you encounter an Acceptability question associated with any of the games throughout the remainder of this book. You will soon get to the point where you can confidently answer these questions in a matter of 30 seconds or less.

LSAT STRATEGY

Whenever you find the correct answer to an Acceptability question, jot it down on your scratch paper and label it with the Question number. Make this a habit. You may be able to use the correct answer to the Acceptability questions to eliminate wrong answers in a Must Be False question and, by having it on the scratch paper, you won't have to click back to the Acceptability question on the computer screen.

A Note on Complete and Accurate List Questions

One of the model question stems in the description of Acceptability questions had the following wording:

> Which one of the following could be a complete and accurate list of employees chosen to attend the company retreat?

That particular wording amounts to asking for an acceptable selection, and the correct answer will represent one possible "solution" to the game.

It's worth noting, however, that the testmaker will occasionally use the phrase "complete and accurate list" for questions that focus on a narrower part of the game. In a Sequencing game, for example, one of these questions might ask for "a complete and accurate list of the days on which Johnson's appointment may be scheduled." In a Distribution game, on the other hand, you might run across a question such as "Which one of the following is a complete and accurate list of all players who could play on Team B?"

For Complete and Accurate List questions such as these, the correct answer must contain any and all of the acceptable slots or entities called for by the question stem. In other words, each wrong answer will either be incomplete—it will not contain all of the days on which Johnson's appointment can be scheduled, or it will be missing players who are eligible for Team B—or the wrong answer will be inaccurate—it will include days on which Johnson's appointment cannot be scheduled or players ineligible for Team B. That makes sense when you think about the question. If the right answer is "complete and accurate," all four wrong answers must be incomplete or inaccurate (or both).

You will recognize Complete and Accurate List questions from question stems like the following, but don't spend too much time trying to hunt down examples of this rare question type.

> Which one of the following is a complete and accurate list of the cars any one of which could be among the cars washed on Tuesday?

> Which one of the following is a complete and accurate list of the days on which Isobel could shop for groceries?

When you do come across Complete and Accurate List questions, don't panic or change your strategic approach to logic games. These questions are too rare to be a type that makes or breaks your score. Just distinguish them from Acceptability questions and remember that the wrong answers are always inaccurate or incomplete (or both). Once you've characterized the answer choices, you just consult the Master Sketch to eliminate the violators and find the right answer.

Must Be/Could Be Questions

The majority of games in any administration of the LSAT have at least one, and often two or more, Must Be/Could Be questions. These questions simply test what must, can, or cannot be true of the arrangement or selection of the entities in the game. Must Be/Could Be question stems do not add any additional conditions or stipulations to the game's original rules and restrictions, and thus, they can always be answered with reference to the Master Sketch containing all of the game's available deductions.

Identifying Must Be/Could Be Questions

Some Must Be/Could Be question stems are straightforward and easy to recognize:

> Which one of the following must be true?
>
> Which one of the following could be true?
>
> Which one of the following must be false?
>
> Which one of the following could be false?

Other Must Be/Could Be question stems ask for the same types of analyses by introducing a negative term:

> Each of the following could be false EXCEPT: (Note that the correct answer here *must be true*)
>
> Which one of the following CANNOT be true? (Note that the correct answer here *must be false*)
>
> Each of the following must be true EXCEPT: (Note that the correct answer here *could be false*)

Finally, some Must Be/Could Be questions include information that is specific to the setup or entities in the game:

> Which one of the following lists a pair of doctors who must work at the same clinic?
>
> Which one of the following is a patient that the dentist CANNOT see at 2:00 PM?

Must Be/Could Be questions are easy to identify. The challenge in these questions is to make sure that you are absolutely clear about the characteristics of the correct and incorrect answers.

Characterizing the Answer Choices in Must Be/Could Be Questions

In real life, you rarely think in "negatives" as you make decisions. It would seem strange, for example, to look at a menu and ask, "Which one of these sandwiches can I *not* choose for lunch?" Even on most tests you've taken in school, the *correct* answer has always equated to the *true* answer. On the LSAT, however, many questions ask for what must be false or what could be false, so you must characterize what you are looking for before evaluating the answer choices.

LOGIC GAMES STRATEGY

On the LSAT, never confuse *true* and *false* statements with *right* and *wrong* answers. Always characterize what you're looking for before evaluating the answer choices.

Some LSAT experts even find it helpful to note what they're looking for on the scratch paper. For example, for a Must Be False question, they might jot down "1 MBF/4 CBT" to signify that the correct answer must be false while the four incorrect answer choices could be true.

Even when the characteristics of the correct answer are clear in your mind, it may be easier to identify incorrect answers as you are evaluating the choices. You've seen a variation of this in Acceptability questions, where applying the rules makes it faster to eliminate the four *unacceptable* choices than it would be to ask repeatedly "Is this answer choice acceptable? How about this one?" and so on.

In Logic Games, the answer choices are never equivocal; there is one choice that meets the criteria of the question stem, and four choices that do not. LSAT experts always identify the characteristics of both the correct and incorrect answers before evaluating the answer choices. The following chart shows how the right and wrong answer characteristics line up.

When the correct answer . . .	Then, the wrong answers . . .
Must Be True	Could Be False*
Could Be True	Must Be False
Must Be False	Could Be True**
Could Be False	Must Be True

*Any answer choice that must be false would qualify as a wrong answer in this case. After all, any statement that must be false certainly could be false.
**Any answer choice that must be true would qualify as a wrong answer in this case. After all, any statement that must be true certainly could be true.

Having that chart memorized will help you avoid costly mistakes on test day. If you evaluate an answer choice and conclude that the statement it contains *must be true*, the chart indicates whether that choice is correct or incorrect. To see this in action, consider the following scenario:

In Country X, exactly one person serves as president at any given time. Thompkins was Country X's first president. Evaluate the truth value of the following statements:

- Jerome was the first president of Country X. [Must be false]
- Jerome was the second president of Country X. [Could be true or false]
- Jerome was not the first president of Country X. [Must be true]

Now, imagine that a question asked, "Which one of the statements must be true?" In that case, the correct answer would be the third statement, and the first two statements would be incorrect. On the other hand, if the question asked, "Which one of the statements must be false?" then the first statement would be the correct answer while the second and third would be incorrect.

Try your hand at characterizing the one right and four wrong answer choices in a handful of question stems. When you're finished, compare your analysis to that of an LSAT expert.

Exercise

Directions: For each of the following question stems, characterize the one correct and the four incorrect answer choices. An LSAT expert's analysis is shown on the pages following the exercise.

Question Stem		My Analysis
1. Which of the following must be true?	→	The correct answer: The four wrong answer choices:
2. Which of the following could be false?	→	The correct answer: The four wrong answer choices:
3. Which of the following applicants CANNOT be selected for the managerial position?	→	The correct answer: The four wrong answer choices:
4. If the painting is the fourth item sold, which of the following could be the fifth item sold?	→	The correct answer: The four wrong answer choices:
5. Each of the following could be true EXCEPT:	→	The correct answer: The four wrong answer choices:
6. Which of the following is an acceptable order in which the cars are repaired?	→	The correct answer: The four wrong answer choices:

Question Stem		My Analysis
7. Alexander could be placed on a team with any of the following EXCEPT:	→	The correct answer: The four wrong answer choices:
8. Which of the following is a pair of items that CANNOT both be included in the display?	→	The correct answer: The four wrong answer choices:
9. Each of the following must be false EXCEPT:	→	The correct answer: The four wrong answer choices:
10. If Brianna is assigned to the history project, then which of the following students must be assigned to the science project?	→	The correct answer: The four wrong answer choices:
11. Which of the following speeches could be presented third?	→	The correct answer: The four wrong answer choices:
12. Which of the following musicians must perform on Monday if Evan performs on Friday?	→	The correct answer: The four wrong answer choices:
13. If Samantha travels to France, then Taylor must travel to	→	The correct answer: The four wrong answer choices:

Question Stem		My Analysis
14. Which of the following could be a complete and accurate assignment of interns to the company's departments?	→	The correct answer: The four wrong answer choices:
15. The color of the fourth garment purchased CANNOT be	→	The correct answer: The four wrong answer choices:
16. The violinist must be seated immediately next to	→	The correct answer: The four wrong answer choices:
17. If astronomy is offered, it could be offered on any day of the week EXCEPT:	→	The correct answer: The four wrong answer choices:
18. Which of the following pieces of furniture could be placed with the divan in the Woodcrest Room?	→	The correct answer: The four wrong answer choices:
19. Which of the following dogs could be scheduled for the first appointment?	→	The correct answer: The four wrong answer choices:
20. Bacon must be included in which of the following meals?	→	The correct answer: The four wrong answer choices:

Expert Analysis

Here's how an LSAT expert would characterize the correct and incorrect answer choices for each of those question stems.

Question stem		Analysis
1. Which of the following must be true?	→	The correct answer must be true. The four wrong answer choices could be false (or must be false).
2. Which of the following could be false?	→	The correct answer could be false. The four wrong answer choices must be true.
3. Which of the following applicants CANNOT be selected for the managerial position?	→	The correct answer must be false. Here, that means someone who must not be selected for the managerial position. Wrong answer choices will list applicants who could or must be selected for the managerial position.
4. If the painting is the fourth item sold, which of the following could be the fifth item sold?	→	The correct answer could be true, which in this case means could be sold fifth. Wrong answer choices must be false, which means they must not be sold fifth.
5. Each of the following could be true EXCEPT:	→	The correct answer must be false. Wrong answer choices could be true (or must be true).
6. Which of the following is an acceptable order in which the cars are repaired?	→	An "acceptable order" is one that could be true. Wrong answer choices will be unacceptable, which means they must be false.

Question		Explanation
7. Alexander could be placed on a team with any of the following EXCEPT:	→	The correct answer must be false, which here means a person with whom Alexander must not be teamed. Wrong answer choices will list people who could (or must) be on a team with Alexander.
8. Which of the following is a pair of items that CANNOT both be included in the display?	→	The correct answer must be false, which here means the two items must not be included together. They may be included individually, but not *together*. Wrong answer choices will list pairs of items that could be included together.
9. Each of the following must be false EXCEPT:	→	The correct answer could (or must) be true. Wrong answer choices must be false.
10. If Brianna is assigned to the history project, then which of the following students must be assigned to the science project?	→	The correct answer must be true, which here means someone who must be assigned to the science project. Wrong answer choices could be false, i.e., students who may not (or cannot) be assigned to the science project.
11. Which of the following speeches could be presented third?	→	The correct answer could be true. In this case, a speech that could be third. Wrong answer choices must be false, i.e., speeches that must not be third.

Question		Answer
12. Which of the following musicians must perform on Monday if Evan performs on Friday?	→	The correct answer must be true, which here means a musician who must perform on Monday. Wrong answer choices could be false, which means musicians who might not (or cannot) perform on Monday.
13. If Samantha travels to France, then Taylor must travel to	→	The correct answer must be true, which here means a place to which Taylor must travel. Wrong answer choices could be false, which means places to which Taylor may not (or does not) travel.
14. Which of the following could be a complete and accurate assignment of interns to the company's departments?	→	The correct answer could be true, which here means an acceptable assignment of interns. Wrong answer choices must be false, which means they describe assignments that are impossible.
15. The color of the fourth garment purchased CANNOT be	→	The correct answer must be false, which here means a color that fourth garment must not be. Wrong answer choices could be true, which means they list colors the fourth garment could be.
16. The violinist must be seated immediately next to	→	The correct answer must be true, which here means someone who must sit next to the violinist. Wrong answer choices could be false, which means people who might not (or do not) sit next to the violinist.
17. If astronomy is offered, it could be offered on any day of the week EXCEPT:	→	The correct answer must be false, which here means a day on which astronomy must not be offered. Wrong answer choices could be true, which means days on which astronomy could be offered.

18. Which of the following pieces of furniture could be placed with the divan in the Woodcrest Room?	→	The correct answer could be true, which here means a piece of furniture that could be placed in the Woodcrest Room along with the divan. Wrong answer choices must be false, which means pieces of furniture that cannot be placed in the Woodcrest Room along with the divan.
19. Which of the following dogs could be scheduled for the first appointment?	→	The correct answer could be true, which here means a dog that could be scheduled first. Wrong answer choices must be false, which means dogs that must not be scheduled first.
20. Bacon must be included in which of the following meals?	→	The correct answer must be true, which here means a meal which must include bacon. Wrong answer choices could be false, which means meals that might not (or definitely do not) include bacon.

Once you are comfortable characterizing the answer choices in Must Be/Could Be questions, the hardest part is over. Most of these questions can be answered simply by consulting the Master Sketch.

Answering Must Be/Could Be Questions Strategically

Must Be/Could Be questions reveal how important Steps 1 through 4 of the Logic Games Method are. By taking the time to sketch out a framework for the game's action, draw the rules into or underneath it, and make the available deductions, you uncover all that can be known about what must, could, and cannot be true within the game. Now, you can evaluate any answer choice in a Must Be/Could Be question by comparing it to the Master Sketch: "Can this statement be true? Does it have to be false?" and so on.

In some cases, your sketch will be so precise that you can even anticipate what the testmaker might ask. Imagine a Sequencing game in which you can deduce that a dentist's second appointment is with Matt. It's common, in such cases, for the test to ask a Must Be True question for which the correct answer is "The dentist sees Matt second." Likewise, in a Distribution game, you may be able to deduce that Catherine is never on Team 2. That deduction would lend itself perfectly to a Must Be False question.

Even when questions don't relate quite so obviously to the deductions, the Master Sketch contains the information you need to evaluate the answer choices. You can see this in the two Must Be/Could Be questions associated with the Truck Arrivals game from Chapter 1.

Refresh (Activate Prior Knowledge)

The first Must Be/Could Be question in the Truck Arrivals game was a Must Be False variant. That question asked for a pair of trucks that could *not* both be red. Review the LSAT expert's analysis of the question.

In a single day, exactly seven trucks—S, T, U, W, X, Y, and Z—are the only arrivals at a warehouse. No truck arrives at the same time as any other truck, and no truck arrives more than once that day. Each truck is either green or red (but not both). The following conditions apply:

No two consecutive arrivals are red.
Y arrives at some time before both T and W.
Exactly two of the trucks that arrive before Y are red.
S is the sixth arrival.
Z arrives at some time before U.

PrepTest37 Sec3 Q7

Step 5: A Must Be False question: Consult the Master Sketch to evaluate the answer choices.

2. For which one of the following pairs of trucks is it the case that they CANNOT both be red?

(A) S and X
(B) T and S
(C) U and W
(D) W and T
(E) X and Z

Step 5 (cont.): The Trucks in the correct answer cannot both be red. The Trucks in the wrong answers *could* both be red.
(B) is correct. T and S will be in consecutive slots (whether T is fifth or seventh). Rule 1 prevents consecutive trucks from both being red. T and S *cannot* both be red.

Steps 1–4:

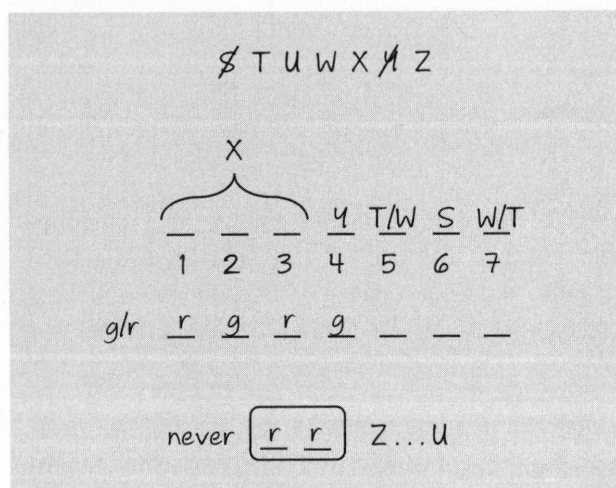

Wrong answers: (A) S could be red if the trucks in slots 5 and 7 are green, and X could be in slot 1 or 3. Both could be red. (C) W could be red in either the fifth or seventh slot, as long as slot 6 is green, and U could be in slot 3. Both could be red. (D) Slots 5 and 7 could both be red, as long as slot 6 is green. Both could be red. (E) Z could be in slot 1 and X could be in slot 3. Both could be red.

Notice how the LSAT expert characterized the one right and four wrong answers before evaluating the choices. Because the LSAT expert has recorded Rule 1 (which prevents consecutive trucks from both being red) and has added Trucks S and T to the Master Sketch, it is clear that choice (B) must be false, and is, therefore, correct.

The final question from that game was another Must Be False variant. Review the expert's analysis.

In a single day, exactly seven trucks—S, T, U, W, X, Y, and Z—are the only arrivals at a warehouse. No truck arrives at the same time as any other truck, and no truck arrives more than once that day. Each truck is either green or red (but not both). The following conditions apply:

No two consecutive arrivals are red.
Y arrives at some time before both T and W.
Exactly two of the trucks that arrive before Y are red.
S is the sixth arrival.
Z arrives at some time before U.

PrepTest37 Sec3 Q11

Step 5: A Must Be False question: Test each answer choice against the Master Sketch.

6. Which one of the following pairs of trucks CANNOT arrive consecutively at the warehouse?

(A) U and Y
(B) X and Y
(C) Y and T
(D) Y and W
(E) Y and Z

Step 5 (cont.): Eliminate any choice in which the pair of trucks *could* arrive consecutively. The correct answer cites a pair of trucks that *cannot* arrive consecutively. (E) is correct; Truck Y is always in slot 4. Truck Z can be only in slots 1 or 2. These trucks can never be consecutive.

Steps 1–4:

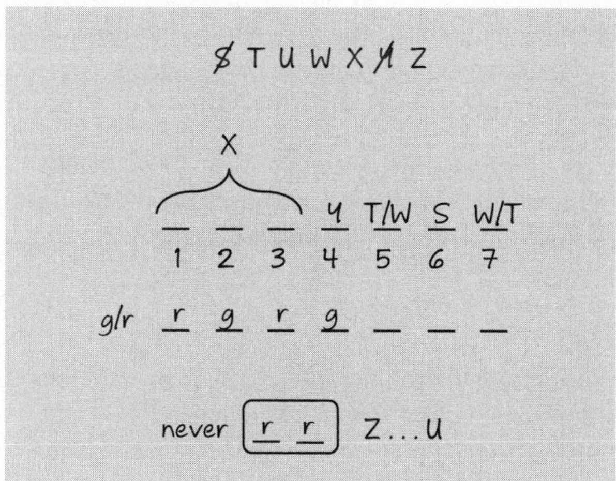

Wrong answers: (A) Truck Y is always in slot 4. Truck U could be in slot 3. (B) Truck Y is always in slot 4. Truck X could be in slot 3. (C) Truck Y is always in slot 4. Truck T could be in slot 5. (D) Truck Y is always in slot 4. Truck W could be in slot 5.

Once again, adding the deductions to the Master Sketch proves decisive. Once the LSAT expert has characterized the correct answer (a pair of trucks that *cannot* arrive consecutively), choice (E) is clearly the winner. By also characterizing the four wrong answer choices (a pair of trucks that can arrive consecutively), the expert can quickly eliminate (A), (B), (C), and (D).

Evaluating the Answer Choices by Making Sketches

Every once in a while, you may encounter a Must Be/Could Be question in which you need to sketch out the implications of an answer choice to know for certain whether it must, can, or cannot be true. In such cases, first eliminate any answers that are clearly incorrect based on the Master Sketch. As you do so, you may locate the correct answer, in which case, you're done, and there is no reason to continue checking the remaining choices. If, however, you still need to test two or more answer choices, quickly copy the Master Sketch framework, and fill in the information from one of the remaining answer choices so that you can evaluate that choice against the criteria of the correct and incorrect answers. Continue this process until you have spotted the right answer, or you have eliminated all four wrong answers.

Don't fall into the pattern of always sketching out every answer choice. That is unnecessarily time consuming. Look first to test the answer choices against the Master Sketch. In most cases, that will be sufficient.

Evaluating Conditional Answer Choices

One rare case that calls for new sketches happens when a Must Be/Could Be question has answer choices that are conditional. For example, you might see something like this:

> Which one of the following must be true?
>
> (A) If the dentist sees Joanna third, then he must see Kim fifth.
>
> (B) If the dentist sees Kim at some time after he sees Matt, then he must see Carlton fourth.
>
> (C) . . . .

While it may be possible for you to picture the condition described in the first clause of each answer choice in your mind and to see its implications, it is safer to quickly copy the Master Sketch and to add the condition in writing. Once you've made any additional deductions triggered by the condition, you can evaluate your new sketch against the rules to determine if the statement in the second clause of the answer choice must, can, or cannot be true.

If all five of the answer choices are conditional (an extremely rare case, indeed), these questions can be quite time consuming. You may find it more strategic to skip the question and come back to it only if you have time remaining for the game. If not, you are probably better off guessing on a question like this and saving your time for the next game and all of its questions.

Evaluating Answer Choices by Using Previous Work

If you are stuck on a particular Must Be/Could Be question, you may be able to use the work you've done on another question to help you evaluate one or more of the answer choices. For example, once you have completed an Acceptability question, its correct answer serves as one acceptable "solution" for the game. Thus, any arrangement seen in that answer choice *could be true*. Thus, if an answer choice in a subsequent Must Be False question describes an arrangement seen in the correct answer of the Acceptability question, that answer choice will be *incorrect* in the Must Be False question.

The Special Feature that follows this chapter goes into the strategy of Using Previous Work in detail and illustrates it with a game you haven't seen before in this book. If you have time in your study schedule, read that Special Feature section and watch the accompanying video. The LSAT Channel expert will show you the ins and outs of using this strategy.

New-"If" Questions

New-"If" questions are the most common question type in every Logic Games section. Most (though not all) games have two or more New-"If" questions. Such a question is distinguished by the first clause of its question stem, which always adds a condition to the game's original setup and rules. While this makes the question stem longer (and seemingly more complicated) than most Must Be/Could Be question stems, the additional restriction serves to limit the number of acceptable arrangements in the game, and thus, often makes New-"If" questions even easier to answer.

Identifying New-"If" Questions

These questions are easy to spot; their question stems almost always begin with the word "If." Every once in a while, you might see "Suppose" or another synonym for "If" at the beginning of the stem, but once you spot the fact that the stem is adding a new condition, you'll know you have a question of this type. Here are some model New-"If" question stems:

> If the dentist sees Kim third, then which one of the following must be false?

> If two doctors are assigned to work at Clinic 3, then each of the following could be false EXCEPT

> Suppose that Karl is chosen to attend the company retreat; in that case, which one of the following is a pair of employees who CANNOT both attend the retreat?

In each case, it is the stem's first clause—the newly added condition—that distinguishes these as New-"If" questions.

Characterizing the Answer Choices in New-"If" Questions

It may have struck you that the second clause in each of those stems sounds like a Must Be/Could Be question. That's typical, and it means that once you are comfortable characterizing the one right and four wrong answers in Must Be/Could Be questions, you can do so just as efficiently and effectively in New-"If" questions, too. Here's how an LSAT expert would characterize the answer choices for the question stems you just saw.

> If the dentist sees Kim third, then which one of the following must be false?

Given this question's new condition (Kim has the third appointment), the correct answer must be false, and the four wrong answers could (or must) be true.

> If two doctors are assigned to work at Clinic 3, then each of the following could be false EXCEPT

Given this question's new condition (two doctors serve at Clinic 3), the correct answer must be true, and the four wrong answers could be false.

> Suppose that Karl is chosen to attend the company retreat; in that case, which one of the following is a pair of employees who CANNOT both attend the retreat?

Given this question's new condition (Karl is selected), the correct answer is a pair of employees who cannot both be selected, and the four wrong answers are pairs of employees who *can* both be selected.

Answering New-"If" Questions Strategically

The strategic aspect of dealing with New-"If" questions relates to how you account for the question's new condition. In most cases, you will do so by creating a new sketch for each specific New-"If" question. The best approach is to copy your Master Sketch framework next to the New-"If" question, add in the new rule or restriction given in the question stem, and make any additional deductions available. Once it's complete, you can use the resulting sketch to evaluate the New-"If" question's answer choices.

Don't balk at the prospect of making these new sketches; doing so actually *saves* time. Every time you add a rule or restriction to a logic game, it reduces the number of acceptable outcomes in the game. The sketches that result from New-"If" question stems usually have very little ambiguity, so you can be quick and confident when evaluating the answer choices. Trying to hold all of the game's information in your head along with the question's new condition will lead to hesitation and mistakes. Note: It's a good idea to label your new sketches with the question number to which they apply so that you don't accidentally use a new sketch for one question to evaluate the answer choices in another.

Refresh (Activate Prior Knowledge)

The Truck Arrivals game had two New-"If" questions, and both of them illustrate the new sketch strategy. Take a few minutes to review the expert's work on the first of these questions.

Step 5: A New-"If" question: Copy the Master Sketch, add this question's new condition, make all available deductions, and use the resulting sketch to evaluate the answer choices.

In a single day, exactly seven trucks—S, T, U, W, X, Y, and Z—are the only arrivals at a warehouse. No truck arrives at the same time as any other truck, and no truck arrives more than once that day. Each truck is either green or red (but not both). The following conditions apply:

No two consecutive arrivals are red.

Y arrives at some time before both T and W.

Exactly two of the trucks that arrive before Y are red.

S is the sixth arrival.

Z arrives at some time before U.

PrepTest37 Sec3 Q8

3. If X is the third arrival, then which one of the following trucks must be green?

(A) S

(B) T

(C) U

(D) W

(E) Z

Step 5 (cont.): (C) is correct. Under this question's conditions, Truck U must be green. Placing Truck X in slot 3 means than Truck Z must take slot 1 and Truck U must take slot 2.

S T U W X Y Z

Z U X Y T/W S W/T

1 2 3 4 5 6 7

g/r r g r g _ _ _

Thus, truck U must be green.

Steps 1–4:

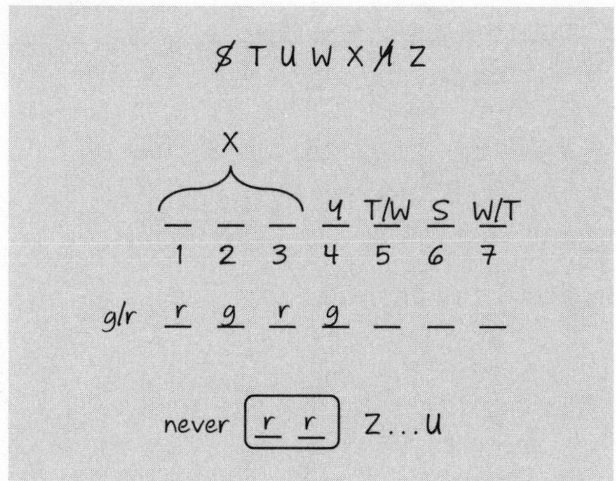

Wrong answers: (A) Truck S could be either green or red. (B) Truck T could be either green or red. (D) Truck W could be either green or red. (E) Under this question's conditions, Truck Z must be red.

In that question, the new condition (placing Truck X third) resulted in five of the seven trucks' positions being firmly established. Evaluating the choices took the expert only a few seconds with the new sketch in place.

The second New-"If" question in that game required a bit more in the way of deductions, but the results were equally clear. Take a few minutes to look it over again now.

Step 5: A New-"If" question: Copy the Master Sketch, add this question's new condition, make all available deductions, and use the resulting sketch to evaluate the answer choices.

In a single day, exactly seven trucks—S, T, U, W, X, Y, and Z—are the only arrivals at a warehouse. No truck arrives at the same time as any other truck, and no truck arrives more than once that day. Each truck is either green or red (but not both). The following conditions apply:

> No two consecutive arrivals are red.
> Y arrives at some time before both T and W.
> Exactly two of the trucks that arrive before Y are red.
> S is the sixth arrival.
> Z arrives at some time before U.

PrepTest37 Sec3 Q9

3. If exactly three of the trucks are green, then which one of the following trucks must be green?

(A) S
(B) T
(C) U
(D) W
(E) Z

Steps 1–4:

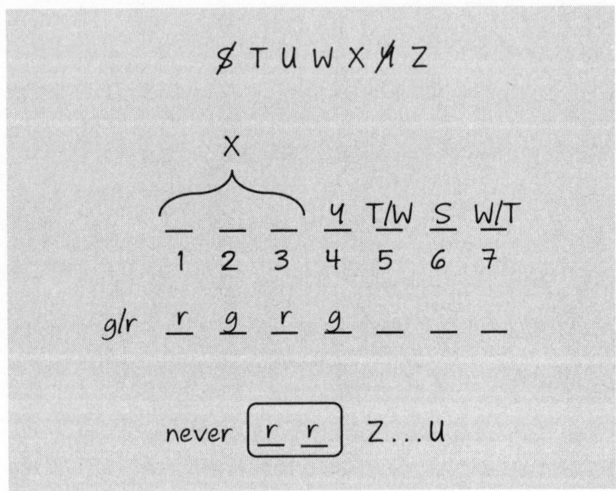

Step 5 (cont.): (A) is correct. Under this question's conditions, Truck S must be green. The trucks in slots 2 and 4 are always green. If there is to be just one more green truck, it will have to take slot 6 to prevent having any red trucks arrive consecutively (Rule 1).

S T U W X Y Z
X
Y T/W S W/T
1 2 3 4 5 6 7
g/r r g r g r g r
Z...U

Thus, Truck S must be green.

Wrong answers: (B) Under this question's conditions, Truck T must be red, whether it is fifth or seventh. (C) Truck U could be either green or red. (D) Under this question's conditions, Truck W must be red, whether it is fifth or seventh. (E) Truck Z could be either green or red.

This time, the new condition fell on the line accounting for the trucks' colors rather than the one designating their arrival order. However, once the new sketch was in place, the expert could see the color that corresponds to each position, and again, evaluating the answer choices was a snap. Those questions are representative of most New-"If" questions you will encounter, and you will have ample opportunity to practice more New-"If"s on almost every game throughout this book.

One more word of caution: Some untrained test takers are tempted to add a New-"If" question's new condition into the Master Sketch and to work out the condition's implications there. The problem with this approach is that the New-"If" question's condition applies *only* to that specific question. Once you finish working on the New-"If" question, you would need to erase its specific conditions and try to restore the Master Sketch to its original state. That leads to confusion and mistakes, and doesn't really save any time in the long run.

Answering New-"If" Questions Using Limited Options

One case in which you may be able to avoid creating new sketches for New-"If" questions is when the game's deductions break down into Limited Options. Because Limited Options deductions lead to dual Master Sketches covering each of the game's two fundamental patterns, many of the game's New-"If" questions will lead you directly to one of the two options. Then, depending on the level of certainty you've been able to deduce, you may be able to use the appropriate option's sketch to evaluate the answer choices.

The Special Feature at the end of Chapter 3 covers Limited Options deductions in detail. If you have time, and you haven't already watched the video accompanying that Special Feature, do so now. Not every game breaks down into Limited Options, but it's not unusual to see it once (or, if you're lucky, twice) per test.

Other Question Types

Completely Determine Questions

From time to time, the LSAT will pose a question asking you for a statement that would completely determine the sequence, selection, matching, or distribution of all entities in the game. Completely Determine questions are not common—among the 60 logic games (345 questions) released from 2014 through 2018, there were only 12 of these questions.

Should you run into one of these questions, you can recognize it from a question stem like one of these:

> The order of the dentist's appointments for the day is completely determined if which one of the following is true?

> The assignment of doctors to the three clinics is completely determined if which one of the following pairs of doctors is assigned to Clinic 2?

Characterizing the answer choices is straightforward in Completely Determine questions. The correct answer is the only one that, if true, provides a complete solution to the game (all entities sequenced, distributed, matched, or selected). The wrong answer choices all leave one or more of the entities' placements undetermined.

Unfortunately, there is usually no way to avoid testing the answer choices one by one, usually by making new sketches. Nonetheless, you can be strategic by testing certain entities first. Because they are the hardest entities to pin down in any game, an unrestricted *floater* entity is often your prime suspect. Test any answer choice that establishes the placement of a floater first. If it completely determines the game's arrangement, you're done.

If none of the answer choices places a floater, or if the answer choice(s) placing a floater doesn't completely determine the arrangement, move on to answer choices placing entities that restrict numerous other entities. For example, imagine you have the following rules in a Strict Sequencing game:

> P will speak sometime after S, but sometime before L.
> P and M will deliver consecutive speeches.

S... M/P ...L

Here, the placement of M or P is much more likely to completely the determine the sequence than are the placements of S or L. Establishing the position of S or L might force the string of entities to move into earlier or later positions, but will not determine the order of M and P. A strategic test taker would evaluate answer choices establishing the position of M or P before evaluating answer choices that address S or L.

You actually used the same reasoning skills associated with Completely Determine questions in the Practice exercise in Chapter 1. Take a look back at question 15 in that exercise, the one that asked "Placing Engle in which slot would completely determine the team's pitching rotation?" The explanation for that question illustrates an analysis identical to what you would use for a Completely Determine question.

Numerical Questions

In earlier chapters, you saw several ways in which the the number restrictions on a game's setup could help you set up a game, make deductions, and answer questions. Numerical questions focus directly on the number limits within a game.

Minimum/Maximum Questions

The test might, for example, ask you to determine the minimum or maximum number of entities that may be selected (in a Selection game) or placed within a certain group (in a Distribution game, for instance). The question stem will be worded more or less like this one:

> What is the maximum number of employees who may be selected for the company retreat?

A question like this one would, of course, be part of the question set for a Selection game. You will use your expertise in Formal Logic to determine the maximum number of students you could choose. Any rule of the type "If A →~B" reduces the maximum number of entities that may be selected. Rules in that pattern translate to "Never AB."

Because you must exclude one of the two entities, the maximum available for selection has been reduced by one. On the flip side, rules fitting the pattern "If ~C → D" establish that at least one of C and D must be selected and so increase the minimum by one. (See Chapter 6 on Formal Logic and Selection games; there, you'll also find a Special Feature on the types of rules that decrease the maximum or increase the minimum number of entities that may be selected.)

The answer choices are always listed in numerical order, either lowest to highest or the other way around. The correct answer cites the precise minimum or maximum number. The wrong answers are either too high or too low.

In terms of strategy, you will always be able to use the rules to establish the minimum or maximum number of entities selected or placed within a particular group. Figure out that number and select the correct answer choice.

It is also possible that you will see a variant of the Minimum/Maximum question that has a New-"If" condition. Here's an example:

> If Milos is chosen to attend the company retreat, what is the maximum number of employees who could be chosen to attend the retreat?

Treat the first part of a question like that one just as you would a conventional New-"If" question. Copy the Master Sketch next to the question, add the new condition, and make any newly available deductions. Use the resulting sketch to determine what the correct answer will be.

On tests released from 2014 to 2018, there was only one Minimum/Maximum questions, and it had a New-"If" condition preceding the question.

Earliest/Latest Questions

In Sequencing games (and Hybrid games with a Sequencing action), you may see a similar question type: the Earliest/Latest question. The question stems are straightforward:

> The earliest that Kim's appointment could be scheduled is

The correct answer gives the precise position that represents the earliest or latest that the entity in question may appear. The incorrect answers are either too early or too late. Like those in Minimum/Maximum questions, the answer choices will be arranged in order, in this case from earliest to latest.

Treat these questions just as you would a Minimum/Maximum question. Simply consult the Master Sketch to determine the correct answer. Keep in mind that you could see a New-"If" variation of this question type, too.

Earliest/Latest questions are easy to understand, and if you've made all of the deductions during Step 4 of the Logic Games Method, they can turn into a quick point on test day. It's too bad you're not more likely to see one. On released tests from 2012 to 2016, there were only two Earliest/Latest questions.

"How Many" Questions

These questions ask you about numbers that can be firmly established in the game. There's little chance you'll misinterpret one of these stems. They tend to be extremely straightforward:

> How many of the interviews are there that could be the one given on Tuesday morning?

> How many of the dentist's patients are there any one of whom could be scheduled for an appointment at 1:00 PM?

> Exactly how many of the state senators are there any one of whom could be assigned to the Highways committee?

The correct answer gives the correct number, and the four wrong answers are either too high or too low. After consulting the Master Sketch, you should be able to predict the correct answer precisely before evaluating the choices.

Refresh (Activate Prior Knowledge)

The question set for the Truck Arrivals game featured one "How Many" question. Take a few minutes to review the LSAT expert's analysis. Note how the expert was able to determine the correct answer before checking the answer choices.

In a single day, exactly seven trucks—S, T, U, W, X, Y, and Z—are the only arrivals at a warehouse. No truck arrives at the same time as any other truck, and no truck arrives more than once that day. Each truck is either green or red (but not both). The following conditions apply:

No two consecutive arrivals are red.
Y arrives at some time before both T and W.
Exactly two of the trucks that arrive before Y are red.
S is the sixth arrival.
Z arrives at some time before U.

PrepTest37 Sec3 Q10

Step 5: A "How Many" question: Use the Master Sketch to determine the value of the correct answer.

5. For exactly how many of the seven trucks can one determine exactly how many trucks arrived before it?

(A) One
(B) two
(C) three
(D) four
(E) five

Step 5 (cont.): (B) is correct; The placements of Trucks S and Y are completely determined. Rule 4 established the placement of Truck S. Combining Rule 2 with Rules 1 and 4 established that Truck Y must take slot 4. Those are the only two trucks whose placement is determined once and for all.

Steps 1–4:

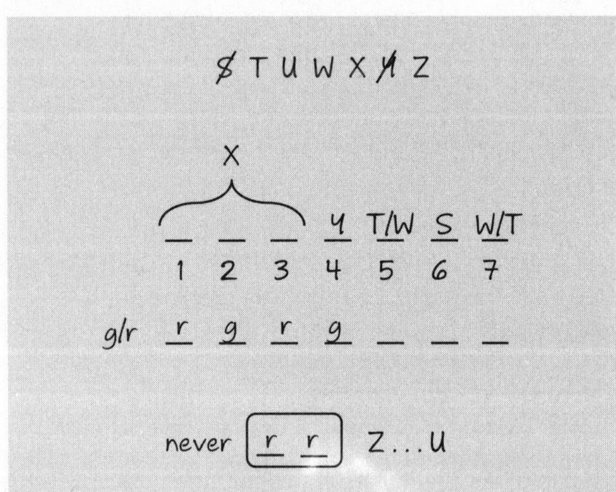

Among the tests released between 2014 and 2018 (with a total of 345 Logic Games questions), there were ten "How Many" questions, four of which were of the New-"If" variety. Here's an example:

If Dr. Shelby is assigned to Clinic 2, exactly how many of the doctors are assigned to Clinic 1?

Should you encounter one of these questions in practice or on test day, treat the first clause of the question stem as you would any other New-"If" question. Copy the Master Sketch, add in the new condition, and make all newly available deductions. Consult the resulting sketch to determine the correct answer.

Rule Alteration Questions

Some tests feature no questions from this subcategory, and historically, those that do almost always have exactly one. That's good news because these questions tend to be difficult for most test takers, and they are time-consuming even for those who get them right.

Rule Substitution Questions

These questions didn't make their debut on the LSAT until PrepTest 57 (administered in June 2009). Since that time, there has been exactly one on each released administration of the exam except for PrepTests 60, 67, 68, and 79 (on which there were none), and PrepTest 71, 81, and 83 (on which there were two). In a Rule Substitution question, the stem asks you to find a rule that would have the same effect on the game that one of the game's original rules has. For example:

> Which one of the following, if substituted for the condition that Barbara's appointment is later than Matt's appointment, would have the same effect on the game?

The correct answer will state a rule that has exactly the same effect on the game as the rule cited in the question stem. That is, the rule in the correct answer will restrict all of the entities restricted by the original rule, and in exactly the same ways. To illustrate this, imagine that the game associated with the model question stem had the following rules:

> Barbara's appointment is later than Matt's appointment.
> Matt and Rebekkah have consecutive appointments.

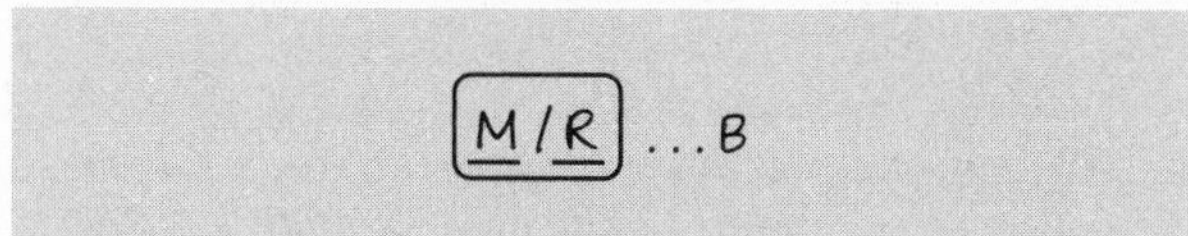

In that case, an answer choice that stated "Rebekkah's appointment is earlier than Barbara's appointment" would have precisely the same effect on the game as the rule cited in the question stem, and would be correct. The rules stated in the four wrong answers will leave something restricted by the original rule unrestricted, or will over-restrict the entities in a way that the original rule did not.

To answer these questions, consult the original rule within the context of the Master Sketch. Ask which entities it explicitly restricts, and which entities it restricts as a result of additional deductions. Then test the answer choices by substituting them for the rule in question. If an answer choice does not create the same restrictions for all entities concerned (or if it over-restricts them), eliminate it. Once you find the rule that produces the exact effects produced by the original rule, you're done.

Analyzing the effect of the rules stated in the answer choices can be complicated, and sometimes, you'll need to redraw the sketch to work out the new rule's exact effects. That's a good way to proceed, but it can become time consuming. If the work required to answer a Rule Substitution question threatens to cut into the time you'll need to tackle additional games, your best strategy may be to guess and move on. Never take so much time answering one question that you run out of time for five to ten additional questions on later games.

Rule Change Questions

In times past, Rule Change questions were more common than they have been in recent years. In fact, between 2014 and 2018, there were no Rule Change questions among all 60 released logic games. (It seems possible that Rule Substitution questions have replaced them permanently.) There's a strong chance that you won't encounter a question of this type on test day. On the off chance that you do—every once in a while, the testmaker brings back questions or games that have not been used in a long time—here's what you should know. Rule Change question stems tell you to ignore one of the rules cited in the game's setup and to use another rule (described in the stem) instead. Then, based on these altered circumstances, the stem will usually pose a Must Be/Could Be-type question. Here is an example that you will work with shortly in the Practice section of this chapter:

Assume that the original condition that the linen dress hangs immediately to the right of the silk dress is replaced by the condition that the wool dress hangs immediately to the right of the silk dress. If all the other initial conditions remain in effect, which one of the following must be false?

PrepTest 41 Sec2 Q7

Notice that the question stem's final clause tells you how to characterize the answer choices. In this case, treat the answer choices just as you would in a Must Be False question.

Since the opening sentence of the question stem changes the game's rules, you can think of Rule Change questions as a cousin of the New-"If" question. The main difference is that New-"If" questions add an additional restriction while preserving the original rules, whereas Rule Change questions alter or suspend one of the original rules. Should you happen across a Rule Change question, your instinct should be to create a new sketch and consult it as you evaluate the answer choices. Just make sure you actively undo the part of the Master Sketch suspended in the Rule Change question stem along with any deductions you drew using that rule.

Supply the "If" Questions

There's one more very rare question type: the Supply the "If" question. Between 2012 and 2016, there was only one of these questions among the 60 logic games released by the LSAC. It is pretty unlikely that you'll see one. If you do, you can recognize it from question stems like these:

> Joanna's appointment must be at 4:00 PM if which one of the following is true?

> Team H will compete later than Team J if which one of the following is true?

Perhaps the best way to think about these unusual questions is that they are New-"If" questions in reverse. The question stem gives you the necessary result and asks you for the sufficient condition. Thus, the correct answer will supply a condition that ensures the result cited in the question stem. The four wrong answers will supply conditions in which the result cited in the question stem could be false.

LSAT experts know that the best approach is to use the Master Sketch to see the possibilities for the entity or slot in question, and then use that analysis to determine the kind of additional restriction that would guarantee the desired result.

As you've learned, the questions covered in this "Other Question Types" section are not common. You're best served by trying these questions if and when they appear among your practice games and tests but not by spending time trying to find more examples of them in older tests. It is your facility with Acceptability, Must Be/Could Be, and New-"If" questions that will make or break your LSAT logic games performance. In contrast, you'll likely see only a single example of one or two of these rare question types on your official LSAT. If you do, analyze the question stem patiently, consult your Master Sketch, and remember that the testmaker always includes all of the information you need to answer every question the test asks.

Practice

Now it's time to practice what you've learned about Logic Games questions. There are three Practice sets. The first is an exercise with 12 question stems. For each stem, you will need to identify the question type, characterize the correct and incorrect answers, and note how to answer the question strategically. The second and third practice sets are the full question sets for two officially released logic games that you have worked with in previous chapters, in which you can practice answering the questions in context.

Expert analysis follows the third Practice set.

Practice 1

Directions: Read the question stems and provide the following analyses: 1) identify the question type, 2) characterize the one correct and four incorrect answer choices, and 3) outline the strategy to answer the question efficiently and effectively. For this Practice set, take your time and answer each question thoroughly.

Question		Analysis
1. If the acrobat is wearing a yellow jacket, which of the following must be true?	→	
2. Which of the following could be an acceptable schedule of the doctor's appointments from first through seventh?	→	
3. If the brown vase is in position 2, then what is the maximum number of vases that could be in position 5?	→	
4. Each of the following could be true EXCEPT	→	
5. Which of the following is a complete and accurate list of the participants, any one of whom could attend the conference on Day 1?	→	
6. If Emerson gives the fifth audition, which of the following could be true?	→	
7. Which of the following dishes must be selected?	→	

8. If K is in position 4, which of the following CANNOT be in position 6? →

9. Which of the following, if true, would completely determine the order of the houses from left to right? →

10. Which of the following could be a complete and accurate ranking of the songs from most to least popular? →

11. Which of the following, if substituted for the condition that Johnson must perform after Landry, would have the same effect in determining the order of the performances? →

12. If pasta is one of the dishes selected, which of the following dishes could be excluded? →

Practice 2

Directions: You have seen this game's setup, rules, and deductions in the preceding chapters of this book. First, review the Master Sketch and reconstruct the work you did in Steps 1-4 of the Logic Games Method. Then, answer the game's questions. For practice, take time to analyze each question thoroughly and enter your analysis for each step and answer choice blank. Complete worked example expert analysis can be found in your online resources.

Question 1:

A closet contains exactly six hangers—1, 2, 3, 4, 5, and 6—hanging, in that order, from left to right. It also contains exactly six dresses—one gauze, one linen, one polyester, one rayon, one silk, and one wool—a different dress on each of the hangers, in an order satisfying the following conditions:

The gauze dress is on a lower-numbered hanger than the polyester dress.
The rayon dress is on hanger 1 or hanger 6.
Either the wool dress or the silk dress is on hanger 3.
The linen dress hangs immediately to the right of the silk dress.

PrepTest41 Sec2 Q1

Steps 1–4:

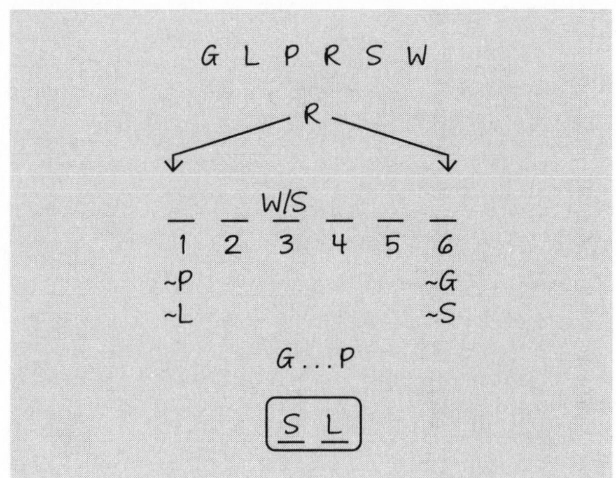

Step 5:

1. Which one of the following could be an accurate matching of the hangers to the fabrics of the dresses that hang on them?

(A) 1: wool; 2: gauze; 3: silk; 4: linen; 5: polyester; 6: rayon
(B) 1: rayon; 2: wool; 3: gauze; 4: silk; 5: linen; 6: polyester
(C) 1: polyester; 2: gauze; 3: wool; 4: silk; 5: linen; 6: rayon
(D) 1: linen; 2: silk; 3: wool; 4: gauze; 5: polyester; 6: rayon
(E) 1: gauze; 2: rayon; 3: silk; 4: linen; 5: wool; 6: polyester

Step 5 (cont.):

Question 2:

Step 5:

A closet contains exactly six hangers—1, 2, 3, 4, 5, and 6—hanging, in that order, from left to right. It also contains exactly six dresses—one gauze, one linen, one polyester, one rayon, one silk, and one wool—a different dress on each of the hangers, in an order satisfying the following conditions:

The gauze dress is on a lower-numbered hanger than the polyester dress.
The rayon dress is on hanger 1 or hanger 6.
Either the wool dress or the silk dress is on hanger 3.
The linen dress hangs immediately to the right of the silk dress.

PrepTest41 Sec2 Q2

2. If both the silk dress and the gauze dress are on odd-numbered hangers, then which one of the following could be true?

(A) The polyester dress is on hanger 1.
(B) The wool dress is on hanger 2.
(C) The polyester dress is on hanger 4.
(D) The linen dress is on hanger 5.
(E) The wool dress is on hanger 6.

Step 5 (cont.):

Steps 1–4:

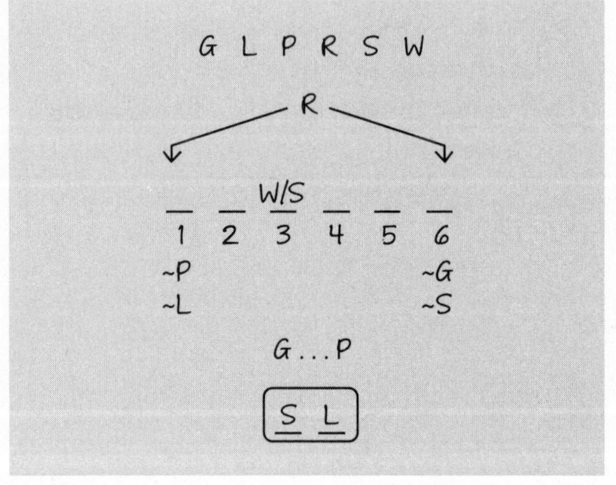

Question 3:

Step 5:

A closet contains exactly six hangers—1, 2, 3, 4, 5, and 6—hanging, in that order, from left to right. It also contains exactly six dresses—one gauze, one linen, one polyester, one rayon, one silk, and one wool—a different dress on each of the hangers, in an order satisfying the following conditions:

The gauze dress is on a lower-numbered hanger than the polyester dress.
The rayon dress is on hanger 1 or hanger 6.
Either the wool dress or the silk dress is on hanger 3.
The linen dress hangs immediately to the right of the silk dress.

PrepTest41 Sec2 Q3

3. If the silk dress is on an even-numbered hanger, which one of the following could be on the hanger immediately to its left?
   (A) the gauze dress
   (B) the linen dress
   (C) the polyester dress
   (D) the rayon dress
   (E) the wool dress

Step 5 (cont.):

Steps 1–4:

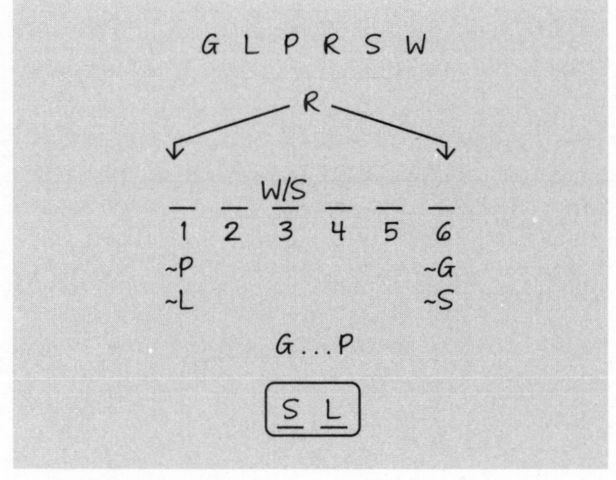

Question 4:

A closet contains exactly six hangers—1, 2, 3, 4, 5, and 6—hanging, in that order, from left to right. It also contains exactly six dresses—one gauze, one linen, one polyester, one rayon, one silk, and one wool—a different dress on each of the hangers, in an order satisfying the following conditions:

The gauze dress is on a lower-numbered hanger than the polyester dress.
The rayon dress is on hanger 1 or hanger 6.
Either the wool dress or the silk dress is on hanger 3.
The linen dress hangs immediately to the right of the silk dress.

PrepTest41 Sec2 Q4

Steps 1–4:

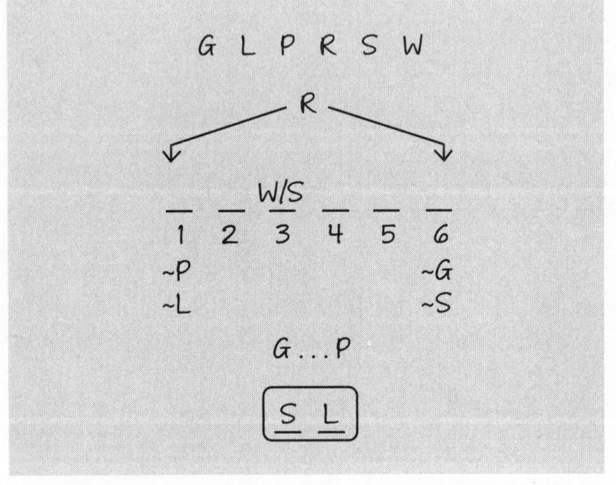

Step 5:

4. If the polyester dress is on hanger 2, then which one of the following must be true?

(A) The silk dress is on hanger 1.
(B) The wool dress is on hanger 3.
(C) The linen dress is on hanger 4.
(D) The linen dress is on hanger 5.
(E) The rayon dress is on hanger 6.

Step 5 (cont.):

Question 5:

Step 5:

A closet contains exactly six hangers—1, 2, 3, 4, 5, and 6—hanging, in that order, from left to right. It also contains exactly six dresses—one gauze, one linen, one polyester, one rayon, one silk, and one wool—a different dress on each of the hangers, in an order satisfying the following conditions:

The gauze dress is on a lower-numbered hanger than the polyester dress.

The rayon dress is on hanger 1 or hanger 6.

Either the wool dress or the silk dress is on hanger 3.

The linen dress hangs immediately to the right of the silk dress.

PrepTest41 Sec2 Q5

5. Which one of the following CANNOT be true?

(A) The linen dress hangs immediately next to the gauze dress.

(B) The polyester dress hangs immediately to the right of the rayon dress.

(C) The rayon dress hangs immediately to the left of the wool dress.

(D) The silk dress is on a lower-numbered hanger than the gauze dress.

(E) The wool dress is on a higher-numbered hanger than the rayon dress.

Steps 1–4:

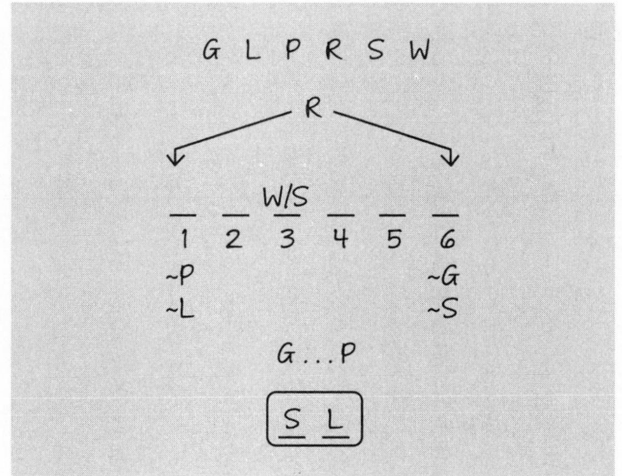

Step 5 (cont.):

Question 6:

Step 5:

A closet contains exactly six hangers—1, 2, 3, 4, 5, and 6—hanging, in that order, from left to right. It also contains exactly six dresses—one gauze, one linen, one polyester, one rayon, one silk, and one wool—a different dress on each of the hangers, in an order satisfying the following conditions:

The gauze dress is on a lower-numbered hanger than the polyester dress.

The rayon dress is on hanger 1 or hanger 6.

Either the wool dress or the silk dress is on hanger 3.

The linen dress hangs immediately to the right of the silk dress.

PrepTest41 Sec2 Q6

6. Which one of the following CANNOT hang immediately next to the rayon dress?

(A) the gauze dress

(B) the linen dress

(C) the polyester dress

(D) the silk dress

(E) the wool dress

Step 5 (cont.):

Steps 1–4:

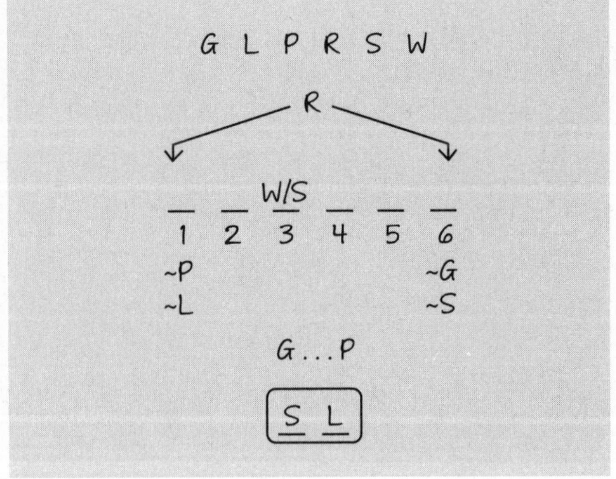

Question 7:

Step 5:

A closet contains exactly six hangers—1, 2, 3, 4, 5, and 6—hanging, in that order, from left to right. It also contains exactly six dresses—one gauze, one linen, one polyester, one rayon, one silk, and one wool—a different dress on each of the hangers, in an order satisfying the following conditions:

The gauze dress is on a lower-numbered hanger than the polyester dress.
The rayon dress is on hanger 1 or hanger 6.
Either the wool dress or the silk dress is on hanger 3.
The linen dress hangs immediately to the right of the silk dress.

PrepTest41 Sec2 Q7

7. Assume that the original condition that the linen dress hangs immediately to the right of the silk dress is replaced by the condition that the wool dress hangs immediately to the right of the silk dress. If all the other initial conditions remain in effect, which one of the following must be false?

(A) The linen dress is on hanger 1.
(B) The gauze dress is on hanger 2.
(C) The wool dress is on hanger 4.
(D) The silk dress is on hanger 5.
(E) The polyester dress is on hanger 6.

Steps 1–4:

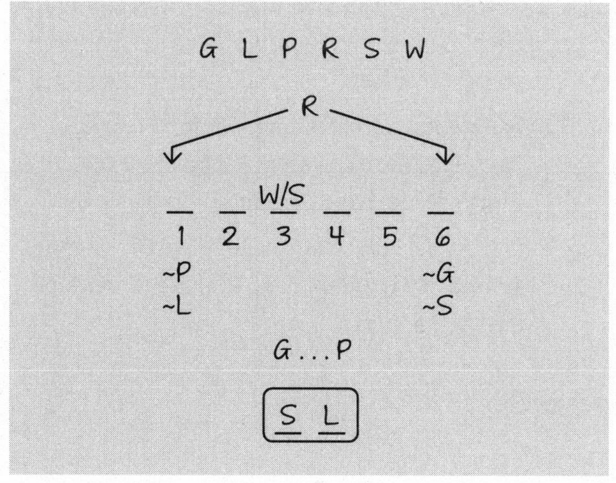

Step 5 (cont.):

Practice 3

Directions: You have seen this game's setup, rules, and deductions in the preceding chapters of this book. First, review the Master Sketch and reconstruct the work you did in Steps 1–4 of the Logic Games Method. Then, answer the game's questions. For practice, take time to analyze each question thoroughly and enter your analysis for each step and answer choice blank. Complete worked example expert analysis can be found in your online resources.

Question 1:

Step 5:

Exactly six people—Lulu, Nam, Ofelia, Pachai, Santiago, and Tyrone—are the only contestants in a chess tournament. The tournament consists of four games, played one after the other. Exactly two people play in each game, and each person plays in at least one game. The following conditions must apply:

Tyrone does not play in the first or third game.
Lulu plays in the last game.
Nam plays in only one game and it is not against Pachai.
Santiago plays in exactly two games, one just before and one just after the only game that Ofelia plays in.

PrepTest45 Sec3 Q7

Steps 1–4:

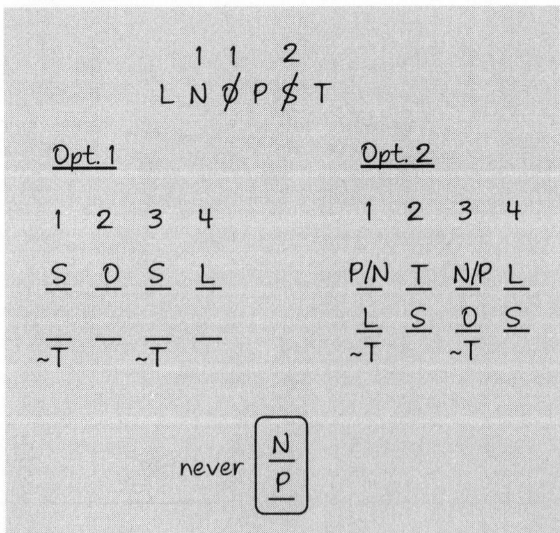

1. Which one of the following could be an accurate list of the contestants who play in each of the four games?

(A) first game: Pachai, Santiago; second game: Ofelia, Tyrone; third game: Pachai, Santiago; fourth game: Lulu, Nam

(B) first game: Lulu, Nam; second game: Pachai, Santiago; third game: Ofelia, Tyrone; fourth game: Lulu, Santiago

(C) first game: Pachai, Santiago; second game: Lulu, Tyrone; third game: Nam, Ofelia; fourth game: Lulu, Nam

(D) first game: Nam, Santiago; second game: Nam, Ofelia; third game: Pachai, Santiago; fourth game: Lulu, Tyrone

(E) first game: Lulu, Nam; second game: Santiago, Tyrone; third game: Lulu, Ofelia; fourth game: Pachai, Santiago

Step 5 (cont.):

Question 2:

Step 5:

Exactly six people—Lulu, Nam, Ofelia, Pachai, Santiago, and Tyrone—are the only contestants in a chess tournament. The tournament consists of four games, played one after the other. Exactly two people play in each game, and each person plays in at least one game. The following conditions must apply:

Tyrone does not play in the first or third game.
Lulu plays in the last game.
Nam plays in only one game and it is not against Pachai.
Santiago plays in exactly two games, one just before and one just after the only game that Ofelia plays in.

PrepTest45 Sec3 Q7

Steps 1–4:

1 1 2
L N Ø P $ T

Opt. 1

1	2	3	4
S	O	S	L
~T		~T	

Opt. 2

1	2	3	4
P/N	T	N/P	L
L	S	O	S
~T		~T	

never N/P

2. Which one of the following contestants could play in two consecutive games?

(A) Lulu
(B) Nam
(C) Ofelia
(D) Santiago
(E) Tyrone

Step 5 (cont.):

Question 3:

Step 5:

Exactly six people—Lulu, Nam, Ofelia, Pachai, Santiago, and Tyrone—are the only contestants in a chess tournament. The tournament consists of four games, played one after the other. Exactly two people play in each game, and each person plays in at least one game. The following conditions must apply:

Tyrone does not play in the first or third game.
Lulu plays in the last game.
Nam plays in only one game and it is not against Pachai.
Santiago plays in exactly two games, one just before and one just after the only game that Ofelia plays in.

PrepTest45 Sec3 Q9

3. If Tyrone plays in the fourth game, then which one of the following could be true?
   (A) Nam plays in the second game.
   (B) Ofelia plays in the third game.
   (C) Santiago plays in the second game.
   (D) Nam plays a game against Lulu.
   (E) Pachai plays a game against Lulu.

Step 5 (cont.):

Steps 1–4:

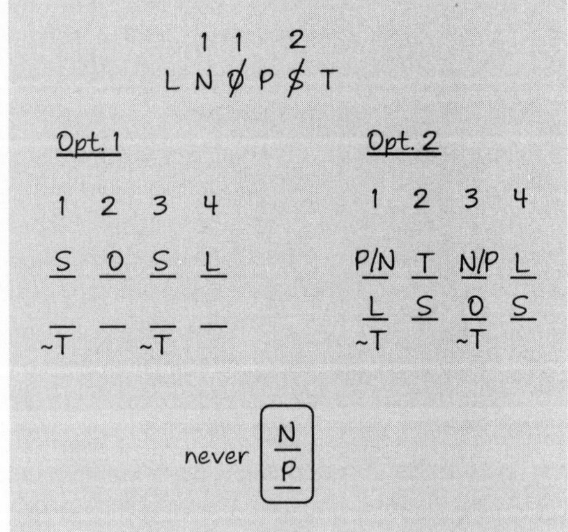

Question 4:

Step 5:

Exactly six people—Lulu, Nam, Ofelia, Pachai, Santiago, and Tyrone—are the only contestants in a chess tournament. The tournament consists of four games, played one after the other. Exactly two people play in each game, and each person plays in at least one game. The following conditions must apply:

Tyrone does not play in the first or third game.
Lulu plays in the last game.
Nam plays in only one game and it is not against Pachai.
Santiago plays in exactly two games, one just before and one just after the only game that Ofelia plays in.

PrepTest45 Sec3 Q10

Steps 1–4:

1 1 2
L N Ø P S̸ T

Opt. 1

1	2	3	4
S	O	S	L
__	__	__	__
~T		~T	

Opt. 2

1	2	3	4
P/N	T	N/P	L
L	S	O	S
~T		~T	

never N/P

4. Which one of the following could be true?

(A) Pachai plays against Lulu in the first game.
(B) Pachai plays against Nam in the second game.
(C) Santiago plays against Ofelia in the second game.
(D) Pachai plays against Lulu in the third game.
(E) Nam plays against Santiago in the fourth game.

Step 5 (cont.):

Question 5:

Step 5:

Exactly six people—Lulu, Nam, Ofelia, Pachai, Santiago, and Tyrone—are the only contestants in a chess tournament. The tournament consists of four games, played one after the other. Exactly two people play in each game, and each person plays in at least one game. The following conditions must apply:

Tyrone does not play in the first or third game.

Lulu plays in the last game.

Nam plays in only one game and it is not against Pachai.

Santiago plays in exactly two games, one just before and one just after the only game that Ofelia plays in.

PrepTest45 Sec3 Q11

5. Which one of the following is a complete and accurate list of the contestants who CANNOT play against Tyrone in any game?

   (A) Lulu, Pachai
   (B) Nam, Ofelia
   (C) Nam, Pachai
   (D) Nam, Santiago
   (E) Ofelia, Pachai

Step 5 (cont.):

Steps 1–4:

1 1 2
L N Ø P S̸ T

Opt. 1

1	2	3	4
S	O	S	L
__	__	__	__
~T		~T	

Opt. 2

1	2	3	4
P/N	T	N/P	L
L	S	O	S
~T		~T	

never N/P

Question 6:

Step 5:

Exactly six people—Lulu, Nam, Ofelia, Pachai, Santiago, and Tyrone—are the only contestants in a chess tournament. The tournament consists of four games, played one after the other. Exactly two people play in each game, and each person plays in at least one game. The following conditions must apply:

Tyrone does not play in the first or third game.

Lulu plays in the last game.

Nam plays in only one game and it is not against Pachai.

Santiago plays in exactly two games, one just before and one just after the only game that Ofelia plays in.

PrepTest45 Sec3 Q12

Steps 1–4:

1 1 2
L N Ø P $ T

Opt. 1

1	2	3	4
S	O	S	L
__	__	__	__
~T		~T	

Opt. 2

1	2	3	4
P/N	T	N/P	L
L	S	O	S
~T		~T	

never N/P

5. If Ofelia plays in the third game, which one of the following must be true?

(A) Lulu plays in the third game.

(B) Nam plays in the third game.

(C) Pachai plays in the first game.

(D) Pachai plays in the third game.

(E) Tyrone plays in the second game.

Step 5 (cont.):

Explanations

Compare your work to that of an LSAT expert. Pay close attention to how the expert identified each question type, characterized the one correct and four incorrect answer choices, and chose the best strategy for answering the question efficiently and effectively.

Practice 1

Question		Analysis
1. If the acrobat is wearing a yellow jacket, which of the following must be true?	→	Q-type: New-"If"/Must Be True. Correct answer: must be true; four incorrect choices: could be or must be false. Strategy: Create a new sketch, add the rule from the stem, and make any deductions. The correct answer will be something that is drawn into the new sketch or that must happen within the new sketch.
2. Which of the following could be an acceptable schedule of the doctor's appointments from first through seventh?	→	Q-type: Acceptability. Correct answer: could be true; four incorrect choices: must be false. Strategy: Apply the rules one by one; four incorrect choices violate one or more rules (or, in rare cases, a deduction). The one remaining choice will be correct.
3. If the brown vase is in position 2, what is the maximum number of vases that could be in position 5?	→	Q-type: New-"If"/Maximum. Correct answer: the total number of entities that can be in position 5. Strategy: Create a new sketch, add the rule from the stem, and make any deductions. Determine which entities *cannot* be in position 5 given the new If, in order to determine how many (i.e., the remaining entities) *could* be.
4. Each of the following could be true EXCEPT	→	Q-type: Must Be False. Correct answer: must be false; four incorrect choices: could be true. Strategy: Find a choice that is impossible in the Master Sketch (the correct answer), or use previous work to eliminate choices that could be true (four incorrect choices).
5. Which of the following is a complete and accurate list of the participants, any one of whom could attend the conference on Day 1?	→	Q-type: Complete and Accurate List. The correct answer will list all of the entities who could attend the conference on Day 1, and only those entities. The incorrect choices will include entities who could not attend the conference on Day 1, or exclude entities who could. Strategy: Save for later in the game, after the New-"If" questions. Use previous work to eliminate choices.
6. If Emerson gives the fifth audition, which of the following could be true?	→	Q-type: New-"If"/Could Be True. Correct answer: could be true, given the new If; four wrong choices: must be false. Strategy: Create a new sketch, add the rule from the stem, and make any deductions. Compare the choices to the sketch, eliminating the four that are impossible given the question's new condition.

Question		Analysis
7. Which of the following dishes must be selected?	→	Q-type: Must Be True. In this case, "true" means "included." The correct answer is an entity that must be included according to the game's rules and restrictions; four incorrect choices are entities that could be excluded. Strategy: Look for a deduction made in the Master Sketch, or use previous work to eliminate the choices that could be "false," or excluded.
8. If K is in position 4, which of the following CANNOT be in position 6?	→	Q-type: New-"If"/Must Be False. Correct answer: an entity that cannot be in position 6; four incorrect choices: entities that could be in position 6. Strategy: Create a new sketch, add the rule from the stem, and make any deductions. Eliminate the choices that list entities acceptable for position 6.
9. Which of the following, if true, would completely determine the order of the houses from left to right?	→	Q-type: Completely Determine. Correct answer will allow for only one possible placement for each entity, while four incorrect choices will allow for multiple possibilities. Strategy: Test answer choices, starting with choices that definitively place any floaters.
10. Which of the following could be a complete and accurate ranking of the songs from most to least popular?	→	Q-type: Acceptability (if ranking is the only action) or Partial Acceptability (if it is a Hybrid that requires you to rank the songs and then match some attribute to each one). Correct answer is a possible ranking; four wrong choices violate one or more rules. Strategy: Apply the rules one by one; eliminate the answer choices that violate each rule.
11. Which of the following, if substituted for the condition that Johnson must perform after Landry, would have the same effect in determining the order of the performances?	→	Q-type: Rule Substitution. The correct answer will have exactly the same effect on the game as the original rule, while wrong answer choices will either restrict an entity or placement not restricted by the original rule, or fail to restrict an entity in the same way that the original rule does. Strategy: Do this one last in the set, or even consider skipping it if short on time.
12. If pasta is one of the dishes selected, which of the following dishes could be excluded?	→	Q-type: New-"If"/Could Be False. The correct answer is an entity that does not have to be selected; the four incorrect choices are entities that must be selected, given the new If. Strategy: Create a new sketch, add the rule from the stem, and make any deductions. Compare the choices to the sketch, eliminating those that must be selected.

Practice 2

Answer Key

1. (A)
2. (B)
3. (E)
4. (E)
5. (B)
6. (D)
7. (D)

Practice 3

Answer Key

1. (A)
2. (A)
3. (A)
4. (A)
5. (C)
6. (E)

Worked example explanations of these questions with complete expert analysis can be found in your Online Study Plan under Chapter 4. View or download the PDF titled "Chapter 4 Practice Full Games Explanations."

Perform

Now, assess your skill level in the strategies and tactics associated with answering logic games questions.

Perform 1

Directions: Take no more than 12 minutes to read the question stems and provide the following analyses: 1) identify the question type, 2) characterize the one correct and four incorrect answer choices, and 3) outline the strategy to answer the question efficiently and **effectively.**

Question		Analysis
1. If Holmes does not travel to Norway, which of the following could be true?	→	
2. Which of the following is NOT an acceptable matching of animals to habitats?	→	
3. Each of the following must be false EXCEPT	→	
4. If the fourth cake baked is chocolate, which of the following CANNOT be the first cake baked?	→	
5. What are the minimum and maximum numbers of people who can serve on the Board at the same time?	→	
6. Which of the following could be a complete and accurate list of the projects assigned to Group A?	→	

Question		Analysis
7. If the fourth phone call is from Lisa, which of the following must be true?	→	
8. If no cars of the same color can be placed consecutively, then in exactly how many distinct orders can the cars be arranged?	→	
9. The matching of tutors to students would be completely determined if which of the following were true?	→	
10. If roses are not selected, what is the maximum number of flowers that can be in the bouquet?	→	
11. Suppose that the condition that Ames and Barnes serve on the same committee is replaced with a condition stating that Ames and Barnes may not serve on the same committee. If all other conditions remain the same, which of the following must be true?	→	
12. Suppose that J can never be the fourth audition and K can never be the first audition. Which of the following must be false?	→	

Perform 2

Directions: You have seen this game's setup, rules, and deductions in the preceding chapters of this book. Take two minutes to review the Master Sketch and reconstruct the work you did in Steps 1–4 of the Logic Games Method. Then, take no more than seven minutes to answer the game's questions. Complete worked example expert analysis can be found in your online resources.

Question 1:

Step 5:

On one afternoon, Patterson meets individually with each of exactly five clients—Reilly, Sanchez, Tang, Upton, and Yansky—and also goes to the gym by herself for a workout. Patterson's workout and her five meetings each start at either 1:00, 2:00, 3:00, 4:00, 5:00, or 6:00. The following conditions must apply:

Patterson meets with Sanchez at some time before her workout.

Patterson meets with Tang at some time after her workout.

Patterson meets with Yansky either immediately before or immediately after her workout.

Patterson meets with Upton at some time before she meets with Reilly.

PrepTest45 Sec3 Q1

Steps 1–4:

R S T U Y W

S/U	__	__	__	__	T/R
1	2	3	4	5	6
~T	~T	~T	~S	~S	~S
~W					~W
~Y					~Y
~R					~U

S... [W/Y] ...T

U...R

1. Which one of the following could be an acceptable schedule of Patterson's workout and meetings, in order from 1:00 to 6:00?

(A) Yansky, workout, Upton, Reilly, Sanchez, Tang
(B) Upton, Tang, Sanchez, Yansky, workout, Reilly
(C) Upton, Reilly, Sanchez, workout, Tang, Yansky
(D) Sanchez, Yansky, workout, Reilly, Tang, Upton
(E) Sanchez, Upton, workout, Yansky, Tang, Reilly

Step 5 (cont.):

Question 2:

Step 5:

On one afternoon, Patterson meets individually with each of exactly five clients—Reilly, Sanchez, Tang, Upton, and Yansky—and also goes to the gym by herself for a workout. Patterson's workout and her five meetings each start at either 1:00, 2:00, 3:00, 4:00, 5:00, or 6:00. The following conditions must apply:

Patterson meets with Sanchez at some time before her workout.

Patterson meets with Tang at some time after her workout.

Patterson meets with Yansky either immediately before or immediately after her workout.

Patterson meets with Upton at some time before she meets with Reilly.

PrepTest45 Sec3 Q2

Steps 1–4:

R S T U Y W

S/U	__	__	__	__	T/R
1	2	3	4	5	6
~T	~T	~T	~S	~S	~S
~W					~W
~Y					~Y
~R					~U

S... [W/Y] ...T

U...R

2. How many of the clients are there, any one of whom could meet with Patterson at 1:00?

(A) one

(B) two

(C) three

(D) four

(E) five

Step 5 (cont.):

Question 3:

Step 5:

On one afternoon, Patterson meets individually with each of exactly five clients—Reilly, Sanchez, Tang, Upton, and Yansky—and also goes to the gym by herself for a workout. Patterson's workout and her five meetings each start at either 1:00, 2:00, 3:00, 4:00, 5:00, or 6:00. The following conditions must apply:

Patterson meets with Sanchez at some time before her workout.

Patterson meets with Tang at some time after her workout.

Patterson meets with Yansky either immediately before or immediately after her workout.

Patterson meets with Upton at some time before she meets with Reilly.

PrepTest45 Sec3 Q3

3. Patterson CANNOT meet with Upton at which one of the following times?

   (A) 1:00
   (B) 2:00
   (C) 3:00
   (D) 4:00
   (E) 5:00

Step 5 (cont.):

Steps 1–4:

R S T U Y W

S/U	__	__	__	__	T/R
1	2	3	4	5	6
~T	~T	~T	~S	~S	~S
~W					~W
~Y					~Y
~R					~U

S... [W/Y] ...T

U...R

Question 4:

Step 5:

On one afternoon, Patterson meets individually with each of exactly five clients—Reilly, Sanchez, Tang, Upton, and Yansky—and also goes to the gym by herself for a workout. Patterson's workout and her five meetings each start at either 1:00, 2:00, 3:00, 4:00, 5:00, or 6:00. The following conditions must apply:

Patterson meets with Sanchez at some time before her workout.

Patterson meets with Tang at some time after her workout.

Patterson meets with Yansky either immediately before or immediately after her workout.

Patterson meets with Upton at some time before she meets with Reilly.

PrepTest45 Sec3 Q4

4. If Patterson meets with Sanchez the hour before she meets with Yansky, then each of the following could be true EXCEPT:

(A) Patterson meets with Reilly at 2:00.

(B) Patterson meets with Yansky at 3:00.

(C) Patterson meets with Tang at 4:00.

(D) Patterson meets with Yansky at 5:00.

(E) Patterson meets with Tang at 6:00.

Steps 1–4:

R S T U Y W

S/U _ _ _ _ T/R
1 2 3 4 5 6
~T ~T ~T ~S ~S ~S
~W ~W
~Y ~Y
~R ~U

S... [W/Y] ...T

U...R

Step 5 (cont.):

Question 5:

Step 5:

On one afternoon, Patterson meets individually with each of exactly five clients—Reilly, Sanchez, Tang, Upton, and Yansky—and also goes to the gym by herself for a workout. Patterson's workout and her five meetings each start at either 1:00, 2:00, 3:00, 4:00, 5:00, or 6:00. The following conditions must apply:

Patterson meets with Sanchez at some time before her workout.

Patterson meets with Tang at some time after her workout.

Patterson meets with Yansky either immediately before or immediately after her workout.

Patterson meets with Upton at some time before she meets with Reilly.

PrepTest45 Sec3 Q5

5. If Patterson meets with Tang at 4:00, then which one of the following must be true?

(A) Patterson meets with Reilly at 5:00.
(B) Patterson meets with Upton at 5:00.
(C) Patterson meets with Yansky at 2:00.
(D) Patterson meets with Yansky at 3:00.
(E) Patterson's workout is at 2:00.

Step 5 (cont.):

Steps 1–4:

R S T U Y W

S/U	__	__	__	__	T/R
1	2	3	4	5	6
~T	~T	~T	~S	~S	~S
~W					~W
~Y					~Y
~R					~U

S... [W/Y] ...T

U...R

Question 6:

Step 5:

On one afternoon, Patterson meets individually with each of exactly five clients—Reilly, Sanchez, Tang, Upton, and Yansky—and also goes to the gym by herself for a workout. Patterson's workout and her five meetings each start at either 1:00, 2:00, 3:00, 4:00, 5:00, or 6:00. The following conditions must apply:

Patterson meets with Sanchez at some time before her workout.

Patterson meets with Tang at some time after her workout.

Patterson meets with Yansky either immediately before or immediately after her workout.

Patterson meets with Upton at some time before she meets with Reilly.

PrepTest45 Sec3 Q6

6. Which one of the following could be the order of Patterson's meetings, from earliest to latest?

   (A) Upton, Yansky, Sanchez, Reilly, Tang
   (B) Upton, Reilly, Sanchez, Tang, Yansky
   (C) Sanchez, Yansky, Reilly, Tang, Upton
   (D) Sanchez, Upton, Tang, Yansky, Reilly
   (E) Sanchez, Upton, Reilly, Yansky, Tang

Step 5 (cont.):

Steps 1–4:

R S T U Y W

S/U	__	__	__	__	T/R
1	2	3	4	5	6
~T	~T	~T	~S	~S	~S
~W					~W
~Y					~Y
~R					~U

S . . . [W/Y] . . . T

U . . . R

Perform 3

Directions: You have seen this game's setup, rules, and deductions in the preceding chapters of this book. Take two minutes to review the Master Sketch and reconstruct the work you did in Steps 1-4 of the Logic Games Method. Then, take no more than seven minutes to answer the game's questions. Complete worked example expert analysis can be found in your online resources.

Question 1:

A showroom contains exactly six new cars—T, V, W, X, Y, and Z—each equipped with at least one of the following three options: power windows, leather interior, and sunroof. No car has any other options. The following conditions must apply:

V has power windows and a sunroof.
W has power windows and a leather interior.
W and Y have no options in common.
X has more options than W.
V and Z have exactly one option in common.
T has fewer options than Z.

PrepTest35 Sec3 Q6

Steps 1–4:

(1) T	V	W	X	Y	(2) Z
	(pw)	(pw)	(pw)	(sr)	(li)
	(sr)	(li)	(li)	~li	
	~li	~sr	(sr)	~pw	

pw or sr
not both

Step 5:

1. For exactly how many of the six cars is it possible to determine exactly which options each one has?

   (A) two
   (B) three
   (C) four
   (D) five
   (E) six

Step 5 (cont.):

Question 2:

Step 5:

A showroom contains exactly six new cars—T, V, W, X, Y, and Z—each equipped with at least one of the following three options: power windows, leather interior, and sunroof. No car has any other options. The following conditions must apply:

V has power windows and a sunroof.
W has power windows and a leather interior.
W and Y have no options in common.
X has more options than W.
V and Z have exactly one option in common.
T has fewer options than Z.

PrepTest35 Sec3 Q7

2. Which one of the following must be false?

   (A) Exactly five of the six cars have leather interiors.

   (B) Exactly five of the six cars have sunroofs.

   (C) Exactly four of the six cars have leather interiors.

   (D) Exactly four of the six cars have power windows.

   (E) Exactly four of the six cars have sunroofs.

Steps 1–4:

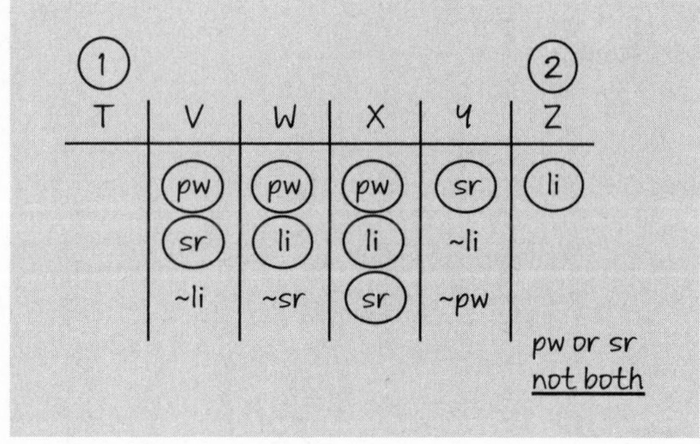

Step 5 (cont.):

Question 3:

Step 5:

A showroom contains exactly six new cars—T, V, W, X, Y, and Z—each equipped with at least one of the following three options: power windows, leather interior, and sunroof. No car has any other options. The following conditions must apply:

V has power windows and a sunroof.
W has power windows and a leather interior.
W and Y have no options in common.
X has more options than W.
V and Z have exactly one option in common.
T has fewer options than Z.

PrepTest35 Sec3 Q8

3. If all the cars that have leather interiors also have power windows, which one of the following must be false?

   (A) T has power windows.
   (B) T has a sunroof.
   (C) V has power windows.
   (D) Z has power windows.
   (E) Z has a sunroof.

Step 5 (cont.):

Steps 1–4:

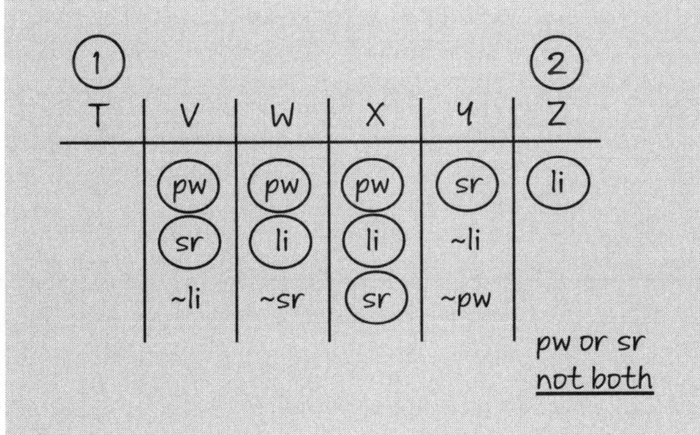

Question 4:

Step 5:

A showroom contains exactly six new cars—T, V, W, X, Y, and Z—each equipped with at least one of the following three options: power windows, leather interior, and sunroof. No car has any other options. The following conditions must apply:

V has power windows and a sunroof.
W has power windows and a leather interior.
W and Y have no options in common.
X has more options than W.
V and Z have exactly one option in common.
T has fewer options than Z.

PrepTest35 Sec3 Q9

4. If Z has no options in common with T but has at least one option in common with every other car, then which one of the following must be false?

(A) T has power windows.
(B) Z has a sunroof.
(C) Exactly four of the six cars have power windows.
(D) Exactly four of the six cars have leather interiors.
(E) Exactly four of the six cars have sunroofs.

Steps 1–4:

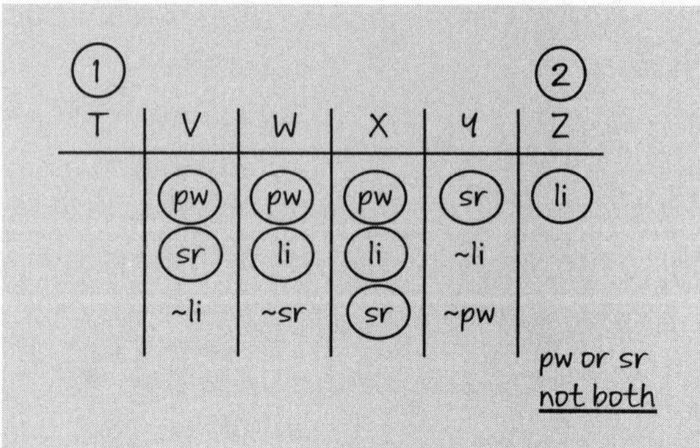

Step 5 (cont.):

Question 5:

Step 5:

A showroom contains exactly six new cars—T, V, W, X, Y, and Z—each equipped with at least one of the following three options: power windows, leather interior, and sunroof. No car has any other options. The following conditions must apply:

V has power windows and a sunroof.
W has power windows and a leather interior.
W and Y have no options in common.
X has more options than W.
V and Z have exactly one option in common.
T has fewer options than Z.

PrepTest35 Sec3 Q10

5. Suppose that no two cars have exactly the same options as one another. In that case, each of the following could be true EXCEPT:

   (A) Exactly three of the six cars have power windows.

   (B) Exactly four of the six cars have power windows.

   (C) Exactly three of the six cars have sunroofs.

   (D) Exactly four of the six cars have sunroofs.

   (E) Exactly four of the six cars have leather interiors.

Steps 1–4:

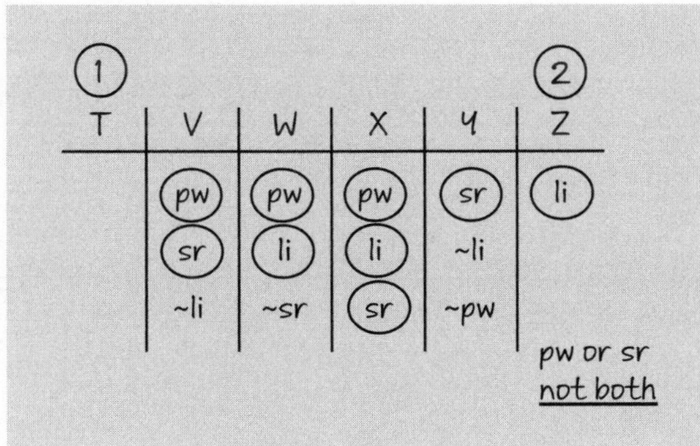

Step 5 (cont.):

Question 6:

Step 5:

A showroom contains exactly six new cars—T, V, W, X, Y, and Z—each equipped with at least one of the following three options: power windows, leather interior, and sunroof. No car has any other options. The following conditions must apply:

V has power windows and a sunroof.
W has power windows and a leather interior.
W and Y have no options in common.
X has more options than W.
V and Z have exactly one option in common.
T has fewer options than Z.

PrepTest35 Sec3 Q11

6. If exactly four of the six cars have leather interiors, and exactly four of the six cars have power windows, then each of the following must be true EXCEPT:

(A) T and V have no options in common.
(B) T and Y have no options in common.
(C) T and Z have exactly one option in common.
(D) W and Z have exactly one option in common.
(E) Y and Z have no options in common.

Step 5 (cont.):

Steps 1–4:

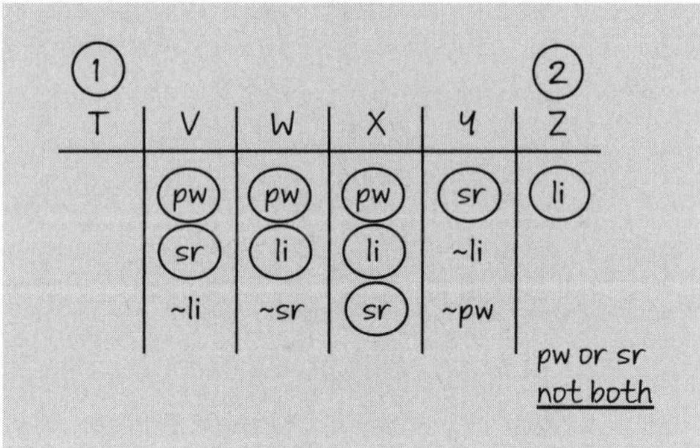

Question 7:

Step 5:

A showroom contains exactly six new cars—T, V, W, X, Y, and Z—each equipped with at least one of the following three options: power windows, leather interior, and sunroof. No car has any other options. The following conditions must apply:

V has power windows and a sunroof.
W has power windows and a leather interior.
W and Y have no options in common.
X has more options than W.
V and Z have exactly one option in common.
T has fewer options than Z.

PrepTest35 Sec3 Q12

Steps 1–4:

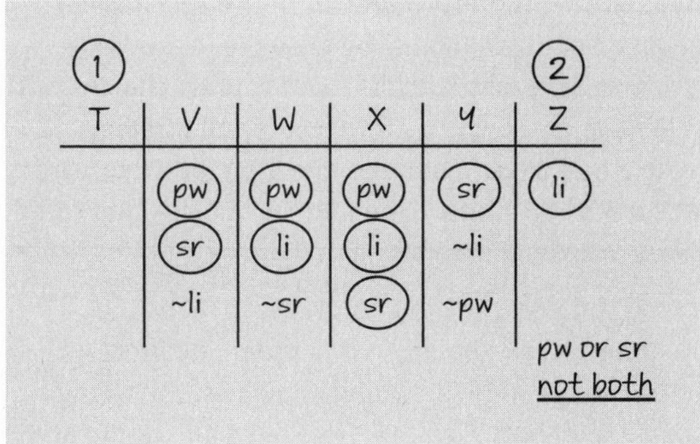

7. Suppose that the condition requiring that X has more options than W is replaced by a new condition requiring that X and W have exactly two options in common. If all of the other original conditions remain in effect, which one of the following must be false?

Ⓐ T and X have no options in common.
Ⓑ V and X have exactly one option in common.
Ⓒ V and X have exactly two options in common.
Ⓓ X and Z have no options in common.
Ⓔ X and Z have exactly two options in common.

Step 5 (cont.):

Explanations

Perform 1

Question		Analysis
1. If Holmes does not travel to Norway, which of the following could be true?	⟶	Q-type: New-"If"/Could Be True. Correct answer: could be true (given the new If); four incorrect choices: must be false. Strategy: Create a new sketch, add the rule from the stem, and make any deductions. Compare the choices to the sketch, eliminating the four that are impossible.
2. Which of the following is NOT an acceptable matching of animals to habitats?	⟶	Q-type: Acceptability EXCEPT. The correct answer violates one or more rules (i.e., must be false). The four incorrect choices could be true. Strategy: Test the rules one by one against the answer choices. If you don't find a rule violator, then check for a choice that violates a deduction.
3. Each of the following must be false EXCEPT	⟶	Q-type: Could Be True. Correct answer: could be or must be true; four incorrect choices: must be false. Strategy: Eliminate choices that are impossible under the Master sketch and rules.
4. If the fourth cake baked is chocolate, which of the following CANNOT be the first cake baked?	⟶	Q-type: New-"If"/Must Be False. The correct answer will list an entity that must be false (i.e., cannot be first), given the new If, while four incorrect choices will list entities that could be true (i.e., first). Strategy: Create a new sketch, add the rule from the stem, and make any deductions. Eliminate the choices that could or must be true (i.e., first).
5. What are the minimum and maximum numbers of people who can serve on the Board at the same time?	⟶	Q-type: Min/Max. The correct answer will list the minimum and maximum, in that order. Incorrect choices will include the wrong minimum, the wrong maximum, or both. Strategy: Use rules and deductions to find either the minimum or the maximum first, and narrow the options accordingly.

Question		Analysis
6. Which of the following could be a complete and accurate list of the projects assigned to Group A?	→	Q-type: Complete and Accurate List. The correct answer includes one possible complete assignment of projects to Group A. Incorrect choices will typically list incompatible entities or force incompatible pairings among entities NOT assigned to Group A. Strategy: First, apply the rules one by one; eliminate any answer choices that violate one or more rules. If more than one choice remains, consider what impact the choice will have on the remaining group(s) and eliminate any choices that would force a violation of the rules.
7. If the fourth phone call is from Lisa, which of the following must be true?	→	Q-type: New-"If"/Must Be True. Correct answer: must be true, given the new "If"; four wrong choices could be false. Strategy: Create a new sketch, add the rule from the stem, and make any deductions. The correct answer will be something drawn into the new sketch or that must happen within the new sketch. Eliminate any choices that must be false or are merely possible.
8. If no cars of the same color can be placed consecutively, then in exactly how many distinct orders can the cars be arranged?	→	Q-type: New-"If"/Could Be True. The correct answer identifies the number of orders that could be true, given the new If. Strategy: Create a new sketch, add the rule from the stem, and make any deductions. Determine how many arrangements do not violate the new rule and/or the other rules of the game.
9. The matching of tutors to students would be completely determined if which of the following were true?	→	Q-type: Completely Determine. The correct answer provides a new rule that allows you to match all tutors and students; four incorrect choices will leave entities unmatched or uncertain. Strategy: Test answer choices, starting with choices that definitively place any floaters.

	Question		Analysis
10.	If roses are not selected, what is the maximum number of flowers that can be in the bouquet?	⟶	Q-type: New-"If"/Maximum. The correct answer will identify the maximum possible number of flowers, given the new "If." Incorrect choices will be too high or too low. Strategy: Create a new sketch, add the rule from the stem, and make any deductions. The correct answer will reflect every entity that can be selected without violating the new and existing rules.
11.	Suppose that the condition that Ames and Barnes serve on the same committee is replaced with a condition stating that Ames and Barnes may not serve on the same committee. If all other conditions remain the same, which of the following must be true?	⟶	Q-type: Rule Change/Must Be True. Correct answer: must be true, given the rule change; incorrect answers: could be false. Strategy: Rework Master Sketch to reflect the change in the rule. Make any deductions based on the rule change. Find something that must be true given the changed rule. Eliminate choices that could be false. Because of the time involved, save for last in the question set.
12.	Suppose that J can never be the fourth audition and K can never be the first audition. Which of the following must be false?	⟶	Q-type: New-"If"/Must Be False. Correct answer: must be false, given the two new conditions; four incorrect choices: could be true. Strategy: Create a new sketch, add the two rules from the stem, and make any deductions. Eliminate the choices that could or must be true.

Perform 2

Answer Key

1. (E)
2. (B)
3. (C)
4. (D)
5. (B)
6. (E)

Perform 3

Answer Key

1. (C)
2. (A)
3. (E)
4. (D)
5. (C)
6. (D)
7. (D)

Worked example explanations of these questions with complete expert analysis can be found in your Online Study Plan under Chapter 4. View or download the PDF titled "Chapter 4 Perform Full Games Explanations."

Assess

Evaluate your performance according to the following criteria:

Logic Games Question Types (Perform 1)

If you correctly identified and analyzed:

10–12 of the question stems: Excellent work! You have a solid understanding of the various question types and of how to approach them. Take time to identify those you missed and review the discussion of them in the Prepare portion of this part of Chapter 4.

7–9 of the question stems: Review your work critically. Check the types of question stems you misidentified or mischaracterized and study their definitions and illustrations in the Prepare portion of this chapter. As you review your performance on the two full games (Perform 2 and Perform 3), check to see whether you answered questions of those types correctly. If not, review the expert analyses carefully, and make a note to review questions of those types whenever you encounter them until you are confident that you can identify and answer them without hesitation.

0–6 of the question stems: Reinforce your fundamental knowdedge of logic games question types and strategies. First, review the Prepare portion of this chapter. Second, review the question stems you misidentified or mischaracterized to ensure that they make sense to you. Third, complete the Fundamentals of Question Types and Strategies quiz in your online center. On test day, you need to know what each question is asking, and how to characterize the one correct and four incorrect answers so that you can choose the best strategy for approaching the question quickly and confidently.

To stay sharp, practice the drills in the Logic Games Training Camp for this chapter in your Online Study Plan. Training Camp drills are divided into Fundamentals, Mid-Level, and Advanced sets.

Full-Games and Question Sets (Perform 2 and Perform 3)

If you correctly answered:

11–13 of the questions in the two games: Outstanding! You're well on your way to a strong logic games performance on test day. Consider whether there were questions that took you too long to answer (even if you got the right answer). On those questions, review the expert analysis to see if there was a more efficient strategy or approach you might have used.

7–10 of the questions in the two games: You're off to a good start. Consider ways in which to build on this performance. First, review the expert analysis of the games thoroughly. If you missed the majority of questions in one of the two games, review the game setup, rules, and deductions as they were analyzed in earlier chapters. Make a note study this game type thoroughly in Part II. If, on the other hand, you recognize that a particular question type (as opposed to game type) is giving you trouble, review the description and illustration of that question type in the Prepare portion of this chapter, and make a note to review your performance on questions of this type going forward. Mostly, practice, practice, practice. Part II of this book has hundreds of questions and exercises to help you develop and refine your skills, and recommendations for dozens of additional games appropriate to your skill level.

0–6 of the questions in the two games: It's time to dig in and create a plan to establish the foundation of strong logic games performance on which you can build your expertise. Here are the recommended steps. 1) Review the Perform games, questions thoroughly, those you got right as well as those you got wrong. This will help you identify the parts of the games you understood and distinguish those that gave you trouble. 2) In your online resources, complete the quiz titled "Question Type Fundamentals." 3) Diagnose the source of your misunderstanding. Did you comprehend the game's setup, rules, and deductions, but struggle with the questions? If so, review the question types and practice characterizing right and wrong answer choices. Or, did you miss something in the Master Sketch? If that's the case, review Chapters 2 and 3 as they relate to the game you're reviewing, and then try the questions again. 4) When you move into Part II of this book, begin with Chapter 5 (on basic Strict Sequencing games). Then, move on to Chapters 7 and 9 (on Loose Sequencing and Matching and Distribution games, respectively) to keep your focus on the most common game types you will encounter on test day. There is enormous opportunity for you to improve your logic games performance, and steady practice is the surest path to expertise.

Reflect

Think back over the work you've been doing in Chapter 4.

- Are you able to distinguish among the common Logic Games question types?
- Do you consistently answer Acceptability questions strategically, by applying the rules one by one to the answer choices?
- When answering a Must Be/Could Be question, can you quickly and accurately characterize the one correct and four incorrect answer choices?
- How do you approach New-"If" questions? Can you calmly create a new sketch, add in the question's new condition, and make the available deductions?
- How does a Limited Options sketch help you save time analyzing and answering some questions?

In the coming days and weeks, take note of real-life cases in which people ask you questions similar to those found in LSAT logic games. You'll find that people are constantly posing Must Be/Could Be and New-"If" type questions:

- If Jamie doesn't have to work on Saturday, what do you guys want to do?
- Who could we have work on the Martinez account next week?
- If they are out of prawns, what will you order?

Pay special attention to whether you are answering these questions by speculating or stating your opinion. The primary distinction between day-to-day questions and those on the LSAT is that LSAT logic games questions will always provide information sufficient to provide a single, correct answer. Reflecting on the information you use to answer real-life questions—by distinguishing speculation and opinion from reasoning and deduction, as it were—can help make you aware of instances on the LSAT in which you are speculating rather than making deductions.

The LSAT Channel Spotlight

Using Previous Work

By Bobby Gautam

Watch the video lesson for this Spotlight in your online Study Plan.

Occasionally, an opportunity will arise for you to make short work of a question or two by using work you've done on previous questions. In the Special Feature video that accompanies this page, one of The LSAT Channel instructors will show you the strategy in action on a complex Strict Sequencing game. The following example illustrates the strategy so that you'll know how it works and be able to spot chances to use it.

Take a couple minutes to set up this simple model Strict Sequencing game.

A vice-principal is arranging six trophies—one each for baseball, chess, debate, golf, lacrosse, and softball—on six pedestals, numbered 1 through 6, in her school's trophy case. The arrangement of the trophies is subject to the following constraints:

> The baseball trophy cannot be placed on Pedestal 1.
> The softball trophy is placed on a pedestal numbered higher than the pedestal on which the debate trophy is placed.
> The golf trophy is placed on Pedestal 3.
> The trophies for chess and debate are placed on consecutively numbered pedestals.

Your Master Sketch should look something like this:

B C D ~~G~~ L S

__ __ G __ __ __
1 2 3 4 5 6
~B

[C/D] . . . S

It would be quite common for the first question in this game's question set to be an Acceptability question. To cut to the chase, assume its correct answer is (C), as shown.

1. Which one of the following could be an acceptable arrangement of the trophies on the pedestals?

   (A)
   (B)
   (C) chess, debate, golf, softball, baseball, lacrosse
   (D)
   (E)

You have already learned to solve Acceptability questions quickly by applying the rules to the answer choices. Use the rules to knock out the wrong answers

and you have a point on this game. But, more importantly for our present purposes, you now have at least one acceptable arrangement of the trophies. That's why it's a good idea to jot down the correct answer to an Acceptability question on your scratch paper.

1) C, D, G, S, B, L

Remember that when you come across a question like this one.

4. Which one of the following must be false?

   (A) The chess trophy is placed on Pedestal 1.
   (B) The debate trophy is placed on Pedestal 1.
   (C) The softball trophy is placed on a pedestal numbered lower than the pedestal on which the lacrosse trophy is placed.
   (D) The debate trophy is placed on a pedestal numbered lower than the pedestal on which the baseball trophy is placed.
   (E) . . .

For many test takers, the first instinct on a question like this one is to test the answer choices one by one until they find the one that must be false. An LSAT expert, on the other hand, will characterize the question's wrong answers: They could be true. The expert also knows that he has at least one place—the correct answer to the Acceptability question—to check a pattern that could be true. He can see quickly that answer choices (A), (C), and (D) are all present in the Acceptability question's correct answer. Thus, they are all wrong answers for this Must Be False question. That leaves only choices (B) and (E). Indeed, once he notices that chess and debate can always swap positions, he can even eliminate choice (B) as one that could be true in Question 4, leaving (E) as the correct answer. It doesn't even matter what choice (E) says. He has eliminated the four demonstrably wrong answers, so it must be false, and therefore, correct.

To use previous work effectively, you will need to 1) know where you have found acceptable solutions, 2) be able to characterize the correct and incorrect answer choices in later questions, and 3) be able to accurately compare answer choices to previously identified patterns. Because the LSAT expert was able to do those three things, his analysis of Question 4 in the example was far more efficient than writing out sketches to test each answer choice.

Follow along with the game on the following pages, as The LSAT Channel expert takes you even deeper into this helpful strategy.

Questions 19–24

A swim team with exactly five members—Jacobson, Kruger, Lu, Miller, Ortiz—swims a ten-lap relay race. Each team member swims exactly two of the laps: one swims laps 1 and 6, one swims laps 2 and 7, one swims laps 3 and 8, one swims laps 4 and 9, and one swims laps 5 and 10. The following conditions apply:

Neither of Kruger's laps is immediately before either of Lu's.

Jacobson does not swim lap 9.

Ortiz's first lap is after (but not necessarily immediately after) Miller's.

At least one of Jacobson's laps is immediately after one of Ortiz's laps.

19. Which one of the following could be an accurate list of the swimmers of the first five laps, in order from lap 1 through lap 5?

(A) Jacobson, Kruger, Miller, Lu, Ortiz

(B) Kruger, Miller, Ortiz, Jacobson, Lu

(C) Lu, Miller, Jacobson, Kruger, Ortiz

(D) Ortiz, Kruger, Miller, Lu, Jacobson

(E) Miller, Ortiz, Jacobson, Kruger, Lu

20. If Jacobson swims lap 8, then for exactly how many of the ten laps can one determine which team member swims the lap?

    (A) ten
    (B) eight
    (C) six
    (D) four
    (E) two

21. If Ortiz swims lap 4, then which one of the following could be true?

    (A) Jacobson swims lap 1.
    (B) Jacobson swims lap 3.
    (C) Kruger swims lap 5.
    (D) Lu swims lap 3.
    (E) Miller swims lap 5.

22. Which one of the following could be true?

    (A) Jacobson swims lap 4.
    (B) Kruger swims lap 5.
    (C) Lu swims lap 5.
    (D) Miller swims lap 10.
    (E) Ortiz swims lap 6.

23 Jacobson CANNOT swim which one of the following laps?

    (A) lap 1
    (B) lap 2
    (C) lap 3
    (D) lap 6
    (E) lap 10

24. Which one of the following could be an accurate list of the swimmers of the last five laps, in order from lap 6 through lap 10?

    (A) Jacobson, Miller, Kruger, Ortiz, Lu
    (B) Jacobson, Miller, Kruger, Ortiz, Lu
    (C) Lu, Kruger, Miller, Ortiz, Jacobson
    (D) Miller, Kruger, Ortiz, Jacobson, Lu
    (E) Ortiz, Jacobson, Kruger, Miller, Lu

PrepTest37 Sec3 Qs 19–24

Complete answers and explanations are provided in The LSAT Channel Spotlight video "Limited Options" in your online Study Plan.

PART TWO

Game Types Unlocked

In this part of the book, each chapter focuses on one or more specific game types.

- Chapter 5: Basic Strict Sequencing Games Unlocked
- Chapter 6: Complex Strict Sequencing Games Unlocked
- Chapter 7: Loose Sequencing Games Unlocked
- Chapter 8: Formal Logic and Selection Games Unlocked
- Chapter 9: Matching and Distribution Games Unlocked
- Chapter 10: Hybrid Games Unlocked
- Chapter 11: Rare Games Unlocked: Process and Mapping

Sequencing games are so common on the LSAT that they are broken up into three chapters to give you the practice you'll need to master all of the Sequencing varieties. In the chapter on Selection games, you'll also find a section that thoroughly covers the aspects of Formal Logic ("If → then" statements) tested in LSAT Logic Games. Matching and Distribution games are similar to one another, and so, are covered together in Chapter 9.

In Chapters 5–10, the Learning Objective is to apply all five steps of the Logic Games Method to the various game types. You will begin with an overall Prepare that introduces the definitions and information you need about the patterns in each game type. Then, you'll have the opportunity to practice on each of Steps 1–4 of the Method. Finally, you will assess your skills with a comprehensive Perform section containing several full, official LSAT games of the type covered in the chapter. Thus, each of these chapters has five sections.

- In Real Life: Prepare for the chapter with a brief section illustrating real-life tasks that mirror the actions found in LSAT logic games.
- Tasks and Sketches: Practice on Steps 1 and 2 of the Logic Games Method, analyzing the game Overview and creating initial sketches.
- Rules: Practice on Step 3 of the Logic Games Method, analyzing and drawing the rules.
- Deductions: Practice on Step 4 of the Logic Games Method, combining rules and restrictions to reveal valid deductions within the game.
- Full Games with Questions: Assess your skill in the game type with several officially released Logic Games, followed by complete explanations and expert analysis.

(Note: In Chapter 7, due to the unusual characteristics of Loose Sequencing games, the sections on Steps 1–4 of the Logic Games Method are combined, but you will still practice all of the steps.)

These chapters will give you the ability to drill down into the specifics and details of specific game types while reinforcing your skills in each step of the Logic Games Method. You can use any of these chapters independently. To focus on the game types most commonly featured on the test, work through Chapters 5, 7, and 9. If you have limited time before test day, make sure to prioritize those important game types.

Chapter 11 is shorter than any of Chapters 5–10. The rare games featured there have appeared very infrequently in recent years, but they are included for students who want the most complete Logic Games preparation possible.

Throughout this part of the book, you'll find a number of LSAT Channel Special Feature pages as well, each accompanied by a video lesson from an LSAT Channel expert.

- At the end of Chapter 6, there is a special feature on Circular Sequencing, a rare but challenging Sequencing variation.
- Along with the Formal Logic section in Chapter 8, there is a special feature on Minimum Increasers and Maximum Decreasers, two of the most important "If → then" statements used in Selection games.
- At the end of Chapter 10, there is a special feature on the Dinosaur Game, a Selection-Matching Hybrid game considered by many to be the most difficult LSAT logic game of all time.
- Along with the discussion of Process games in Chapter 11, there is a special feature on a Process game from PrepTest 80 (administered in December 2016), the first Process game to appear on an official, released LSAT in more than 20 years.

CHAPTER 5

Basic Strict Sequencing Games Unlocked

LEARNING OBJECTIVES

In this chapter, you'll learn to

- Apply the Logic Games Method to basic Strict Sequencing games.

Prepare

By far, the most common game type is Strict Sequencing. Over the past five years, over one-third of the games on all officially released tests have been Strict Sequencing games.

Types of Games By Percentage, 2014–2018

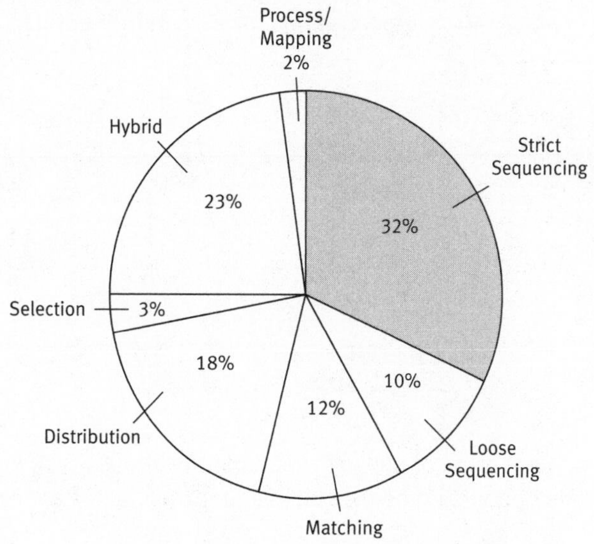

**PrepTests 72–86; released 2014–2018*

Given their prominence, Strict Sequencing games are central to your score in the Logic Games section of the LSAT.

Strict Sequencing games run the gamut from some of the easiest games on the test to some of the hardest. Strict Sequencing actions on the easier end of the spectrum tend to be simple and concrete, e.g., you are asked to place six entities in order in six numbered positions, one entity per position.

A B C D E F

__ __ __ __ __ __
1 2 3 4 5 6

Alternatively, your task could be scheduling one appointment for each of seven entities over the course of seven days, one appointment per day.

G H J K L N O

__ __ __ __ __ __ __
Su M Tu W Th F Sa

Along with this kind of simple action, the easiest Strict Sequencing games also tend to have quite restrictive rules that allow for solid deductions. We'll cover these basic Strict Sequencing games in this chapter.

Harder Strict Sequencing games often include variations that make the action more complex, e.g., over the course of five days, you will need to schedule two separate appointments for each of four entities, with a maximum of two appointments per day.

T_1 U_1 X_1 Y_1
T_2 U_2 X_2 Y_2

M Tu W Th F

__ __ __ __ __
__ __ __ __ __

Not only is this setup more complex, but it also contains some ambiguity about which days will have two appointments and which will have one or none. Complex Strict Sequencing games are covered in Chapter 6.

On recent tests, you've been virtually guaranteed to see one (or more) Strict Sequencing games, so work through Chapter 5 regardless of your skill level. Even if Strict Sequencing is your strong suit, practice with this important game type is essential.

BASIC STRICT SEQUENCING IN REAL LIFE

If you think about it, you'll realize that there's probably not a day in your adult life in which you don't sequence something. Every time you alphabetize, schedule, rank, or decide the order of steps in a process, you're sequencing.

The most common scenario—the default, if you will—is that things in the sequence happen one at a time or that items are ranked without ties, one per space. If asked to rank your 10 favorite songs, you probably wouldn't ask, "Are three songs supposed to be tied at number 2?" or "Should I avoid repeating the same song twice in my list?" You might have difficulty ranking your favorites, but you'd assume that the list is intended to have 10 songs and 10 slots with one song per slot.

Many real-world Sequencing tasks have obvious, or even visual, criteria that would make the task too easy to use on the LSAT. It wouldn't be much of a challenge, for example, to arrange six spice jars on a shelf *alphabetically*: "allspice is before basil"; "basil is before cumin"; and so on. But the test could give you a sequencing game that mimics the steps in a recipe: "add basil before adding allspice"; "add cumin fourth"; and so on.

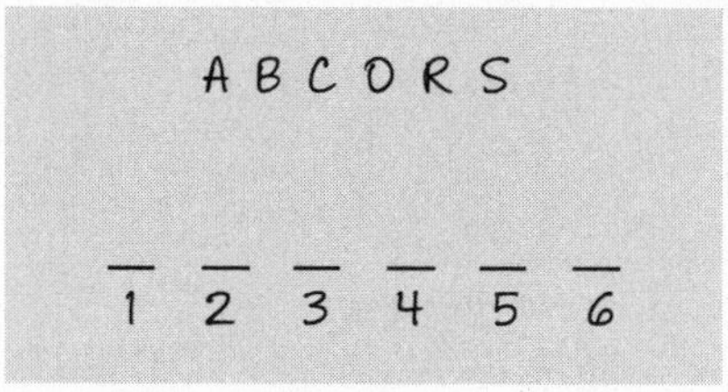

A B C O R S

_ _ _ _ _ _
1 2 3 4 5 6

Never assume anything on LSAT logic games. While it's true that a large majority of Sequencing games contain one-at-a-time, one-per-space restrictions, the testmaker must be, and will be, explicit about all restrictions that are to apply. Make sure you always pay attention to the overall limitations that affect a game's action and account for them in your sketch.

Even in basic Strict Sequencing, your assumptions can lead you astray. If the test asked you to create a sequence of six departments' offices in a certain company, your default would almost certainly be to start with a sketch like this:

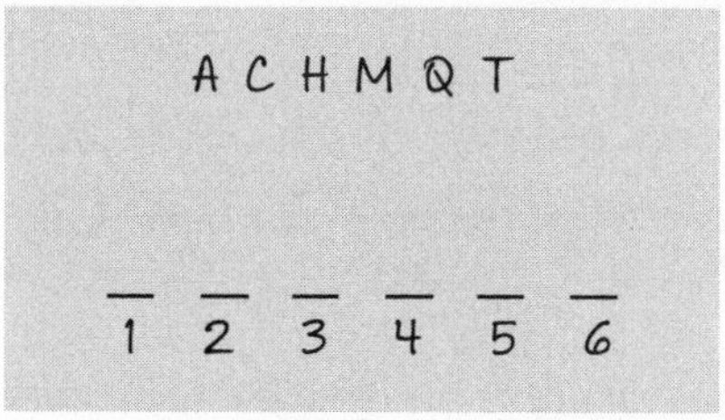

A C H M Q T

_ _ _ _ _ _
1 2 3 4 5 6

Our default orientations are generally left to right or top to bottom. Now, imagine that the six departments occupy one floor each in an six-story building. If the test includes a rule like "Human Resources occupies a higher floor than Marketing," your sketch needs to be numbered from the bottom up. You would have no problem with this task if it were part of your real-world job because you would already be thinking about your company's offices. But, on the test, you need to read the setup carefully before creating your initial sketch.

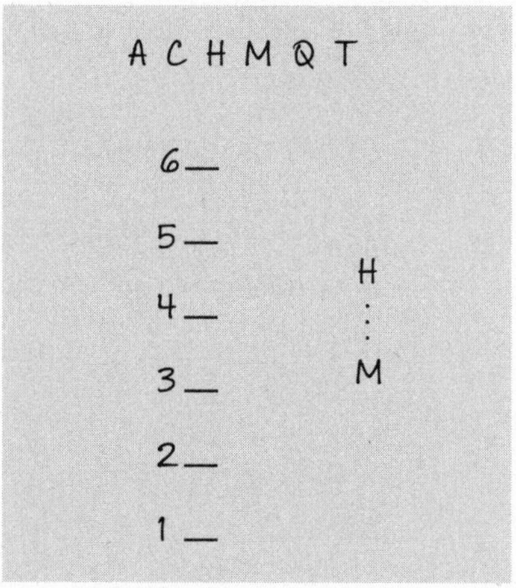

A C H M Q T

6 _
5 _ H
4 _ ⋮
3 _ M
2 _
1 _

The same confusion can be avoided by paying attention to the differences between games that mirror two more real-world tasks: ranking versus ordering. Consider two examples: If a game setup tells you that seven salespeople will be ranked on their performance over the past quarter, a rule such as "Barber ranks lower than Carty" should be depicted like this:

A B C D E F G

1 2 3 4 5 6 7

C . . . B

or

1 —
2 —
3 — C
4 — B
5 —
6 —
7 —

Being ranked lower means taking a position closer to number seven.

On the other hand, if the game asks you to assign seven salespeople to seven offices, numbered 1 through 7, the rule "Baker is assigned a lower-numbered office than the office to which Carty is assigned" should be written like this:

A B C D E F G

1 2 3 4 5 6 7

B . . . C

Here, having a lower-numbered office means taking an office closer to number 1.

The testmaker can even reward you for paying attention to the criterion on which items are ranked. Imagine a game show host telling you, "Put these five products in order by price"; you'd make sure to know whether you are supposed to arrange the products from cheapest to most expensive, or vice versa. In the real world, when the gym teacher says, "Line up by height," she might gesture in a way that makes it clear whether you are supposed to go from tallest to shortest or the other way around. The testmaker must, and will, always be explicit about the order you're supposed to use. Over the years, there have been many examples of relatively simple Strict Sequencing games that challenged or confused test takers who failed to catch these distinctions.

As you conduct an Overview analysis in Step 1 of the Logic Games Method, use the real-world scenario described in the game's setup to your advantage. Ask the logical questions about your task and make sure you reflect all of the game's restrictions or definitions in your sketch framework. It's better to jot down "Cheapest" at the top of your sketch and "Most Expensive" at the bottom than to set up the whole game incorrectly and have to start over from scratch.

BASIC STRICT SEQUENCING GAMES TASKS AND SKETCHES

LEARNING OBJECTIVES

In this section of the chapter, you'll practice

- Applying Steps 1 and 2 of the Logic Games Method to basic Strict Sequencing games by
  - Asking the SEAL questions to analyze the game's Overview, and then
  - Creating a simple, useful Sketch framework

Prepare

Although the scenario may vary, Sequencing games always task you with putting people, places, or items in order.

LOGIC GAMES STRATEGY

Sequencing games ask you to put things in order

- Chronologically—either using units of time such as years, weeks, days, or hours, or simply using the ideas of "earlier" and "later"
- Spatially—horizontally or vertically; imagine runners about to run a race taking their positions in numbered lanes, or a wedding cake with different layers, one on top of the other
- By rank—similar to a top 10 list, or the finishing order of a competition
- By size or amount—imagine a wish list with items arranged from most to least expensive

In basic Strict Sequencing, the entities are arranged one per position, and the number of entities is equal to the number of positions.

On one evening at a political convention, six politicians—Jones, Kasim, Laurence, Marcos, Nguyen, and Pearson—will give speeches. Each politician will speak once, and only one politician will speak at a time. The order of the speeches is determined in accordance with the following considerations:

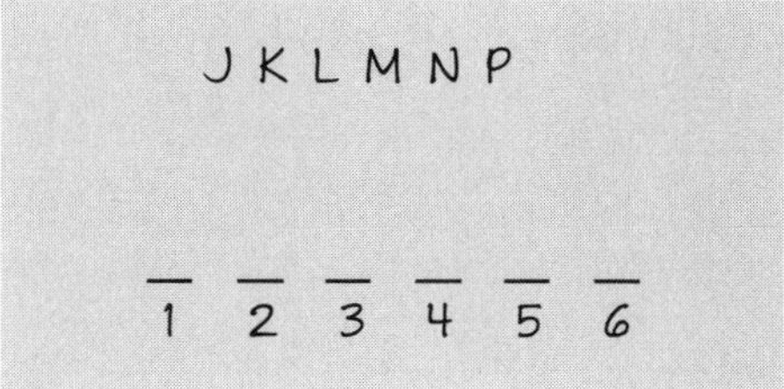

Try Steps 1 and 2 on the model game setups that follow.

Practice

Directions: Conduct an Overview of each game's setup by asking the SEAL questions, and create an initial sketch framework for the game's action.

Practice 1

A novelty-item sales representative is tasked with arranging on a shelf six new products—an art kit, a bandanna, a charm bracelet, a disco ball, a pair of earrings, and a fleece pullover—bearing the logo of a popular band. Strict company guidelines dictate that in arranging the items from left to right, one at a time, the sales representative must conform to the following restrictions:

1. [Step 1] Conduct an Overview analysis:
    - What is this game's Situation?
    - Who or what are the game's Entities?
    - What is the game's Action?
    - What are the Limitations explicit in the game setup?
2. [Step 2] Create an initial Sketch:

Practice 2

A park ranger surveyed different parks in her district for various species of medium-sized predators—bobcat, coyote, lynx, marten, ocelot and wolverine—and ranked them from most to least common, with no ties. The results indicated:

1. [Step 1] Conduct an Overview analysis:
    - What is this game's Situation?
    - Who or what are the game's Entities?
    - What is the game's Action?
    - What are the Limitations explicit in the game setup?
2. [Step 2] Create an initial Sketch:

Practice 3

Note: To complete Steps 1 and 2 for this game, you will need to use one of the rules.

Throughout the course of a day, an executive will attend exactly seven different business presentations. Each of the presentations is on exactly one of four topics: Distribution, Logistics, Marketing, and Sales. She attends the meetings according to the following constraints:

She attends exactly three presentations on Logistics, exactly two presentations on Marketing, and exactly one presentation each on Distribution and Sales.

1. [Step 1] Conduct an Overview analysis:
   - What is this game's Situation?
   - Who or what are the game's Entities?
   - What is the game's Action?
   - What are the Limitations explicit in the game setup?

2. [Step 2] Create an initial Sketch:

Explanations

Compare your work to that of an LSAT expert. Keep track of any case in which you incorrectly characterized the action described in the setup, and any case in which you drew a sketch framework that does not match the details of the game's situation.

Practice 1

A novelty-item sales representative is tasked with arranging on a shelf six new products—an art kit, a bandanna, a charm bracelet, a disco ball, a pair of earrings, and a fleece pullover—bearing the logo of a popular band. Strict company guidelines dictate that in arranging the items from left to right, one at a time, the sales representative must conform to the following restrictions:

1. [Step 1] Conduct an Overview analysis:
    - What is this game's Situation? *A sales representative is arranging six items in order along a shelf.*
    - Who or what are the game's Entities? *Six types of items—A, B, C, D, E, and F—each bearing a band's logo.*
    - What is the game's Action? *Sequencing (assuming that any of the rules mention specific positions or numbers of positions between entities, this is Strict Sequencing)*
    - What are the Limitations explicit in the game setup? *"One at a time," i.e., one item per position*
2. [Step 2] Create an initial Sketch:

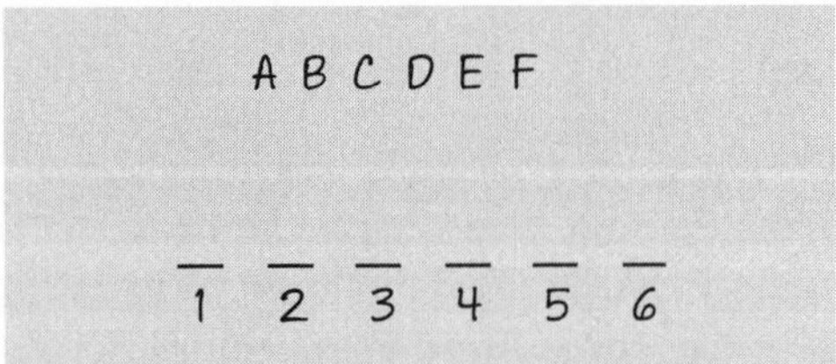

Practice 2

A park ranger surveyed different parks in her district for various species of medium-sized predators—bobcat, coyote, lynx, marten, ocelot and wolverine—and ranked them from most to least common, with no ties. The results indicated:

1. [Step 1] Conduct an Overview analysis:
    - What is this game's Situation? *A survey of the populations of six animal species in various parks.*
    - Who or what are the game's Entities? *The six animal species—B, C, L, M, O, and W*
    - What is the game's Action? *Sequencing (assuming that any of the rules mention specific positions or numbers of positions between entities, this is Strict Sequencing)*
    - What are the Limitations explicit in the game setup? *"with no ties," i.e., one species per position in the ranking*
2. [Step 2] Create an initial Sketch:

B C L M O W

1 2 3 4 5 6

or

1 —
2 —
3 —
4 —
5 —
6 —

Practice 3

Note: To complete Steps 1 and 2 for this game, you will need to use one of the rules.

> Throughout the course of a day, an executive will attend exactly seven different business presentations. Each of the presentations is on exactly one of four topics: Distribution, Logistics, Marketing, and Sales. She attends the meetings according to the following constraints:
>
> > She attends exactly three presentations on Logistics, exactly two presentations on Marketing, and exactly one presentation each on Distribution and Sales.

1. [Step 1] Conduct an Overview analysis:
   - What is this game's Situation? *An executive's itinerary of seven presentations on one day of a business conference.*
   - Who or what are the game's Entities? *Four presentation topics—D, L, M, and S; because of the game's first rule, you know topics of all seven presentations that the executive will attend—D, L_1, L_2, L_3, M_1, M_2, and S.*
   - What is the game's Action? *Sequencing (assuming that any of the rules mention specific positions or numbers of positions between entities, this is Strict Sequencing)*
   - What are the Limitations explicit in the game setup? *Each presentation is on one of the topics.*

2. [Step 2] Create an initial Sketch:

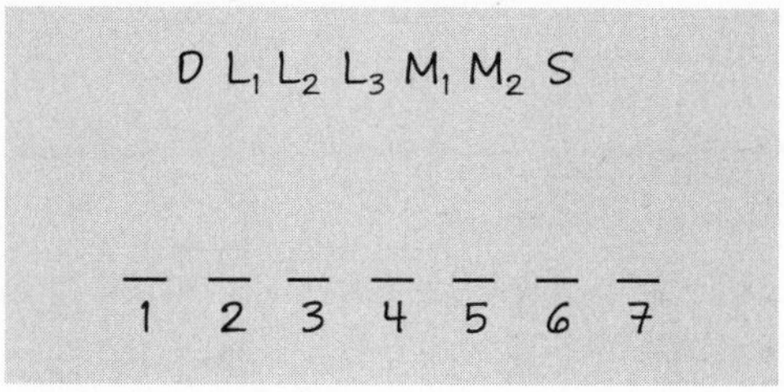

D L_1 L_2 L_3 M_1 M_2 S

_ _ _ _ _ _ _
1 2 3 4 5 6 7

You'll see these model game setups again as you practice Step 3, analyzing and drawing the rules, and Step 4, making deductions in basic Strict Sequencing games.

BASIC STRICT SEQUENCING GAMES RULES

LEARNING OBJECTIVES

In this section of the chapter, you'll practice

- Applying Step 3 of the Logic Games Method to basic Strict Sequencing games by analyzing and sketching the rules

Prepare

Strict Sequencing games ask you to assign entities to specific positions. Knowing that should help you anticipate the kinds of rules you'll encounter in these games.

LOGIC GAMES STRATEGY

Strict Sequencing rules basically tell you one or more of the following:

- The order in which two or more entities are placed
- The number of spaces between two or more entities
- The slot(s) in which a given entity can or cannot be placed

In Strict Sequencing, a few types of rules may be drawn directly into the sketch framework.

> C is in position 3.
>
> D is either in position 1 or else in position 6.
>
> F is not in position 5.

→

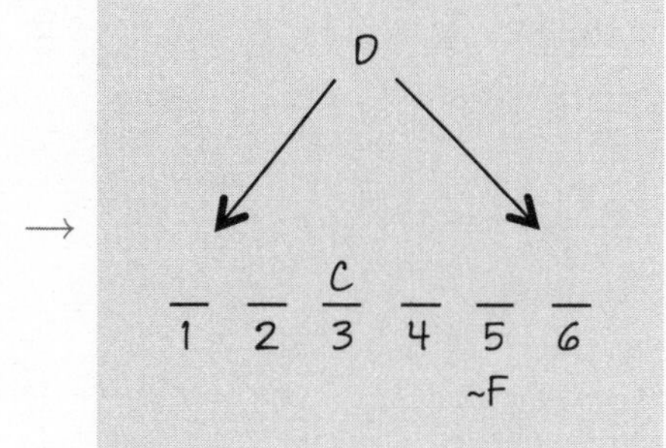

Most Strict Sequencing rules, however, stipulate the relative order or distance (or both) between two entities, and will be depicted underneath the sketch.

> H occupies a higher-numbered position than J.
>
> L and M occupy adjacent positions.
>
> P's position is at least two spaces earlier than Q's position.

→

1 2 3 4 5 6

J...H

[L M] or [M L]

P _ ... Q

Very rarely, you may see a conditional Formal Logic rule in a Strict Sequencing game; for example:

> If R is delivered sixth, then Q is delivered second.

If R6 → Q2
If ~Q2 → ~R6

A rule like this only applies in two situations: when R *is* in the sixth slot (in which case Q must be in the second slot), or when Q is *not* in the second slot (in which case, R *cannot* be in the sixth slot). Formal Logic is most common in Selection games, and the process of analyzing and diagramming Formal Logic is discussed in detail in Chapter 8 along with the Selection games deep dive.

The following chart shows a handful of common Strict Sequencing rules and suggested drawings for each.

Rule		Analysis
C and D must be next to each other.	→	[C/D D/C] or: [C D] or [D C]
There are at least two people in line after A but before B.	→	A _ _ . . . B
E appears on some day before F.	→	E . . . F
C's appointment is on the day before D's appointment.	→	[C D]
There is exactly one day between C's lecture and D's lecture.	→	[C/D _ D/C] or: [C _ D] or [D _ C]
Either V comes before W or V comes before X, but not both.	→	W . . . V . . . X or X . . . V . . . W
E performs some time before both F and G.	→	E . . . F E . . . G or E / \\ F G
If A is in position 2, B is in position 5.	→	If A2 → B5 If ~B5 → ~A2
C and D cannot be adjacent to each other.	→	never [C D] never [D C]
A must appear before B, but after C.	→	C . . . A . . . B

Practice

Now, practice Strict Sequencing rules by completing four exercises. In the first, you'll see rules listed out as in the preceding table. Your job is to analyze and draw them accurately. The next three exercises add rules to the three Strict Sequencing game setups you sketched earlier. Analyze the rules, answer the questions about them, and draw them into or underneath the sketch frameworks.

Practice 1

Directions: Analyze and draw each of the following Strict Sequencing game rules.

Rule	My Analysis
1. There are exactly three appointments between D's appointment and C's appointment.	
2. There is, at most, one spot between H's spot and J's spot.	
3. If L is the second car, then M is the first car.	
4. J and K both have lower-numbered positions than H, or H has a lower-numbered position than both J and K.	
5. D is in position 4.	
6. C is immediately after D but before E.	
7. S is after both T and V.	
8. P finishes later than Q, but earlier than R.	
9. M's position is at least two positions later than J's position.	
10. N arrives exactly two hours before Z arrives.	
11. X is either in position 1 or position 6.	
12. B is not fifth.	

Practice 2

Directions: Take a couple of minutes to review the game setup, summarize your Overview analysis, and recreate the initial Sketch. Then, one at a time, analyze the rules, answer the questions about each one, and draw the rule either inside or underneath the sketch framework.

A novelty-item sales representative is tasked with arranging on a shelf six new products—an art kit, a bandanna, a charm bracelet, a disco ball, a pair of earrings, and a fleece pullover—bearing the logo of a popular band. Strict company guidelines dictate that in arranging the items from left to right, one at a time, the sales representative must conform to the following restrictions:

The art kit must be in one of the two middle spaces.
The charm bracelet must be in a space next to one of the end spaces.
The fleece pullover must be two spaces to the left of the disco ball.
The art kit must never be placed immediately to the left of the fleece pullover.
The earrings must be somewhere to the left of the bandanna.

1. [Step 1] Summarize your Overview analysis:

2. [Step 2] Create an initial Sketch:

3. [Step 3] Analyze and draw the Rules:
    - For each rule, answer the following questions and draw the rule in the appropriate box.
        - What does the rule restrict, and what does it leave open?
        - What are the rule's negative implications, if any?
        - Can the rule be depicted inside the sketch framework?

Rule 1:	Rule 4:
Rule 2:	Rule 5:
Rule 3:	

Practice 3

Directions: Take a couple of minutes to review the game setup, summarize your Overview analysis, and recreate the initial Sketch. Then, one at a time, analyze the rules, answer the questions about each one, and draw the rule either inside or underneath the sketch framework.

A park ranger surveyed different parks in her district for various species of medium-sized predators—bobcat, coyote, lynx, marten, ocelot and wolverine—and ranked them from most to least common, with no ties. The results indicated:

In all parks, coyotes were the most or second most common species.
Bobcat and lynx were never both among the three most common species in the same park.
In every park, both bobcat and lynx were more common than both marten and wolverine.

1. [Step 1] Summarize your Overview analysis:

2. [Step 2] Create an initial Sketch:

3. [Step 3] Analyze and draw the Rules:
   - For each rule, answer the following questions and draw the rule in the appropriate box.
     - What does the rule restrict, and what does it leave open?
     - What are the rule's negative implications, if any?
     - Can the rule be depicted inside the sketch framework?

Rule 1:	Rule 3:
Rule 2:	

Practice 4

Directions: Take a couple of minutes to review the game setup, summarize your Overview analysis, and recreate the initial Sketch. Then, one at a time, analyze the rules, answer the questions about each one, and draw the rule either inside or underneath the sketch framework.

Throughout the course of a day, an executive will attend exactly seven different business presentations. Each of the presentations is on exactly one of four topics: Distribution, Logistics, Marketing, and Sales. She attends the meetings according to the following constraints:

She attends exactly three presentations on Logistics, exactly two presentations on Marketing, and exactly one presentation each on Distribution and Sales.
She never attends consecutive meetings on Logistics.
She attends the meeting on Sales immediately after she attends the meeting on Distribution.
Either the first or last presentation she attends, or both, will be a Marketing presentation.

1. [Step 1] Summarize your Overview analysis:

2. [Step 2] Create an initial Sketch:

3. [Step 3] Analyze and draw the Rules:
   - For each rule, answer the following questions and draw the rule in the appropriate box.
     - What does the rule restrict, and what does it leave open?
     - What are the rule's negative implications, if any?
     - Can the rule be depicted inside the sketch framework?

Rule 1:	Rule 3:
Rule 2:	Rule 4:

Explanations

Compare your work to that of an LSAT expert. Pay close attention to how the expert analyzed each rule and then depicted it within or beneath the game's initial sketch.

Practice 1

Rule		My Analysis
1. There are exactly three appointments between D's appointment and C's appointment.	→	D/C _ _ _ C/D
2. There is, at most, one spot between H's spot and J's spot.	→	[H/J] or H/J _ J/H
3. If L is the second car, then M is the first car.	→	If L2 → M1 If M~1 → L~2
4. J and K both have lower-numbered positions than H or H has a lower-numbered position than both J and K.	→	J, K ... H or H ... J, K
5. D is in position 4.	→	_ _ _ D _ _ (1 2 3 4 5 6)
6. C is immediately after D but before E.	→	[D C] ... E
7. S is after both T and V.	→	T, V ... S
8. P finishes later than Q, but earlier than R.	→	Q...P...R
9. M's position is at least two positions later than J's position.	→	J _ ...M
10. N arrives exactly two hours before Z arrives.	→	[N _ Z]
11. X is in either position 1 or position 6.	→	X → 1 or 6 (_ _ _ _ _ _ 1 2 3 4 5 6)
12. B is not fifth.	→	_ _ _ _ _ _ (1 2 3 4 5 6), ~B under 5

Practice 2

A novelty-item sales representative is tasked with arranging on a shelf six new products—an art kit, a bandanna, a charm bracelet, a disco ball, a pair of earrings, and a fleece pullover—bearing the logo of a popular band. Strict company guidelines dictate that in arranging the items from left to right, one at a time, the sales representative must conform to the following restrictions:

The art kit must be in one of the two middle spaces.
The charm bracelet must be in a space next to one of the end spaces.
The fleece pullover must be two spaces to the left of the disco ball.
The art kit must never be placed immediately to the left of the fleece pullover.
The earrings must be somewhere to the left of the bandanna.

1. [Step 1] Summarize your Overview analysis: *A Strict Sequencing game in which a sales rep is placing six items in order from left to right, one per position, along a shelf.*

2. [Step 2] Create an initial Sketch:

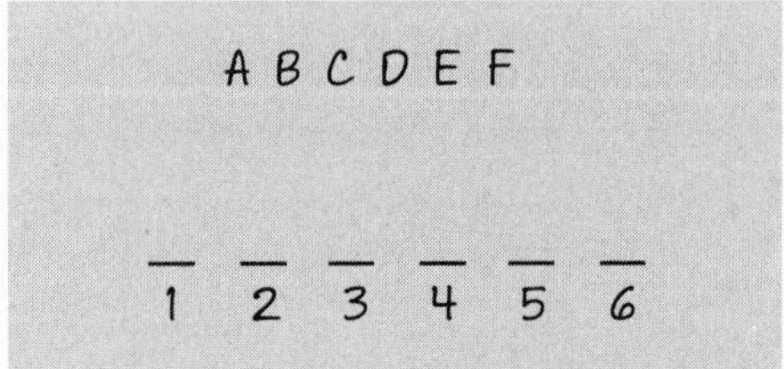

3. [Step 3] Analyze and draw the Rules:
   - Rule 1:
     - What does the rule restrict, and what does it leave open? *This rule restricts A to one of two positions (slot 3 or slot 4).*
     - What are the rule's negative implications, if any? *Simply that A won't be in slots 1, 2, 5, or 6.*
     - Can the rule be depicted inside the sketch framework? *Yes.*
     - Draw the rule:

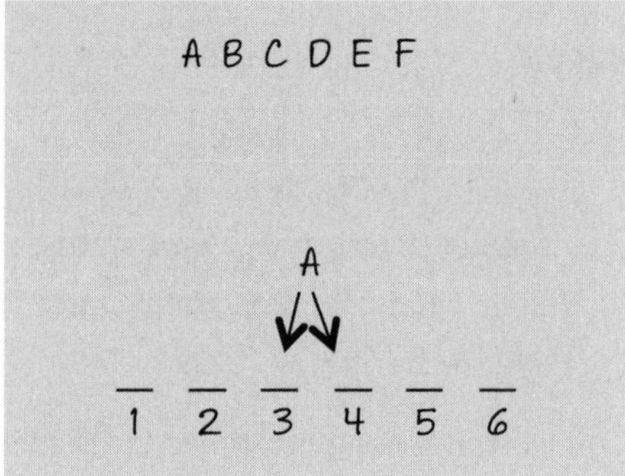

   - Rule 2:
     - What does the rule restrict, and what does it leave open? *This rule restricts C to one of two positions (slot 2 or slot 5).*
     - What are the rule's negative implications, if any? *Simply that C will not be in slots 1, 3, 4, or 6.*
     - Can the rule be depicted inside the sketch framework? *Yes.*
     - Draw the rule:

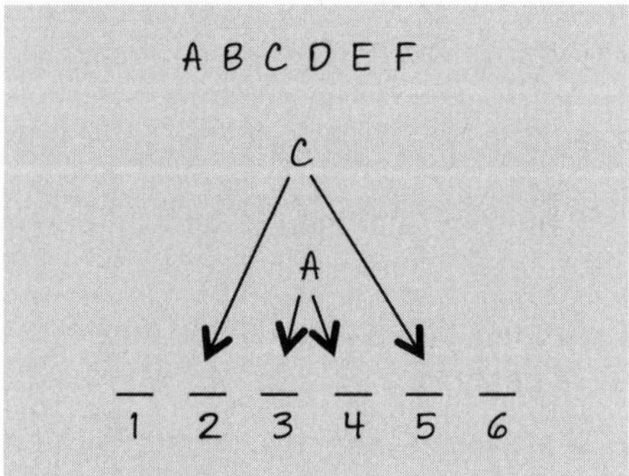

   - Rule 3:
     - What does the rule restrict, and what does it leave open? *This rule determines the order and distance between D and F: F will be exactly two slots to the left of D.*
     - What are the rule's negative implications, if any? *None beyond the fact that the relationship between D and F cannot be otherwise.*

- Can the rule be depicted inside the sketch framework? *No.*
- Draw the rule:

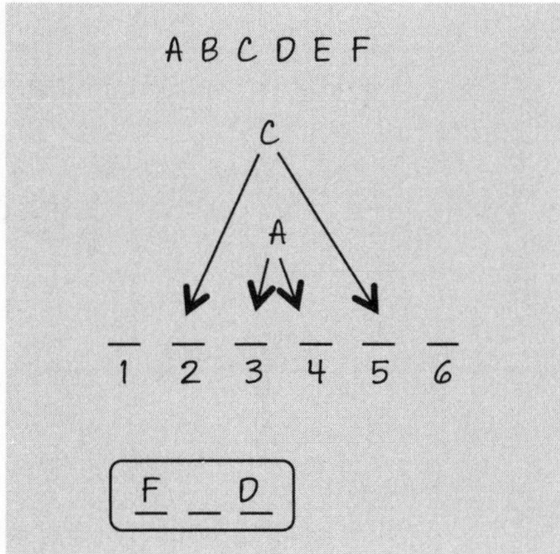

- Rule 4:
  - What does the rule restrict, and what does it leave open? *This is a negative rule that prevents A from being immediately to the left of F.*
  - What are the rule's negative implications, if any? *Either F is to the left of A, or A is two or more spaces to the left of F.*
  - Can the rule be depicted inside the sketch framework? *No.*
  - Draw the rule:

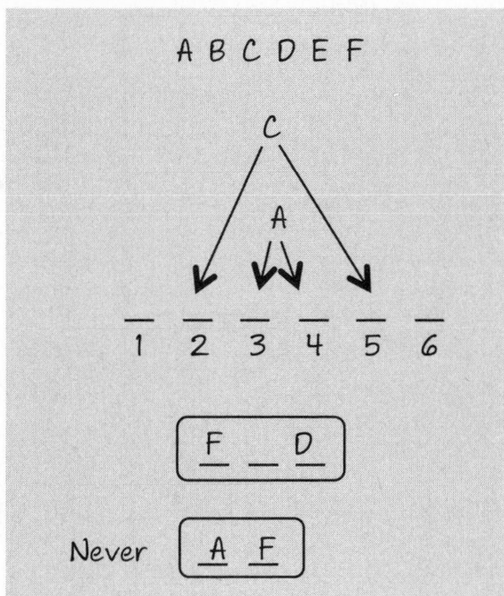

- Rule 5:
  - What does the rule restrict, and what does it leave open? *This creates a "loose" block: E . . . B. It says nothing about how close or far apart E and B are from one another.*
  - What are the rule's negative implications, if any? *B is never to the left of E.*
  - Can the rule be depicted inside the sketch framework? *No.*
  - Draw the rule:

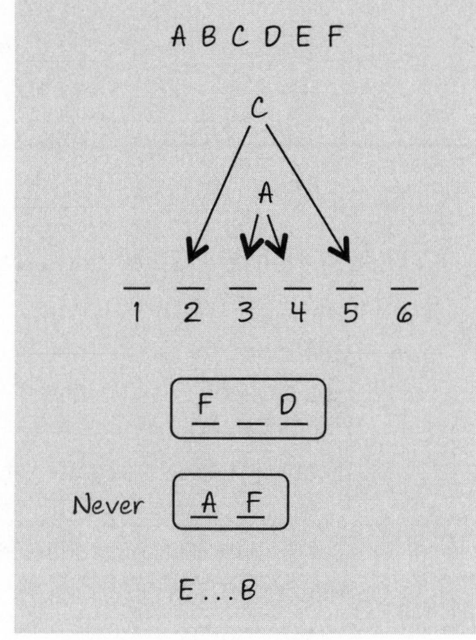

Practice 3

A park ranger surveyed different parks in her district for various species of medium-sized predators—bobcat, coyote, lynx, marten, ocelot and wolverine—and ranked them from most to least common, with no ties. The results indicated:

In all parks, coyotes were the most or second most common species.
Bobcat and lynx were never both among the three most common species in the same park.
In every park, both bobcat and lynx were more common than both marten and wolverine.

1. [Step 1] Summarize your Overview analysis: *A Strict Sequencing game that accounts for the population sizes of six animal species in various parks.*

2. [Step 2] Create an initial Sketch: *Earlier, you saw this game depicted both horizontally and vertically. While either layout is fine, you'll see only the horizontal layout in the remainder of this chapter.*

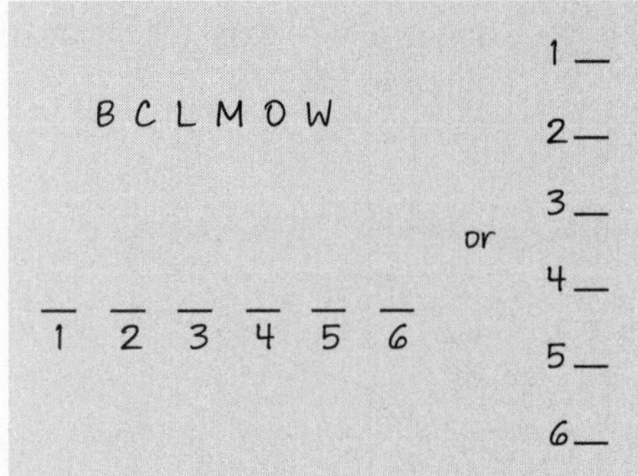

3. [Step 3] Analyze and draw the Rules:
   - Rule 1:
     - What does the rule restrict, and what does it leave open? *This rule places C in either slot 1 or slot 2.*
     - What are the rule's negative implications, if any? *Simply that C is not in slots 3–6.*
     - Can the rule be depicted inside the sketch framework? *Yes.*
     - Draw the rule:

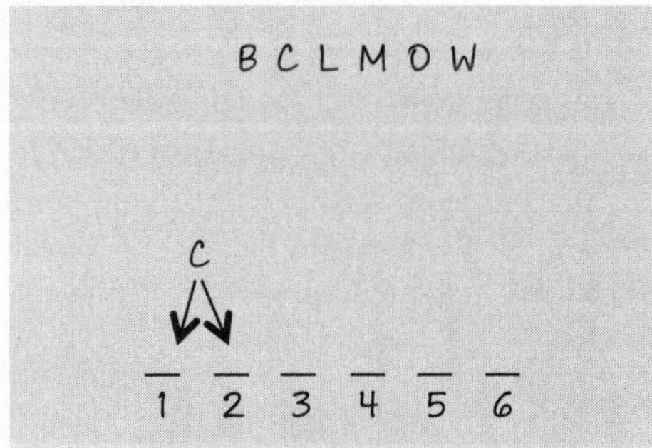

   - Rule 2:
     - What does the rule restrict, and what does it leave open? *This rule forbids both B and L from being among the top three slots. Note: The rule does not require either B or L to be among the top three; it simply says that if one of them is among the top three, the other will not be among the top three.*
     - What are the rule's negative implications, if any? *The top three spots will not consist of B, C, and L.*
     - Can the rule be depicted inside the sketch framework? *Yes, at least in a negative sense.*
     - Draw the rule:

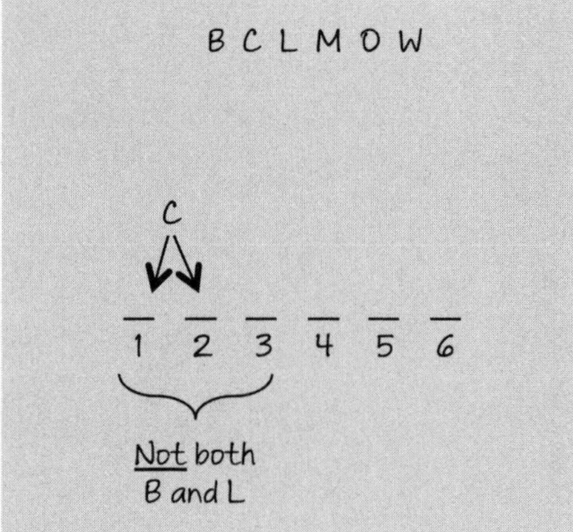

   - Rule 3:
     - What does the rule restrict, and what does it leave open? *This is really two rules in one: B is ranked higher than M and W, and L is ranked higher than M and W. It does not give the relative order between B and L, or between M and W, nor does it restrict the distances among any of these entities.*
     - What are the rule's negative implications, if any? *Neither M nor W can be ranked higher than either B or L; neither M nor W can ever be ranked first or second, and neither B nor L can be ranked fifth or sixth.*
     - Can the rule be depicted inside the sketch framework? *No.*
     - Draw the rule:

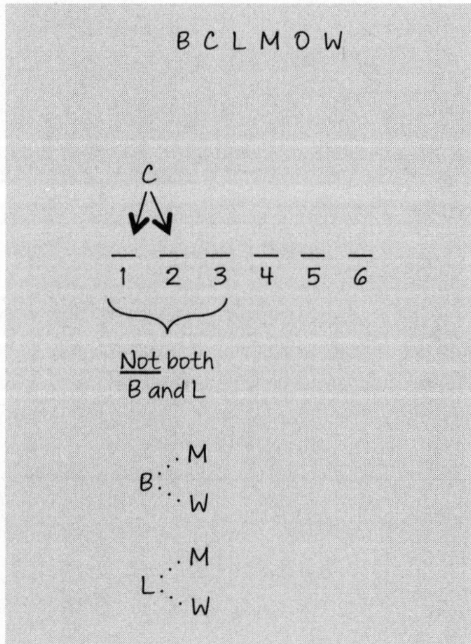

Practice 4

Throughout the course of a day, an executive will attend exactly seven different business presentations. Each of the presentations is on exactly one of four topics: Distribution, Logistics, Marketing, and Sales. She attends the meetings according to the following constraints:

She attends exactly three presentations on Logistics, exactly two presentations on Marketing, and exactly one presentation each on Distribution and Sales.
She never attends consecutive meetings on Logistics.
She attends the meeting on Sales immediately after she attends the meeting on Distribution.
Either the first or last presentation she attends, or both, will be a Marketing presentation.

1. [Step 1] Summarize your Overview analysis: *A Strict Sequencing game that accounts for an executive's itinerary of seven presentations over the course of one day. There are four types of presentations—D, L, M, and S—but we don't know the number of each type of presentation that the executive will see until Rule 1.*

2. [Step 2] Create an initial Sketch:

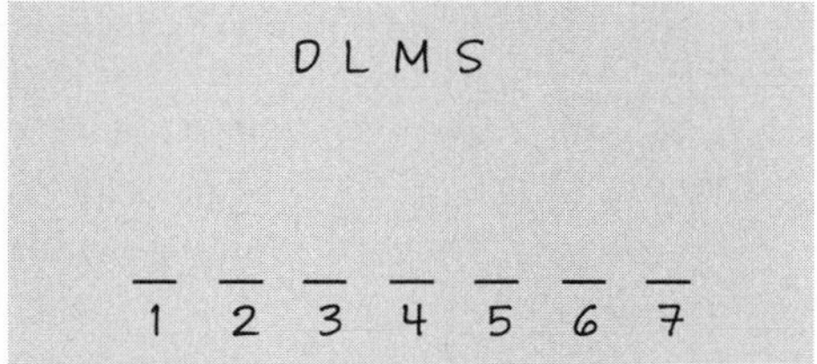

3. [Step 3] Analyze and draw the Rules:
   - Rule 1:
     - What does the rule restrict, and what does it leave open? *This rule defines the number of each type of presentation the executive will see—one D, three Ls, two Ms, and an S.*
     - What are the rule's negative implications, if any? *None. The number of each meeting type is now completely determined.*
     - Can the rule be depicted inside the sketch framework? No, *but this rule's details can be added to the roster of entities.*
     - Draw the rule:

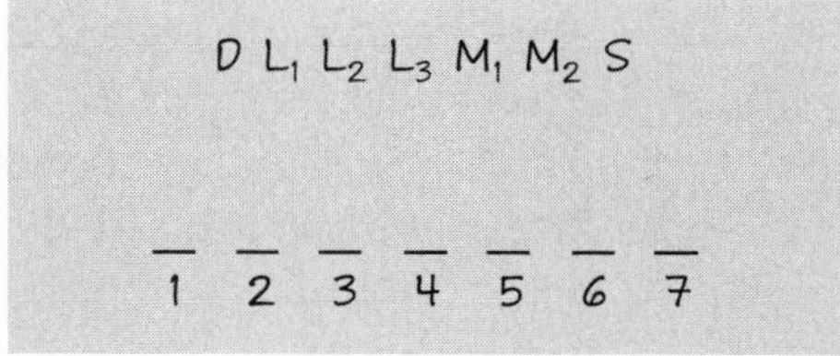

   - Rule 2:
     - What does the rule restrict, and what does it leave open? *This rule forbids consecutive presentations on Logistics.*
     - What are the rule's negative implications, if any? *At least one other type of presentation will always intervene between two Logistics presentations.*
     - Can the rule be depicted inside the sketch framework? *No.*
     - Draw the rule:

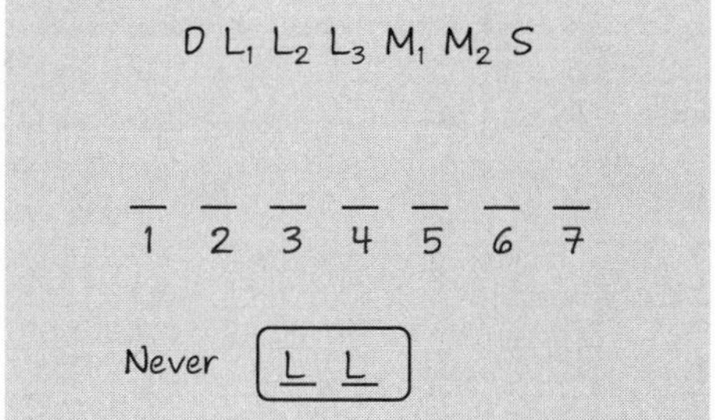

   - Rule 3:
     - What does the rule restrict, and what does it leave open? *This rule creates a block of entities: D-S.*
     - What are the rule's negative implications, if any? *S cannot come before D, and the two can never be separated.*
     - Can the rule be depicted inside the sketch framework? *No.*
     - Draw the rule:

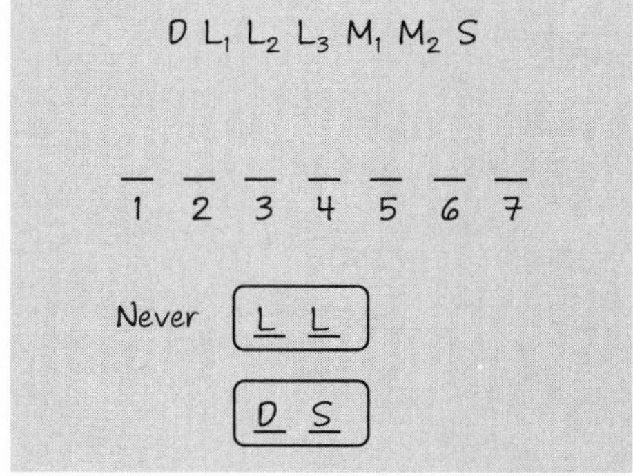

- Rule 4:
    - What does the rule restrict, and what does it leave open? *This rule dictates that Marketing will be the first presentation, the last presentation, or both.*
    - What are the rule's negative implications, if any? *None.*
    - Can the rule be depicted inside the sketch framework? *Partially—It is easy to show that an M needs to be in either slot 1 or slot 7, but the "or both" should be noted separately, as well.*
- Draw the rule:

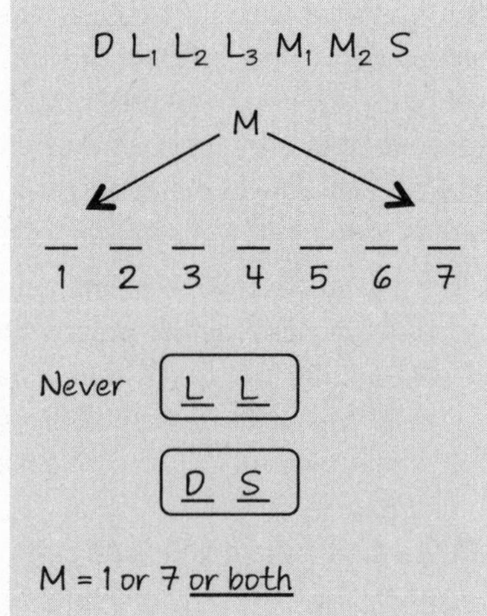

With the rules in place, you may already be anticipating the deductions that can be made in each of these practice game setups. You'll have a chance to add those in the next section of this chapter covering Step 4 of the Logic Games Method in basic Strict Sequencing games.

BASIC STRICT SEQUENCING GAMES DEDUCTIONS

LEARNING OBJECTIVES

In this section of the chapter, you'll practice

- Applying Step 4 of the Logic Games Method to Simple Strict Sequencing games by combining rules and restrictions to make all valid deductions in the game.

Prepare

Strict Sequencing games involve putting entities in order in numbered or named positions. It stands to reason, then, that the most concrete restrictions within these games come from rules that place an entity precisely (Established Entities) and those involving the relative positions of two or more entities (Blocks of Entities).

Keep in mind, though, that a rule such as "Brianna is placed exactly one position after Feng" is much more restrictive than one saying "Brianna's position is at some point after Feng's position." The first of those rules creates a block of entities that must occupy two consecutive positions, and depending on the other rules in the game, there may be only one or two places within the game's framework where you can find two consecutive open slots.

Whenever you're making deductions in a Strict Sequencing game, look for Duplications (rules that can be combined because they share a common entity). Knowing, for example, that L comes before J or that N comes before L is helpful, of course. But knowing that the three entities are all related (N . . . L . . . J), and thus all restrict one another, is far more restrictive within the game, and will lead to further deductions.

LOGIC GAMES STRATEGY

In Sequencing games, deductions are most likely to stem from:

- **Blocks of Entities**—Two or more entities that are linked together; when one is placed, the other's placement is determined or restricted.
- **Duplications**—Entities shared by two or more rules; duplications are always at the heart of Loose Sequencing games.
- **Established Entities**—Entities placed into a specific position; even if no rule directly provides for an Established Entity, you may be able to determine an entity's exact position by combining other rules.

In Sequencing games, deductions may involve:

- **Limited Options**—The situation arises when a Block of Entities or a key player (an entity affecting the positions of other entities) is restricted to either of two positions; when this occurs, draw dual Limited Options sketches.
- **Number Restrictions**—Limitations or rules affecting the number of entities that can be placed in a given position; this is rare in Sequencing games—typically, the stated limitation is one entity per position.

Practice

Directions: In each game setup, first reacquaint yourself with the setup and rules. Then, combine the rules and restrictions to make all available deductions, recording your analyses as indicated. Finally, test your deductions by answering the questions that accompany each game. You can find expert analysis and explanations at the end of the Practice section.

Practice 1

A novelty-item sales representative is tasked with arranging on a shelf six new products—an art kit, a bandanna, a charm bracelet, a disco ball, a pair of earrings, and a fleece pullover—bearing the logo of a popular band. Strict company guidelines dictate that in arranging the items from left to right, one at a time, the sales representative must conform to the following restrictions:

The art kit must be in one of the two middle spaces.
The charm bracelet must be in a space next to one of the end spaces.
The fleece pullover must be two spaces to the left of the disco ball.
The art kit must never be placed immediately to the left of the fleece pullover.
The earrings must be somewhere to the left of the bandanna.

Steps 1–3:

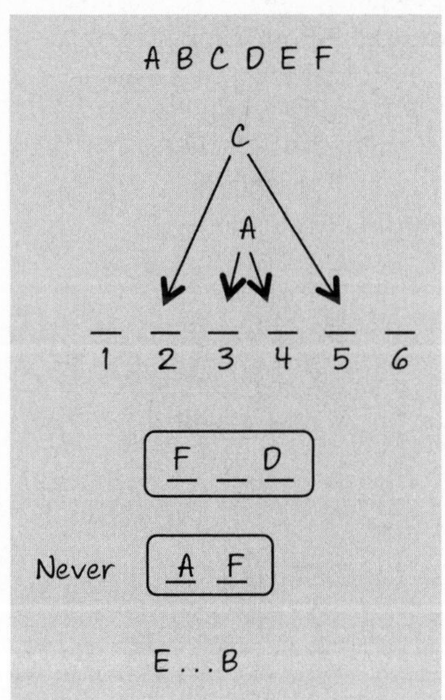

1. Which entities or positions are the most restricted in this game? Why?

2. Which elements from the BLEND checklist can you identify in this game? Are there
   - Blocks of entities? If so, what are they?
   - Limited Options? If so, which rule(s) trigger them?
   - Established Entities? If so, which ones?
   - Number Restrictions? If so, describe them.
   - Duplications? If so, which rules share an entity?
3. Combine the rules and restrictions to create a Master Sketch depicting all of the deductions available in this game:

4. Evaluate your sketch by answering the following questions:
   - Write out a complete and accurate list of the entities that could acceptably occupy position 1.
   - If the art kit is in position 3, which entity or entities could be in position 5?
   - If the art kit is in position 4, which entity or entities could be in position 2?
   - How many entities could acceptably occupy position 6?

Practice 2

A park ranger surveyed different parks in her district for various species of medium-sized predators—bobcat, coyote, lynx, marten, ocelot and wolverine—and ranked them from most to least common, with no ties. The results indicated:

In all parks, coyotes were the most or second most common species.
Bobcat and lynx were never both among the three most common species in the same park.
In every park, both bobcat and lynx were more common than both marten and wolverine.

Steps 1–3:

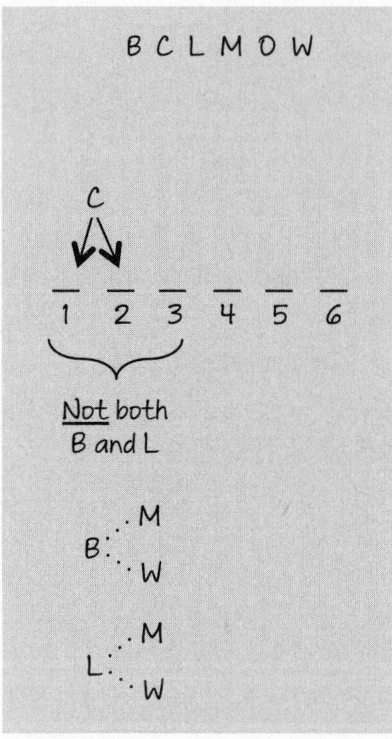

1. Which entities or positions are the most restricted in this game? Why?

2. Which elements from the BLEND checklist can you identify in this game? Are there
   - Blocks of entities? If so, what are they?
   - Limited Options? If so, which rule(s) trigger them?
   - Established Entities? If so, which ones?
   - Number Restrictions? If so, describe them.
   - Duplications? If so, which rules share an entity?

3. Combine the rules and restrictions to create a Master Sketch depicting all of the deductions available in this game:

4. Evaluate your sketch by answering the following questions:
   - Write out a complete and accurate list of species that could be the fourth most common at one of the parks.
   - Write out a complete and accurate list of the positions that martens could acceptably occupy.
   - Write out a complete and accurate list of the species that could be the most common at one of the parks.
   - If bobcats are the second most common species at one of the parks, what else *must be true* about species population at that park?

Practice 3

Throughout the course of a day, an executive will attend exactly seven different business presentations. Each of the presentations is on exactly one of four topics: Distribution, Logistics, Marketing, and Sales. She attends the meetings according to the following constraints:

She attends exactly three presentations on Logistics, exactly two presentations on Marketing, and exactly one presentation each on Distribution and Sales.
She never attends consecutive meetings on Logistics.
She attends the meeting on Sales immediately after she attends the meeting on Distribution.
Either the first or last presentation she attends, or both, will be a Marketing presentation.

Steps 1–3:

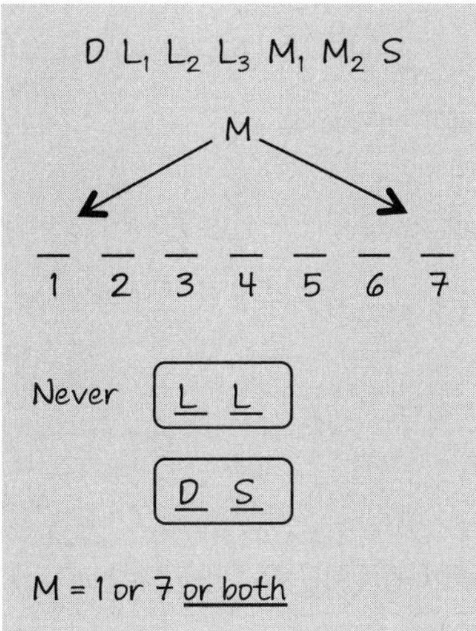

1. Which entities or positions are the most restricted in this game? Why?

2. Which elements from the BLEND checklist can you identify in this game? Are there
   - Blocks of entities? If so, what are they?
   - Limited Options? If so, which rule(s) trigger them?
   - Established Entities? If so, which ones?
   - Number Restrictions? If so, describe them.
   - Duplications? If so, which rules share an entity?
3. Combine the rules and restrictions to create a Master Sketch depicting all of the deductions available in this game:

4. Evaluate your sketch by answering the following questions:
   - If the executive sees the Sales presentation fourth, for how many of the positions can the topic of the presentation be precisely determined?
   - If the executive sees a Logistics presentation second, in which positions could she see the Distribution presentation?
   - If the executive sees a Marketing presentation first, which of the topics could be the topic she sees in the seventh presentation?
   - Write out a complete and accurate list of all the topics that could not be the topic covered by the first presentation.

Explanations

Compare your work to that of an LSAT expert. Pay close attention to how the expert combined the rules and restrictions to make additional deductions, and to how the expert depicted the deductions within the sketch framework.

Practice 1

A novelty-item sales representative is tasked with arranging on a shelf six new products—an art kit, a bandanna, a charm bracelet, a disco ball, a pair of earrings, and a fleece pullover—bearing the logo of a popular band. Strict company guidelines dictate that in arranging the items from left to right, one at a time, the sales representative must conform to the following restrictions:

The art kit must be in one of the two middle spaces.
The charm bracelet must be in a space next to one of the end spaces.
The fleece pullover must be two spaces to the left of the disco ball.
The art kit must never be placed immediately to the left of the fleece pullover.
The earrings must be somewhere to the left of the bandanna.

Steps 1–3:

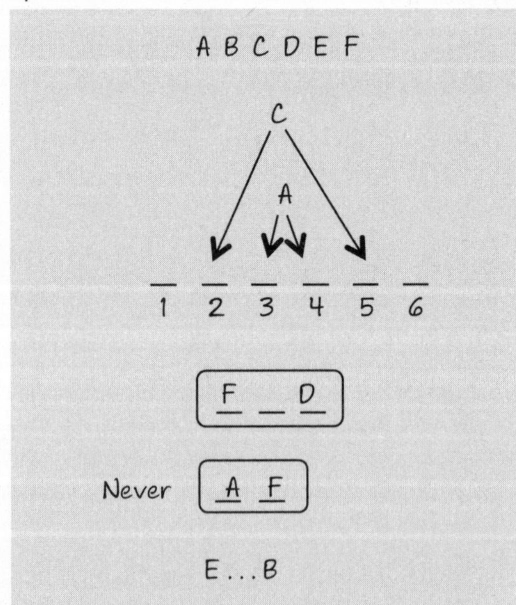

1. Which entities or positions are the most restricted in this game? Why? *Both A and C are restricted to just two positions each (Rules 1 and 2), but A is even more restricted because it cannot be to the immediate left of F (Rule 4).*
2. Which elements from the BLEND checklist can you identify in this game? Are there
   - Blocks of entities? If so, what are they? *Rule 3 creates a block of two entities over three positions: F_D. Rule 5 creates a "loose" block: E . . . B.*
   - Limited Options? If so, which rule(s) trigger them? *Both Rules 1 and 2 create potential Limited Options scenarios by limiting A and C to just two positions each. Test Rule 1 first, however, because Rule 4 also restricts A in relationship to F, which is, in turn restricted by D (Rule 3).*
   - Established Entities? If so, which ones? *N/A*
   - Number Restrictions? If so, describe them. *N/A, entities are placed one per position.*
   - Duplications? If so, which rules share an entity? *Rules 1 and 4 share A, and Rules 3 and 4 share F.*
3. Combine the rules and restrictions to create a Master Sketch depicting all of the deductions available in this game: *Begin by recording the negative implications of the blocks of entities. Because of Rule 3, D will never take positions 1 or 2, and F will never take positions 5 or 6. Likewise, because of Rule 5, B will never take position 1 and E will never take position 6. Add those deductions to the sketch.*

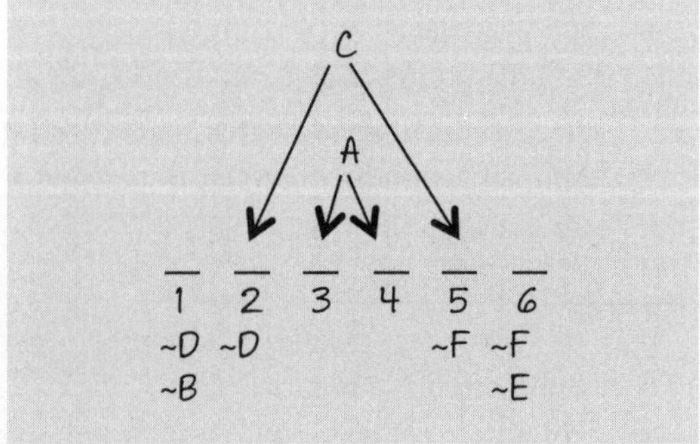

The only entities available for position 1 are thus E and F, and the only entities available for position 6 are thus B and D.

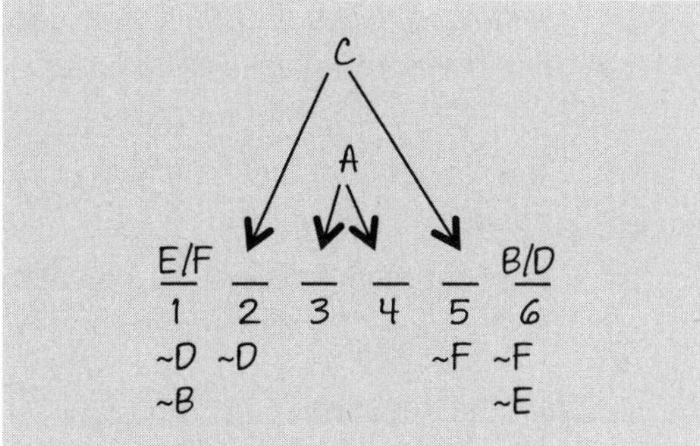

Now, because Rule 1 limits A to positions 3 or 4, and because the placement of A triggers another restriction in Rule 4, make a Limited Options framework to test out each of A's potential positions.

	1	2	3	4	5	6
Opt. I	E/F		A			B/D
Opt. II	E/F			A		B/D

First, explore Option I. Because of Rule 4, F cannot occupy position 4 with A in position 3. Where could the F_D block be placed in this option? It can go only in positions 2 and 4. That means E will take position 1, and B will take position 6. In this option, C must take position 5, the only position that remains open.

	1	2	3	4	5	6
Opt. I	E	F	A	D	C	B

Now, work out the deductions in Option II. With A in position 4, the F_D block could fit in positions 1 and 3, or in positions 3 and 5. In either case, B will take position 6.

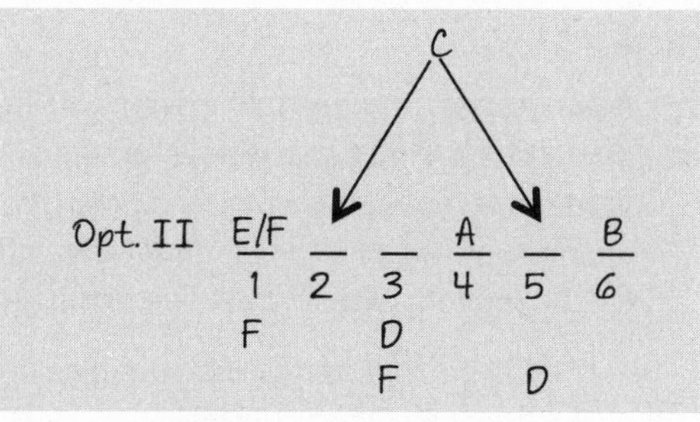

With the two options worked out to that degree, you should be able to answer any question that the test might throw at you about this game.

Note: If you wanted to, you could continue to push the deductions in Option II even further. For example, when the F_D block takes positions 1 and 3, then C and E will take positions 2 and 5 in either order. And when the F_D block takes positions 3 and 5, then E must take position 1 and C must take position 2. The decision to take the deductions that far on test day would be a matter of time, and of how much additional help you think it would be in answering the questions.

	1	2	3	4	5	6
Opt. II	F	C/E	D	A	E/C	B
	E	C	F	A	D	B

4. Evaluate your sketch by answering the following questions:
   - Which entities could acceptably occupy position 1? *The earrings or the fleece pullover.*
   - If the art kit is in position 3, which entity or entities could be in position 5? *Only the charm bracelet.*
   - If the art kit is in position 4, which entity or entities could be in position 2? *The earrings or the charm bracelet.*
   - How many entities could acceptably occupy position 6? *Just one, the bandanna.*

Practice 2

A park ranger surveyed different parks in her district for various species of medium-sized predators—bobcat, coyote, lynx, marten, ocelot and wolverine—and ranked them from most to least common, with no ties. The results indicated:

In all parks, coyotes were the most or second most common species.
Bobcat and lynx were never both among the three most common species in the same park.
In every park, both bobcat and lynx were more common than both marten and wolverine.

Steps 1–3:

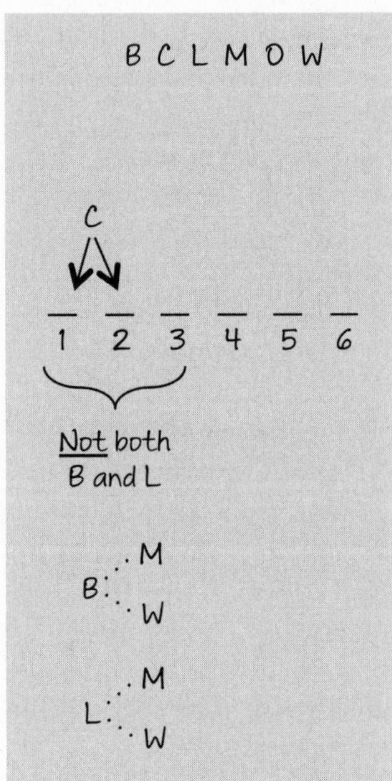

1. Which entities or positions are the most restricted in this game? Why? *While C is restricted to just two acceptable positions (Rule 1), B and L are both restricted by two rules (Rules 2 and 3). Both B and L must have larger populations than M and W, but only one of B or L is permitted to be among the top three largest populations.*

2. Which elements from the BLEND checklist can you identify in this game? Are there
   - Blocks of entities? If so, what are they? *Rule 3 creates two loose blocks: B is larger than M and W, and L is larger than M and W.*
   - Limited Options? If so, which rule(s) trigger them? *N/A*
   - Established Entities? If so, which ones? *C is restricted to two positions, but no entity's position is completely established.*
   - Number Restrictions? If so, describe them. *N/A; the arrangement is already one per position ("no ties").*
   - Duplications? If so, which rules share an entity? *Rules 2 and 3 share B and L.*

3. Combine the rules and restrictions to create a Master Sketch depicting all of the deductions available in this game: *The duplication of two entities in Rules 2 and 3 make B and L the focus of the deductions here. Because both B and L must rank higher than M and W, the lowest B or L could be is fourth. Because only one of B or L is allowed to among the top three species, you know that either B or L is always fourth.*

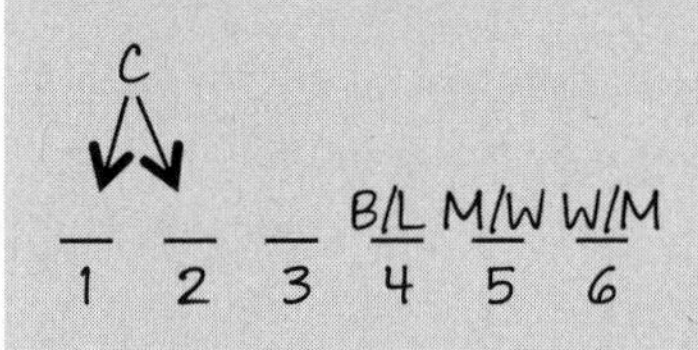

That sketch also shows that M and W will be fifth and sixth, in either order, because both of them must be ranked lower than either B or L.

With one of B or L in fourth place, you can deduce that the other will be among the top three species. You already know (from Rule 1) that C is either first or second. That means that O, the only remaining entity, will also be among the top three.

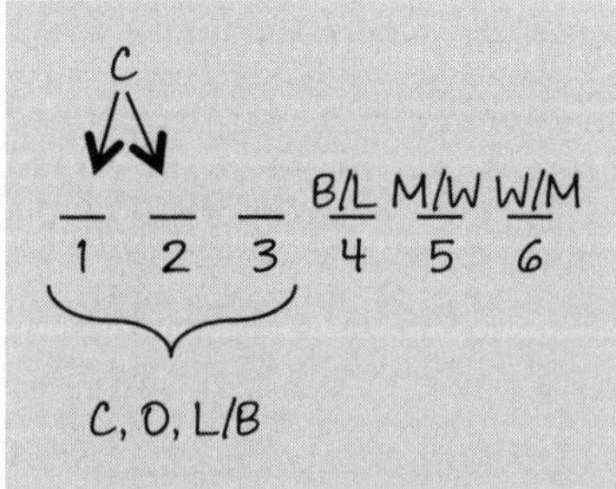

It is not worth the time it would take to work out all the possible arrangements of the first through third spots. Those positions would come

into play in New-"If" questions, and the question stem would give you the information necessary to work out what you would need to know.

4. Evaluate your sketch by answering the following questions:
    - Write out a complete and accurate list of species that could be the fourth most common at one of the parks. *Bobcat and lynx.*
    - Write out a complete and accurate list of the positions that martens could acceptably occupy. *Fifth or sixth.*
    - Write out a complete and accurate list of the species that could be the most common at one of the parks. *Bobcat, coyote, lynx, and ocelot.*
    - If bobcats are the second most common species at one of the parks, what else *must be true* about species population at that park? *In that case, 1) coyotes are the most common species, 2) ocelots are the third most common species, and 3) lynx are the fourth most common species at that park.*

Practice 3

Throughout the course of a day, an executive will attend exactly seven different business presentations. Each of the presentations is on exactly one of four topics: Distribution, Logistics, Marketing, and Sales. She attends the meetings according to the following constraints:

> She attends exactly three presentations on Logistics, exactly two presentations on Marketing, and exactly one presentation each on Distribution and Sales.
> She never attends consecutive meetings on Logistics.
> She attends the meeting on Sales immediately after she attends the meeting on Distribution.
> Either the first or last presentation she attends, or both, will be a Marketing presentation.

Steps 1–3:

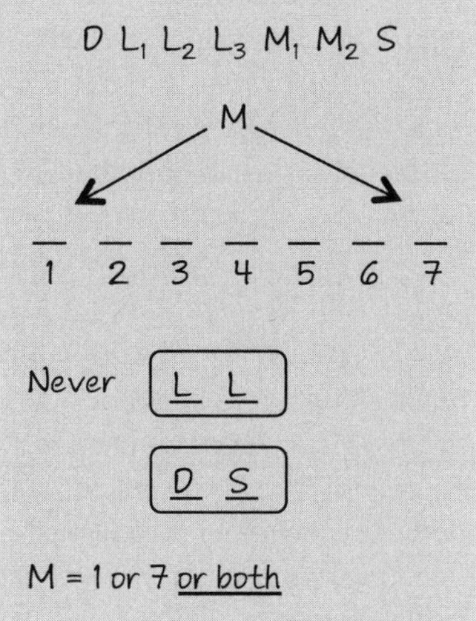

1. Which entities or positions are the most restricted in this game? Why? *With the unusual set of entities in this game, the place to begin will be with the three presentations on Logistics (noted as L_1, L_2, and L_3 in the sketch), none of which can be consecutive.*

2. Which elements from the BLEND checklist can you identify in this game? Are there
    - Blocks of entities? If so, what are they? *Rule 3 creates a strict block: D-S.*
    - Limited Options? If so, which rule(s) trigger them? *N/A*
    - Established Entities? If so, which ones? *N/A*
    - Number Restrictions? If so, describe them. *N/A; although the assignment of entities to positions is one-to-one, Rule 1 creates a quasi-number restriction by stipulating that there are three Logistics presentations and two Marketing presentations.*
    - Duplications? If so, which rules share an entity? *All four entities appear in Rule 1 and in one other rule (Logistics in Rule 2, Distribution and Sales in Rule 3, and Marketing in Rule 4).*

3. Combine the rules and restrictions to create a Master Sketch depicting all of the deductions available in this game: *Start with the combination of Rules 1 and 2. If there are to be three Ls, and if none of them can be consecutive, they can be depicted like this:*

L _ ... L _ ... L

Note that the string of Ls takes up at least five of the game's seven positions. Next, consider the two Ms. At least one of them must be first or seventh, and Rule 3 allows for them to be both first and seventh. However, if Ms were both first and seventh, you would find yourself in this situation:

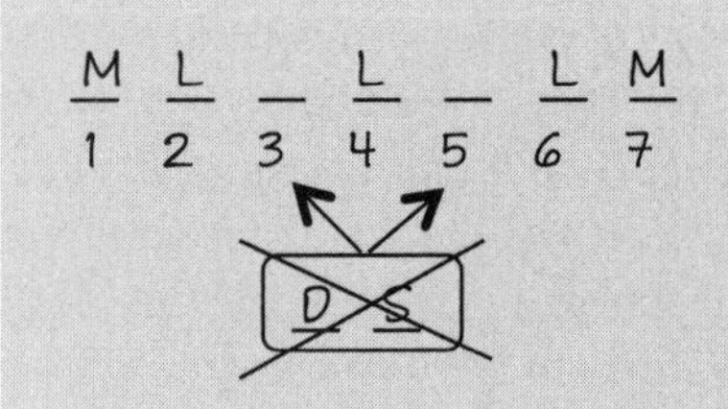

In that case, there is no place for the D-S block. You now know that if one M is first, the other cannot be seventh, and vice versa. To find room for the D-S block, it will need to go in between two Ls, and one of the Ms will also have to go in between two Ls.

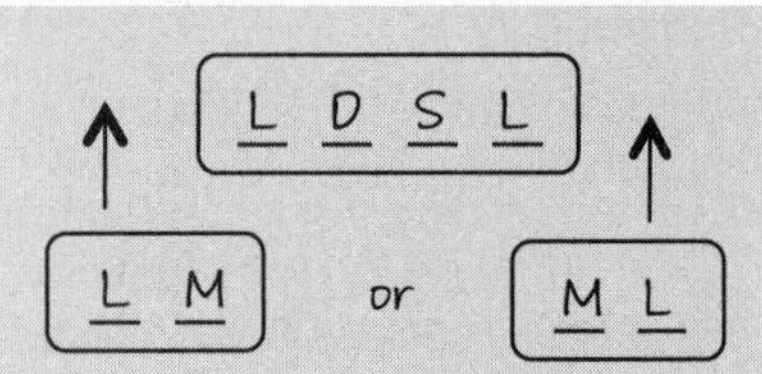

The remaining M can go on either side of one of these six-entity blocks. That helps you to see that whenever M is first, an L will be seventh, and whenever an M is seventh, an L will be first.

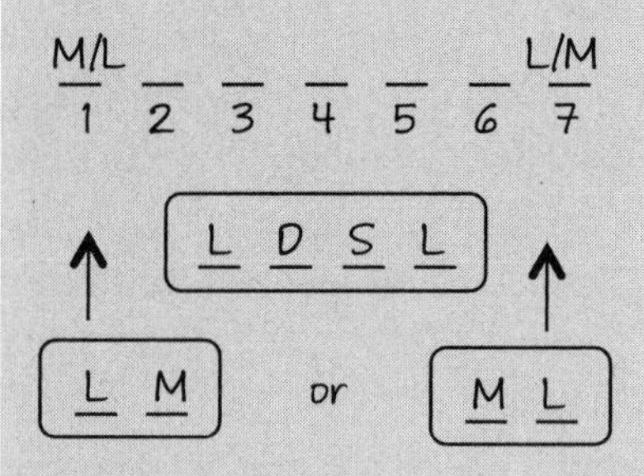

4. Evaluate your sketch by answering the following questions:
   - If the executive sees the Sales presentation fourth, for how many of the positions can the topic of the presentation be precisely determined? *All seven positions can be determined. With S in the fourth position, the only acceptable arrangement is: M, L, D, S, L, M, L*
   - If the executive sees a Logistics presentation second, in which positions could she see the Distribution presentation? *If an L is second, there are two acceptable arrangements, either M, L, D, S, L, M, L or M, L, M, L, D, S, L; thus, with an L in the second position, the D could be third or fifth.*
   - If the executive sees a Marketing presentation first, which of the topics could be the topic she sees in the seventh presentation? *If an M is first, an L must be seventh.*
   - Write out a complete and accurate list of all the topics that could not be the topic covered by the first presentation. *The first presentation must be an M or an L. Thus, D and S are the topics that cannot be first.*

The number of deductions available in Strict Sequencing games varies widely. In some, the deductions are so concrete that you will be left with only a handful of acceptable arrangements by the time you've finished Step 4. In others, the testmaker leaves much more ambiguity among the entities and within the framework. In games with fewer deductions, expect to see more New-"If" questions, as each of those questions' stems introduces a new rule or restriction into the mix. If you find yourself feeling stuck in Step 4, glance at the questions. If almost all of them are New-"If"s, you may have found all of the deductions available. Move on, creating new sketches for each of the New-"If" scenarios, and make the deductions for each question there.

In the next (and final) section of this chapter, put all of your skills together to handle some full basic Strict Sequencing games and their questions.

BASIC STRICT SEQUENCING GAMES—FULL GAMES WITH QUESTIONS

LEARNING OBJECTIVES

In this section, you'll assess your ability to

- Apply the Logic Games Method to basic Strict Sequencing games.

Perform

Here is your opportunity to put all of the pieces together and assess your skills on basic Strict Sequencing games. On the following pages, you'll find three full-length games along with their question sets. All of these games are from officially released LSAT tests, and all are representative of basic Strict Sequencing games you could see on test day. You can take the games one at a time or all together, but for your self-evaluation to be as accurate as possible, adhere to the timing guidelines set forth in the directions.

An answer key follows the games. Complete worked example analyses can be found in your online resources.

After you complete and review all three games, assess your performance using the evaluation guidelines. There you'll find recommendations for additional Easy, Medium, and Hard basic Strict Sequencing games from officially released LSAT exams that you can practice to continue honing your skills and raising your score.

Directions: Take no more than 9 minutes per game to complete the following three games and all of their questions.

Perform 1

Questions 1–5

A producer is positioning exactly seven music pieces—F, G, H, J, K, L, and M—one after another on a music recording, not necessarily in that order. Each piece will fill exactly one of the seven sequential tracks on the recording, according to the following conditions:

F must be second.

J cannot be seventh.

G can come neither immediately before nor immediately after H.

H must be in some track before that of L.

L must be in some track before that of M.

1. Which one of the following could be the order, from first to seventh, of the pieces on the recording?

(A) F, K, G, J, H, L, M

(B) G, F, H, K, L, J, M

(C) G, F, H, K, L, M, J

(D) K, F, G, H, J, L, M

(E) K, F, L, J, H, M, G

2. If M fills some track before that of J and also before that of K on the recording, which one of the following must be true?

   (A) G is first.
   (B) K is seventh.
   (C) L is third.
   (D) H comes either immediately before or immediately after F.
   (E) L comes either immediately before or immediately after G.

3. Which one of the following is a complete and accurate list of the pieces any of which could be first on the recording?

   (A) G, J, K
   (B) G, H, J, K
   (C) G, H, J, L
   (D) G, J, K, L
   (E) H, J, K, L, M

4. The earliest track that M can fill is the

   (A) first
   (B) third
   (C) fourth
   (D) fifth
   (E) sixth

5. If G is to come immediately before H but all the other conditions remain in effect, any of the following could be true EXCEPT:

   (A) J comes immediately before F.
   (B) K comes immediately before G.
   (C) J comes immediately after L.
   (D) J comes immediately after K.
   (E) K comes immediately after M.

PrepTest23 Sec1 Qs 1-5

Perform 2

Questions 6–10

Five people—Harry, Iris, Kate, Nancy, and Victor—are to be scheduled as contestants on a television show, one contestant per day, for five consecutive days from Monday through Friday. The following restrictions governing the scheduling of contestants must be observed:

Nancy is not scheduled for Monday.

If Harry is scheduled for Monday, Nancy is scheduled for Friday.

If Nancy is scheduled for Tuesday, Iris is scheduled for Monday.

Kate is scheduled for the next day after the day for which Victor is scheduled.

6. Victor can be scheduled for any day EXCEPT

(A) Monday

(B) Tuesday

(C) Wednesday

(D) Thursday

(E) Friday

7. If Iris is scheduled for the next day after Harry, which one of the following lists all those days any one of which could be the day for which Harry is scheduled?

   (A) Monday, Tuesday
   (B) Monday, Wednesday
   (C) Monday, Thursday
   (D) Monday, Tuesday, Wednesday
   (E) Monday, Wednesday, Thursday

8. If Kate is scheduled for Wednesday, which one of the following could be true?

   (A) Iris is scheduled for Friday.
   (B) Nancy is scheduled for Tuesday.
   (C) Nancy is scheduled for an earlier day than the day for which Harry is scheduled.
   (D) Nancy is scheduled for an earlier day than the day for which Iris is scheduled.
   (E) Nancy is scheduled for an earlier day than the day for which Kate is scheduled.

9. If Kate is scheduled for Friday, which one of the following must be true?

   (A) Harry is scheduled for Tuesday.
   (B) Harry is scheduled for Wednesday.
   (C) Iris is scheduled for Monday.
   (D) Iris is scheduled for Wednesday.
   (E) Nancy is scheduled for Wednesday.

10. If Iris is scheduled for Wednesday, which one of the following must be true?

   (A) Harry is scheduled for an earlier day than the day for which Nancy is scheduled.
   (B) Harry is scheduled for an earlier day than the day for which Kate is scheduled.
   (C) Kate is scheduled for an earlier day than the day for which Harry is scheduled.
   (D) Nancy is scheduled for an earlier day than the day for which Kate is scheduled.
   (E) Nancy is scheduled for an earlier day than the day for which Iris is scheduled.

PrepTest13 Sec1 Qs 7-11

Perform 3

Questions 11–17

During a period of six consecutive days—day 1 through day 6—each of exactly six factories—F, G, H, J, Q, and R—will be inspected. During this period, each of the factories will be inspected exactly once, one factory per day. The schedule for the inspections must conform to the following conditions:

F is inspected on either day 1 or day 6.

J is inspected on an earlier day than Q is inspected.

Q is inspected on the day immediately before R is inspected.

If G is inspected on day 3, Q is inspected on day 5.

11. Which one of the following could be a list of the factories in the order of their scheduled inspections, from day 1 through day 6?

(A) F, Q, R, H, J, G

(B) G, H, J, Q, R, F

(C) G, J, Q, H, R, F

(D) G, J, Q, R, F, H

(E) J, H, G, Q, R, F

12. Which one of the following must be false?

    (A) The inspection of G is scheduled for day 4.
    (B) The inspection of H is scheduled for day 6.
    (C) The inspection of J is scheduled for day 4.
    (D) The inspection of Q is scheduled for day 3.
    (E) The inspection of R is scheduled for day 2.

13 The inspection of which one of the following CANNOT be scheduled for day 5?

    (A) G
    (B) H
    (C) J
    (D) Q
    (E) R

14. The inspection scheduled for day 3 and day 5, respectively, could be those of

    (A) G and H
    (B) G and R
    (C) H and G
    (D) R and J
    (E) R and H

15. If the inspection of R is scheduled for the day immediately before the inspection of F, which one of the following must be true about the schedule?

    (A) The inspection of either G or H is scheduled for day 1.
    (B) The inspection of either G or J is scheduled for day 1.
    (C) The inspection of either G or J is scheduled for day 2.
    (D) The inspection of either H or J is scheduled for day 3.
    (E) The inspection of either H or J is scheduled for day 4.

16. If the inspection of G and of H are scheduled, not necessarily in that order, for days as far apart as possible, which one of the following is a complete and accurate list of the factories any one of which could be scheduled for inspection for day 1?

    (A) F, J
    (B) G, H
    (C) G, H, J
    (D) F, G, H
    (E) F, G, H, J

17. If the inspection of G is scheduled for the day immediately before the inspection of Q, which one of the following could be true?

    (A) The inspection of G is scheduled for day 5.
    (B) The inspection of H is scheduled for day 6.
    (C) The inspection of J is scheduled for day 2.
    (D) The inspection of Q is scheduled for day 4.
    (E) The inspection of R is scheduled for day 3.

PrepTest19 Sec1 Qs 1-7

Answer Key

Perform 1

1. (B)
2. (D)
3. (B)
4. (C)
5. (D)

Perform 2

6. (E)
7. (E)
8. (C)
9. (C)
10. (C)

Perform 3

11. (B)
12. (E)
13. (C)
14. (E)
15. (D)
16. (D)
17. (C)

Worked example explanations of these questions with complete expert analysis can be found in your Online Study Plan under Chapter 5. View or download the PDF titled "Chapter 5 Perform Full Games Explanations."

Assess

Use the following criteria to evaluate your results on the Perform games.

If, under timed conditions, you correctly answered

14–17 of the questions: Outstanding! You have demonstrated a strong skill level in basic Strict Sequencing games. For further practice in basic Strict Sequencing, use any of the Recommended Additional Practice sets, including the Advanced set. Then, move on to Chapter 6 on complex Strict Sequencing.

10–13 of the questions: Good work! You have a solid foundation in basic Strict Sequencing games. For further practice in basic Strict Sequencing, begin with the Foundations or Mid-Level Recommended Additional Practice set. Then, move on to Chapter 6 on complex Strict Sequencing. If you have time before test day, try the Advanced Recommended Additional Practice set, as well.

0–9 of the questions: Keep working. Strict Sequencing games are central to your logic games performance, and continued practice will help you improve your score. Begin by reviewing this chapter. Then, try the games in the Foundations Recommended Additional Practice set. As you continue to progress, move on to the Mid-Level Recommended Additional Practice set, and then to Chapter 6 on complex Strict Sequencing games.

To stay sharp, practice the drills in the Logic Games Training Camp for this chapter in your Online Study Plan. Training Camp drills are divided into Fundamentals, Mid-Level, and Advanced sets.

Recommended Additional Practice: Basic Strict Sequencing

All of the following games will provide good practice on basic Strict Sequencing games. They are grouped by difficulty as determined from empirical student practice results. All PrepTests included are available on LawHub with an LSAC Prep Plus subscription.

Foundations

PrepTest 70, Section 3, Game 1: Benefit Concert

PrepTest 67, Section 3, Game 2: Literary Theory Lectures

PrepTest 63, Section 2, Game 2: Skydiving Team

PrepTest 62, Section 3, Game 4: Testifying Witnesses

PrepTest 57, Section 1, Game 1: Student Activities

Mid-Level

PrepTest 66, Section 3, Game 2: Shopping Center Businesses

PrepTest 64, Section 2, Game 1: Employee Parking

PrepTest 62, Section 3, Game 1: Motel Service Appointments

PrepTest 56, Section 1, Game 1: Saxophone Auditions

PrepTest 54, Section 3, Game 3: Cake Layers

Advanced

PrepTest 71, Section 2, Game 4: Paintings in a Museum

PrepTest 69, Section 2, Game 1: Manuscript Ages

PrepTest 63, Section 2, Game 3: Vehicle Service

PrepTest 59, Section 1, Game 2: Museum Photographs

PrepTest 59, Section 1, Game 4: Organization's Annual Meetings

Complete explanations and analysis for all of the more-than-70 official LSAT tests on LawHub that come with an LSAC LSAT Prep Plus subscription are available in Kaplan's LSAT Link and Link+ tools. Visit **www.kaptest.com/lsat** to learn more or to purchase LSAT Link or Link+.

Reflect

Think back over the study and practice you did in this chapter.

- Are you able to identify basic Strict Sequencing games from their setups?
- Do you have a default sketch framework for Strict Sequencing actions?
- What kinds of rules do you anticipate seeing in Strict Sequencing games?
- Are you comfortable analyzing Strict Sequencing rules and determining whether to record them within or underneath the sketch framework?
- Are you making the available deductions efficiently and effectively in Strict Sequencing games?

In the coming days and weeks before test day, take note of real-world tasks that reflect basic Strict Sequencing tasks. Consider how they mirror the setups and questions in LSAT Strict Sequencing, and how they differ. Try to reframe real-life sequencing tasks using the terms, rules, and restrictions used by the testmaker.

CHAPTER 6

Complex Strict Sequencing Games Unlocked

LEARNING OBJECTIVES

In this chapter, you'll learn to

- Apply the Logic Games Method to complex Strict Sequencing games.

Prepare

On LSATs administered over the past five years, around 60 percent of all Strict Sequencing games qualify as "complex." Now, just because a Strict Sequencing game is complex doesn't mean that it's hard. While the complex Strict Sequencing variants are, on average, somewhat more challenging than their basic counterparts, they nevertheless run the gamut from games on the easier end of the spectrum to games that are among the hardest found on the LSAT. Don't be intimidated by a complex setup. Once these games are familiar—and nothing builds familiarity like practice does—you'll be able to apply the Logic Games Method just as you do on other game types. And, remember, the LSAT always provides all of the information you need to answer the questions.

The defining characteristic of basic Strict Sequencing games is a one-to-one matchup of entities to positions. Complex Strict Sequencing games alter the setup in a variety of ways. Some may ask you to sequence the entities two (or even three) times. Imagine a game in which five hurdlers at a track meet will take different starting positions in each of three heats.

A B C D E

Heat

Heat					
1	_ 1	_ 2	_ 3	_ 4	_ 5
2	_ 1	_ 2	_ 3	_ 4	_ 5
3	_ 1	_ 2	_ 3	_ 4	_ 5

Another common variant has different numbers of entities and positions. You could be asked, for example, to schedule seven entities over the course of five days, with one *or two* each day.

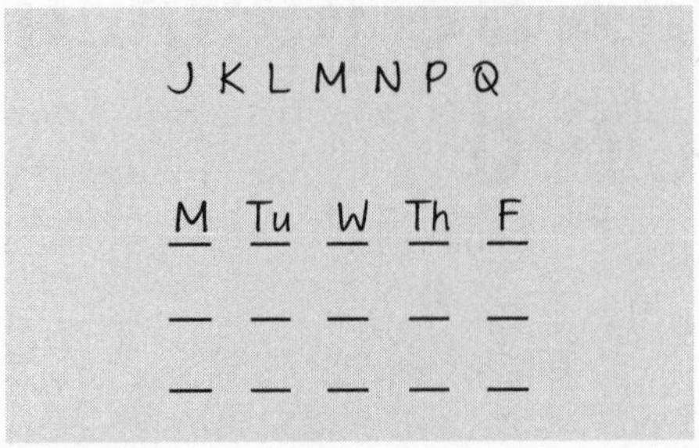

J K L M N P Q

M Tu W Th F

Alternatively, the setup might call for you to figure out when each of six events occurred over the course of eight years.

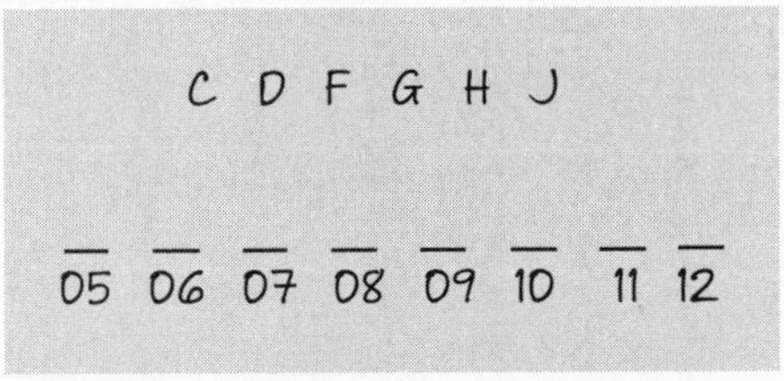

C D F G H J

05 06 07 08 09 10 11 12

Perhaps the most common complex Strict Sequencing variant is one in which the framework is doubled. This could involve two different people performing the same tasks in different orders.

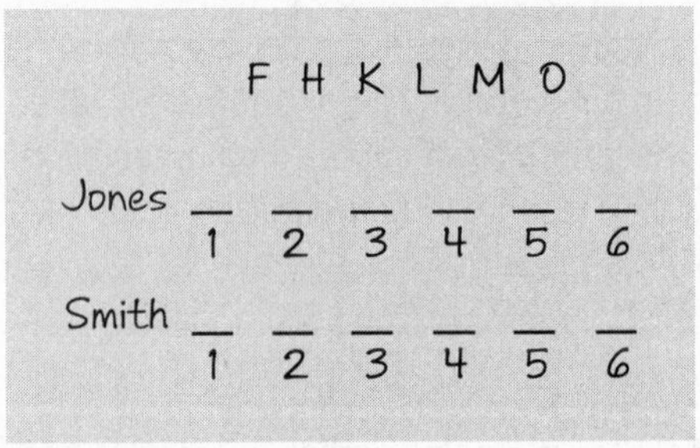

F H K L M O

Jones 1 2 3 4 5 6

Smith 1 2 3 4 5 6

It could also be a schedule of appointments with morning and afternoon meeting times.

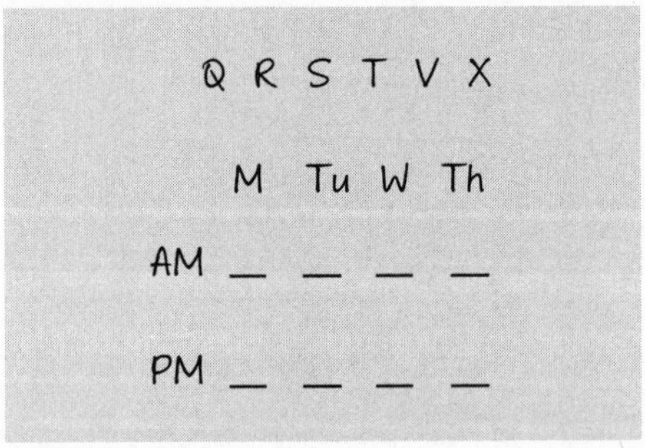

Q R S T V X

M Tu W Th

AM

PM

There is one complex Strict Sequencing setup so rare that it warrants a separate discussion. In the Special Feature that follows this chapter, you'll learn about Circular Sequencing, in which the entities are arranged around a table, or in some other type of round scenario. While it's unlikely that you'll see a Circular Sequencing game, those that were released in the past were challenging, and students who want the most comprehensive Logic Games preparation will enjoy the video in which a Kaplan LSAT Channel instructor takes you through one of the toughest complex Sequencing games ever to appear on the LSAT.

The Overview step of the Logic Games Method takes on added importance in complex games. You'll want to quickly understand the situation and have a clear picture of the task before you create your initial sketch.

COMPLEX STRICT SEQUENCING IN REAL LIFE

When you think about Sequencing tasks in real life, you likely default to those corresponding to basic Strict Sequencing—a group of people or items arranged in a row, one at a time. You won't have to brainstorm too long, however, to come up with real-life scenarios that mirror the LSAT's complex Strict Sequencing tasks.

In one or more of your college classes, you probably had to meet with a professor more than one time during the semester. For example, a professor may have required one meeting to discuss and approve your research topic, a second meeting to approve your list of sources, and then a third to review your first draft. Stick that scenario into a logic game that describes a seminar course with six students, and you have a ready-made complex Strict Sequencing game.

A C J L S V

meetings

	1	2	3	4	5	6
1	__	__	__	__	__	__
2	__	__	__	__	__	__
3	__	__	__	__	__	__

A class schedule presents another easily understandable variation. It might be that a law student has some classes only on Tuesdays and Thursdays, and others only on Mondays, Wednesdays, and Fridays. For good measure, throw one of those long, once-per-week classes into the mix. You have no problem interpreting this student's schedule at a glance.

	M	Tu	W	Th	F
9:30AM	Torts	__	Torts	__	Torts
10:30AM	__	CivPro	__	CivPro	__
1PM	__	Property	__	Property	__
2:30-5:30PM	Crim Law	__	__	__	__

In real-life sequencing tasks, you sometimes have to account for subgroups among the people or things you're putting in order. In a photograph or a game, for example, you may want to arrange people "boy-girl-boy-girl." If you have six pictures to hang on a wall, you would take into account the fact that three have blue backgrounds and three have red backgrounds. You might want to keep those with the same background color together, or you might want to intersperse them with pictures of the other color. Either way, you would not ignore the differences in the groups. The LSAT sometimes mirrors these real-life situations by subdividing the entities in a Sequencing game. You might run into a game in which you are deciding the speaking order of seven foreign policy experts: four who specialize in the Balkans—A, B, C, and D—and three who specialize in North Africa—M, P, S.

Bal	N.Afr
A B C D	m p s

__	__	__	__	__	__	__
1	2	3	4	5	6	7

Because the entities are subdivided, that game would qualify as "complex" Strict Sequencing, even though the ratio of entities to slots is one-to-one. When you encounter a situation like this, expect the rules or restrictions to explicitly group or break up entities in one or both of the subgroups within the sequence.

Even if a game asks you to use some entities multiple times, to leave some slots open, or to account for subdivisions among the entities, it's nothing you haven't done before. In the next section of this chapter, you'll have the chance to practice Steps 1 and 2 of the Logic Games Method on a handful of complex Strict Sequencing games. Pay close attention as you conduct your overview, and see if you can translate the situation described there into a clear, helpful sketch.

COMPLEX STRICT SEQUENCING GAMES TASKS AND SKETCHES

LEARNING OBJECTIVES

In this section of the chapter, you'll practice

- Applying Steps 1 and 2 of the Logic Games Method to complex Strict Sequencing games by
  - Asking the SEAL questions to analyze the game's Overview, and then
  - Creating a simple, useful Sketch framework

Prepare

While the situations described in complex Strict Sequencing setups offer an additional layer to action, the underlying tasks are identical to those in basic Strict Sequencing.

LOGIC GAMES STRATEGY

Sequencing games ask you to put things in order in one of the following ways:

- Chronologically—either using units of time such as years, weeks, days, or hours, or simply using the ideas of "earlier" and "later"
- Spatially—horizontally or vertically; imagine runners about to run a race taking their positions in numbered lanes, or a wedding cake with different layers, one on top of the other
- By rank—similar to a top 10 list, or the finishing order of a competition
- By size or amount—imagine a wish list with items arranged from most to least expensive

In complex Strict Sequencing, pay special attention to the list of entities—are the entities used once, twice, or three times each?—and to the description of the framework for the game—can each position in the game accommodate one or more than one entity?

> At a chili cook-off, two judges—Rodriguez and Stanton—will each sample chili prepared by six contestants—Berghoff, Charlton, Dominguez, Ellis, Ferguson, and Gascon—although not necessarily in the same order. Each judge samples one bowl of chili from each contestant. The order in which each judge samples the chili will conform to the following restrictions:

B C D E F G

Rod __ __ __ __ __ __
1 2 3 4 5 6

Stan __ __ __ __ __ __
1 2 3 4 5 6

In that game, each of the entities will be used twice, once in each judge's row.

Try Steps 1 and 2 of the Logic Games Method on the following game setups. Be on the lookout for the variations that make them examples of *complex* Strict Sequencing.

Practice

Directions: Conduct an Overview of each game's setup by asking the SEAL questions, and create an initial sketch framework for the game's action.

Practice 1

A committee of teachers at Lakeside High School is planning the spring exam schedule for first-year and second-year students for a given week, Monday through Friday. The committee must schedule four first-year student exams—algebra, biology, English 1, and world history; four second-year student exams—chemistry, English 2, geometry, and US history; and no other exams. Each exam will be administered once during the week, either at 8 AM or at 11 AM, and no exams may be administered simultaneously. The following conditions must be met:

1. [Step 1] Conduct an Overview analysis:
   - What is this game's Situation?
   - Who or what are the game's Entities?
   - What is the game's Action?
   - What are the Limitations explicit in the game setup?
2. [Step 2] Create an initial Sketch:

Practice 2

An apartment building has five floors. Each floor has either one or two apartments. There are exactly eight apartments in the building. The residents of the building are J, K, L, M, N, O, P, and Q, who each live in a different apartment.

PrepTest2 Sec3 Qs 6–12

1. [Step 1] Conduct an Overview analysis:
   - What is this game's Situation?
   - Who or what are the game's Entities?
   - What is the game's Action?
   - What are the Limitations explicit in the game setup?
2. [Step 2] Create an initial Sketch:

Practice 3

Exactly seven professors—Madison, Nilsson, Orozco, Paton, Robinson, Sarkis, and Togo—were hired in the years 1989 through 1995. Each professor has one or more specialties, and any two professors hired in the same year or in consecutive years do not have a specialty in common. The professors were hired according to the following conditions:

PrepTest35 Sec3 Qs 18–23

1. [Step 1] Conduct an Overview analysis:
   - What is this game's Situation?
   - Who or what are the game's Entities?
   - What is the game's Action?
   - What are the Limitations explicit in the game setup?
2. [Step 2] Create an initial Sketch:

Explanations

Compare your work to that of an LSAT expert. Keep track of any case in which you incorrectly characterized the action described in the setup, and any case in which you drew a sketch framework that does not match the details of the game's situation.

Practice 1

A committee of teachers at Lakeside High School is planning the spring exam schedule for first-year and second-year students for a given week, Monday through Friday. The committee must schedule four first-year student exams—algebra, biology, English 1 and world history; four second-year student exams—chemistry, English 2, geometry and US history; and no other exams. Each exam will be administered once during the week, either at 8 AM or at 11 AM, and no exams may be administered simultaneously. The following conditions must be met:

1. [Step 1] Conduct an Overview analysis:
   - What is this game's Situation? *The task here is to schedule eight different exams—four each for two different groups of students—over the course of one school week.*
   - Who or what are the game's Entities? *Eight exams—A, B, E_1, and G for the first-year student, and C, E_2, G, and U for the second-year students.*
   - What is the game's Action? *Complex Strict Sequencing—there may be one or two exams per day given at 8 AM or 11 AM.*
   - What are the Limitations explicit in the game setup? *No exams given simultaneously.*
2. [Step 2] Create an initial Sketch:

```
1st-4          2nd-4
a b e1 w       C E2 G U

     M   Tu   W   Th   F

8    _   _    _   _    _
11   _   _    _   _    _
```

Practice 2

An apartment building has five floors. Each floor has either one or two apartments. There are exactly eight apartments in the building. The residents of the building are J, K, L, M, N, O, P, and Q, who each live in a different apartment.

PrepTest2 Sec3 Qs 6–12

1. [Step 1] Conduct an Overview analysis:
   - What is this game's Situation? *The task is to figure out which of five floors of an apartment building eight different people live on.*
   - Who or what are the game's Entities? *Eight residents—J, K, L, M, N, O, P, and Q.*
   - What is the game's Action? *Complex Strict Sequencing—some floors will have more than one resident.*
   - What are the Limitations explicit in the game setup? *Each floor has either one or two apartments, and each resident lives alone.*
2. [Step 2] Create an initial Sketch:

```
J K L M N O P Q

5  _  (_)
4  _  (_)
3  _  (_)
2  _  (_)
1  _  (_)
```

Practice 3

Exactly seven professors—Madison, Nilsson, Orozco, Paton, Robinson, Sarkis, and Togo—were hired in the years 1989 through 1995. Each professor has one or more specialties, and any two professors hired in the same year or in consecutive years do not have a specialty in common. The professors were hired according to the following conditions:

PrepTest35 Sec3 Qs 18–23

1. [Step 1] Conduct an Overview analysis:
   - What is this game's Situation? *The task is to determine the hiring year of seven professors who were each hired between 1989 and 1995.*
   - Who or what are the game's Entities? *Seven professors—M, N, O, P, R, S, and T.*
   - What is the game's Action? *Complex Strict Sequencing—more than one professor may have been hired in a given year (the setup offers qualifications for "any two professors hired in the same year"), and thus, some years may have no hirings.*
   - What are the Limitations explicit in the game setup? *Some of the professors share specialties, a characteristic that will prevent them from being hired in the same year or consecutive years to professors with the same specialty.*
2. [Step 2] Create an initial Sketch:

M N O P R S T

89 90 91 92 93 94 95

You'll see these model game setups again as you practice Step 3, analyzing and drawing the rules, and Step 4, making deductions in basic Strict Sequencing games. When you come back to the Professors' Hire Dates game, pay special attention to the rules that describe professors who share specialties. When logic games introduce unique terms (like "specialties" in that game), they will always define the term and use it to create restrictions within the game.

COMPLEX STRICT SEQUENCING RULES

LEARNING OBJECTIVES

In this section of the chapter, you'll practice

- Applying Step 3 of the Logic Games Method to complex Strict Sequencing games by analyzing and sketching the rules

Prepare

The rules in complex Strict Sequencing games aren't much different than those found in basic Strict Sequencing. In both, the rules restrict entities in relationship to specific positions or relative to one another.

LOGIC GAMES STRATEGY

Strict Sequencing rules basically tell you one or more of the following:

- The order in which two or more entities are placed
- The number of spaces between two or more entities
- The slot(s) in which a given entity can or cannot be placed

There are a couple of instances in which a complex Strict Sequencing sketch framework can work a little differently than its standard counterpart. Consider what the following rules mean in a game in which you are asked to schedule appointments for either a morning or an afternoon from Monday to Friday.

> Becky's appointment is some time before Craig's appointment.
> Greg's appointment is on an earlier day of the week than Rachel's appointment.

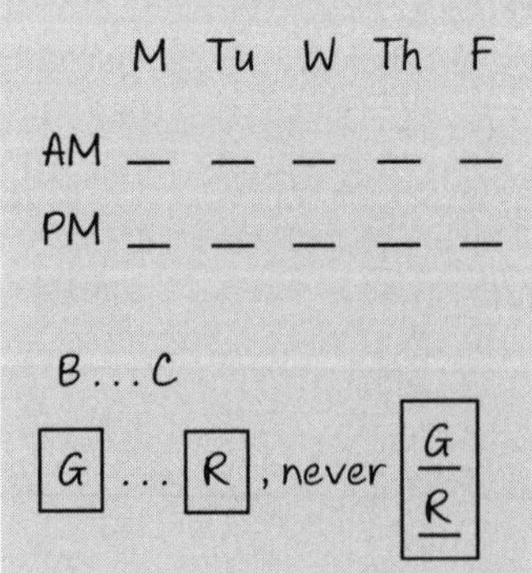

In the first of those rules, Becky's appointment could be in the morning of the same day on which Craig has an appointment in the afternoon. In the second rule, that case would be unacceptable.

If a game asks you to schedule entities more than one time apiece, pay close attention to the wording of rules that stipulate one of the entity's positions. For example, in a game where six employees are scheduled for two shifts each, you could see rules like the following:

> The second day on which Carlos works is Wednesday.
> Firuz works on Thursday.

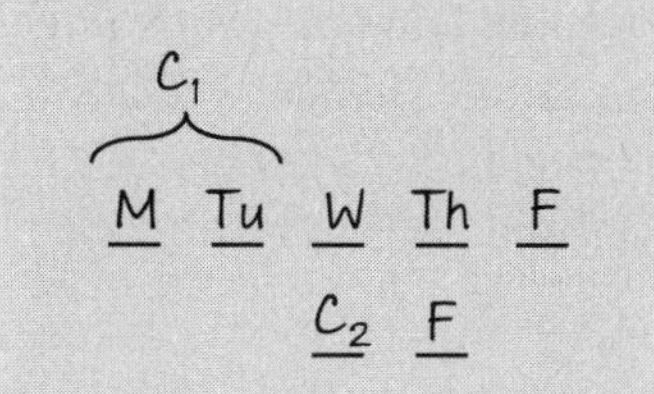

Did you catch the distinction? The first rule states that Carlos's second shift is on Wednesday, meaning that his first shift must be on Monday or Tuesday. In Firuz's case, however, you learn only that *one of* his shifts is on Thursday, but not whether it is his first or second shift.

In the following exercises, the rules have been added to the three setups you analyzed in the previous section of this chapter. Practice analyzing and drawing the rules in the context of each setup.

Practice

Directions: Take a couple minutes to review each game's setup, summarize your Overview analysis, and recreate the initial Sketch. Then, one at a time, analyze the rules, answer the questions about each one, and draw the rule either inside or underneath the sketch framework.

Practice 1

A committee of teachers at Lakeside High School is planning the spring exam schedule for first-year and second-year students for a given week, Monday through Friday. The committee must schedule four first-year student exams—algebra, biology, English 1 and world history; four second-year student exams—chemistry, English 2, geometry and US history; and no other exams. Each exam will be administered once during the week, either at 8 AM or at 11 AM, and no exams may be administered simultaneously. The following conditions must be met:

No two first-year student exams may be given on the same day.
Exactly one first-year student exam is administered at 8 AM.
The geometry exam and the US history exam must be administered on the same day.
No exam will be administered on Friday at 11 AM.
The algebra exam and the biology exam must be administered at the same time of day on consecutive days.

1. [Step 1] Summarize your Overview analysis:

2. [Step 2] Create an initial Sketch:

3. [Step 3] Analyze and draw the Rules:
    - For each rule, answer the following questions and draw the rule in the appropriate box.
        - What does the rule restrict, and what does it leave open?
        - What are the rule's negative implications, if any?
        - Can the rule be depicted inside the sketch framework?

Rule 1:	Rule 2:
Rule 3:	Rule 4:
Rule 5:	

Practice 2

An apartment building has five floors. Each floor has either one or two apartments. There are exactly eight apartments in the building. The residents of the building are J, K, L, M, N, O, P, and Q, who each live in a different apartment.

J lives on a floor with two apartments.
K lives on the floor directly above P.
The second floor is made up of only one apartment.
M and N live on the same floor.
O does not live on the same floor as Q.
L lives in the only apartment on her floor.
Q does not live on the first or second floor.

PrepTest2 Sec3 Qs 6–12

1. [Step 1] Summarize your Overview analysis:

2. [Step 2] Create an initial Sketch:

3. [Step 3] Analyze and draw the Rules:
   - For each rule, answer the following questions and draw the rule in the appropriate box.
     - What does the rule restrict, and what does it leave open?
     - What are the rule's negative implications, if any?
     - Can the rule be depicted inside the sketch framework?

Rule 1:	Rule 2:
Rule 3:	Rule 4:
Rule 5:	Rule 6:
Rule 7:	

Practice 3

Exactly seven professors—Madison, Nilsson, Orozco, Paton, Robinson, Sarkis, and Togo—were hired in the years 1989 through 1995. Each professor has one or more specialties, and any two professors hired in the same year or in consecutive years do not have a specialty in common. The professors were hired according to the following conditions:

Madison was hired in 1993, Robinson in 1991.
There is at least one specialty that Madison, Orozco, and Togo have in common.
Nilsson shares a specialty with Robinson.
Paton and Sarkis were each hired at least one year before Madison and at least one year after Nilsson.
Orozco, who shares a specialty with Sarkis, was hired in 1990.

PrepTest35 Sec3 Qs 18–23

1. [Step 1] Summarize your Overview analysis:

2. [Step 2] Create an initial Sketch:

3. [Step 3] Analyze and draw the Rules:
   - For each rule, answer the following questions and draw the rule in the appropriate box.
     - What does the rule restrict, and what does it leave open?
     - What are the rule's negative implications, if any?
     - Can the rule be depicted inside the sketch framework?

Rule 1:	Rule 2:
Rule 3:	Rule 4:
Rule 5:	

Explanations

Compare your work to that of an LSAT expert. Pay close attention to how the expert analyzed each rule and then depicted it within or beneath the game's initial sketch.

Practice 1

A committee of teachers at Lakeside High School is planning the spring exam schedule for first-year and second-year students for a given week, Monday through Friday. The committee must schedule four first-year student exams—algebra, biology, English 1 and world history; four second-year student exams—chemistry, English 2, geometry and US history; and no other exams. Each exam will be administered once during the week, either at 8 AM or at 11 AM, and no exams may be administered simultaneously. The following conditions must be met:

No two first-year student exams may be given on the same day.
Exactly one first-year student exam is administered at 8 AM.
The geometry exam and the US history exam must be administered on the same day.
No exam will be administered on Friday at 11 AM.
The algebra exam and the biology exam must be administered at the same time of day on consecutive days.

1. [Step 1] Summarize your Overview analysis: *The task is to schedule eight exams—four each for two different groups of students—over the course of one week, with either one or two exams per day (and no exams administered at the same time).*

2. [Step 2] Create an initial Sketch:

1st-4 2nd-4
a b e_1 w C E_2 G U

M Tu W Th F

8 _ _ _ _ _
11 _ _ _ _ _

3. [Step 3] Analyze and draw the Rules:
   - Rule 1:
     - What does the rule restrict, and what does it leave open? *This rule forbids scheduling two first-year student exams for the same day.*
     - What are the rule's negative implications, if any? *Because this rule is phrased negatively, its corollary is positive: All first-year student exams will be on different days.*
     - Can the rule be depicted inside the sketch framework? *No.*
   - Draw the rule:

   - Rule 2:
     - What does the rule restrict, and what does it leave open? *This limits the number of first-year student exams at 8 AM to just one. This means that three of the first-year student exams will be at 11 AM. You can record that now or in Step 4 when making the deductions.*
     - What are the rule's negative implications, if any? *N/A*
     - Can the rule be depicted inside the sketch framework? *Next to the 8 AM line*
     - Draw the rule:

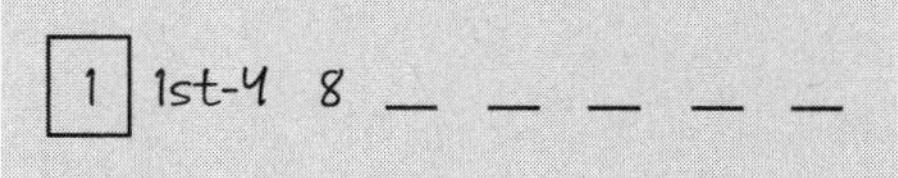

   - Rule 3:
     - What does the rule restrict, and what does it leave open? *This rule creates a vertical block of G and U, in either order.*
     - What are the rule's negative implications, if any? *G and U can never be on different days.*
     - Can the rule be depicted inside the sketch framework? *No.*

- Draw the rule:

- Rule 4:
  - What does the rule restrict, and what does it leave open? *This prevents any exams from being scheduled at 11 AM on Friday.*
  - What are the rule's negative implications, if any? *N/A*
  - Can the rule be depicted inside the sketch framework? *Yes.*
  - Draw the rule:

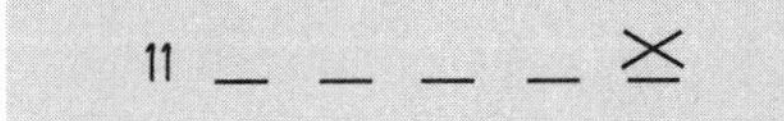

- Rule 5:
  - What does the rule restrict, and what does it leave open? *This rule creates a horizontal block for* a *and* b. *They will be at the same time on consecutive days.*
  - What are the rule's negative implications, if any? *Tests* a *and* b *cannot be on the same day nor at different times than one another.*
  - Can the rule be depicted inside the sketch framework? *No.*
  - Draw the rule:

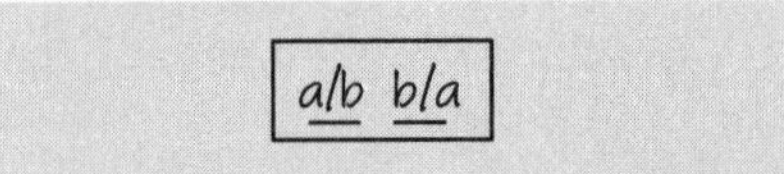

Here is the sketch with all of the rules depicted.

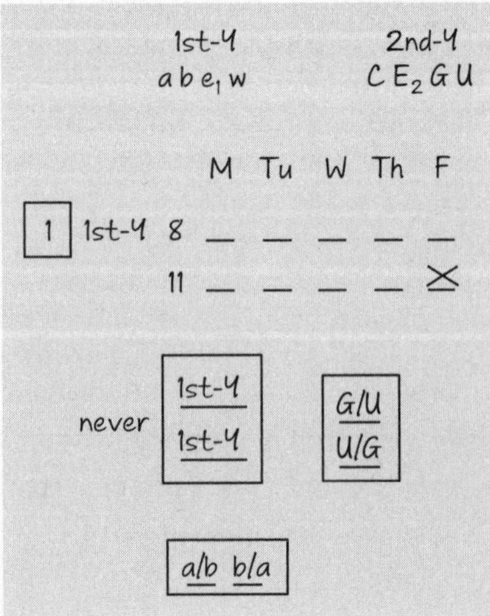

Practice 2

An apartment building has five floors. Each floor has either one or two apartments. There are exactly eight apartments in the building. The residents of the building are J, K, L, M, N, O, P, and Q, who each live in a different apartment.

J lives on a floor with two apartments.
K lives on the floor directly above P.
The second floor is made up of only one apartment.
M and N live on the same floor.
O does not live on the same floor as Q.
L lives in the only apartment on her floor.
Q does not live on the first or second floor.

PrepTest2 Sec3 Qs 6–12

1. [Step 1] Summarize your Overview analysis: *The task is to determine which of five floors in an apartment building eight residents live on. Each floor has one or two apartments, and each resident lives alone in one of the apartments.*

2. [Step 2] Create an initial Sketch:

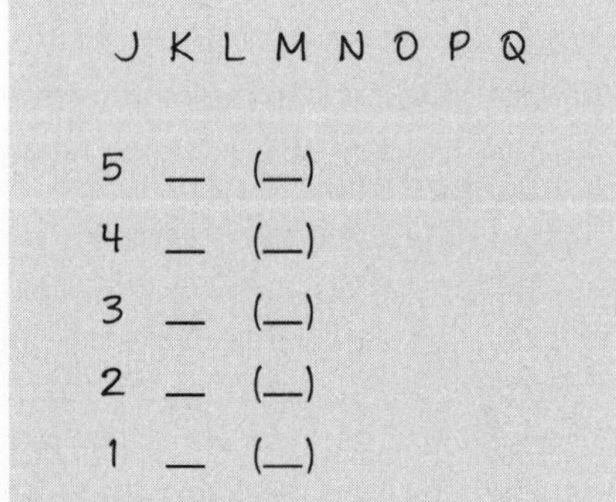

3. [Step 3] Analyze and draw the Rules:
   - Rule 1:
     - What does the rule restrict, and what does it leave open? *This rule stipulates that resident J has a neighbor on the same floor. Without more information, you have no idea which floor this may or may not be.*
     - What are the rule's negative implications, if any? *Resident J cannot live on a floor that has only one apartment.*
     - Can the rule be depicted inside the sketch framework? *No.*

- Draw the rule:

- Rule 2:
    - What does the rule restrict, and what does it leave open? *This creates a vertical block of entities: K is one floor above P. Without more information, however, it does not determine which floor either lives on.*
    - What are the rule's negative implications, if any? *K cannot be on floor 1 and P cannot be on floor 5.*
    - Can the rule be depicted inside the sketch framework? *No.*
    - Draw the rule:

- Rule 3:
    - What does the rule restrict, and what does it leave open? *This rule restricts floor 2 to only one apartment.*
    - What are the rule's negative implications, if any? *Anyone who lives on a floor with two apartments cannot live on floor 2. Note: If you notice that this affects resident J (Rule 1), you can eliminate J from floor 2 now. If not, you will catch that interaction in Step 4, when making the deductions.*
    - Can the rule be depicted inside the sketch framework? *Yes.*
    - Draw the rule:

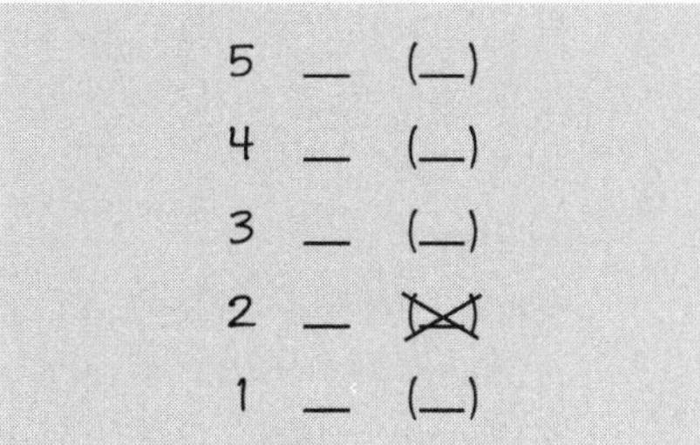

- Rule 4:
    - What does the rule restrict, and what does it leave open? *This rule creates a horizontal block: residents M and N are same-floor neighbors.*
    - What are the rule's negative implications, if any? *Residents M and N cannot live on any floor that has only one apartment. Note: Here, again, if you notice that this rule interacts with Rule 3, you can eliminate residents M and N from floor 2. If not, you'll catch this deduction in Step 4.*
    - Can the rule be depicted inside the sketch framework? *No.*
    - Draw the rule:

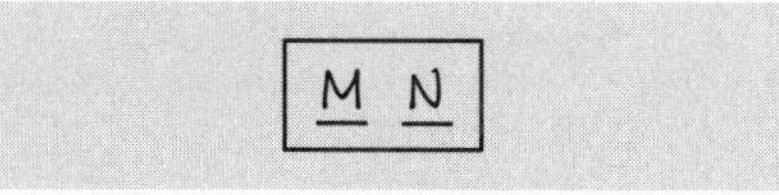

- Rule 5:
    - What does the rule restrict, and what does it leave open? *This rule creates a horizontal "anti-block": residents O and Q do not live on the same floor.*
    - What are the rule's negative implications, if any? *None. Residents O and Q could live on any floor, and they may or may not have same-floor neighbors (just not each other).*
    - Can the rule be depicted inside the sketch framework? *No.*
    - Draw the rule:

- Rule 6:
    - What does the rule restrict, and what does it leave open? *This rule means that resident L lives on a floor with only one apartment. Floor 2 is a possibility, but not a certainty, for resident L's apartment.*
    - What are the rule's negative implications, if any? *Resident L cannot live on a floor with two apartments.*
    - Can the rule be depicted inside the sketch framework? *No.*
    - Draw the rule:

- Rule 7:
  - What does the rule restrict, and what does it leave open? *This negative rule prevents Q from taking an apartment on floors 1 or 2. The other floors remain open to him.*
  - What are the rule's negative implications, if any? *The rule is phrased negatively. Its affirmative implication is that Q lives on one of floors 3, 4, or 5.*
  - Can the rule be depicted inside the sketch framework? *Yes.*
  - Draw the rule:

5 __ (__)
4 __ (__)
3 __ (__)
~Q 2 __ (☒)
~Q 1 __ (__)

Here is the sketch at the end of Step 3, with all of the rules depicted.

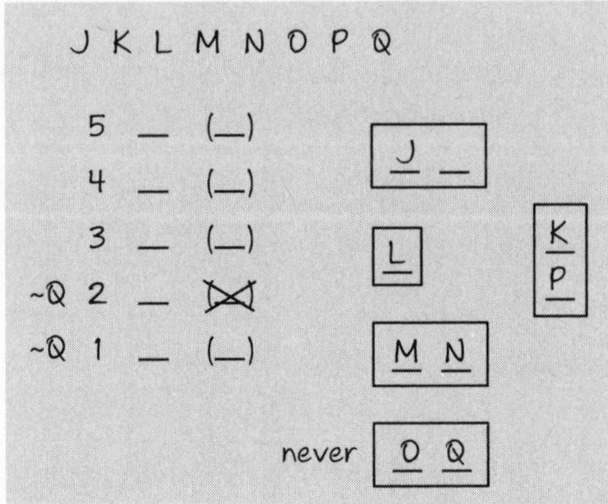

Practice 3

Exactly seven professors—Madison, Nilsson, Orozco, Paton, Robinson, Sarkis, and Togo—were hired in the years 1989 through 1995. Each professor has one or more specialties, and any two professors hired in the same year or in consecutive years do not have a specialty in common. The professors were hired according to the following conditions:

Madison was hired in 1993, Robinson in 1991.

There is at least one specialty that Madison, Orozco, and Togo have in common.

Nilsson shares a specialty with Robinson.

Paton and Sarkis were each hired at least one year before Madison and at least one year after Nilsson.

Orozco, who shares a specialty with Sarkis, was hired in 1990.

PrepTest35 Sec3 Qs 18–23

[Steps 1 and 2] Here is this game's Overview and initial Sketch: *The task is to figure out the year (from 1989 to 1995) in which each of seven professors were hired. More than one professor may be hired during a given year, meaning that some years may have seen no professors hired. The professors have specialties, and cannot be hired during the same year or in years consecutive to other professors with the same specialty.*

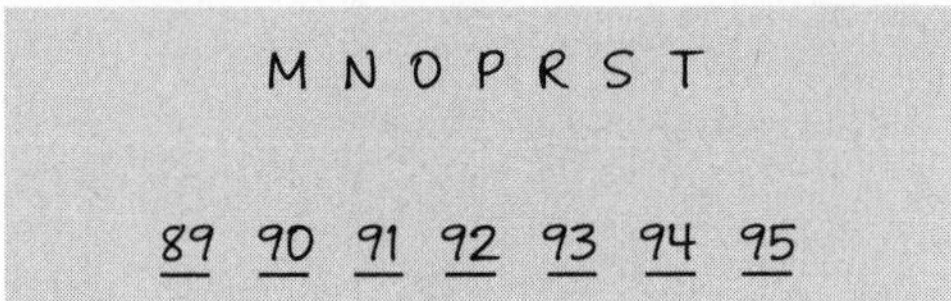

1. [Step 3] Analyze and draw the Rules:
   - Rule 1:
     - What does the rule restrict, and what does it leave open? *This rule creates two established entities: M was hired in 1993, and R was hired in 1991. Remember, other professors may have been hired during those years, too.*
     - What are the rule's negative implications, if any? *N/A*
     - Can the rule be depicted inside the sketch framework? *Yes.*
     - Draw the rule:

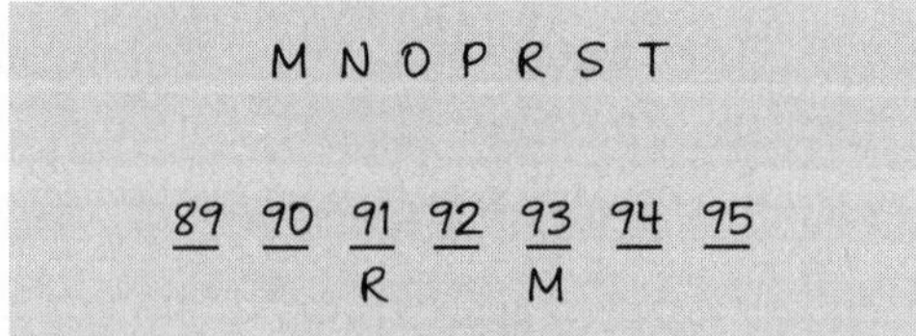

   - Rule 2:
     - What does the rule restrict, and what does it leave open? *This rule tells you that three professors—M, O, and T—share a specialty. Remember that this means they were not hired during the same year, nor in adjacent years.*
     - What are the rule's negative implications, if any? *Remember that this sharing a specialty*

means none of these professors were hired during the same year, nor in adjacent years.

- Can the rule be depicted inside the sketch framework? *No.*
- Draw the rule:

M N O P R S T

89 90 91 92 93 94 95
R M

share spec
M = O = T

- Rule 3:
  - What does the rule restrict, and what does it leave open? *This is another rule about shared specialties, this time between N and R.*
  - What are the rule's negative implications, if any? *Remember that this sharing a specialty means that these professors were not hired during the same year, nor in adjacent years.*
  - Can the rule be depicted inside the sketch framework? *No.*
  - Draw the rule:

M N O P R S T

89 90 91 92 93 94 95
R M

share spec
M = O = T
N = R

- Rule 4:
  - What does the rule restrict, and what does it leave open? *This rule provides the relative order of hiring among four of the professors: N was hired before P and S, and M was hired after P and S. The rule does not state the relationship between P and S.*
  - What are the rule's negative implications, if any? *N/A*
  - Can the rule be depicted inside the sketch framework? *No.*
  - Draw the rule:

M N O P R S T

89 90 91 92 93 94 95
R M

share spec
M = O = T
N = R

N < P, S < M

- Rule 5:
  - What does the rule restrict, and what does it leave open? *This rule establishes professor O's position—1990—and adds that O shares a specialty with professor S.*
  - What are the rule's negative implications, if any? *Remember that this sharing a specialty means that these professors were not hired during the same year, nor in adjacent years.*
  - Can the rule be depicted inside the sketch framework? *Partially. Write in O under the 1990 slot, and record the specialty rule with the rest of the shared specialty list.*
  - Draw the rule:

M N O P R S T

89 90 91 92 93 94 95
O R M

share spec
M = O = T
N = R
O = S

N < P, S < M

The Professors' Hire Dates game initially appeared to be quite complicated. After all, more than one professor may be hired in a given year, some years may be empty, and the setup introduced the unique term *specialty*. The rules, however, have already established the positions of three of the seven entities, reducing the game's complexity dramatically. By the time you add all of the deductions that stem from the "shared specialty" rules, this one won't seem so bad at all.

With the rules in place, you may already be anticipating the deductions that can be made in each of those practice game setups. You'll have a chance to add those in the next section of this chapter covering Step 4 of the Logic Games Method in basic Strict Sequencing games.

COMPLEX STRICT SEQUENCING GAMES DEDUCTIONS

LEARNING OBJECTIVES

In this section of the chapter, you'll practice

- Applying Step 4 of the Logic Games Method to complex Strict Sequencing games by combining rules and restrictions to make all valid deductions in the game.

Prepare

The added complexity in the games in this chapter means that you have to be especially careful and precise with setup and sketch framework to be sure that you are correctly interpreting and representing the situation described. That extra scrutiny will often pay off in Step 4, where extra complexity may produce several key deductions.

LOGIC GAMES STRATEGY

In Sequencing games, deductions are most likely to stem from:

- **Blocks of Entities**—Two or more entities that are linked together; when one is placed, the other's placement is determined or restricted
- **Duplications**—Entities shared by two or more rules; duplications are always at the heart of Loose Sequencing games.
- **Established Entities**—Entities placed into a specific position; even if no rule directly provides for an Established Entity, you may be able to determine an entity's exact position by combining other rules.

In Sequencing games, deductions may involve:

- **Limited Options**—The situation arises when a Block of Entities or a key player (an entity affecting the positions of other entities) is restricted to either of two positions; when this occurs, draw dual Limited Options sketches.
- **Number Restrictions**—Limitations or rules affecting the number of entities that can be placed in a given position; this is rare in Sequencing games—typically, the stated limitation is one entity per position.

The kinds of deductions you're looking for in these games are not much different than those in basic Strict Sequencing, but with all the moving parts in these games, you'll want to make sure you are able to get them all.

Practice Step 4 on the setups you've been working with throughout this chapter.

Practice

Directions: In each game setup, first reacquaint yourself with the setup and rules. Then, combine the rules and restrictions to make all available deductions, recording your analyses as indicated. Finally, test your deductions by answering the questions that accompany each game. You can find expert analysis and explanations at the end of the Practice section.

Practice 1

A committee of teachers at Lakeside High School is planning the spring exam schedule for first-year and second-year students for a given week, Monday through Friday. The committee must schedule four first-year student exams—algebra, biology, English 1 and world history; four second-year student exams—chemistry, English 2, geometry and US history; and no other exams. Each exam will be administered once during the week, either at 8 AM or at 11 AM, and no exams may be administered simultaneously. The following conditions must be met:

No two first-year student exams may be given on the same day.
Exactly one first-year student exam is administered at 8 AM.
The geometry exam and the US history exam must be administered on the same day.
No exam will be administered on Friday at 11 AM.
The algebra exam and the biology exam must be administered at the same time of day *on consecutive days*.

Steps 1–3:

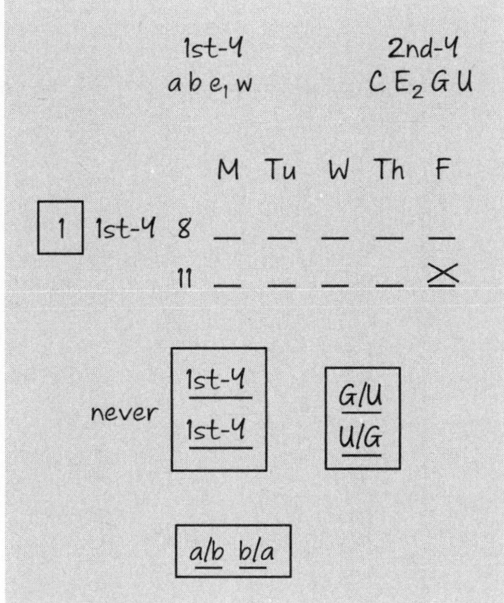

1. Which entities or positions are the most restricted in this game? Why?
2. Which elements from the BLEND checklist can you identify in this game? Are there
   - Blocks of entities? If so, what are they?
   - Limited Options? If so, which rule(s) trigger them?
   - Established Entities? If so, which ones?
   - Number Restrictions? If so, describe them.
   - Duplications? If so, which rules share an entity?
3. Combine the rules and restrictions to create a Master Sketch depicting all of the deductions available in this game:

4. Evaluate your sketch by answering the following questions:
   - How many of the exams will be administered at 11 AM?
   - Which exams could be the one administered at 8 AM on Friday?
   - How many second-year student exams must be administered at 8 AM?
   - Which first-year student exams must be administered at 11 AM?

Practice 2

An apartment building has five floors. Each floor has either one or two apartments. There are exactly eight apartments in the building. The residents of the building are J, K, L, M, N, O, P, and Q, who each live in a different apartment.

J lives on a floor with two apartments.
K lives on the floor directly above P.
The second floor is made up of only one apartment.
M and N live on the same floor.
O does not live on the same floor as Q.
L lives in the only apartment on her floor.
Q does not live on the first or second floor.

PrepTest2 Sec3 Qs 6–12

Steps 1–3:

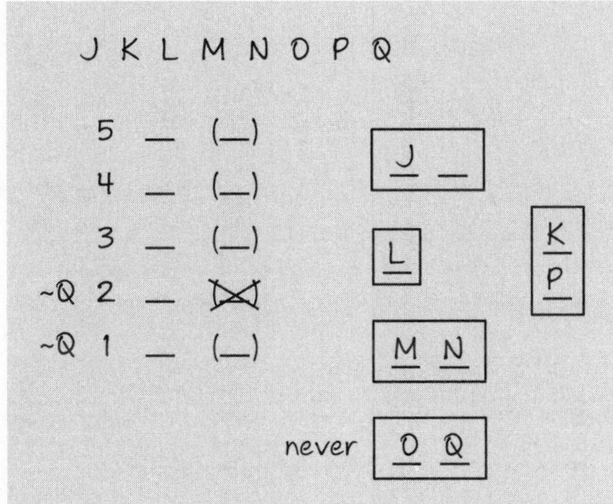

1. Which entities or positions are the most restricted in this game? Why?

2. Which elements from the BLEND checklist can you identify in this game? Are there
   - Blocks of entities? If so, what are they?
   - Limited Options? If so, which rule(s) trigger them?
   - Established Entities? If so, which ones?
   - Number Restrictions? If so, describe them.
   - Duplications? If so, which rules share an entity?

3. Combine the rules and restrictions to create a Master Sketch depicting all of the deductions available in this game:

4. Evaluate your sketch by answering the following questions:
   - Write a complete and accurate list of the residents who could live on the second floor.
   - If resident L lives on the third floor, and resident M lives on the fifth floor, what can you deduce about resident K?
   - Write a complete and accurate list of the residents who may not live on the first floor.
   - If resident P lives on the second floor, who are the residents who cannot live on the third floor?

Practice 3

Exactly seven professors—Madison, Nilsson, Orozco, Paton, Robinson, Sarkis, and Togo—were hired in the years 1989 through 1995. Each professor has one or more specialties, and any two professors hired in the same year or in consecutive years do not have a specialty in common. The professors were hired according to the following conditions:

> Madison was hired in 1993, Robinson in 1991.
> There is at least one specialty that Madison, Orozco, and Togo have in common.
> Nilsson shares a specialty with Robinson.
> Paton and Sarkis were each hired at least one year before Madison and at least one year after Nilsson.
> Orozco, who shares a specialty with Sarkis, was hired in 1990.

PrepTest35 Sec3 Qs 18–23

Steps 1–3:

M N O P R S T

89 90 91 92 93 94 95
O R M

share spec
M = O = T
N = R
O = S

N P S M

1. Which entities or positions are the most restricted in this game? Why?

2. Which elements from the BLEND checklist can you identify in this game? Are there
   - Blocks of entities? If so, what are they?
   - Limited Options? If so, which rule(s) trigger them?
   - Established Entities? If so, which ones?
   - Number Restrictions? If so, describe them.
   - Duplications? If so, which rules share an entity?

3. Combine the rules and restrictions to create a Master Sketch depicting all of the deductions available in this game:

4. Evaluate your sketch by answering the following questions:
   - For how many of the seven professors can the exact year in which they were hired be determined? Who are they?
   - In which of the seven years is it possible that none of the professors were hired?
   - In which of the seven years is it possible that more than one of the professors were hired?
   - If Paton and Orozco share a specialty, in how many of the seven years could Paton have been hired? Which one(s)?

Explanations

Compare your work to that of an LSAT expert. Pay close attention to how the expert combined the rules and restrictions to make additional deductions, and to how the expert depicted the deductions within the sketch framework.

Practice 1

A committee of teachers at Lakeside High School is planning the spring exam schedule for first-year and second-year students for a given week, Monday through Friday. The committee must schedule four first-year student exams—algebra, biology, English 1 and world history; four second-year student exams—chemistry, English 2, geometry and US history; and no other exams. Each exam will be administered once during the week, either at 8 AM or at 11 AM, and no exams may be administered simultaneously. The following conditions must be met:

No two first-year student exams may be given on the same day.
Exactly one first-year student exam is administered at 8 AM.
The geometry exam and the US history exam must be administered on the same day.
No exam will be administered on Friday at 11 AM.
The algebra exam and the biology exam must be administered at the same time of day *on consecutive days.*

1. Which entities or positions are the most restricted in this game? Why? *The entire category of first-year student tests is highly restricted. One must be at 8 AM, three at 11:00 AM. Moreover, Tests a and b have to be at the same time (which you can now deduce will be at 11:00 AM).*

2. Which elements from the BLEND checklist can you identify in this game? Are there
   - Blocks of entities? If so, what are they? *Tests* G *and* U *are a vertical block; they must be on the same day. Tests* a *and* b *are a horizontal block; they must be at the same time on consecutive days.*
   - Limited Options? If so, which rule(s) trigger them? *N/A*
   - Established Entities? If so, which ones? *None; Friday at 11 AM has been established as a time at which no test may be scheduled.*
   - Number Restrictions? If so, describe them. *Because exactly one first-year student exam is at 8 AM, three first-year student exams are at 11 AM (Rule 1).*
   - Duplications? If so, which rules share an entity? *Rules 1, 2, and 5 are all about first-year student exams.*

3. Combine the rules and restrictions to create a Master Sketch depicting all of the deductions available in this game: *Consider where the first-year student block a/b (Rule 5) may be placed: since only one first-year student exam may be given at 8 AM, the algebra and biology exams must be given at 11 AM.*

```
              M   Tu   W   Th   F
[1] 1st-Y  8  __  __   __  __   __
          11  __  __   __  __   X    [a/b b/a]
```

Another 11 AM slot must be taken up by one of G and U:

```
              M   Tu   W   Th   F                 [G/U]
[1] 1st-Y  8  __  __   __  __   __
          11  __  __   __  __   X    [a/b b/a]   [U/G]
```

This leaves one remaining 11 AM slot for a third first-year student exam:

```
              M   Tu   W   Th   F                 [G/U]
[1] 1st-Y  8  __  __   __  __   __
          11  __  __   __  __   X    [a/b b/a]   [U/G]   e1/w
```

Now, consider when the 8 AM *first-year student exam could be given. Three 11* AM *slots are taken by first-year student exams, and the other one is occupied by a second-year student exam (G/U) that must be preceded in the 8* AM *slot by another second-year student exam (U/G). Therefore, the only day that the 8* AM *first-year student exam could be given is on Friday:*

M Tu W Th F
1 | 1st-4 8 — — — — w/e_1 | G/U
11 — — — — X | a/b b/a | U/G | e_1/w

The remaining two second-year student exams—chemistry and English 2—must be offered at 8 AM*, and one 8* AM *slot will remain open:*

M Tu W Th F
1 | 1st-4 8 — — — — w/e_1 C E_2 | G/U | X
11 — — — — X | a/b b/a | U/G | e_1/w

4. Evaluate your sketch by answering the following questions:
   - How many of the exams will be administered at 11 AM? *Four; three of the first-year student exams (including Tests* a *and* b*), and one second-year student exam (either Test* G *or* U*) will be administered at 11* AM.
   - Which exams could be the one administered at 8 AM on Friday? *Either Test* e_1 *or Test* w *must be administered at 8* AM *on Friday.*
   - How many second-year student exams must be administered at 8 AM? *Three; one of* G *or* U *must be administered at 11* AM*. The other of* G *or* U*, plus* C *and* E_2*, must be administered at 8* AM.
   - Which first-year student exams must be administered at 11 AM? *Because of Rules 1, 2, and 5, Tests* a *and* b *must be administered at 11* AM*. One more first-year student exam must also be administered at 11* AM*, but there is no way to say which one that is.*

Practice 2

An apartment building has five floors. Each floor has either one or two apartments. There are exactly eight apartments in the building. The residents of the building are J, K, L, M, N, O, P, and Q, who each live in a different apartment.

J lives on a floor with two apartments.
K lives on the floor directly above P.
The second floor is made up of only one apartment.
M and N live on the same floor.
O does not live on the same floor as Q.
L lives in the only apartment on her floor.
Q does not live on the first or second floor.

PrepTest2 Sec3 Qs 6–12

Steps 1–3:

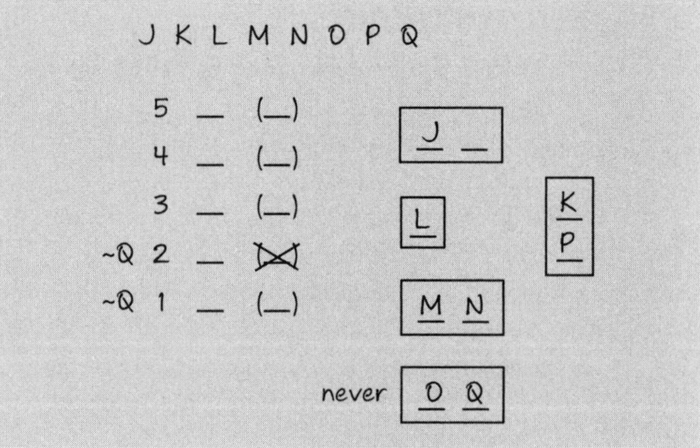

1. Which entities or positions are the most restricted in this game? Why? *The most restricted position is floor 2, which can have only one apartment. All of the entities have some restriction, but none stands out yet as central to the deduction-making process.*

2. Which elements from the BLEND checklist can you identify in this game? Are there
   - Blocks of entities? If so, what are they? *Rule 2 created a vertical block—K above P. Rule 4 created a horizontal block—M and N on the same floor. Rule 1 creates a quasi-block because J has a same-floor neighbor, but the rule doesn't specify who that neighbor is.*
   - Limited Options? If so, which rule(s) trigger them? *N/A*

- Established Entities? If so, which ones? *N/A*
- Number Restrictions? If so, describe them. *Rule 3 requires that floor 2 have only one apartment.*
- Duplications? If so, which rules share an entity? *1) Rule 3, which restricts floor 2 to one apartment, interacts with Rules 1 and 4, which dictate that residents J, M, and N live on floors with two apartments. 2) While resident Q appears in Rules 5 and 7, there isn't much to deduce from this Duplication because both of those rules are negative.*

3. Combine the rules and restrictions to create a Master Sketch depicting all of the deductions available in this game: *Start with floor 2. It can have only one apartment (Rule 3). Record the negative implications of Rules 1 and 4 here. J, M, and N cannot live on floor 2.*

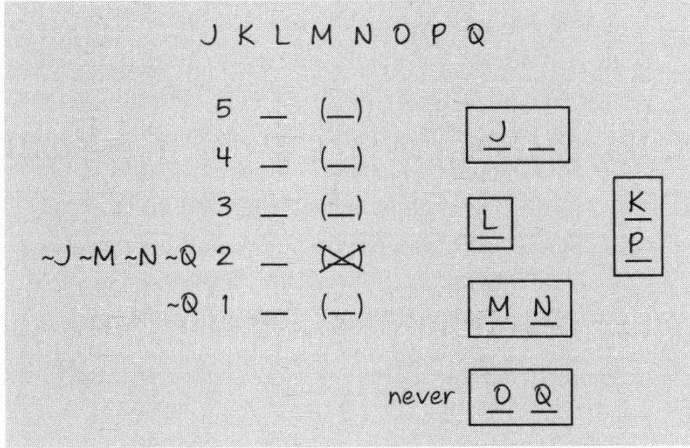

Don't forget to record the negative implications of the vertical block created by Rule 2: Resident P cannot live on floor 5, and resident K cannot live on floor 1.

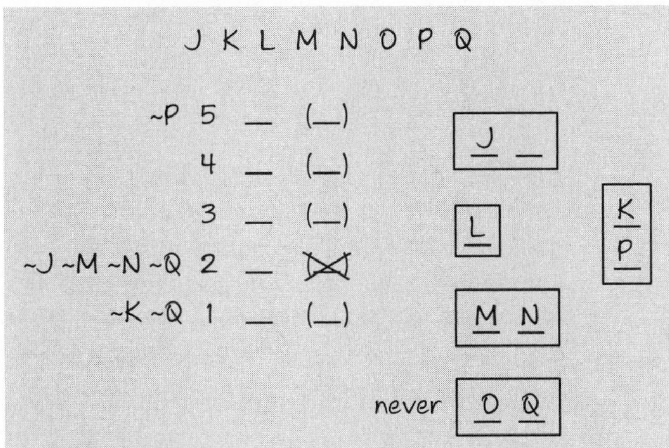

Beyond this point, deduction gives way to speculation. There are dozens of "What if . . . ?" questions that you could ask at this point, but none of them lead to any additional certainties. You can be confident that the sketch above has all of the information you will need to answer the questions.

4. Evaluate your sketch by answering the following questions:
   - Write a complete and accurate list of the residents who could live on the second floor. *Residents K, L, O, and P could live on floor 2.*
   - If resident L lives on the third floor, and resident M lives on the fifth floor, what can you deduce about resident K? *Because L must live on a floor with one apartment (Rule 6), and because M must live on the same floor as N (Rule 4), the only place that the vertical K-P block (Rule 2) would fit is floors 1 and 2. Thus, under this question's conditions, K must live on floor 2.*
   - Write a complete and accurate list of the residents who may <u>not</u> live on the first floor. *Residents Q (Rule 7) and K (Rule 2) cannot live on floor 1.*
   - If resident P lives on the second floor, who are the residents who <u>cannot</u> live on the third floor? *If resident P lives on floor 2, then resident K will live on floor 3 (Rule 2). With K living on floor 3, residents L (Rule 6), M, and N (Rule 4) cannot live on floor 3.*

Practice 3

Exactly seven professors—Madison, Nilsson, Orozco, Paton, Robinson, Sarkis, and Togo—were hired in the years 1989 through 1995. Each professor has one or more specialties, and any two professors hired in the same year or in consecutive years do not have a specialty in common. The professors were hired according to the following conditions:

> Madison was hired in 1993, Robinson in 1991.
> There is at least one specialty that Madison, Orozco, and Togo have in common.
> Nilsson shares a specialty with Robinson.
> Paton and Sarkis were each hired at least one year before Madison and at least one year after Nilsson.
> Orozco, who shares a specialty with Sarkis, was hired in 1990.

PrepTest35 Sec3 Qs 18–23

Steps 1–3:

M N O P R S T

89 90 91 92 93 94 95
O R M (under 90, 91, 93)

share spec
M = O = T
N = R
O = S

P
N M
S

1. Which entities or positions are the most restricted in this game? Why? *Professor T, who shares a specialty with two established entities (Professors O and M).*

2. Which elements from the BLEND checklist can you identify in this game? Are there
   - Blocks of entities? If so, what are they? *Rule 4 created a long, loose string: N before P and S, and P and S before M. Each shared specialty rule (Rules 2, 3, and 5) create "anti-blocks" that prevent professors who share specialties from being hired in the same or adjacent years.*
   - Limited Options? If so, which rule(s) trigger them? *N/A*
   - Established Entities? If so, which ones? *Professors M (Rule 1), O (Rule 5), and R (Rule 1) are all locked in.*
   - Number Restrictions? If so, describe them. *N/A; remember that more than one professor may be hired in the same year, and that there may be years in which no professors were hired.*
   - Duplications? If so, which rules share an entity? *Yes, five of them: 1) Rules 1, 2, and 4 all share M; 2) Rules 1 and 3 share R; 3) Rules 2 and 5 share O; 4) Rules 3 and 4 share N; and 5) Rules 4 and 5 share S.*

3. Combine the rules and restrictions to create a Master Sketch depicting all of the deductions available in this game: *Start with Professor T. Because T shares a specialty with O (Rule 2), T could not have been hired in '89, '90, or '91. Because T shares a specialty with M (also Rule 2), T could not have been hired in '92, '93, or '94. Thus, T must have been hired in 1995. Add T under '95 and cross out all of the established entities in the roster of entities above the sketch framework.*

~~M~~ N ~~O~~ P ~~R~~ S ~~T~~

89 90 91 92 93 94 95
O R M T (under 90, 91, 93, 95)

share spec
M = O = T
N = R
O = S

P
N M
S

Next, turn to Professor S, who shares a specialty with O (Rule 5) and must be after N and before M (Rule 4). Because S shares a specialty with O, S could not have been hired in '89, '90, or '91. That leaves only '92 as a year before M's hire date in which S could have been hired. Write S under '92, and cross out S in the roster of entities.

M N O P R S T

89	90	91	92	93	94	95
	O	R	S	M		T

share spec
M = O = T
N = R
O = S

N < P, S < M

Determining that Professor S was hired in '92 means that Professor N could only have been hired in '89, '90 or '91 (Rule 4). However, remember that N shares a specialty with R (Rule 3), ruling out '90 or '91 as N's hire date. That means that N was hired in '89. Write in N under '89 and cross out N in the roster of entities.

M N O P R S T

89	90	91	92	93	94	95
N	O	R	S	M		T

share spec
M = O = T
N = R
O = S

N < P, S < M

Remarkably, six of the seven professors' hire dates are now determined once and for all. Only Professor P remains. Rule 4 places P's hire date between those of N and M, in other words, between '90 and '92. Professor P has no other restrictions, so simply indicate the acceptable range of dates for P, and you're done.

M N O P R S T

89	90	91	92	93	94	95
N	O	R	S	M		T

P (90–92)

share spec
M = O = T
N = R
O = S

N < P, S < M

4. Evaluate your sketch by answering the following questions:
   - For how many of the seven professors can the exact year in which they were hired be determined? Who are they? *Six: N in '89, O in '90, R in '91, S in '92, M in '93, and T in '95.*
   - In which of the seven years is it possible that none of the professors were hired? *1994.*
   - In which of the seven years is it possible that more than one of the professors were hired? *1990, 1991, and 1992.*
   - If Paton and Orozco share a specialty, in how many of the seven years could Paton have been hired? Which one(s)? *Only one: 1992.*

Because the game setups in Practice 2 and Practice 3 come from officially released LSAT tests, you will have the opportunity to practice answering their questions in the next section of this chapter. After that, in the Perform section, you'll see two brand new games that you can use to assess your overall skill level on complex Strict Sequencing games.

COMPLEX STRICT SEQUENCING GAMES—FULL GAMES WITH QUESTIONS

LEARNING OBJECTIVES

In this section of the chapter, you'll practice and assess your ability to

- Apply the Logic Games Method to complex Strict Sequencing games.

In this section of the chapter, you will practice full-length complex Strict Sequencing games accompanied by their question sets. Look for all of the question types you encountered in Chapter 4, and apply the appropriate strategies to answer each as efficiently and accurately as possible. Given the complex nature of these games' setups and deductions, look for opportunities to turn the Master Sketch into quick points on Must Be/Could Be questions.

The two games in the Practice exercise are Apartment Floors and Professors' Hire Dates, games on which you've already worked through Steps 1–4. If you skipped the sections on those steps, go back and work through the practice exercises there.

Then, in the Perform section, you'll see two new games. On those, you can assess your skill level at applying all five steps of the Logic Games Method to complex Strict Sequencing.

Practice

Directions: You have seen this game's setup, rules, and deductions in the preceding sections of this chapter. For each question, first review the Master Sketch and reconstruct the work you did in Steps 1–4 of the Logic Games Method. Then, answer the question. For practice, take time to analyze each question thoroughly and enter your analysis for each step and answer choice blank. Complete, worked example expert analyses can be found in your Online Study Plan in the PDF labeled "Chapter 6 Full Game Practice Explanations."

Question 1:

An apartment building has five floors. Each floor has either one or two apartments. There are exactly eight apartments in the building. The residents of the building are J, K, L, M, N, O, P, and Q, who each live in a different apartment.

J lives on a floor with two apartments.
K lives on the floor directly above P.
The second floor is made up of only one apartment.
M and N live on the same floor.
O does not live on the same floor as Q.
L lives in the only apartment on her floor.
Q does not live on the first or second floor.

PrepTest2 Sec3 Q6

Steps 1–4:

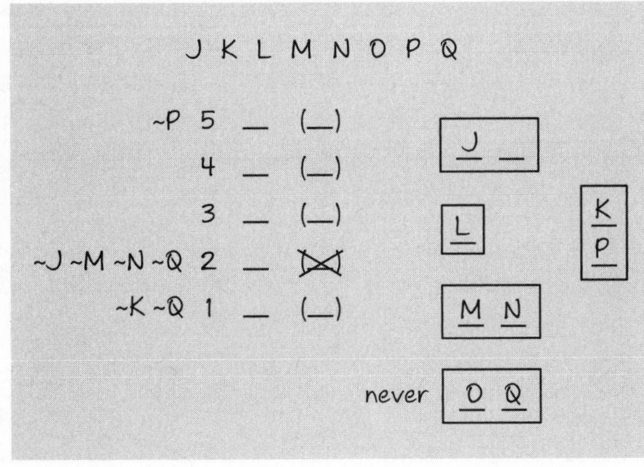

Step 5:

1. Which one of the following must be true?

   (A) Q lives on the third floor.
   (B) Q lives on the fifth floor.
   (C) L does not live on the fourth floor.
   (D) N does not live on the second floor.
   (E) J lives on the first floor.

Step 5 (cont.):

Question 2:

An apartment building has five floors. Each floor has either one or two apartments. There are exactly eight apartments in the building. The residents of the building are J, K, L, M, N, O, P, and Q, who each live in a different apartment.

J lives on a floor with two apartments.
K lives on the floor directly above P.
The second floor is made up of only one apartment.
M and N live on the same floor.
O does not live on the same floor as Q.
L lives in the only apartment on her floor.
Q does not live on the first or second floor.

PrepTest2 Sec3 Q7

Steps 1–4:

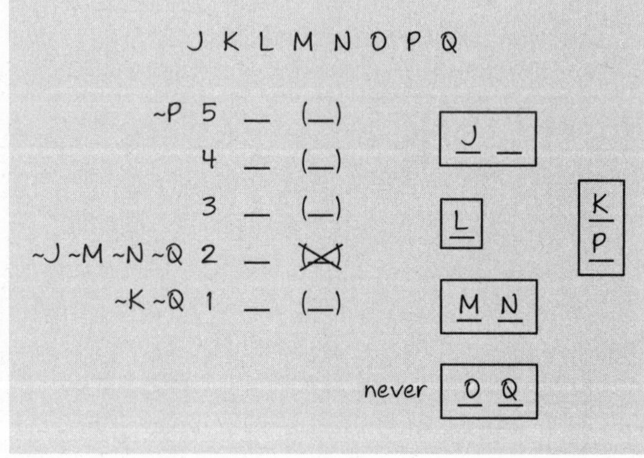

Step 5:

2. Which one of the following CANNOT be true?

(A) K lives on the second floor.
(B) M lives on the first floor.
(C) N lives on the fourth floor.
(D) O lives on the third floor.
(E) P lives on the fifth floor.

Step 5 (cont.):

Question 3:

An apartment building has five floors. Each floor has either one or two apartments. There are exactly eight apartments in the building. The residents of the building are J, K, L, M, N, O, P, and Q, who each live in a different apartment.

J lives on a floor with two apartments.

K lives on the floor directly above P.

The second floor is made up of only one apartment.

M and N live on the same floor.

O does not live on the same floor as Q.

L lives in the only apartment on her floor.

Q does not live on the first or second floor.

PrepTest2 Sec3 Q8

Steps 1–4:

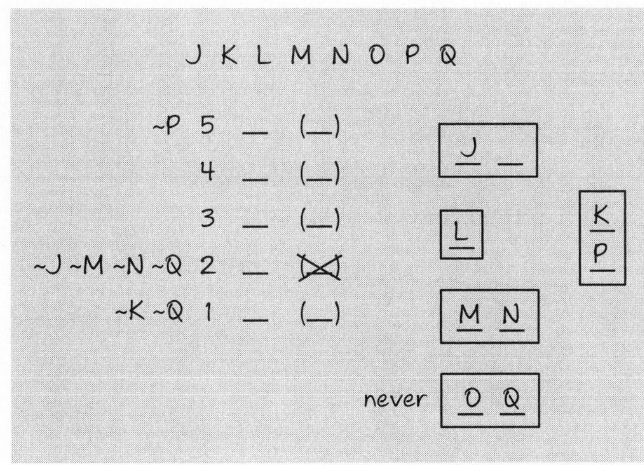

Step 5:

3. If J lives on the fourth floor and K lives on the fifth floor, which one of the following can be true?

(A) O lives on the first floor.

(B) Q lives on the fourth floor.

(C) N lives on the fifth floor.

(D) L lives on the fourth floor.

(E) P lives on the third floor.

Step 5 (cont.):

Question 4:

Step 5:

An apartment building has five floors. Each floor has either one or two apartments. There are exactly eight apartments in the building. The residents of the building are J, K, L, M, N, O, P, and Q, who each live in a different apartment.

J lives on a floor with two apartments.

K lives on the floor directly above P.

The second floor is made up of only one apartment.

M and N live on the same floor.

O does not live on the same floor as Q.

L lives in the only apartment on her floor.

Q does not live on the first or second floor.

PrepTest2 Sec3 Q9

4. If O lives on the second floor, which one of the following CANNOT be true?

   (A) K lives on the fourth floor.

   (B) K lives on the fifth floor.

   (C) L lives on the first floor.

   (D) L lives on the third floor.

   (E) L lives on the fourth floor.

Step 5 (cont.):

Steps 1–4:

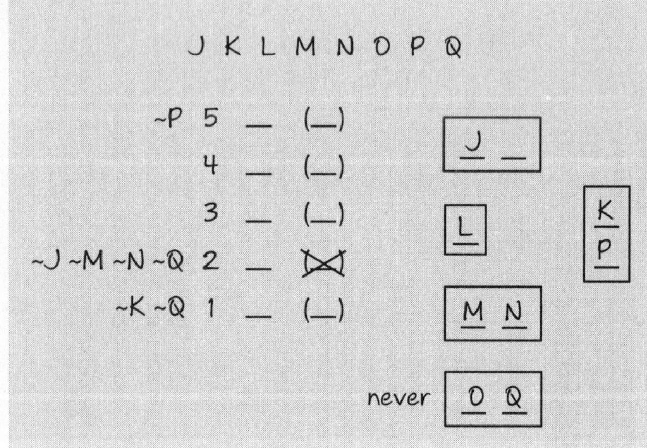

Question 5:

Step 5:

An apartment building has five floors. Each floor has either one or two apartments. There are exactly eight apartments in the building. The residents of the building are J, K, L, M, N, O, P, and Q, who each live in a different apartment.

J lives on a floor with two apartments.
K lives on the floor directly above P.
The second floor is made up of only one apartment.
M and N live on the same floor.
O does not live on the same floor as Q.
L lives in the only apartment on her floor.
Q does not live on the first or second floor.

PrepTest2 Sec3 Q10

5. If M lives on the fourth floor, which one of the following must be false?

(A) O lives on the fifth floor.
(B) J lives on the first floor.
(C) L lives on the second floor.
(D) Q lives on the third floor.
(E) P lives on the first floor.

Step 5 (cont.):

Steps 1–4:

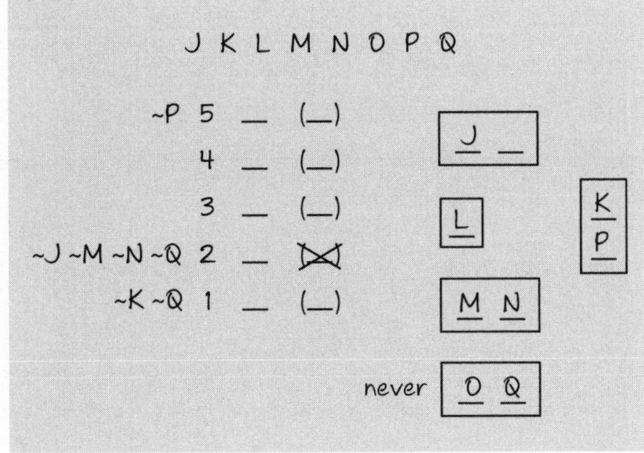

Question 6:

Step 5:

An apartment building has five floors. Each floor has either one or two apartments. There are exactly eight apartments in the building. The residents of the building are J, K, L, M, N, O, P, and Q, who each live in a different apartment.

J lives on a floor with two apartments.
K lives on the floor directly above P.
The second floor is made up of only one apartment.
M and N live on the same floor.
O does not live on the same floor as Q.
L lives in the only apartment on her floor.
Q does not live on the first or second floor.

PrepTest2 Sec3 Q11

Steps 1–4:

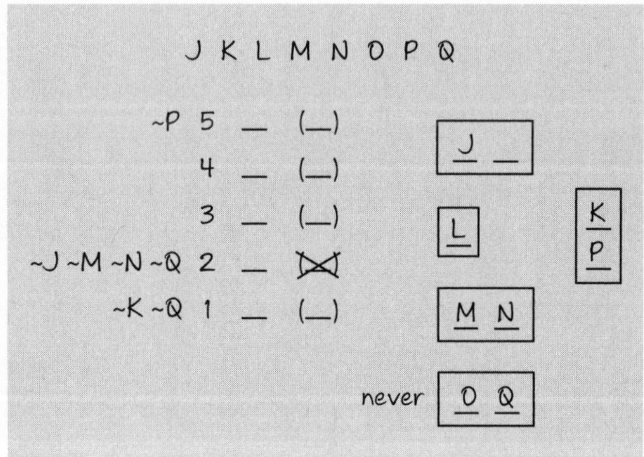

6. Which one of the following must be true?

   (A) If J lives on the fourth floor, then Q does not live on the fifth floor.

   (B) If O lives on the second floor, then L does not live on the fourth floor.

   (C) If N lives on the fourth floor, then K does not live on the second floor.

   (D) If K lives on the third floor, then O does not live on the fifth floor.

   (E) If P lives on the fourth floor, then M does not live on the third floor.

Step 5 (cont.):

Question 7:

An apartment building has five floors. Each floor has either one or two apartments. There are exactly eight apartments in the building. The residents of the building are J, K, L, M, N, O, P, and Q, who each live in a different apartment.

J lives on a floor with two apartments.
K lives on the floor directly above P.
The second floor is made up of only one apartment.
M and N live on the same floor.
O does not live on the same floor as Q.
L lives in the only apartment on her floor.
Q does not live on the first or second floor.

PrepTest2 Sec3 Q12

Steps 1–4:

J K L M N O P Q

~P 5 __ (__)
4 __ (__)
3 __ (__)
~J ~M ~N ~Q 2 __ (X)
~K ~Q 1 __ (__)

[J __]
[L]
[K / P]
[M N]
never [O Q]

Step 5:

7. If O lives on the fourth floor and P lives on the second floor, which one of the following must be true?

(A) L lives on the first floor.
(B) M lives on the third floor.
(C) Q lives on the third floor.
(D) N lives on the fifth floor.
(E) Q lives on the fifth floor.

Step 5 (cont.):

Practice 2

Directions: You have seen this game's setup, rules, and deductions in the preceding sections of this chapter. For each question, first review the Master Sketch and reconstruct the work you did in Steps 1–4 of the Logic Games Method. Then, answer the question. For practice, take time to analyze each question thoroughly and enter your analysis for each step and answer choice blank. Complete expert analysis can be found in your Online Study Plan in the PDF labeled "Chapter 6 Full Game Practice Explanations."

Question 8:

Exactly seven professors—Madison, Nilsson, Orozco, Paton, Robinson, Sarkis, and Togo—were hired in the years 1989 through 1995. Each professor has one or more specialties, and any two professors hired in the same year or in consecutive years do not have a specialty in common. The professors were hired according to the following conditions:

> Madison was hired in 1993, Robinson in 1991.
>
> There is at least one specialty that Madison, Orozco, and Togo have in common.
>
> Nilsson shares a specialty with Robinson.
>
> Paton and Sarkis were each hired at least one year before Madison and at least one year after Nilsson.
>
> Orozco, who shares a specialty with Sarkis, was hired in 1990.

PrepTest35 Sec3 Q18

Steps 1–4:

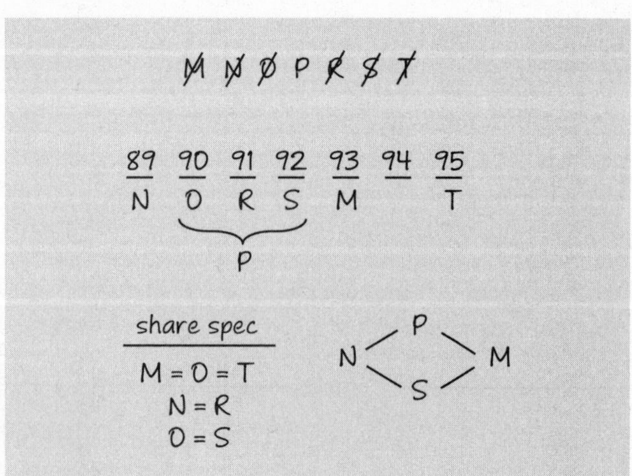

Step 5:

8. Which one of the following is a complete and accurate list of the professors who could have been hired in the years 1989 through 1991?

(A) Nilsson, Orozco, Robinson
(B) Orozco, Robinson, Sarkis
(C) Nilsson, Orozco, Paton, Robinson
(D) Nilsson, Orozco, Paton, Sarkis
(E) Orozco, Paton, Robinson, Sarkis

Step 5 (cont.):

Question 9:

Step 5:

Exactly seven professors—Madison, Nilsson, Orozco, Paton, Robinson, Sarkis, and Togo—were hired in the years 1989 through 1995. Each professor has one or more specialties, and any two professors hired in the same year or in consecutive years do not have a specialty in common. The professors were hired according to the following conditions:

Madison was hired in 1993, Robinson in 1991.
There is at least one specialty that Madison, Orozco, and Togo have in common.
Nilsson shares a specialty with Robinson.
Paton and Sarkis were each hired at least one year before Madison and at least one year after Nilsson.
Orozco, who shares a specialty with Sarkis, was hired in 1990.

PrepTest35 Sec3 Q19

Steps 1–4:

M N O P R S T

89	90	91	92	93	94	95
N	O	R	S	M		T

(P: 90–92)

share spec
M = O = T
N = R
O = S

N — P — M; N — S — M

9. If exactly one professor was hired in 1991, then which one of the following could be true?

(A) Madison and Paton share a specialty.
(B) Robinson and Sarkis share a specialty.
(C) Paton was hired exactly one year after Orozco.
(D) Exactly one professor was hired in 1994.
(E) Exactly two professors were hired in 1993.

Step 5 (cont.):

Question 10:

Step 5:

Exactly seven professors—Madison, Nilsson, Orozco, Paton, Robinson, Sarkis, and Togo—were hired in the years 1989 through 1995. Each professor has one or more specialties, and any two professors hired in the same year or in consecutive years do not have a specialty in common. The professors were hired according to the following conditions:

Madison was hired in 1993, Robinson in 1991.

There is at least one specialty that Madison, Orozco, and Togo have in common.

Nilsson shares a specialty with Robinson.

Paton and Sarkis were each hired at least one year before Madison and at least one year after Nilsson.

Orozco, who shares a specialty with Sarkis, was hired in 1990.

PrepTest35 Sec3 Q20

10. Which one of the following must be false?

    (A) Nilsson was hired in 1989.

    (B) Paton was hired in 1990.

    (C) Paton was hired in 1991.

    (D) Sarkis was hired in 1992.

    (E) Togo was hired in 1994.

Step 5 (cont.):

Steps 1–4:

M N O P R S T

89	90	91	92	93	94	95
N	O	R	S	M		T

P (90–92)

share spec

M = O = T
N = R
O = S

N – P – M
N – S – M

Question 11:

Exactly seven professors—Madison, Nilsson, Orozco, Paton, Robinson, Sarkis, and Togo—were hired in the years 1989 through 1995. Each professor has one or more specialties, and any two professors hired in the same year or in consecutive years do not have a specialty in common. The professors were hired according to the following conditions:

> Madison was hired in 1993, Robinson in 1991.
>
> There is at least one specialty that Madison, Orozco, and Togo have in common.
>
> Nilsson shares a specialty with Robinson.
>
> Paton and Sarkis were each hired at least one year before Madison and at least one year after Nilsson.
>
> Orozco, who shares a specialty with Sarkis, was hired in 1990.

PrepTest35 Sec3 Q21

Steps 1–4:

M N O P R S T

89	90	91	92	93	94	95
N	O	R	S	M		T

P (90–92)

share spec
M = O = T
N = R
O = S

N — P — M
N — S — M

Step 5:

11. Which one of the following must be true?

(A) Orozco was hired before Paton.

(B) Paton was hired before Sarkis.

(C) Sarkis was hired before Robinson.

(D) Robinson was hired before Sarkis.

(E) Madison was hired before Sarkis.

Step 5 (cont.):

Question 12:

Step 5:

Exactly seven professors—Madison, Nilsson, Orozco, Paton, Robinson, Sarkis, and Togo—were hired in the years 1989 through 1995. Each professor has one or more specialties, and any two professors hired in the same year or in consecutive years do not have a specialty in common. The professors were hired according to the following conditions:

Madison was hired in 1993, Robinson in 1991.
There is at least one specialty that Madison, Orozco, and Togo have in common.
Nilsson shares a specialty with Robinson.
Paton and Sarkis were each hired at least one year before Madison and at least one year after Nilsson.
Orozco, who shares a specialty with Sarkis, was hired in 1990.

PrepTest35 Sec3 Q22

Steps 1–4:

M N O P R S T

89	90	91	92	93	94	95
N	O	R	S	M		T

P (under 90–92)

share spec
M = O = T
N = R
O = S

N < P, S < M

12. If exactly two professors were hired in 1992, then which one of the following could be true?

(A) Orozco, Paton, and Togo share a specialty.
(B) Madison, Paton, and Togo share a specialty.
(C) Exactly two professors were hired in 1991.
(D) Exactly two professors were hired in 1993.
(E) Paton was hired in 1991.

Step 5 (cont.):

Question 13:

Step 5:

Exactly seven professors—Madison, Nilsson, Orozco, Paton, Robinson, Sarkis, and Togo—were hired in the years 1989 through 1995. Each professor has one or more specialties, and any two professors hired in the same year or in consecutive years do not have a specialty in common. The professors were hired according to the following conditions:

> Madison was hired in 1993, Robinson in 1991.
>
> There is at least one specialty that Madison, Orozco, and Togo have in common.
>
> Nilsson shares a specialty with Robinson.
>
> Paton and Sarkis were each hired at least one year before Madison and at least one year after Nilsson.
>
> Orozco, who shares a specialty with Sarkis, was hired in 1990.

PrepTest35 Sec3 Q23

Steps 1–4:

M N O P R S T

89	90	91	92	93	94	95
N	O	R	S	M		T

P (90–92)

share spec
M = O = T
N = R
O = S

N → P → M
N → S → M

13. If Paton and Madison have a specialty in common, then which one of the following must be true?

(A) Nilsson does not share a specialty with Paton.
(B) Exactly one professor was hired in 1990.
(C) Exactly one professor was hired in 1991.
(D) Exactly two professors were hired in each of two years.
(E) Paton was hired at least one year before Sarkis.

Step 5 (cont.):

Answer Key

Practice 1

1. (D)
2. (E)
3. (A)
4. (E)
5. (C)
6. (B)
7. (C)

Practice 2

8. (C)
9. (A)
10. (E)
11. (D)
12. (A)
13. (E)

Worked example explanations of these questions with complete expert analysis can be found in your Online Study Plan under Chapter 6. View or download the PDF titled "Chapter 6 Practice Full Games Explanations."

Perform

Here is your opportunity to put all of the pieces together and assess your skills on complex Strict Sequencing games. On the following pages, you'll find two full-length games along with their question sets. All of these games are from officially released LSAT tests, and all are representative of complex Strict Sequencing games you could see on test day. You can take the games one at a time or all together, but for your self-evaluation to be as accurate as possible, adhere to the timing guidelines set forth in the directions.

An answer key follows the games. Complete worked example expert analyses can be found in your online resources.

After you complete and review both games, assess your performance using the evaluation guidelines. There, you'll find recommendations for additional Easy, Medium, and Hard complex Strict Sequencing games from officially released LSAT exams that you can practice to continue honing your skills and raising your score.

Directions: Take no more than 9 minutes per game to complete the following two games and all of their questions.

Perform 1

Questions 1–7

A committee ranks five towns—Palmdale, Quietville, Riverdale, Seaside, Tidetown—from first (best) to fifth (worst) on each of three criteria: climate, location, friendliness.

For each of the three criteria, none of the five towns receives the same ranking as any other town does.

In climate, Tidetown is ranked third and Seaside fourth.

In location, Quietville is ranked second, Riverdale third, and Palmdale fourth.

In friendliness, Tidetown's ranking is better than Palmdale's, Quietville is ranked fourth and Seaside fifth.

Riverdale receives a better ranking in climate than in friendliness.

Quietville's three rankings are all different from each other.

1. Which of the following is a complete and accurate list of the rankings any one of which could be the ranking on climate given to Riverdale?

   (A) first
   (B) first, second
   (C) first, fifth
   (D) second, fifth
   (E) first, second, fifth

2. Which of the following is a town that CANNOT be ranked fifth on any one of the three criteria?

(A) Palmdale
(B) Quietville
(C) Riverdale
(D) Seaside
(E) Tidetown

3. Which of the following could be true?

(A) Palmdale is ranked first in both climate and friendliness.
(B) Quietville is ranked second in both climate and location.
(C) Riverdale is ranked first in climate and third in both location and friendliness.
(D) Seaside is ranked fifth in friendliness and fourth in both climate and location.
(E) Tidetown is ranked third in both climate and friendliness.

4. If Quietville is ranked first in climate, then it must be true that

(A) Palmdale is ranked second in climate
(B) Palmdale is ranked third in friendliness
(C) Riverdale is ranked second in friendliness
(D) Riverdale is ranked third in friendliness
(E) Tidetown is ranked fifth in location

5. If Palmdale is ranked second in climate, then which one of the following can be true?

(A) Palmdale is ranked second in friendliness.
(B) Quietville is ranked first in climate.
(C) Riverdale is ranked first in friendliness.
(D) Riverdale is ranked fifth in climate.
(E) Tidetown is ranked third in friendliness.

6. If Tidetown is ranked first in location and Riverdale is ranked second in friendliness, then it is possible to deduce with certainty all three rankings for exactly how many of the towns?

(A) One
(B) Two
(C) Three
(D) Four
(E) Five

7. Which one of the following statements CANNOT be true?

(A) Palmdale is ranked first in climate.
(B) Quietville is ranked fifth in climate.
(C) Riverdale is ranked third in friendliness.
(D) Seaside is ranked first in location.
(E) Tidetown is ranked second in friendliness.

PrepTest5 Sec2 Qs 18–24

Perform 2

Questions 8–13

A disc jockey will play a sequence consisting of exactly seven different songs: three ballads—F, G, and H—and four dance tunes—R, S, V, and X. The following conditions must be met:

No dance tune can be played immediately after another dance tune.

H must be played earlier in the sequence than V.

V and S must be separated from each other by exactly one song.

S must be played immediately before or immediately after F.

F must be played immediately after R, unless G is played earlier than R.

8. Which one of the following could be the order of the songs in the sequence?

(A) G, H, S, X, V, F, R

(B) R, H, X, G, S, F, V

(C) S, F, X, G, R, H, V

(D) V, F, S, H, X, G, R

(E) X, G, R, H, S, F, V

9. Which one of the following must be true about the sequence?

   (A) The first song is X.
   (B) The fifth song is S.
   (C) No ballad is played immediately after a dance tune.
   (D) No ballad is played immediately after another ballad.
   (E) No dance tune is played immediately after a ballad.

10. Which one of the following could be the fourth song in the sequence?

   (A) G
   (B) R
   (C) S
   (D) V
   (E) X

11. Which one of the following could be the first song in the sequence?

   (A) R
   (B) S
   (C) V
   (D) F
   (E) G

12. If the third song in the sequence is S, which one of the following must be the sixth song?

   (A) G
   (B) H
   (C) R
   (D) V
   (E) X

13. If the seventh song in the sequence is R, which one of the following could be the fifth song?

   (A) F
   (B) G
   (C) H
   (D) V
   (E) X

PrepTest25 Sec3 Qs 19–24

Answer Key

Perform 1

1. (B)
2. (C)
3. (C)
4. (D)
5. (A)
6. (E)
7. (E)

Perform 2

8. (E)
9. (D)
10. (A)
11. (A)
12. (A)
13. (D)

Worked example explanations of these questions with complete expert analysis can be found in your Online Study Plan under Chapter 6. View or download the PDF titled "Chapter 6 Perform Full Games Explanations."

Assess

Use the following criteria to evaluate your results on the Perform games.

If, under timed conditions, you correctly answered

11–13 of the questions: Outstanding! You have demonstrated a strong skill level in complex Strict Sequencing games. For further practice in complex Strict Sequencing, use any of the Recommended Additional Practice sets, including the Advanced set. Then, move on to Chapter 7 on Loose Sequencing.

8–11 of the questions: Good work! You have a solid foundation in complex Strict Sequencing games. For further practice in complex Strict Sequencing, begin with the Foundations or Mid-Level Recommended Additional Practice set. Then, move on to Chapter 7 on Loose Sequencing. If you have time before test day, try the Advanced Recommended Additional Practice set, as well.

0–7 of the questions: Keep working. Strict Sequencing games are central to your logic games performance, and continued practice will help you improve your score. Begin by reviewing this chapter. Then, try the games in the Foundations Recommended Additional Practice set. As you continue to progress, move on to the Mid-Level Recommended Additional Practice set, and then to Chapter 7 on Loose Sequencing games.

To stay sharp, practice the drills in the Logic Games Training Camp for this chapter in your Online Study Plan. Training Camp drills are divided into Fundamentals, Mid-Level, and Advanced sets.

Recommended Additional Practice: Complex Strict Sequencing

All of the following games will provide good practice on complex Strict Sequencing games. They are grouped by difficulty as determined from empirical student practice results. All PrepTests included are available on LawHub with an LSAC Prep Plus subscription.

Foundations

PrepTest 69, Section 2, Game 2: Storing Petri Dishes (Vertical/Multiple Entities per Slot)

PrepTest 68, Section 4, Game 1: Realtor Showings (Slot Groupings)

PrepTest 65, Section 2, Game 2: Crafts Presentations (Entity Subsets)

PrepTest 64, Section 2, Game 4: Bookcase Shelves (Vertical/Multiple Entities per Slot)

PrepTest 60, Section 2, Game 1: Arts and Crafts Workshops (Calendar)

Mid-Level

PrepTest 69, Section 2, Game 3: Juice and Snack Deliveries (Double Sequencing)

PrepTest 67, Section 3, Game 3: Toy Store Aisles (Multiple Entities per Slot)

PrepTest 54, Section 3, Game 2: CD Star Ratings (Entities Repeat/Multiple Entities per Slot)

Advanced

PrepTest 68, Section 4, Game 4: Article Editing (Entity Subsets)

PrepTest 65, Section 2, Game 4: TV Scheduling (Entity Sizes Vary)

PrepTest 63, Section 2, Game 4: Street Entertainer (Vertical/Entities Repeat)

Complete explanations and analysis for all of the more-than-70 official LSAT tests on LawHub that come with an LSAC LSAT Prep Plus subscription are available in Kaplan's LSAT Link and Link+ tools. Visit **www.kaptest.com/lsat** to learn more or to purchase LSAT Link or Link+.

Reflect

Think back over the study and practice you did in this chapter.

- Are you able to identify complex Strict Sequencing games from their setups?
- Do you have default sketch frameworks for various complex Strict Sequencing variations?
- What kinds of rules do you anticipate seeing in complex Strict Sequencing games? In what ways are they similar to or different from those in basic Strict Sequencing?
- Are you comfortable analyzing complex Strict Sequencing rules and determining whether to record them within or underneath the sketch framework?
- Are you making the available deductions efficiently and effectively in complex Strict Sequencing games?

In the coming days and weeks before test day, take note of real-world tasks that reflect complex Strict Sequencing tasks. Consider how they mirror the setups and questions in LSAT Strict Sequencing, and how they differ. Try to reframe real-life sequencing tasks using the terms, rules, and restrictions employed by the testmaker.

The LSAT Channel Spotlight

Circular Sequencing

By Jeff Boudreau

Watch the video lesson for this Spotlight in your online Study Plan.

Of all the variations on Strict Sequencing that the LSAT has featured, the most unusual is Circular Sequencing. At the time of this edition of this book, Circular Sequencing has appeared on released LSAT tests only three times, most recently on PrepTest 88 (September 2019), before that on PrepTest 41 (October 2003), and way back on PrepTest 1 (June 1991). From those dates, it looks like Circular Sequencing comes around no more than once in a decade, but it also seems that the testmaker has never fully abandoned this variant.

Circular Sequencing is just what it sounds like. The game's setup calls for you to determine the order of a set of entities, but instead of arranging them in a line, you must place them at points around a circle. In both of the Circular Sequencing games that have been officially released, the situation described people sitting around a circular table. It's not too hard to imagine other scenarios the testmaker might use—people taking their spots for a circle dance, items arranged around the points of a sundial, or maybe decorative flowers around the rim of a wedding cake—but, so far, it has always been people sitting at a round table.

In PrepTest 1's Circular Sequencing game, six trade representatives were seated in numbered chairs (1 through 6), and all of the rules centered around entities that were required to or prevented from sitting in adjacent seats. The only real trick there was remembering that, because the table is round, Seats 1 and 6 are adjacent seats. Okay, no more spoilers about that game in case you want to try it after this Special Feature.

The Circular Sequencing game from PrepTest 41 was less concrete. Notably, the seats in this case were not numbered.

Eight people—Fiona, George, Harriet, Ingrid, Karl, Manuel, Olivia, and Peter—are sitting, evenly spaced, around a circular picnic table. Any two of them are said to be sitting directly across from one another if and only if there are exactly three other people sitting between them, counting in either direction around the table. The following conditions apply:

> Fiona sits directly across from George.
> Harriet sits immediately next to neither Fiona nor Karl.
> Ingrid sits immediately next to, and immediately clockwise from, Olivia.

PrepTest41 Sec2 Qs 18-24

You may have noticed that this complex game has only three rules, and that they restrict only six of the eight entities. It's not surprising, then, that student results demonstrate that this is a difficult logic game.

In the video that accompanies this page, an LSAT Channel expert will walk you through the Picnic Table game, which is printed in full on the following pages. Try it on your own first, if you like. The expert's lesson provides a great example of how the Logic Games Method allows you to effectively tackle even unusual and unexpected games.

Questions 18–24

Eight people—Fiona, George, Harriet, Ingrid, Karl, Manuel, Olivia, and Peter—are sitting, evenly spaced, around a circular picnic table. Any two of them are said to be sitting directly across from one another if and only if there are exactly three other people sitting between them, counting in either direction around the table. The following conditions apply:

Fiona sits directly across from George.

Harriet sits immediately next to neither Fiona nor Karl.

Ingrid sits immediately next to, and immediately clockwise from, Olivia.

18. Which one of the following could be the order in which four of the people are seated, with no one else seated between them, counting clockwise around the table?

(A) George, Peter, Karl, Fiona

(B) Harriet, Olivia, Ingrid, Karl

(C) Ingrid, Fiona, Peter, Manuel

(D) Olivia, Manuel, Karl, George

(E) Peter, Harriet, Karl, Fiona

19. If Harriet and Olivia each sits immediately next to George, then which one of the following could be the two people each of whom sits immediately next to Peter?

(A) Fiona and Karl
(B) Fiona and Olivia
(C) Harriet and Ingrid
(D) Harriet and Karl
(E) Karl and Manuel

20. If George does not sit immediately next to Harriet, then which one of the following could be the two people each of whom sits immediately next to Manuel?

(A) Fiona and Harriet
(B) Fiona and Peter
(C) George and Karl
(D) George and Peter
(E) Harriet and Peter

21. If Manuel sits immediately next to Olivia, then which one of the following people must sit immediately next to Fiona?

(A) Harriet
(B) Ingrid
(C) Karl
(D) Manuel
(E) Peter

22. What is the minimum possible number of people sitting between Ingrid and Manuel, counting clockwise from Ingrid around the table?

(A) zero
(B) one
(C) two
(D) three
(E) four

23. If Karl sits directly across from Ingrid, then each of the following people could sit immediately next to Olivia EXCEPT:

(A) Fiona
(B) George
(C) Harriet
(D) Manuel
(E) Peter

24. If Karl sits directly across from Harriet, then what is the minimum possible number of people sitting between George and Karl, counting clockwise from George to Karl?

(A) zero
(B) one
(C) two
(D) three
(E) four

PrepTest41 Sec2 Qs 18–24

Complete answers and explanations are provided in The LSAT Channel Spotlight video "Limited Options" in your online Study Plan.

CHAPTER 7

Loose Sequencing Games Unlocked

LEARNING OBJECTIVES

In this chapter, you'll learn to

- Apply the Logic Games Method to Loose Sequencing games.

Prepare

Loose Sequencing games are far less common than the Strict Sequencing games you've seen in the two preceding chapters. Even so, Loose Sequencing has accounted for around 10 percent of all logic games on LSAT tests released in recent years.

Types of Games By Percentage, 2014–2018

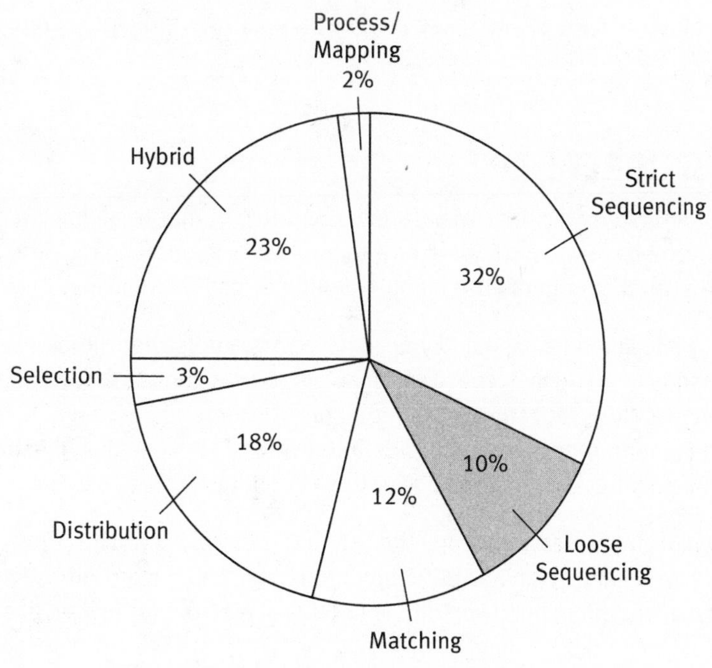

The opening paragraph of a Loose Sequencing game—its setup, if you will—is often no different than that of any other Sequencing game. The setup will define an ordering task such as ranking or scheduling, and it will always use language that tells you that the entities are to be arranged one per position with no ties.

> At a retirement party, exactly seven employees—Arias, Barnhard, Carmichael, Deng, Evans, Furillo, and Gillis—will give toasts honoring a retiring coworker. The employees will give their toasts one at a time in an order subject to the following considerations:

So far, that looks like any basic Strict Sequencing game.

The defining characteristic of Loose Sequencing games appears in the rules. All of the rules will stipulate the relative positions between or among the entities. For example:

> Gillis will give a toast before Carmichael and Furillo give toasts.
> Deng will give a toast after Carmichael.
> Arias gives a toast at some time before Carmichael, but at some time later than Barnhard.
> Evans will give a toast at some time before Gillis.

Notice, too, that every entity in the game is mentioned in at least one rule, and some are mentioned in two. This is typical of Loose Sequencing, and it leads to a special sketch framework that you'll learn for this game type.

Loose Sequencing games never present a rule that establishes an entity in a particular named or numbered position, that stipulates the exact number of positions by which two entities are separated, or that dictates that two entities are in adjacent positions. You might, on occasion, see a conditional rule (e.g., "If A ranks higher than C, then D ranks lower than F") or one that gives two alternative orders (e.g., "Either G ranks higher than B and lower than E, or G ranks lower than B and higher than A"). Rules like these are rare, and always indicate a more difficult Loose Sequencing game.

LOOSE SEQUENCING IN REAL LIFE

Because Loose Sequencing is defined by the relative nature of the rules, finding analogies in day-to-day life means thinking about the information you have when deciding how to put things in order. In real life, ranking things—deciding which ones you like better than others—often approximates Loose Sequencing.

Imagine you are relaxing with a social media page and you come across a poll titled "Rank the Greatest Classic Rock Bands." The poll lists seven bands—call them A, B, K, L, P, R, and W. As you look over the list, you probably don't think "I'll put W and L in consecutive positions, but I might like either one better than the other." Almost certainly, you don't think "I haven't considered the other bands here, but R is definitely third," or "K is ranked exactly two positions lower than W." Those "strict" rules seem inherently out of place in this kind of task.

Given the "loose" nature of ranking favorites, you study the list, and probably start with thoughts such as, "Well, I like L better than A, but not as well as R," and "I have to put R higher than W," and so on. For a simple task like this, you probably wouldn't need to sketch anything, but if you did, your "rules" would start to look like this:

```
R—L—A
 \
  W
```

At this point, you've ranked W relative to R, but not yet relative to L or A. Likewise, A is ranked relative to R and L, but not relative to W. In the real-life game, you will add more of these relative decisions—your "rules," if you like—until, in the end, you'll decide on a specific order, first through seventh.

On the LSAT, a Loose Sequencing game will stop short of giving you enough information to decide on just one final order. To see what a Master Sketch will look like on the test, add a couple more decisions to your classic rock list: "B and P both rank higher than R" and "K ranks below W." Here's what you know so far:

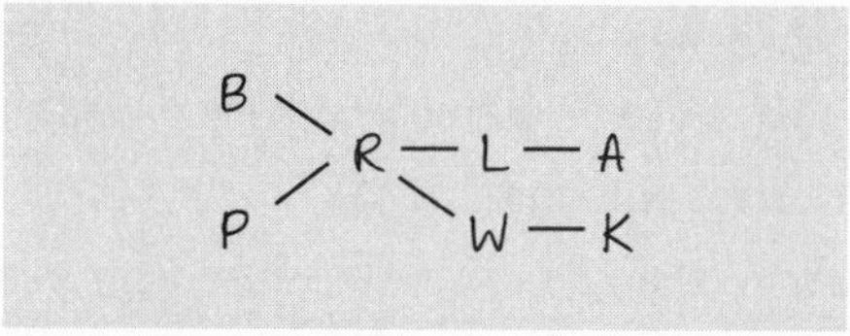

```
B \
   > R — L — A
P /    \
        W — K
```

At this point, you know that one of B or P is your favorite among the seven bands, and the other is your second favorite. You've now determined that R is, for sure, your third favorite. Band A might be your least favorite of the seven, but it could still wind up as high as fifth because you haven't yet ranked it against W or K.

The sketch represents a typical LSAT Loose Sequencing game's Master Sketch, including all of the rules and deductions. By giving you that much information, the game's questions can ask you about any number of cases that must, could, or cannot be true. Given the "rules" recorded so far, for example, it must be true that you like P more than W, but it could be true or false that you like W more than L. The test may also ask New-"If" questions by giving conditions that further restrict something so far undetermined within the game: "If L is your fourth favorite of the seven bands, which one of the following must/could be true/false?"

When you notice sequencing tasks in your everyday routine, stop to consider whether the "rules" inherent in them are "strict" or "loose." Keep in mind that, on the LSAT, most Strict Sequencing games contain one or more loose, relative-relationship rules along with those that mention named or numbered positions and others that provide for strict relationships among the entities. LSAT Loose Sequencing games, however, provide only relative relationships. In the next section, you'll learn how LSAT experts handle sketches and deductions a little differently in Loose Sequencing than they do in other game types.

LOOSE SEQUENCING GAMES RULES

LEARNING OBJECTIVES

In this section of the chapter, you'll practice

- Applying Steps 1 and 2 of the Logic Games Method to Loose Sequencing games by
  - Asking the SEAL questions to analyze the game's Overview, and then
  - Building the rules into a simple, useful framework
- Applying Step 3 of the Logic Games Method to Loose Sequencing games by analyzing and sketching the rules
- Applying Step 4 of the Logic Games Method to Loose Sequencing games by combining rules and restrictions to make all valid deductions in the game

Prepare

Steps 1, 2, and 3 in Loose Sequencing Games

Because Loose Sequencing setups are often indistinguishable from their Strict counterparts, there isn't much to add about Step 1. As you ask the SEAL questions, you'll discover a game that asks you to put people or items in order or to schedule them, one per position with no ties. As a result, your instinct in Step 2 will be to draw out a standard Strict Sequencing sketch framework. That's fine. But, when you turn to the rules and find out you have a Loose Sequencing game—that is, when you discover that *all* of the rules provide *only* relative relationships among the entities—you'll know that you are going to build the rules into a branching "tree" of relationships, and won't depict any of them within a framework of numbered slots.

LOGIC GAMES STRATEGY

To distinguish Loose Sequencing games from Strict Sequencing games, modify **SEAL** to **SEAL'R**. In other words, if your answers to the SEAL questions in the Step 1 produce the following results:

- The **S**ituation poses an ordering or scheduling task,
- The roster of **E**ntities has no subdivisions,
- The **A**ction is Sequencing, and
- The **L**imitations specify a one per position/no ties arrangement

then quickly review the **R**ules.

- If all of the rules provide only relative relationships between or among the entities, this is a Loose Sequencing game.
- If any of the rules establishes an entity's position, provide an exact number of spaces between two (or more) entities, or stipulate that two entities are adjacent, this is a Strict Sequencing game.

As you practice, you'll begin to instinctively add that quick review of the rules to the Overview step. Most of the time, the rules will reveal a basic Strict Sequencing game (they are simply more common on the LSAT), but from time to time, you'll uncover a Loose Sequencing game.

To make the distinction concrete, consider the setup from the introduction to this chapter.

> At a retirement party, exactly seven employees—Arias, Barnhard, Carmichael, Deng, Evans, Furillo, and Gillis—will give toasts honoring a retiring coworker. The employees will give their toasts one at a time in an order subject to the following considerations:

While it is clear that the Action here is basic Sequencing, you don't yet know whether it is Strict or Loose. Now, consider two potential sets of rules to accompany that setup:

Rule Set I

> Deng gives the seventh toast.
> Exactly one employee gives a toast between Gillis and Carmichael.
> Barnhard's toast is some time before Arias's toast.
> Gillis's toast is before Evans's toast but after Furillo's.

```
A B C D E F G

                        D
_  _  _  _  _  _  _
1  2  3  4  5  6  7

G/C _ C/G

B...A
F...G...E
```

The first two rules distinguish Set I as belonging to a Strict Sequencing game. Rule 1 is depicted directly within the sketch framework, and Rule 2 is written out to reflect the spacing and orientation of the framework.

Rule Set II

> Gillis will give a toast before Carmichael and Furillo give toasts.
> Deng will give a toast after Carmichael.
> Arias gives a toast at some time before Carmichael, but at some time later than Barnhard.
> Evans will give a toast at some time before Gillis.

```
A B C D E F G

B — A \
       C — D
      /
E — G \
       F
```

Rule Set II indicates a Loose Sequencing game. All of the rules outline relative relationships among the entities. In another distinguishing characteristic of Loose Sequencing games, notice that all of the game's entities are mentioned in at least one of the rules. The resulting sketch doesn't correspond to a framework, but it contains all of the information needed to answer the game's questions.

Steps 3 and 4 in Loose Sequencing Games

While examining the Loose Sequencing example provided by Rule Set II, it may have struck you that the LSAT expert combined all of the rules into a single "tree" of relationships. In essence, the expert combined Steps 3 and 4 while writing out the rules. To see how that happened, take the rules one at a time, and note how the expert adds each rule to the existing branches of the "tree":

> At a retirement party, exactly seven employees—Arias, Barnhard, Carmichael, Deng, Evans, Furillo, and Gillis—will give toasts honoring a retiring coworker. The employees will give their toasts one at a time in an order subject to the following considerations:
>
> Gillis will give a toast before Carmichael and Furillo give toasts.

A B C D E F G

G — C
G — F

> Deng will give a toast after Carmichael.

A B C D E F G

G — C — D
G — F

> Arias gives a toast at some time before Carmichael, but at some time later than Barnhard.

A B C D E F G

B — A — C — D
G — C
G — F

> Evans will give a toast at some time before Gillis.

A B C D E F G

B — A — C — D
E — G — C
G — F

The value of a tree-like depiction of Loose Sequencing rules is that the resulting sketch allows you to determine the acceptable positions for every entity. To do this, count the number of entities that must come before, and the number of entities that must come after, the entity in question.

Take Gillis, for example, in the Retirement Toasts game: Gillis must follow Evans, and must precede Furillo, Carmichael, and Deng. Thus, Gillis could be no earlier than second, and no later than fourth. None of the rules relates Gillis directly to Barnhard or Arias. Gillis may give a toast earlier than both of them, later than both of them, or in between the two.

Now, consider Carmichael. What is the earliest and latest she could give her toast?

Carmichael must follow Evans, Gillis, Barnhard, and Arias, so the earliest toast she could give is fifth. Carmichael must precede Deng, so the latest toast she could give is sixth. The only employee not directly related to Carmichael by the rules is Furillo. Carmichael could give her toast before or after Furillo's toast.

For good measure, try one more. Determine the earliest and latest positions that are acceptable for Arias.

Arias must be preceded by Barnhard, so the earliest Arias could give a toast is second. Arias must be followed by Carmichael and Deng, so the latest Arias could give a toast is fifth. Note that Arias is not related to Evans, Gillis, or Furillo in any way by the rules.

Most Loose Sequencing games contain straightforward rules that state the relative order of two or three entities. From time to time, the LSAT will increase the complexity of Loose Sequencing games by adding conditional rules, or rules that allow for more than one order among certain entities.

LOGIC GAMES STRATEGY

In Loose Sequencing games, the rules basically tell you:

- The order in which two or more entities are positioned.

Occasionally, Loose Sequencing rules give you:

- A condition under which the order between entities can change; e.g., If C ranks higher than D, then F ranks higher than E.
- Two alternative orders among three entities; e.g., P ranks higher than either M or N, but not both. (This means that either of M-P-N or N-P-M is acceptable, but in no case can both M and N precede or follow P.)

Because Loose Sequencing games use so few types of rules, the deductions come from a limited number of sources.

LOGIC GAMES STRATEGY

In Loose Sequencing games, deductions are most likely to stem from:

- **"Loose" Blocks of Entities**—Two or more entities that must appear in a particular order, but are not restricted by the number of spaces between them, and
- **Duplications**—Entities shared by two or more rules; duplications are always at the heart of Loose Sequencing games.

In Loose Sequencing games, deductions may involve:

- **Limited Options**—The situation arises when a "loose" Block of Entities is restricted to either of two acceptable orders; when this occurs, draw dual Limited Options sketches.

In Loose Sequencing games, deductions never involve:

- **Established Entities**—Entities placed into a specific position.
- **Number Restrictions**—Limitations or rules affecting the number of entities that can be placed in a given position.

To see how the test might construct a complex Loose Sequencing game that results in Limited Options, revisit the "real-life" scenario of ranking classic rock bands.

> Carla is ranking seven classic rock bands—A, B, K, L, P, R, and W—and no others from most to least favorite. She will rank each band once, with no ties. Her rankings correspond to the following considerations:
>
> She ranks P higher than she ranks R.
> She ranks B lower than she ranks L.
> She ranks A higher than she ranks both P and W.
> She ranks one of L or A, but not both, higher than she ranks K.

In this game, Rule 4 provides exactly two ways in which Karen might rank A, K, and L.

A — K — L or L — K — A

That provides a perfect starting point from which to build out dual Limited Options sketches. Because Rule 3 and Rule 4 share A, you can attach Rule 3 to both options.

Opt. I: A — K — L (A — P, A — W)

Opt. II: L — K — A (A — P, A — W)

Likewise, because Rule 2 and Rule 4 share L, you can attach Rule 2 to each option.

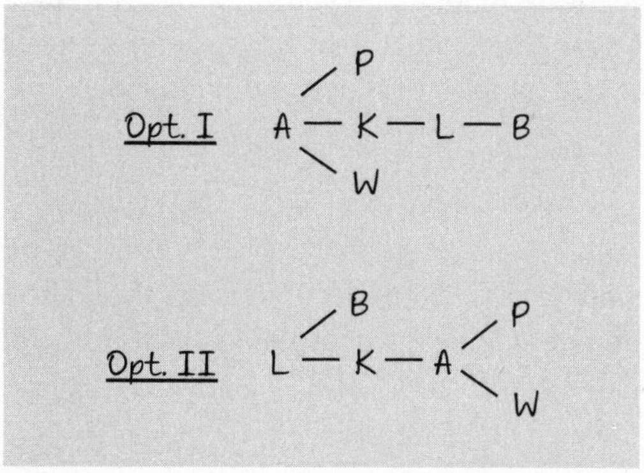

And, finally, because P is already placed in each option, there are clear places to attach Rule 1 to the "trees."

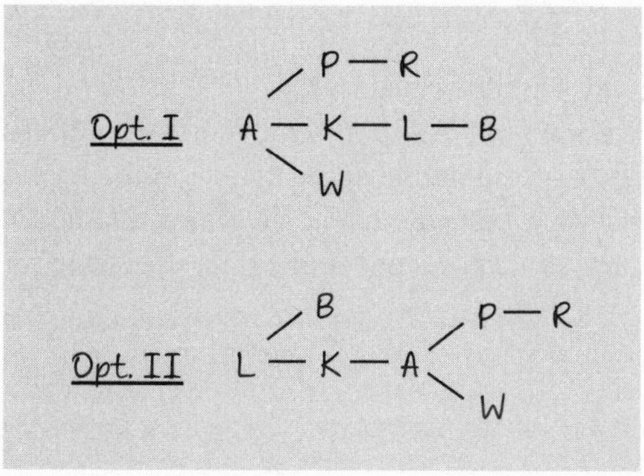

Rule 4 clearly makes this game more complex than a Loose Sequencing game without any rules that provide for alternative orders. Within each of the two options, however, you can still determine the highest or lowest that a given entity might appear.

Consider K, for example. In Option I, K is preceded by only A, so K could be ranked as high as second. In Option I, K is followed by only L and B, and could thus rank as low as fifth. In this option, K is not directly related to P, R, or W.

In Option II, K is preceded only by L, and again, could rank as high as second. However, in the second option, K is followed by A, P, R, and W, and so can only rank as low as third. In this option, K is directly related to every entity except B.

Remember that Loose Sequencing games with Limited Options are pretty rare. Should you see one, however, you will really appreciate being able to quickly and accurately assess the dual sketches. If a New-"If" question opened with "If Carla ranks K fifth . . . ", then you would know you are in Option I (because K can't rank fifth in Option II), you would know that A ranks first (because it always does in Option I), and you would know that L ranks sixth and that B ranks seventh (because they must follow K in Option I). You could quickly draw a sketch for that question, and you would have high confidence that you could assess what must, could, and cannot be true as a result.

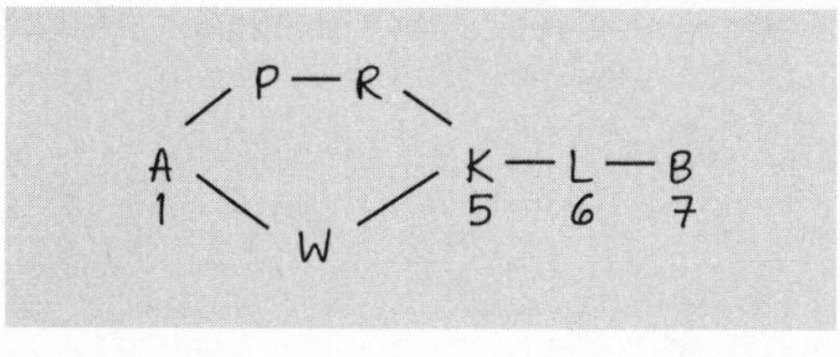

Now, it's time for a little practice with Loose Sequencing setups, rules, and deductions. You already know what you're going to see in the setup—a basic Sequencing action—and you know that, because these are Loose Sequencing games, you won't need a sketch framework. Therefore, the practice exercises focus on Steps 3 and 4, and especially on your ability to "read" the tree-like sketch (or sketches) that you will build.

Practice

Directions: In each practice exercise, work through Steps 1 through 4 of the Logic Games Method. After you complete your Master Sketch, assess its utility by determining the acceptable positions for each of the game's entities.

Practice 1

The order of presentation of six film award categories—comedy, documentary, foreign, historical, independent, and nature—at an annual film festival always adheres to the following guidelines established by the festival advisory committee:

No two award presentations will be made concurrently.
The award for foreign films is always presented at some time before the award for comedies.
The award for comedies is always presented at some time after the award for documentaries.
The award for foreign films is always presented at some time after the awards for historical and nature films.
The award for independent films is always presented before the award for historical films.

1. [Steps 1–4] Record your Master Sketch in the following space:

2. Evaluate your sketch by answering the following questions:
   - What are the earliest and latest positions in which the award for comedy may be presented?
   - What are the earliest and latest positions in which the award for documentary may be presented?
   - What are the earliest and latest positions in which the award for foreign film may be presented?
   - What are the earliest and latest positions in which the award for historical film may be presented?
   - What are the earliest and latest positions in which the award for independent film may be presented?
   - What are the earliest and latest positions in which the award for nature film may be presented?
   - If the nature film award is the third award presented, how many categories of awards are there that could be the second award category presented? Which categories are they?
   - If the foreign film award is the fourth award presented, which category of awards is presented fifth?
   - If the historical film award is the second award presented, how many categories of awards are there that could be the third award category presented? Which categories are they?

Practice 2

A music producer is sequencing seven instrumental music pieces—*Atmosphere, Botanica, Clouds, Dynamic, Ecologica, Fireflies,* and *Gyrate*—for a New Age relaxation CD. Each piece will appear exactly one time, and none of the pieces overlap. In order to achieve a harmonic progression in mood, the producer will adhere to the following guidelines:

Botanica can neither appear earlier on the CD than *Fireflies* nor later on the CD than *Dynamic.*
Atmosphere must appear earlier on the CD than *Fireflies* in any sequence in which *Gyrate* appears earlier than *Dynamic.*
Ecologica must appear earlier on the CD than both *Clouds* and *Fireflies.*
Dynamic must appear earlier on the CD than *Atmosphere.*

1. [Steps 1–4] Record your Master Sketch in the following space:

2. Evaluate your sketch by answering the following questions:
   - What are the earliest and latest positions in which *Atmosphere* may appear on the CD?
   - What are the earliest and latest positions in which *Botanica* may appear on the CD?
   - What are the earliest and latest positions in which *Clouds* may appear on the CD?
   - What are the earliest and latest positions in which *Dynamic* may appear on the CD?
   - What are the earliest and latest positions in which *Ecologica* may appear on the CD?
   - What are the earliest and latest positions in which *Fireflies* may appear on the CD?
   - What are the earliest and latest positions in which *Gyrate* may appear on the CD?
   - If *Botanica* is the fourth track on the CD, how many tracks are there that could be second track? Which ones are they?
   - If *Dynamic* is the fourth track on the CD, how many tracks are there that could be the fifth track? Which ones are they?

Explanations

Compare your work to that of an LSAT expert. Make sure that your sketch accurately reflects all of the restrictions given in the rules. Then, compare your answers to those of the expert on each of the assessment questions. If your answers differ, review the rules and your sketch to see why your analysis was mistaken.

Practice 1

The order of presentation of six film award categories—comedy, documentary, foreign, historical, independent, and nature—at the annual film festival always adheres to the following guidelines established by the festival advisory committee:

No two award presentations will be made concurrently.
The award for foreign films is always presented at some time before the award for comedies.
The award for comedies is always presented at some time after the award for documentaries.
The award for foreign films is always presented at some time after the awards for historical and nature films.
The award for independent films is always presented before the award for historical films.

1. [Steps 1–4] Record your Master Sketch in the following space:

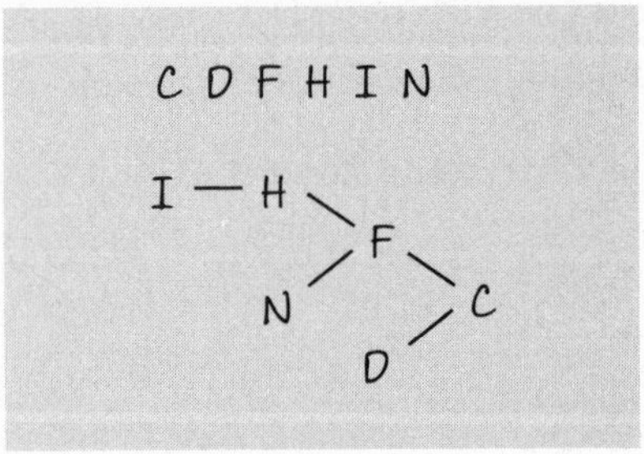

C D F H I N

I — H
N → F → C
D → C

2. Evaluate your sketch by answering the following questions:
   - What are the earliest and latest positions in which the award for comedy may be presented? *The comedy award must be presented sixth; it is preceded by all five of the other entities.*
   - What are the earliest and latest positions in which the award for documentary may be presented? *The earliest that the documentary award may be presented is first (no entities must precede it); the latest the documentary award may be presented is fifth (it is followed by comedy).*
   - What are the earliest and latest positions in which the award for foreign film may be presented? *The earliest that the foreign film award may be presented is fourth (it is preceded by independent, historical, and nature); the latest the foreign film award may be presented is fifth (it is followed by comedy).*
   - What are the earliest and latest positions in which the award for historical film may be presented? *The earliest that the historical film award may be presented is second (it is preceded by independent); the latest the historical film award may be presented is fourth (it is followed by foreign film and comedy).*
   - What are the earliest and latest positions in which the award for independent film may be presented? *The earliest that the independent film award may be presented is first (no entities must precede it); the latest the independent award may be presented is third (it is followed by historical film, foreign film, and comedy).*
   - What are the earliest and latest positions in which the award for nature film may be presented? *The earliest that the nature film award may be presented is first (no entities must precede it); the latest the nature award may be presented is fourth (it is followed by foreign film and comedy).*
   - If the nature film award is the third award presented, how many categories of awards are there that could be the second award category presented? Which categories are they? *When the nature film award is presented third, there are three categories that could be presented second: documentary, historical, and independent. Presenting the nature film award third allows for either of these sequence patterns:*

```
(1-2)
I
  \
   N — H — F — C
  / 3   4   5   6
D
(1-2)
```

```
            (4-5)
              F
            /   \
I — H — N         C
1   2   3 \     / 6
            D
          (4-5)
```

- If the foreign film award is the fourth award presented, which category of awards is presented fifth? *When the foreign film award is fourth, then the fifth award must be for documentary.*

```
(1-2) (2-3)
I  —  H
        \
         F — D — C
        / 4   5   6
      N
    (1-3)
```

- If the historical film award is the second award presented, how many categories of awards are there that could be the third award category presented? Which categories are they? *When the historical film award is presented second, there are two categories that could be presented third: nature film or documentary.*

```
I — H  (4-5)
1   2 \ F
      /   \
    N       C
 (3-4)    / 6
       D
     (3-5)
```

Practice 2

A music producer is sequencing seven instrumental music pieces—*Atmosphere, Botanica, Clouds, Dynamic, Ecologica, Fireflies,* and *Gyrate*—for a New Age relaxation CD. Each piece will appear exactly one time, and none of the pieces overlap. In order to achieve a harmonic progression in mood, the producer will adhere to the following guidelines:

> *Botanica* can neither appear earlier on the CD than *Fireflies* nor later on the CD than *Dynamic.*
>
> *Atmosphere* must appear earlier on the CD than *Fireflies* in any sequence in which *Gyrate* appears earlier than *Dynamic.*
>
> *Ecologica* must appear earlier on the CD than both *Clouds* and *Fireflies.*
>
> *Dynamic* must appear earlier on the CD than *Atmosphere.*

1. [Steps 1–4] Record your Master Sketch in the following space: *Rule 1 translates into the following sketch:*

```
F — B — D
```

Rule 2 is conditional. For the moment, write it off to the side.

```
F — B — D

If G — D → A — F

If F — A → D — G
```

Rules 3 and 4 can be attached to Rule 1.

```
   / F — B — D — A
E
   \
     C

If G — D → A — F

If F — A → D — G
```

Now, consider Rule 2 in light of what the sketch reveals about A and F. For G to be earlier than D, A must be earlier than F. But, A is locked into a position later than F. That means that G can never be in a position earlier than D. Add G to the sketch following D.

```
   / F — B — D — A
E              \
   \             G
     C
```

At this point, the sketch is complete, and you can use it to determine acceptable positions for each entity.

2. Evaluate your sketch by answering the following questions:
   - What are the earliest and latest positions in which *Atmosphere* may appear on the CD? Atmosphere *can take any position from fifth through seventh. It is preceded by E, F, B, and D, but is unrelated to C and G.*
   - What are the earliest and latest positions in which *Botanica* may appear on the CD? Botanica *can be third or fourth. It is preceded by E and F, followed by D, A, and G, and is unrelated to C.*
   - What are the earliest and latest positions in which *Clouds* may appear on the CD? Clouds *can take any position from second through seventh. It is preceded by E, but is unrelated to any other entity.*
   - What are the earliest and latest positions in which *Dynamic* may appear on the CD? Dynamic *can be fourth or fifth. It is preceded by E, F, and B, followed by A and G, and is unrelated to C.*
   - What are the earliest and latest positions in which *Ecologica* may appear on the CD? Ecologica *must be the first track on the CD. It is followed by every other piece of music.*
   - What are the earliest and latest positions in which *Fireflies* may appear on the CD? Fireflies *could be second or third. It is preceded by E, followed by B, D, A, and G, and is unrelated to C.*
   - What are the earliest and latest positions in which *Gyrate* may appear on the CD? Gyrate *can take any position from fifth through seventh. It is preceded by E, F, B, and D, but is unrelated to C and A.*
   - If *Botanica* is the fourth track on the CD, how many tracks are there that could be second track? Which ones are they? *When* Botanica *is fourth, there are two options for the second track:* Fireflies *and* Clouds.

```
    (2-3)            (6-7)
   / F \            / A
E        B — D
1  \    / 4   5  \
     C             G
   (2-3)           (6-7)
```

   - If *Dynamic* is the fourth track on the CD, how many tracks are there that could be the fifth track? Which ones are they? *When* Dynamic *is fourth, there are three options for track five:* Atmosphere, Clouds, *and* Gyrate.

```
                 / A (5-7)
E — F — B — D — G (5-7)
1   2   3   4 \
                 C (5-7)
```

Now that you've learned the ins and outs of setting up Loose Sequencing games, test your skills on two officially released LSAT games in the Perform section.

LOOSE SEQUENCING GAMES—FULL GAMES WITH QUESTIONS

LEARNING OBJECTIVES

In this section of the chapter, you'll assess your ability to

- Apply the Logic Games Method to Loose Sequencing games.

Perform

Here is your opportunity to put all of the pieces together and assess your skills on Loose Sequencing games. On the following pages, you'll find two full-length games along with their question sets. Both of these games are from officially released LSAT tests, and are representative of Loose Sequencing games you could see on test day. You can take the games one at a time or together, but for your self-evaluation to be as accurate as possible, adhere to the timing guidelines set forth in the directions.

An answer key follows the games. Complete worked example expert analyses can be found in your online resources.

After you complete and review both games, assess your performance using the evaluation guidelines. There, you'll find recommendations for additional Easy, Medium, and Hard Loose Sequencing games from officially released LSAT exams that you can practice to continue honing your skills and raising your score.

Directions: Take no more than 9 minutes per game to complete the following two games and all of their questions.

Perform 1

Questions 1–7

A rowing team uses a boat with exactly six seats arranged in single file and numbered sequentially 1 through 6, from the front of the boat to the back. Six athletes—Lee, Miller, Ovitz, Singh, Valerio, and Zita—each row at exactly one of the seats. The following restrictions must apply:

Miller rows closer to the front than Singh.

Singh rows closer to the front than both Lee and Valerio.

Valerio and Zita each row closer to the front than Ovitz.

1. Which one of the following could be an accurate matching of athletes to seats?

   (A) Miller: seat 1; Valerio: seat 5; Lee: seat 6

   (B) Singh: seat 3; Valerio: seat 4; Zita: seat 5

   (C) Miller: seat 1; Valerio: seat 3; Lee: seat 6

   (D) Lee: seat 3; Valerio: seat 4; Ovitz: seat 5

   (E) Zita: seat 2; Valerio: seat 3; Ovitz: seat 6

2. If Valerio rows at seat 5, then which one of the following must be true?

   (A) Miller rows at seat 1.
   (B) Singh rows at seat 2.
   (C) Zita rows at seat 3.
   (D) Lee rows at seat 4.
   (E) Ovitz rows at seat 6.

3. If Lee rows at seat 3, then each of the following could be true EXCEPT:

   (A) Zita rows immediately behind Valerio.
   (B) Ovitz rows immediately behind Valerio.
   (C) Ovitz rows immediately behind Zita.
   (D) Valerio rows immediately behind Lee.
   (E) Singh rows immediately behind Zita.

4. Which one of the following CANNOT be true?

   (A) Ovitz rows closer to the front than Singh.
   (B) Zita rows closer to the front than Miller.
   (C) Lee rows closer to the front than Valerio.
   (D) Singh rows closer to the front than Zita.
   (E) Valerio rows closer to the front than Lee.

5. Exactly how many different seats could be the seat occupied by Zita?

   (A) two
   (B) three
   (C) four
   (D) five
   (E) six

6. If Valerio rows closer to the front than Zita, then which one of the following must be true?

   (A) Miller rows immediately in front of Singh.
   (B) Lee rows immediately in front of Valerio.
   (C) Zita rows immediately in front of Ovitz.
   (D) Singh rows immediately in front of Lee.
   (E) Singh rows immediately in front of Valerio.

7. Suppose the restriction that Miller rows closer to the front than Singh is replaced by the restriction that Singh rows closer to the front than Miller. If the other two restrictions remain in effect, then each of the following could be an accurate matching of athletes to seats EXCEPT:

   (A) Singh: seat 1; Zita: seat 2; Miller: seat 6
   (B) Singh: seat 1; Valerio: seat 3; Ovitz: seat 5
   (C) Singh: seat 3; Lee: seat 4; Valerio: seat 5
   (D) Valerio: seat 3; Miller: seat 4; Lee: seat 5
   (E) Valerio: seat 4; Miller: seat 5; Ovitz: seat 6

PrepTest43 Sec4 Qs 6–12

Perform 2

Questions 8–12

Each of seven television programs—H, J, L, P, Q, S, V—is assigned a different rank: from first through seventh (from most popular to least popular). The ranking is consistent with the following conditions:

J and L are each less popular than H.
J is more popular than Q.
S and V are each less popular than L.
P and S are each less popular than Q.
S is not seventh.

8. Which one of the following could be the order of the programs, from most popular to least popular?

(A) J, H, L, Q, V, S, P
(B) H, L, Q, J, S, P, V
(C) H, J, Q, L, S, V, P
(D) H, J, V, L, Q, S, P
(E) H, L, V, J, Q, P, S

9. If J is more popular than L, and S is more popular than P, then which one of the following must be true of the ranking?

   (A) J is second.
   (B) J is third.
   (C) L is third.
   (D) Q is third.
   (E) P is seventh.

10. Which one of the following programs CANNOT be ranked third?

   (A) L
   (B) J
   (C) Q
   (D) V
   (E) P

11. If V is more popular than Q and J is less popular than L, then which one of the following could be true of the ranking?

   (A) P is more popular than S.
   (B) S is more popular than V.
   (C) P is more popular than L.
   (D) J is more popular than V.
   (E) Q is more popular than V.

12. If Q is more popular than L, then each of the following must be true of the ranking EXCEPT:

   (A) H is first.
   (B) L is fourth.
   (C) V is not fourth.
   (D) J is not third.
   (E) Q is third.

PrepTest33 Sec4 Qs 1–5

Answer Key

Perform 1

1. (C)
2. (E)
3. (E)
4. (A)
5. (D)
6. (A)
7. (C)

Perform 2

8. (C)
9. (A)
10. (E)
11. (D)
12. (B)

Worked example explanations of these questions with complete expert analysis can be found in your Online Study Plan under Chapter 7. View or download the PDF titled "Chapter 7 Perform Full Games Explanations."

Assess

Use the following criteria to evaluate your results on the Perform games.

If, under timed conditions, you correctly answered

10–12 of the questions: Outstanding! You have demonstrated a strong skill level in Loose Sequencing games. For further practice in Loose Sequencing, use any of the Recommended Additional Practice sets, including the Advanced set. Then, move on to either Chapter 8 on Selection games, or if you have limited time before test day, skip to Chapter 9 on Matching and Distribution games.

7–9 of the questions: Good work! You have a solid foundation in Loose Sequencing games. For further practice in Loose Sequencing, begin with the Foundations or Mid-Level Recommended Additional Practice set. If you have ample time before test day, try the Advanced Recommended Additional Practice set, as well. Then, move on to either Chapter 8 on Selection games, or if you have limited time before test day, skip to Chapter 9 on Matching and Distribution games.

0–6 of the questions: Keep working. Loose Sequencing games are not as central to your logic games performance as Strict Sequencing games are, but they appear regularly, and continued practice will help you improve your score. Begin by reviewing this chapter. Then, try the games in the Foundations Recommended Additional Practice set. As you continue to progress, move on to the Mid-Level Recommended Additional Practice set, and then on to Chapter 8 on Selection games, or if you have limited time before test day, skip to Chapter 9 on Matching and Distribution games.

To stay sharp, practice the drills in the Logic Games Training Camp for this chapter in your Online Study Plan. Training Camp drills are divided into Fundamentals, Mid-Level, and Advanced sets.

Recommended Additional Practice: Loose Sequencing

All of the following games will provide good practice on Loose Sequencing. They are grouped by difficulty as determined from empirical student practice results. All PrepTests included are available on LawHub with an LSAC Prep Plus subscription.

Foundations

PrepTest 71, Section 2, Game 1: Film Releases

PrepTest 65, Section 2, Game 1: Piano Recital Solos

Mid-Level

PrepTest 61, Section 3, Game 2: Ancient Artifacts

PrepTest 60, Section 2, Game 2: Actors in Opening Credits

Advanced

PrepTest 52, Section 2, Game 1: Water Valves

PrepTest 52, Section 2, Game 4: Bread Truck Deliveries

Complete explanations and analysis for all of the more-than-70 official LSAT tests on LawHub that come with an LSAC LSAT Prep Plus subscription are available in Kaplan's LSAT Link and Link+ tools. Visit **www.kaptest.com/lsat** to learn more or to purchase LSAT Link or Link+.

Reflect

Think back over the study and practice you did in this chapter.

- Are you able to distinguish Loose Sequencing games from Strict Sequencing? What makes the difference?
- Do you understand why LSAT experts combine Steps 3 and 4 of the Logic Games Method in Loose Sequencing?
- What kinds of rules do you anticipate seeing in complex Loose Sequencing games? In what ways are they similar to or different from those in basic Strict Sequencing?
- Are you making the available deductions efficiently and effectively in Loose Sequencing games?

In the coming days and weeks before test day, take note of real-world tasks that reflect Loose Sequencing tasks, especially those that ask you to rank things. Consider how the day-to-day tasks mirror the setups and questions in LSAT Loose Sequencing, and how they differ. Try to reframe real-life sequencing tasks using the terms, rules, and restrictions employed by the testmaker.

CHAPTER 8

Formal Logic and Selection Games Unlocked

LEARNING OBJECTIVES

In this chapter, you'll learn to

- Apply the Logic Games Method to Selection games
- Identify, translate, and apply Formal Logic statements used in logic games rules

On recent LSATs, Selection games have been rare, accounting for just 3 percent of the games on tests released over the last five years. Of the 60 games that appeared in released LSATs during that period, only two were true Selection games.

Types of Games By Percentage, 2014–2018

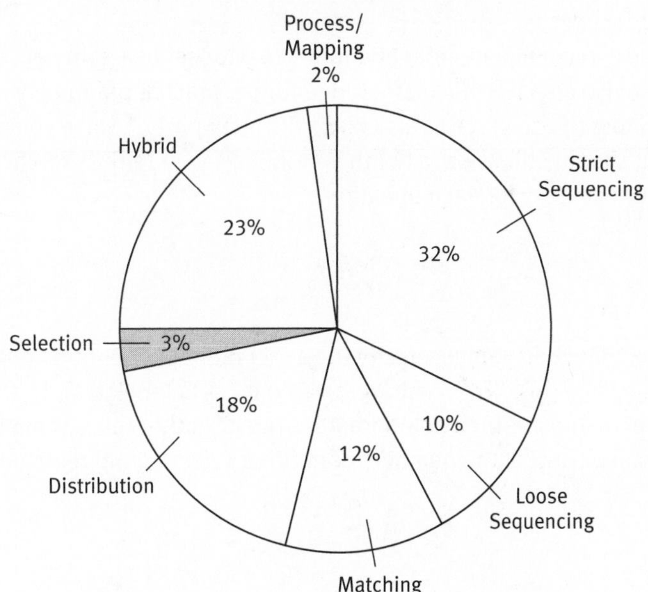

*PrepTests 72–86; released 2014–2018

That number is unusually low compared to earlier periods in the LSAT's history, so it may be that the coming years will see the percentage shift back toward the mean. It's also worth noting that 5 of the 12 Hybrid games to appear on tests released in the past five years had a Selection element. So, the work you do in this chapter will not be for nothing. (If you have very little time between now and test day, however, you should probably complete Chapter 9 on the more common Matching and Distribution games first).

Another reason that this chapter is important to your LSAT performance is that this is where you'll learn to analyze, interpret, and sketch out Formal Logic. On the LSAT, Formal Logic is primarily tested through conditional (or "If-then") statements. The reason Formal Logic is covered in this chapter is that virtually all Selection game rules are conditional. Even when they aren't explicitly stated with an "if" clause and a "then" clause, they can be translated into that format for easy analysis. As an aside, the work you do on Formal Logic may turn out to be a bigger help to you in the LSAT's Logical Reasoning section than in Logic Games. On a typical LSAT, around 38 percent of the questions touch on Formal Logic in some way, and unless you run into a Selection game, the large majority of those questions are in Logical Reasoning.

The defining characteristic of Selection games is a setup that provides you with a list of entities, and then asks you to choose some of those entities to form a smaller group. You can easily recognize this action from verbs like *select*, *choose*, or *pick*.

The main variations in Selection games arise from how specific a game's setup is about the number of entities you will choose. In a little under half of games, the test gives no guidance at all. The setup simply says something along the lines of "From among seven photographs—A, B, C, D, E, F, and G—Karen will choose which to post on her home page." The rules will help to define how few or how many she selects, of course, but the setup itself will provide no limitations. For a game of this type, the best sketch is simply a list of the entities. Circle those she chooses, and cross out those she rejects for any given question.

A B Ⓒ D Ⓔ ~~F~~ G

Occasionally, the test will provide a maximum number of entities to choose. In a game of this type, the setup might say, "From among seven flavors of ice cream—chocolate, fudge ripple, mocha, praline pecan, rocky road, strawberry, and vanilla—Jack will choose at most five to serve at his child's birthday party." Since you don't know the exact number selected or rejected, you should still use a list of the entities as your initial sketch. It's easy to copy, and you can circle or cross out entities as necessary for each question.

C ~~F~~ Ⓜ Ⓟ R ~~S~~ V

A little more than half of the time, Selection games specify the exact number of entities to be selected. A typical setup of this type would contain phrasing like this: "From among seven data sets labeled M, N, O, P, Q, R, and S, a statistician will select exactly four to analyze for a demographic study." In this case, some LSAT experts prefer to use an "in-out" sketch to help them keep track of the numbers of entities selected and rejected.

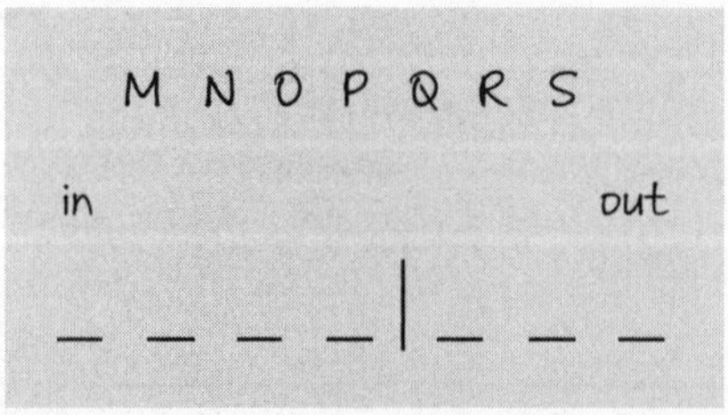

M N O P Q R S

in   out

_ _ _ _ | _ _ _

You'll have the chance to work with setups and games in which the number to be selected is defined and others in which that number is left open-ended. In both types, your ability to accurately analyze and sketch rules written in Formal Logic will be the key to your success.

SELECTION GAMES IN REAL LIFE

You make selections all the time in your day-to-day life. You might be deciding which guests to invite to a wedding or a dinner. At work, you might need to choose which of six employees to send to a conference or meeting. Preparing to go to the conference, you might need to choose which of your suits or dresses to pack for the trip. Often, the toughest part of real-life selection lies in figuring out what not to include. That's true on the LSAT as well. Always remember that coming up with a complete and accurate list of which entities are not chosen is just as valuable as the list of which ones are. In real life, these tasks involve wildly different numbers of choices, professional considerations, and even personal feelings. Fortunately, the LSAT always limits you to choosing from among a limited set of options, typically from among five to nine entities.

Real-life selection tasks mirror the variations that the testmaker uses when designing these games. Here's a typical case: Imagine that you and a roommate are going to throw a party; maybe you have friends coming over to watch a big football game. One of you asks, "What snacks should we have?" In real life, that question is open-ended. You could have as many or as few snacks as you like. As you try to make your decision, it's likely that your first question will be, "How many kinds of snacks will we serve?" When the answer to that question is not inherent in the task, it's up to you to come up with a minimum or maximum number. Likewise, when LSAT Selection games do not provide you with a specific number of entities to choose, one or more of the questions accompanying the game will ask you to determine the minimum or maximum number of entities that may be chosen.

In the real-life version of the task, there are sometimes additional considerations. You could, for example, buy all of the snacks for the party, make all of them at home, or decide on some combination of the two. You and your roommate might say, "We're too busy to make anything; let's just buy the snacks." Or you might decide, "Let's make two snacks and buy two others." It will always be important to note whether the testmaker has designated subdivisions within the entities. In turning this scenario into a logic game, the testmaker could, for example, say simply, "The roommates will choose from among eight snacks: almonds, cupcakes, garlic bread, licorice, meatballs, pretzels, tortilla chips, and wings." Or they could put the snacks into two categories, like so: "The roommates will choose from among four homemade snacks—cupcakes, garlic bread, meatballs, and wings—and four store-bought snacks—almonds, licorice, pretzels, and tortilla chips." When the testmaker subdivides the entities, look for restrictions based on those categories, with rules like "At least two homemade snacks and at least two store-bought snacks must be served."

However the entity set is constructed, you can anticipate the types of rules that will be used. They're the same kinds of "rules" that guide your real-world decision. You might say, "If we serve pretzels, let's not have tortilla chips," or "If we have wings, then we have to have garlic bread." That leads to one of the friendliest features of Selection games: your sketch is basically no different than what you'd do in real life. "Okay, let's list out our potential snacks. We'll circle the ones we're going to serve and cross out the ones we're not."

Selection tasks are probably more common in everyday life than Selection games are on the test. This is one area where you should have no trouble spotting analogies to what you'll see on the LSAT. Take advantage of your experience when the opportunity arises. Recontextualizing a seemingly difficult LSAT task by seeing it reflected in a simple, real-life scenario will help you build confidence, and improve your performance on test day.

SELECTION GAMES TASKS AND SKETCHES

LEARNING OBJECTIVES

In this section of the chapter, you'll practice

- Applying Steps 1 and 2 of the Logic Games Method to Selection games by
  - Asking the SEAL questions to analyze the game's Overview, and then
  - Creating a simple, useful Sketch framework

Prepare

Selection tasks are straightforward, and there is little chance that you will miss the action. Fortunately, the key question about Selection games' limitations is almost instinctive as well: "How many can I/must I choose?"

LOGIC GAMES STRATEGY

Selection games ask you to choose a smaller group of entities out of a larger one; the number you'll choose may be

- Open-ended—the game's setup will tell you that "some" or "at least one" of the entities is selected, but gives you no further guidance,
- A minimum of *y* and/or a maximum of *x*—the game's setup will set a floor or ceiling (or both) on the number of entities that may be selected, but will not state a specific number, or
- A specific number—the game's setup will explicitly state a limitation such as "five of the nine" or "four out of seven."

As discussed in the introduction to this chapter, your choice of sketch will depend largely on how clear-cut the number restrictions are in the game's setup. When the number selected is unclear, simply copy the list of entities, and circle those selected and cross out those rejected in each question.

A B Ⓒ D Ⓔ ~~F~~ G

When the game's setup provides a precise number of entities to select out of the initial list, you may choose to employ an "in-out" sketch.

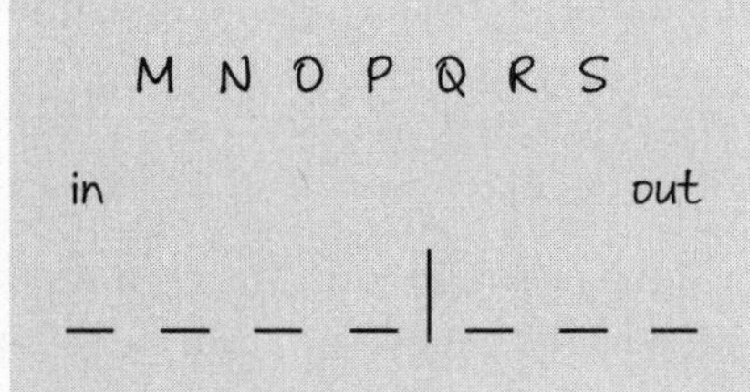

Practice applying Steps 1 and 2 of the Logic Games Method to some Selection games setups. Keep an eye out for the verb that signals the Selection task. Use the limitations on the number of entities to be selected to help you decide which sketch framework to use.

Practice

Directions: Conduct an Overview of each game's setup by asking the SEAL questions, and create an initial sketch framework for the game's action.

Practice 1

A graphic designer must choose colors for a new logo from among the seven—fuchsia, grapefruit, hibiscus, indigo, jade, kiwi, and lemon—suggested by the client. The color selection must conform to the following conditions:

1. [Step 1] Conduct an Overview analysis:
   - What is this game's Situation?
   - Who or what are the game's Entities?
   - What is the game's Action?
   - What are the Limitations explicit in the game setup?
2. [Step 2] Create an initial Sketch:

Practice 2

Melanie is planning a series of performances to promote her new relaxation CD. At each performance, she will play at least four of the pieces—*Atmosphere*, *Beats*, *Clouds*, *Dynamic*, *Ecologica*, *Firefly*, and *Glaciers*—that appear on the CD. Her selection for each performance is based on the following conditions:

1. [Step 1] Conduct an Overview analysis:
   - What is this game's Situation?
   - Who or what are the game's Entities?
   - What is the game's Action?
   - What are the Limitations explicit in the game setup?
2. [Step 2] Create an initial Sketch:

Practice 3

Writers for a science magazine submitted eight articles to their editor, each on a different topic—anatomy, biochemistry, climatology, ecology, genetics, hydrology, immunology, and neuroscience. The editor will select exactly four of the articles for publication in the next issue, based on the following guidelines:

1. [Step 1] Conduct an Overview analysis:
   - What is this game's Situation?
   - Who or what are the game's Entities?
   - What is the game's Action?
   - What are the Limitations explicit in the game setup?
2. [Step 2] Create an initial Sketch:

Explanations

Compare your work to that of an LSAT expert. Keep track of any case in which you incorrectly characterized the action described in the setup, and any case in which you drew a sketch framework that does not match the details of the game's situation.

Practice 1

A graphic designer must choose colors for a new logo from among the seven—fuchsia, grapefruit, hibiscus, indigo, jade, kiwi, and lemon—suggested by the client. The color selection must conform to the following conditions:

1. [Step 1] Conduct an Overview analysis:
   - What is this game's Situation? *A graphic designer choosing colors for a new logo.*
   - Who or what are the game's Entities? *Seven colors—F, G, H, I, J, K, and L.*
   - What is the game's Action? *Selection.*
   - What are the Limitations explicit in the game setup? *None; no minimum or maximum is provided.*
2. [Step 2] Create an initial Sketch:

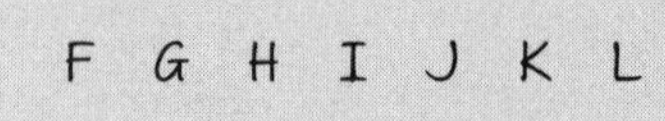

Practice 2

Melanie is planning a series of performances to promote her new relaxation CD. At each performance, she will play at least four of the pieces—*Atmosphere*, *Beats*, *Clouds*, *Dynamic*, *Ecologica*, *Firefly*, and *Glaciers*—that appear on the CD. Her selection for each performance is based on the following conditions:

1. [Step 1] Conduct an Overview analysis:
   - What is this game's Situation? *A musician scheduling a series of performances.*
   - Who or what are the game's Entities? *Seven songs—A, B, C, D, E, F, and G.*
   - What is the game's Action? *Selection; while the overview suggests multiple performances, the goal is to figure out which songs are selected for any given performance.*
   - What are the Limitations explicit in the game setup? *At least four songs will be used, but no maximum.*
2. [Step 2] Create an initial Sketch:

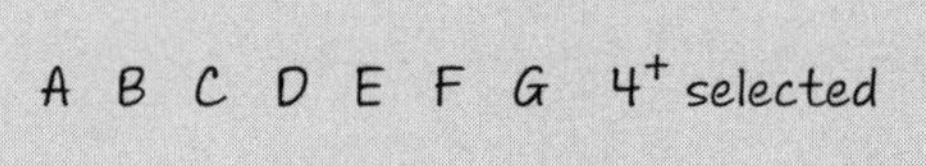

Practice 3

Writers for a science magazine submitted eight articles to their editor, each on a different topic—anatomy, biochemistry, climatology, ecology, genetics, hydrology, immunology, and neuroscience. The editor will select exactly four of the articles for publication in the next issue, based on the following guidelines:

1. [Step 1] Conduct an Overview analysis:
   - What is this game's Situation? *An editor of a science magazine deciding which articles to publish.*
   - Who or what are the game's Entities? *Eight articles, by topic—A, B, C, E, G, H, I, and N.*
   - What is the game's Action? *Selection.*
   - What are the Limitations explicit in the game setup? *Exactly four will be selected, which means the other four will not.*
2. [Step 2] Create an initial Sketch:

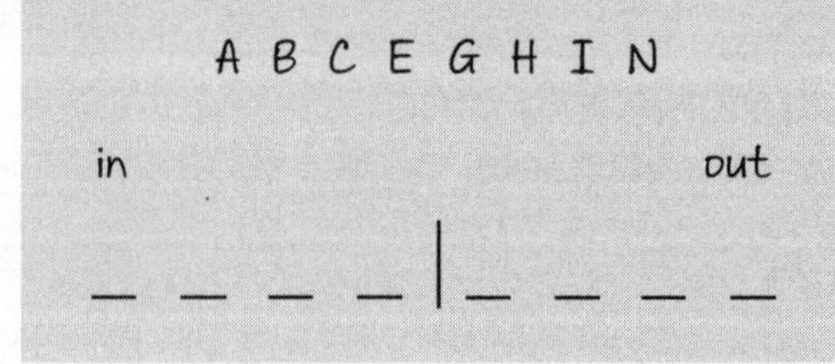

The most important work you'll do on Selection games happens in Step 3. Interpreting and drawing out the Formal Logic contained in these games' rules is crucial to answering the questions efficiently and effectively. The next section of this chapter goes into detail and provides ample practice on everything you need to know about conditional statements in LSAT logic games.

If you are already a master of "If-then" statements and contrapositives, you may choose to skip the next section and move on to practicing with Selection rules in context. If not, you'll want to work through the next section carefully. Do all of the practice exercises and review them with the expert analysis that follows. Then, assess your own skill level with the Perform quizzes. Formal Logic can seem tricky at first, but with practice and review, you can master the fundamentals of conditional statements and contrapositives and use these reasoning principles with great confidence on the LSAT.

FORMAL LOGIC IN LSAT LOGIC GAMES

LEARNING OBJECTIVES

In this section, you'll learn to:

- Identify what is and what is not a conditional statement (that is, understand what it means for a statement to be a conditional statement)

Before you can work with conditional statements to make valid deductions and inferences (and answer questions), you must be able to identify such statements.

This section of Chapter 8 contains nine Learning Objectives that, taken together, cover the breadth of knowledge you'll need to use Formal Logic in LSAT logic games. Each Learning Objective builds upon the ones before it, so you are encouraged to take them in the order presented.

Conditional Statements

In some Logic Games, and always in Selection games, the rules provided can be written as conditional statements. These statements always have two parts—a sufficient term and a necessary result or requirement—and can always be translated into an "If-then" format.

Conditional statements will appear in LSAT questions in all three sections of the test, but are most important in Logical Reasoning and Logic Games. The following chart shows the relative importance of Formal Logic on the LSAT.

LSAT Qs Testing Formal Logic, 2014–18

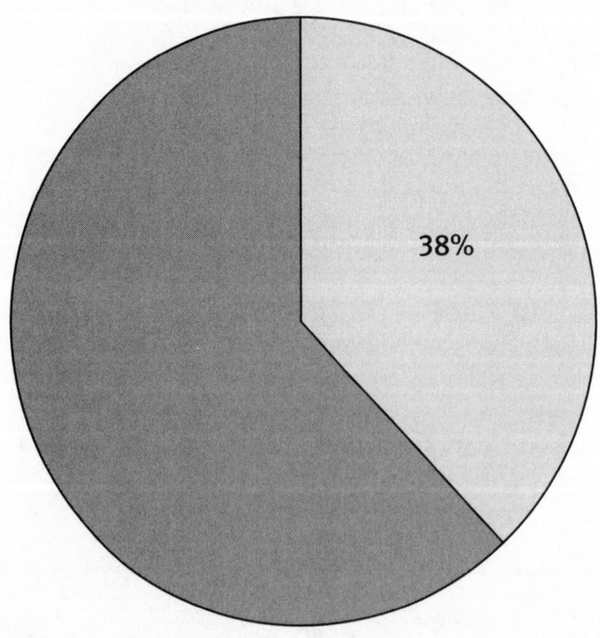

PrepTests 72–86, released 2014–2018

LOGIC GAMES STRATEGY

Although Formal Logic appears in a minority of Logic Games, its importance is heightened by two considerations:

Most test takers have not refined the skill of understanding Formal Logic prior to preparing for the LSAT. Familiarity with Formal Logic will give you a competitive advantage.

Expertise in understanding and applying Formal Logic makes the correct answer to many LSAT questions unequivocal. There is little room for doubt or error if you have analyzed conditional statements correctly.

Identify Conditional Statements

Prepare

LOGIC GAMES STRATEGY

Every conditional statement has two parts:

- A *sufficient term*, also known as the "trigger" or "If" term.
- A *necessary term*, also known as the "result/requirement" or "then" term.

Consider this conditional statement:

If the flashlight is working, then it must have batteries.

The flashlight working is a *sufficient* condition. That means knowing the flashlight works provides sufficient (i.e., enough) information to logically make a deduction: that it has batteries.

Batteries are a *necessary* condition. That means the batteries are required for the sufficient term to be present. In this case, the batteries are needed for the flashlight to work. If there were no batteries, the flashlight couldn't work.

But be careful. The sufficient condition is not required. In other words, the flashlight does not need to work in order for there to be batteries. Similarly, the necessary condition does not guarantee anything. It's possible for batteries to be installed without the flashlight working; after all, the light bulb could be broken.

Conditional relationships can be expressed in many ways other than "If . . . then" sentence structure. The key is to look for an absolute condition—either a condition that is always sufficient to produce a particular result, or one that is always necessary for something else to happen. Take a look at how an LSAT expert identifies conditional statements.

Premises		Analysis
Is each of the following a conditional statement?		
Every person who orders a cheeseburger also orders french fries.	→	Yes; the word *every* indicates that french fries will be ordered any time someone orders a cheeseburger. Ordering a cheeseburger is a *sufficient* condition.
John will participate in the race only if he runs first.	→	Yes; if John participates in the race, then he must run first. The phrase *only if* indicates that being first is a *necessary* condition for John to participate.
Apples, grapes, and strawberries are available for use in the fruit salad.	→	No; this just defines what is available, but nothing is sufficient to use these fruits and nothing is required.
Any Picasso painting in the exhibit must be placed directly to the left of a Renoir painting.	→	Yes; if a Picasso is included, then there must be a Renoir directly to its right. This is true for *any* Picasso painting. So including a Picasso is a *sufficient* condition, triggering its placement next to a Renoir.

Practice

In the following exercise, read each statement and decide whether it expresses a conditional relationship. If it does, which term is *sufficient* and which is *necessary*?

Premises	My Analysis
1. Square-shaped blocks are always placed in box 1.	→
2. Each member assigned to the advisory council is a college graduate.	→
3. The carpenter may receive several requests for estimates.	→
4. Robert will present in the Gold Room only if Jenson presents in the Black Room.	→

Explanations

Here's how an LSAT expert would analyze those statements.

Premises		Analysis
1. Square-shaped blocks are always placed in box 1.	→	Yes; the word *always* indicates that every square-shaped block is placed in box 1. This could be written: *If it's square-shaped, then it is placed in box 1.* Knowing that a block is square-shaped is *sufficient* to determine that it is placed in the box 1. And being placed in the box 1 is a *necessary* condition of all square-shaped blocks.
2. Each member assigned to the advisory council is a college graduate.	→	Yes; the word *each* indicates that being assigned to the advisory council is *sufficient* to know that that person is a college graduate. This could be written: *If a person is assigned to the advisory council, then he is a college graduate.* Being a college graduate is *necessarily* true of all of the members of the advisory council.
3. The carpenter may receive several requests for estimates.	→	No; conditional statements are statements of certainty. The use of language such as *may* and *several* often indicate that a statement is not conditional. Ask yourself: Is this statement saying that if one thing is true, then another thing must be true? No, this statement is just describing what might happen.
4. Robert will present in the Gold Room only if Jenson presents in the Black Room.	→	Yes; the phrase "only if" indicates that Jenson presenting in the Black Room is a *requirement* for Robert presenting in the Gold Room. This could be written: *If Robert presents in the Gold Room, then Jenson will present in the Black Room.* Robert presenting in the Gold Room is *sufficient* to know that Jenson is presenting in the Black Room.

Perform

In the following exercise, read each statement and decide whether it expresses a conditional relationship. If it does, which term is *sufficient* and which is *necessary*?

Premises	My Analysis
5. Certain medications can be prescribed to the patient.	→
6. Kaylie will not participate in the Denver chess tournament unless she participates in at least two other tournaments.	→
7. Robert will watch a movie at 8:00 PM if he does not go to the gym at 6:00 PM.	→
8. The zebra will be transferred to the zoo only if the giraffe is also transferred.	→

Explanations

Here's how an LSAT expert would analyze those statements.

Premises		Analysis
5. Certain medications can be prescribed to the patient.	→	No; conditional statements are statements of certainty. Just because medications "can" be prescribed doesn't mean they necessarily will. Ask yourself: Is this statement saying that if one thing is true, then another thing must be true? Here, the answer is no.
6. Kaylie will not participate in the Denver chess tournament unless she participates in at least two other tournaments.	→	Yes; the word *unless* indicates that Kaylie participating in at least two other tournaments is *necessary* for her to participate in the Denver chess tournament. This could be written: *If Kaylie competes in the Denver chess tournament, then she also participates in at least two other tournaments.* Knowing that Kaylie participates in the Denver tournament is *sufficient* to know that she will participate in at least two other tournaments.
7. Robert will watch a movie at 8:00 PM if he does not go to the gym at 6:00 PM.	→	Yes; the word *if* indicates a *sufficient* condition. This could be written: *If Robert does not go to the gym at 6:00 PM, then he will watch a movie at 8:00 PM.* Watching a movie at 8 PM is a *necessary* result of Robert not going to the gym at 6 PM.
8. The zebra will be transferred to the zoo only if the giraffe is also transferred.	→	Yes; the phrase "only if" indicates that the giraffe being transferred is *necessary* for the zebra to be transferred. This could be written: *If the zebra is transferred, then the giraffe is also transferred.* The zebra being transferred would be *sufficient* to know that the giraffe was also transferred.

Understand Conditional Statements with *And* and *Or*

LEARNING OBJECTIVES

In this section, you'll learn to:

- Understand conditional statements that include *and* or *or*

Some conditional statements will also contain the words *and* or *or*. The two terms have quite different effects in conditional statements.

Prepare

LOGIC GAMES STRATEGY

In Formal Logic:

And means both terms are needed for a sufficient condition to trigger a result or for a necessary condition to be fulfilled.

Or means that at least one of the terms (the first or the second or both) is needed for a sufficient condition to trigger a result or for a necessary condition to be fulfilled.

Note how an LSAT expert analyzes conditional statements containing *and* or *or*.

Conditional Statement		Analysis
If Anthony and Brendan attend the concert, then so does Evan.	→	One way to guarantee Evan attending the concert is to have Anthony and Brendan attend. Having Anthony or Brendan attend without the other does not guarantee that Evan will attend.
If the tour includes the planetarium, then it also includes the meteorite exhibit and the space shuttle exhibit.	→	When the planetarium is included, it is guaranteed that both the meteorite and the space shuttle exhibits are included. It's not possible to include the planetarium and then include only one of the other exhibits.

If Luisa or Steve performs in the orchestra, then Fiona performs in the choir.	→	If either Luisa or Steve joins the orchestra, it is guaranteed that Fiona will join the choir. Even if *both* Luisa and Steve join the orchestra, it is still guaranteed Fiona will join the choir. And if Luisa and Steve *don't* join the orchestra, it's still possible for Fiona to join the choir.
If the factory does not manufacture chairs, then it must manufacture bookshelves or easels.	→	If chairs are not made, then it's guaranteed that either bookshelves or easels are. It's also possible that both bookshelves *and* easels are made. And if chairs *are* made, then nothing is known about bookshelves and easels. It's possible that all three products are made in the factory.

Practice

Check your understanding by analyzing the following conditional statements.

Conditional Statement	My Analysis
If Manny and Nouman are both assigned to Honduras, then Peggy will be assigned to Belize.	
9. What do we know if we are told that Manny is assigned to Honduras?	→
10. What do we know if we are told that Peggy is assigned to Belize?	→
11. What do we know if we are told that Peggy is not assigned to Belize?	→
Any person who takes a picture by the tide pools will also take a picture by the lighthouse or by the harbor.	
12. What do we know if we are told that Bonnie takes a picture by the lighthouse?	→
13. What do we know if we are told that Porter does not take a picture by the tide pools?	→
14. What do we know if we are told that Tamara takes a picture by neither the lighthouse nor the harbor?	→

Explanations

Here's how an LSAT expert would analyze the questions about each conditional statement in the exercise.

Conditional Statement		Analysis
If Manny and Nouman are both assigned to Honduras, then Peggy will be assigned to Belize.		
9. What do we know if we are told that Manny is assigned to Honduras?	→	Nothing additional; we need to know that Manny and Nouman are *both* assigned to Honduras before we can confirm that Peggy must be assigned to Belize.
10. What do we know if we are told that Peggy is assigned to Belize?	→	Nothing additional; Peggy being assigned to Belize is a result of Manny and Nouman being assigned to Honduras. But Peggy being assigned to Belize does not, by itself, trigger anything.
11. What do we know if we are told that Peggy is not assigned to Belize?	→	If this is true, then there is no way that both Manny and Nouman are assigned to Honduras. So, we know that either Manny or Nouman (or both) is not assigned to Honduras.
Any person who takes a picture by the tide pools will also take a picture by the lighthouse or by the harbor.		
12. What do we know if we are told that Bonnie takes a picture by the lighthouse?	→	Nothing additional; taking a picture by the lighthouse is not sufficient to know anything else about Bonnie.
13. What do we know if we are told that Porter does not take a picture by the tide pools?	→	Nothing additional; it is still possible that Porter takes a picture by the lighthouse and the harbor.
14. What do we know if we are told that Tamara takes a picture by neither the lighthouse nor the harbor?	→	In this case, we would know that Tamara also does not take a picture by the tide pools; otherwise, she would have taken a picture by either the lighthouse or the harbor.

Perform

Check your understanding by analyzing the following conditional statements.

Conditional Statement	My Analysis
If a blue jelly bean is added to the jar, then a red jelly bean and a green jelly bean will also be added to the jar.	
15. What do we know if we are told that no red jelly beans are added to the jar?	→
16. What do we know if we are told that no blue jelly beans are added to the jar?	→
17. What do we know if we are told both red and green jelly beans are added to the jar?	→
Whenever a motorcycle or a bicycle is advertised in the magazine, there must be at least one advertisement for helmets.	
18. What do we know if we are told that the magazine contains an advertisement for helmets?	→
19. What do we know if we are told that the magazine features advertisements for both motorcycles and bicycles?	→
20. What do we know if we are told that there are no helmets advertised in the magazine?	→

Explanations

Here's how an LSAT expert would analyze the questions about each conditional statement in the exercise.

Conditional Statement		Analysis
If a blue jelly bean is added to the jar, then a red jelly bean and a green jelly bean will also be added to the jar.		
15. What do we know if we are told that no red jelly beans are added to the jar?	→	If no red jelly beans are added to the jar, then no blue jelly beans can be added to the jar. Otherwise, there would have to be red jelly beans (along with green ones).
16. What do we know if we are told that no blue jelly beans are added to the jar?	→	Nothing additional; even without blue jelly beans, it's still possible that red and green jelly beans are added.
17. What do we know if we are told both red and green jelly beans are added to the jar?	→	Nothing additional; blue jelly beans may or may not be added to the jar.
Whenever a motorcycle or a bicycle is advertised in the magazine, there must be at least one advertisement for helmets.		
18. What do we know if we are told that the magazine contains an advertisement for helmets?	→	Nothing additional; while it's possible that the magazine features advertisements for a motorcycle or a bicycle, it's also possible that there are only ads for helmets (or perhaps other products).
19. What do we know if we are told that the magazine features advertisements for both motorcycles and bicycles?	→	The magazine will also include at least one other advertisement for helmets.
20. What do we know if we are told that there are no helmets advertised in the magazine?	→	If there are no advertisements for helmets, then the magazine features ads for neither motorcycles nor bicycles. Otherwise, there would have been a helmet advertisement.

Translate Conditional Statements into If-Then Format

LEARNING OBJECTIVES

In this section, you'll learn to:

- Translate a sentence that expresses a conditional relationship into If-Then format.

Prepare

It's helpful to develop a simple system of notation for conditional statements. Whenever you see a conditional statement in Logic Games, translate it into something that looks like this:

If Trigger (sufficient) → Result/Requirement (necessary)

Write the sufficient term on the left, the necessary term on the right, and an arrow in the middle pointing from left to right (to indicate the direction in which the logic flows).

Here's how an LSAT expert takes several conditional statements and turns them into "If-then" statements.

Conditional Statement		Analysis
If Ricardo is in the tournament, then he's on the blue team.	→	If Ricardo in → Blue team "If" indicates the sufficient condition, with "blue team" being the necessary result.
Copper is used in every experiment that includes acetone.	→	If acetone → copper The word *every* indicates the sufficient condition. The presence of acetone is enough to guarantee the presence of copper.
The project will involve glue only if it involves cotton balls.	→	If glue → cotton balls The phrase "only if" indicates cotton balls are a necessary condition. They are required for glue to be used.
The platter is not selected unless the tureen or the gravy boat is selected.	→	If platter → tureen OR gravy boat The word *unless* indicates that a tureen or gravy boat is necessary in order for the platter to be selected.
Any two people who are assigned to the same group must be of the same rank.	→	If same group → same rank *Any* indicates sufficiency, and *must* indicates necessity. Being in the same group is enough to deduce that two people are of the same rank. That's required.

Translating The Prose of Common Conditional Statements

Conditional statements can be phrased in many different ways; you'll see that some of those are more common than others in Logic Games, but they all appear from time to time. You will need to learn to quickly distill the language into a notation like the following.

Formal Logic Statement		Analysis
If A, then B	→	If A → B
All C are D	→	If C → D
Every E is F	→	If E → F
If G, then not H	→	If G → ~H
No I are J	→	If I → ~J
Only K are L	→	If L → K
M only if N	→	If M → N
The only O are P	→	If O → P
No Q unless R	→	If Q → R
S unless T	→	If ~S → T
No U without V	→	If U → V
Without W, no X	→	If X → W
Y if, but only if, Z	→	If Y → Z If Z → Y
AA if, and only if, BB	→	If AA → BB If BB → AA
If CC, then neither DD nor EE	→	If CC → ~DD and ~EE
FF if GG	→	If GG → FF
HH is always II	→	If HH → II

It's okay if your shorthand is different from what is shown here, but it must be consistent and accurate to ensure your success on the test.

Practice

Using the previous statements as reference, translate each of the following statements, each of which expresses a sufficient and necessary relationship, into simple shorthand.

Formal Logic Statement		My Analysis
21. None of the first three songs on the album are country songs.	→	
22. Only red bicycles can be placed in the fourth storage shed.	→	
23. Monica will not go fishing unless Charlie goes dancing.	→	
24. All of the photographs in Norton Hall are panoramas.	→	
25. Anna is going to attend the basketball game only if Beth also attends.	→	
26. Every bowl on the third shelf is ceramic.	→	
27. Students may attend the conference unless they are currently on academic probation.	→	
28. Danielle will play golf tomorrow at 7 AM if Esther goes swimming at 9 AM.	→	
29. The only banks with secure vaults are on the north side of the street.	→	
30. Peg will order the pork chop if, but only if, she orders the collard greens.	→	

Explanations

This is how an LSAT expert might abbreviate each of the statements from the exercise.

Formal Logic Statement		Analysis
21. None of the first three songs on the album are country songs.	→	If one of first three songs on album → not country song
22. Only red bicycles can be placed in the fourth storage shed.	→	If in 4th shed → red bicycle
23. Monica will not go fishing unless Charlie goes dancing.	→	If Monica fishing → Charlie dancing
24. All of the photographs in Norton Hall are panoramas.	→	If Norton Hall → panorama
25. Anna is going to attend the basketball game only if Beth also attends.	→	If Anna attends → Beth attends
26. Every bowl on the third shelf is ceramic.	→	If bowl on third shelf → ceramic
27. Students may attend the conference unless they are currently on academic probation.	→	If a student can't attend the conference → that student is on academic probation
28. Danielle will play golf tomorrow at 7 AM if Esther goes swimming at 9 AM.	→	If Esther swimming 9 AM → Danielle golf 7 AM
29. The only banks with secure vaults are on the north side of the street.	→	If bank has secure vault → north side of street
30. Peg will order the pork chop if, but only if, she orders the collard greens.	→	If Peg orders pork chop → orders collard greens If Peg orders collard greens → orders pork chop

Perform

Using the previous statements as reference, translate each of the following statements, each of which expresses a sufficient and necessary relationship, into simple shorthand.

Formal Logic Statement		My Analysis
31. Whenever the orangutan pulls the blue lever, she is given a pear.	→	
32. Euchre club is always on Friday.	→	
33. The photographer cannot go to Peru without an editor also going to Peru.	→	
34. The purple book is placed in the bedroom only when the red book is placed in the den.	→	
35. All of the cookies in the small jar were made by Julia.	→	
36. Pamela won't join the bowling team if Zoe is on the team.	→	
37. Every time the band visits Columbus, they play "Groovy."	→	
38. Unless the batteries are to the right of the candle, the dagger is to the left of the gizmo.	→	
39. Only divers who have previously won a local diving competition will be invited to the state tournament.	→	
40. If the park does not have a slide, then it will have a jungle gym.	→	

Explanations

This is how an LSAT expert might abbreviate each of the statements from the exercise.

Formal Logic Statement		Analysis
31. Whenever the orangutan pulls the blue lever, she is given a pear.	→	If pull blue lever → pear
32. Euchre club is always on Friday.	→	If Euchre club → Friday
33. The photographer cannot go to Peru without an editor also going to Peru.	→	If photographer Peru → editor Peru
34. The purple book is placed in the bedroom only when the red book is placed in the den.	→	If purple book in bedroom → red book in den
35. All of the cookies in the small jar were made by Julia.	→	If cookie in small jar → made by Julia
36. Pamela won't join the bowling team if Zoe is on the team.	→	If Zoe on bowling team → Pamela not on bowling team
37. Every time the band visits Columbus, they play "Groovy."	→	If band visits Columbus → play "Groovy"
38. Unless the batteries are to the right of the candle, the dagger is to the left of the gizmo.	→	If dagger not left of the gizmo → batteries right of the candle
39. Only divers who have previously won a local diving competition will be invited to the state tournament.	→	If invited to state tourn. → previously won local comp.
40. If the park does not have a slide, then it will have a jungle gym.	→	If no slide → jungle gym

Make Valid Deductions from Conditional Statements

LEARNING OBJECTIVES

In this section, you'll learn to:

- Make deductions on the basis of conditional statements

Prepare

LOGIC GAMES STRATEGY

Any time the necessary or "result" clause of one statement matches the sufficient or "If" clause of another, the two statements can be combined. For example:

If B → ~D
If ~D → ~F
If B → ~D → ~F

Deduction:

If B → ~F

Connecting Conditional Statements

Now that you understand conditional relationships and how to spot them, you're ready to think about how to combine them to make new deductions.

Formal Logic Statements		Analysis
If A then B If B then C	→	If A → B → C
If D then E If F then E	→	If D OR F → E
If G then H If G then I	→	If G → H and I

Practice

Translate the given conditional statements and use them to create a chain of logic. Then, answer questions about what we must know, given the chain.

Formal Logic Statements		My Analysis
(1) If the zebra is chosen, then so is the antelope	→	
(2) If the tortoise is chosen, then so is the zebra	→	
(3) If the antelope is chosen, then so is the gorilla	→	
Chain of logic:		
What do we know if . . .		
41. the zebra is chosen?	→	
42. the gorilla is chosen?	→	
43. the tortoise is chosen?	→	

Explanations

Here's how an LSAT expert would translate and combine the conditional statements in the previous exercise.

Formal Logic Statements		Analysis
(1) If the zebra is chosen, then so is the antelope	→	If Z → A
(2) If the tortoise is chosen, then so is the zebra	→	If T → Z
(3) If the antelope is chosen, then so is the gorilla	→	If A → G
Chain of logic:	→	If T → Z → A → G
What do we know if . . .		
41. the zebra is chosen?	→	If the zebra is chosen, then the antelope and the gorilla are chosen. Z → A → G
42. the gorilla is chosen?	→	Choosing the gorilla does not lead to any further deduction.
43. the tortoise is chosen?	→	If the tortoise is chosen, then all of the animals in the list will be chosen. T → Z → A → G

Perform

Translate the given conditional statements and use them to create a chain of logic. Then, answer questions about what we must know, given the chain.

Formal Logic Statements		My Analysis
(1) If Craig brings his map, then he also brings his compass	→	
(2) If Craig brings his compass, then he also brings his notebook and his binoculars	→	
(3) If Craig does not bring his binoculars, then he does not bring his journal.	→	
(4) If Craig brings his binoculars, then he also brings his guidebook.	→	
Chain of logic:		
What do we know if . . .		
44. Craig brings his notebook?	→	
45. Craig brings his compass?	→	
46. Craig brings his binoculars?	→	

Explanations

Here's how an LSAT expert would translate and combine the conditional statements in the previous exercise.

Formal Logic Statements		Analysis
(1) If Craig brings his map, then he also brings his compass	→	If M → C
(2) If Craig brings his compass, then he also brings his notebook and his binoculars	→	If C → N and B
(3) If Craig does not bring his binoculars, then he does not bring his journal.	→	If ~B → ~J
(4) If Craig brings his binoculars, then he also brings his guidebook.	→	If B → G
Chain of logic:	→	If M → C → N and B If B → G
What do we know if . . .		
44. Craig brings his notebook?	→	Nothing else can be determined. Having the notebook is not sufficient to know anything else.
45. Craig brings his compass?	→	If Craig brings the compass, then he also brings the notebook and binoculars. And bringing the binoculars means he brings the guidebook. If C → N and B If B → G
46. Craig brings his binoculars?	→	If Craig brings the binoculars, then he also brings the guidebook. If B → G

Contrapositives

LEARNING OBJECTIVES

In this section, you'll learn to:

- Translate a conditional statement into its contrapositive
- Make valid deductions from the contrapositive of a conditional statement
- Make valid deductions from conditional statements containing *And* and *Or*
- Make valid deductions from conditional statements containing an "Exclusive Or" provision

Despite the many ways to express conditional statements, the logic underlying conditional statements is remarkably consistent. One more feature of these statements that is crucial for making deductions is the contrapositive.

Translating "If-then" Statements into Contrapositives: The contrapositive of a conditional statement is just another way of phrasing the sufficient/necessary relationship described in that statement. Take the following statement as an example:

All team leaders must be an adult.

If team leader → adult

Now, what happens if a team member is not an adult? Well, that person can't be team leader. That's the contrapositive of the statement. It looks like this:

If NOT adult → NOT team leader

That's the basis for the contrapositive: What happens if the *necessary* condition is negated, if it cannot happen? In that case, the sufficient condition cannot happen either. Every contrapositive is formed in exactly that way.

Conditional statements with two terms in the necessary condition: When the necessary term of a conditional statement has two terms, check to see whether both are necessary (B *and* C) or whether just one or the other is necessary (B *or* C). If both are necessary, then the absence of either will make the sufficient term impossible. In short, the "and" in the necessary term becomes "or" in the sufficient term of the contrapositive. If just one of the terms is necessary, then it is the absence of both that will render the sufficient term impossible. In other words, the "or" in the necessary clause becomes "and" in the sufficient clause of the contrapositive. For example:

Roberts will not be assigned to the project unless Tang and Wilhelm are assigned.

Abbreviate that statement in Formal Logic shorthand:

If Roberts → Tang AND Wilhelm

Now, what happens if either one of the two necessary conditions is not met?

If NO Tang → NO Roberts

If NO Wilhelm → NO Roberts

Thus, to form the contrapositive of the first statement, the *and* in the necessary condition must become *or* in the sufficient condition of the contrapositive:

If NO Tang OR NO Wilhelm → NO Roberts

Translating "If"-Then Statements into Contrapositives

LEARNING OBJECTIVES

In this section, you'll learn to:

- Translate a conditional statement into its contrapositive

Prepare

LOGIC GAMES STRATEGY

To form the contrapositive:

- Reverse the sufficient and necessary terms.
- Negate each term.
- Change *and* to *or* and change *or* to *and* (whenever applicable).

Here is a chart of the most common Formal Logic statements and their contrapositives.

Formal Logic Statements		Analysis
All A are B	→	If A → B If ~B → ~A
No C are D	→	If C → ~D If D → ~C
E unless F	→	If ~E → F If ~F → E
If G, then neither H nor I	→	If G → ~H and ~I If H or I → ~G
If J or K, then no L	→	If J or K → ~L If L → ~J and ~K

Practice

Translate each of the following statements into simple shorthand, and form the correct contrapositive of each.

Formal Logic Statement	My Analysis
47. None of the attendees at the programming seminar are enrolled in a four-week course.	→
48. The chef won't add onions to any salad that doesn't also contain tomatoes.	→
49. Businesses with offices on the third floor must also have offices on the fifth floor.	→
50. If the red car is not chosen for display, then the green car will be chosen.	→

51. Jake will finish fourth if and only if Nancy finishes sixth.

→

52. The Spanish club will not go to Mexico unless the French club goes to Cameroon and the Portuguese club goes to Brazil.

→

53. Only those with a severe condition will be allowed to participate in Trial B.

→

54. All of the members of the kayaking team have orange helmets.

→

55. There must be at least three members on any committee to which Jolene is assigned.

→

Explanations

Here's how an LSAT expert might abbreviate the statements and form the contrapositives.

Formal Logic Statement		Analysis
47. None of the attendees at the programming seminar are enrolled in a four-week course.	→	If at programming seminar → ~ 4-week course If 4-week course → ~ at programming seminar
48. The chef won't add onions to any salad that doesn't also contain tomatoes.	→	If ~ tomatoes in salad → ~ onions If onions in salad → tomatoes
49. Businesses with offices on the third floor must also have offices on the fifth floor.	→	If bus. has 3rd floor office → 5th floor office If ~ 5th floor office → ~ 3rd floor office
50. If the red car is not chosen for display, then the green car will be chosen.	→	If ~ red car → green car If ~ green car → red car
51. Jake will finish fourth if and only if Nancy finishes sixth.	→	If Jake 4th → Nancy 6th If ~ Nancy 6th → ~ Jake 4th If Nancy 6th → Jake 4th If ~ Jake 4th → ~ Nancy 6th
52. The Spanish club will not go to Mexico unless the French club goes to Cameroon and the Portuguese club goes to Brazil.	→	If Spanish club to Mexico → French club to Cameroon AND Portuguese club to Brazil If ~French club to Cameroon OR ~ Portuguese club to Brazil → ~ Spanish club to Mexico
53. Only those with a severe condition will be allowed to participate in Trial B.	→	If in Trial B → severe condition If ~ severe condition → ~ Trial B
54. All of the members of the kayaking team have orange helmets.	→	If on kayaking team → orange helmet If ~ orange helmet → ~ on kayaking team
55. There must be at least three members on any committee to which Jolene is assigned.	→	If Jolene on committee → 3+ members on that committee If ~ 3+ members on committee → ~ Jolene on that committee

Perform

Translate each of the following statements into simple shorthand, and form the correct contrapositive of each.

Formal Logic Statement	My Analysis
56. Janine is a member of every club that Marie is a member of.	→
57. Every tree planted in Big Park is either a magnolia or a gingko.	→
58. Allison will select a mauve dress if she selects either the black shoes or the white necklace.	→
59. The purple rug is selected only if the yellow rug is selected.	→
60. Unless medication A is prescribed, medication B will be prescribed.	→
61. If the first track is hip-hop, the second track will be country or jazz.	→
62. Whenever Bob and Jerami are both on Team A, Taina is on Team D.	→
63. All of the passengers in row 3 are wearing blue shirts.	→
64. The only kind of snack in the first bag is pretzels.	→

Explanations

Here's how an LSAT expert might abbreviate the statements and form the contrapositives.

Formal Logic Statement		Analysis
56. Janine is a member of every club that Marie is a member of.	→	If Marie in club → Janine in club If ~ Janine in club → ~ Marie in club
57. Every tree planted in Big Park is either a magnolia or a gingko.	→	If planted in Big Park → magnolia OR gingko If ~ magnolia AND ~ gingko → ~ planted in Big Park
58. Allison will select a mauve dress if she selects either the black shoes or the white necklace.	→	If black shoes OR white necklace → mauve dress If ~ mauve dress → ~ black shoes AND ~ white necklace
59. The purple rug is selected only if the yellow rug is selected.	→	If purple rug → yellow rug If ~ yellow rug → ~ purple rug
60. Unless medication A is prescribed, medication B will be prescribed.	→	If ~ medication B → medication A If ~ medication A → medication B
61. If the first track is hip-hop, the second track will be country or jazz.	→	If hip-hop 1st → country 2nd OR jazz 2nd If ~ country 2nd AND ~ jazz 2nd → ~ hip-hop 1st
62. Whenever Bob and Jerami are both on Team A, Taina is on Team D.	→	If Bob on Team A AND Jerami on Team A → Taina on Team D If ~ Taina on Team D → ~ Bob on Team A OR ~ Jerami on Team A
63. All of the passengers in row 3 are wearing blue shirts.	→	If in row 3 → blue shirt If ~ blue shirt → ~ in row 3
64. The only kind of snack in the first bag is pretzels.	→	If snack in first bag → pretzels If ~ pretzels → ~ snack in first bag

Make Valid Deductions from the Contrapositives of Conditional Statements

LEARNING OBJECTIVES

In this section, you'll learn to:

- Make valid deductions from the contrapositive of a conditional statement

In the previous section, you learned how to make contrapositives. You can use the contrapositive of any Formal Logic statement to help in making deductions about what must be true.

Prepare

When the contrapositive is formed, it provides a second sufficient condition (i.e., trigger). If that new sufficient condition is triggered, then the arrow can be followed to deduce the necessary result of that logic. Deductions can only be made when a sufficient condition is triggered. When a necessary condition (or result) is met, it cannot be logically deduced that the sufficient condition was met.

Conditional Statement		Analysis
If the clown has blue balloons, then she also has red balloons.	→	If blue → red If ~ red → ~ blue
What do we know if . . .		
the clown has blue balloons?	→	If the clown has blue balloons, that is sufficient to deduce that the clown also has red balloons.
the clown does not have blue balloons?	→	Nothing; blue balloons are sufficient, but they are not necessary. It is possible for the clown to have red balloons without blue balloons.
the clown has red balloons?	→	Nothing; red balloons are merely a necessary result of having blue balloons. However, having red balloons is not sufficient, and thus does not trigger any result.
the clown does not have red balloons?	→	The red balloons are necessary. An absence of red balloons, triggers the contrapositive, resulting in the deduction that the clown cannot have blue balloons.

Practice

Review the deduction exercise you tried earlier, and then complete the practice on the next page.

Formal Logic Statements		Analysis
(1) If the zebra is chosen, then so is the antelope.	→	If Z → A
(2) If the tortoise is chosen, then so is the zebra.	→	If T → Z
(3) If the antelope is chosen, then so is the gorilla.	→	If A → G
Chain of logic:	→	If T → Z → A → G
What do we know if . . .		
the zebra is chosen?	→	If the zebra is chosen, then the antelope and the gorilla are chosen. If Z → A → G
the gorilla is chosen?	→	Choosing the gorilla does not lead to any further deduction.
the tortoise is chosen?	→	If the tortoise is chosen, then all of the animals in the list will be chosen. If T → Z → A → G

For each of the following statements, form the contrapositive of the statement and add it to the My Analysis column. Then answer the questions that follow.

Formal Logic Statements		My Analysis
(1) If the zebra is chosen, then so is the antelope.	→	If Z → A
(2) If the tortoise is chosen, then so is the zebra.	→	If T → Z
(3) If the antelope is chosen, then so is the gorilla.	→	If A → G
Chain of logic:	→	If T → Z → A → G

What do we know if . . .

65. the zebra is not chosen? →

66. the gorilla is not chosen? →

67. the tortoise is not chosen? →

68. the antelope is not chosen? →

Explanations

Here's how an LSAT expert would analyze the previous statements and answer the associated questions.

Formal Logic Statements		Analysis
(1) If the zebra is chosen, then so is the antelope.	→	If Z → A If ~A → ~Z
(2) If the tortoise is chosen, then so is the zebra.	→	If T → Z If ~Z → ~T
(3) If the antelope is chosen, then so is the gorilla.	→	If A → G If ~G → ~A
Chain of logic:	→	If T → Z → A → G If ~G → ~A → ~Z → ~T
What do we know if . . .		
65. the zebra is not chosen?	→	If the zebra is not chosen, then the tortoise cannot be chosen. If ~Z → ~T
66. the gorilla is not chosen?	→	Not choosing the gorilla means that none of the other animals can be selected either. If ~G → ~A → ~Z → ~T
67. the tortoise is not chosen?	→	If the tortoise is not chosen, no further deduction can be made.
68. the antelope is not chosen?	→	If the antelope is not chosen, then the zebra is not chosen, which means the tortoise is also not chosen. If ~A → ~Z → ~T

In the practice sets on the following pages, you will need to make the initial translations and abbreviations for the conditional statements, and then form the contrapositives before moving on to answer the questions.

Perform

For each of the following statements, turn it into shorthand, form the contrapositive, and then make notes about how each can be combined with other conditional statements in the same set to make deductions.

Formal Logic Statements		My Analysis
(1) If the vitamins are selected, the spinach will not be selected.	→	
(2) If the tea is selected, the vitamins will be selected.	→	
(3) If the milk is selected, the spinach will be selected.	→	
Chain of logic:	→	
What do we know if . . .		
69. the spinach is selected?	→	
70. the milk is not selected?	→	
71. the vitamins are not selected?	→	
72. the tea is not selected?	→	

Explanations

Here's how an LSAT expert would analyze the previous statements and answer the associated questions.

Formal Logic Statements		Analysis
(1) If the vitamins are selected, the spinach will not be selected.	→	If V → ~S If S → ~V
(2) If the tea is selected, the vitamins will be selected.	→	If T → V If ~V → ~T
(3) If the milk is selected, the spinach will be selected.	→	If M → S If ~S → ~M
Chain of logic:	→	If T → V → ~S → ~M If M → S → ~V → ~T
What do we know if ...		
69. the spinach is selected?	→	If the spinach is selected, then the vitamins are not selected and the tea is not selected. If S → ~V → ~T
70. the milk is not selected?	→	Nothing additional can be deduced.
71. the vitamins are not selected?	→	If the vitamins are not selected, then the tea is not selected. If ~V → ~T
72. the tea is not selected?	→	Nothing additional can be deduced.

Make Valid Deductions from Conditional Statements Containing *And* and *Or*

LEARNING OBJECTIVES

In this section, you'll learn to:

- Make valid deductions from conditional statements containing *And* and *Or*

Prepare

Earlier in this chapter, you learned that when a conditional statement includes an *and* or an *or* in one of its conditions, you must swap *and* for *or* (and vice versa) when forming the contrapositive. Here's another example to refresh your memory.

Whenever lentil soup is offered on Tuesday, then minestrone or gumbo is offered on Wednesday.

In a Formal Logic abbreviation, that statement would become:

If lentil on Tue. → minestrone on Wed. OR gumbo on Wed.

To form the contrapositive, reverse and negate the terms and swap the *or* for *and*.

NO minestrone on Wed. AND NO gumbo on Wed. → NO lentil on Tue.

So, consider what you know in each of the following cases:

If we know that ...		then we also know that ...
lentil soup is offered on Tuesday	→	at least one of minestrone or gumbo is offered on Wednesday, perhaps both.
lentil soup is not offered on Tuesday	→	we cannot deduce anything. Lentil soup is sufficient, not necessary. It's possible to have minestrone or gumbo on Wednesday even without lentil soup on Tuesday.
minestrone is offered on Wednesday, but not gumbo	→	we cannot deduce anything. Minestrone on Wednesday is merely a necessary condition. It is not sufficient by itself to guarantee lentil soup on Tuesday.
gumbo is offered on Wednesday, but not minestrone	→	we cannot deduce anything. Gumbo on Wednesday is merely a necessary condition. It is not sufficient by itself to guarantee lentil soup on Tuesday.
both gumbo and minestrone are offered on Wednesday	→	we cannot deduce anything. Gumbo and/or minestrone on Wednesday is merely a necessary condition. It is not sufficient by itself to guarantee lentil soup on Tuesday.
neither gumbo nor minestrone is offered on Wednesday	→	lentil soup cannot be offered on Tuesday.

The following chart shows the correct contrapositives for a variety of complex conditional statements.

Formal Logic Statement		Contrapositive
If A → B or C	→	If ~B and ~C → ~A
If D → E and F	→	If ~E or ~F → ~D
If G or H → J	→	If ~J → ~G and ~H
If K and L → M	→	If ~M → ~K or ~L
If N and O → P and R	→	If ~P or ~R → ~N or ~O
If S or T → U and V	→	If ~U or ~V → ~S and ~T
If W and X → Y or Z	→	If ~Y and ~Z → ~W or ~X
If AA or BB → CC or DD	→	If ~CC and ~DD → ~AA and ~BB

Here is an example of an LSAT expert's analysis of the implications of a complex conditional statement that contains two terms in its necessary clause.

Conditional Statement		Analysis
Whenever Ezra performs, Gloria and Horatio also perform.	→	If E → G and H If ~G or ~H → ~E
Is each of the following an acceptable group of people who perform?		
Ezra, Gloria, and Horatio together	→	Yes
Ezra and Gloria, but not Horatio	→	No
Ezra and Horatio, but not Gloria	→	No
Gloria and Horatio, but not Ezra	→	Yes
Ezra alone	→	No
Gloria alone	→	Yes
Horatio alone	→	Yes

Practice

In this exercise, translate the conditional statement to Formal Logic abbreviations and form the correct contrapositive of the statement. Then, answer the questions beneath the statement using your work.

Conditional Statement		My Analysis
Yolanda will not join the sales team unless Xavier joins the accounting team and Wanda joins the development team.	→	
73. If Xavier joins the accounting team and Wanda joins the development team, will Yolanda join the sales team?	→	
74. If Xavier and Wanda both join the development team (and no other teams), will Yolanda join the sales team?	→	
75. If Yolanda does not join the sales team, do you know anything about where Xavier or Wanda can or cannot be assigned?	→	

Explanations

Here's how an LSAT expert would analyze the previous statements and answer the questions.

Conditional Statement		Analysis
Yolanda will not join the sales team unless Xavier joins the accounting team and Wanda joins the development team.	→	If Ys → Xa AND Wd If ~Xa OR ~Wd → ~Ys
73. If Xavier joins the accounting team and Wanda joins the development team, will Yolanda join the sales team?	→	This could happen, but it doesn't have to happen. Knowing the teams that Xavier and Wanda join is necessary but not sufficient for knowing the team that Yolanda joins.
74. If Xavier and Wanda both join the development team (and no other teams), will Yolanda join the sales team?	→	No, she won't. If Xavier does not join the accounting team, then Yolanda cannot join the sales team.
75. If Yolanda does not join the sales team, do you know anything about where Xavier or Wanda can or cannot be assigned?	→	No, nothing is known. If Yolanda were assigned to sales, we would know where Xavier and Wanda are assigned. But since Yolanda is not assigned there, we don't know anything about Xavier and Wanda.

Perform

In this exercise, translate the conditional statements to Formal Logic abbreviations and form the correct contrapositive of the statement. Then, answer the questions beneath the statement using your work.

Conditional Statement	My Analysis
Every gumdrop in the third bowl is red and apple-flavored.	→
76. If a gumdrop is blue, can it be apple flavored?	→
77. If a gumdrop is not apple-flavored, can it be in the third bowl?	→
78. If a gumdrop is red and apple-flavored, must it be in the third bowl?	→

Explanations

Here's how an LSAT expert would analyze the previous statements and answer the questions.

Conditional Statement		Analysis
Every gumdrop in the third bowl is red and apple-flavored.	→	If gumdrop in bowl 3 → red AND apple If ~ apple OR ~ red → ~ gumdrop in bowl 3
76. If a gumdrop is blue, can it be apple flavored?	→	This is possible. We don't know anything about gumdrops that are in other bowls.
77. If a gumdrop is not apple-flavored, can it be in the third bowl?	→	No, this isn't possible. Every gumdrop in the third bowl is apple-flavored.
78. If a gumdrop is red and apple-flavored, must it be in the third bowl?	→	No. It could be in the third bowl, but it could also be in other bowls.

Make Valid Deductions from Conditional Statements Containing an "Exclusive Or" Provision

LEARNING OBJECTIVES

In this section, you'll learn to:

- Make valid deductions from conditional statements containing an "Exclusive Or" provision

Prepare

So far, you've learned the fact that *or*, by itself, does not denote mutual exclusivity in conditional Formal Logic statements. However, if the LSAT adds a phrase such as "but not both," then, and only then, does it become a case of mutual exclusivity. Such statements are rare on the LSAT, but they warrant enough practice that you won't be thrown by them on test day.

Here's how an LSAT expert would translate such statements:

Formal Logic Statements		Analysis
If A, then B or C, but not both.	→	If A → B or C If ~B and ~C → ~A If A → ~(B and C) If B and C → ~A The sufficient condition results in the selection of exactly one entity (not both).
If D or E, but not both, then F.	→	If exactly one of D or E → F If ~F → (D and E) or (~D and ~E) [both or neither] The selection of exactly one triggers the result. Without the necessary result, then either both conditions occurred or both did not occur.

Practice

Record each of the following statements in If-Then format, and form both parts of their contrapositive.

Formal Logic Statements		My Analysis
79. Each member who attends the purchasing conference will also attend the sales conference or the marketing conference, but not both.	→	
80. Students who take exactly one of either math or economics will also take biology.	→	

Explanations

Here's how an LSAT expert might analyze the statements on the previous page.

Formal Logic Statements		Analysis
79. Each member who attends the purchasing conference will also attend the sales conference or the marketing conference, but not both.	→	If purchasing → sales OR marketing (but not both) If ~ sales AND ~ marketing → ~ purchasing If sales AND marketing → ~ purchasing
80. Students who take exactly one of either math or economics will also take biology.	→	If math or econ. (but not both) → bio If ~ bio → either [both math AND econ] OR [~ math AND ~ econ]

Perform

In this exercise, take each of the Formal Logic statements, turn it into "If-then" format, and make both parts of the contrapositive.

Formal Logic Statements	My Analysis
81. If Orson joins the dance team, he will also join the chess club or the glee club, but not both.	→
82. Whenever a box contains a peanut or a cashew (but not both), that box will be painted black.	→

Explanations

Here's how an LSAT expert might analyze the statements on the previous page.

Formal Logic Statements		My Analysis
81. If Orson joins the dance team, he will also join the chess club or the glee club, but not both.	→	If dance → chess or glee (but not both) If ~ chess AND ~ glee → ~ dance If chess AND glee → ~ dance
82. Whenever a box contains a peanut or a cashew (but not both), that box will be painted black.	→	If peanut OR cashew (but not both) → black box If ~ black box → either [no peanuts AND no cashews] OR [peanuts AND cashews]

Numerical Deductions from Conditional Statements

LEARNING OBJECTIVES

In this section, you'll learn to:

- Determine the valid deduction from If X → ~Y and from If ~X → Y

Prepare

Numerical deductions are often rewarded on the LSAT, especially in Logic Games. This section highlights two such deductions that frequently arise from conditional Formal Logic statements.

Determining the Valid Deduction From If X → ~Y

The trigger involves something that *does* happen, and the result is something else that *cannot* happen. This reduces the number of terms by at least one.

In this case, the deduction is this: You cannot have both. (And you might have neither.)

If the contracting company services plumbing, it does not service roofing.

If plumbing	→	~ roofing
If roofing	→	~ plumbing

The company will not service both. It can service just plumbing, just roofing, or neither.

Determining the Valid Deduction From If ~X → Y

The trigger involves something that *doesn't* happen, and the result is something that *must* happen. This increases the number of terms chosen by at least one.

In this case, the deduction is this: You must have at least one. (And you might have both.)

If the story does not include metaphors, then it must include symbolism.

If ~ metaphor	→	symbolism
If ~ symbolism	→	metaphor

The story will definitely include at least one of those two literary devices. It will include symbolism, metaphor, or possibly both.

LOGIC GAMES STRATEGY

The triggers of a Formal Logic statement and its contrapositive can never occur simultaneously. You can have the sufficient and necessary terms of the original statement, the sufficient and necessary terms of the contrapositive, or both necessary terms—but never both sufficient terms at once.

Formal Logic Statements		Analysis
No X are Y	→	If X → ~Y You cannot have both X and Y. You may have X without Y, Y without X, or neither X nor Y.
If no U, then V	→	If ~U → V You must have at least one of U or V. You can either have just U, just V, or both U and V.
All those with J don't have K	→	If J → ~K You cannot have both J and K. You may have J without K, have K without J, or have neither J nor K.
R unless S	→	If ~R → S You must have at least one of R and S. You can either have just R, just S, or both R and S.

Practice

For each of the following statements, write out the statement in shorthand, and indicate whether a numerical deduction can be made based on the statement.

Formal Logic Statements		My Analysis
83. If the arrow is not selected, the hammer will be selected.	→	
84. Any time the bake sale has brownies, it does not have cupcakes.	→	
85. The oak tree will be planted in the orchard only if the maple tree is also planted in the orchard.	→	

Explanations

Here's how an LSAT expert might translate and analyze the statements in the exercise.

Formal Logic Statements		Analysis
83. If the arrow is not selected, the hammer will be selected.	→	If ~ arrow → hammer If ~ hammer → arrow This statement increases the minimum of selected items by one. At the very least, either the hammer or the arrow will always be selected. It's possible that both are selected.
84. Any time the bake sale has brownies, it does not have cupcakes.	→	If brownies → ~ cupcakes If cupcakes → ~ brownies This statement decreases the maximum number of items at the bake sale. It will never have both brownies and cupcakes. It's possible the sale has neither.
85. The oak tree will be planted in the orchard only if the maple tree is also planted in the orchard.	→	If oak → maple If ~ maple → ~ oak No numerical deduction can be made here. It's possible to plant both trees in the park, it's possible to plant neither of the trees in the park, and it's also possible to plant a maple tree and not an oak tree.

Perform

For each of the following statements, write out the statement in shorthand, and indicate whether a numerical deduction can be made based on the statement.

Formal Logic Statements	My Analysis
86. Whenever the photographer is not selected, the writer is not selected.	→
87. Kyle is on every committee that Hector is not on.	→
88. If the poppy is included in the painting, then the rose will not be included.	→

Explanations

Here's how an LSAT expert might translate and analyze the statements in the exercise.

Formal Logic Statements		My Analysis
86. Whenever the photographer is not selected, the writer is not selected.	→	If ~ photographer → ~ writer If writer → photographer No numerical deduction can be made here. It's possible that both are selected, it's possible that neither are selected, and it's possible that the photographer is selected but not the writer.
87. Kyle is on every committee that Hector is not on.	→	If ~ Hector → Kyle If ~ Kyle → Hector This statement assures that every committee will have at least one member—either Hector or Kyle. As soon as one of them is NOT on a committee, the other person is assigned to that committee. It's also possible that they are on a committee together.
88. If the poppy is included in the painting, then the rose will not be included.	→	If poppy → ~ rose If rose → ~ poppy The painting cannot include both the poppy and the rose, so the maximum number of flowers in the painting is reduced by one. It's possible that the painting contains neither the rose nor the poppy.

Although this last learning objective about numerical deductions in Formal Logic comes all the way at the end of the section, the types of rules discussed here are very valuable when they appear in Selection games. In The LSAT Channel Special Feature that follows this section, a Kaplan expert will explain why these rules are so important, and illustrate them in action in a classic open-ended Selection game. If you want to push your mastery of LSAT Formal Logic over the top, don't miss this Special Feature.

Assess

Mastering Formal Logic takes repetition. No matter how you did on the exercises in this section, hone your edge and stay sharp by doing the Formal Logic drills in the Logic Games Training Camp in your online Study Plan.

Reflect

Look back over your practice:

Did you take the time to understand each conditional statement before noting it down in shorthand?

If you couldn't immediately see how to write it down in one sentence, did you translate it into "If-then" form and make the contrapositive? (If so, that's great!)

When forming contrapositives, did you remember to always negate and reverse the terms? Did you always remember that the result (the necessary condition) can occur without the trigger (the sufficient condition), but not vice versa?

Minimum Increasers and Maximum Decreasers

By Hannah Gist

Watch the video lesson for this Spotlight in your online Study Plan.

While a conditional Formal Logic rule could appear in almost any game type, Formal Logic is at the heart of Selection games. Nearly all of the rules in Selection games will provide triggers and results based on the selection or rejection of an entity; e.g., "If A is selected, then B is also selected" or "C is not selected unless D is also selected." The lengthy section of Chapter 8 that precedes this Special Feature is dedicated to helping you build mastery and confidence with just these types of statements.

Even with that work under your belt, there are two Formal Logic rules that deserve extra attention:

> If G is selected, then H is not selected.

and

> If L is not selected, M is selected.

These rules appear frequently in Selection games, and they are frequently misunderstood, leading to confusion and wrong answers. That's unfortunate, of course, but there is a bright side. When these rules are handled correctly, they not only help you solve the questions, they also give you direct insight into the minimum and maximum number of entities that may be selected. Here's the how and why of it.

Take the first rule: If G is selected, then H is not selected. This pattern—if positive, then negative—is a "maximum decreaser." It simply means that G and H cannot both be selected. Putting the rule into Formal Logic shorthand demonstrates this:

If G → ~H

Reverse and negate to get the contrapositive:

If H → ~G

Any time G or H is selected, the other is rejected. The maximum number of entities that may be selected is reduced by one. Some LSAT experts just cut to the chase and jot down the rule like this:

~GH

That insight is almost certain to help you get points in a Selection game featuring this rule. But, the rule has a pitfall, a simple mistake that many students make that costs them points: They think the rule means that either G or H must be selected. It does not. Selecting G or selecting H are the triggers. The rule says nothing about rejecting them. Memorize the results of "maximum decreasers" like this: If G → ~H means that we could 1) select G and reject H, 2) select H and reject G, or 3) reject both G and H. We cannot, however, select both G and H.

The other rule, illustrated with the previous example "If L is not selected, then M is selected," has the inverse pattern—negative to positive. This is a "minimum increaser." Again, write it out in Formal Logic shorthand:

If ~L → M

and form the contrapositive:

If ~M → L

You could shorten this one to:

At least one of M or L

or

M, L, or ML

Now, the minimum number of entities that must be selected is increased by one. Any time L is rejected, M is selected. And any time M is rejected, L is selected. Since the "minimum increaser" is the inverse of the "maximum decreaser," test takers are at risk of making the inverse mistake. That is, they mistakenly assume that at least one of the two entities must be rejected. Nope. The triggers this time are the rejection, not selection, of one of the entities. It's possible that both are selected, simply because selecting one of the entities does not trigger anything (nothing prevents the selection of both entities).

Memorize the results of "minimum increasers" like this: If ~L → M means that we could 1) reject L and select M, 2) reject M and select L, or 3) select both L and M. We cannot, however, reject both L and M.

In the video that accompanies this Special Feature, an LSAT Channel expert will demonstrate a game that features both a maximum decreaser and a minimum increaser. The game is printed on the next two pages. Try it out on your own, if you like, but pay special attention to the rules that operate just like the ones discussed here. They are key to unlocking the game you're about to do.

Questions 6–12

Bird-watchers explore a forest to see which of the following six kinds of birds—grosbeak, harrier, jay, martin, shrike, wren—it contains. The findings are consistent with the following conditions:

> If harriers are in the forest, then grosbeaks are not.
>
> If jays, martins, or both are in the forest, then so are harriers.
>
> If wrens are in the forest, then so are grosbeaks.
>
> If jays are not in the forest, then shrikes are.

6. Which one of the following could be a complete and accurate list of the birds NOT in the forest?

   (A) jays, shrikes
   (B) harriers, grosbeaks
   (C) grosbeaks, jays, martins
   (D) grosbeaks, martins, shrikes, wrens
   (E) martins, shrikes

7. If both martins and harriers are in the forest, then which one of the following must be true?

   (A) Shrikes are the only other birds in the forest.
   (B) Jays are the only other birds in the forest.
   (C) The forest contains neither jays nor shrikes.
   (D) There are at least two other kinds of birds in the forest.
   (E) There are at most two other kinds of birds in the forest.

8. If jays are not in the forest, then which one of the following must be false?

   (A) Martins are in the forest.
   (B) Harriers are in the forest.
   (C) Neither martins nor harriers are in the forest.
   (D) Neither martins nor shrikes are in the forest.
   (E) Harriers and shrikes are the only birds in the forest.

9. Which one of the following is the maximum number of the six kinds of birds the forest could contain?

   (A) two
   (B) three
   (C) four
   (D) five
   (E) six

10. Which one of the following pairs of birds CANNOT be among those birds contained in the forest?

    (A) jays, wrens
    (B) jays, shrikes
    (C) shrikes, wrens
    (D) jays, martins
    (E) shrikes, martins

11. If grosbeaks are in the forest, then which one of the following must be true?

    (A) Shrikes are in the forest.
    (B) Wrens are in the forest.
    (C) The forest contains both wrens and shrikes.
    (D) At most two kinds of birds are in the forest.
    (E) At least three kinds of birds are in the forest.

12. Suppose the condition is added that if shrikes are in the forest, then harriers are not. If all other conditions remain in effect, then which one of the following could be true?

    (A) The forest contains both jays and shrikes.
    (B) The forest contains both wrens and shrikes.
    (C) The forest contains both martins and shrikes.
    (D) Jays are not in the forest, whereas martins are.
    (E) Only two of the six kinds of birds are not in the forest.

PrepTest33 Sec4 Qs 6–12

Complete answers and explanations are provided in The LSAT Channel Spotlight video "Limited Options" in your online Study Plan.

SELECTION GAMES RULES

LEARNING OBJECTIVES

In this section of the chapter, you'll practice

- Applying Step 3 of the Logic Games Method to Selection games by analyzing and sketching the rules

Prepare

Now that you've worked through the section of this chapter on Formal Logic, there's not much more to say about Selection games rules. Aside from the occasional "established entity" rule (e.g., "Y is selected"), virtually everything you'll see will be expressed in conditional ("If"-then) terms.

LOGIC GAMES STRATEGY

Selection rules tell you one or more of the following:

- One entity's selection is dependent on another entity being selected.
- At least one of two entities must be selected.
- At least one of two entities must be rejected.
- Two entities must be selected or rejected as a pair (one cannot be selected and the other rejected).

Before moving on to the practice exercises, take a few moments to review some of the most common Selection rules.

In the expert analysis you'll see them written in Formal Logic shorthand, and accompanied by their contrapositives.

Rules		Analysis
R is never selected without W.	→	If R → W If ~W → ~R
If A is chosen, then Z will not be chosen.	→	If A → ~Z If Z → ~A or Never AZ
T will be selected for the display if G is not selected.	→	If ~G → T If ~T → G or Must have G or T (or both)
H will be chosen only if T is chosen.	→	If H → T If ~T → ~H
If B is chosen, then either C or D (but not both) will also be chosen.	→	If B → C or D If B → ~[both C and D] If ~C and ~D → ~B If C and D → ~B
At least one of either K or L will be selected.	→	If ~K → L If ~L → K or Must have K or L (or both)
Whenever J is not chosen, P is not chosen.	→	~J → ~P P → J
Only when O and X are selected is E selected.	→	E → O and X ~O or ~X → ~E
F and Y cannot both be selected.	→	If F → ~Y If Y → ~F or Never FY
M is a member of every group of which N is a member.	→	If N → M If ~M → ~N

In a Selection game in which the entities are subdivided, you may see number restrictions expressed in the rules. For example, in a game that tasks you with selecting a team of researchers from among four biologists and four chemists, a rule such as "Exactly two biologists will be selected for the research team" is likely. Such rules are almost always straightforward and easy to add to your sketch by simply noting the number above that subgroup of entities.

There are four practice exercises. In the first, you'll analyze and draw out 12 rules. In the next three, you'll see the model game setups you worked with in the section of this chapter covering Steps 1 and 2, but now accompanied by their rules. Analyze the rules, answer the questions posed about them, and draw them as you would on test day.

Practice

Practice 1

Directions: Analyze and draw each of the following Selection game rules, and record their contrapositives.

Rules	Analysis
1. If Dan is picked for the dance team, then Elaine will also be picked for the dance team.	→
2. The blue toy will be selected only if the red toy is not selected.	→
3. If A is chosen, then neither B nor C is chosen.	→
4. Juan will become a member only if Levi becomes a member.	→
5. If X is not selected for inclusion, then Z will be selected.	→
6. Nanda will not be selected unless Opal is selected.	→
7. Uriah cannot be chosen for the group without either Van or Walker being chosen.	→
8. If D is picked, then T is not picked.	→
9. Glen must be selected for the medical trial unless Jack is not selected for the medical trial.	→
10. Only if Z is chosen will K be chosen.	→
11. Patty will be selected if Ben is not selected.	→
12. If R and S are selected, then Q is selected.	→

Practice 2

Directions: Take a couple of minutes to review the game setup, summarize your Overview analysis, and recreate the initial Sketch. Then, one at a time, analyze the rules, answer the questions about each one, and draw the rule either inside or underneath the sketch framework.

A graphic designer must choose colors for a new logo from among the seven—fuchsia, grapefruit, hibiscus, indigo, jade, kiwi, and lemon—suggested by the client. The color selection must conform to the following conditions:

If grapefruit is used, then lemon cannot be used.
If jade is used, then indigo must also be used.
If indigo is used, then lemon must also be used.
If fuchsia is not used, then grapefruit must be used.
Hibiscus and kiwi cannot both be used.

1. [Step 1] Summarize your Overview analysis:

2. [Step 2] Create an initial Sketch:

3. [Step 3] Analyze and draw the Rules:
   - For each rule, answer the following questions and draw the rule in the appropriate box.
     - What does the rule restrict, and what does it leave open?
     - What are the rule's negative implications, if any?
     - Can the rule be depicted inside the sketch framework?

Rule 1:	Rule 2:
Rule 3:	Rule 4:
Rule 5:	

Practice 3

Directions: Take a couple of minutes to review the game setup, summarize your Overview analysis, and recreate the initial Sketch. Then, one at a time, analyze the rules, answer the questions about each one, and draw the rule either inside or underneath the sketch framework.

Melanie is planning a series of performances to promote her new relaxation CD. At each performance, she will play at least four of the pieces—*Atmosphere*, *Beats*, *Clouds*, *Dynamic*, *Ecologica*, *Firefly*, and *Glaciers*—that appear on the CD. Her selection for each performance is based on the following conditions:

Beats must be played at any performance that includes *Glaciers*.
Firefly will not be played at any performance that includes *Glaciers*.
Ecologica will not be played at any performance that includes both *Beats* and *Glaciers*.
If *Dynamic* is played, then *Atmosphere* is as well.
Clouds will be played at every performance.

1. [Step 1] Summarize your Overview analysis:

2. [Step 2] Create an initial Sketch:

3. [Step 3] Analyze and draw the Rules:
   - For each rule, answer the following questions and draw the rule in the appropriate box.
     - What does the rule restrict, and what does it leave open?
     - What are the rule's negative implications, if any?
     - Can the rule be depicted inside the sketch framework?

Rule 1:	Rule 2:
Rule 3:	Rule 4:
Rule 5:	

Practice 4

Directions: Take a couple of minutes to review the game setup, summarize your Overview analysis, and recreate the initial Sketch. Then, one at a time, analyze the rules, answer the questions about each one, and draw the rule either inside or underneath the sketch framework.

> Writers for a science magazine submitted eight articles to their editor, each on a different topic—anatomy, biochemistry, climatology, ecology, genetics, hydrology, immunology, and neuroscience. The editor will select exactly four of the articles for publication in the next issue, based on the following guidelines:
>
> The issue will include an article on either climatology or neuroscience, but not both.
> If the article on biochemistry is not included, then the article on ecology will be included.
> The article on genetics will not be included unless the article on immunology is included.
> If the article on hydrology is included, then the article on anatomy is not included.
> The article on ecology will be included if, but only if, the article on anatomy is included.

1. [Step 1] Summarize your Overview analysis:

2. [Step 2] Create an initial Sketch:

3. [Step 3] Analyze and draw the Rules:
   - For each rule, answer the following questions and draw the rule in the appropriate box.
     - What does the rule restrict, and what does it leave open?
     - What are the rule's negative implications, if any?
     - Can the rule be depicted inside the sketch framework?

Rule 1:	Rule 2:
Rule 3:	Rule 4:
Rule 5:	

Explanations

Compare your work to that of an LSAT expert. Pay close attention to how the expert analyzed each rule and then depicted it within or beneath the game's initial sketch.

Practice 1

Rules		Analysis
1. If Dan is picked for the dance team, then Elaine will also be picked for the dance team.	→	If D → E If ~E → ~D
2. The blue toy will be selected only if the red toy is not selected.	→	If B → ~R If R → ~B or Never BR
3. If A is chosen, then neither B nor C is chosen.	→	If A → ~B and ~C If B or C → ~A or Never AB Never AC
4. Juan will become a member only if Levi becomes a member.	→	If J → L If ~L → ~J
5. If X is not selected for inclusion, then Z will be selected.	→	If ~X → Z If ~Z → X or Must have X or Z (or both)
6. Nanda will not be selected unless Opal is selected.	→	If N → O If ~O → ~N
7. Uriah cannot be chosen for the group without either Van or Walker being chosen.	→	If U → V or W If ~V and ~W → ~U
8. If D is picked, then T is not picked.	→	If D → ~T If T → ~D or Never DT
9. Glen must be selected for the medical trial unless Jack is not selected for the medical trial.	→	If J → G If ~G → ~J
10. Only if Z is chosen will K be chosen.	→	If K → Z If ~Z → ~K
11. Patty will be selected if Ben is not selected.	→	If ~B → P If ~P → B or Must have B or P (or both)
12. If R and S are selected, then Q is selected.	→	If R and S → Q If ~Q → ~R or ~S

Practice 2

A graphic designer must choose colors for a new logo from among the seven—fuchsia, grapefruit, hibiscus, indigo, jade, kiwi, and lemon—suggested by the client. The color selection must conform to the following conditions:

If grapefruit is used, then lemon cannot be used.
If jade is used, then indigo must also be used.
If indigo is used, then lemon must also be used.
If fuchsia is not used, then grapefruit must be used.
Hibiscus and kiwi cannot both be used.

1. [Step 1] Summarize your Overview analysis: *A Selection game in which an unspecific number of colors will be chosen by a graphic designer for a new logo.*
2. [Step 2] Create an initial Sketch:

   F G H I J K L

3. [Step 3] Analyze and draw the Rules:
   - Rule 1:
     - What does the rule restrict, and what does it leave open? *If grapefruit is selected, then lemon is not.*
     - What are the rule's negative implications, if any? *By contrapositive, if lemon is selected, then grapefruit is not. This means the designer cannot select both.*
     - Can the rule be depicted inside the sketch framework? *No.*
     - Draw the rule:

       If G → ~L
       If L → ~G
       Never [G L]

   - Rule 2:
     - What does the rule restrict, and what does it leave open? *If jade is selected, then indigo is selected.*
     - What are the rule's negative implications, if any? *If indigo is not selected, then jade is not selected.*
     - Can the rule be depicted inside the sketch framework? *No.*
     - Draw the rule:

       If J → I
       If ~I → ~J

   - Rule 3:
     - What does the rule restrict, and what does it leave open? *If indigo is selected, then lemon is selected.*
     - What are the rule's negative implications, if any? *If lemon is not selected, then indigo is not selected.*
     - Can the rule be depicted inside the sketch framework? *No.*
     - Draw the rule:

       If I → L
       If ~L → ~I

   - Rule 4:
     - What does the rule restrict, and what does it leave open? *If fuchsia is not selected, then grapefruit is.*
     - What are the rule's negative implications, if any? *If grapefruit is not selected, then fuchsia is. This means at least one (if not both) of these colors will be selected.*
     - Can the rule be depicted inside the sketch framework? *No.*
     - Draw the rule:

       If ~F → G
       If ~G → F
       F or G (or both)

   - Rule 5:
     - What does the rule restrict, and what does it leave open? *Hibiscus and kiwi cannot both be selected, but it's also possible they're both left out.*
     - What are the rule's negative implications, if any? *N/A*
     - Can the rule be depicted inside the sketch framework? *No.*
     - Draw the rule:

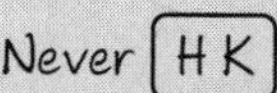

Practice 3

Melanie is planning a series of performances to promote her new relaxation CD. At each performance, she will play at least four of the pieces—*Atmosphere*, *Beats*, *Clouds*, *Dynamic*, *Ecologica*, *Firefly*, and *Glaciers*—that appear on the CD. Her selection for each performance is based on the following conditions:

Beats must be played at any performance that includes *Glaciers*.
Firefly will not be played at any performance that includes *Glaciers*.
Ecologica will not be played at any performance that includes both *Beats* and *Glaciers*.
If *Dynamic* is played, then *Atmosphere* is as well.
Clouds will be played at every performance.

1. [Step 1] Summarize your Overview analysis: *A Selection game in which a musician selects at least four pieces of music for each of her performances.*

2. [Step 2] Create an initial Sketch:

A B C D E F G 4^+ selected

3. [Step 3] Analyze and draw the Rules:
   - Rule 1:
     - What does the rule restrict, and what does it leave open? *If Glaciers is performed, then so is Beats.*
     - What are the rule's negative implications, if any? *If Beats is not performed, then Glaciers is not.*
     - Can the rule be depicted inside the sketch framework? *No.*
     - Draw the rule:

       If G → B
       If ~B → ~G

   - Rule 2:
     - What does the rule restrict, and what does it leave open? *If Glaciers is performed, then Firefly is not performed.*
     - What are the rule's negative implications, if any? *If Firefly is performed, then Glaciers is not.*
     - Can the rule be depicted inside the sketch framework? *No.*
     - Draw the rule:

       If G → ~F
       If F → ~G
       Never FG

   - Rule 3:
     - What does the rule restrict, and what does it leave open? *If both Beats and Glaciers are performed, then Ecologica is not.*
     - What are the rule's negative implications, if any? *If Ecologica is performed, then either Beats or Glaciers is not performed. It's also possible none of these pieces are played. The one certainty is that all three pieces cannot be performed.*
     - Can the rule be depicted inside the sketch framework? *No.*
     - Draw the rule:

       If B and G → ~E
       If E → ~B or ~G
       Never BGE

   - Rule 4:
     - What does the rule restrict, and what does it leave open? *If Dynamic is performed, then so is Atmosphere.*
     - What are the rule's negative implications, if any? *If Atmosphere is not performed, then neither is Dynamic.*
     - Can the rule be depicted inside the sketch framework? *No.*
     - Draw the rule:

       If D → A
       If ~A → ~D

- Rule 5:
  - What does the rule restrict, and what does it leave open? *Clouds is always performed.*
  - What are the rule's negative implications, if any? *N/A*
  - Can the rule be depicted inside the sketch framework? *Yes.*
  - Draw the rule:

Practice 4

Writers for a science magazine submitted eight articles to their editor, each on a different topic—anatomy, biochemistry, climatology, ecology, genetics, hydrology, immunology, and neuroscience. The editor will select exactly four of the articles for publication in the next issue, based on the following guidelines:

> The issue will include an article on either climatology or neuroscience, but not both.
> If the article on biochemistry is not included, then the article on ecology will be included.
> The article on genetics will not be included unless the article on immunology is included.
> If the article on hydrology is included, then the article on anatomy is not included.
> The article on ecology will be included if, but only if, the article on anatomy is included.

1. [Step 1] Summarize your Overview analysis: *A Selection game in which exactly four articles will be selected for inclusion in a magazine. The other four articles will be left out.*

2. [Step 2] Create an initial Sketch:

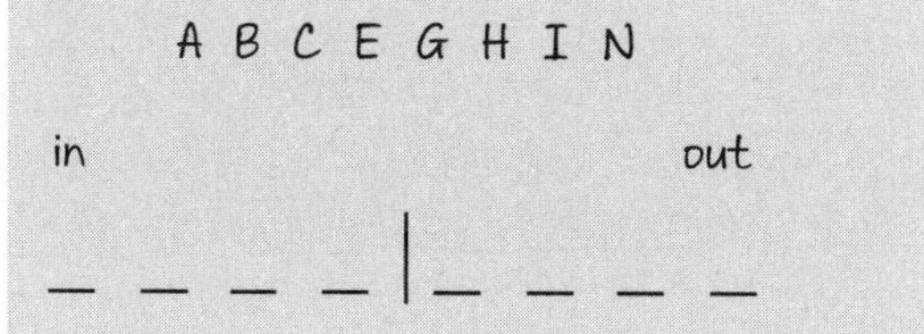

3. [Step 3] Analyze and draw the Rules:
   - Rule 1:
     - What does the rule restrict, and what does it leave open? *Of climatology and neuroscience, exactly one will be selected.*
     - What are the rule's negative implications, if any? *One of them will be out.*
     - Can the rule be depicted inside the sketch framework? *Yes.*
     - Draw the rule:

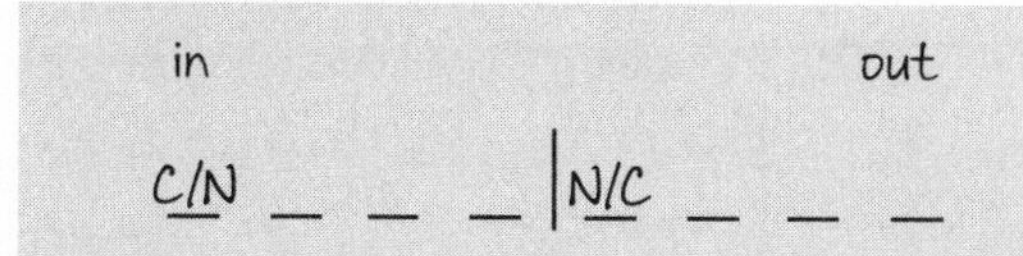

   - Rule 2:
     - What does the rule restrict, and what does it leave open? *If the biochemistry article is not selected, then the ecology article is.*
     - What are the rule's negative implications, if any? *If the ecology article is not selected, then the biochemistry article is. That means at least one of them (or both) must be selected.*
     - Can the rule be depicted inside the sketch framework? *Yes, along with the Formal Logic.*
     - Draw the rule:

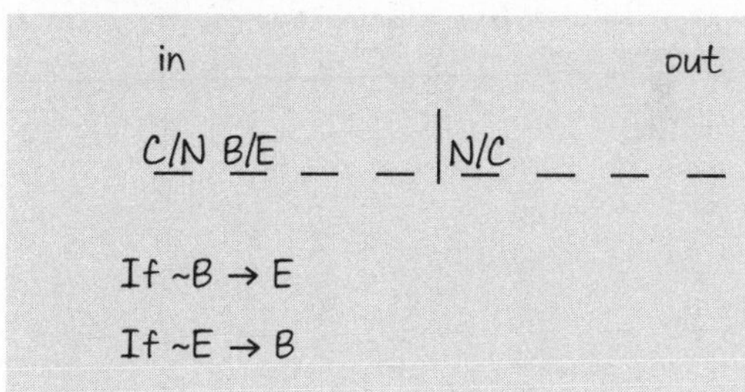

   - Rule 3:
     - What does the rule restrict, and what does it leave open? *If the genetics article is selected, then so is the immunology article.*
     - What are the rule's negative implications, if any? *If the immunology article is not selected, then the genetics article is not.*
     - Can the rule be depicted inside the sketch framework? *No.*
     - Draw the rule:

If G → I

If ~I → ~G

- Rule 4:
  - What does the rule restrict, and what does it leave open? *If the hydrology article is selected, then the anatomy article is not.*
  - What are the rule's negative implications, if any? *If the anatomy article is selected, then the hydrology article is not. Essentially, they cannot both be selected. There could be just one, or perhaps neither one.*
  - Can the rule be depicted inside the sketch framework? *Yes, along with the Formal Logic.*
  - Draw the rule:

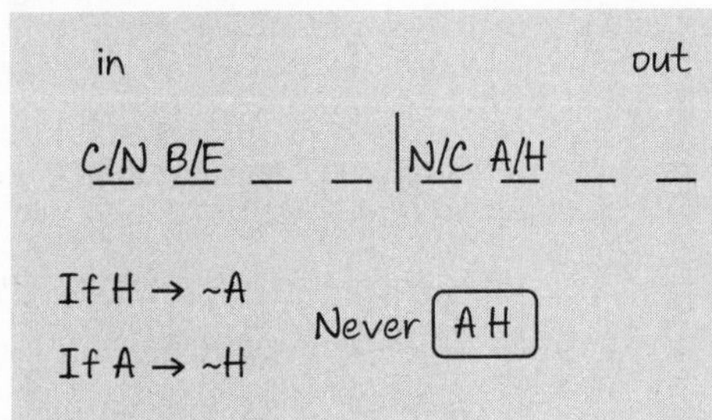

- Rule 5:
  - What does the rule restrict, and what does it leave open? *If the ecology article is selected, then so is the anatomy article . . . and vice versa: if the anatomy article is selected, then the ecology must be, too.*
  - What are the rule's negative implications, if any? *By contrapositive of both parts of the logic, if either one is not selected, then the other one is out, too. In short, either both are selected, or they're both out.*
  - Can the rule be depicted inside the sketch framework? *No.*
  - Draw the rule:

AE or neither

As you worked with all of those rules, you may already have noticed rules that can be combined into strings because the result of one matches the trigger of another. In some Selection games, these strings will grow to four or five entities long, and the same thing with their contrapositives in the other direction. You'll practice decoding those strings, and determining which rules do or don't combine, in the next section of this chapter on Step 4 of the Logic Games Method.

SELECTION GAMES DEDUCTIONS

LEARNING OBJECTIVES

In this section of the chapter, you'll practice

- Applying Step 4 of the Logic Games Method to Selection games by combining rules and restrictions to make all valid deductions in the game.

Prepare

The most common pattern of deductions in Selection games occurs when the result of one conditional rule matches the trigger of another conditional rule. This allows the rules to be combined into a "string" or "chain" of deductions. This is easily illustrated with two rules:

If A → B
If B → C

Because the result of the first rule matches the trigger of the second, these two rules combine into a string:

If A → B → C

Yielding the deduction:

If A → C

Don't forget that in every such case, the rules' contrapositives can also be combined:

If ~B → ~A
If ~C → ~B

Because the result of the second rule's contrapositive matches the trigger of the first rule's contrapositive, the two rules combine into a string:

If ~C → ~B → ~A

Yielding the deduction:

If ~C → ~A

LOGIC GAMES STRATEGY

In Selection games, deductions are likely to stem from:

- **Duplications**—Entities shared by two or more rules; Selection games often feature "strings" or "chains" of deductions from Formal Logic statements that can be linked by shared entities.
- **Numbers Restrictions**—Restrictions or limitations on the number of entities to be selected or determinations of the minimum or maximum numbers that can be selected given the game's rules.

In Selection games, deductions may involve:

- **Limited Options**—The situation that arises when a rule specifies that exactly two selection patterns are possible (e.g., either G is selected and F is not selected, or F is selected and G is not selected, in every case)
- **Blocks of Entities**—Two or more entities that must be selected or rejected as a pair
- **Established Entities**—Entities that must be selected or rejected; this is very rare in Selection games where all or most rules are conditional; occasionally, the Numbers Restrictions will allow you to determine that a specific entity can never be selected.

There is a debate among LSAT experts about whether to actually write out all of the strings that can be found among a Selection game's rules. While writing out all of the deductions may help you spot all of the chains, it can be time consuming, and if the chains are long, stringing together three or four rules, your Master Sketch can become too cluttered. As long as you have written the rules neatly, and have lined up the "If"s and the "then"s of your Formal Logic, you should be able to spot any case in which one rule (or contrapositive) triggers another rule (or contrapositive).

Any time that LSAT experts disagree, it means that there is no one "correct" or "proper" way to do something on the test. (After all, the experts all got very high scores on the LSAT by doing it their own ways, right?) During practice, experiment a little with Selection rules and deductions. Try one game by writing out the chains of logic you discover. Then, try another by leaving your rules as-is and spotting the chains as they arise during the questions. You'll discover what works best for you when you are actually working in context.

You can try that out here, as you revisit the model games you've been working on throughout this chapter.

Practice

Directions: In each game setup, first reacquaint yourself with the setup and rules. Then, combine the rules and restrictions to make all available deductions, recording your analyses as indicated. Finally, test your deductions by answering the questions that accompany each game. You can find expert analysis and explanations at the end of the Practice section.

Practice 1

A graphic designer must choose colors for a new logo from among the seven—fuchsia, grapefruit, hibiscus, indigo, jade, kiwi, and lemon—suggested by the client. The color selection must conform to the following conditions:

If grapefruit is used, then lemon cannot be used.
If jade is used, then indigo must also be used.
If indigo is used, then lemon must also be used.
If fuchsia is not used, then grapefruit must be used.
Hibiscus and kiwi cannot both be used.

1. Which entities or positions are the most restricted in this game? Why?

2. Which elements from the BLEND checklist can you identify in this game? Are there
   - Blocks of entities? If so, what are they?
   - Limited Options? If so, which rule(s) trigger them?
   - Established Entities? If so, which ones?
   - Number Restrictions? If so, describe them.
   - Duplications? If so, which rules share an entity?
3. Combine the rules and restrictions to create a Master Sketch depicting all of the deductions available in this game:

4. Evaluate your sketch by answering the following questions:
   - What is the maximum number of colors that could be selected?
   - If just one color was used, what could it be?
   - Which colors directly guarantee the selection of another color?
   - If lemon is used, what other color(s) must ultimately be used?

Practice 2

Melanie is planning a series of performances to promote her new relaxation CD. At each performance, she will play at least four of the pieces—*Atmosphere*, *Beats*, *Clouds*, *Dynamic*, *Ecologica*, *Firefly*, and *Glaciers*—that appear on the CD. Her selection for each performance is based on the following conditions:

Beats must be played at any performance that includes *Glaciers*.
Firefly will not be played at any performance that includes *Glaciers*.
Ecologica will not be played at any performance that includes both *Beats* and *Glaciers*.
If *Dynamic* is played, then *Atmosphere* is as well.
Clouds will be played at every performance.

1. Which entities or positions are the most restricted in this game? Why?

2. Which elements from the BLEND checklist can you identify in this game? Are there
   - Blocks of entities? If so, what are they?
   - Limited Options? If so, which rule(s) trigger them?
   - Established Entities? If so, which ones?
   - Number Restrictions? If so, describe them.
   - Duplications? If so, which rules share an entity?
3. Combine the rules and restrictions to create a Master Sketch depicting all of the deductions available in this game:

4. Evaluate your sketch by answering the following questions:
   - What is the maximum number of pieces at any performance?
   - What is the maximum number of pieces that are *not* performed at any performance?
   - What pieces must be performed?
   - What piece(s) cannot be performed if *Firefly* is performed?

Practice 3

Writers for a science magazine submitted eight articles to their editor, each on a different topic—anatomy, biochemistry, climatology, ecology, genetics, hydrology, immunology, and neuroscience. The editor will select exactly four of the articles for publication in the next issue, based on the following guidelines:

The issue will include an article on either climatology or neuroscience, but not both.
If the article on biochemistry is not included, then the article on ecology will be included.
The article on genetics will not be included unless the article on immunology is included.
If the article on hydrology is included, then the article on anatomy is not included.
The article on ecology will be included if, but only if, the article on anatomy is included.

1. Which entities or positions are the most restricted in this game? Why?

2. Which elements from the BLEND checklist can you identify in this game? Are there
   - Blocks of entities? If so, what are they?
   - Limited Options? If so, which rule(s) trigger them?
   - Established Entities? If so, which ones?
   - Number Restrictions? If so, describe them.
   - Duplications? If so, which rules share an entity?
3. Combine the rules and restrictions to create a Master Sketch depicting all of the deductions available in this game:

4. Evaluate your sketch by answering the following questions:
   - How many of the submitted articles will not be included?
   - Which article(s) must be selected?
   - If the ecology article is selected, which other article(s) must also be selected?
   - Which articles cannot be selected if the climatology article is selected?

Explanations

Compare your work to that of an LSAT expert. Pay close attention to how the expert combined the rules and restrictions to make additional deductions, and to how the expert depicted the deductions within the sketch framework.

Practice 1

A graphic designer must choose colors for a new logo from among the seven—fuchsia, grapefruit, hibiscus, indigo, jade, kiwi, and lemon—suggested by the client. The color selection must conform to the following conditions:

If grapefruit is used, then lemon cannot be used.
If jade is used, then indigo must also be used.
If indigo is used, then lemon must also be used.
If fuchsia is not used, then grapefruit must be used.
Hibiscus and kiwi cannot both be used.

1. Which entities or positions are the most restricted in this game? Why? *Lots of entities are mentioned multiple times, so no single entity stands out as the most significant.*

2. Which elements from the BLEND checklist can you identify in this game? Are there
   - Blocks of entities? If so, what are they? *N/A*
   - Limited Options? If so, which rule(s) trigger them? *N/A*
   - Established Entities? If so, which ones? *N/A*
   - Number Restrictions? If so, describe them. *Rule 1 prevents two colors from being together, dropping the maximum to six total colors. Rule 5 prevents two other colors from being together, dropping the maximum to five total colors.*
   - Duplications? If so, which rules share an entity? *Rules 1 and 3 mention lemon. Rules 1 and 4 mention grapefruit. Rules 2 and 3 mention indigo.*

3. Combine the rules and restrictions to create a Master Sketch depicting all of the deductions available in this game: *It's possible to combine various pieces of logic. For example, if lemon is used, then grapefruit is not, which then means fuchsia is. However, when every rule (or almost every rule) is based on Formal Logic, it's often not worth drawing every possible string. Simply have the triggers lined up. If a trigger produces a result, see if that new result triggers another piece of logic.*

F G H I J K L

If G → ~L
If L → ~G
Never [G L]

If J → I
If ~I → ~J

If I → L
If ~L → ~I

If ~F → G
If ~G → F
F or G (or both)

Never [H K]

4. Evaluate your sketch by answering the following questions:
   - What is the maximum number of colors that could be selected? *Five. Of the seven, the selection can't have both grapefruit and lemon, and can't have both hibiscus and kiwi.*
   - If just one color was used, what could it be? *Fuchsia or grapefruit.*
   - Which colors directly guarantee the selection of another color? *Jade (which guarantees indigo) and indigo (which guarantees lemon).*
   - If lemon is used, what other color(s) must ultimately be used? *Fuchsia; with lemon, there can be no grapefruit, which means fuchsia must be used.*

Practice 2

Melanie is planning a series of performances to promote her new relaxation CD. At each performance, she will play at least four of the pieces—*Atmosphere, Beats, Clouds, Dynamic, Ecologica, Firefly,* and *Glaciers*—that appear on the CD. Her selection for each performance is based on the following conditions:

Beats must be played at any performance that includes *Glaciers.*
Firefly will not be played at any performance that includes *Glaciers.*
Ecologica will not be played at any performance that includes both *Beats* and *Glaciers.*
If *Dynamic* is played, then *Atmosphere* is as well.
Clouds will be played at every performance.

1. Which entities or positions are the most restricted in this game? Why? *Glaciers is mentioned in each of the first three rules, so it will have the most impact.*

2. Which elements from the BLEND checklist can you identify in this game? Are there
   - Blocks of entities? If so, what are they? *N/A*
   - Limited Options? If so, which rule(s) trigger them? *N/A*
   - Established Entities? If so, which ones? *Rule 5 established Clouds as selected.*
   - Number Restrictions? If so, describe them. *Rule 2 prevents two pieces from being together, reducing the maximum to 6 pieces. Rule 3 also prevents every piece from being used, but the repeated use of Glaciers does not allow for further reductions after Rule 2.*
   - Duplications? If so, which rules share an entity? *Rules 1, 2, and 3 mention Glaciers. Rules 1 and 3 mention Beats.*

3. Combine the rules and restrictions to create a Master Sketch depicting all of the deductions available in this game: *Although Clouds is selected, that leads to no further deductions. The rest of the rules are based on Formal Logic, so no concrete deductions can be made. Any remaining song can be selected or not, depending on what else is selected.*

A B (C) D E F G 4-6 selected

If G → B
If ~B → ~G

If G → ~F
If F → ~G
Never [G F]

If B and G → ~E
If E → ~B or ~G
Never [B G E]

If D → A
IF ~A → ~D

4. Evaluate your sketch by answering the following questions:
   - What is the maximum number of pieces at any performance? *Six; Glaciers would prevent other pieces from being performed. However, if Glaciers is out, everything else could be in without violating any rules.*
   - What is the maximum number of pieces that are *not* performed at any performance? *Three; at least four are in, so only three can be out.*
   - What pieces must be performed? *Only Clouds; everything else can be in or out, depending on what else is performed.*
   - What piece(s) cannot be performed if *Firefly* is performed? *Glaciers.*

Practice 3

Writers for a science magazine submitted eight articles to their editor, each on a different topic—anatomy, biochemistry, climatology, ecology, genetics, hydrology, immunology, and neuroscience. The editor will select exactly four of the articles for publication in the next issue, based on the following guidelines:

> The issue will include an article on either climatology or neuroscience, but not both.
> If the article on biochemistry is not included, then the article on ecology will be included.
> The article on genetics will not be included unless the article on immunology is included.
> If the article on hydrology is included, then the article on anatomy is not included.
> The article on ecology will be included if, but only if, the article on anatomy is included.

1. Which entities or positions are the most restricted in this game? Why? *Anatomy and ecology, as the last rule severely restricts their selection and each one affects the selection of other entities.*

2. Which elements from the BLEND checklist can you identify in this game? Are there
   - Blocks of entities? If so, what are they? *Rule 5 effectively makes anatomy and ecology a block, as they will be both in or both out.*
   - Limited Options? If so, which rule(s) trigger them? *Rule 5 provides two outcomes: either anatomy and ecology are both in, or they're both out.*
   - Established Entities? If so, which ones? *Rule 1 establishes one of the articles as either climatology or neuroscience.*
   - Number Restrictions? If so, describe them. *The Overview sets the numbers of exactly four in and four out.*
   - Duplications? If so, which rules share an entity? *Rules 2 and 5 mention ecology, while rules 4 and 5 mention anatomy.*

3. Combine the rules and restrictions to create a Master Sketch depicting all of the deductions available in this game:

The last rule creates two options. In the first option, both the anatomy and ecology articles are selected. That means the hydrology article is out.

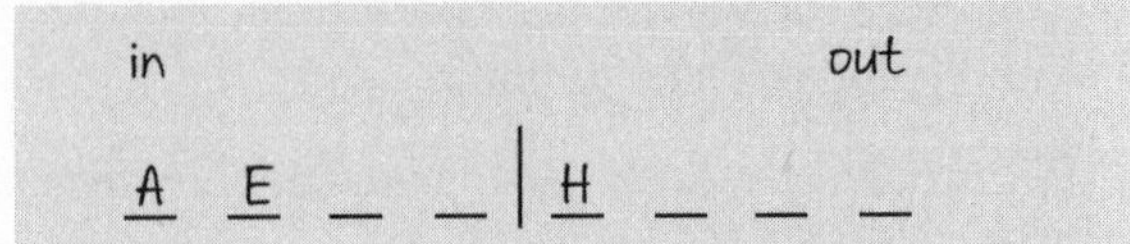

In that case, a third article included will be on either climatology or neuroscience. The other will be a second article out.

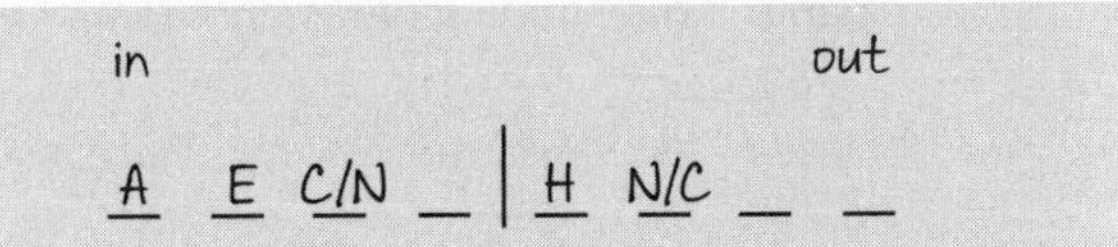

One more article needs to be included. All that remains are biochemistry, genetics, and immunology. However, genetics can't be included without immunology, so genetics must be out. The last article will be either biochemistry or immunology.

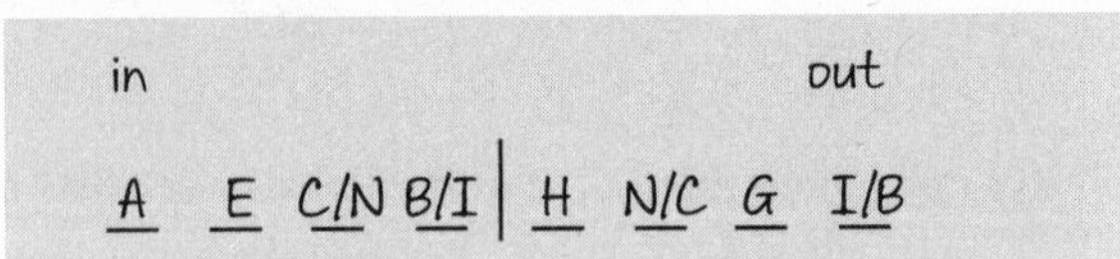

In the second option, the anatomy and ecology articles are both out.

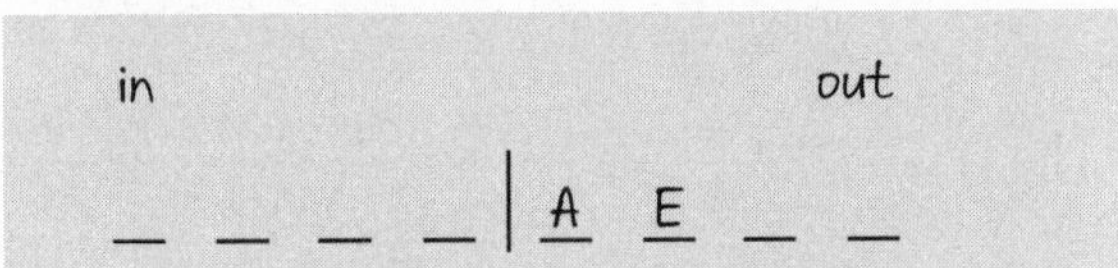

That means the biochemistry article must be included. A second article included will be on either climatology or neuroscience. The other will be a third article out.

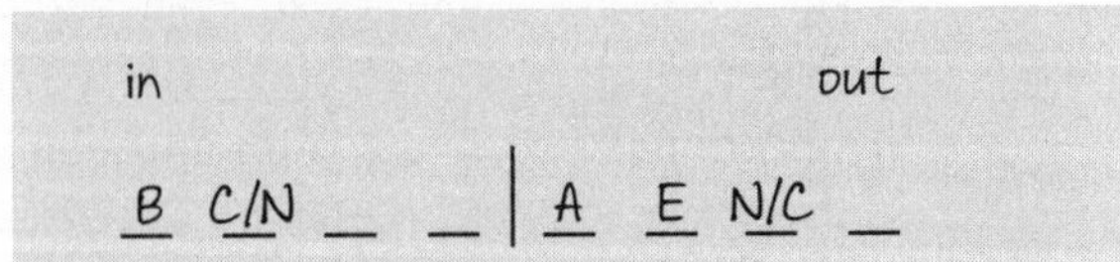

That leaves genetics, hydrology, and immunology. Only one more can be left out. However, immunology can't be left out without also leaving out genetics. So, immunology must be included, along with either genetics or hydrology. The remaining article will be the final one out.

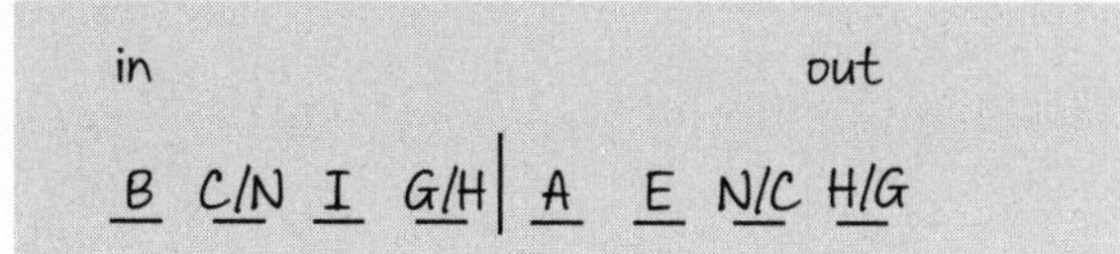

4. Evaluate your sketch by answering the following questions:
   - How many of the submitted articles will not be included? *Four.*
   - Which article(s) must be selected? *None; each of the eight articles could be selected depending on what else is selected.*
   - If the ecology article is selected, which other article(s) must also be selected? *Anatomy.*
   - Which articles cannot be selected if the climatology article is selected? *Neuroscience.*

You've done a lot of work building up your expertise in Selection games, especially so if you started this chapter as a Formal Logic novice. In the last section of Chapter 8, evaluate your mastery of these new skills with two officially released Selection games.

SELECTION GAMES—FULL GAMES WITH QUESTIONS

LEARNING OBJECTIVES

In this section, you'll assess your ability to

- Apply the Logic Games Method to Selection games.

Perform

Here is your opportunity to put all of the pieces together and assess your skills on Selection games. On the following pages, you'll find two full-length games along with their question sets. Both of these games are from officially released LSAT tests, and are representative of Selection games you could see on test day. You can take the games one at a time or together, but for your self-evaluation to be as accurate as possible, adhere to the timing guidelines set forth in the directions.

An answer key follows the games. Complete worked example expert analyses can be found in your online resources.

After you complete and review both games, assess your performance using the evaluation guidelines. There, you'll find recommendations for additional Easy, Medium, and Hard Selection games from officially released LSAT exams that you can practice to continue honing your skills and raising your score.

Directions: Take no more than 9 minutes per game to complete the following two games and all of their questions.

Perform 1

Questions 1–6

Fu, Gunsel, Jackson, Kowalski, Lee, Mayer, and Ordoveza are the only applicants being considered for some positions at a nonprofit organization. Only applicants who are interviewed will be hired. The hiring process must meet the following constraints:

If Gunsel is interviewed, Jackson is interviewed.
If Jackson is interviewed, Lee is interviewed.
Fu is interviewed.
Fu is not hired, unless Kowalski is interviewed.
Kowalski is not hired, unless Mayer is interviewed.
If Mayer is hired, and Lee is interviewed, Ordoveza is hired.

1. Which one of the following could be a complete and accurate list of the applicants that are interviewed?

(A) Fu, Gunsel
(B) Fu, Jackson
(C) Fu, Lee
(D) Fu, Gunsel, Lee
(E) Fu, Gunsel, Jackson

2. Which one of the following could be true?

   (A) Lee and Mayer are the only applicants interviewed.

   (B) Fu, Jackson, and Kowalski are the only applicants interviewed.

   (C) Gunsel and one other applicant are the only applicants interviewed.

   (D) Gunsel and two other applicants are the only applicants interviewed.

   (E) Gunsel and three other applicants are the only applicants interviewed.

3. If Mayer is not interviewed, which one of the following must be true?

   (A) Kowalski is not interviewed.

   (B) Kowalski is interviewed but not hired.

   (C) Fu is not hired.

   (D) Fu is hired but Kowalski is not hired.

   (E) Fu is interviewed but Kowalski is not hired.

4. If Gunsel and five other applicants are the only applicants interviewed, and if exactly three applicants are hired, then which one of the following could be an accurate list of the applicants hired?

   (A) Fu, Lee, Mayer

   (B) Fu, Kowalski, Mayer

   (C) Kowalski, Lee, Ordoveza

   (D) Gunsel, Jackson, Mayer

   (E) Gunsel, Jackson, Lee

5. If every applicant that is interviewed is hired, and if Lee is hired, then each of the following applicants must be interviewed EXCEPT:

   (A) Fu

   (B) Jackson

   (C) Kowalski

   (D) Mayer

   (E) Ordoveza

6. If Ordoveza is not interviewed, and if exactly four applicants are hired, then which one of the following must be false?

   (A) Lee is hired.

   (B) Mayer is hired.

   (C) Jackson is interviewed.

   (D) Kowalski is interviewed.

   (E) Gunsel is interviewed.

PrepTest23 Sec1 Qs 6–11

Perform 2

Questions 7–12

From a group of seven people—J, K, L, M, N, P, and Q—exactly four will be selected to attend a diplomat's retirement dinner. Selection must conform to the following conditions:

Either J or K must be selected, but J and K cannot both be selected.

Either N or P must be selected, but N and P cannot both be selected.

N cannot be selected unless L is selected.

Q cannot be selected unless K is selected.

7. Which one of the following could be the four people selected to attend the retirement dinner?

(A) J, K, M, P

(B) J, L, N, Q

(C) J, M, N, Q

(D) K, M, P, Q

(E) L, M, N, P

8. Among the people selected to attend the retirement dinner there must be

   (A) K or Q or both
   (B) L or M or both
   (C) N or M or both
   (D) N or Q or both
   (E) P or Q or both

9. Which one of the following is a pair of people who CANNOT both be selected to attend the retirement dinner?

   (A) J and N
   (B) L or M or both
   (C) K and L
   (D) K and N
   (E) N and Q

10. If M is not selected to attend the retirement dinner, the four people selected to attend must include which one of the following pairs of people?

    (A) J and Q
    (B) K and L
    (C) K and P
    (D) L and P
    (E) N and Q

11. If P is not selected to attend the retirement dinner, then exactly how many different groups of four are there each of which would be an acceptable selection?

    (A) one
    (B) two
    (C) three
    (D) four
    (E) five

12. There is only one acceptable group of four that can be selected to attend the retirement dinner if which one of the following pairs of people is selected?

    (A) J and L
    (B) K and M
    (C) L and N
    (D) L and Q
    (E) M and Q

PrepTest9 Sec3 Qs 8–13

Answer Key

Perform 1

1. (C)
2. (E)
3. (E)
4. (E)
5. (B)
6. (B)

Perform 2

7. (D)
8. (B)
9. (B)
10. (B)
11. (C)
12. (E)

Worked example explanations of these questions with complete expert analysis can be found in your Online Study Plan under Chapter 8. View or download the PDF titled "Chapter 8 Perform Full Games Explanations."

Assess

Use the following criteria to evaluate your results on the Perform games.

If, under timed conditions, you correctly answered

10–12 of the questions: Outstanding! You have demonstrated a strong skill level in Selection games. For further practice in Selection, use any of the Recommended Additional Practice sets, including the Advanced set. Then, move on to Chapter 9 on Matching and Distribution games.

7–9 of the questions: Good work! You have a solid foundation in Selection games. For further practice in basic Selection, begin with the Foundations or Mid-Level Recommended Additional Practice set. Then, move on to Chapter 9 on Matching and Distribution games. If you have time before test day, try the Advanced Recommended Additional Selection Practice set, as well.

0–6 of the questions: Keep working. Selection games do not show up frequently, but the practice with Formal Logic will pay off in other game types and on Logical Reasoning as well. Continued practice will help you improve your score. Begin by reviewing this chapter. Then, try the games in the Foundations Recommended Additional Practice set. As you continue to progress, move on to the Mid-Level Recommended Additional Practice set. Then, move on to Chapter 9 on Matching and Distribution games.

To stay sharp, practice the drills in the Logic Games Training Camp for this chapter in your Online Study Plan. Training Camp drills are divided into Fundamentals, Mid-Level, and Advanced sets.

Recommended Additional Practice: Selection

All of the following games will provide good practice on Selection. They are grouped by difficulty as determined from empirical student practice results. All PrepTests included are available on LawHub with an LSAC Prep Plus subscription.

Foundations

PrepTest 58, Section 3, Game 2: Day Care Volunteers

PrepTest 54, Section 3, Game 1: Dancers on Stage

Mid-Level

PrepTest 70, Section 3, Game 2: Corporate Research Team

PrepTest 65, Section 2, Game 3: Luncheon Foods

Advanced

PrepTest 59, Section 1, Game 3: Alicia's Courses

PrepTest 58, Section 3, Game 4: Summer School Courses

Complete explanations and analysis for all of the more-than-70 official LSAT tests on LawHub that come with an LSAC LSAT Prep Plus subscription are available in Kaplan's LSAT Link and Link+ tools. Visit **www.kaptest.com/lsat** to learn more or to purchase LSAT Link or Link+.

Reflect

Think back over the study and practice you did in this chapter.

- Are you able to identify Selection games from their setups?
- Do you have a default sketch framework for Selection actions?
- What kinds of rules do you anticipate seeing in Selection games?
- Are you comfortable analyzing Selection rules, translating them to Formal Logic and writing their contrapositives?
- Are you making the available deductions efficiently and effectively when a rule is triggered in a Selection game?

In the coming days and weeks before test day, take note of real-world tasks that reflect Selection tasks. Consider how they mirror the setups and questions in LSAT Selection, and how they differ. Try to reframe real-life sequencing tasks using the terms, rules, and restrictions used by the testmaker.

CHAPTER 9

Matching and Distribution Games Unlocked

LEARNING OBJECTIVES

In this chapter, you'll learn to

- Apply the Logic Games Method to Matching games
- Apply the Logic Games Method to Distribution games

Taken together, Matching and Distribution games have been about as common as Strict Sequencing games on LSAT tests released over the past five years. This is due largely to the recent popularity of Distribution games, which have accounted for about 18 percent of games on the 15 LSATs released from 2014 through 2018. That's a dramatic increase from 2007 to 2011, during which time Distribution accounted for just under seven percent of all games. Matching games haven't seen a similar increase in recent years, but they account for just under 12 percent of all games on tests released from 2014 through 2018.

Types of Games By Percentage, 2014–2018

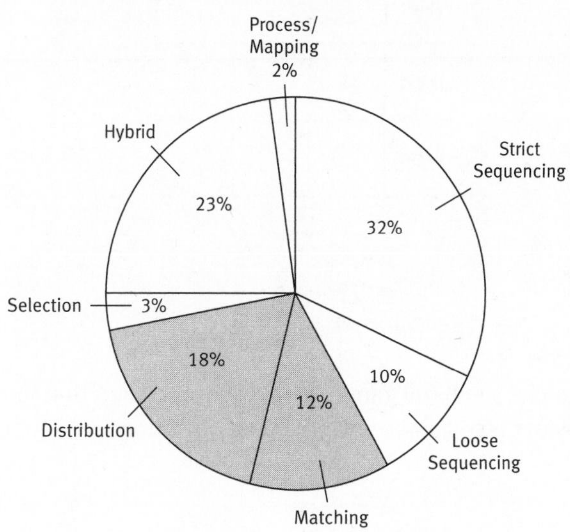

There is a reason to cover Matching and Distribution games in the same chapter. They are similar, so much so that LSAT experts will sometimes argue about which of the two categories a particular game falls into. Both involve grouping entities under two or more headings, and at times, their initial sketches can look quite similar. There is, however, an important distinction between the two game types, and covering them side by side will help you spot it and appreciate its importance.

The primary distinction between the two game types concerns the number of times each of the entities may be used in the game. In a standard Distribution game, you are tasked with dividing up a set of entities into two or more groups or teams. In most Distribution games, once an entity is placed into a group, the entity cannot be placed anywhere else. If Johnny plays for the Red Team, it stands to reason that he can't play for the Blue Team at the same time.

Blue	Red
—	J
—	—
—	—

In Matching, on the other hand, you have two sets of entities, and your job is to assign items or attributes in one set to each of the individuals in the other set. Matching tasks allow you assign the same item or attribute more than once. In a game in which you are matching colors to pieces of clothing, for example, nothing seems inherently strange about saying that two skiers both wear blue parkas.

	S	T	V
hat			
parka	b		b
gloves			

b = blue
g = gold
r = red

As you work through the practice exercises and full games in this chapter, keep that fundamental difference between the two game types in mind. Mastery of these games will provide a huge boost to your success in the Logic Games section of the LSAT.

MATCHING AND DISTRIBUTION GAMES IN REAL LIFE

Real-life Matching

Like all logic game tasks, Matching games correspond to real-life situations that you deal with regularly. Making decisions about what each of several guests will have for dinner provides a perfect illustration. Imagine you have five friends or family members coming over for a meal; call them A, B, C, D, and E. You've prepared plenty of food for everyone. You have two kinds of soup: split pea and minestrone. You have three different entrées: ham, pasta, and roast beef. You've even made a dessert. In real life, absent any artificial rules, your guests could say, "Oh, I want to try both soups," or "I'll have a little ham and a little of the pasta." Some of your guests will have dessert, and some might be too full. Your main concern—and this is what corresponds with the Matching task in a logic game—is that there's plenty for everyone. You can give B ham and still have some left to serve to D and E if they'd like to have it, too. Nothing (except running out) prevents you from serving everyone the roast beef, or anything else.

Now, you can see how the LSAT imposes restrictions on this kind of game. The testmaker can limit the number of entrées each guest has. (The simplest games would simply say, "Each guest will have exactly one kind of soup and exactly one entrée.") They could set restrictions among the guests, e.g., "C will not have any kind of food that A has," or, "B and D will have the same kind of soup." Likewise, they can impose restrictions based on the foods, e.g., "Any guest who has the split pea soup will have ham for an entrée," or, "No guest will have both the minestrone soup and the pasta." Number restrictions are just as important in Matching games as they are in Selection games—or, as you will soon see, Distribution games—but because the items to be matched can be reused, the numbers will play out along two dimensions of the game. In our dinner example, you'll need to pay attention to how many kinds of food you serve to individual guests and how many servings of each kind of food you serve. It's always valuable in Matching to have a clear orientation (an *x*-axis and *y*-axis, if you will) for each part of your task.

	A	B	C	D	E
m/sp	__	__	__	__	__
h/p/rb	__	__	__	__	__
des y/n	__	__	__	__	__

Record the number restrictions along the appropriate rows and columns. That diagram isn't tough to understand, although this fictional menu is more complicated than any Matching game that has actually appeared on the LSAT over the last 10 years.

Real-life Distribution

You engage in Distribution tasks whenever you choose teams for a game, decide which piece of clothing goes in which drawer, assign people to certain locations, or even when you deal out cards from a deck. The key thing to notice is that, in Distribution tasks, once you assign someone or something to a team or a place, you cannot simultaneously assign it somewhere else; the grey suit can't hang in the hall closet and the bedroom closet at the same time; Joe can't be at the New York office and the Boston office concurrently. Think of the entities in Distribution games as individual physical beings or objects. You might move the green chair from the living room to the den, but it can't be in both places at once.

Because real-world models for Distribution so often spring from activities like games and sports, your default assumption will often be that the teams or groups must be made up of equal numbers of players or entities. In most real-world games, each player gets the same number of cards or playing pieces to start. As you've already read (and will again), check your assumptions at the door when you approach logic games. The testmaker must be explicit about number restrictions in Distribution games. If they aren't, don't impose your own limitations.

While there are examples of Distribution tasks that follow an "equal groups" model, there are plenty that don't. A real-world model for Distribution games with unequal teams is a work assignment in which your boss tells you to assign eight employees to three different projects—logistics, marketing, and real estate, let's say—one project per person.

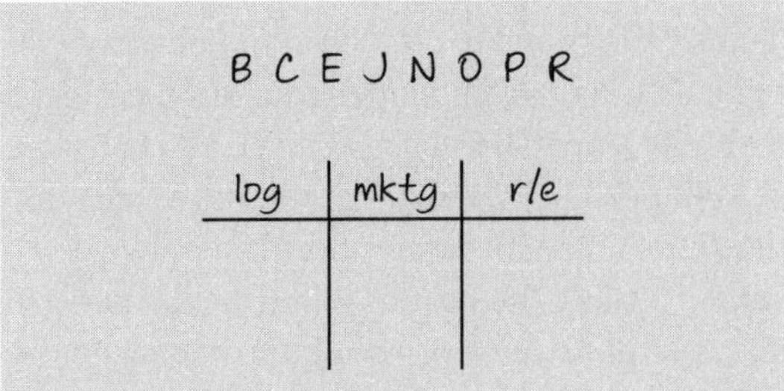

Your first question might be, "How many people do you want on each task?" But your boss responds, "You tell me. I want those projects finished ASAP. If the marketing initiative needs more bodies than the real estate plan, so be it." Like a Distribution setup on the test, your boss might impose some limits without giving you exact numbers: for example, "Just don't put more than four people on the real estate plan."

B C E J N O P R
(max 4)
log
mktg
r/e

You might wish that your boss would be more definite, but you wouldn't let this response stop you from making the proposed assignments. Don't let the lack of numbers stop you from attacking a Distribution game, either.

What's definite in almost any real-world Distribution task is that there are certain people or items you'll want to keep together and certain ones you'll want to keep apart. In choosing basketball teams, you might say, "Tom and Dave are team captains," in order to keep the two tallest guys from being on the same team. Arranging your furniture, you might think, "The chair could go in the living room or the den, but either way, the ottoman has to go with it."

Even your boss might tell you, "I don't care which project you put Peggy on, but don't assign Chuck to the same one," or, "Just make sure Evelyn and Nancy are working together; they're a good team."

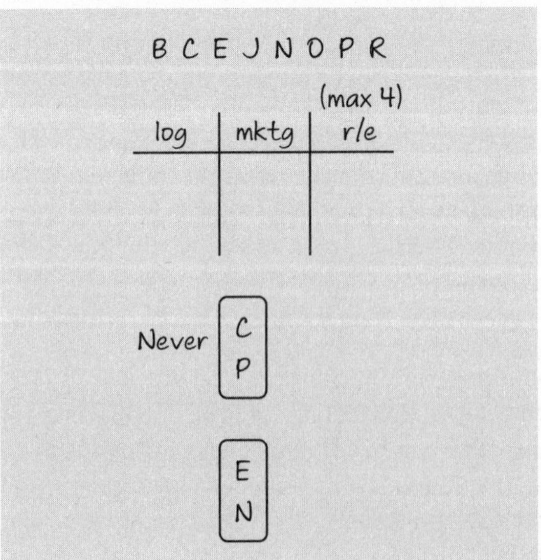

Thinking about how common such restrictions are in real life should take a lot of the sting out of the Formal Logic rules that sometimes appear in Distribution games. It's unlikely that you'd wring your hands or get confused if your boss said, "Look, if you assign Evelyn to the marketing campaign, then put Rosa on the real estate planning team."

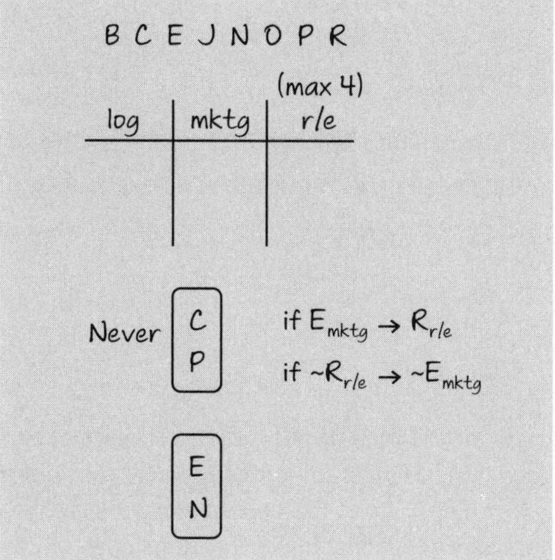

Don't let the testmaker undermine your confidence by using formal conditions, either.

Keep these everyday tasks in mind as you practice Steps 1–4 on Matching and Distribution setups. Logic Games setups almost always present tasks that you would feel confident handling in real life.

MATCHING GAMES TASKS AND SKETCHES

LEARNING OBJECTIVES

In this section of the chapter, you'll practice

- Applying Steps 1 and 2 of the Logic Games Method to Matching games by
  - Asking the SEAL questions to analyze the game's Overview, and then
  - Creating a simple, useful Sketch framework

Prepare

The key to recognizing a Matching game is to find what appears to be two sets of entities. One set is unchanging—the "anchor" set of the game, if you will—and is made up of the people, places, or things receiving items or attributes from the second set. The second set is flexible; some of the people or places in the first set will get all of the items or attributes in the second set, while others may get only some of the items or attributes. Most importantly, in Matching games, the items or attributes in the second set can be matched to more than one of the "anchor" entities.

LOGIC GAMES STRATEGY

Matching games ask you to match

- Attributes, items, or tasks to a certain set of people, places, or things, or
- Attributes (such as color) to a set of items belonging to a certain set of people.

To make the definition of Matching tasks more concrete, consider the following game setup, and consider how an LSAT expert decided to depict its initial sketch.

> In downtown Farlow, there are three doughnut shops, one each on H Street, J Street, and L Street. Each of the shops sells between two and four of the following kinds of doughnuts—crullers, glazed, old fashioned, and sprinkles. The following conditions apply:

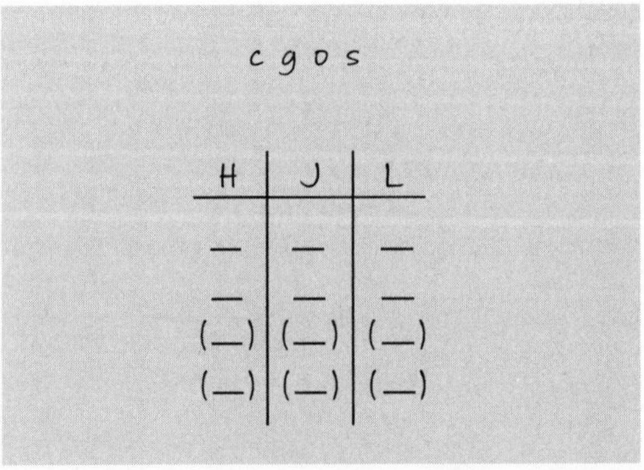

c g o s

H	J	L
—	—	—
—	—	—
(—)	(—)	(—)
(—)	(—)	(—)

The game's task is to determine the types of doughnuts sold at each of three shops. The shops serve as the "anchor" set of entities. They are unchanging. The doughnuts are the items that will be matched to each shop. The shops can have different numbers of doughnuts. Some may sell one or more types sold in another shop. This is a classic Matching game task.

For the record, that game (and virtually all Matching games) could also be depicted with a grid sketch. LSAT experts vary on which type of sketch they prefer. Whenever high scorers use slightly different tactics with equal success, it's a good idea for you to practice a bit with both approaches to see which works best for you.

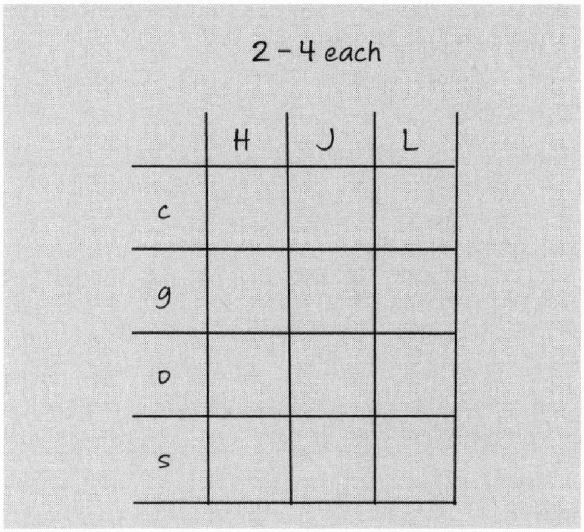

2 – 4 each

	H	J	L
c			
g			
o			
s			

As an aside, students often ask how they can know which set of entities should go on the *x*-axis of their sketch and which should go on the *y*-axis. The answer is that it really doesn't matter as long it's consistent throughout the game. Most people instinctively place the "anchor" set horizontally along the *x*-axis. But, as a practical matter, if you find that the orientation of your sketch is confusing you, stop. Redraw the sketch in the way you've discovered makes more sense, and then get back to the game. Struggling through a game for several minutes with a sketch your brain doesn't fully comprehend will cost you time and, potentially, points on the test. Taking a few seconds to "fix" the sketch is well worth the small effort it takes.

Practice identifying and sketching Matching tasks with the model game setups that follow. Complete expert analysis can be found on the pages following the exercise.

Practice

Directions: Conduct an Overview of each game's setup by asking the SEAL questions, and create an initial sketch framework for the game's action.

Practice 1

A chef will prepare each of three entrées—K, L, and M—each of which will contain at least three of the following ingredients—buttermilk, garlic, onion, paprika, and salt. Each ingredient is used at least once. Preparation of the entrées must also conform to the following conditions:

1. [Step 1] Conduct an Overview analysis:
   - What is this game's Situation?
   - Who or what are the game's Entities?
   - What is the game's Action?
   - What are the Limitations explicit in the game setup?
2. [Step 2] Create an initial Sketch:

Practice 2

A financial advisor is meeting with four clients—Jordan, Klaus, Lisa, and Marie. Each client is investing in at least one of five mutual funds—energy, financials, gold, healthcare, and international—and no others. Investing choices must conform to the following conditions:

1. [Step 1] Conduct an Overview analysis:
   - What is this game's Situation?
   - Who or what are the game's Entities?
   - What is the game's Action?
   - What are the Limitations explicit in the game setup?
2. [Step 2] Create an initial Sketch:

Practice 3

A video game designer is creating a game for young children that involves players progressing through four separate levels, from level 1 to level 4. On each level, players are offered at least one reward—an apple, a bagel, or a cookie—and will encounter at least one obstacle—a mud pit, an oil slick, or quicksand. The designer is limited by the following constraints:

1. [Step 1] Conduct an Overview analysis:
   - What is this game's Situation?
   - Who or what are the game's Entities?
   - What is the game's Action?
   - What are the Limitations explicit in the game setup?
2. [Step 2] Create an initial Sketch:

Explanations

Compare your work to that of an LSAT expert. Keep track of any case in which you incorrectly characterized the action described in the setup, and any case in which you drew a sketch framework that does not match the details of the game's situation.

Practice 1

A chef will prepare each of three entrées—K, L, and M—each of which will contain at least three of the following ingredients—buttermilk, garlic, onion, paprika, and salt. Each ingredient is used at least once. Preparation of the entrées must also conform to the following conditions:

1. [Step 1] Conduct an Overview analysis:
   - What is this game's Situation? *A chef preparing three entrées.*
   - Who or what are the game's Entities? *Three entrées—K, L, and M—and five ingredients—b, g, o, p, and s.*
   - What is the game's Action? *Matching; determine which ingredients will be used in each entrée.*
   - What are the Limitations explicit in the game setup? *Each entrée will receive at least three ingredients. Each ingredient needs to be used at least once.*
2. [Step 2] Create an initial Sketch:

Practice 2

A financial advisor is meeting with four clients—Jordan, Klaus, Lisa, and Marie. Each client is investing in at least one of five mutual funds—energy, financials, gold, healthcare, and international—and no others. Investing choices must conform to the following conditions:

1. [Step 1] Conduct an Overview analysis:
   - What is this game's Situation? *Clients making investments into mutual funds.*
   - Who or what are the game's Entities? *Four clients—J, K, L, and M—and five mutual funds—e, f, g, h, i.*
   - What is the game's Action? *Matching; determine the mutual funds in which each person invests.*
   - What are the Limitations explicit in the game setup? *Each person invested in at least one fund, but there's no limit to how many people can invest in each fund. It's possible some funds go unused.*
2. [Step 2] Create an initial Sketch:

Practice 3

A video game designer is creating a game for young children that involves players progressing through four separate levels, from level 1 to level 4. On each level, players are offered at least one reward—an apple, a bagel, or a cookie—and will encounter at least one obstacle—a mud pit, an oil slick, or quicksand. The designer is limited by the following constraints:

1. [Step 1] Conduct an Overview analysis:
   - What is this game's Situation? *A video game designer creating levels for a kid's game.*
   - Who or what are the game's Entities? *Four levels—1, 2, 3, and 4—and six items—rewards A, B, and C; obstacles m, o, and q.*
   - What is the game's Action? *Matching; for each level, determine which rewards and/or obstacles will appear.*
   - What are the Limitations explicit in the game setup? *Each floor will include at least one reward and at least one obstacle. No limits are set, so it's possible that some rewards or obstacles will not appear in the game.*

2. [Step 2] Create an initial Sketch:

	1	2	3	4	
rew:	__	__	__	__	A B C
obst:	__	__	__	__	m o q

With your sketches in place, it's time to add in the rules. Practice applying Step 2 of the Logic Games Method to Matching games in the next section.

MATCHING GAMES RULES

LEARNING OBJECTIVES

In this section of the chapter, you'll practice

- Applying Step 3 of the Logic Games Method to Matching games by analyzing and sketching the rules

Prepare

Numbers are at the heart of Matching games, and it's likely that one or more rules will present some restriction on how many attributes can be matched to particular "anchor" entities, and that other rules will establish or limit the number of "anchor" entities to which a particular attribute can be matched. Those number restrictions—along with simpler rules that stipulate that a particular anchor must or cannot have a given attribute, or that certain attributes must or cannot be matched to the same "anchor"—usually lead to important deductions during Step 4 in Matching games.

LOGIC GAMES STRATEGY

Matching rules tell you one or more of the following:

- Attributes that must or cannot be matched to the same entity.
- The number of attributes that must, can, or cannot be assigned to an entity, or the relative numbers among entities (e.g., Frances is assigned to review more books than Greg is).
- Conditions triggering the assignment of an attribute to a particular entity (e.g., if Horace's painting has blue in it, then Inez's painting has red in it).

How you choose to depict the rules in Matching games depends a lot on how you chose to draw the initial sketch. To see this in action, here is the doughnut-shop setup along with four typical Matching rules.

> In downtown Farlow, there are three doughnut shops, one each on H Street, J Street, and L Street. Each of the shops sells between two and four of the following kinds of doughnuts—crullers, glazed, old fashioned, and sprinkles. The following conditions apply:
>
> > Exactly two shops sell old fashioned doughnuts.
> > Any shop that sells crullers does not sell glazed doughnuts.
> > The shop on L Street sells more kinds of doughnuts than the shop on J Street.
> > The shop on H Street sells glazed doughnuts.

Take a look at those rules depicted in the sketch you saw in the preceding section.

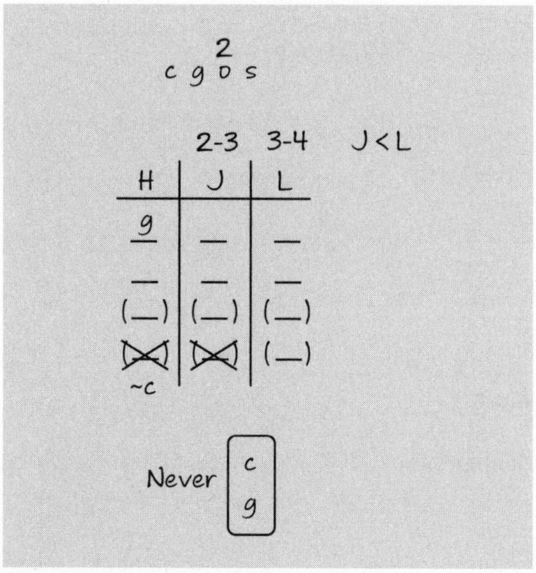

The LSAT expert noted Rule 1 above the “o” (for old fashioned) in the roster of entities to be matched. The expert jotted down Rule 2 in shorthand underneath the sketch. The LSAT expert noted Rule 3 just to the side of the columns representing the “anchor” entities, and it is built into the sketch in two ways: first, J’s fourth slot is crossed off (if L sells more types of doughnuts than J, then J does not sell all four), and the possible numbers of doughnut types for J and L are recorded above their respective columns. Finally, Rule 4 was drawn directly into H’s column. The expert even anticipated one of the deductions in this game. Because H sells glazed doughnuts, Rule 2 prevents it from selling crullers. Most rules in Matching games can be depicted in and around the initial sketch in ways that logically relate them to the entities they restrict.

Here’s how those rules would appear in a grid sketch. Notice that the expert follows the same principles—depicting the rules in and around the entities they restrict—even though the sketch framework is slightly different.

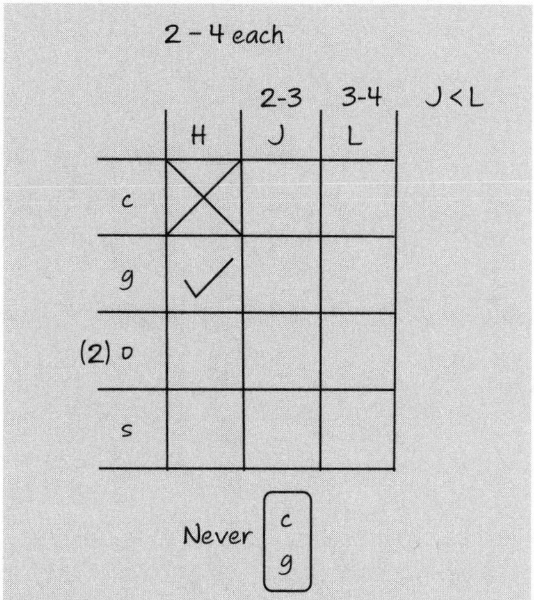

Review the following expert analyses of a handful of other common Matching game rules. Here, again, pay attention to how the rules are depicted in ways that fit the game’s sketch.

Rule	Analysis
A game in which three theaters—1, 2 and 3—each show at least one of five movies—a comedy, a drama, a fantasy, a horror film, and a mystery.	

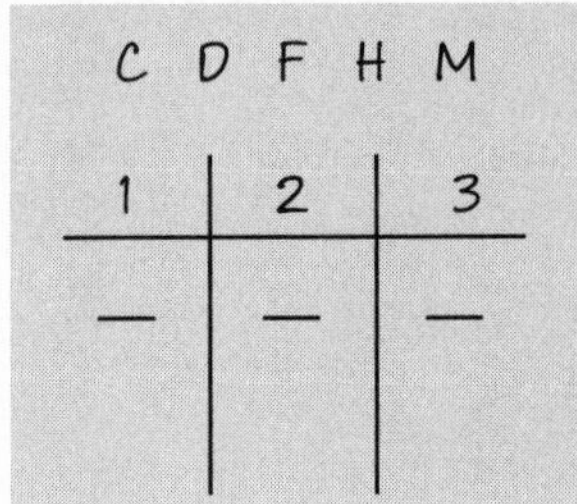

Rule		Analysis
Exactly two theaters will show the fantasy.	→	F = 2x
Exactly two films will be shown in theater 1.	→	1 | 2 | 3 (theater 1: two slots; theaters 2 and 3: one slot each)
If theater 2 shows the horror film, then theater 3 shows the comedy.	→	If H in 2 → C in 3 If ~C in 3 → ~H in 2

A game in which four athletes—J, K, L, and M—each participate in at least one of three sports—rugby, soccer, or tennis.

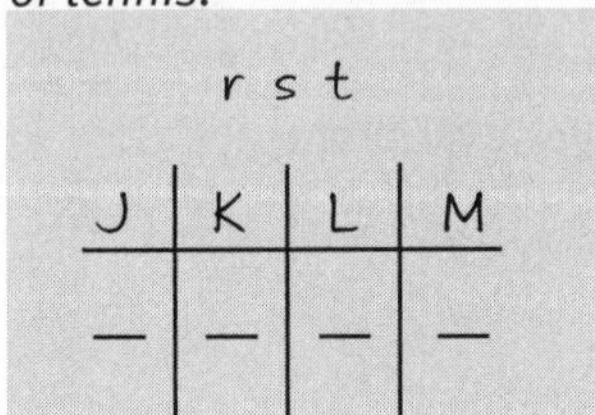

Rule		Analysis
M participates in rugby.	→	J | K | L | M (r in M's column)
J participates in exactly the same sports as K.	→	J = K
If L participates in soccer, then M participates in tennis.	→	If L = s → M = t If M ≠ t → L ≠ s

Now, practice analyzing and drawing Matching game rules. There are four exercises. The first provides 12 Matching game rules associated with four simple descriptions of the setups with which they are associated. Then, you'll see three exercises that add full sets of rules to each of the three setups you worked with in the previous section of this chapter.

Practice

Practice 1

Directions: Analyze and draw each of the following Matching game rules. Use the brief game description to guide your depiction of the game's framework.

Rule		My Analysis
A game in which three riders—L, M, and N—each ride at least one of six horses—a black horse, a champagne horse, a gray horse, a roan horse, a sorrel horse, and a white horse.		
1. L rides the grey horse.	→	
2. The champagne horse and the white horse are never ridden by the same person.	→	
3. M rides exactly two of the horses.	→	
A game in which each of six albums—R, S, T, V, W, and X—contains at least one of three musical genres—classical, jazz, and opera.		
4. If R contains jazz, then S contains classical.	→	
5. T and X have no musical genres in common.	→	
6. Exactly three of the albums contain jazz.	→	
A game in which four dresses each use at least one of six colors—green, orange, red, white, violet, and yellow.		
7. Any dress that contains red also contains white.	→	
8. A dress contains yellow if, and only if, it contains green.	→	
9. No dress can contain both orange and violet.	→	
A game in which five houses—1, 2, 3, 4, and 5—each contain at least one of four features—balcony, fireplace, patio, and skylight.		
10. House 2 contains neither a patio nor a skylight.	→	
11. No house contains both a balcony and a patio.	→	
12. Houses 1 and 4 have no features in common.	→	

Practice 2

Directions: Take a couple of minutes to review the game setup, summarize your Overview analysis, and recreate the initial Sketch. Then, one at a time, analyze the rules, answer the questions about each one, and draw the rule either inside or underneath the sketch framework.

A chef will prepare each of three entrées—K, L, and M—each of which will contain at least three of the following ingredients—buttermilk, garlic, onion, paprika, and salt. Each ingredient is used at least once. Preparation of the entrées must also conform to the following conditions:

No entrée contains all five ingredients.
Entrée L does not contain onion.
Garlic is used in exactly two of the entrées.
Entrée L contains more of these ingredients than entrée K.

1. [Step 1] Summarize your Overview analysis:

2. [Step 2] Create an initial Sketch:

3. [Step 3] Analyze and draw the Rules:
   - For each rule, answer the following questions and draw the rule in the appropriate box.
     - What does the rule restrict, and what does it leave open?
     - What are the rule's negative implications, if any?
     - Can the rule be depicted inside the sketch framework?

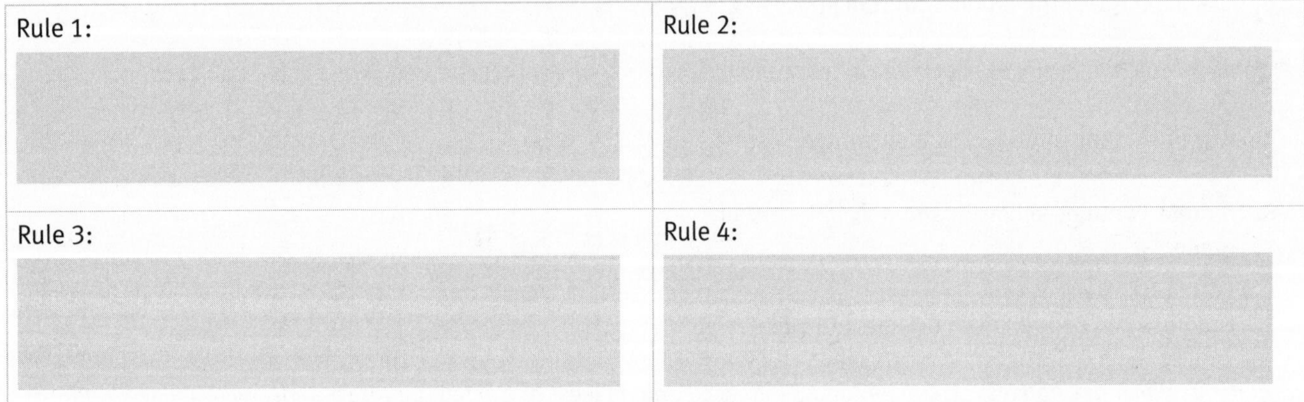

Practice 3

Directions: Take a couple of minutes to review the game setup, summarize your Overview analysis, and recreate the initial Sketch. Then, one at a time, analyze the rules, answer the questions about each one, and draw the rule either inside or underneath the sketch framework.

A financial advisor is meeting with four clients—Jordan, Klaus, Lisa, and Marie. Each client is investing in at least one of five mutual funds—energy, financials, gold, healthcare, and international—and no others. Investing choices must conform to the following conditions:

Lisa invests in gold.
Klaus invests in neither energy nor healthcare.
At least three of the clients invest in financials.
Klaus invests in every fund that Marie invests in.

1. [Step 1] Summarize your Overview analysis:

2. [Step 2] Create an initial Sketch:

3. [Step 3] Analyze and draw the Rules:
   - For each rule, answer the following questions and draw the rule in the appropriate box.
     - What does the rule restrict, and what does it leave open?
     - What are the rule's negative implications, if any?
     - Can the rule be depicted inside the sketch framework?

Rule 1:	Rule 2:
Rule 3:	Rule 4:

Practice 4

Directions: Take a couple of minutes to review the game setup, summarize your Overview analysis, and recreate the initial Sketch. Then, one at a time, analyze the rules, answer the questions about each one, and draw the rule either inside or underneath the sketch framework.

A video game designer is creating a game for young children that involves players progressing through four separate levels, from level 1 to level 4. On each level, players are offered at least one reward—an apple, a bagel, or a cookie—and will encounter at least one obstacle—a mud pit, an oil slick, or quicksand. The designer is limited by the following constraints:

No reward or obstacle can appear more than once on any level.
No reward can appear on three consecutive levels.
Level 2 has an apple, and level 3 has both a mud pit and quicksand.
Level 4 has a greater combined total of rewards and obstacles than does level 2.
Level 2 has a greater number of obstacles than each of level 3 and level 4.

1. [Step 1] Summarize your Overview analysis:

2. [Step 2] Create an initial Sketch:

3. [Step 3] Analyze and draw the Rules:
    - For each rule, answer the following questions and draw the rule in the appropriate box.
        - What does the rule restrict, and what does it leave open?
        - What are the rule's negative implications, if any?
        - Can the rule be depicted inside the sketch framework?

Rule 1:	Rule 2:
Rule 3:	Rule 4:
Rule 5:	

Explanations

Compare your work to that of an LSAT expert. Pay close attention to how the expert analyzed each rule and then depicted it within or beneath the game's initial sketch.

Practice 1

Rule	Analysis
A game in which three riders—L, M, and N, each ride at least one of six horses—a black horse, a champagne horse, a gray horse, a roan horse, a sorrel horse, and a white horse.	

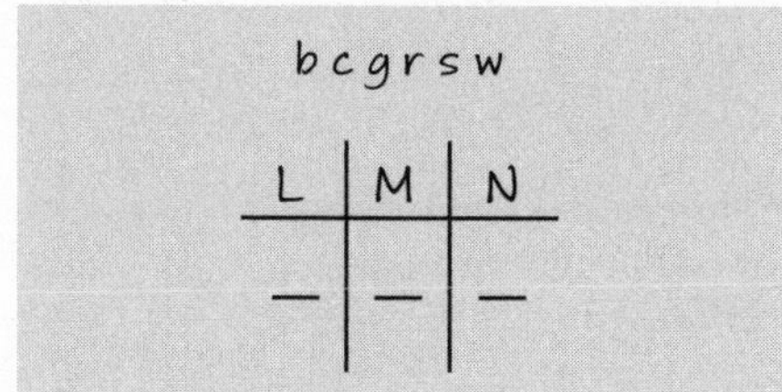

Rule	Analysis
1. L rides the gray horse.	→ L | M | N; g | — | —
2. The champagne horse and the white horse are never ridden by the same person.	→ never [c w]
3. M rides exactly two of the horses.	→ L | M | N; — | — | —; = under M
A game in which each of six albums—R, S, T, V, W, and X—contains at least one of three musical genres—classical, jazz, and opera.	

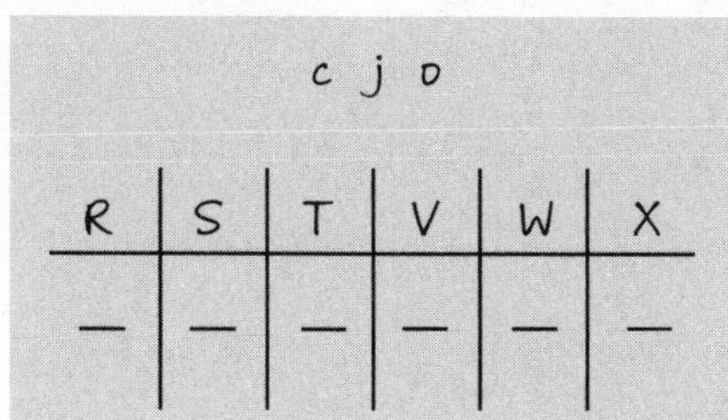

Rule	Analysis
4. If R contains jazz, then S contains classical.	→ If R = j → S = c If S ≠ c → R ≠ j
5. T and X have no musical genres in common.	→ T ≠ X
6. Exactly three of the albums contain jazz.	→ c j o / j / j / = OR: exactly 3 j

A game in which four dresses each use at least one of six colors—green, orange, red, white, violet, and yellow.

G O R W V Y

1	2	3	4
—	—	—	—

7. Any dress that contains red also contains white. → If R → W; If ~W → ~R

8. A dress contains yellow if, and only if, it contains green. → If Y → G; If G → Y; If ~G → ~Y; If ~Y → ~G; OR [G Y] or neither

9. No dress can contain both orange and violet. → never [O V]

A game in which each of five houses—1, 2, 3, 4, and 5—contains at least one of four features—balcony, fireplace, patio, and skylight.

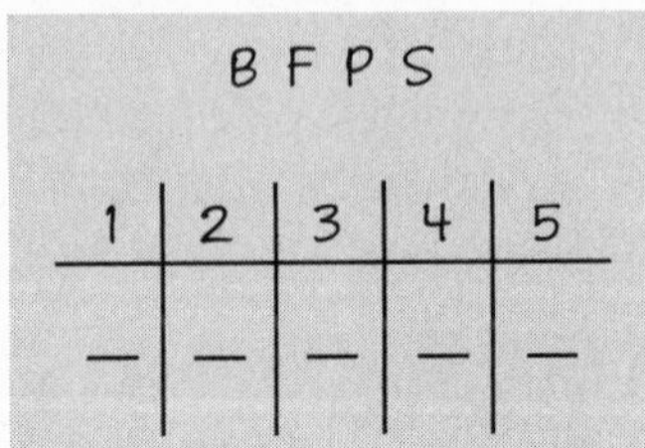

10. House 2 contains neither a patio nor a skylight. →

1	2	3	4	5
—	B/F — ~P ~S (BF?)	—	—	—

11. No house contains both a balcony and a patio. → never [B P]

12. Houses 1 and 4 have no features in common. → 1 ≠ 4

Practice 2

A chef will prepare each of three entrées—K, L, and M—each of which will contain at least three of the following ingredients—buttermilk, garlic, onion, paprika, and salt. Each ingredient is used at least once. Preparation of the entrées must also conform to the following conditions:

> No entrée contains all five ingredients.
> Entrée L does not contain onion.
> Garlic is used in exactly two of the entrées.
> Entrée L contains more of these ingredients than entrée K.

1. [Step 1] Summarize your Overview analysis: *A Matching game in which a chef will use at least three of five ingredients in each of three entrées. Ingredients can be used in multiple entrées, and each ingredient will be used at least once.*

2. [Step 2] Create an initial Sketch:

3. [Step 3] Analyze and draw the Rules:
   - Rule 1:
     - What does the rule restrict, and what does it leave open? *The rule prevents any entrée from having all five ingredients.*
     - What are the rule's negative implications, if any? *Because an entrée has at least three but can't have all five, an entrée is limited to either three or four ingredients.*
     - Can the rule be depicted inside the sketch framework? *No.*
     - Draw the rule:

never all 5 ing.

   - Rule 2:
     - What does the rule restrict, and what does it leave open? *Entrée L won't get onion, but it could still get anything else.*
     - What are the rule's negative implications, if any? *Either entrée K or M gets onion, if not both.*
     - Can the rule be depicted inside the sketch framework? *Yes.*
     - Draw the rule:

   - Rule 3:
     - What does the rule restrict, and what does it leave open? *Exactly two entrées get garlic, but it could be any pair.*
     - What are the rule's negative implications, if any? *One entrée will not get garlic.*
     - Can the rule be depicted inside the sketch framework? *No.*
     - Draw the rule:

b g o p s
g

Or: exactly 2g

   - Rule 4:
     - What does the rule restrict, and what does it leave open? *Entrée L gets more ingredients than K.*
     - What are the rule's negative implications, if any? *Entrée L cannot have the minimum of three.*
     - Can the rule be depicted inside the sketch framework? *Yes; add a fourth slot to L, and draw a double line under K's three slots to indicate that it cannot have more ingredients.*

- Draw the rule:

Practice 3

A financial advisor is meeting with four clients—Jordan, Klaus, Lisa, and Marie. Each client has decided to invest in at least one of five mutual funds—energy, financials, gold, healthcare, and international—and no others. Investing choices must conform to the following conditions:

> Lisa invests in gold.
> Klaus invests in neither energy nor healthcare.
> At least three of the clients invest in financials.
> Klaus invests in every fund that Marie invests in.

1. [Step 1] Summarize your Overview analysis: *A Matching game in which four people invest in one or more of five different mutual funds.*

2. [Step 2] Create an initial Sketch:

3. [Step 3] Analyze and draw the Rules:
   - Rule 1:
     - What does the rule restrict, and what does it leave open? *Lisa invests in gold, but could invest in other funds. Also, other people can invest in gold, too.*
     - What are the rule's negative implications, if any? *N/A*
     - Can the rule be depicted inside the sketch framework? *Yes.*
     - Draw the rule:

J | K | L | M
g

   - Rule 2:
     - What does the rule restrict, and what does it leave open? *Energy and healthcare are ruled out for Klaus.*
     - What are the rule's negative implications, if any? *Klaus still has to invest in at least one of financials, gold, or international.*
     - Can the rule be depicted inside the sketch framework? *Yes.*
     - Draw the rule:

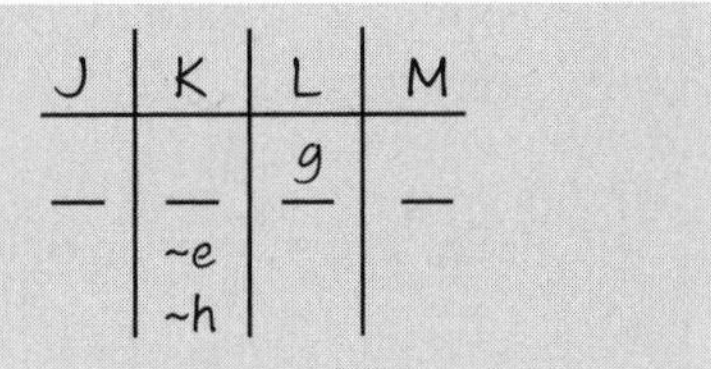

   - Rule 3:
     - What does the rule restrict, and what does it leave open? *At least three of the clients invest in financials, but it could be any of the three or all four.*
     - What are the rule's negative implications, if any? *At most, only one of the investors will not invest in financials.*
     - Can the rule be depicted inside the sketch framework? *No; remember that the rule says "at least three," not exactly three.*
     - Draw the rule:

at least 3 f

   - Rule 4:
     - What does the rule restrict, and what does it leave open? *If Marie invests in something, then so does Klaus. Klaus could invest in more, but has to have at least as many investments as Marie.*
     - What are the rule's negative implications, if any? *By contrapositive, if Klaus doesn't invest in a particular fund, then Marie can't invest in that fund.*

- Can the rule be depicted inside the sketch framework? *No.*
- Draw the rule:

If M → K

If ~K → ~M

Practice 4

A video game designer is creating a game for young children that involves players progressing through four separate levels, from level 1 to level 4. On each level, players are offered at least one reward—an apple, a bagel, or a cookie—and will encounter at least one obstacle—a mud pit, an oil slick, or quicksand. The designer is limited by the following constraints:

No reward or obstacle can appear more than once on any level.

No reward can appear on three consecutive levels.

Level 2 has an apple, and level 3 has both a mud pit and quicksand.

Level 4 has a greater combined total of rewards and obstacles than does level 2.

Level 2 has a greater number of obstacles than each of level 3 and level 4.

1. [Step 1] Summarize your Overview analysis: *A Matching game in which at least one of three rewards and at least one of three obstacles are assigned to each of four levels in a kids' video game. Rewards and obstacles can be repeated on different levels.*

2. [Step 2] Create an initial Sketch:

	1	2	3	4	
rew:	_	_	_	_	A B C
obst:	_	_	_	_	m o q

3. [Step 3] Analyze and draw the Rules:
   - Rule 1:
     - What does the rule restrict, and what does it leave open? *Entities can be used only once on each level.*
     - What are the rule's negative implications, if any? *Entities cannot appear multiple times on any given level.*
     - Can the rule be depicted inside the sketch framework? *No.*
     - Draw the rule:

       no dupl. in level

   - Rule 2:
     - What does the rule restrict, and what does it leave open? *No reward can appear on three consecutive levels. This does not put the same restriction on obstacles.*
     - What are the rule's negative implications, if any? *No reward will appear on all four levels. And if a reward is used three times in the game, it would be on levels 1, 2, and 4 or levels 1, 3, and 4.*
     - Can the rule be depicted inside the sketch framework? *No.*
     - Draw the rule:

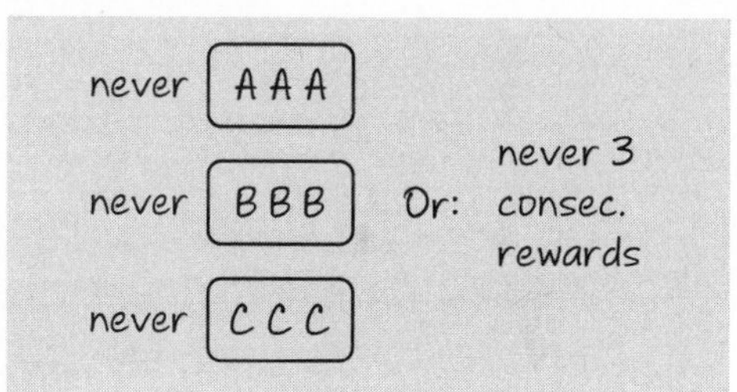

   - Rule 3:
     - What does the rule restrict, and what does it leave open? *A reward is established in level 2 and two obstacles are established in level 3. Level 2 still needs an obstacle and level 3 still needs a reward.*
     - What are the rule's negative implications, if any? *N/A*
     - Can the rule be depicted inside the sketch framework? *Yes.*
     - Draw the rule:

	1	2	3	4	
rew:	_	A	_	_	A B C
obst:	_	_	m q	_	m o q

- Rule 4:
  - What does the rule restrict, and what does it leave open? *The total number of items in level 4 is greater than the total number of items in level 2. The exact numbers are unknown.*
  - What are the rule's negative implications, if any? *Level 2 cannot get everything. It has a maximum of five items.*
  - Can the rule be depicted inside the sketch framework? *No.*
  - Draw the rule:

total: 4 > 2

- Rule 5:
  - What does the rule restrict, and what does it leave open? *Level 2 has more obstacles than level 3 and level 4. So, level 2 will have at least two obstacles, but it could be any two—or all three.*
  - What are the rule's negative implications, if any? *Neither level 3 nor level 4 will get all three obstacles.*
  - Can the rule be depicted inside the sketch framework? *No.*
  - Draw the rule:

obst: 2 > 3

obst: 2 > 4

Matching games typically have multiple deductions, often centered around the number restrictions and duplications among the various entities. You may have spotted some of them already as you were analyzing and drawing out the rules. If there were any you missed, you'll have the chance to discover them as you rigorously apply Step 4 of the Logic Games Method to these games in the next section of this chapter.

MATCHING GAMES DEDUCTIONS

LEARNING OBJECTIVES

In this section of the chapter, you'll practice

- Applying Step 4 of the Logic Games Method to Matching games by combining rules and restrictions to make all valid deductions in the game.

Prepare

In the section on Matching games rules, you saw the importance of drawing the rules in ways that reflect the visual orientation of the game's setup. Whether you prefer to use list-style or grid-style sketch frameworks for Matching games, continue that emphasis on accurate visual depiction of the game as you add the deductions.

LOGIC GAMES STRATEGY

In Matching games, deductions are likely to stem from:

- **Duplications**—Entities shared by two or more rules; one rule might match a certain attribute to entity X, and another might tell you that entity Y has more attributes to it than X does.
- **Number Restrictions**—Limitations on the number of attributes that can be assigned to a given entity of limitations on the number of entities to which an attribute can be matched.
- **Established Entities**—Matches between entities and attributes that must be maintained throughout the game (e.g., Luis uses blueberries in his pie); Established Entities are quite common in Matching games.

In Matching games, deductions may involve:

- **Blocks of Entities**—Two or more entities that must be assigned a given attribute, or two or more attributes that must be assigned to the same entity or entities; Blocks are somewhat rare in Matching games.
- **Limited Options**—The situation that arises when a rule or a combination of rules makes all acceptable arrangements fall into one of two patterns; Limited Options is a rare deduction to find in Matching games.

In any Matching game, pay attention to numbers restrictions that affect multiple entities. For example, in the model setup about the three doughnut shops, Rule 3 required L to sell more kinds of doughnuts than J. From that, the LSAT expert was able to deduce that J could not sell all four kinds of doughnuts mentioned in the game, and built that deduction into the sketch at the same time as the expert recorded the rule.

> In downtown Farlow, there are three doughnut shops, one each on H Street, J Street, and L Street. Each of the shops sells between two and four of the following kinds of doughnuts—crullers, glazed, old fashioned, and sprinkles. The following conditions apply:
>
> Exactly two shops sell old fashioned doughnuts.
> Any shop that sells crullers does not sell glazed doughnuts.
> The shop on L Street sells more kinds of doughnuts than the shop on J Street.
> The shop on H Street sells glazed doughnuts.

2
c g o s

2-3 3-4 J<L

H J L

g

~c

Never c g

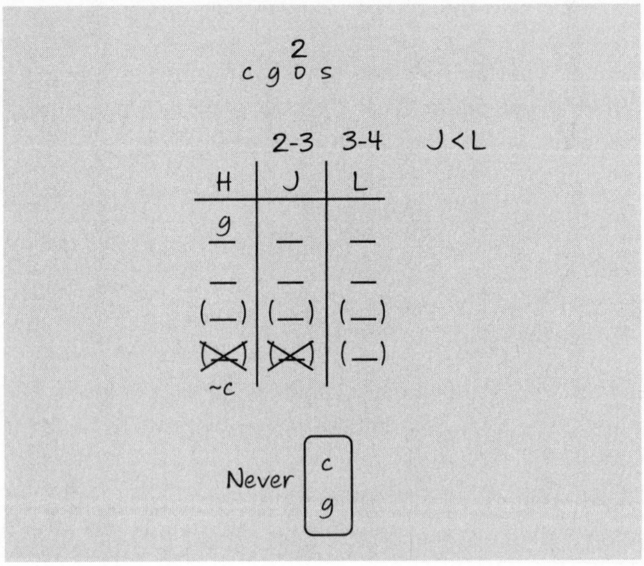

The expert also made a deduction from the duplication of *g* in Rules 2 and 4, that H cannot sell crullers because it sells glazed doughnuts.

You'll spot similar deductions as you practice applying Step 4 of the Logic Games Method to the now familiar model game setups you've been working with. Just as the LSAT expert did with the doughnut shop game, you may already have spotted some of these deductions as you were analyzing and drawing the rules.

Practice

Directions: In each game setup, first reacquaint yourself with the setup and rules. Then, combine the rules and restrictions to make all available deductions, recording your analyses as indicated. Finally, test your deductions by answering the questions that accompany each game. You can find expert analysis and explanations at the end of the Practice section.

Practice 1

A chef will prepare each of three entrées—K, L, and M—each of which will contain at least three of the following ingredients—buttermilk, garlic, onion, paprika, and salt. Each ingredient is used at least once. Preparation of the entrées must also conform to the following conditions:

No entrée contains all five ingredients.
Entrée L does not contain onion.
Garlic is used in exactly two of the entrées.
Entrée L contains more of these ingredients than entrée K.

b g o p s
g

K	L	M
—	—	—
—	—	—
—	—	—
	~o	

never all 5 ing.
L > K
exactly 2g

1. Which entities or positions are the most restricted in this game? Why?

2. Which elements from the BLEND checklist can you identify in this game? Are there
   - Blocks of entities? If so, what are they?
   - Limited Options? If so, which rule(s) trigger them?
   - Established Entities? If so, which ones?
   - Number Restrictions? If so, describe them.
   - Duplications? If so, which rules share an entity?

3. Combine the rules and restrictions to create a Master Sketch depicting all of the deductions available in this game:

4. Evaluate your sketch by answering the following questions:
   - How many entrées can include onion?
   - Which ingredients can be used in all three entrées?
   - Which ingredients can entrées K and M have in common?
   - What is the maximum total number of ingredients that can be used in all three entrées?

Practice 2

A financial advisor is meeting with four clients—Jordan, Klaus, Lisa, and Marie. Each client is investing in at least one of five mutual funds—energy, financials, gold, healthcare, and international—and no others. Investing choices must conform to the following conditions:

Lisa invests in gold.
Klaus invests in neither energy nor healthcare.
At least three of the clients invest in financials.
Klaus invests in every fund that Marie invests in.

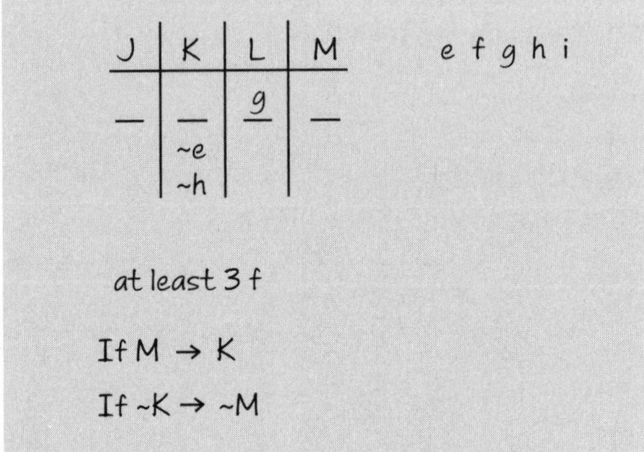

1. Which entities or positions are the most restricted in this game? Why?

2. Which elements from the BLEND checklist can you identify in this game? Are there
   - Blocks of entities? If so, what are they?
   - Limited Options? If so, which rule(s) trigger them?
   - Established Entities? If so, which ones?
   - Number Restrictions? If so, describe them.
   - Duplications? If so, which rules share an entity?

3. Combine the rules and restrictions to create a Master Sketch depicting all of the deductions available in this game:

4. Evaluate your sketch by answering the following questions:
   - What is the maximum number of investments that Marie can make?
   - Which clients can invest in energy?
   - Which funds can be invested in by all four clients?
   - Who can invest in financials if Lisa invests in only one fund?

Practice 3

A video game designer is creating a game for young children that involves players progressing through four separate levels, from level 1 to level 4. On each level, players are offered at least one reward—an apple, a bagel, or a cookie—and will encounter at least one obstacle—a mud pit, an oil slick, or quicksand. The designer is limited by the following constraints:

No reward or obstacle can appear more than once on any level.
No reward can appear on three consecutive levels.
Level 2 has an apple, and level 3 has both a mud pit and quicksand.
Level 4 has a greater combined total of rewards and obstacles than does level 2.
Level 2 has a greater number of obstacles than each of level 3 and level 4.

	1	2	3	4	
rew:	_	A	_	_	ABC
obst:	_	_	m q	_	moq

never AAA
never BBB
never CCC

no dupl. in level
total: 4 > 2
obst: 2 > 3
obst: 2 > 4

1. Which entities or positions are the most restricted in this game? Why?

2. Which elements from the BLEND checklist can you identify in this game? Are there
   - Blocks of entities? If so, what are they?
   - Limited Options? If so, which rule(s) trigger them?
   - Established Entities? If so, which ones?
   - Number Restrictions? If so, describe them.
   - Duplications? If so, which rules share an entity?

3. Combine the rules and restrictions to create a Master Sketch depicting all of the deductions available in this game:

4. Evaluate your sketch by answering the following questions:
   - Which rewards can appear on level 3?
   - Which rewards or obstacles can appear on all four levels?
   - Which levels can include both a cookie and an oil slick?
   - What is the maximum total rewards and obstacles for any level?

Explanations

Compare your work to that of an LSAT expert. Pay close attention to how the expert combined the rules and restrictions to make additional deductions, and to how the expert depicted the deductions within the sketch framework.

Practice 1

A chef will prepare each of three entrées—K, L, and M—each of which will contain at least three of the following ingredients—buttermilk, garlic, onion, paprika, and salt. Each ingredient is used at least once. Preparation of the entrées must also conform to the following conditions:

No entrée contains all five ingredients.
Entrée L does not contain onion.
Garlic is used in exactly two of the entrées.
Entrée L contains more of these ingredients than entrée K.

Which entities or positions are the most restricted in this game? Why? *Entrée L, because it needs more ingredients than entrée K yet cannot use onion.*

1. Which elements from the BLEND checklist can you identify in this game? Are there
    - Blocks of entities? If so, what are they? *N/A*
    - Limited Options? If so, which rule(s) trigger them? *N/A*
    - Established Entities? If so, which ones? *N/A*
    - Number Restrictions? If so, describe them. *Rule 1 reduces the maximum number of ingredients in a entrée. Rule 3 limits garlic to just two entrées. Rule 4 gives entrée L more ingredients than entrée K.*
    - Duplications? If so, which rules share an entity? *Rules 2 and 4 both mention entrée L.*
2. Combine the rules and restrictions to create a Master Sketch depicting all of the deductions available in this game:

    K has to have at least three ingredients. L has to have more, so it has to have at least four, but it can't have all five. So L has exactly four, limiting K to just three.

3.

K	L	M
—	—	—
—	—	—
—	—	—
=	—	
	=	

L cannot have onion, so its four ingredients must be buttermilk, garlic, paprika, and salt.

K	L	M
—	b	—
—	g	—
—	p	—
=	s	
	=	

L has garlic, which means only one more entrée—K or M—will have garlic.

4. Evaluate your sketch by answering the following questions:
    - How many entrées can include onion? *Two; it's not in entrée L, but it could be in both K and M.*
    - Which ingredients can be used in all three entrées? *Buttermilk, paprika, and salt; garlic is in only two entrées, and L doesn't use onion.*
    - Which ingredients can entrées K and M have in common? *Any three of buttermilk, onion, paprika, and salt.*
    - What is the maximum total number of ingredients that can be used in all three entrées? *Eleven; K and L are set at three and four, respectively. M cannot have all five, but can have four.*

Practice 2

A financial advisor is meeting with four clients—Jordan, Klaus, Lisa, and Marie. Each client is investing in at least one of five mutual funds—energy, financials, gold, healthcare, and international—and no others. Investing choices must conform to the following conditions:

Lisa invests in gold.
Klaus invests in neither energy nor healthcare.
At least three of the clients invest in financials.
Klaus invests in every fund that Marie invests in.

1. Which entities or positions are the most restricted in this game? Why? *Klaus, who cannot have energy or healthcare, but needs to share investments with Marie.*

2. Which elements from the BLEND checklist can you identify in this game? Are there
   - Blocks of entities? If so, what are they? *N/A*
   - Limited Options? If so, which rule(s) trigger them? *N/A*
   - Established Entities? If so, which ones? *Rule 1 establishes gold for Lisa.*
   - Number Restrictions? If so, describe them. *Rule 3 sets a minimum of three clients getting the financials fund.*
   - Duplications? If so, which rules share an entity? *Rules 2 and 4 mention Klaus.*

3. Combine the rules and restrictions to create a Master Sketch depicting all of the deductions available in this game: *By the contrapositive of Rule 4, if Klaus doesn't invest in a fund, then Marie can't invest in that fund. That means Marie can't invest in energy or healthcare.*

J	K	L	M
—	—	g	—
	~e		~e
	~h		~h

The contrapositive also affects financials. If Klaus didn't invest in financials, then Marie couldn't. That would leave just two clients who could invest in financials, which would not be enough to satisfy Rule 3. So, Klaus must invest in financials.

J	K	L	M
—	f	g	—
	~e		~e
	~h		~h

4. Evaluate your sketch by answering the following questions:
   - What is the maximum number of investments that Marie can make? *Three—financials, gold, and international.*
   - Which clients can invest in energy? *Jordan and Lisa.*
   - Which funds can be invested in by all four clients? *Financials, gold, and international.*
   - Who must invest in financials if Lisa invests in only one fund? *Jordan, Klaus, and Marie; three people must invest in financials, and Lisa must invest in gold.*

Practice 3

A video game designer is creating a game for young children that involves players progressing through four separate levels, from level 1 to level 4. On each level, players are offered at least one reward—an apple, a bagel, or a cookie—and will encounter at least one obstacle—a mud pit, an oil slick, or quicksand. The designer is limited by the following constraints:

No reward or obstacle can appear more than once on any level.
No reward can appear on three consecutive levels.
Level 2 has an apple, and level 3 has both a mud pit and quicksand.
Level 4 has a greater combined total of rewards and obstacles than does level 2.
Level 2 has a greater number of obstacles than each of level 3 and level 4.

1. Which entities or positions are the most restricted in this game? Why? *Level 2, which is limited by what's on levels 3 and 4.*

2. Which elements from the BLEND checklist can you identify in this game? Are there
   - Blocks of entities? If so, what are they? *N/A*
   - Limited Options? If so, which rule(s) trigger them? *N/A*
   - Established Entities? If so, which ones? *Rule 3 establishes three items on two of the levels.*
   - Number Restrictions? If so, describe them. *Rules 4 and 5 require some levels to have more of certain items than others.*
   - Duplications? If so, which rules share an entity? *Rules 3, 4, and 5 all mention level 2; Rules 3 and 5 mention level 3; and Rules 4 and 5 mention level 4.*

3. Combine the rules and restrictions to create a Master Sketch depicting all of the deductions available in this game: *Level 3 has two obstacles to begin with. That means level 2 must get all three obstacles.*

	1	2	3	4
rew:	_	A	_	_
obst:	_	m o q	m q	_

That gives level 2 at least four items total (one reward and three obstacles). So level 4 has to have at least five items total. However, level 4 cannot have all three obstacles, so it must have exactly five items: all three rewards and just two obstacles.

	1	2	3	4
rew:	_	A	_	A B C
obst:	_	m o q	m q	_ _ ||

Level 2 is thus done with four items total. Level 3 cannot have any more obstacles, but can have more rewards. Level 1 is unlimited. Levels 2 and 4 both contain the apple as a reward, so level 3 cannot contain an apple.

	1	2	3	4
rew:	_	A ||	_	A B C
obst:	_	m o q ||	m q || ~A	_ _ ||

4. Evaluate your sketch by answering the following questions:
   - Which rewards can appear on level 3? *Bagel or cookie, or both.*
   - Which rewards or obstacles can appear on all four levels? *Mud pit or quicksand, or both.*
   - Which levels can include both a cookie and an oil slick? *Levels 1 or 4, or both; level 2 doesn't offer a cookie, and level 3 has no oil slick.*
   - What is the maximum total rewards and obstacles for any level? *Six; level 1 is unlimited and thus can offer everything.*

Now, put your Matching games skills to the test. In the next section, you can evaluate your performance and get recommendations for further practice.

MATCHING GAMES—FULL GAMES WITH QUESTIONS

LEARNING OBJECTIVES

In this section, you'll assess your ability to

- Apply the Logic Games Method to Matching games.

Perform

Here is your opportunity to put all of the pieces together and assess your skills on Matching games. On the following pages, you'll find two full-length games along with their question sets. Both of these games are from officially released LSAT tests, and all are representative of Matching games you could see on test day. You can take the games one at a time or both together, but for your self-evaluation to be as accurate as possible, adhere to the timing guidelines set forth in the directions.

An answer key follows the games. Complete worked example expert analyses can be found in your online resources.

After you complete and review both games, assess your performance using the evaluation guidelines. There, you'll find recommendations for additional Easy, Medium, and Hard Matching games from officially released LSAT exams that you can practice to continue honing your skills and raising your score.

Directions: Take no more than 9 minutes per game to complete the following two games and all of their questions.

Perform 1

Questions 1–7

Three couples—John and Kate, Lewis and Marie, and Nat and Olive have dinner in a restaurant together. Kate, Marie, and Olive are women; the other three are men. Each person orders one and only one of the following kinds of entrees: pork chops, roast beef, swordfish, tilefish, veal cutlet. The six people order in a manner consistent with the following conditions:

The two people in each couple do not order the same kind of entree as each other.

None of the men orders the same kind of entree as any of the other men.

Marie orders swordfish.

Neither John nor Nat orders a fish entree.

Olive orders roast beef.

1. Which one of the following is a complete and accurate list of the entrees any one of which Lewis could order?

   (A) pork chops, roast beef

   (B) pork chops, veal cutlet

   (C) pork chops, swordfish, veal cutlet

   (D) pork chops, roast beef, tilefish, veal cutlet

   (E) pork chops, roast beef, swordfish, tilefish, veal cutlet

2. Which one of the following statements could be true?

   (A) John orders the same kind of entree as Marie does.

   (B) Kate orders the same kind of entree as Nat does.

   (C) Lewis orders the same kind of entree as Nat does.

   (D) Marie orders the same kind of entree as Olive does.

   (E) Nat orders the same kind of entree as Olive does.

3. Which one of the following statements must be true?

   (A) One of the men orders pork chops or veal cutlet.

   (B) One of the men orders swordfish or veal cutlet.

   (C) Two of the women order tilefish.

   (D) None of the men orders a fish entree.

   (E) Exactly one of the women orders a fish entree.

4. If John orders veal cutlet, then which one of the following statements must be true?

   (A) Kate orders roast beef.

   (B) Kate orders swordfish.

   (C) Lewis orders tilefish.

   (D) Lewis orders veal cutlet.

   (E) Nat orders pork chops.

5. If none of the six people orders pork chops, then which one of the following statements must be true?

   (A) John orders veal cutlet.

   (B) Kate orders tilefish.

   (C) Lewis orders tilefish.

   (D) One of the men orders swordfish.

   (E) One of the women orders tilefish.

6. If Lewis orders pork chops, then which one of the following is a complete and accurate list of the entrees any one of which John could order?

   (A) roast beef

   (B) veal cutlet

   (C) roast beef, veal cutlet

   (D) roast beef, swordfish

   (E) pork chops, roast beef, swordfish

7. Suppose that the people in each couple both order the same kind of entree as each other rather than order different kinds of entrees. If all other conditions remain the same, and no two women order the same kind of entree, then which one of the following statements could be true?

   (A) John orders roast beef.

   (B) John orders swordfish.

   (C) Kate orders roast beef.

   (D) Two of the people order pork chops.

   (E) Two of the people order tilefish.

PrepTest3 Sec1 Qs 1–7

Perform 2

Questions 8–12

A store sells shirts only in small, medium, and large sizes, and only in red, yellow, and blue colors. Casey buys exactly three shirts from the store.

A shirt type consists of both a size and a color.

Casey does not buy two shirts of the same type.

Casey does not buy both a small shirt and a large shirt.

No small red shirts are available.

No large blue shirts are available.

8. Which one of the following must be false?

(A) Two of the shirts that Casey buys are small and two are red.

(B) Two of the shirts that Casey buys are medium and two are red.

(C) Two of the shirts that Casey buys are large and two are red.

(D) Two of the shirts that Casey buys are small, one is yellow, and one is blue.

(E) Two of the shirts that Casey buys are medium, one is yellow, and one is blue.

9. If Casey buys a small blue shirt, which one of the following must be false?

   (A) Casey buys two blue shirts.
   (B) Casey buys two red shirts.
   (C) Casey buys two yellow shirts.
   (D) Casey buys two small shirts.
   (E) Casey buys two medium shirts.

10. If Casey does not buy a medium yellow shirt, which one of the following must be true?

    (A) Casey buys either a medium red shirt or a small blue shirt.
    (B) Casey buys either a medium red shirt or a medium blue shirt.
    (C) Casey buys either a large red shirt or a small blue shirt.
    (D) Casey buys either a large red shirt or a medium red shirt.
    (E) Casey buys either a large yellow shirt or a small yellow shirt.

11. If Casey buys exactly one medium shirt and does not buy two shirts of the same color, then she cannot buy which one of the following?

    (A) a medium red shirt
    (B) a medium yellow shirt
    (C) a medium blue shirt
    (D) a large red shirt
    (E) a large yellow shirt

12. If neither large red shirts nor small blue shirts are available, which one of the following must Casey buy?

    (A) a red shirt
    (B) a medium yellow shirt
    (C) either a large shirt or a small shirt
    (D) either a medium red shirt or a medium blue shirt
    (E) either a large yellow shirt or a medium blue shirt

PrepTest5 Sec2 Qs 7–11

Answer Key

Perform 1

1. (D)
2. (B)
3. (A)
4. (E)
5. (C)
6. (A)
7. (D)

Perform 2

8. (A)
9. (B)
10. (B)
11. (B)
12. (D)

Worked example explanations of these questions with complete expert analysis can be found in your Online Study Plan under Chapter 9. View or download the PDF titled “Chapter 9 Matching Perform Full Games Explanations.”

Assess

Use the following criteria to evaluate your results on the Perform games.

If, under timed conditions, you correctly answered

10–12 of the questions: Outstanding! You have demonstrated a strong skill level in Matching games. For further practice in Matching, use any of the Recommended Additional Practice sets, including the Advanced set. Then, move on to the Distribution section of this chapter and to Chapter 10 on Hybrid games.

7–9 of the questions: Good work! You have a solid foundation in Matching games. For further practice in Matching, begin with the Foundations or Mid-Level Recommended Additional Practice set. Then, move on to the Distribution section of this chapter and to Chapter 10 on Hybrid games. If you have time before test day, try the Advanced Recommended Additional Matching Practice set, as well.

0–6 of the questions: Keep working. Matching, along with its close cousin Distribution, shows up on more than a third of games as a pure action or as part of a hybrid. Continued practice will help you improve your score. Begin by reviewing this chapter. Then, try the games in the Foundations Recommended Additional Practice set. As you continue to progress, move on to the Mid-Level Recommended Additional Practice set. Then, move on to the Distribution section of this chapter and to Chapter 10 on Hybrid games.

To stay sharp, practice the drills in the Logic Games Training Camp for this chapter in your Online Study Plan. Training Camp drills are divided into Fundamentals, Mid-Level, and Advanced sets.

Recommended Additional Practice: Matching

All of the following games will provide good practice on Matching. They are grouped by difficulty as determined from empirical student practice results. All PrepTests included are available on LawHub with an LSAC Prep Plus subscription.

Foundations

PrepTest 67, Section 3, Game 1: Student Speeches

PrepTest 56, Section 1, Game 3: Parks and Trees

Mid-Level

PrepTest 64, Section 2, Game 3: Bicycle Testers

PrepTest 62, Section 3, Game 2: Stained Glass Windows

PrepTest 56, Section 1, Game 2: Furniture Moving

Advanced

PrepTest 68, Section 4, Game 3: Maintenance Service Targets

PrepTest 67, Section 3, Game 4: Development Zones

Complete explanations and analysis for all of the more-than-70 official LSAT tests on LawHub that come with an LSAC LSAT Prep Plus subscription are available in Kaplan's LSAT Link and Link+ tools. Visit **www.kaptest.com/lsat** to learn more or to purchase LSAT Link or Link+.

Reflect

Think back over the study and practice you did in this chapter.

- Are you able to identify Matching games from their setups?
- Do you have a default sketch framework for Matching actions?
- What kinds of rules do you anticipate seeing in Matching games?
- Are you comfortable analyzing Matching rules and determining whether to record them within or underneath the sketch framework?
- Are you making the available deductions efficiently and effectively in Matching games?

In the coming days and weeks before test day, take note of real-world tasks that reflect Matching tasks. Consider how they mirror the setups and questions in LSAT Matching, and how they differ. Try to reframe real-life sequencing tasks using the terms, rules, and restrictions used by the testmaker.

DISTRIBUTION GAMES TASKS AND SKETCHES

LEARNING OBJECTIVES

In this section of the chapter, you'll practice

- Applying Steps 1 and 2 of the Logic Games Method to Distribution games by
  - Asking the SEAL questions to analyze the game's Overview, and then
  - Creating a simple, useful Sketch framework

Prepare

As soon as you discern that the situation in a game involves splitting the entities into groups, you know that you have a Distribution game. You will almost instinctively ask the two questions that will guide how you set up the game: "How many groups/teams are there?" and "How many items/people go into each group?" The setup will almost always answer the first question, and will usually provide names for the groups or teams involved. In some games, the setup will answer the second question as well—e.g., "three teams, each with three players"—but, in other games, you will need to use the rules or limitations to determine the number of entities acceptable within each group. In many real-life situations, we assume that we want groups or teams with equal numbers. That is not the case in Distribution games *unless* the setup or rules explicitly establish that condition.

LOGIC GAMES STRATEGY

Distribution games ask you to

- Divide an initial set of entities into two, three, or four groups

In Distribution games, there are two things to keep in mind about the entities. First, unlike the attributes or items you are matching to other entities in Matching games, each of the entities in most Distribution games can be assigned to just one group or team. Think of them as physical individuals that cannot exist in two places at once.

Second, always note when the game's setup subdivides the entities. Most Distribution setups will provide an undifferentiated list of entities, in which all of them are to be treated equally. When the setup designates subgroups, however, it will always supply rules that treat entities in the two subgroups differently. For example, if a Distribution game tasks you with dividing a group of eight hikers into two smaller groups with four hikers each *and* tells you that three of the hikers are experienced and five are inexperienced, then there will almost certainly be a rule requiring at least one experienced hiker on each team.

Keep these considerations in mind as you apply Steps 1 and 2 to three model Distribution setups in the following practice section.

Practice

Directions: Conduct an Overview of each game's setup by asking the SEAL questions, and create an initial sketch framework for the game's action.

Practice 1

A homeowner has purchased exactly seven fruit trees—a kiwi tree, a lemon tree, a mango tree, a nectarine tree, an orange tree, a plum tree, and a quince tree—to plant in his front and back yards. The planting of trees must adhere to the following guidelines:

1. [Step 1] Conduct an Overview analysis:
   - What is this game's Situation?
   - Who or what are the game's Entities?
   - What is the game's Action?
   - What are the Limitations explicit in the game setup?
2. [Step 2] Create an initial Sketch:

Practice 2

Seven graduate students—Arroyo, Baxter, Chen, Domingo, Erickson, Farrel, and Goya—are being assigned as teaching assistants for three professors—Sheffield, Tran, and Umberto. Each student will be assigned to exactly one professor, and each professor will receive at least one student. Arroyo, Baxter, Domingo, and Erickson are studying mathematics, while Chen, Farrel, and Goya are studying physics. The following restrictions apply:

1. [Step 1] Conduct an Overview analysis:
   - What is this game's Situation?
   - Who or what are the game's Entities?
   - What is the game's Action?
   - What are the Limitations explicit in the game setup?
2. [Step 2] Create an initial Sketch:

Practice 3

A theater director is scheduling auditions for seven actors—Anh, Behn, Chang, Dien, Enge, Fein, and Gus. The actors will audition either alone or in groups. The director will schedule at most four auditions, with each actor attending exactly one audition. The final schedule will be based on the following determinations:

1. [Step 1] Conduct an Overview analysis:
   - What is this game's Situation?
   - Who or what are the game's Entities?
   - What is the game's Action?
   - What are the Limitations explicit in the game setup?
2. [Step 2] Create an initial Sketch:

Explanations

Compare your work to that of an LSAT expert. Keep track of any case in which you incorrectly characterized the action described in the setup, and any case in which you drew a sketch framework that does not match the details of the game's situation.

Practice 1

A homeowner has purchased exactly seven fruit trees—a kiwi tree, a lemon tree, a mango tree, a nectarine tree, an orange tree, a plum tree, and a quince tree—to plant in his front and back yards. The planting of trees must adhere to the following guidelines:

1. [Step 1] Conduct an Overview analysis:
   - What is this game's Situation? *A homeowner planting trees in his front and back yards.*
   - Who or what are the game's Entities? *Seven trees—K, L, M, N, O, P, and Q.*
   - What is the game's Action? *Distribution. Determine in which yard each tree is planted.*
   - What are the Limitations explicit in the game setup? *There are "exactly seven trees," so no tree will be repeated. Thus, each tree will be assigned to just one yard—front or back.*
2. [Step 2] Create an initial Sketch:

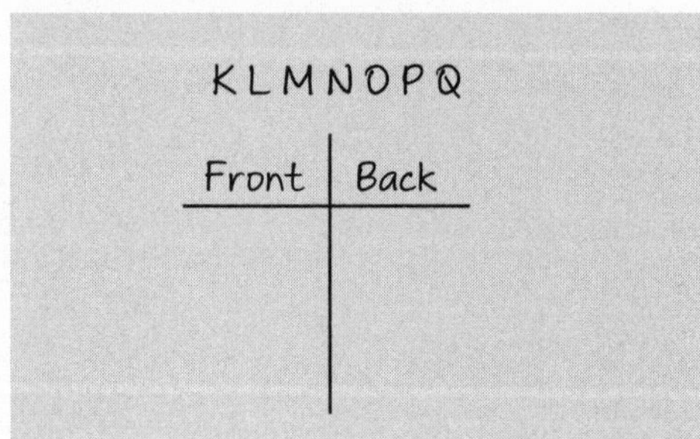

Practice 2

Seven graduate students—Arroyo, Baxter, Chen, Domingo, Erickson, Farrel, and Goya—are being assigned as teaching assistants for three professors—Sheffield, Tran, and Umberto. Each student will be assigned to exactly one professor, and each professor will receive at least one student. Arroyo, Baxter, Domingo, and Erickson are studying mathematics, while Chen, Farrel, and Goya are studying physics. The following restrictions apply:

1. [Step 1] Conduct an Overview analysis:
   - What is this game's Situation? *Students being assigned as teaching assistants to a group of professors.*
   - Who or what are the game's Entities? *Seven students—math students A, B, D, and E; physics students c, f, and g.*
   - What is the game's Action? *Distribution; assign the students to the professors.*
   - What are the Limitations explicit in the game setup? *Each student is assigned to exactly one professor, and each professor gets at least one student.*
2. [Step 2] Create an initial Sketch:

Math — ABDE
Phys — cfg

Shef	Tran	Umb
—	—	—

Practice 3

A theater director is scheduling auditions for seven actors—Anh, Behn, Chang, Dien, Enge, Fein, and Gus. The actors will audition either alone or in groups. The director will schedule at most four auditions, with each actor attending exactly one audition. The final schedule will be based on the following determinations:

1. [Step 1] Conduct an Overview analysis:
   - What is this game's Situation? *A director scheduling auditions for a play.*
   - Who or what are the game's Entities? *Seven actors—A, B, C, D, E, F, and G.*
   - What is the game's Action? *Distribution; putting actors in groups for auditions.*

- What are the Limitations explicit in the game setup? *There are "at most four auditions," which means there could be fewer. For any audition, there's no limit. There could be one actor or it could be multiple actors—perhaps all seven. However, each actor will only be assigned to one audition.*

2. [Step 2] Create an initial Sketch:

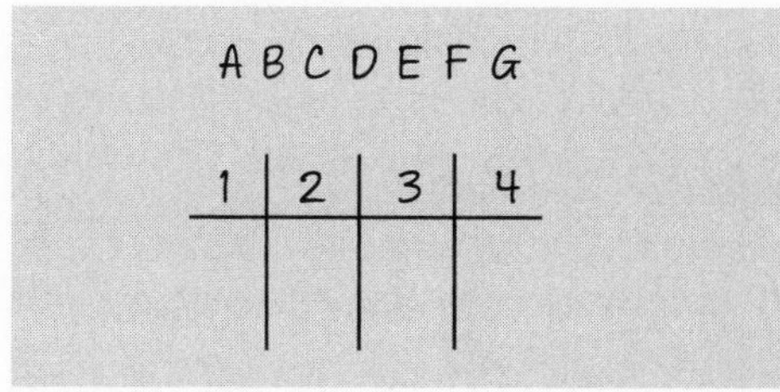

In the next section of this chapter, we'll add the rules to these setups. There, you'll practice applying Step 3 of the Logic Games Method to Distribution games by analyzing and drawing the rules.

DISTRIBUTION GAMES RULES

LEARNING OBJECTIVES

In this section of the chapter, you'll practice

- Applying Step 3 of the Logic Games Method to Distribution games by analyzing and sketching the rules

Prepare

LOGIC GAMES STRATEGY

Distribution rules tell you one or more of the following:

- Entities that must or cannot be assigned to the same group.
- The number of entities that must, can, or cannot be assigned to a group, or the relative sizes among groups (e.g., the lighting crew must have more members than the props crew).
- Conditions triggering the assignment of an entity to a particular group (e.g., if the vase is exhibited in Percy Hall, then the sculpture is exhibited in Rowe Hall).

In both Distribution and Matching games, the setup and sketch have a big influence over how you will depict the rules. In Distribution, this is especially true of games with different numbers of groups. Consider the following rule:

Dan does not play on the Blue Team.

You will draw that rule differently in a game with two teams than you would in a game with three teams.

Red	Blue
D	—
—	—

Red	Blue	Green
—	—	—
—	—	—
	~D	

With only two teams, the rule forbidding Dan from playing on the Blue Team means that he will play on the Red Team. With three teams in the mix, however, the best you can do is to record the negative restriction on Dan beneath the Blue Team's column.

Take a look at an expert's analysis and drawing of common Distribution rules in a couple more game contexts.

Rules		Analysis
A game in which seven volunteers—A, B, C, D, E, F, and G—are each assigned to exactly one group—1, 2, or 3.		
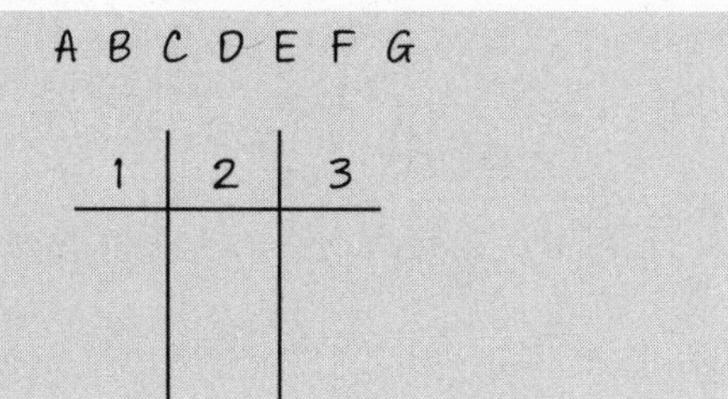		
If A is assigned to group 1, then B is assigned to group 2	→	If A = 1 → B = 2 If B ≠ 2 → A ≠ 1
E and F cannot be assigned to the same group.	→	never [E / F]
C and D are assigned to the same group.	→	[C / D]
A game in which six workers—J, K, L, M, N, and O—are each assigned to work on exactly one of two projects—1 or 2.		
J K L M N O 1 | 2		
If J is assigned to project 1, then K is assigned to project 1.	→	If J = 1 → K = 1 If K = 2 → J = 2
K and L are assigned to different projects.	→	1 | 2 K/L | L/K
Either exactly two or exactly three workers are assigned to project 1.	→	1 | 2: two slots | four slots 1 | 2: three slots | three slots

Now, practice that kind of rule analysis and depiction in four exercises. The first is similar to the table, where the rules are grouped under brief game descriptions. In the next three practice exercises, full sets of rules are provided for the game setups you analyzed in the preceding section of this chapter.

Practice

Directions: Analyze and draw each of following Distribution game rules. Use the brief game description to guide your depiction of the game's framework.

Practice 1

Rules		Analysis
A game distributing seven animals—B, D, F, G, H, J, and K—into three habitats—1, 2, and 3, each of which must have at least one animal.		
1. B and D must be assigned to the same habitat.	→	
2. If J is in habitat 1, then G is in habitat 3.	→	
3. Habitat 2 has exactly twice as many animals as does habitat 1.	→	
A game distributing five pieces of furniture—a bookcase, a couch, a hutch, an ottoman, and a table—into three rooms—a dining room, a living room, and a study.		
4. The table and the couch are placed in the same room.	→	
5. If the couch is placed in the living room, the bookcase must go in the dining room.	→	
6. The hutch is placed in the study.	→	
A game in which six accountants—D, E, F, G, H, and I—are each assigned to exactly one of two projects—billing or collection.		
7. If D is not assigned to billing, then E must be.	→	
8. If G is assigned to billing, then H is assigned to collection.	→	
9. E and F must be assigned to different projects.	→	
A game in which six departments—bedding, kitchen, lighting, pets, swimwear, and toys—are each placed on exactly one of three floors in a building—1, 2, and 3.		
10. Exactly one department will be on Floor 2.	→	
11. Swimwear and toys will be assigned to different floors.	→	
12. Lighting is not assigned to Floor 3.	→	

Practice 2

Directions: Take a couple minutes to review the game setup, summarize your Overview analysis, and recreate the initial Sketch. Then, one at a time, analyze the rules, answer the questions about each one, and draw the rule either inside or underneath the sketch framework.

A homeowner has purchased exactly seven fruit trees—a kiwi tree, a lemon tree, a mango tree, a nectarine tree, an orange tree, a plum tree, and a quince tree—to plant in his front and back yards. The planting of trees must adhere to the following guidelines:

The kiwi tree and the mango tree cannot be planted in the same yard.
The quince tree and the orange tree cannot be planted in the same yard.
The lemon tree and the orange tree must be planted in the same yard.
If the nectarine tree is planted in the front yard, then the plum tree must also be planted in the front yard.
The quince tree must be planted in the front yard.

1. [Step 1] Summarize your Overview analysis:

2. [Step 2] Create an initial Sketch:

3. [Step 3] Analyze and draw the Rules:
   - For each rule, answer the following questions and draw the rule in the appropriate box.
     - What does the rule restrict, and what does it leave open?
     - What are the rule's negative implications, if any?
     - Can the rule be depicted inside the sketch framework?

Rule 1:	Rule 2:
Rule 3:	Rule 4:
Rule 5:	

Practice 3

Directions: Take a couple minutes to review the game setup, summarize your Overview analysis, and recreate the initial Sketch. Then, one at a time, analyze the rules, answer the questions about each one, and draw the rule either inside or underneath the sketch framework.

Seven graduate students—Arroyo, Baxter, Chen, Domingo, Erickson, Farrel, and Goya—are being assigned as teaching assistants for three professors—Sheffield, Tran, and Umberto. Each student will be assigned to exactly one professor, and each professor will receive at least one student. Arroyo, Baxter, Domingo, and Erickson are studying mathematics, while Chen, Farrel, and Goya are studying physics. The following restrictions apply:

No student studying physics can be assigned to the same professor as another student studying physics.
Baxter and Domingo will be assigned to the same professor.
Tran will be assigned more teaching assistants than will Sheffield.
If Erickson is assigned to Tran, then Arroyo cannot be assigned to Tran.

1. [Step 1] Summarize your Overview analysis:

2. [Step 2] Create an initial Sketch:

3. [Step 3] Analyze and draw the Rules:
   - For each rule, answer the following questions and draw the rule in the appropriate box.
     - What does the rule restrict, and what does it leave open?
     - What are the rule's negative implications, if any?
     - Can the rule be depicted inside the sketch framework?

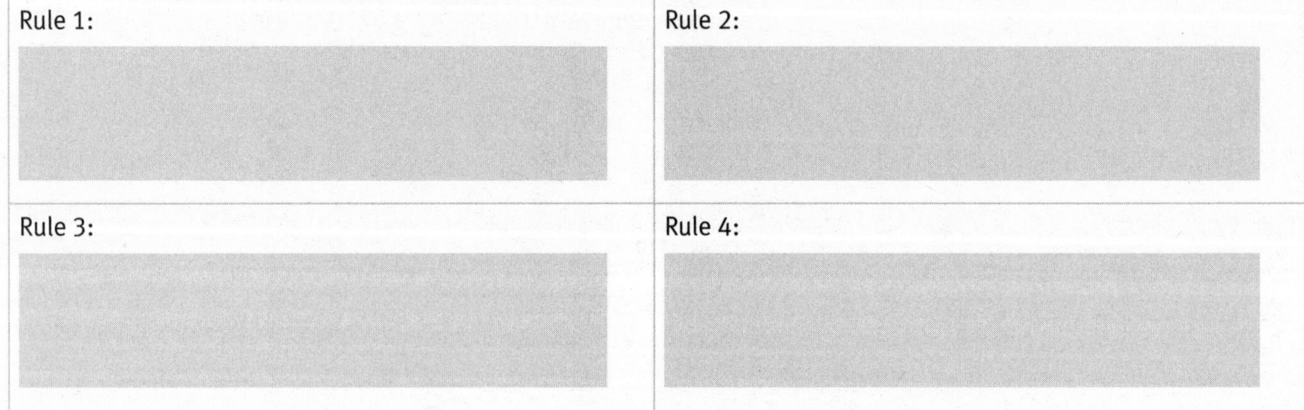

Rule 1:	Rule 2:
Rule 3:	Rule 4:

Practice 4

Directions: Take a couple of minutes to review the game setup, summarize your Overview analysis, and recreate the initial Sketch. Then, one at a time, analyze the rules, answer the questions about each one, and draw the rule either inside or underneath the sketch framework.

A theater director is scheduling auditions for seven actors—Anh, Behn, Chang, Dien, Enge, Fein, and Gus. The actors will audition either alone or in groups. The director will schedule at most four auditions, with each actor attending exactly one audition. The final schedule will be based on the following determinations:

Fein will audition alone.
Anh and Enge will not be scheduled for the same audition.
Chang and Enge will be not be scheduled for the same audition.
Anh and Chang will not audition together unless Behn and Chang audition together.
Dien and Anh will not audition together unless Behn auditions alone.

1. [Step 1] Summarize your Overview analysis:

2. [Step 2] Create an initial Sketch:

3. [Step 3] Analyze and draw the Rules:
   - For each rule, answer the following questions and draw the rule in the appropriate box.
     - What does the rule restrict, and what does it leave open?
     - What are the rule's negative implications, if any?
     - Can the rule be depicted inside the sketch framework?

Rule 1:	Rule 2:
Rule 3:	Rule 4:
Rule 5:	

Explanations

Compare your work to that of an LSAT expert. Pay close attention to how the expert analyzed each rule and then depicted it within or beneath the game's initial sketch.

Practice 1

Rules		Analysis

A game distributing seven animals—B, D, F, G, H, J, and K—into three habitats—1, 2, and 3, each of which must have at least one animal.

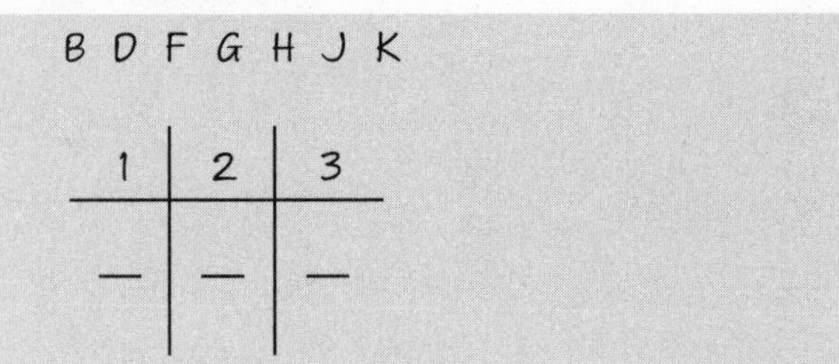

1. B and D must be assigned to the same habitat. → [B D]

2. If J is in habitat 1, then G is in habitat 3. → If J = 1 → G = 3; If G ≠ 3 → J ≠ 1

3. Habitat 2 has exactly twice as many animals as does habitat 1. →

1	2	3
—	—	—
	—	—
		—
		—

1	2	3
—	—	—
—	—	
	—	
	—	

A game distributing five pieces of furniture—a bookcase, a couch, a hutch, an ottoman, and a table—into three rooms—a dining room, a living room, and a study.

B C H O T

dr	lr	st

4. The table and the couch are placed in the same room. → [T C]

5. If the couch is placed in the living room, the bookcase must go in the dining room. → If C = lr → B = dr; If B ≠ dr → C ≠ lr

6. The hutch is placed in the study. →

dr	lr	st
		H

A game in which six accountants—D, E, F, G, H, and I—are each assigned to exactly one of two projects—billing or collection.

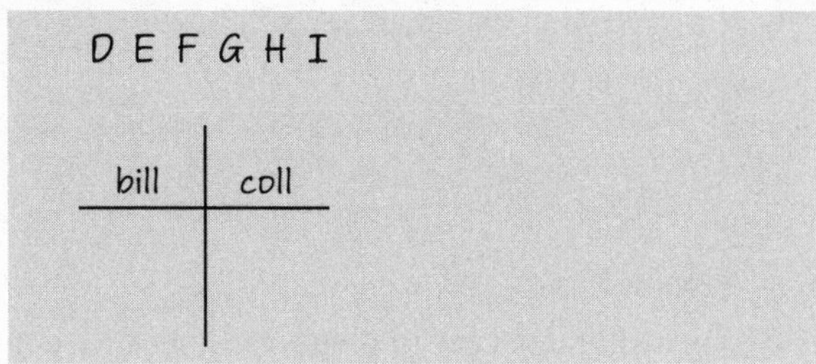

7. If D is not assigned to billing, then E must be. → If D = coll → E = bill; If E = coll → D = bill

8. If G is assigned to billing, then H is assigned to collection. → If G = bill → H = coll; If H = bill → G = coll

9. E and F must be assigned to different projects. →

bill	coll
E/F	F/E

A game in which six departments—bedding, kitchen, lighting, pets, swimwear, and toys—are each placed on exactly one of three floors in a building—1, 2, and 3.

B K L P S T

3:
2:
1:

10. Exactly one department will be on Floor 2. →

3:
2: __ ||
1:

11. Swimwear and toys will be assigned to different floors. → never [S T]

12. Lighting is not assigned to Floor 3. →

3: ~L
2: __ ||
1:

Practice 2

A homeowner has purchased exactly seven fruit trees—a kiwi tree, a lemon tree, a mango tree, a nectarine tree, an orange tree, a plum tree, and a quince tree—to plant in his front and back yards. The planting of trees must adhere to the following guidelines:

> The kiwi tree and the mango tree cannot be planted in the same yard.
> The quince tree and the orange tree cannot be planted in the same yard.
> The lemon tree and the orange tree must be planted in the same yard.
> If the nectarine tree is planted in the front yard, then the plum tree must also be planted in the front yard.
> The quince tree must be planted in the front yard.

1. [Step 1] Summarize your Overview analysis: *A Distribution game in which each of seven trees will be planted in exactly one of two yards. There is no limit, minimum or maximum, for each yard.*

2. [Step 2] Create an initial Sketch:

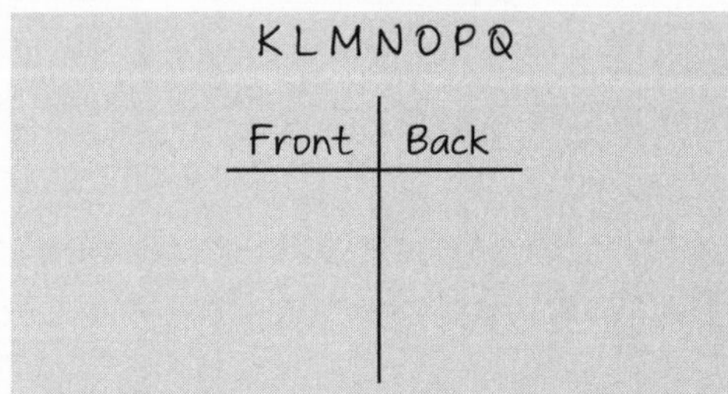

3. [Step 3] Analyze and draw the Rules:
   - Rule 1:
     - What does the rule restrict, and what does it leave open? *The kiwi and the mango trees cannot be together.*
     - What are the rule's negative implications, if any? *They must be in different yards. Since there are only two yards, one must be in the front, and one must be in the back.*
     - Can the rule be depicted inside the sketch framework? *Yes.*
     - Draw the rule:

Front	Back
K/M	M/K

   - Rule 2:
     - What does the rule restrict, and what does it leave open? *The quince and the orange trees cannot be in the same yard.*
     - What are the rule's negative implications, if any? *They must be in different yards. Since there are only two yards, one must be in the front, and one must be in the back.*
     - Can the rule be depicted inside the sketch framework? *Yes.*
     - Draw the rule:

Front	Back
K/M	M/K
O/Q	Q/O

   - Rule 3:
     - What does the rule restrict, and what does it leave open? *The lemon and orange trees are in the same yard, but it could be either yard.*
     - What are the rule's negative implications, if any? *These trees cannot be split up.*
     - Can the rule be depicted inside the sketch framework? *No.*
     - Draw the rule:

   - Rule 4:
     - What does the rule restrict, and what does it leave open? *If the nectarine is in the front yard, then the plum must be there, too. If the nectarine is in the back yard, the rule doesn't apply and the plum could be in either yard.*

- What are the rule's negative implications, if any? *By contrapositive, if the plum is not in the front yard (i.e., if it's in the back yard), then the nectarine can't be in the front yard (i.e., it must be in the back yard). Again, if the plum is in the front yard, the rule doesn't apply, and the nectarine could be in either yard.*
- Can the rule be depicted inside the sketch framework? *No.*
- Draw the rule:

If N = front → P = front

If P = back → N = back

- Rule 5:
  - What does the rule restrict, and what does it leave open? *The quince tree is established in the front yard.*
  - What are the rule's negative implications, if any? *It's not in the back yard.*
  - Can the rule be depicted inside the sketch framework? *Yes.*
  - Draw the rule:

Front	Back
Q	

Practice 3

Seven graduate students—Arroyo, Baxter, Chen, Domingo, Erickson, Farrel, and Goya—are being assigned as teaching assistants for three professors—Sheffield, Tran, and Umberto. Each student will be assigned to exactly one professor, and each professor will receive at least one student. Arroyo, Baxter, Domingo, and Erickson are studying mathematics, while Chen, Farrel, and Goya are studying physics. The following restrictions apply:

No student studying physics can be assigned to the same professor as another student studying physics.

Baxter and Domingo will be assigned to the same professor.

Tran will be assigned more teaching assistants than will Sheffield.

If Erickson is assigned to Tran, then Arroyo cannot be assigned to Tran.

1. [Step 1] Summarize your Overview analysis: *This is a Distribution game in which seven students will each be assigned to exactly one of three professors. Each professor will get at least one student. The students are split into two subgroups: math students and physics students.*

2. [Step 2] Create an initial Sketch:

Math	Phys
A B D E	c f g

Shef	Tran	Umb
—	—	—

3. [Step 3] Analyze and draw the Rules:
   - Rule 1:
     - What does the rule restrict, and what does it leave open? *None of the physics students (Chen, Farrel, and Goya) can be assigned to the same professor.*
     - What are the rule's negative implications, if any? *They each must be assigned to a different professor.*
     - Can the rule be depicted inside the sketch framework? *Yes. There are three physics students, and only three professors. Each professor must get one of the physics students. One each of* c, f, *and* g *will be with each professor.*
     - Draw the rule:

Shef	Tran	Umb
c/f/g	c/f/g	c/f/g

   - Rule 2:
     - What does the rule restrict, and what does it leave open? *Baxter and Domingo must be together, but they could be assigned to any teacher.*
     - What are the rule's negative implications, if any? *Baxter and Domingo cannot be separated.*

- Can the rule be depicted inside the sketch framework? *No.*
- Draw the rule:

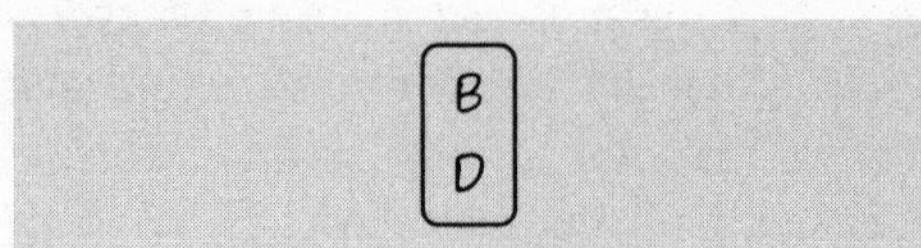

- Rule 3:
    - What does the rule restrict, and what does it leave open? *Tran will get more students than Sheffield, but it's unknown how many more.*
    - What are the rule's negative implications, if any? *Tran cannot have just one student, so Tran will get at least two.*
    - Can the rule be depicted inside the sketch framework? *Generally, no; however, a second space can be added to Tran's column.*
    - Draw the rule:

(1-2) <

Shef	Tran	Umb
—	—	—
	—	

- Rule 4:
    - What does the rule restrict, and what does it leave open? *If Erickson is assigned to Tran, then Arroyo is not.*
    - What are the rule's negative implications, if any? *By contrapositive, if Arroyo is assigned to Tran, Erickson is not. Essentially, they can't both be assigned to Tran—although they could be together with another professor.*
    - Can the rule be depicted inside the sketch framework? *No, but you can draw an anti-block under the Tran column.*
    - Draw the rule:

If E = Tran → A ≠ Tran

If A = Tran → E ≠ Tran

Practice 4

A theater director is scheduling auditions for seven actors—Anh, Behn, Chang, Dien, Enge, Fein, and Gus. The actors will audition either alone or in groups. The director will schedule at most four auditions, with each actor attending exactly one audition. The final schedule will be based on the following determinations:

Fein will audition alone.
Anh and Enge will not be scheduled for the same audition.
Chang and Enge will be not be scheduled for the same audition.
Anh and Chang will not audition together unless Behn and Chang audition together.
Dien and Anh will not audition together unless Behn auditions alone.

1. [Step 1] Summarize your Overview analysis: *A Distribution game in which seven actors will each be assigned to exactly one of four auditions. There's a maximum of four auditions, so there could be fewer than four. There's no limit to the number of actors at each audition. The auditions don't have labels, so call them 1, 2, 3, and 4.*

2. [Step 2] Create an initial Sketch:

3. [Step 3] Analyze and draw the Rules:
    - Rule 1:
        - What does the rule restrict, and what does it leave open? *Fein will be alone.*
        - What are the rule's negative implications, if any? *Nobody could be with Fein, so there must be at least a second audition for the other actors.*
        - Can the rule be depicted inside the sketch framework? *No.*
        - Draw the rule:

- Rule 2:
  - What does the rule restrict, and what does it leave open? *Anh and Enge will not be together.*
  - What are the rule's negative implications, if any? *They must attend different auditions.*
  - Can the rule be depicted inside the sketch framework? *No.*
  - Draw the rule:

- Rule 3:
  - What does the rule restrict, and what does it leave open? *Chang and Enge will not be together.*
  - What are the rule's negative implications, if any? *They must attend different auditions.*
  - Can the rule be depicted inside the sketch framework? *No.*
  - Draw the rule:

- Rule 4:
  - What does the rule restrict, and what does it leave open? *If Anh and Cheng are to audition together, then Behn would also have to audition with Cheng, i.e., they would all be together.*
  - What are the rule's negative implications, if any? *By contrapositive, if Behn and Cheng auditioned separately, then Anh and Cheng are separate, too.*
  - Can the rule be depicted inside the sketch framework? *No.*
  - Draw the rule:

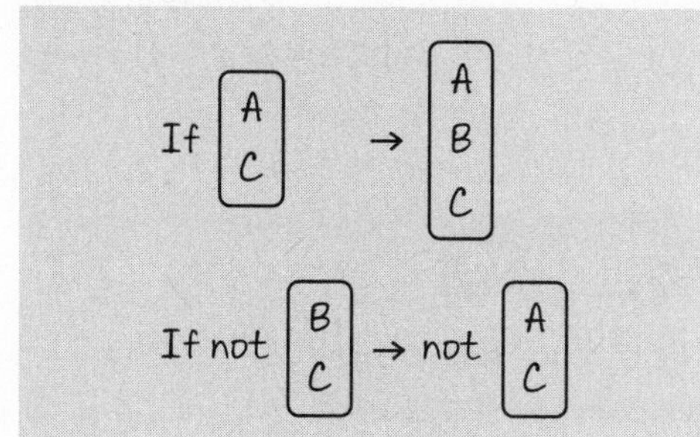

- Rule 5:
  - What does the rule restrict, and what does it leave open? *If Ahn and Dien audition together, then Behn must audition alone.*
  - What are the rule's negative implications, if any? *By contrapositive, if Behn auditions with anybody else, then Ahn and Dien must audition separately.*
  - Can the rule be depicted inside the sketch framework? *No.*
  - Draw the rule:

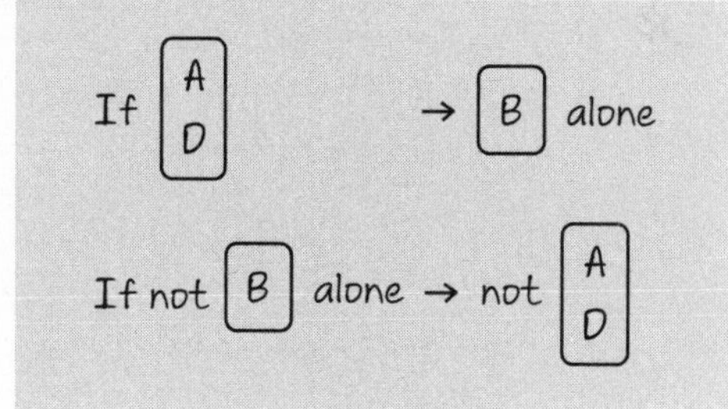

Rule analysis reveals another way in which Distribution and Matching games are similar. In both, deductions can often be made "on the fly" as you are analyzing and drawing out the rules. It is always fine to add a deduction to your sketch during Step 3 if you notice it as you are drawing out the rules. However, you should still take a moment to catalog the rules using the BLEND checklist to be sure you've made all of the available deductions. Practice that step in the next section of this chapter.

DISTRIBUTION GAMES DEDUCTIONS

LEARNING OBJECTIVES

In this section of the chapter, you'll practice

- Applying Step 4 of the Logic Games Method to Distribution games by combining rules and restrictions to make all valid deductions in the game.

Prepare

Distribution games are distinguished from Matching games because, instead of featuring attributes that can be assigned to multiple entities, Distribution games ask you to dole out individual entities among a number of groups. In Distribution games, once you've distributed an entity (assigned it to a group), the entity is "done," and you cannot assign it to a second group. This difference in task makes for a slight difference in where the LSAT expert expects to spot the game's deductions. In all Distribution games, Numbers Restrictions are paramount. If a game's Overview establishes the number of entities per group up front (e.g., three boats with three seats each), then the key deductions will involve entities that must stay together (Blocks of Entities) or must be assigned to different groups. When the game doesn't establish the number of entities per group up front, the LSAT expert focuses on rules that help establish or limit the possibilities. For example, if the game has two teams and you're told that X and Y must be assigned to different teams and that P and Q must be assigned to different teams, you now know that each team has at least two entities.

LOGIC GAMES STRATEGY

In Distribution games, deductions are likely to stem from:

- **Numbers Restrictions—**Limitations on the number of entities per group or determinations of the minimum and maximum number of entities per group; in Distribution games, rules preventing entities from being assigned to the same group may act as *de facto* Numbers Restrictions (e.g., Raul and Sylvia must be assigned to different groups; ergo, two groups have at least one person). Another Numbers Restriction involves games with only two groups: The binary structure of such games means that if an entity is not in one group, it must be in the other.
- **Blocks of Entities—**Two or more entities that must be placed in the same group.
- **Limited Options—**The situation that arises when there are only two possible patterns for the number of entities per group (e.g., either five students are assigned to project X and four students to project Y, or four students are assigned to project X and five students to project Y); In Distribution games, you can sometimes determine a Limited Options numbers scenario by applying other rules to the game's overall framework. Limited Options sketches may also be created if a Block of Entities is influential enough to warrant two or three sketches.
- **Duplications—**Entities shared by two or more rules; a common occurrence in Distribution games is one rule that says A and B will be in the same group and another rule that says A and C cannot be in the same group—from this, you can deduce that B and C cannot be in the same group.

In Distribution games, deductions may involve:

- **Established Entities—**Entities that are assigned to one group for the entire game; this is not very common in Distribution games.

Maintain your focus on numbers deductions and on rules that create blocks of entities (or forbid two entities from ever becoming a block) as you practice Step 4 by making the deductions in the model game setups you've been working with earlier in this chapter.

Practice

Directions: In each game setup, first reacquaint yourself with the setup and rules. Then, combine the rules and restrictions to make all available deductions, recording your analyses as indicated. Finally, test your deductions by answering the questions that accompany each game. You can find expert analysis and explanations at the end of the Practice section.

Practice 1

A homeowner has purchased exactly seven fruit trees—a kiwi tree, a lemon tree, a mango tree, a nectarine tree, an orange tree, a plum tree, and a quince tree—to plant in his front and back yards. The planting of trees must adhere to the following guidelines:

The kiwi tree and the mango tree cannot be planted in the same yard.
The quince tree and the orange tree cannot be planted in the same yard.
The lemon tree and the orange tree must be planted in the same yard.
If the nectarine tree is planted in the front yard, then the plum tree must also be planted in the front yard.
The quince tree must be planted in the front yard.

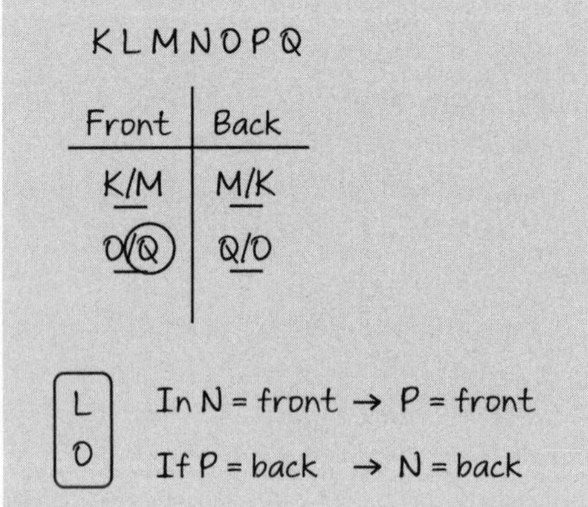

1. Which entities or positions are the most restricted in this game? Why?

2. Which elements from the BLEND checklist can you identify in this game? Are there
    - Blocks of entities? If so, what are they?
    - Limited Options? If so, which rule(s) trigger them?
    - Established Entities? If so, which ones?
    - Number Restrictions? If so, describe them.
    - Duplications? If so, which rules share an entity?

3. Combine the rules and restrictions to create a Master Sketch depicting all of the deductions available in this game:

4. Evaluate your sketch by answering the following questions:
    - Which trees could be planted in either yard?
    - What is the minimum number of trees that must be planted in the front yard?
    - What is the maximum number of trees that could be planted in the same yard as the orange tree (not including the orange tree itself)?
    - If only two trees are planted in the front yard, what could they be?

Practice 2

Seven graduate students—Arroyo, Baxter, Chen, Domingo, Erickson, Farrel, and Goya—are being assigned as teaching assistants for three professors—Sheffield, Tran, and Umberto. Each student will be assigned to exactly one professor, and each professor will receive at least one student. Arroyo, Baxter, Domingo, and Erickson are studying mathematics, while Chen, Farrel, and Goya are studying physics. The following restrictions apply:

> No student studying physics can be assigned to the same professor as another student studying physics.
> Baxter and Domingo will be assigned to the same professor.
> Tran will be assigned more teaching assistants than will Sheffield.
> If Erickson is assigned to Tran, then Arroyo cannot be assigned to Tran.

Math	Phys
A B D E	c f g

(1-2)

Shef	Tran	Umb
c/f/g	c/f/g	c/f/g
__	__	__
	__	

[B D]

Tran > Shef

If E = Tran → A ≠ Tran

If A = Tran → E ≠ Tran

1. Which entities or positions are the most restricted in this game? Why?

2. Which elements from the BLEND checklist can you identify in this game? Are there
   - Blocks of entities? If so, what are they?
   - Limited Options? If so, which rule(s) trigger them?
   - Established Entities? If so, which ones?
   - Number Restrictions? If so, describe them.
   - Duplications? If so, which rules share an entity?

3. Combine the rules and restrictions to create a Master Sketch depicting all of the deductions available in this game:

4. Evaluate your sketch by answering the following questions:
   - Which math students can be assigned to any of the three professors?
   - Which professor could get both Arroyo and Erickson together?
   - What is the maximum number of students that could be assigned to Umberto?
   - If Umberto is assigned one student, who could it be?

Practice 3

A theater director is scheduling auditions for seven actors—Anh, Behn, Chang, Dien, Enge, Fein, and Gus. The actors will audition either alone or in groups. The director will schedule at most four auditions, with each actor attending exactly one audition. The final schedule will be based on the following determinations:

Fein will audition alone.
Anh and Enge will not be scheduled for the same audition.
Chang and Enge will be not be scheduled for the same audition.
Anh and Chang will not audition together unless Behn and Chang audition together.
Dien and Anh will not audition together unless Behn auditions alone.

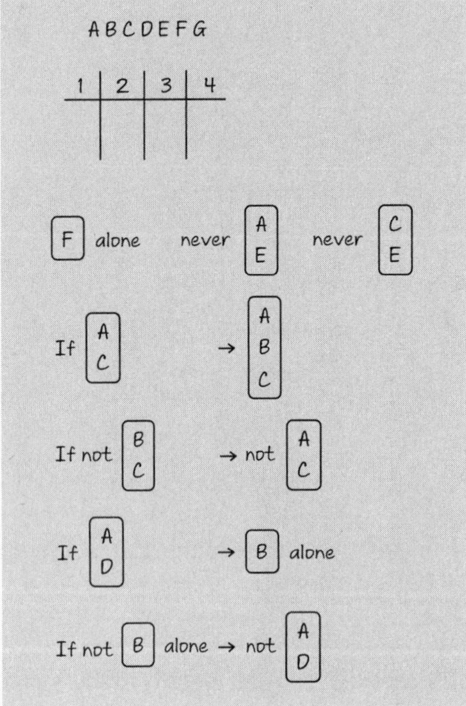

1. Which entities or positions are the most restricted in this game? Why?

2. Which elements from the BLEND checklist can you identify in this game? Are there
   - Blocks of entities? If so, what are they?
   - Limited Options? If so, which rule(s) trigger them?
   - Established Entities? If so, which ones?
   - Number Restrictions? If so, describe them.
   - Duplications? If so, which rules share an entity?

3. Combine the rules and restrictions to create a Master Sketch depicting all of the deductions available in this game:

4. Evaluate your sketch by answering the following questions:
   - What is the minimum number of auditions that must be held?
   - Who could Enge audition with?
   - Who could Chang audition with?
   - What is the maximum number of people in any audition?

Explanations

Compare your work to that of an LSAT expert. Pay close attention to how the expert combined the rules and restrictions to make additional deductions, and to how the expert depicted the deductions within the sketch framework.

Practice 1

A homeowner has purchased exactly seven fruit trees—a kiwi tree, a lemon tree, a mango tree, a nectarine tree, an orange tree, a plum tree, and a quince tree—to plant in his front and back yards. The planting of trees must adhere to the following guidelines:

The kiwi tree and the mango tree cannot be planted in the same yard.
The quince tree and the orange tree cannot be planted in the same yard.
The lemon tree and the orange tree must be planted in the same yard.
If the nectarine tree is planted in the front yard, then the plum tree must also be planted in the front yard.
The quince tree must be planted in the front yard.

1. Which entities or positions are the most restricted in this game? Why? *The quince tree, which is established in the front yard, and the orange tree, which cannot be with the quince tree but must be with the lemon tree.*

2. Which elements from the BLEND checklist can you identify in this game? Are there
   - Blocks of entities? If so, what are they? *Rule 3 requires the lemon and orange trees to be together.*
   - Limited Options? If so, which rule(s) trigger them? *N/A*
   - Established Entities? If so, which ones? *Rule 5 establishes the quince tree in the front yard.*
   - Number Restrictions? If so, describe them. *Rules 1 and 2 each place one tree in each yard. Together, they establish at least two trees in each yard.*
   - Duplications? If so, which rules share an entity? *Rules 2 and 5 both mention the quince tree. Rules 2 and 3 both mention the orange tree.*

3. Combine the rules and restrictions to create a Master Sketch depicting all of the deductions available in this game: *Start with the quince tree, which is established in the front yard. That means the orange tree (and thus also the lemon tree) must be in the back yard.*

Front	Back
Q	O
	L

The kiwi and mango trees are split, but either can be planted in either yard.

Front	Back
Q	O
K/M	L
	M/K

4. Evaluate your sketch by answering the following questions:
   - Which trees could be planted in either yard? *Kiwi, mango, nectarine, and plum.*
   - What is the minimum number of trees that must be planted in the front yard? *Two.*
   - What is the maximum number of trees that could be planted in the same yard as the orange tree (not including the orange tree itself)? *Four; lemon, nectarine, plum, and one more—either the kiwi or the mango.*
   - If only two trees are planted in the front yard, what could they be? *The quince and the kiwi, or the quince and the mango.*

Practice 2

Seven graduate students—Arroyo, Baxter, Chen, Domingo, Erickson, Farrel, and Goya—are being assigned as teaching assistants for three professors—Sheffield, Tran, and Umberto. Each student will be assigned to exactly one professor, and each professor will receive at least one student. Arroyo, Baxter, Domingo, and Erickson are studying mathematics, while Chen, Farrel, and Goya are studying physics. The following restrictions apply:

> No student studying physics can be assigned to the same professor as another student studying physics.
>
> Baxter and Domingo will be assigned to the same professor.
>
> Tran will be assigned more teaching assistants than will Sheffield.
>
> If Erickson is assigned to Tran, then Arroyo cannot be assigned to Tran.

1. Which entities or positions are the most restricted in this game? Why? *Sheffield, who must have fewer entities than Tran.*

2. Which elements from the BLEND checklist can you identify in this game? Are there
   - Blocks of entities? If so, what are they? *Rule 2 puts Baxter and Domingo together.*
   - Limited Options? If so, which rule(s) trigger them? *Not directly, but the Block from Rule 2 and the numbers of Rule 3 are restricted enough to present two options each.*
   - Established Entities? If so, which ones? *Rule 1 establishes a physics student with each professor.*
   - Number Restrictions? If so, describe them. *Rule 4 gives Tran at least two students, and limits Sheffield to fewer than Tran.*
   - Duplications? If so, which rules share an entity? *Rules 3 and 4 both mention Tran, but not in a way that can be easily combined.*

3. Combine the rules and restrictions to create a Master Sketch depicting all of the deductions available in this game:

   Sheffield has to have fewer students than Tran. Sheffield can just have one student (a physics student) or two. If Sheffield got three students, Tran would need four, leaving nobody for Umberto. So Sheffield is limited to just one or two students.

(1-2) <

Shef	Tran	Umb
c/f/g	c/f/g	c/f/g
	—	

One of Sheffield's students must be a physics student. So, even if Sheffield got two students, it couldn't be both Baxter and Domingo.

There are two opportunities for Limited Options. The first is based on the Block of Baxter and Domingo, which can only be assigned to Tran or Umberto. If they were assigned to Tran, that would set up five slots in the sketch, and nothing else.

Shef	Tran	Umb
c/f/g	c/f/g	c/f/g
	B	
	D	

However, if Baxter and Domingo were assigned to Umberto, that would set up six slots. The second student for Tran would be Arroyo or Erickson.

Shef	Tran	Umb
c/f/g	c/f/g	c/f/g
	A/E	B
		D

Tran cannot get both Arroyo and Erickson, so Tran will be finished with two students. That means Sheffield has just one. Whichever student Tran doesn't get (Arroyo or Erickson) will have to be assigned to Umberto.

Shef	Tran	Umb
c/f/g	c/f/g	c/f/g
	A/E	B
		D
		A/E

The second opportunity for Limited Options is based on the number—whether Sheffield gets one or two students. If Sheffield gets just one student, that has no further effect on the numbers. Baxter and Domingo can be assigned to Tran or Umberto. Arroyo and Erickson cannot both be assigned to Tran, so at least one of them (if not both) must be assigned to Umberto.

Shef	Tran	Umb
c/f/g	c/f/g	c/f/g
	—	A/E

If Sheffield gets two students, then Tran gets at least three. Umberto could then only get one extra math student, so Baxter and Domingo must be assigned to Tran. Sheffield's second student will be Arroyo or Erickson. Whichever one is not assigned to Sheffield could go to Tran or Umberto.

Shef	Tran	Umb
c/f/g	c/f/g	c/f/g
A/E	B	
	D	

4. Evaluate your sketch by answering the following questions:
   - Which math students can be assigned to any of the three professors? *Arroyo or Erickson.*
   - Which professor could get both Arroyo and Erickson together? *Umberto.*
   - What is the maximum number of students that could be assigned to Umberto? *Four.*
   - If Umberto is assigned one student, who could it be? *It must be a physics student: Chen, Farrel, or Goya.*

Practice 3

A theater director is scheduling auditions for seven actors—Anh, Behn, Chang, Dien, Enge, Fein, and Gus. The actors will audition either alone or in groups. The director will schedule at most four auditions, with each actor attending exactly one audition. The final schedule will be based on the following determinations:

Fein will audition alone.
Anh and Enge will not be scheduled for the same audition.
Chang and Enge will be not be scheduled for the same audition.
Anh and Chang will not audition together unless Behn and Chang audition together.
Dien and Anh will not audition together unless Behn auditions alone.

1. Which entities or positions are the most restricted in this game? Why? *Anh, Chang, and Enge; Enge cannot be with the other two, and both Anh and Chang potentially affect other actors.*

2. Which elements from the BLEND checklist can you identify in this game? Are there
   - Blocks of entities? If so, what are they? *N/A*
   - Limited Options? If so, which rule(s) trigger them? *N/A*
   - Established Entities? If so, which ones? *Rule 1 establishes F in an audition alone.*
   - Number Restrictions? If so, describe them. *Rule 1 established that one audition will have exactly one actor, meaning there must be at least a second audition. Rules 2 and 3 also split up actors, requiring multiple auditions.*

- Duplications? If so, which rules share an entity? *Rules 2, 4, and 5 all mention Anh. Rules 2 and 3 mention Enge. Rules 3 and 4 mention Chang. Rules 4 and 5 mention Behn.*

3. Combine the rules and restrictions to create a Master Sketch depicting all of the deductions available in this game:

   The auditions are never referred to by name, and there's no order to the auditions. So, the audition labels are arbitrary, and actors can be placed into any audition at any time. So, start by placing Fein in audition 1 and closing it off.

1	2	3	4
F (closed)			

   After that, Anh and Enge must be separated, so put Ang in audition 2 and Enge in audition 3. Chang cannot go into audition 3 with Enge.

1	2	3	4
F (closed)	A	E	
		~C	

   That means there will be at least three auditions. Everything else is dependent on the Formal Logic. It can be noted that the result of each Formal Logic rule triggers the contrapositive of the other. In other words, if Anh and Chang are together, then Behn is with them and thus not alone. So, Anh and Dien would be separate. Similarly, if Anh and Dien were separate, then Behn would be alone and thus couldn't be with Chang. That would mean Anh and Chang would have to be separate.

4. Evaluate your sketch by answering the following questions:
   - What is the minimum number of auditions that must be held? *Three.*
   - Who could Enge audition with? *Behn, Dien, or Gus.*
   - Who could Chang audition with? *Anh, Behn, Dien, or Gus.*
   - What is the maximum number of people in any audition? *Four; nobody can be with Fein, and Enge can't audition with Chang. The remaining five (Anh, Behn, Chang, Dien, and Gus) cannot all be together. If Anh and Dien were together, Behn would have to be alone. However, If Dien was elsewhere, Anh, Behn, Chang and Gus could all be together.*

In both Matching and Distribution games, the deductions step can make or break your ability to answer the questions quickly and accurately. With all of the deductions in place, you can often handle the question set quite quickly and confidently. Make sure to give Step 4 due diligence, however, as you evaluate your skills in all five steps of the Logic Games Method on the full-length Distribution games in the next section of this chapter.

DISTRIBUTION GAMES—FULL GAMES WITH QUESTIONS

LEARNING OBJECTIVES

In this section, you'll assess your ability to

- Apply the Logic Games Method to Distribution games.

Perform

Here is your opportunity to put all of the pieces together and assess your skills on Distribution games. On the following pages, you'll find two full-length games along with their question sets. Both of these games are from officially released LSAT tests, and all are representative of Distribution games you could see on test day. You can take the games one at a time or both together, but for your self-evaluation to be as accurate as possible, adhere to the timing guidelines set forth in the directions.

An answer key follows the games. Complete worked example expert analyses can be found in your online resources.

After you complete and review both games, assess your performance using the evaluation guidelines. There, you'll find recommendations for additional Easy, Medium, and Hard Distribution games from officially released LSAT exams that you can practice to continue honing your skills and raising your score.

Directions: Take no more than 9 minutes per game to complete the following two games and all of their questions.

Perform 1

Questions 1–5

Planes 1, 2, 3, and 4—and no others—are available to fly in an air show.

Pilots Anna, Bob, and Cindy are all aboard planes that are flying in the show and they are the only qualified pilots in the show.

Copilots Dave, Ed, and Fran are all aboard planes that are flying in the show and they are the only qualified copilots in the show.

No plane flies in the show without a qualified pilot aboard.

No one but qualified pilots and qualified copilots flies in the show.

Anna will only fly in either plane 1 or plane 4.

Dave will only fly in either plane 2 or plane 3.

1. If Anna flies in plane 4 and Dave flies in plane 2, which one of the following must be true?

(A) Cindy flies in either plane 1 or plane 3.

(B) If Cindy flies in plane 3, Bob flies in plane 2.

(C) Bob and one other person fly in plane l.

(D) If Bob is aboard plane 4, Cindy flies in plane 3.

(E) If Cindy is in plane 2, Bob flies in plane 3.

2. If Bob and Anna fly on the same plane, which one of the following must be true?

   (A) Cindy flies with Dave and Ed.
   (B) Cindy flies with Ed.
   (C) Dave flies with Cindy.
   (D) Dave flies with Cindy, Ed, and Fran.
   (E) Fran flies with Ed.

3. If Cindy and Fran are the only people in one of the planes, which one of the following must be true?

   (A) Bob flies with Anna.
   (B) Dave flies with Ed.
   (C) Dave and Ed fly with Bob.
   (D) Dave flies with Bob.
   (E) Ed flies with Anna.

4. If plane 1 is used, its crew could consist of

   (A) Anna, Bob, Cindy, Fran
   (B) Anna, Bob, Ed, Fran
   (C) Bob, Cindy, Ed, Fran
   (D) Bob, Cindy, Dave, Ed
   (E) Bob, Dave, Ed, Fran

5. If as many of the pilots and copilots as possible fly in plane 4, that group will consist of

   (A) exactly two people
   (B) exactly three people
   (C) exactly four people
   (D) exactly five people
   (E) three pilots and two copilots

PrepTest3 Sec1 Qs 20–24

Perform 2

Questions 6–11

Eight camp counselors—Fran, George, Henry, Joan, Kathy, Lewis, Nathan, and Olga—must each be assigned to supervise exactly one of three activities—swimming, tennis, and volleyball. The assignment of counselors must conform to the following conditions:

Each activity is supervised by at least two, but not more than three, of the eight counselors.

Henry supervises swimming.

Neither Kathy nor Olga supervises tennis.

Neither Kathy nor Nathan supervises the same activity as Joan.

If George supervises swimming, both Nathan and Olga supervise volleyball.

6. Which one of the following is an acceptable assignment of the counselors to the activities?

(A) Swimming: Fran, George, Henry; Tennis: Joan, Lewis; Volleyball: Kathy, Nathan, Olga

(B) Swimming: George, Henry, Olga; Tennis: Fran, Joan, Lewis; Volleyball: Kathy, Nathan

(C) Swimming: Henry; Tennis: Fran, George, Joan, Lewis; Volleyball: Kathy, Nathan, Olga

(D) Swimming: Henry, Joan, Kathy; Tennis: George, Nathan; Volleyball: Fran, Lewis, Olga

(E) Swimming: Henry, Nathan; Tennis: Fran, Kathy, Lewis; Volleyball: George, Joan, Olga

7. Which one of the following is a pair of counselors who could be two of three counselors assigned to supervise swimming?

   (A) George and Nathan
   (B) George and Olga
   (C) Joan and Kathy
   (D) Joan and Nathan
   (E) Joan and Olga

8. Which one of the following is a pair of counselors who could together be assigned to supervise tennis?

   (A) Fran and Kathy
   (B) George and Nathan
   (C) Henry and Lewis
   (D) Joan and Nathan
   (E) Joan and Olga

9. If George and Kathy are two of three counselors assigned to supervise swimming, which one of the following could be true of the assignment?

   (A) Fran supervises swimming.
   (B) Henry supervises tennis.
   (C) Joan supervises volleyball.
   (D) Lewis supervises volleyball.
   (E) Nathan supervises tennis.

10. If Fran and Lewis are two of three counselors assigned to supervise swimming, which one of the following must be true of the assignment?

   (A) George supervises volleyball.
   (B) Henry supervises volleyball.
   (C) Joan supervises tennis.
   (D) Kathy supervises swimming.
   (E) Nathan supervises tennis.

11. If Joan is assigned to supervise the same activity as Olga, which one of the following CANNOT be true of the assignment?

   (A) Fran supervises swimming.
   (B) George supervises swimming.
   (C) Kathy supervises volleyball.
   (D) Lewis supervises volleyball.
   (E) Nathan supervises tennis.

PrepTest11 Sec1 Qs 1–6

Answer Key

Perform 1

1. (B)
2. (C)
3. (D)
4. (B)
5. (C)

Perform 2

6. (A)
7. (E)
8. (B)
9. (D)
10. (C)
11. (B)

Worked example explanations of these questions with complete expert analysis can be found in your Online Study Plan under Chapter 9. View or download the PDF titled "Chapter 9 Distribution Perform Full Games Explanations."

Assess

Use the following criteria to evaluate your results on the Perform games.

If, under timed conditions, you correctly answered

9–11 of the questions: Outstanding! You have demonstrated a strong skill level in Distribution games. For further practice in Distribution, use any of the Recommended Additional Practice sets, including the Advanced set. Then, move on to Chapter 10 on Hybrid games.

6–8 of the questions: Good work! You have a solid foundation in Distribution games. For further practice in Distribution, begin with the Foundations or Mid-Level Recommended Additional Practice set. Then, move on to Chapter 10 on Hybrid games. If you have time before test day, try the Advanced Recommended Additional Distribution Practice set, as well.

0–5 of the questions: Keep working. Distribution, along with its close cousin Matching, shows up on more than a third of games as a pure action or as part of a hybrid. Continued practice will help you improve your score. Begin by reviewing this chapter. Then, try the games in the Foundations Recommended Additional Practice set. As you continue to progress, move on to the Mid-Level Recommended Additional Practice set. Then, move on to Chapter 10 on Hybrid games.

To stay sharp, practice the drills in the Logic Games Training Camp for this chapter in your Online Study Plan. Training Camp drills are divided into Fundamentals, Mid-Level, and Advanced sets.

Recommended Additional Practice: Distribution

All of the following games will provide good practice on Distribution. They are grouped by difficulty as determined from empirical student practice results. All PrepTests included are available on LawHub with an LSAC Prep Plus subscription.

Foundations

PrepTest 68, Section 4, Game 2: Two Days of Witness Testimony

PrepTest 63, Section 2, Game 1: Judicial Appointments

Mid-Level

PrepTest 71, Section 2, Game 2: Application Evaluation

PrepTest 66, Section 3, Game 3: Software Company Sales Zones

PrepTest 61, Section 3, Game 1: Business Convention

Advanced

PrepTest 69, Section 2, Game 4: Cases for Paralegals

PrepTest 52, Section 2, Game 2: Field Trip Chaperones

Complete explanations and analysis for all of the more-than-70 official LSAT tests on LawHub that come with an LSAC LSAT Prep Plus subscription are available in Kaplan's LSAT Link and Link+ tools. Visit **www.kaptest.com/lsat** to learn more or to purchase LSAT Link or Link+.

Reflect

Think back over the study and practice you did in this chapter.

- Are you able to identify Distribution games from their setups?
- Do you have a default sketch framework for Distribution actions?
- What kinds of rules do you anticipate seeing in Distribution games?
- Are you comfortable analyzing Distribution rules and determining whether to record them within or underneath the sketch framework?
- Are you making the available deductions efficiently and effectively in Distribution games?

In the coming days and weeks before test day, take note of real-world tasks that reflect Distribution tasks. Consider how they mirror the setups and questions in LSAT Distribution, and how they differ. Try to reframe real-life distribution tasks using the terms, rules, and restrictions used by the testmaker.

CHAPTER 10

Hybrid Games Unlocked

LEARNING OBJECTIVES

In this chapter, you'll learn to

- Apply the Logic Games Method to Hybrid Games

Hybrid games have made up more than 20 percent of the games on official LSATs released over the past five years.

Types of Games By Percentage, 2014–2018

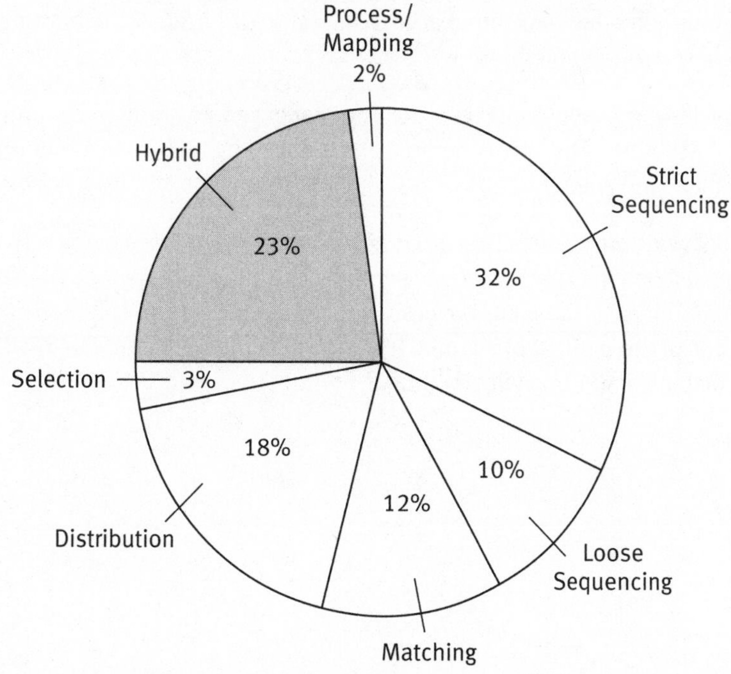

That looks like a lot, but don't think that you have to learn more than one-fifth of the Logic Games section in this chapter. In reality, you've learned most of what you'll be doing in this chapter already. That's because Hybrid games combine two (or, very rarely, three) of the standard game actions: Sequencing, Distribution, Matching, and Selection.

In theory, the test could combine any of the standard actions, but in practice, there are just four Hybrids that regularly appear on the LSAT. A look at the breakdown of Hybrid games on LSATs released from 2014 to 2018 show you what they are.

Hybrid Actions	**# of games on LSATs released 2014–2018**
Selection-Sequencing	4
Distribution-Sequencing	3
Matching-Sequencing	3
Selection-Distribution	3
Distribution-Matching	1

In the next section of this chapter, you'll see default sketch frameworks suggested for each of those Hybrid actions.

Hybrid games have a reputation for being complicated, confusing, and downright hard. That's fair to an extent—Hybrids are, on average, slightly harder than other game types—but the difficulty of Hybrids is often exaggerated. The individual actions in Hybrid games are often quite simple. In a Sequencing-Matching Hybrid, for example, you might be asked to put six figurines in a row, one per position, and then assign each figurine one of two colors, black or tan. (By the way, did it strike you that the game just described is very similar to the Truck Arrivals game from Chapter 1? That, too, was a Sequencing-Matching Hybrid game.)

After the work you've already done, a six-entity basic Strict Sequencing game shouldn't sound too bad. Nor should a matching game with just two attributes. The only complexity introduced by this game's Hybrid nature is that you must account for each entity's position and color.

Throughout this chapter, you'll work with games that provide examples of the four common Hybrids. At the end of the chapter, there is an LSAT Channel Special Feature on one example of a rare Hybrid game—Selection-Matching—that has only appeared twice in LSAT history. The game covered in that Special Feature is famous (well, as famous as an LSAT logic game can be) as one of the hardest of all time. It's known as the Dinosaur game, and you will definitely want to check out The LSAT Channel experts giving their take on it.

HYBRID GAMES IN REAL LIFE

If you think about it, almost everything you do in real life is a Hybrid task. To make this statement concrete, think of the jobs involved in planning a wedding. You have to decide whom you'll invite. That's Selection. You have to plan who will (or won't) sit together at dinner, like a huge Distribution game. You even have to decide the pairs in the wedding party and the order in which they'll walk down the aisle; that's a Sequencing-Matching game. As you plan that task, you and your spouse-to-be will have some "rules" to determine who enters first, second, third, and so on, and other "rules" to determine who will walk with whom. This is exactly what the test would outline in a comparable logic game.

Ask anyone who has ever planned a wedding and they'll tell you it is a very complex task. While the wedding scenarios provide some helpful analogies, LSAT Hybrid games keep your job much simpler. The LSAT will never ask you to sequence seven bridesmaids and to assign each of them between one and three types of clothing, jewelry, and bouquets. They don't expect even the most expert test takers to able to complete a game like that in eight and half minutes. As you practice with the games in this chapter, take note of how the testmaker limits the scope of one or both of the tasks.

Here are four more real-life tasks that illustrate the standard sketch frameworks associated with the LSAT's most common Hybrid game types.

Sequencing-Matching

Arrange six plants labeled A, B, C, D, E, and F from left to right in a planter box with six spaces, one plant per space. Each plant flowers in exactly one of three colors—red, white, or yellow.

A B C D E F

__ __ __ __ __ __
1 2 3 4 5 6
r/w/y __ __ __ __ __ __

In real life, you'd have practical or aesthetic reasons for how you arrange the plants. Maybe the left side of the window box will get more sun. Or maybe you want flowers of the same color kept together or apart. In any case, the factors that go into your decisions translate easily into logic games rules: "Plants with the same color flowers cannot be in adjacent spaces" or "C is placed to the right of E."

Selection-Sequencing

From an envelope containing six family photos—one of mom, one of dad, one with mom and dad together, one of your sister as a baby, one of your sister as a teen, and one of your brother—choose four to display on the hallway wall. Then, choose the order in which to display them, one at a time, from left to right.

M, D, MD, S_1, S_2, B (4 of 6)

__ __ __ __
1 2 3 4

You can already imagine how the rules might work. You will select only one picture of your sister. If you select both individual pictures of your mom and dad, you won't select the one of them together. You will hang the pictures of your siblings on either side of pictures of your parents. Simply substitute letters like A, B, C, and D for the pictures, and you have a ready-made Selection-Sequencing Hybrid game.

Selection-Distribution

From 10 articles of clothing—three blouses: one each in blue, red, and white; two dresses: one each in blue and white; two pairs of jeans: one each in blue and white; and three sweaters: one each in blue, red, and white—choose seven articles to keep. For each of the pieces kept, decide whether to hang it in the closet or put it in a drawer.

B_b B_r B_w J_b J_w
D_b D_w S_b S_r S_w Choose 7 of 10

Closet	Drawer

This task might be hard in real life for emotional reasons ("oh, man, I love those jeans"), but it's pretty easy to picture, and certainly doesn't seem complicated. It's also pretty easy to see how your own rules—"I'll keep two of the three sweaters," "I'll keep two of the white things," or "Any dress I keep has to go in the closet"—would work in the context of an LSAT logic game.

This scenario actually has more entities and options than any recent Selection-Distribution game featured on the LSAT. It's good to remember how many factors there are in the everyday things we do, and use that to remind ourselves that LSAT logic games have quite limited and concrete tasks.

Distribution-Sequencing

From a group of eight sprinters—Q, R, S, T, W, X, Y, and Z—create two relay teams of four runners each. Assign each runner to run one leg—1st, 2nd, 3rd, or 4th—in the race.

Q R S T W X Y Z

	Team 1	Team 2
1	—	—
2	—	—
3	—	—
4	—	—

This task would be routine for any track coach or PE teacher. In real life, you might have your reasons for making the two teams as equal as possible, or for making one much stronger than the other. Whatever your motive, the rules are easy to imagine: "Q and R will run on the same team," or "W is the fastest sprinter here, so she will run the anchor leg regardless of the team she's on."

With some grounding in the everyday nature of these tasks, and a good idea of the standard Hybrid sketches, you're ready to start analyzing these setups and games in the context that you'll see them on the LSAT.

HYBRID GAMES TASKS AND SKETCHES

LEARNING OBJECTIVES

In this section of the chapter, you'll learn to

- Apply Steps 1 and 2 of the Logic Games Method to Hybrid games by
  - Asking the SEAL questions to analyze the game's Overview, and then
  - Creating a simple, useful Sketch framework

Prepare

By reading the section on Hybrid Games in Real Life and taking careful note of the sample sketches, you've done the preparation needed to practice applying Steps 1 and 2 to Hybrid games.

LOGIC GAMES STRATEGY

Hybrid games ask you to combine two (or, rarely, three) of the standard game actions. The most common Hybrid games are

- Sequencing-Matching
- Distribution-Sequencing
- Selection-Sequencing
- Selection-Distribution

Not every Hybrid game fits one of the standard sketch frameworks exactly, of course. You've seen how LSAT experts adapt their default sketches to account for small "twists" or variations in all of the standard game types. The same thing applies here. Memorize the standard sketch formats—add them to your mental "library," if you will—and then be open to altering them as necessary to fit the situations described in various game setups.

Practice

Directions: Conduct an Overview of each game's setup by asking the SEAL questions, and create an initial sketch framework for the game's action.

Practice 1

Six witnesses—B, C, D, E, F, and G—are scheduled to testify in a court case. Three witnesses will be examined by the plaintiff's lead litigator, while the other three will be examined by the assistant attorney. Each witness will be examined once. The order in which they testify, and who examines them, are restricted by the following conditions:

Witness C will testify immediately after witness D.
Witness G will testify before witness F but after witness C.
Witness E will testify after witness D.
The lead litigator will examine the first and last witnesses.
The lead litigator will examine C.
The assistant attorney will not examine three consecutive witnesses.

1. [Step 1] Conduct an Overview analysis:
   - What is this game's Situation?
   - Who or what are the game's Entities?
   - What is the game's Action?
   - What are the Limitations explicit in the game setup?
2. [Step 2] Create an initial Sketch:

Practice 2

A company is conducting a quarterly review. Eight employees—Grant, Heather, Julia, Kendra, Lauren, Matthew, Nathan, and Oliver—will each attend a meeting with a supervisor on either Thursday or Friday of this week. One employee at a time will attend each meeting. The arrangement of the meetings is subject to the following restrictions:

If Heather attends her meeting on Thursday, then Lauren and Nathan will both attend their meetings on Friday.
Grant will attend his meeting on a different day than Matthew.
Julia will attend her meeting after Oliver and on the same day.
Friday will have no more than three meeting slots.
Julia's meeting is never the last meeting of the day.

1. [Step 1] Conduct an Overview analysis:
   - What is this game's Situation?
   - Who or what are the game's Entities?
   - What is the game's Action?
   - What are the Limitations explicit in the game setup?
2. [Step 2] Create an initial Sketch:

Practice 3

A senior partner is deciding how to organize the firm's associates for a new class action. Six of the eight associates—Ann, Brian, Courtney, David, Edwin, Frank, Gina, and Hannah—will be selected for either the Support team or the Trial team, each team needing at least two associates. The selection is governed by the following conditions:

There are at most three associates selected for the Support team.
If Edwin is on the Trial team, then Ann is on the Support team and David is not selected for either.
If Ann is selected, then Hannah and Ann are placed on the same team.
Brian and Courtney will never be placed on the same team.
If Frank is placed on the Support team, then David is also placed on the Support team.

1. [Step 1] Conduct an Overview analysis:
   - What is this game's Situation?
   - Who or what are the game's Entities?
   - What is the game's Action?
   - What are the Limitations explicit in the game setup?
2. [Step 2] Create an initial Sketch:

Explanations

Compare your work to that of an LSAT expert. Keep track of any case in which you incorrectly characterized the action described in the setup, and any case in which you drew a sketch framework that does not match the details of the game's situation.

Practice 1

Six witnesses—B, C, D, E, F, and G—are scheduled to testify in a court case. Three witnesses will be examined by the plaintiff's lead litigator, while the other three will be examined by the assistant attorney. Each witness will be examined once. The order in which they testify, and who examines them, are restricted by the following conditions:

Witness C will testify immediately after witness D.
Witness G will testify before witness F but after witness C.
Witness E will testify after witness D.
The lead litigator will examine the first and last witnesses.
The lead litigator will examine witness C.
The assistant attorney will not examine three consecutive witnesses.

1. [Step 1] Conduct an Overview analysis:
   - What is this game's Situation? *Witnesses testifying in a court case.*
   - Who or what are the game's Entities? *Six witnesses—B, C, D, E, F, and G—and two examiners—a (assistant attorney) and l (lead litigator).*
   - What is the game's Action? *Sequencing-Matching Hybrid. Determine the order in which the witnesses testify (Sequencing) and determine who examines each witness (Matching).*
   - What are the Limitations explicit in the game setup? *Each witness is examined once, making this standard one-to-one Sequencing. For the Matching action, each witness will be examined by one person; three by the lead litigator, and three by the assistant attorney.*

2. [Step 2] Create an initial Sketch:

```
1  2  3  4  5  6
_  _  _  _  _  _   BCDEFG
                   aaalll
```

Practice 2

A company is conducting a quarterly review. Eight employees—Grant, Heather, Julia, Kendra, Lauren, Matthew, Nathan, and Oliver—will each attend a meeting with a supervisor on either Thursday or Friday of this week. One employee at a time will attend each meeting. The arrangement of the meetings is subject to the following restrictions:

If Heather attends her meeting on Thursday, then Lauren and Nathan will both attend their meetings on Friday.
Grant will attend his meeting on a different day than Matthew.
Julia will attend her meeting after Oliver and on the same day.
Friday will have no more than three meeting slots.
Julia's meeting is never the last meeting of the day.

1. [Step 1] Conduct an Overview analysis:
   - What is this game's Situation? *Employees getting their quarterly reviews.*
   - Who or what are the game's Entities? *Eight employees—G, H, J, K, L, M, N, and O.*
   - What is the game's Action? *Distribution-Sequencing Hybrid; determine the day on which each employee has a meeting (Distribution), followed by the order in which they have their meetings on each day (Sequencing).*
   - What are the Limitations explicit in the game setup? *Each employee will attend*

"a meeting," so that's one each, and they meet "one . . . at a time," so the sequencing is one-to-one.

2. [Step 2] Create an initial Sketch:

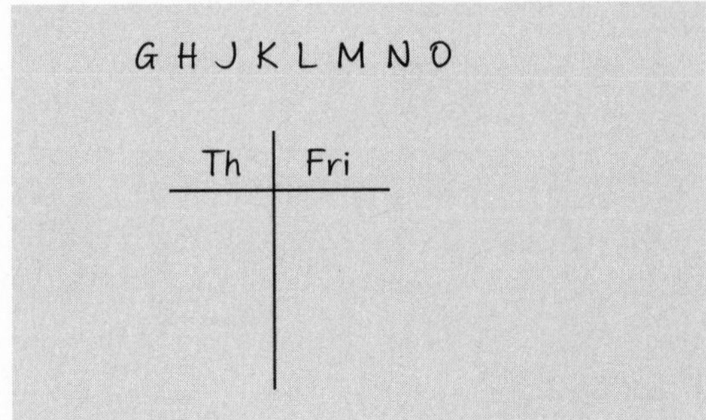

Practice 3

A senior partner is deciding how to organize the firm's associates for a new class action. Six of the eight associates—Ann, Brian, Courtney, David, Edwin, Frank, Gina, and Hannah—will be selected for either the Support or the Trial team, each team needing at least two associates. The selection is governed by the following conditions:

There are at most three associates selected for the Support team.

If Edwin is on the Trial team, then Ann is on the Support team and David is not selected for either.

If Ann is selected, then Hannah and Ann are placed on the same team.

Brian and Courtney will never be placed on the same team.

If Frank is placed on the Support team, then David is also placed on the Support team.

1. [Step 1] Conduct an Overview analysis:
   - What is this game's Situation? *A law firm putting together teams of associates for a new class action.*
   - Who or what are the game's Entities? *Eight associates—A, B, C, D, E, F, G, and H—and two teams—Support and Trial.*
   - What is the game's Action? *Selection-Distribution Hybrid; determine which associates are going to be assigned to teams (Selection), then determine the team to which they will be assigned (Distribution).*
   - What are the Limitations explicit in the game setup? *Exactly six of the eight are selected, so two will be out. The six that are selected will each be assigned to exactly one team.*
2. [Step 2] Create an initial Sketch:

ABCDEFGH

Supp | Trial | Out

Once you have your sketch in place for Hybrid games, take note of how each rule affects one or both of the Hybrid's two actions. Where and how you depict each rule will have much to do with the part(s) of the game it restricts. Keep that in mind as you turn to the next section and apply Step 3 to Hybrid games.

HYBRID GAMES RULES

LEARNING OBJECTIVES

In this section of the chapter, you'll practice

- Applying Step 3 of the Logic Games Method to Hybrid games by analyzing and sketching the rules

Prepare

The rules in Hybrid games will be of the same types as those in their single-action counterparts. The only difference is that within a Hybrid game, you will see a mix of different types of rules.

LOGIC GAMES STRATEGY

Hybrid rules tell you one of the following:

- How one action of the game is restricted
- How the actions are restricted simultaneously

When you are analyzing the rules in Hybrid games, pay attention to which of the actions each rule affects. In a Sequencing-Matching Hybrid, for example, some rules will exclusively apply to the Sequencing element, some to the Matching, and a couple may overlap. Here's the "real-life" game about flowers in the window box with several logic games-style rules appended to it.

> An apartment dweller is arranging six plants—labeled A, B, C, D, E, and F—from left to right in a planter box with six spaces, with one plant occupying each space. Each plant flowers in exactly one of three colors—red, white, or yellow. His arrangement of the plants will correspond to the following considerations:
>
> A and C are placed in adjacent boxes.
> F is placed in a space to the left of D.
> Plant E has yellow flowers.
> Plant D does not have white flowers.
> Plant C will occupy a space between two plants that have white flowers.

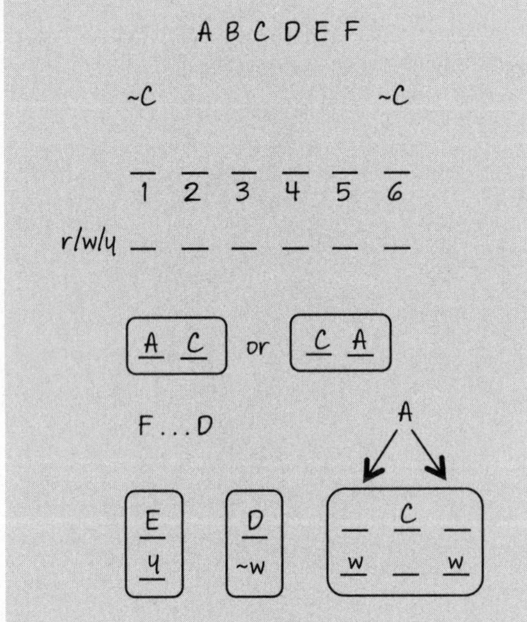

In this scenario, Rules 1 and 2 apply specifically to the Sequencing action. Rules 3 and 4 apply exclusively to the Matching action. Rule 5, however, touches both the Sequencing and Matching lines of the initial sketch. Because Rule 5 is a true "Hybrid rule," at least two deductions result from it: 1) It prevents C from being in either Space 1 or Space 6, and 2) it establishes A as having white flowers, because Rule 1 places A adjacent to C on the Sequencing line.

As you review the sample Hybrid rules in the following table, assess which part of the Hybrid games described each rule affects. Make a note of how the LSAT expert analyzes and draws "Hybrid rules" that affect both of the game's actions.

Rules		Analysis
A Sequencing-Matching Hybrid in which racers T, V, W, X, Y, and Z are arranged in six consecutive lanes at the starting line, and each one is wearing one brand of shoe—k, l, or m.		
V does not wear *k* unless X is in lane 6.	→	If $\frac{V}{k}$ → X = 6 If X ≠ 6 → ~ $\frac{V}{k}$
Only one racer is wearing brand *m*, and that racer is in a higher-numbered lane than T and a lower-numbered lane than W	→	$\frac{T}{k/l}$ . . . $\frac{\ }{m}$ . . . $\frac{W}{k/l}$
Z wears brand *l* in lane 4, and no racer in a higher-numbered lane wears brand *l*.	→	1 2 3 4 5 6 _ _ _ $\frac{Z}{l}$ $\frac{\ }{k/m}$ $\frac{\ }{k/m}$
A Selection-Sequencing Hybrid in which six out of eight collectibles—B, D, F, G, H, M, N, and P—are selected and arranged in 6 positions labeled 1 to 6 from left to right.		
F cannot appear to the left of G.	→	Never F . . . G
B is chosen only if D is not in position 6.	→	If B selected → D ≠ 6 If D = 6 → B not selected
If M appears to the right of P, then N is in position 3.	→	If P . . . M → N = 3 If N ≠ 3 → ~(P . . . M)
A Distribution-Selection game in which six of nine workers—F, G, H, J, K, L, M, N and P—are selected and assigned to either the front or back area.		
L does not work in the front area.	→	Front | Back ~L
If H is assigned to the front area, then G is assigned to the back area.	→	If H = Front → G = Back If G ≠ Back → H ≠ Front

Now, get in some practice analyzing and drawing rules in Hybrid games. In the first exercise, consider the brief game descriptions to help you determine how best to draw the rules that follow. In exercises 2–4, you'll revisit the game setups you saw in the previous section of this chapter, now accompanied by full sets of rules.

Practice

Practice 1

Directions: Analyze and draw each of following Hybrid game rules. Use the brief game description to guide your depiction of the game's framework.

Rules		Analysis
A Sequencing-Matching Hybrid in which six cars—B, C, D, E, F, and G—are exhibited in order at a car show, and each car is from a different decade—1970s, 1980s, or 1990s.		
1. The third and sixth car must be from different decades.	⟶	
2. If C is presented before B, then the second car must be from an earlier decade than the sixth car.	⟶	
3. F is not from the 1970s unless D is immediately before E.	⟶	
A Distribution-Sequencing Hybrid in which six students—P, Q, R, S, T, and U—are each assigned to exactly one class—art or music—and are arranged in order of the presentations they give in class.		
4. Q is assigned to the music class.	⟶	
5. If T is assigned to the art class, then P and U must be assigned to the music class, with P presenting some time before U.	⟶	
6. R is assigned to the art class if S gives the last presentation in the music class.	⟶	
A Selection-Sequencing Hybrid that selects five out of eight artifacts—S, T, U, V, W, X, Y, and Z—and arranges them in order of presentation.		
7. V is selected only if X is presented at some time before it.	⟶	
8. T is not selected unless U and W are presented consecutively.	⟶	
9. S cannot be one of the first three artifacts presented.	⟶	
A Selection-Matching Hybrid in which exactly six of eight canvasses—A, B, C, D, E, F, G, and H—are selected and matched to exactly one of three colors—red, silver, or tan.		
10. B cannot be selected if it is red.	⟶	
11. If C and D are selected, then exactly two of the canvasses selected are silver.	⟶	
12. Exactly three of the canvasses selected are tan.	⟶	

Practice 2

Directions: Take a couple minutes to review the game setup, summarize your Overview analysis, and recreate the initial Sketch. Then, one at a time, analyze the rules, answer the questions about each one, and draw the rule either inside or underneath the sketch framework.

Six witnesses—B, C, D, E, F, and G—are scheduled to testify in a court case. Three witnesses will be examined by the plaintiff's lead litigator, while the other three will be examined by the assistant attorney. Each witness will be examined once. The order in which they testify, and who examines them, are restricted by the following conditions:

Witness C will testify immediately after witness D.
Witness G will testify before witness F but after witness C.
Witness E will testify after witness D.
The lead litigator will examine the first and last witnesses.
The lead litigator will examine C.
The assistant attorney will not examine three consecutive witnesses.

1. [Step 1] Summarize your Overview analysis:

2. [Step 2] Create an initial Sketch:

3. [Step 3] Analyze and draw the Rules:
   - For each rule, answer the following questions and draw the rule in the appropriate box.
     - What does the rule restrict, and what does it leave open?
     - What are the rule's negative implications, if any?
     - Can the rule be depicted inside the sketch framework?

Rule 1:	Rule 2:
Rule 3:	Rule 4:
Rule 5:	Rule 6:

Practice 3

Directions: Take a couple minutes to review the game setup, summarize your Overview analysis, and recreate the initial Sketch. Then, one at a time, analyze the rules, answer the questions about each one, and draw the rule either inside or underneath the sketch framework.

A company is conducting a quarterly review. Eight employees—Grant, Heather, Julia, Kendra, Lauren, Matthew, Nathan, and Oliver—will each attend a meeting with a supervisor on either Thursday or Friday of this week. One employee at a time will attend each meeting. The arrangement of the meetings is subject to the following restrictions:

If Heather attends her meeting on Thursday, then Lauren and Nathan will both attend their meetings on Friday.
Grant will attend his meeting on a different day than Matthew.
Julia will attend her meeting after Oliver and on the same day.
Friday will have no more than three meeting slots.
Julia's meeting is never the last meeting of the day.

1. [Step 1] Summarize your Overview analysis:

2. [Step 2] Create an initial Sketch:

3. [Step 3] Analyze and draw the Rules:
   - For each rule, answer the following questions and draw the rule in the appropriate box.
     - What does the rule restrict, and what does it leave open?
     - What are the rule's negative implications, if any?
     - Can the rule be depicted inside the sketch framework?

Rule 1:	Rule 2:
Rule 3:	Rule 4:
Rule 5:	

Practice 4

Directions: Take a couple minutes to review the game setup, summarize your Overview analysis, and recreate the initial Sketch. Then, one at a time, analyze the rules, answer the questions about each one, and draw the rule either inside or underneath the sketch framework.

A senior partner is deciding how to organize the firm's associates for a new class action. Six of the eight associates—Ann, Brian, Courtney, David, Edwin, Frank, Gina, and Hannah—will be selected for either the Support team or the Trial team, each team needing at least two associates. The selection is governed by the following conditions:

There are at most three associates selected for the Support team.
If Edwin is on the Trial team, then Ann is on the Support team and David is not selected for either.
If Ann is selected, then Hannah and Ann are placed on the same team.
Brian and Courtney will never be placed on the same team.
If Frank is placed on the Support team, then David is also placed on the Support team.

1. [Step 1] Summarize your Overview analysis:

2. [Step 2] Create an initial Sketch:

3. [Step 3] Analyze and draw the Rules:
   - For each rule, answer the following questions and draw the rule in the appropriate box.
     - What does the rule restrict, and what does it leave open?
     - What are the rule's negative implications, if any?
     - Can the rule be depicted inside the sketch framework?

Rule 1:	Rule 2:
Rule 3:	Rule 4:
Rule 5:	

Explanations

Compare your work to that of an LSAT expert. Pay close attention to how the expert analyzed each rule and then depicted it within or beneath the game's initial sketch.

Practice 1

Rules		Analysis
A Sequencing-Matching Hybrid in which six cars—B, C, D, E, F, and G—are exhibited in order at a car show, and each car is from a different decade—1970s, 1980s, or 1990s.		
1. The third and sixth car must be from different decades.	→	Dec: $3^{rd} \neq 6^{th}$
2. If C is presented before B, then the second car must be from an earlier decade than the sixth car.	→	If C . . . B → $2^{nd} < 6^{th}$ (Dec) If $2^{nd} > 6^{th}$ (Dec) → B . . . C
3. F is not from the 1970s unless D is immediately before E.	→	If $\frac{F}{70}$ → [DE] If ~[DE] → ~ $\frac{F}{70}$
A Distribution-Sequencing Hybrid in which six students—P, Q, R, S, T, and U—are each assigned to exactly one class—art or music—and are arranged in order of the presentations they give in class.		
4. Q is assigned to the music class.	→	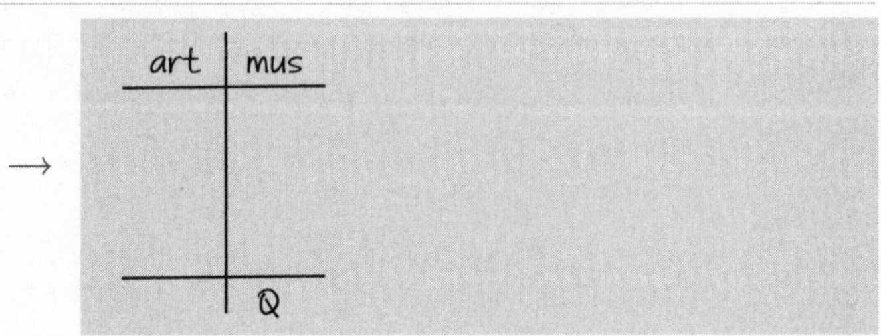
5. If T is assigned to the art class, then P and U must be assigned to the music class, with P presenting some time before U.	→	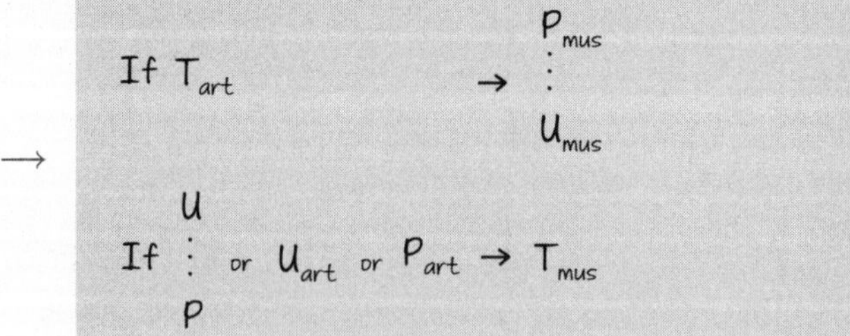
6. R is assigned to the art class if S gives the last presentation in the music class.	→	If $S_{mus\ (last)}$ → R_{art} If R_{mus} → $S_{mus\ (not\ last)\ or\ art}$

A Selection-Sequencing Hybrid that selects five out of eight artifacts—S, T, U, V, W, X, Y, and Z—and arranges them in order of presentation.

7. V is selected only if X is presented at some time before it. →

   If V = Sel → X . . . V

   If X = 5 or X ≠ Sel → V ≠ Sel

8. T is not selected unless U and W are presented consecutively. →

   If T = Sel → [UW] or [WU]

   If ~[UW] and ~[WU] → T ≠ Sel

   If U ≠ Sel or W ≠ Sel → T ≠ Sel

9. S cannot be one of the first three artifacts presented. →

   S T U V W X Y Z

   _ _ _ _ _ | _ _ _
   1 2 3 4 5 | out
   ~S ~S ~S

A Selection-Matching Hybrid in which exactly six of eight canvasses—A, B, C, D, E, F, G, and H—are selected and matched to exactly one of three colors—red, silver, or tan.

10. B cannot be selected if it is red. →

    never [B / r]

11. If C and D are selected, then exactly two of the canvasses selected are silver. →

12. Exactly three of the canvasses selected are tan. →

    Exactly 3 t

    or

    r s t
    t
    t

Practice 2

Six witnesses—B, C, D, E, F, and G—are scheduled to testify in a court case. Three witnesses will be examined by the plaintiff's lead litigator, while the other three will be examined by the assistant attorney. Each witness will be examined once. The order in which they testify, and who examines them, are restricted by the following conditions:

Witness C will testify immediately after witness D.
Witness G will testify before witness F but after witness C.
Witness E will testify after witness D.
The lead litigator will examine the first and last witnesses.
The lead litigator will examine C.
The assistant attorney will not examine three consecutive witnesses.

1. [Step 1] Summarize your Overview analysis: *A Sequencing-Matching Hybrid that asks for the order in which six witnesses testify at a court case, as well as which one of the two lawyers will examine them. Three witnesses will be examined by the lead litigator, and three by the assistant attorney.*
2. [Step 2] Create an initial Sketch:

```
1 2 3 4 5 6
                  BCDEFG
_ _ _ _ _ _
                  aaalll
```

3. [Step 3] Analyze and draw the Rules:
   - Rule 1:
     - What does the rule restrict, and what does it leave open? *D and C will be in that order, consecutively.*
     - What are the rule's negative implications, if any? *C cannot be first and D cannot be last.*
     - Can the rule be depicted inside the sketch framework? *No.*
     - Draw the rule:

```
[DC]
```

   - Rule 2:
     - What does the rule restrict, and what does it leave open? *In order, C, then G, then F will testify, but not necessarily consecutively.*
     - What are the rule's negative implications, if any? *With two people after, C cannot go fifth or sixth. G is in the middle, so cannot be first or sixth. F has to come after two people, so F cannot go first or second.*
     - Can the rule be depicted inside the sketch framework? *No.*
     - Draw the rule:

```
C...G...F
```

   - Rule 3:
     - What does the rule restrict, and what does it leave open? *D will go before E, but with any amount of space in between.*
     - What are the rule's negative implications, if any? *D cannot go last and E cannot go first.*
     - Can the rule be depicted inside the sketch framework? *No.*
     - Draw the rule:

```
D...E
```

   - Rule 4:
     - What does the rule restrict, and what does it leave open? *This establishes the lead litigator in the first and sixth positions, but does not state who the witnesses will be.*
     - What are the rule's negative implications, if any? *N/A*
     - Can the rule be depicted inside the sketch framework? *Yes.*
     - Draw the rule:

```
1 2 3 4 5 6
_ _ _ _ _ _
l         l
```

   - Rule 5:
     - What does the rule restrict, and what does it leave open? *This matches C to the lead*

litigator, but does not establish when it will occur.

- What are the rule's negative implications, if any? *C will not be examined by the assistant attorney.*
- Can the rule be depicted inside the sketch framework? *No.*
- Draw the rule:

- Rule 6:
  - What does the rule restrict, and what does it leave open? *The assistant attorney will not appear in three consecutive positions.*
  - What are the rule's negative implications, if any? *The lead litigator will have to examine at least one witness in between the assistant attorney's witnesses.*
  - Can the rule be depicted inside the sketch framework? *No.*
  - Draw the rule:

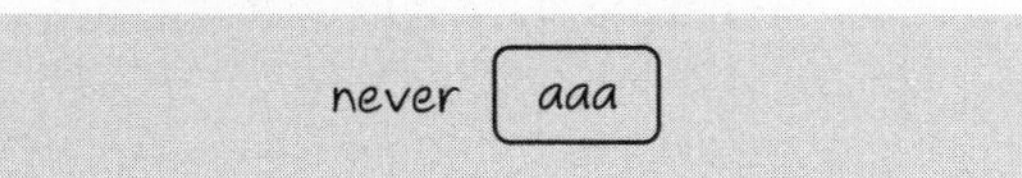

Practice 3

A company is conducting a quarterly review. Eight employees—Grant, Heather, Julia, Kendra, Lauren, Matthew, Nathan, and Oliver—will each attend a meeting with a supervisor on either Thursday or Friday of this week. One employee at a time will attend each meeting. The arrangement of the meetings is subject to the following restrictions:

If Heather attends her meeting on Thursday, then Lauren and Nathan will both attend their meetings on Friday.
Grant will attend his meeting on a different day than Matthew.
Julia will attend her meeting after Oliver and on the same day.
Friday will have no more than three meeting slots.
Julia's meeting is never the last meeting of the day.

1. [Step 1] Summarize your Overview analysis: *A Distribution-Sequencing Hybrid in which eight employees will be assigned to either a Thursday or Friday meeting, and the employees on each day will be arranged in order. Each employee meets on just one day, but there is no limit to the number of employees on either day.*
2. [Step 2] Create an initial Sketch:

3. [Step 3] Analyze and draw the Rules:
   - Rule 1:
     - What does the rule restrict, and what does it leave open? *If Heather is on Thursday, then Lauren and Nathan are both on Friday.*
     - What are the rule's negative implications, if any? *By contrapositive, if either Lauren or Nathan is not on Friday (i.e., is on Thursday), then Heather is not on Thursday (i.e., is on Friday).*
     - Can the rule be depicted inside the sketch framework? *No.*
     - Draw the rule:

       If H = Th → L = Fr and N = Fr
       If L = Th or N = Th → H = Fr

   - Rule 2:
     - What does the rule restrict, and what does it leave open? *Grant and Matthew cannot be on the same day.*
     - What are the rule's negative implications, if any? *They must be on different days. With only two days, that means Grant is on one and Matthew is on the other.*
     - Can the rule be depicted inside the sketch framework? *Yes.*

- Draw the rule:

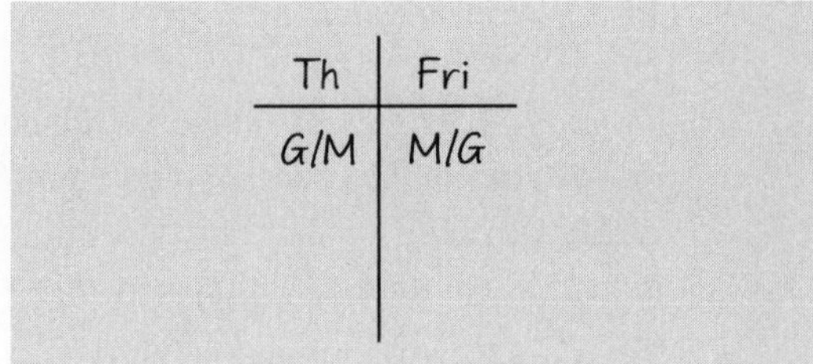

- Rule 3:
  - What does the rule restrict, and what does it leave open? *Julia and Oliver are on the same day, with Oliver going before Julia. This still could happen on either day.*
  - What are the rule's negative implications, if any? *Julia will not be first on either day, and Oliver will not be last.*
  - Can the rule be depicted inside the sketch framework? *No.*
  - Draw the rule:

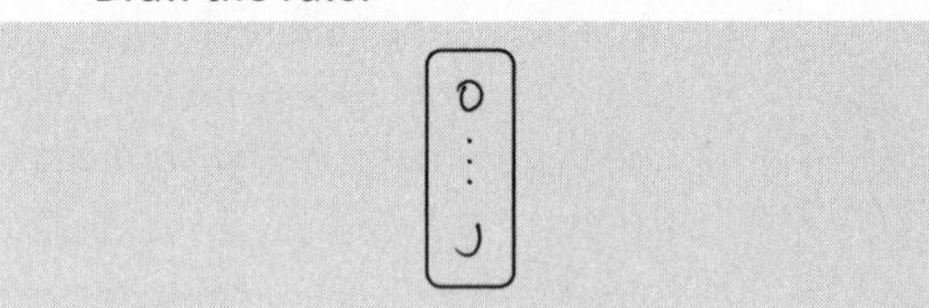

- Rule 4:
  - What does the rule restrict, and what does it leave open? *This sets a maximum of three spaces for Friday.*
  - What are the rule's negative implications, if any? *At least five employees have to be on Thursday, otherwise there would be too many left for Friday.*
  - Can the rule be depicted inside the sketch framework? *Not entirely; add the minimum slots to Thursday, and write in the minimum and maximum numbers above Thursday and Friday columns, respectively.*
  - Draw the rule:

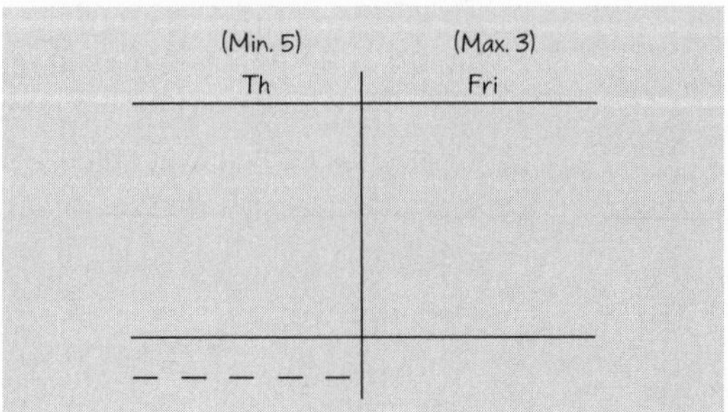

- Rule 5:
  - What does the rule restrict, and what does it leave open? *Julia cannot be last.*
  - What are the rule's negative implications, if any? *At least one person must come after Julia, regardless of the day.*
  - Can the rule be depicted inside the sketch framework? *No.*
  - Draw the rule:

Practice 4

A senior partner is deciding how to organize the firm's associates for a new class action. Six of the eight associates—Ann, Brian, Courtney, David, Edwin, Frank, Gina, and Hannah—will be selected for either the Trial team or Support team, each team needing at least two associates. The selection is governed by the following conditions:

There are at most three associates selected for the Support team.
If Edwin is on the Trial team, then Ann is on the Support team and David is not selected for either.
If Ann is selected, then Hannah and Ann are placed on the same team.
Brian and Courtney will never be placed on the same team.
If Frank is placed on the Support team, then David is also placed on the Support team.

1. [Step 1] Summarize your Overview analysis: *A Selection-Distribution Hybrid in which six of eight associates are selected, and each one is placed on one of two teams: Trial or Support. Each team needs at least two associates, and exactly two associates will go unselected.*
2. [Step 2] Create an initial Sketch:

A B C D E F G H

Supp	Trial	Out
—	—	—
—	—	—

3. [Step 3] Analyze and draw the Rules:
   - Rule 1:
     - What does the rule restrict, and what does it leave open? *The support team will have a maximum of three associates.*
     - What are the rule's negative implications, if any? *The support team has to have at least two associates, so it can only have two or three. If it had two, the Trial team would get four associates. If support had three, the Trial team would get three.*
     - Can the rule be depicted inside the sketch framework? *It can be drawn to the side, or incorporated into Limited Options.*
     - Draw the rule:

Supp	Trial	Out
—	—	—
—	—	—
	—	
	—	

or

Supp	Trial	Out
—	—	—
—	—	—
—	—	

or

Supp: Max. 3

   - Rule 2:
     - What does the rule restrict, and what does it leave open? *If Edwin is on the Trial team, then Ann is on the Support team and David is out.*
     - What are the rule's negative implications, if any? *By contrapositive, if Ann is not on the Support team or if David is not out, then Edwin cannot be on the Trial team.*
     - Can the rule be depicted inside the sketch framework? *No.*
     - Draw the rule:

If E_{Tr} → A_{Sup} and D_{Out}

If ~D_{Out} or ~A_{Sup} → ~E_{Tr}

   - Rule 3:
     - What does the rule restrict, and what does it leave open? *If Ann is selected, then Hannah is also selected and on her team.*
     - What are the rule's negative implications, if any? *If Hannah is not selected, then neither is Ann—which would mean everyone else is.*
     - Can the rule be depicted inside the sketch framework? *No.*
     - Draw the rule:

If $A_{Sup\ or\ Tr}$ → [A H]

If H_{Out} → A_{Out}

   - Rule 4:
     - What does the rule restrict, and what does it leave open? *Brian and Courtney will never be assigned to the same team.*
     - What are the rule's negative implications, if any? *Don't assume they're just on separate teams. It's possible one is just not selected—or maybe they're both out!*
     - Can the rule be depicted inside the sketch framework? *No.*
     - Draw the rule:

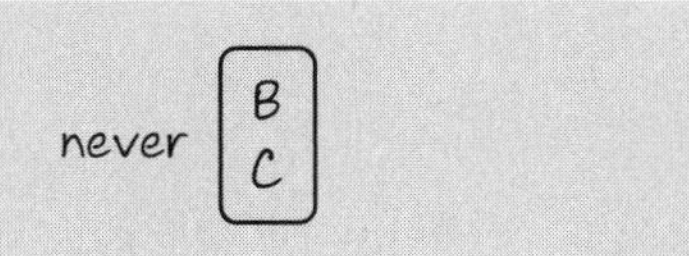

- Rule 5:
  - What does the rule restrict, and what does it leave open? *If Frank is on the Support team, then so is David.*
  - What are the rule's negative implications, if any? *If David is not on the Support team, then neither is Frank. That doesn't mean they're on the Trial team. One or both of them could be out.*
  - Can the rule be depicted inside the sketch framework? *No.*
  - Draw the rule:

$\text{If } F_{Sup} \rightarrow D_{Sup}$

$\text{If } {\sim}D_{Sup} \rightarrow {\sim}F_{Sup}$

As you've seen, the rules vary a great deal in Hybrid games that combine different actions. Once the rules are in place, however, deductions will turn out to spring from the same sources you've seen in all of the single-action games you've practiced. The BLEND checklist is still your go-to source for making all of the game's available deductions. Practice applying it to Hybrids in the next section of this chapter.

HYBRID GAMES DEDUCTIONS

LEARNING OBJECTIVES

In this section of the chapter, you'll practice

- Applying Step 4 of the Logic Games Method to Hybrid games by combining rules and restrictions to make all valid deductions in the game.

Prepare

The notion of Hybrid deductions is a bit of a misnomer. Because Hybrid games combine the actions of two (or occasionally three) of the standard logic games actions, the deductions you're likely to encounter correspond to the actions the testmaker has chosen to create the game. Thus, in Sequencing-Matching Hybrids (the most common Hybrid actions), Blocks of Entities are likely to form the basis for Sequencing deductions and Duplications and/or Numbers Restrictions will give you further certainty for the Matching component. On the other hand, if you have a Selection-Sequencing Hybrid game, expect to see Numbers Restrictions informing the Selection action and Blocks of Entities driving the Sequencing action. The one type of deduction unique to Hybrid games comes from rules and restrictions that cross over between the actions, providing deductions in one part of the game based on restrictions in the other.

LOGIC GAMES STRATEGY

In Hybrid games, deductions are likely to stem from:

- **BLEND**—Because Hybrid games may involve any of the standard logic games actions, all five of the BLEND elements are on the table.
- **"Cross Over" rules**—In Hybrid games, keep an eye out for rules that provide restrictions to multiple actions in the game.

Use all that you've learned about deductions thus far as you practice applying Step 4 of the Logic Games Method to Hybrid games.

Practice

Directions: In each game setup, first reacquaint yourself with the setup and rules. Then, combine the rules and restrictions to make all available deductions, recording your analyses as indicated. Finally, test your deductions by answering the questions that accompany each game. You can find expert analysis and explanations at the end of the Practice section.

Practice 1

Six witnesses—B, C, D, E, F, and G—are scheduled to testify in a court case. Three witnesses will be examined by the plaintiff's lead litigator, while the other three will be examined by the assistant attorney. Each witness will be examined once. The order in which they testify, and who examines them, are restricted by the following conditions:

Witness C will testify immediately after witness D.
Witness G will testify before witness F but after witness C.
Witness E will testify after witness D.
The lead litigator will examine the first and last witnesses.
The lead litigator will examine C.
The assistant attorney will not examine three consecutive witnesses.

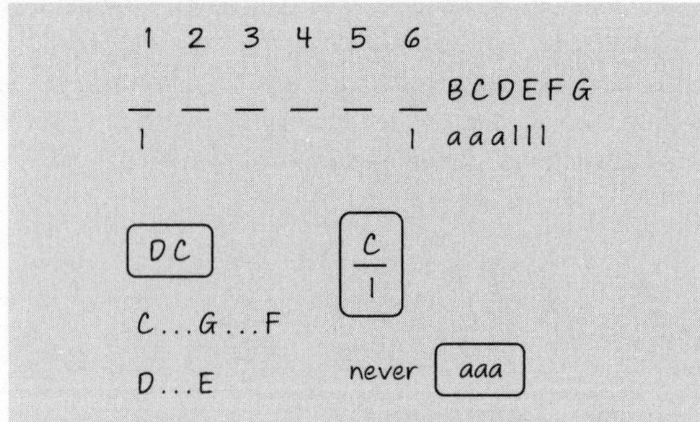

1. Which entities or positions are the most restricted in this game? Why?

2. Which elements from the BLEND checklist can you identify in this game? Are there
   - Blocks of entities? If so, what are they?
   - Limited Options? If so, which rule(s) trigger them?
   - Established Entities? If so, which ones?
   - Number Restrictions? If so, describe them.
   - Duplications? If so, which rules share an entity?

3. Combine the rules and restrictions to create a Master Sketch depicting all of the deductions available in this game:

4. Evaluate your sketch by answering the following questions:
   - Which position could witness F be in?
   - What is the earliest position in which witness E could be scheduled?
   - Which witnesses must be examined by the assistant attorney?
   - Which witnesses must be examined by the lead litigator?

Practice 2

A company is conducting a quarterly review. Eight employees—Grant, Heather, Julia, Kendra, Lauren, Matthew, Nathan, and Oliver—will each attend a meeting with a supervisor on either Thursday or Friday of this week. One employee at a time will attend each meeting. The arrangement of the meetings is subject to the following restrictions:

> If Heather attends her meeting on Thursday, then Lauren and Nathan will both attend their meetings on Friday.
> Grant will attend his meeting on a different day than Matthew.
> Julia will attend her meeting after Oliver and on the same day.
> Friday will have no more than three meeting slots.
> Julia's meeting is never the last meeting of the day.

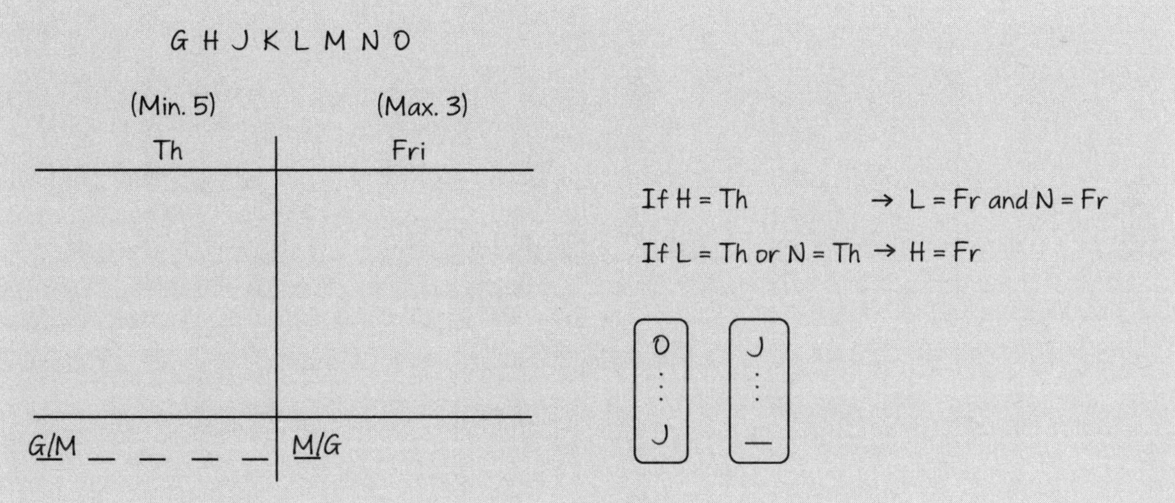

1. Which entities or positions are the most restricted in this game? Why?

2. Which elements from the BLEND checklist can you identify in this game? Are there
   - Blocks of entities? If so, what are they?
   - Limited Options? If so, which rule(s) trigger them?
   - Established Entities? If so, which ones?
   - Number Restrictions? If so, describe them.
   - Duplications? If so, which rules share an entity?

3. Combine the rules and restrictions to create a Master Sketch depicting all of the deductions available in this game:

4. Evaluate your sketch by answering the following questions:
   - What is the minimum number of people whose meetings are on Thursday?
   - On which day(s) could Julia's and Oliver's meetings be?
   - Who could have the last meeting on Thursday?
   - If Heather and Nathan had their meetings on the same day, what day(s) could it be?

Practice 3

A senior partner is deciding how to organize the firm's associates for a new class action. Six of the eight associates—Ann, Brian, Courtney, David, Edwin, Frank, Gina, and Hannah—will be selected for either the Support team or the Trial team, each team needing at least two associates. The selection is governed by the following conditions:

There are at most three associates selected for the Support team.
If Edwin is on the Trial team, then Ann is on the Support team and David is not selected for either.
If Ann is selected, then Hannah and Ann are placed on the same team.
Brian and Courtney will never be placed on the same team.
If Frank is placed on the Support team, then David is also placed on the Support team.

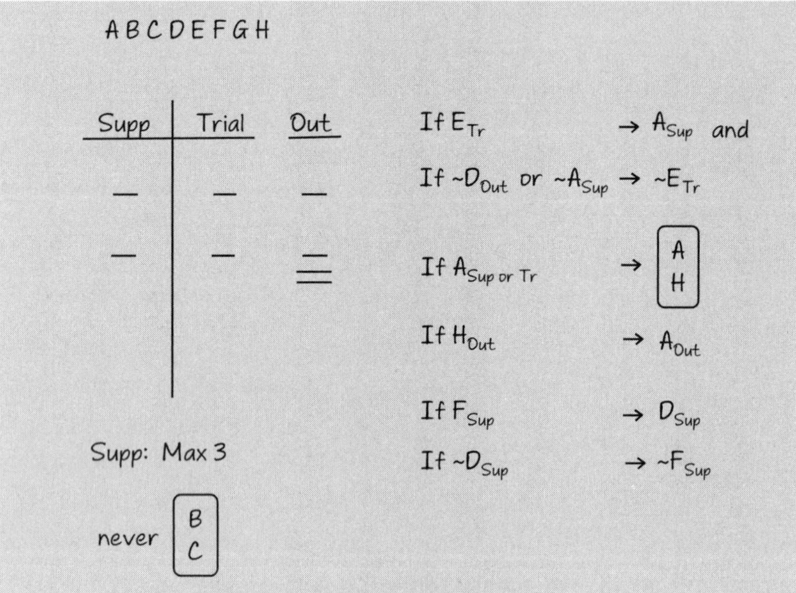

1. Which entities or positions are the most restricted in this game? Why?

2. Which elements from the BLEND checklist can you identify in this game? Are there
   - Blocks of entities? If so, what are they?
   - Limited Options? If so, which rule(s) trigger them?
   - Established Entities? If so, which ones?
   - Number Restrictions? If so, describe them.
   - Duplications? If so, which rules share an entity?

3. Combine the rules and restrictions to create a Master Sketch depicting all of the deductions available in this game:

4. Evaluate your sketch by answering the following questions:
   - What is the minimum number of associates on the Trial team?
   - What team(s), if any, could Hannah be on without Ann?
   - What team(s), if any, could David be on without Frank?
   - If Edwin is on the Trial team, who must be on the Support team?

Explanations

Compare your work to that of an LSAT expert. Pay close attention to how the expert combined the rules and restrictions to make additional deductions, and to how the expert depicted the deductions within the sketch framework.

Practice 1

Six witnesses—B, C, D, E, F, and G—are scheduled to testify in a court case. Three witnesses will be examined by the plaintiff's lead litigator, while the other three will be examined by the assistant attorney. Each witness will be examined once. The order in which they testify, and who examines them, are restricted by the following conditions:

Witness C will testify immediately after witness D.
Witness G will testify before witness F but after witness C.
Witness E will testify after witness D.
The lead litigator will examine the first and last witnesses.
The lead litigator will examine C.
The assistant attorney will not examine three consecutive witnesses.

1. Which entities or positions are the most restricted in this game? Why? *Witness C, who is already matched to the lead litigator and whose order is directly restricted by two other rules.*

2. Which elements from the BLEND checklist can you identify in this game? Are there
   - Blocks of entities? If so, what are they? *Rule 1 provides an absolute Block of D immediately before C.*
   - Limited Options? If so, which rule(s) trigger them? *N/A*
   - Established Entities? If so, which ones? *Rule 4 establishes the lead litigator to positions 1 and 6. Rule 5 establishes C with the lead litigator.*
   - Number Restrictions? If so, describe them. *Rule 6 prevents three consecutive positions with the assistant attorney.*
   - Duplications? If so, which rules share an entity? *Rules 1, 2, and 5 all mention witness C. Rules 1 and 3 mention witness D. Rules 4 and 5 mention the lead litigator.*

3. Combine the rules and restrictions to create a Master Sketch depicting all of the deductions available in this game:

The Block of witnesses D and C must appear before witnesses G and F (in that order), as well as before witness E.

DC ...G...F
E

That means D and C could only be in positions 1 and 2, or in positions 2 and 3. However, C is with the lead litigator. If C was in position 2, that would leave three consecutive positions (3, 4, and 5) for the assistant attorney. So, D and C must be positions 2 and 3.

1	2	3	4	5	6
	D	C			
l		l			l

That means witnesses 2, 4, and 5 will all be examined by the assistant attorney.

1	2	3	4	5	6
	D	C			
l	a	l	a	a	l

E, F, and G will be in the final three spots, with E in any of the three spots, and G and F, in that order, taking up the remaining spots. That leaves B for the first position.

E (positions 4–6)

1	2	3	4	5	6
B	D	C			
l	a	l	a	a	l

G . . . F (positions 4–6)

4. Evaluate your sketch by answering the following questions:
   - Which position could witness F be in? *5th or 6th.*
   - What is the earliest position in which witness E could be scheduled? *4th.*
   - Which witnesses must be examined by the assistant attorney? *D and G. (Note that G can be 4th or 5th, either way certainly being examined by the assistant attorney.)*
   - Which witnesses must be examined by the lead litigator? *B and C.*

Practice 2

A company is conducting a quarterly review. Eight employees—Grant, Heather, Julia, Kendra, Lauren, Matthew, Nathan, and Oliver—will each attend a meeting with a supervisor on either Thursday or Friday of this week. One employee at a time will attend each meeting. The arrangement of the meetings is subject to the following restrictions:

If Heather attends her meeting on Thursday, then Lauren and Nathan will both attend their meetings on Friday.

Grant will attend his meeting on a different day than Matthew.

Julia will attend her meeting after Oliver and on the same day.

Friday will have no more than three meeting slots.

Julia's meeting is never the last meeting of the day.

1. Which entities or positions are the most restricted in this game? Why? *Julia, who must be with Oliver and is the only employee with two restrictions on sequencing. Also, Friday is restricted to a maximum of three out of eight people.*

2. Which elements from the BLEND checklist can you identify in this game? Are there
   - Blocks of entities? If so, what are they? *N/A*
   - Limited Options? If so, which rule(s) trigger them? *The substantial results of the Formal Logic in Rule 1 offer a great opportunity.*
   - Established Entities? If so, which ones? *Rule 2 essentially establishes that Grant or Matthew will occupy a spot on each day.*
   - Number Restrictions? If so, describe them. *Rule 4 restricts the number of employees on Friday, which effectively sets a minimum number of employees on Thursday.*
   - Duplications? If so, which rules share an entity? *Rules 3 and 5 mention Julia.*

3. Combine the rules and restrictions to create a Master Sketch depicting all of the deductions available in this game:

Julia is the only Duplicate. Oliver will be on the same day as her, and before her. There will also be at least one more person after her.

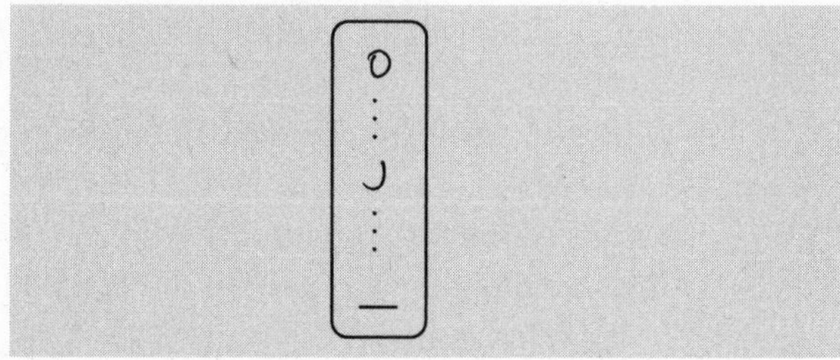

There's plenty of space on Thursday, but Friday's more of a problem. There's a maximum of three employees on Friday, and Grant or Matthew must be one. If Julia and Oliver were on Friday, that would reach the maximum, but that would put Heather on Thursday with Lauren and Nathan. Thats can't happen, so Julia and Oliver must be on Thursday.

If that wasn't immediately clear, it could be discovered by setting up Limited Options based on the first rule. The Formal Logic affects a lot of entities, so set up one sketch if Heather is on Thursday, and one if Heather is on Friday. If she's on Thursday, then Lauren and Nathan are on Friday along with Grant or Matthew. That's the maximum for Friday, so all the remaining employees (Julia, Kendra, and Oliver) are on Thursday.

Th	Fri
O ... J ... —	
H J K O G/M	L N M/G

If Heather is on Friday, the Formal Logic doesn't apply. However, there are now at least two employees on Friday. There's no longer room for both Julia and Oliver, so they must be on Thursday.

Th	Fri
O ⋮ J ⋮ —	
M/G J O — —	G/M H —

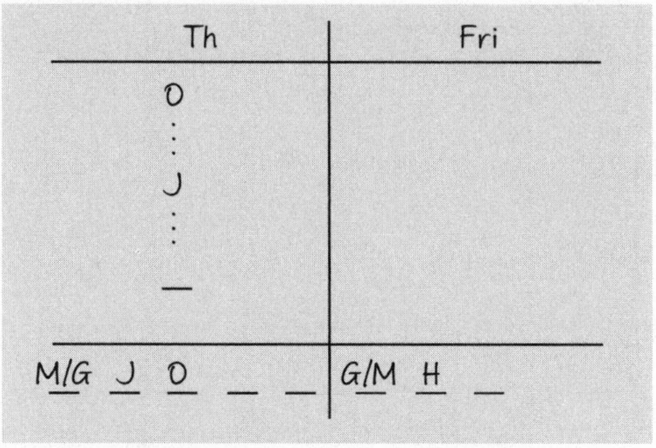

4. Evaluate your sketch by answering the following questions:
    - What is the minimum number of people whose meetings are on Thursday? *Five.*
    - On which day(s) could Julia's and Oliver's meetings be? *They must be on Thursday.*
    - Who could have the last meeting on Thursday? *Grant, Heather, Kendra, Lauren, Matthew, or Nathan; basically, anybody but Oliver and Julia.*
    - If Heather and Nathan had their meetings on the same day, what day(s), if any, could it be? *Friday; if Heather was on Thursday, Nathan would be on Friday. However, Nathan could also be on Friday if Heather is there, too.*

Practice 3

A senior partner is deciding how to organize the firm's associates for a new class action. Six of the eight associates—Ann, Brian, Courtney, David, Edwin, Frank, Gina, and Hannah—will be selected for either the Support team or the Trial team, each team needing at least two associates. The selection is governed by the following conditions:

> There are at most three associates selected for the Support team.
> If Edwin is on the Trial team, then Ann is on the Support team and David is not selected for either.
> If Ann is selected, then Hannah and Ann are placed on the same team.
> Brian and Courtney will never be placed on the same team.
> If Frank is placed on the Support team, then David is also placed on the Support team.

1. Which entities or positions are the most restricted in this game? Why? *The Support team, which is referenced in three of the rules. As for the associates, Ann is the only one duplicated and hence the most limited.*

2. Which elements from the BLEND checklist can you identify in this game? Are there
    - Blocks of entities? If so, what are they? *N/A*
    - Limited Options? If so, which rule(s) trigger them? *Rule 1 sets up only two numerical outcomes.*
    - Established Entities? If so, which ones? *N/A*
    - Number Restrictions? If so, describe them. *Rule 1 has an effect on the numeric distribution.*
    - Duplications? If so, which rules share an entity? *Rules 1, 2, and 5 mention the Support team. Rules 2 and 3 mention Ann.*

3. Combine the rules and restrictions to create a Master Sketch depicting all of the deductions available in this game:

The Support team must have at least two associates, but no more than three. If it has only two, the Trial team will have four. If Support has three, the Trial team will have three. You can draw out both options.

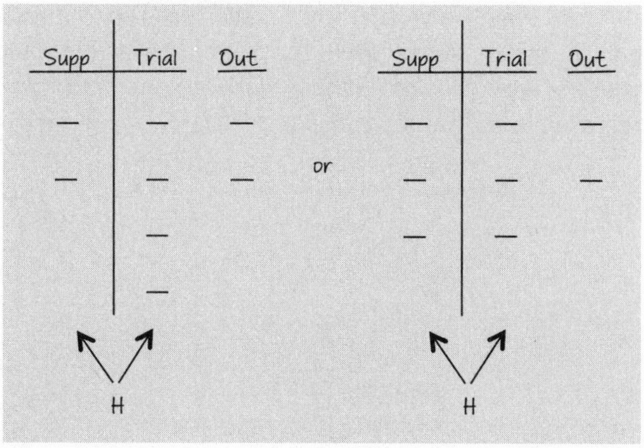

Supp	Trial	Out
—	—	—
—	—	—
	—	
	—	

(↖ ↗ H)

or

Supp	Trial	Out
—	—	—
—	—	—
—	—	

(↖ ↗ H)

Beyond that, the remaining rules are all abstract or conditional. The one rule with the biggest potential impact is the one with Ann and Hannah. If Hannah is out, then Ann must be out, which would mean everyone else is in. Drawing out Limited Options may provide some useful information.

If Hannah is out, then Ann is out, meaning Brian, Courtney, David, Edwin, Frank, and Gina are in. Brian and Courtney can't be together, so one will be on Support and one on Trial.

Supp	Trial	Out
B/C	C/B	A
—	—	H
	—	

With Ann out, Edwin cannot be on Trial, so must be on Support. That leaves only one more possible space on Support. Frank cannot be on Support without David, so Frank would have to be on Trial. At least one more person is on Trial, and that will be either David or Gina. The other person could be on either team.

Supp	Trial	Out
B/C	C/B	A
E	F	H
	—	

If Hannah is in, no concrete deductions can be made, so that would just leave the two numeric outcomes.

Supp	Trial	Out
—	—	—
—	—	—
	—	
	—	

H (Supp or Trial)

or

Supp	Trial	Out
—	—	—
—	—	—
—	—	

H (Supp or Trial)

4. Evaluate your sketch by answering the following questions:
   - What is the minimum number of associates on the Trial team? *Three.*
   - What team(s), if any, could Hannah be on without Ann? *Either Support or Trial; Ann cannot be without Hannah, but Hannah can be without Ann if Ann is out.*
   - What team(s), if any, could David be on without Frank? *Either Support or Trial; David is only required to be with Frank if Frank is on the Support team. If Frank is on the Trial team or out, David can go anywhere.*
   - If Edwin is on the Trial team, who must be on the Support team? *Ann, which would also mean Hannah has to be there.*

As always, the true assessment of your skills comes with Step 5, the Questions. The full game section of this chapter is longer than you've seen previously. That's so that you can evaluate yourself on several different types of Hybrid games. Taking and reviewing those games will help you discover which of the Hybrid actions come more naturally to you, and which you still need to work on. The recommended practice is labeled by the type of Hybrid each game represents, so that you can more efficiently follow up with additional work.

HYBRID GAMES—FULL GAMES WITH QUESTIONS

LEARNING OBJECTIVES

In this section, you'll assess your ability to

- Apply the Logic Games Method to Hybrid games.

Perform

Here is your opportunity to put all of the pieces together and assess your skills on Hybrid games. On the following pages, you'll find five full-length games along with their question sets. All of these games are from officially released LSAT tests, and all are representative of Hybrid games you could see on test day. You can take the games one at a time or all together, but for your self-evaluation to be as accurate as possible, adhere to the timing guidelines set forth in the directions.

An answer key follows the games. Complete worked example expert analyses can be found in your online resources.

After you complete and review these games, assess your performance using the evaluation guidelines. There, you'll find recommendations for additional Easy, Medium, and Hard Hybrid games from officially released LSAT exams that you can practice to continue honing your skills and raising your score.

Directions: Take no more than 9 minutes per game to complete the following five games and all of their questions.

Perform 1

Questions 1–6

An official is assigning five runners—Larry, Ned, Olivia, Patricia, and Sonja—to parallel lanes numbered consecutively 1 through 5. The official will also assign each runner to represent a different charity—F, G, H, J, and K—not necessarily in order of the runners' names as given. The following ordering restrictions apply:

The runner representing K is assigned to lane 4.

Patricia is assigned to the only lane between the lanes of the runners representing F and G.

There are exactly two lanes between Olivia's lane and the lane of the runner representing G.

Sonja is assigned to a higher-numbered lane than the lane to which Ned is assigned.

1. Which one of the following is a possible assignment of runners to lanes by the charity they represent?

	1	2	3	4	5
(A)	F	G	H	K	J
(B)	G	H	J	K	F
(C)	G	K	F	J	H
(D)	H	J	G	K	F
(E)	J	H	F	K	G

2. The lane to which Patricia is assigned must be a lane that is

   (A) next to the lane to which Larry is assigned
   (B) next to the lane to which Ned is assigned
   (C) separated by exactly one lane from the lane to which Ned is assigned
   (D) separated by exactly one lane from the lane to which Olivia is assigned
   (E) separated by exactly one lane from the lane to which Sonja is assigned

3. If Olivia is assigned to lane 2, which one of the following assignments must be made?

	Charity	Lane
(A)	F	1
(B)	G	5
(C)	H	1
(D)	H	3
(E)	J	5

4. Which one of the following is a complete and accurate list of runners each of whom could be the runner representing F?

   (A) Larry, Ned
   (B) Patricia, Sonja
   (C) Larry, Ned, Olivia
   (D) Larry, Ned, Sonja
   (E) Ned, Patricia, Sonja

5. If Ned is the runner representing J, then it must be true that

   (A) the runner representing G is assigned to lane 1
   (B) the runner representing H is assigned to lane 2
   (C) Larry is the runner representing K
   (D) Olivia is the runner representing F
   (E) Patricia is the runner representing H

6. If Larry represents J, which one of the following could be the assignment of runners to lanes?

	1	2	3	4	5
(A)	Larry	Olivia	Ned	Patricia	Sonja
(B)	Larry	Ned	Olivia	Sonja	Patricia
(C)	Larry	Sonja	Patricia	Ned	Olivia
(D)	Ned	Olivia	Larry	Patricia	Sonja
(E)	Ned	Sonja	Olivia	Patricia	Larry

PrepTest7 Sec2 Qs 19-24

Perform 2

Questions 7–12

An art teacher will schedule exactly six of eight lectures—fresco, history, lithography, naturalism, oils, pastels, sculpture, and watercolors—for three days—1, 2, and 3. There will be exactly two lectures each day—morning and afternoon. Scheduling is governed by the following conditions:

Day 2 is the only day for which oils can be scheduled.

Neither sculpture nor watercolors can be scheduled for the afternoon.

Neither oils nor pastels can be scheduled for the same day as lithography.

If pastels is scheduled for day 1 or day 2, then the lectures scheduled for the day immediately following pastels must be fresco and history, not necessarily in that order.

7. Which one of the following is an acceptable schedule of lectures for days 1, 2, and 3, respectively?

   (A) Morning: lithography, history, sculpture
   Afternoon: pastels, fresco, naturalism

   (B) Morning: naturalism, oils, fresco
   Afternoon: lithography, pastels, history

   (C) Morning: oils, history, naturalism
   Afternoon: pastels, fresco, lithography

   (D) Morning: sculpture, lithography, naturalism
   Afternoon: watercolors, fresco, pastels

   (E) Morning: sculpture, pastels, fresco
   Afternoon: lithography, history, naturalism

8. If lithography and fresco are scheduled for the afternoons of day 2 and day 3, respectively, which one of the following is a lecture that could be scheduled for the afternoon of day 1?

   (A) history
   (B) oils
   (C) pastels
   (D) sculpture
   (E) watercolors

9. If lithography and history are scheduled for the mornings of day 2 and day 3, respectively, which one of the following lectures could be scheduled for the morning of day 1?

   (A) fresco
   (B) naturalism
   (C) oils
   (D) pastels
   (E) sculpture

10 If oils and lithography are scheduled for the mornings of day 2 and day 3, respectively, which one of the following CANNOT be scheduled for any day?

   (A) fresco
   (B) history
   (C) naturalism
   (D) pastels
   (E) sculpture

11. If neither fresco nor naturalism is scheduled for any day, which one of the following must be scheduled for day 1?

   (A) history
   (B) lithography
   (C) oils
   (D) pastels
   (E) sculpture

12. If the lectures scheduled for the mornings are fresco, history, and lithography, not necessarily in that order, which one of the following could be true?

   (A) Lithography is scheduled for day 3.
   (B) Naturalism is scheduled for day 2.
   (C) Fresco is scheduled for the same day as naturalism.
   (D) History is scheduled for the same day as naturalism.
   (E) History is scheduled for the same day as oils.

PrepTest13 Sec1 Qs 12-17

Perform 3

Questions 13–19

Exactly six tourists—Harry, Irene, Klaus, Laura, Michael, Norma—are to be assigned to four guides: Valois, Xerxes, Yossarian, Zalamea. Each tourist is assigned to exactly one guide, with at least one tourist assigned to each guide. Valois speaks only French. Xerxes speaks only Turkish and Spanish. Yossarian speaks only French and Turkish. Zalamea speaks only Spanish and Russian. Each tourist speaks exactly one of the languages spoken by his or her guide and speaks no other language.

The following rules govern the assignment of the tourists to the guides:

> At least Harry and Irene are assigned to Yossarian.
> At least Laura is assigned to Zalamea.
> If Klaus is assigned to Xerxes, then Michael speaks French.

13. Each of the following could be true EXCEPT:

    (A) Both Klaus and Harry speak Turkish.
    (B) Both Klaus and Michael speak French.
    (C) Both Klaus and Michael speak Russian.
    (D) Both Klaus and Norma speak French.
    (E) Both Klaus and Norma speak Spanish.

14. Which one of the following must be true?
    (A) Zalamea is assigned fewer than three of the tourists.
    (B) Xerxes is assigned fewer than two of the tourists.
    (C) Yossarian is assigned exactly two of the tourists.
    (D) Valois is assigned exactly one of the tourists.
    (E) Zalamea is assigned exactly one of the tourists.

15. Each of the following could be true of the assignment of tourists to guides EXCEPT:
    (A) It assigns Klaus to Valois and Michael to Xerxes.
    (B) It assigns Klaus to Yossarian and Norma to Zalamea.
    (C) It assigns Laura to Zalamea and Michael to Zalamea.
    (D) It assigns Michael to Valois and Klaus to Zalamea.
    (E) It assigns Michael to Xerxes and Klaus to Zalamea.

16. If Klaus and Laura speak the same language as each other, then which one of the following must be true?
    (A) At least one of Michael and Norma speaks Spanish.
    (B) At least two tourists speak Russian.
    (C) Klaus and Laura speak Russian.
    (D) At least two tourists speak French.
    (E) At least one of Michael and Norma speaks French.

17. If Laura and Norma speak the same language as each other, then the maximum number of the tourists who could speak Turkish is
    (A) two
    (B) three
    (C) four
    (D) five
    (E) six

18. If exactly two tourists are assigned to Xerxes, then which one of the following could be true?
    (A) Norma speaks Russian and Laura speaks Russian.
    (B) Norma speaks French and Michael speaks French.
    (C) Norma speaks French and Klaus speaks Turkish.
    (D) Michael speaks Spanish and Klaus speaks Spanish.
    (E) Michael speaks French and Klaus speaks Spanish.

19. If Harry, Irene, Michael, and Norma all speak the same language as each other, then which one of the following could be true?
    (A) Klaus speaks Russian.
    (B) Exactly two of the tourists speak Russian.
    (C) Exactly three of the tourists speak Spanish.
    (D) Exactly two of the tourists speak Turkish.
    (E) Klaus speaks French.

PrepTest25 Sec3 Qs 6-12

Perform 4

Questions 20–26

Exactly six of seven researchers—three anthropologists: Franklin, Jones, and Marquez; and four linguists: Neil, Osborne, Rice, and Samuels—will be included in two three-person teams—team 1 and team 2. No researcher will be included in more than one team. Each team must include at least one anthropologist and at least one linguist. The teams' composition must conform to the following conditions:

Neither team includes both Franklin and Samuels.

Neither team includes both Neil and Rice.

If a team includes Marquez, it includes neither Rice nor Samuels.

If team 1 includes Jones, team 2 includes Rice.

20. Which one of the following could be the list of the researchers on the two teams?

(A) team 1: Franklin, Marquez, Osborne
team 2: Jones, Neil, Rice

(B) team 1: Franklin, Neil, Samuels
team 2: Jones, Osborne, Rice

(C) team 1: Franklin, Osborne, Rice
team 2: Jones, Neil, Samuels

(D) team 1: Jones, Marquez, Neil
team 2: Osborne, Rice, Samuels

(E) team 1: Jones, Osborne, Rice
team 2: Franklin, Marquez, Neil

21. If Jones is on team 1, which one of the following is a pair of researchers that must be on team 2 together?

(A) Franklin and Rice
(B) Marquez and Osborne
(C) Neil and Osborne
(D) Osborne and Samuels
(E) Rice and Samuels

22. If Neil is on team 1, which one of the following is a pair of researchers that could be on team 1 together with Neil?

(A) Franklin and Jones
(B) Jones and Osborne
(C) Jones and Rice
(D) Jones and Samuels
(E) Osborne and Samuels

23. If Franklin is on the same team as Marquez, which one of the following could be true?

(A) Jones is on team 1.
(B) Rice is on team 1.
(C) Samuels is on team 2.
(D) Both Neil and Osborne are on team 1.
(E) Both Neil and Osborne are on team 2.

24. Each of the following is a pair of researchers that could be on team 2 together EXCEPT:

(A) Franklin and Jones
(B) Franklin and Marquez
(C) Franklin and Rice
(D) Jones and Marquez
(E) Jones and Rice

25. Which one of the following could be true?

(A) Franklin is on team 1 and Neil is on team 2.
(B) Franklin is on team 2 and Jones is not on any team.
(C) Franklin is on team 2 and Marquez is on team 2.
(D) Franklin is not on any team and Jones is on team 1.
(E) Jones is on team 1 and Neil is on team 2.

26. If Marquez is on team 2, which one of the following must also be on team 2?

(A) Franklin
(B) Jones
(C) Osborne
(D) Rice
(E) Samuels

PrepTest23 Sec1 Qs 12-18

Perform 5

Questions 27–31

The members of two committees, a planting committee and a trails committee, are to be selected from among seven volunteers—F, G, H, J, K, L, and M. The following conditions govern the composition of the committees:

> Each committee must have at least three members.
>
> F cannot be on the same committee as K.
>
> If K is on a committee, J must also be on that committee.
>
> M must be on at least one of the committees.
>
> The two committees must have at least one member in common.

27. Which one of the following represents an acceptable selection of volunteers for the committees?

(A) planting: F, G, H; trails: G, J, K, L

(B) planting: F, H, J; trails: G, H, L, M

(C) planting: F, H, M; trails: G, K, L, M

(D) planting: F, G, L, M; trails: F, H

(E) planting: F, H, J, K; trails: H, L, M

28. If the planting committee consists of F, H, L, and M, and if the trails committee consists of G, H, and J, then K could replace which one of the following committee members on a committee without violating any of the conditions governing the composition of the committees?

(A) F

(B) G

(C) H

(D) L

(E) M

29. If the only members of the planting committee are G, H, and L and if the two committees are to have as many members in common as the conditions allow, then which one of the following must be true?

(A) The trails committee and the planting committee have exactly one member in common.

(B) The trails committee and the planting committee have exactly two members in common.

(C) The trails committee and the planting committee have an equal number of members.

(D) The trails committee has at least one more member than the planting committee.

(E) The planting committee has exactly two more members than the trails committee.

30. If K is on both committees and L is also on both committees and if the planting committee has exactly three members, then which one of the following must be true?

(A) F is on the planting committee.

(B) F is on the trails committee.

(C) G is on the planting committee.

(D) M is on the planting committee.

(E) M is on the trails committee.

31. The largest number of members that the planting committee and the trails committee could have in common is

(A) three

(B) four

(C) five

(D) six

(E) seven

PrepTest25 Sec3 Qs 1-5

Answer Key

Perform 1

1. (E)
2. (D)
3. (B)
4. (D)
5. (B)
6. (A)

Perform 2

7. (B)
8. (A)
9. (E)
10. (D)
11. (B)
12. (E)

Perform 3

13. (C)
14. (A)
15. (B)
16. (E)
17. (B)
18. (E)
19. (E)

Perform 4

20. (C)
21. (A)
22. (D)
23. (C)
24. (B)
25. (A)
26. (B)

Perform 5

27. (B)
28. (B)
29. (D)
30. (E)
31. (D)

Worked example explanations of these questions with complete expert analysis can be found in your Online Study Plan under Chapter 10. View or download the PDF titled "Chapter 10 Perform Full Games Explanations."

Assess

Use the following criteria to evaluate your results on the Perform games.

If, under timed conditions, you correctly answered

25–31 of the questions: Outstanding! You have demonstrated a strong skill level in Hybrid games. For further practice in Hybrids, use any of the Recommended Additional Practice sets, including the Advanced set. Then, move on to Chapter 11 on Rare games, if you have time before test day.

17–24 of the questions: Good work! You have a solid foundation in Hybrid games. For further practice in Hybrids, begin with the Foundations or Mid-Level Recommended Additional Practice set. If you have time before test day, try the Advanced Recommended Additional Practice set, as well.

0–16 of the questions: Keep working. Hybrid games historically comprise more than a fifth of all games, so you're likely to see one on test day. Continued practice will help you improve your score. Begin by reviewing this chapter. Then, try the games in the Foundations Recommended Additional Practice set. As you continue to progress, move on to the Mid-Level Recommended Additional Practice set.

To stay sharp, practice the drills in the Logic Games Training Camp for this chapter in your Online Study Plan. Training Camp drills are divided into Fundamentals, Mid-Level, and Advanced sets.

Recommended Additional Practice: Hybrid

All of the following games will provide good practice on Hybrids. They are grouped by difficulty as determined from empirical student practice results. All PrepTests included are available on LawHub with an LSAC Prep Plus subscription.

Foundations

PrepTest 70, Section 3, Game 4: Bird Lectures (Sequencing/Matching)

PrepTest 64, Section 2, Game 2: Ambassador Assignments (Selection/Distribution)

PrepTest 58, Section 3, Game 3: Flyhigh & Getaway Airlines (Sequencing/Matching)

Mid-Level

PrepTest 71, Section 2, Game 3: Literature Course (Sequencing/Matching)

PrepTest 70, Section 3, Game 3: Repertory Theater Screenings (Distribution/Sequencing)

PrepTest 61, Section 3, Game 3: Track Team (Selection/Sequencing)

PrepTest 52, Section 2, Game 3: Sales Conference Seminars (Distribution/Sequencing)

Advanced

PrepTest 66, Section 3, Game 4: Wayne & Zara's Piano Solos (Sequencing/Matching)

PrepTest 60, Section 2, Game 4: Travel Magazine Interns (Distribution/Matching)

PrepTest 56, Section 1, Game 4: Executives and Manufacturing Plants (Distribution/Sequencing)

PrepTest 53, Section 2, Game 3: Burglary Suspects (Sequencing/Matching)

Complete explanations and analysis for all of the more-than-70 official LSAT tests on LawHub that come with an LSAC LSAT Prep Plus subscription are available in Kaplan's LSAT Link and Link+ tools. Visit **www.kaptest.com/lsat** to learn more or to purchase LSAT Link or Link+.

Reflect

Think back over the study and practice you did in this chapter.

- Are you able to identify Hybrid games and their individual actions from their setups?
- Do you have a default sketch framework for each of the common Hybrid action combinations?
- What kinds of rules do you anticipate seeing in Hybrid games?
- Are you comfortable identifying which action a rule describes and determining whether and how to record the rules within the sketch framework?
- Are you making the available deductions efficiently and effectively in Hybrid games?

In the coming days or weeks before test day, take note of real-world tasks that reflect Hybrid task combinations. Consider how they mirror the setups and questions in LSAT Hybrids, and how they differ. Try to reframe real-life hybrid tasks using the terms, rules, and restrictions used by the testmaker.

Turn the page to see an LSAT Channel Spotlight feature on the game many consider the hardest in LSAT history. ▶ ▶ ▶

The LSAT Channel Spotlight

The Dinosaur Game

By Melanie Triebel and Bobby Gautam

Watch the video lesson for this Spotlight in your online Study Plan.

Being asked to arrange a display of five plastic dinosaur toys in different colors doesn't sound so bad, does it? Depending on the mood you're in, it might be downright fun. Well, LSAT test takers in June of 2009 didn't think so. The third logic game on their test—now known as PrepTest 57—had exactly that task, and it stopped some folks in their tracks.

Each of seven toy dinosaurs—an iguanadon, a lambeosaur, a plateosaur, a stegosaur, a tyrannosaur, an ultrasaur, and a velociraptor—is completely colored either green, mauve, red, or yellow. A display is to consist entirely of exactly five of these toys. The display must meet the following specifications:

> Exactly two mauve toys are included.
> The stegosaur is red and is included.
> The iguanadon is included only if it is green.
> The plateosaur is included only if it is yellow.
> The velociraptor is included only if the ultrasaur is not.
> If both the lambeosaur and the ultrasaur are included, at least one of them is not mauve.

PrepTest57 Sec1 Qs 12–17

Given the whimsy of its subject matter, it seems ironic that this is the logic game that has gone down in LSAT folklore as maybe the hardest of all time, a game to fear and panic over. How did it become so notorious? What are the reasons that it strikes people as being so weird, and so difficult? Two factors stand out.

First, it is an unusual Hybrid—Selection and Matching—that had only appeared on a released LSAT once before (on PrepTest B, administered in February 1999) and never since. Not knowing a game's type is paralyzing to some test takers. Familiarity with game types and setups is comforting, and quickly recognizing a game helps you feel that you have a head start on it. Still, you shouldn't feel too intimidated by a Selection game that asks you to choose five of seven toys, or by a Matching game that asks you to match a single color to each of five items. So the game type itself cannot account for all of this game's bad reputation.

The second factor that made the Dinosaur game intimidating is the wording of its rules. The first two are straightforward, but the next three are all Formal Logic, and they have the "only if" construction. Well-trained test takers know that "only if" translates to "then," indicating the necessary clause. But, for any test taker who misunderstands or mistranslates those rules, this game quickly goes off the rails. Whenever you draw a game's rules incorrectly, at least some of the questions will seem to make no sense at all. As if those three "only if" rules weren't enough for one game, the Dinosaur game's final rule offers another unusual construction, and thus, another opportunity to make a mistake. Patient test takers shouldn't be thrown off by the game's final rule, however, as it boils down to a simple prohibition: You can't put a mauve lambeosaur and a mauve ultrasaur together in the display. Come to think of it, maybe this game seemed so tough because nobody can ever remember exactly what color *mauve* is.

Bottom line, the Dinosaur game *is* legitimately challenging. Like all hard games, it demands respect. Likewise, it rewards careful, strategic reading and precision in translating the rules and making deductions. It is a terrific test of your expertise in using the Logic Games Method.

The Dinosaur game is a great example of one more thing that top scorers always develop: the ability to respond to unfamiliar games creatively. Anchored in the Logic Games Method, and confident in the fact that the LSAT always provides all of the information needed to answer every question, LSAT experts don't panic in the face of the unfamiliar (and, remember, even the most experienced LSAT guru could only have seen one of these games before). Indeed, LSAT experts respond to unfamiliar games with the same approach they do run of the mill games: They assess the game's Situation, Entities, Actions, and Limitations, and then create a sketch that will allow them to account for the rules. That is the foundation for success on any LSAT logic game. On unfamiliar games, however, experts know that the sketch they need probably isn't sitting in their standard library of sketches. They adapt the familiar to account for the unique.

On a game as rare as the Dinosaur game, the sketches created by two different experts may not even match one another, but they will both fit the game. And both experts' sketches will be simple, accurate, and useful. In the video that accompanies this Special Feature, two LSAT Channel experts will show you how they handled the Dinosaur game, and how they got its questions right. Try the game yourself on the following pages (but don't expect to be perfect, even if you've been acing the Perform quizzes in this book). Then, let the experts walk you through it their way. Take note of the patterns they spotted, and of how they applied the Logic Games Method to turn the unfamiliar into something manageable. You may never tackle a Selection-Matching Hybrid game again, but the lessons you'll take away from this Spotlight will serve you well whenever you bump up against a game that gives other test takers nightmares.

Questions 12–17

Each of seven toy dinosaurs—an iguanadon, a lambeosaur, a plateosaur, a stegosaur, a tyrannosaur, an ultrasaur, and a velociraptor—is completely colored either green, mauve, red, or yellow. A display is to consist entirely of exactly five of these toys. The display must meet the following specifications:

Exactly two mauve toys are included.
The stegosaur is red and is included.
The iguanadon is included only if it is green.
The plateosaur is included only if it is yellow.
The velociraptor is included only if the ultrasaur is not.
If both the lambeosaur and the ultrasaur are included, at least one of them is not mauve.

12. Which one of the following could be the toys included in the display?

(A) the lambeosaur, the plateosaur, the stegosaur, the ultrasaur, the velociraptor

(B) the lambeosaur, the plateosaur, the stegosaur, the tyrannosaur, the ultrasaur

(C) the iguanadon, the lambeosaur, the plateosaur, the stegosaur, the ultrasaur

(D) the iguanadon, the lambeosaur, the plateosaur, the tyrannosaur, the velociraptor

(E) the iguanadon, the lambeosaur, the stegosaur, the ultrasaur, the velociraptor

13. If the tyrannosaur is not included in the display, then the display must contain each of the following EXCEPT:

(A) a green iguanadon
(B) a mauve velociraptor
(C) a mauve lambeosaur
(D) a mauve ultrasaur
(E) a yellow plateosaur

14. Which one of the following is a pair of toys that could be included in the display together?

(A) a green lambeosaur and a mauve velociraptor
(B) a green lambeosaur and a yellow tyrannosaur
(C) a green lambeosaur and a yellow ultrasaur
(D) a yellow tyrannosaur and a green ultrasaur
(E) a yellow tyrannosaur and a red velociraptor

15. If the display includes a yellow tyrannosaur, then which one of the following must be true?

(A) The iguanadon is included in the display.
(B) The plateosaur is not included in the display.
(C) The display includes two yellow toy dinosaurs.
(D) The display contains a green lambeosaur.
(E) The display contains a mauve velociraptor.

16. If both the iguanadon and the ultrasaur are included in the display, then the display must contain which one of the following?

(A) a mauve tyrannosaur
(B) a mauve ultrasaur
(C) a yellow lambeosaur
(D) a yellow plateosaur
(E) a yellow ultrasaur

17. If the display includes two green toys, then which one of the following could be true?

(A) There is exactly one yellow toy included in the display.
(B) The tyrannosaur is included in the display and it is green.
(C) Neither the lambeosaur nor the velociraptor is included in the display.
(D) Neither the tyrannosaur nor the velociraptor is included in the display.
(E) Neither the ultrasaur nor the velociraptor is included in the display.

PrepTest57 Sec1 Qs 12–17

Complete answers and explanations are provided in The LSAT Channel Spotlight video "Limited Options" in your online Study Plan.

CHAPTER 11

Rare Games Unlocked: Process and Mapping

The rare game types outlined in this chapter are truly rare. Since the LSAT established its current format in 1991, the LSAC has released more than 80 official exams containing more than 320 logic games. Of those, exactly seven have been Process games, and only five have been Mapping games. In recent years, there has been only *one* of either of these game types on a released LSAT, which was a process game on PrepTest 80.

Types of Games By Percentage, 2014–2018

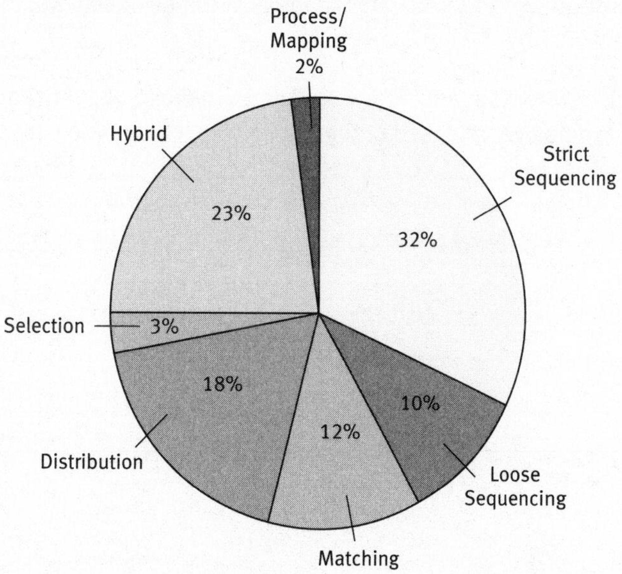

Process/ Mapping 2%
Strict Sequencing 32%
Loose Sequencing 10%
Matching 12%
Distribution 18%
Selection 3%
Hybrid 23%

Process Games By the Numbers

Those meager numbers take on even more significance when you consider the dates of those tests. Of the seven released Process games, six are from tests administered in the 1990s. It is noteworthy that the one Process game that postdates the '90s appeared on the December 2016 LSAT (PrepTest 80). Seeing a Process game on a current administration of the exam surprised many, including LSAT experts. The reemergence of Process was so significant that you'll find an LSAT Channel Special Feature on that game following the discussion of Process games in this chapter. There, you'll have the opportunity to work through that game, and to see an LSAT Channel instructor's approach to it.

In the Special Feature, you'll also discover that Kaplan LSAT experts had taken note of several recent Sequencing games that may have signaled the testmaker's renewed interest in Process games. At present, the game on PrepTest 80 remains an anomaly, and there's no evidence that it foreshadows a new wave of Process games. Still, the return of Process after such a long period of dormancy is intriguing. Process games warrant a small amount of your study time if only for the peace of mind that you'll recognize a Process game should the LSAT decide to include another one on an upcoming administration.

Mapping Games By the Numbers

Of the five Mapping games ever to appear on officially released LSAT tests, the most recent is from PrepTest 40, administered in June 2003. Since that time, Mapping has been a dead letter on released exams, with nothing to suggest its return.

To be clear, the LSAC has never announced that it is abandoning Mapping games, so an unexpected return is not impossible. Nonetheless, if you have limited time between now and test day, and if you have more work to do on any of the important game types covered in earlier chapters of this book, your time will probably be better spent honing your mastery of Sequencing, Distribution, or Hybrid games than it would be seeking out further practice on this rarest of all games.

For true logic games mavens—those who want absolutely complete coverage of every game type—there are complete lists of all Process and Mapping games ever released at the end of each game type's respective section in this chapter.

PROCESS GAMES UNLOCKED

Prepare

In most LSAT logic games, your task is take a list of unassigned entities and place each of them into specific positions or groups. In Process games, the entities start out assigned to positions or groups (or, rarely, New-"If" question stems stipulate initial arrangements), and your task is to reassign them to new positions or groups. Here's a typical Process game setup:

> In a particular area of national forest, there are four fire lookouts—numbered 1 through 4—and a headquarters. In the current winter quarter, five rangers are assigned as follows: Adams is in Lookout 1, Benitez is in Lookout 2, Campbell is in Lookout 3, Davis is in Lookout 4, and Estavez is at headquarters. At the end of each quarter, and only then, the area supervisor will reassign the rangers according to exactly one of the following protocols:

In the Step 1 Overview, an LSAT expert would note three key features of this setup that identify this as a Process game: 1) the fact that an initial arrangement of the entities is provided, 2) the phrase "[a]t the end of each quarter," which indicates an iterative action, and 3) the word "reassign," which establishes the nature of the task.

In Step 2, the expert will sketch out what is given about the initial arrangement. In this case, the setup provides a complete picture of the rangers' initial assignments.

HQ	1	2	3	4
E	A	B	C	D

In Step 3 of a Process game, an LSAT expert will begin by noting what the setup or rules say about how often change takes place. In this game, a reassignment is made "[a]t the end of each quarter." The setup tells you that the initial arrangement represents the winter quarter. That means that after one reassignment is made, you will have the arrangement for the spring quarter. After two reassignments have occurred, it will be summer. And so on. Always make a note of how often change occurs within the game.

After that, Step 3 for Process games is much the same as it is in any other game type. Analyze the rules and draw them out in a helpful shorthand or visual representation of the action.

> In a particular area of national forest, there are four fire lookouts—numbered 1 through 4—and a headquarters. In the current winter quarter, five rangers are assigned as follows: Adams is at Lookout 1, Benitez is at Lookout 2, Campbell is at Lookout 3, Davis is at Lookout 4, and Estavez is at headquarters. At the end of each quarter, the area supervisor will reassign the rangers according to exactly one of the following protocols:
>
> 1. The ranger at headquarters will move to Lookout 1; the ranger at Lookout 1 will move to Lookout 4; and the ranger at Lookout 4 will move to headquarters.
> 2. The rangers in Lookouts 1 and 2 will change positions with one another.
> 3. The rangers in Lookouts 3 and 4 will change positions with one another.

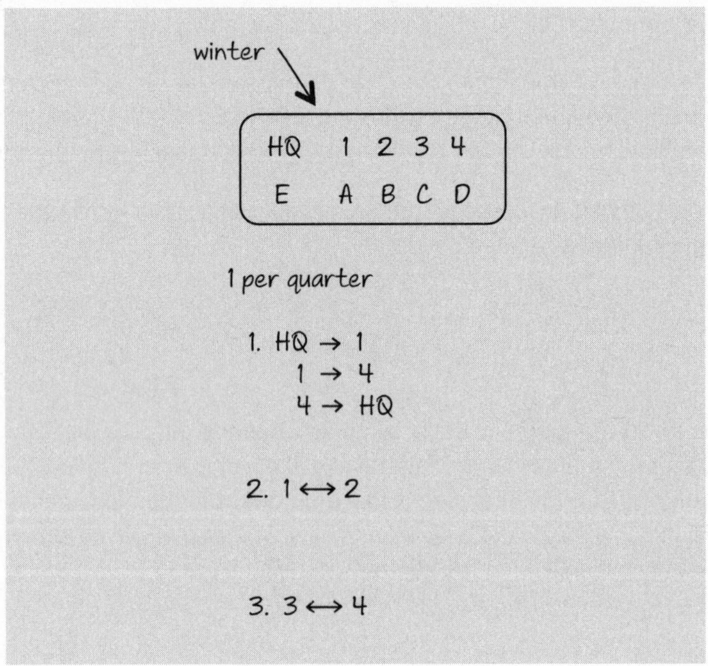

Because of their iterative nature, Process games tend to have few solid deductions to make up front. If you see Duplications among the rules that lead to clear outcomes, you can note them. In this game, for example, you can quickly record the spring arrangements that result from the implementation of each protocol.

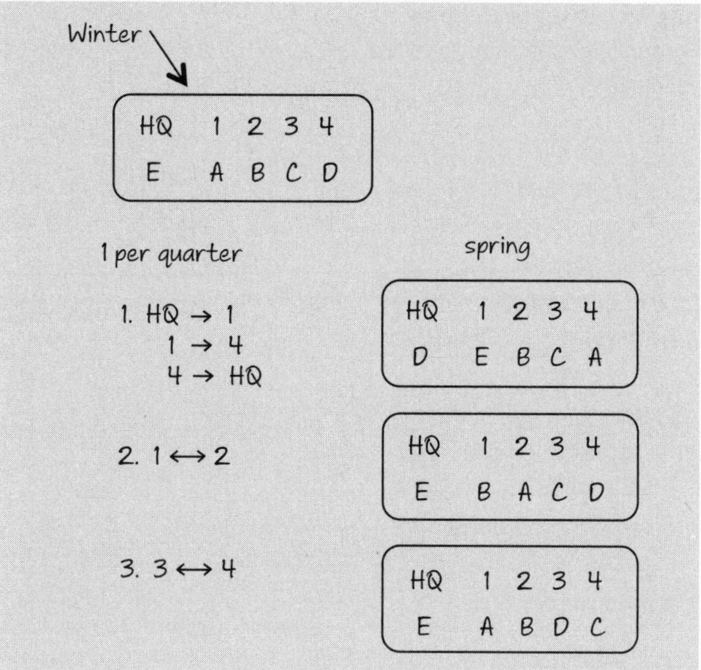

Avoid the inclination to speculate about all of the various ways that entities could be arranged after two or three reassignments. The questions that ask about the state of affairs after two or three iterations will always provide the information you need to determine what happened earlier in the process.

Step 5 in Process games is no different than it is in other game types. Process games are accompanied by all of the standard question types.

- Acceptability—e.g., "Which one of the following could be an acceptable assignment of the rangers during the spring quarter?"
- Must Be/Could Be—e.g., "Which one of the following must be false?" [*A potential correct answer for this question might be "Estavez is at Lookout 3 during the summer." No matter which reassignments the supervisor makes at the end of the winter and spring quarters, there is no way for Estavez to be at Lookout 3 before the fall.*]
- New-"If"—e.g., "If summer is the first quarter in which Adams is assigned to headquarters, which one of the following must have been true of the spring quarter?" [*For Adams to be assigned to headquarters in the summer, he must have been at Lookout 4 in the spring. Because he was assigned to Lookout 1 in the winter, the protocol implemented at the end of the winter must have been protocol 1. That means that in the spring, Davis was at headquarters, Estavez was at Lookout 1, Benitez was at Lookout 2, Campbell was at Lookout 3, and Adams was at Lookout 4. One of those assignments will be stated in the correct answer to this question.*]
- "How Many" or Minimum/Maximum questions—"What is the minimum number of quarters needed for a ranger assigned to Lookout 2 to be reassigned to headquarters?" [*The correct answer will be "three." The quickest way for a ranger to get from Lookout 2 to headquarters is via the implementation of protocol 2, then protocol 1, and then protocol 1 again.*]

Process games tend to expect you to be able to figure out possible arrangements for up to three iterations. In questions accompanying this game, you would almost certainly be asked about the arrangements found in the spring and summer quarters, and maybe even about the fall. It's very unlikely, however, that any question would take you beyond that point.

Practice

Directions: Practice applying the Logic Games Method to a full game and question set. An answer key follows the game. Complete worked example expert analysis can be found in your online resources.

Questions 1–5

Four apprentices—Louis, Madelyn, Nora, and Oliver—are initially assigned to projects Q, R, S, and T, respectively. During the year in which they are apprentices, two reassignments of apprentices to projects will be made, each time according to a different one of the following plans, which can be used in any order:

Plan 1. The apprentice assigned to project Q switches projects with the apprentice assigned to project S and the apprentice assigned to project R switches projects with the apprentice assigned to project T.

Plan 2. The apprentice assigned to project S switches projects with the apprentice assigned to project T.

Plan 3. Louis and Madelyn switch projects with each other.

1. Which one of the following must be true after the second reassignment of apprentices to projects during the year if that reassignment assigns Nora to project T ?

(A) Louis is assigned to project S.
(B) Madelyn is assigned to project R.
(C) Madelyn is assigned to project S.
(D) Oliver is assigned to project R.
(E) Oliver is assigned to project S.

2. Which one of the following could be true after only one reassignment during the year?

   (A) Louis is assigned to project T.
   (B) Nora is assigned to project R.
   (C) Oliver is assigned to project Q.
   (D) Louis and Nora each remain assigned to the same projects as before.
   (E) Nora and Oliver each remain assigned to the same projects as before.

3. If at some time during the year, Louis is reassigned to project R, which one of the following could have been the assignment of apprentices to the projects immediately before the reassignment?

   (A) Q: Louis; R: Madelyn; S: Oliver; T: Nora
   (B) Q: Louis; R: Nora; S: Oliver; T: Madelyn
   (C) Q: Nora; R: Madelyn; S: Louis; T: Oliver
   (D) Q: Nora; R: Olivia; S: Louis; T: Madelyn
   (E) Q: Oliver; R: Nora; S: Louis; T: Madelyn

4. Which one of the following is an acceptable assignment of apprentices to the projects after only one reassignment during the year?

   (A) Q: Louis; R: Madelyn; S: Nora; T: Oliver
   (B) Q: Madelyn; R: Louis; S: Nora; T: Oliver
   (C) Q: Madelyn; R: Oliver; S: Nora; T: Louis
   (D) Q: Nora; R: Louis; S: Oliver; T: Madelyn
   (E) Q: Nora; R: Madelyn; S: Oliver; T: Louis

5. If the first reassignment is made according to plan 1, which one of the following must be true?

   (A) Louis is assigned to project T as a result of the second reassignment.
   (B) Madelyn is assigned to project Q as a result of the second reassignment.
   (C) Madelyn is assigned to project T as a result of the second reassignment.
   (D) Oliver is assigned to project S as a result of the second reassignment.
   (E) Oliver is assigned to project T as a result of the second reassignment.

PrepTest11 Sec1 Qs 20–24

Answer Key

Process Game Practice

1. (E)
2. (E)
3. (A)
4. (B)
5. (A)

Worked example explanations of these questions with complete expert analysis can be found in your Online Study Plan under Chapter 11. View or download the PDF titled "Chapter 11 Process Practice Full Game Explanations."

For further practice on Process games, start with the LSAT Channel Special Feature that follows this section. There, you can practice the one recent Process game (from PrepTest 80, December 2016), and then go to your online center to see an LSAT Channel expert explain the game and provide strategies and tactics for Process games.

For your convenience, here is a list of all of the Process games ever to appear in released LSAT tests. Unless you have ample time before test day, do not spend too much of your time on this rare game type.

Officially Released Process games

PrepTest 18, Section 1, Game 4 (Firm's Annual Review for Promotion)

PrepTest 10, Section 2, Game 3 (Words/Sentences Game)

PrepTest 11, Section 1, Game 4 (Apprentice Re-Assignment to Projects)*

PrepTest 12, Section 2, Game 4 (Four Colored Chemical Flasks)

PrepTest 16, Section 1, Game 4 (Tennis Matches Based on Rankings)

PrepTest 80, Section 3, Game 4 (Trading Buildings)**

*This is the game featured in this chapter. **This is the game featured in the Special Feature that follows this section of this chapter.

The LSAT Channel Spotlight

The Return of Process

By Melanie Triebel

Watch the video lesson for this Spotlight in your online Study Plan.

In December 2016, a remarkable thing happened, but only a few thousand people knew about it. While the rest of the world was focused on holiday shopping, football, and the politics of a new presidential administration, these "lucky" people saw something that had not happened in more than 21 years.

Even in January of the new year, when a document was released that contained this amazing rarity, most of the world ignored it. But for the small group of us who follow the LSAT test, it was a stunner. LSAC PrepTest 80 contained a Process game!

A Process game is one in which the game setup provides an initial arrangement of entities, followed by a set of rules that specify conditions for the *rearrangement* of those entities.

Three real estate companies—RealProp, Southco, and Trustcorp—are considering trading buildings with one another. Each building they own is categorized as either class 1, class 2, or class 3, depending on its approximate value:

RealProp owns the Garza Tower (class 1), the Yates House (class 3), and the Zimmer House (class 3).

Southco owns the Flores Tower (class 1) and the Lynch Building (class 2).

Trustcorp owns the King Building, the Meyer Building, and the Ortiz Building, all of which are class 2.

Each trade must be of exactly one of the following three kinds:

Trading one building for one other building of the same class

Trading one class 1 building for two class 2 buildings

Trading one class 2 building for two class 3 buildings

PrepTest80 Sec3 Qs 19–23

Consider this December 2016 game. In a standard Matching game, you would be given the five towers F, G, T, Y, and Z, and then asked to match them up to the three real estate companies. But, the Process game is different. Its setup *states* the initial match-ups. But those initial match-ups are subject to change. So the rules explain the Process (get it?) by which those towers can be traded among the companies. And the questions, as you'll see when you attempt this game, go on to ask about the new match-ups that could result after one or more trades are made.

For a period of time in the 1990s, the LSAT featured Process games regularly. PrepTest 16 (the LSAT from September 1995) and PrepTest 18 (from December 1992) presented one Process game each. So did all four 1994 exams, published as PrepTests 10–13. Then there was no sign of Process for two decades. The LSAT simply stopped using Process as a game type. By the 2010s, most LSAT experts figured that it would never return.

The first hint that the testmaker might be open to bringing back Process games came in June 2014, when PrepTest 72 included a "quadruple Strict Sequencing" game (Summit Company Workpieces), which reminded LSAT watchers of the old Process games. Then, on PrepTest 77, in December 2015, a hybrid Sequencing/Matching game about office selection showed the influence of Process games. Almost a year later, in September 2016, PrepTest 79's fourth game (Computer Virus) was an unusual "branching Sequencing" game that was hotly debated among the Kaplan LSAT team.

Finally, in December 2016, it happened unequivocally: Process came back. The game was so unusual that we had to include it here. Try it out on the next two pages, and then watch the video that accompanies this Special Feature to see an LSAT Channel instructor take you through the game step-by-step.

Questions 19–23

Three real estate companies—RealProp, Southco, and Trustcorp—are considering trading buildings with one another. Each building they own is categorized as either class 1, class 2, or class 3, depending on its approximate value:

RealProp owns the Garza Tower (class 1), the Yates House (class 3), and the Zimmer House (class 3).

Southco owns the Flores Tower (class 1) and the Lynch Building (class 2).

Trustcorp owns the King Building, the Meyer Building, and the Ortiz Building, all of which are class 2.

Each trade must be of exactly one of the following three kinds:

Trading one building for one other building of the same class

Trading one class 1 building for two class 2 buildings

Trading one class 2 building for two class 3 buildings

19. Which one of the following could be the buildings owned by the three companies after only one trade is made?

(A) RealProp: the Flores Tower and the Garza Tower
Southco: the Lynch Building, the Yates House, and the Zimmer House
Trustcorp: the King Building, the Meyer Building, and the Ortiz Building

(B) RealProp: the Garza Tower, the King Building, and the Ortiz Building
Southco: the Flores Tower and the Lynch Building
Trustcorp: the Meyer Building, the Yates House, and the Zimmer House

(C) RealProp: the Garza Tower and the Lynch Building
Southco: the Flores Tower, the Yates House, and the Zimmer House
Trustcorp: the King Building, the Meyer Building, and the Ortiz Building

(D) RealProp: the Garza Tower, the Meyer Building, and the Yates House
Southco: the Flores Tower and the Lynch Building Trustcorp: the King Building, the Ortiz Building, and the Zimmer House

(E) RealProp: the Garza Tower, the Yates House, and the Zimmer House
Southco: the Lynch Building and the Ortiz Building
Trustcorp: the Flores Tower, the King Building, and the Meyer Building

20. Which one of the following CANNOT be true, no matter how many trades are made?

(A) The buildings owned by RealProp are the Flores Tower and the Garza Tower.

(B) The buildings owned by Southco are the Flores Tower and the Meyer Building.

(C) The buildings owned by Southco are the Garza Tower and the Lynch Building.

(D) The buildings owned by Trustcorp are the Flores Tower and the Ortiz Building.

(E) The buildings owned by Trustcorp are the Garza Tower and the Meyer Building.

21. If RealProp owns only class 2 buildings after some number of trades, which one of the following must be true?

(A) Trustcorp owns a class 1 building.

(B) Trustcorp owns the Meyer Building.

(C) Southco owns a class 2 Building.

(D) Southco owns both of the class 3 buildings.

(E) Southco owns the Flores Tower.

22. If Trustcorp owns no class 2 buildings after some number of trades, which one of the following must be true?

(A) RealProp owns a class 1 building.

(B) Southco owns only class 2 buildings.

(C) Southco has made at least one trade with Trustcorp.

(D) Trustcorp owns the Garza Tower.

(E) Trustcorp owns the Zimmer House.

23. Which one of the following CANNOT be true, no matter how many trades are made?

(A) The buildings owned by RealProp are the Lynch Building, the Meyer Building, and the Ortiz Building.

(B) The buildings owned by Southco are the Garza Tower and the Meyer Building.

(C) The buildings owned by Southco are the King Building, the Meyer Building, and the Ortiz Building.

(D) The buildings owned by Trustcorp are the Flores Tower and the Yates House.

(E) The buildings owned by Trustcorp are the Garza Tower and the Lynch Building.

PrepTest80 Sec3 Qs 19–23

Complete answers and explanations are provided in The LSAT Channel Spotlight video "Limited Options" in your online Study Plan.

MAPPING GAMES UNLOCKED

Prepare

Mapping games, as the name implies, always describe a spatial layout of places, areas, or zones. In some Mapping games, each place is a distinct node connected to other distinct places by a network of paths, roads, or rails. An urban area's subway map provides a good real-world analogy to Mapping games of this type. The model setup you'll see here fits this description.

In other cases, the map may describe overlapping or distinct regions, each with a certain characteristic. A valid real-world example might be a map showing the dominant language groups within a larger region. In some areas, a single language is dominant, while in others, two or even three languages may coexist. As you'll see, the full-length Mapping game used as a practice exercise matches this description quite well.

Take a look at a model Mapping setup of the first type just described. Try to anticipate what an LSAT expert will do when applying Steps 1 and 2 of the Logic Games Method to it.

> On the grounds of a mansion, there is a large garden with exactly six features. Five of the features—a fountain, a gazebo, a pond, and a rose bed, and a topiary display—are arranged in that order in a semicircle from the mansion's left to its right. The hermitage lies outside the semicircle directly behind the pond. Gardeners are constructing paths that will connect features to the mansion or to one another according to the following criteria:

In Step 1, an LSAT expert would immediately notice the description of the physical layout of the garden. The order and positions of the features matter. In some Mapping games, the setup may provide a simple diagram to illustrate the positions of the places named in the setup. When, as here, no diagram is provided, it is incumbent on the test taker to carefully create a diagram that matches the description in the setup. Nothing is more important in Mapping games than having an accurate map.

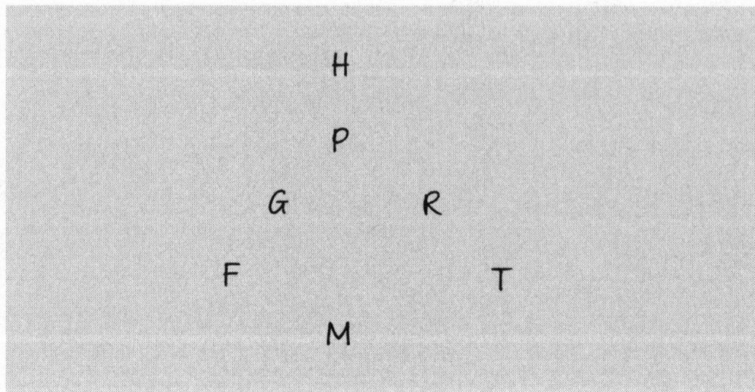

The expert would also note that while the drawing of the map will be based on the features in the garden, the action is based on creating connections—paths in this case—*between* features. From this, the expert can anticipate that the rules will cover how many paths may be built and restrict the features they may connect.

> On the grounds of a mansion, there is a large garden with exactly six features. Five of the features—a fountain, a gazebo, a pond, and a rose bed, and a topiary display—are arranged in that order in a semi-circle from the mansion's left to its right. The hermitage lies outside the semi-circle directly behind the pond. Gardeners are constructing paths that will connect features to the mansion or to one another according to the following criteria:
>
> Neither the mansion nor any of the features is connected by more than two paths.
> Paths will connect the mansion to the fountain and to one other feature.
> Paths will connect the pond to the gazebo and to the hermitage.
> A path will connect the rose bed to the topiary display.
> None of the paths may cross another path.
> All of the paths are straight, and connect exactly two features or connect the mansion with exactly one feature.

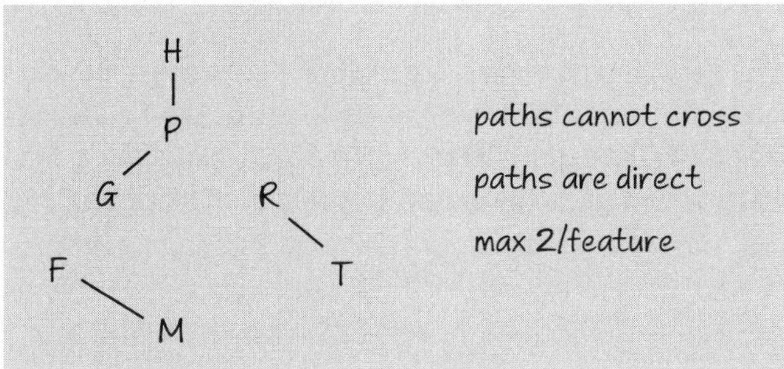

As expected, all of the rules in this game define, limit, or establish paths. Rules 1, 5, and 6 limit how many paths may be built, and provide regulations for how they must be built. Rules 2, 3, and 4 establish four of the paths, which can be drawn directly into the sketch. In any game, it is always preferable to draw the rules inside of the sketch framework. That goes double in Mapping games, in which the visual and spatial elements are so strong.

In Mapping games, deductions will most likely spring from Duplications. When a place on the map is named in more than one rule, or a place is mentioned in one rule and a connection to that place is mentioned in another, there is likely a deduction to be made. In the game you've been exploring, the key Duplication arises in another way. Rule 1 limits the number of paths connecting any feature to two. Rule 3 creates two paths connecting connecting the pond to other features. Thus, the pond's connections are established once and for all in this game. Circle or box in P on your map to indicate this.

H
(P)
G
R
F
T
M
paths cannot cross
paths are direct
max 2/feature

Turning to Step 5, you'll find that the types of questions associated with Mapping games depend a lot on the map itself. In games with points and connections, like the one you've been working on, there is a lot of counting. You could see questions that ask "What is minimum number of additional paths that must be built to walk from the mansion to the pond?" [*The answer would be "one," either by building a path from the mansion to the gazebo or from the fountain to the gazebo. Remember, a path cannot be built directly from the mansion to the pond because the pond has its limit of two paths already.*] New-"If" questions could explore the same territory; e.g., "If a path is built between the rose bed and the hermitage, what additional path must be built for a person to walk from the mansion to the hermitage taking only two paths?" [*The answer would be "a path from the mansion to the rose bed."*] There always seems to be a whiff of Sequencing in these Mapping games because so many of the questions center on the number of connections one must use or the number of points one must pass through to move from one point to another. The difference, of course, is that number of spaces moved is not always in a straight line in Mapping games.

In Mapping games with overlapping areas, the game is more likely to provide entities that must, can, or cannot be placed or stationed within certain areas. Although the basis of these game is still spatial, the action is closer to that in Matching games. As you'll see in the practice game, some entities may be placed in a single named area, while others, by being placed in an area of overlap, are placed in two named areas at the same time.

To get the feel of the second variety of Mapping games, try the practice exercise now. Feel free to compare your work to that of the LSAT expert—found on the pages following the game—in a step-by-step fashion. Complete Steps 1 and 2, and then compare your map to that of the expert. When you're comfortable that you understand the setup, move on to Steps 3 and 4, and then compare your work to the expert's once more before tackling the questions.

Practice

Directions: Practice applying the Logic Games Method to a full game and question set. An answer key follows the game. Complete worked example expert analysis can be found in your online resources.

Questions 1–7

The country of Zendu contains exactly four areas for radar detection: R, S, T, and U. Each detection area is circular and falls completely within Zendu. Part of R intersects T; part of S also intersects T; R does not intersect S. Area U is completely within R and also completely within T. At noon exactly four planes—J, K, L, M—are over Zendu, in a manner consistent with the following statements:

Each plane is in at least one of the four areas.
J is in area S.
K is not in any detection area that J is in.
L is not in any detection area that M is in.
M is in exactly one of the areas.

1. Which one of the following could be a complete listing of the planes located in the four areas at noon, with each plane listed in every area in which it is located?

   (A) R: J, L; S: J, M; T: L; U: L
   (B) R: J, L; S: K; T: M; U: none
   (C) R: K; S: J; T: L; U: M
   (D) R: K, M; S: J, L; T: J; U: none
   (E) R: M; S: J, K; T: J, L; U: none

2. If at noon K is within exactly two of the four areas, then which one of the following CANNOT be true at that time?

 (A) J is within area T.
 (B) K is within area R.
 (C) K is within area T.
 (D) L is within area R.
 (E) L is within area T.

3. Which one of the following is a complete and accurate list of those planes any one of which could be within area T at noon?

 (A) M
 (B) J, L
 (C) J, L, M
 (D) K, L, M
 (E) J, K, L, M

4. Which one of the following statements CANNOT be true at noon about the planes?

 (A) K is within area T.
 (B) K is within area U.
 (C) L is within area R.
 (D) M is within area R.
 (E) M is within area U.

5. It CANNOT be true that at noon there is at least one plane that is within both area

 (A) R and area T
 (B) R and area U
 (C) S and area T
 (D) S and area U
 (E) T and area U

6. If at noon M is within area T, then which one of the following statements CANNOT be true at that time?

 (A) J is within area T.
 (B) L is within area R.
 (C) L is within area S.
 (D) K is within exactly two areas.
 (E) L is within exactly two areas.

7. If at noon plane L is within exactly three of the areas, which one of the following could be true at that time?

 (A) J is within exactly two of the areas.
 (B) J is within exactly three of the areas.
 (C) K is within area S.
 (D) M is within area R.
 (E) M is within area T.

PrepTest15 Sec4 Qs 7–13

Answer Key

Mapping Game Practice

1. (D)
2. (A)
3. (E)
4. (E)
5. (D)
6. (E)
7. (A)

Worked example explanations of these questions with complete expert analysis can be found in your Online Study Plan under Chapter 11. View or download the PDF titled "Chapter 11 Mapping Practice Full Game Explanations."

For further practice on Mapping games, consult the following list. Only five Mapping games have ever appeared on LSAC PrepTests, and even the most recent is more than a decade old (PrepTest 40 was administered in 2003). If you want to do one more, choose that one, but unless you have ample time before test day, do not spend too much of your time on this rare game type.

Officially Released Mapping games

PrepTest 4, Section 3, Game 4 (Ski Chalet Snow Shoveled Paths)

PrepTest 6, Section 4, Game 4 (Island Bridges)

PrepTest 18, Section 1, Game 3 (Five Subway Lines)

PrepTest 15, Section 4, Game 2 (Plane Zones)*

PrepTest 40, Section 2, Game 3 (Zephyr Airlines)

*This game is the game featured in this chapter.

PART THREE

Appendices

APPENDIX I

Logic Games—Timing and Section Management

The Logic Games section is the smallest of the scored sections with only 23 questions, on average. Nonetheless, for most test takers, time is tight in the Logic Games section. You must complete four games (and all of their associated questions) in 35 minutes. That means that you have roughly 8.5 minutes to tackle each game. After spending roughly three minutes to set up a game, you'll have just over a minute to tackle each question. Of course, these numbers rarely break down so evenly. Some games will take longer than others, and some questions take longer than others. Knowing your own strengths and weaknesses, knowing game actions, and knowing question types will put you in a position to strategically move through the games in a way that will ensure you get the most points possible.

In this chapter, we'll talk about how to maximize the time available to you in the Logic Games section. There is no one-size-fits-all strategy here. For some of you, your best bet will be to tackle three of the four games, giving yourself more time to fully understand rules and make valid deductions during the game setup. For others, you'll want to aim to get to all four games but be quick to strategically skip questions that you anticipate will be very difficult or time-consuming. In practice, you'll find the best strategy for you.

For every test taker, there are a few simple rules to keep in mind to help you maximize your performance in this section:

Slow down and think. Success in Logic Games ultimately comes from understanding the action (or actions, in Hybrid Games) in the initial game setup, interpreting rules correctly, and making deductions. Rushing through these steps to get to the questions quickly will lead to a poor understanding of the game, sloppy mistakes, and frustration.

Do the games in the order you want to do them. There is nothing that says that you have to do the games in the order in which they are presented to you. Quickly analyze a game's action(s), rules, and even the question stems themselves to determine if you'd like to do the game now, or save it for later.

Skip questions that you know will be overly difficult or time-consuming. Even easy games can have difficult questions. Some types, like Rule Substitution questions, nearly always have a 4-star difficulty rating. Instead of investing two or three minutes working through such a question, skip it and use that time to set up the next game.

Answer questions that you know are straightforward and simple. Even if you skip a game, ask yourself if you can at least answer that game's Acceptability question. Remember, all you need to do to correctly answer an Acceptability question is to work through the rules and eliminate choices that violate those rules.

Use past work to answer more difficult questions. One of the benefits of creating sketches for "If" questions is that each of those sketches will provide a possible permutation of the game. Label those sketches by question number on your scratch paper and use them to help you quickly select the right answer in a Could be True question, or eliminate wrong answers in Must be False questions.

When in doubt, sketch it out. Imagine you've exhausted your question-specific strategies and you've referred to previous work to help you answer a question, and you're still stuck. Now what? Confident test takers know that there is no value in staring at questions, hoping the right answer magically appears to them. Instead, they aggressively dive into answer choices and sketch out what is and is not possible.

If you practice those strategies, you'll become a better, more efficient test taker. Let's take a look at each strategy in a bit more depth.

Slow Down to Speed Up

It might sound counterintuitive at first: "Slow down to speed up." But that's exactly the right approach to success in Logic Games. Here's why: Most students who struggle with timing in Logic Games do so because they rush through the game setup, then get bogged down in the questions. This is the wrong approach. Without a clear understanding of the game's mechanics, and without at least one or two concrete deductions, every question essentially becomes a completely new puzzle to solve. That is frustrating, and time consuming. You simply don't have time to sketch out possible scenarios for every single answer choice in every question. Instead, there is a better way: Be deliberate and precise in the first four steps of the method.

In Step 1, understanding the the game's action and limitations will help you set up an effective sketch in Step 2. In Step 3, reading and translating each rule is key, of course, but do you also sit with each rule and consider what the rule says *can't* happen? Do you consider *both* the positive and negative implications of every rule? Do you consider how each rule builds on and interacts with other rules in the game? In Step 4, read through the rules again and see if there are deductions you missed. Is this a game where you could set up two master sketches? Were there any duplicate entities that you overlooked? How did the rules modify any number limitations that might be present in the game? Excellent test takers know that it's better to sit and ponder (and, if necessary, sketch!) the answers to these mental questions than to simply rush to the game's questions. Give yourself time. The more clearly you see how the game "works," the better off you're going to be.

In practice, make note cards with the SEAL questions and the BLEND deductions written out on them. Place those note cards over the Acceptability question and force yourself to go through each list before moving on to the questions. After a while, this approach will become second nature to you, and you can start tackling new games without the note cards.

Game Triage

To maximize your performance in the Logic Games section, you also want to consider how strategic you are in your approach to the section as a whole. Everyone understands that the goal in the Logic Games section of the LSAT, like the goal in every other section of the test, is to correctly answer as many questions as possible. Unfortunately, many people interpret this task to mean that they should rush through each game in an effort to get to every question presented. But what many test takers soon discover in practice is that this strategy is actually counterproductive to the goal of getting as many questions correct as possible. By focusing so much on speed, they make crucial errors during the game setup. If this sounds like something that you've fallen victim to in your practice, consider slowing down and tackling fewer games, but spending more time interpreting rules, making deductions, and creating new sketches in the games that you do tackle.

As for the order in which you do the games, there is no rule that says you must do them in the order in which they are presented. Instead, take control of the section, and make it a point to do the games in the order in which *you* choose to do them. On the bar of answer bubbles at the bottom of the screen you'll see lines dividing the questions that belong to each game in the section. This makes it very easy to navigate to the first question for each game so that you can quickly assess the game type and setup.

While it's possible that the first game is the easiest and the fourth game is the most difficult, it doesn't always work out that way. Take a look at the following chart, which breaks down the difficulty level of the questions in the Logic Games section of PrepTest 62.

Game 1 - Strict Sequencing

Question	Difficulty Level
1	★
2	★★
3	★★★
4	★★
5	★
6	★★★★

Game 2 - Matching

Question	Difficulty Level
7	★
8	★★★
9	★★★
10	★★★
11	★★★★
12	★★
13	★★★★

Game 3 - Hybrid: Sequencing-Matching

Question	Difficulty Level
14	★
15	★★★★
16	★★★★
17	★★★
18	★★★★

Game 4 - Strict Sequencing

Question	Difficulty Level
19	★
20	★
21	★
22	★★★
23	★★

Notice that any test taker who simply worked through the section from Game 1 to Game 4 would have had to work through the very difficult Game 3 before getting to the much easier Game 4. A strategic test taker, on the other hand, would have tackled games in the order in which she wanted to do them. Such a test taker would have wisely moved past Game 3, grabbed the easy points available in Game 4, and then returned to Game 3 in the time remaining.

This idea of evaluating the games and then deciding the order in which you choose to tackle them is what we call "game triage." There is no right way to triage games—the important thing is that you at least give yourself the opportunity to choose for yourself which games you are going to do, and the order in which you are going to do them.

Our data suggest that the most difficult game is rarely one of the first two games. Instead, there is a roughly equal chance that it will be Game 3 or Game 4. So, use this knowledge to your advantage. Some test takers make it a point to do Games 1 and 2 first, then stop and consider whether they'd prefer to do Game 3 or Game 4 next. Some test takers decide to triage the entire section by spending the first minute or so looking at all four games and then deciding a route that works for them. And then there are some test takers who simply work through the games in order, but are comfortable moving on from any game that is difficult to set up or in which very few deductions can be made.

When you think about game triage, consider factors that would cause you to tackle a game, or cause you to skip a game. Games that have straightforward actions, simple sketch setups, and rules that allow for many deductions are often going to be easier than games that have multiple actions, a difficult sketch setup, or few overlapping rules. For example, imagine Game 2 is a Selection/Sequencing/Matching Hybrid that involves selecting four or five entities out of eight possible entities, putting them in order and then matching each to a specific color. Game 3, on the other hand, is a Strict Sequencing game that simply involves putting six entities in order. Which game would you prefer to do first, and why? These are the types of questions strategic test takers ask themselves.

Tackling the Questions

Once you've taken the time to understand the game's limitations, rules, and deductions, it's time to get points by answering the questions. But not all questions are created equally. Acceptability questions, for example, are nearly always straightforward and require nothing more than an understanding of the game's rules. Other question types, like Rule Substitution, can be extremely difficult, or time-consuming, or both.

No matter your game triage strategy, try to answer the Acceptability question in each of the four games. These questions can be answered even without a clear understanding of the game's setup and deductions. Simply look at the rules, eliminate choices that violate rules, and pick the choice that is left over.

As for tackling the rest of the questions in a game, your strategy will likely depend on the number of deductions you've been able to make during Steps 3 and 4. If you were able to make a key deduction—something like a certain entity being forced into exactly one spot in a Sequencing game, or discovering that two entities cannot be placed together in the same group in a Distribution game—then look to any Must Be True/False or Could Be True/False questions that directly test your understanding of that deduction.

If, on the other hand, you struggled to make any concrete deductions in a game, there is no need to panic. Instead, head to the "If" questions after tackling the Acceptability question. For each "If" question, sketch the new scenario or the new rule, and push yourself to make as many deductions as possible. Each "If" question is an opportunity to see how one permutation of the game could be constructed. For example, perhaps an "If" question demonstrates that by placing a certainty entity in spot 3, another entity is forced to occupy spot 2. This deduction isn't just helpful in answering that question, it's helpful in your overall understanding of the game.

After tackling the "If" questions, you can then return to any questions you might have skipped. Use all of the sketches you now have on your scratch paper to help you either quickly select the right answer, or quickly eliminate wrong answers, in any Must Be True/False or Could Be True/False questions.

Other question types that are less common—Complete and Accurate List, Rule Substitution—can be left for the end of the game. For rare or uncommon question types, be sure to read carefully to understand the task at hand. If the question is confusing or if it appears that the route to the right answer is going to take too long, consider skipping that question and using the time saved to set up the next game in the section. Flag questions you skip so that you can come back to them time permitting or at least mark a guess before the end of the section.

Using Past Work

Even if you work through a game's setup and its questions strategically, you still might find yourself struggling with one or two questions where the approach to the right answer does not seem obvious. In these questions, see if you can use your work on other questions to answer the question correctly or, at the very least, eliminate clearly wrong answers. For example, imagine a game where seven different people are arranged in a line from left to right, in spots 1 through 7. There is a question that asks:

1. Paul CANNOT be assigned to which of the following spots?
   (A) first
   (B) second
   (C) thid
   (D) fourth
   (E) fifth

You look at your master sketch and notice that because Paul is always to the left of Mary, Paul can never be in the seventh spot. So, you look through the answer choices and... well, "seventh" isn't an answer choice. Now what? Well, first consider what would constitute a wrong answer. In this question, wrong answer choices will represent a spot to which Paul COULD be assigned. Look through the other questions in the set. Imagine that the correct answer to the first question, the Acceptability question, shows an acceptable arrangement in which Paul is ranked second. So, because it is possible for Paul to be ranked second, choice B cannot be correct and can be eliminated. Now look to some of the sketches you created for "If" questions. Perhaps in one "If" question, you've discovered that it's possible for Paul to be in the first spot, and in another "If" question, it is possible to place Paul in the third spot. Eliminate choices A and C. Now you are simply left with two choices: D and E. Test one of them out, following the rules and limitations of the game. Imagine you try choice D, placing Paul in the fourth spot. If you discover that the placement of Paul in that spot *cannot* work, you've found the right answer. If on the other hand you discover that placing Paul in spot 4 is fine, and that the other rules and limitations of the game allow for other entities to be placed elsewhere on the sketch with no violations, then you know that D is incorrect and you can confidently select choice E. Note how all of these strategies reward the test taker who jots down the correct answer to the Acceptability question on scratch paper and who labels the sketches for New-"If" questions.

One of the keys to getting more efficient in Logic Games is trying to do only enough work to get right answers, and no more than that. Relying on previous work is an excellent example of this principle.

When In Doubt, Sketch It Out

For every game, and for every question, you have a strategy, a plan of attack. You are going to do the games in the order in which you want to do them, and you have a system for getting through the questions strategically and efficiently. Even still, there may be times when a question has you stumped. You're not sure what you should do next, or how your past work will help you. When you hit such a roadblock, do one of two things: flag that question and move on or start sketching. Sitting and staring at a question and its answer choices won't help you. The right answer isn't going to magically come to you. You either don't know it (move on!) or you have to figure it out (start sketching!).

While excellent test takers might have slightly different approaches to game types, sketch setups, and question order, they do all tend to have a similar personality trait: a confident attitude of "I'm going to figure out this question." Build this attitude within yourself. When you're stuck on a question, remember: The rules of the game are there on the page in front of you. The deductions you made during the game setup are sound. The "If" sketches you've created show possible avenues down which the game can go. You've got this. You can figure it out. If you need to make a sketch or two to figure out a new deduction, to see if an entity can go in that spot, or to find out if two people can join the same group—do it. Make the sketch. Be confident, and be decisive.

Summing Up

A sound section management strategy in Logic Games will help you maximize your performance in this section. As you practice, remember to:

Slow down and think.

Understand the action(s) in the initial game setup, interpret rules correctly, and make solid, concrete deductions before moving to the questions.

Do the games in the order you want to do them. Analyze a game's action(s), rules, and questions stems to determine if you'd like to do the game now, or save it for later.

Skip difficult questions and tackle easy questions. Make it a point to tackle all of the Acceptability questions in the section, even if you don't have time to do a game fully. Strategically skip Rule Substitution questions that are notoriously difficult.

Use past work. The right answer to an Acceptability question and "If" sketches provide possible acceptable game scenarios. Use that information to quickly find right answers or quickly eliminate wrong answers.

When in doubt, sketch it out. Be confident. In questions where you cannot strategically use past work, aggressively dive into answer choices and sketch out what is and is not possible.

Put These Skills to the Test

The best way to practice the strategies and tactics described in this appendix is to take a timed Logic Games section. If possible, use a released PrepTest for which you have explanations available so that you can do quality self-assessment when you're done. Don't forget: You have access to explanations for PrepTests 71 and 73—the tests included in LSAC's free LSAT Prep tool—in this book's online resources. Complete analysis and explanations for the more than 70 officially released tests on LawHub that come with an LSAC LSAT Prep Plus subscription are available on Kaplan's LSAT Link and Link+ tools. See **kaptest.com/lsat** for more information or to purchase LSAT Link or Link+.

APPENDIX II

Countdown to Test Day

Is it starting to feel like your whole life is a buildup to the LSAT? You've known about it for years, worried about it for months, and now spent weeks in solid preparation for it. As the test gets closer, you may find your anxiety is on the rise. You shouldn't worry. After the preparation you've done, you're in good shape. To calm any pre-test jitters you may have, though, here are a few strategies for the days before the test.

During the COVID-19 pandemic, LSAC adopted a take-at-home version of the LSAT called LSAT-Flex. It had three sections, all scored, and was remotely proctored through ProctorU. As of the time this book went to print, LSAC had announced that all test dates through at least June 2022 would be live, remote-proctored administrations, but now with an experimental section, making the LSAT a four-section experience on test day. If you are getting ready for a test date after June 2022, please check www.lsac.org/lsat for the latest information. Kaplan will make every effort to keep the most current information available on our website and in your online resources as well.

As soon as you've confirmed that your test date will be "take-at-home," check your equipment against the requirements listed on the LSAC website (or linked in the confirmation email for your test registration). If there is any equipment you're lacking or if you have any issues securing a quiet, secure space for testing, contact LSAC. The organization has stated its commitment to helping all test takers acquire the equipment and space they need for a successful test day. Also, make sure to upload your required "passport-style" photo to your LSAC account, and double-check both that the name on your government-issued ID precisely matches the name with which you registered for your test and that your ID will not expire before test day.

Finally, the way that LSAT-Flex has been working, you register for a testing window of a few days, and then about two-weeks prior to the first day of testing in that window, you'll receive an email from **LSACinfo@LSAC.org** with instructions for how to select and sign up for a specific day and time for your test. While there's no reason to think LSAC will change this procedure, Kaplan advises you to confirm the steps you'll need to complete prior to test day to be sure.

THE WEEK BEFORE THE TEST

Your goal during the week before the LSAT is to set yourself up for success on test day. Up until this point, you have been working to build your LSAT potential, but test day is about achievement. That process begins with taking care of your basic needs: food, sleep, and exercise. It's easy to get caught up in the stress of balancing your life with your studying, but if taking an extra hour to study every night leaves you sleep deprived and exhausted on test day, it's hurting you more than helping. Figure out what time you need to go to sleep the night before the exam, and make sure you're in bed at that time every night the week before the exam. This is particularly important if you're a night owl who tends to get a second wind late in the evening. If at all possible, start doing some LSAT work—even if it's only a few problems—at the same time that you will be taking your test. Finally, if you are someone who regularly goes to the gym or engages in other physical activity, this is *not* the week to stop. Physical activity helps lower stress and increases production of dopamine and norepinephrine, two neurotransmitters that play a crucial role in memory, attention, and mood!

You should also decide on and set up the room and desk you'll use to take the test, especially if that space is different at all from the room or desk you normally use to study. Take a practice test (or at least a timed section) with this configuration to ensure that it is as quiet and comfortable as you imagine. If you live with roommates or family members, let them know about your testing schedule and make sure they'll be able to give you the privacy and quiet you'll need on test day. Taking those steps now will pay off by preventing unexpected situations when it matters most.

Also, at least a week prior to your test, make sure to double-check your registration against the government-issued ID you'll be showing to the proctor on camera. Be sure that the names match and that the ID isn't expired! (As of the time this book went to press, LSAC accepts photo IDs that expired *within 90 days* of the test date, but check the LSAC website for the latest information.) If the names don't match, contact LSAC *immediately* so you can remedy the situation. If that isn't fixed by test day, you may not be allowed to take the exam. You will also need a passport-style photograph to upload to your LSAC account. The deadline to upload the photo is approximately one month before test day. Confirm your photo upload deadline by checking the LSAC website. LSAC is strict about the photo requirements, so Kaplan recommends that you have your photos taken professionally at a place that specializes in passport photos.

For a complete list of the LSAC photo requirements, visit LSAC's website, **www.lsac.org/jd/lsat/day-of-test/photo-requirements**.

The kind of practice that you do the week before the exam is important. Resist the temptation to focus on your weaknesses, and instead focus primarily on shoring up your strengths. The reality is that you are more likely to grab a few points in your strengths at the last minute than you are in the areas you struggle with the most. Of course, be sure to work on all three areas during this time: no one section should be fully ignored. Also keep in mind that the actual LSAT is a test of timing and endurance. A majority of your work should be under timed conditions, and you should try to fit in a complete test or two if you have the time in your schedule. Having said that, do not fall into the trap of doing nothing but tests right before the LSAT. As always, there is a balancing act between test taking and review: Taking a test every day can make it difficult to find time to review them, which means you aren't learning from them. You also need to watch your stress levels carefully: Taking too many exams can lead to a stress spiral that is hard to climb out of.

Finally, the week before the exam is the time to decide whether you are ready to take your test. As of the time of writing, LSAC's policy allows you to withdraw your registration all the way up until 11:59 P.M. Eastern time the night before the exam without it showing up on your record. There is no right or wrong answer to the question of whether you are ready to take your exam, but if you are having any doubts, ask yourself two questions:

- What is the lowest score I would be okay with an admissions officer seeing?
- Am I scoring at least that high now?

You can choose your goals in life, but you can't always choose your timelines. If the answer to the second question is a resounding no, then it may be in your best interest to change your test date. Though there is a modest benefit to applying early, submitting a score that is well below a school's median is more likely to result in a faster rejection than a surprise admission. Don't expect any miracles on test day. It's possible that your score will suddenly jump up to an all-time high on the day of the exam, but it isn't likely. More importantly, it's risky. This is especially important if you already have one score or cancellation within the last five years: Admissions officers are understanding about one blemish on your record, but two starts to become a pattern.

LSAT STRATEGY

In the last week before the test:

- Double-check your registration and ID.
- Get your body on schedule for the time of your test.
- Set up and try out your testing area.
- Don't take any practice tests within 48 hours of the test.
- Decide whether you want to take the test or withdraw.

THE DAY BEFORE THE TEST

The day before the test is as important as the six days before that. The first instinct of most test takers is to cram as much as possible in hopes of grabbing a few last-second points. But the LSAT isn't an AP exam or your history final: You cannot "cram" for the LSAT. Think of test day as an experienced athlete thinks of game day. An athlete doesn't try to run 10 miles the day before a big race: She rests up to make sure that she can hit her potential when it counts. Though this advice is hard to follow, trust Kaplan's decades of experience with tens of thousands of students. Make the day before the test a wonderful, relaxing day. There's a good chance that during the last few weeks or months, the stress of balancing prep with the rest of your life has meant you've had less time to yourself or with your family and loved ones. Spend a day with your significant other or kids. Go to the spa or spend the day watching a movie marathon. Whatever you do, make sure the day is as restful and relaxing as possible. Put your LSAT materials away and leave them there because, while you aren't going to cram your way to a good score, you may cram your way to a bad one. Think of how you normally feel when you get a score on something that is less than you hoped for. Now imagine how it would feel the day before the exam and what that kind of anxiety could do to you. The benefits to studying the day before are almost nonexistent, but the risks are sky-high.

Don't forget to cap off the day with a healthy dinner and a good night's sleep. It's not going to be easy to fall asleep the night before the test, so make sure you are in bed on time. Resist the urge to stare at a television or computer screen: They tend to make it even harder to sleep. For what it's worth, however, the most important night's sleep isn't the night before the test; it's two nights before the test. For various reasons, the effects of sleep deprivation tend to skip a day, so getting a great night's sleep two nights before the exam will help make sure that you are well rested the day of the test!

LSAT STRATEGY

On the day before the test:

- Relax! Read a book, watch a movie, go for a walk, etc.
- Make sure you have anything you may need during the test the next day—e.g., water, tissues, pen or pencil, plain scratch paper.
- Eat a healthy dinner and get plenty of sleep.

THE MORNING OF THE TEST

On the morning of the exam, get up early to give yourself some time to wake up, have breakfast, and prepare your testing space. If you have an afternoon testing time, plan your morning accordingly. A relaxed morning is a much better start than a frantic, stressful one. Make sure breakfast has a good balance of protein and carbohydrates. You'll need the energy later!

Dress comfortably in a way you don't mind being seen on camera. The proctors will take your picture and a picture of your photo ID and will be watching you throughout the exam. Remember that you may not wear sunglasses or a hat or hood (unless it is subject to a religious exemption), and that you may not have a purse, bag, briefcase, or backpack in the room with you during your LSAT.

LSAC strictly forbids several other kinds of items from being on the desk or in the room where you are testing. The proctor will have you point your camera around the room to ensure forbidden items are not present.

LSAT FACTS

The following items are prohibited during the test:

- Cell phones (you may use one as a mirror prior to your photograph, but then will be asked to turn it off and put it away)
- Electronic devices of any kind, including tablets, MP3 players, or digital watches
- Headphones and earbuds (you may use plain foam ear plugs as approved by the proctor)
- Backpacks, bags, briefcases, or purses
- Mechanical pencils
- Papers or books (other than five sheets of plain scratch paper, which you will allow the proctor to examine)
- Hats and hoods (other than religious items)

This is not a complete list, so be sure to check the LSAC website to get the most updated information. But do know that once you check in, you may not have any of these items on your person or in the room.

DURING THE TEST

Without a doubt, the best part of the "take-at-home" LSAT experience is the fact that there is no need to travel to a testing site, worry about parking, wait in line to check in, and wait with other nervous test takers for the proctors to distribute tablets, read rules, and answer questions from test takers much less prepared than you will be.

Now, to start your LSAT, you will log in to ProctorU (LSAC will provide instructions for making an account) and click "Start Session." Follow the simple setup process—there's a tech check, photo-ID verification, and installation of a test-recovery app—and then you'll meet a proctor who will direct you to LSAC's LawHub (you'll already be familiar with it from ample practice), where you'll launch your LSAT.

You'll need your LSAC username and password to log in, so make sure you remember them. The proctor will have you read the rules out loud and check a box to indicate your agreement. At this point, the proctor will enter a password that activates a start button on your screen.

Click that, and your LSAT test will begin.

Now let all your practice and preparation take over. Identify the questions and use the Kaplan methods, strategies, and tactics you've learned for each section and question type. Use the expert section-management techniques from your LSAT Channel Spotlight sessions, and rock your LSAT test day.

After the first two sections, you'll have a short break. Follow the proctor's instructions for moving, leaving the room, or anything else you may ask to do. When it's time to resume, start up again with confidence in your preparation and test expertise.

After the fourth section of the test, take a moment to relax and breathe. Congratulations! You have finished the scored sections of the LSAT. The only section that now remains is LSAT Writing, which you will take at some point relatively soon after your test. Though this section is not unimportant, it's nowhere near as important as what you've just accomplished.

LSAT STRATEGY

During the test:

- Use the methods, strategies, and tactics you've learned and practiced for every section and question.
- If you find yourself stressed or distracted, take a deep breath and remind yourself that all the questions you see on test day are just like the ones you've studied and practiced.
- Keep moving through the test and stay focused on the section you're currently in, not those you've already done or the ones coming up.

AFTER THE TEST

If it turns out that test day doesn't go *exactly* as planned, that's all right—it rarely, if ever, does, and the LSAT does not require perfection! All over the country, your fellow test takers will likely experience some level of self-doubt as well; that's typical.

Let's presume your official test goes as well—or better—than you'd hoped. If that's the case, feel free to skip the next section and head to the Post-LSAT Festivities section later in this chapter. If, however, you end up having a disappointing or upsetting test day, you may think about canceling your score. Remember that first-time test takers now have the option to purchase Score Preview. That allows you to see your score before deciding whether to cancel (you have six days to decide after scores are released). You can purchase the Score Preview option prior to your test or, for a slightly higher price, during a designated period after your test day. It's like an insurance policy, but it applies only to your first-ever administration. If you've received an LSAT score or canceled a previous administration after completing the test, you are not eligible for Score Preview.

Canceling your score means that neither you nor the law schools will have access to whatever your score would have been. But here's the rub: Law schools will still know that you took the test at that administration. To avoid having your cancellation raise a red flag for the schools to which you've applied, consider attaching an addendum to your application explaining why you canceled.

The only way to cancel your LSAT score is online, through your account at lsac.org, within six calendar days after the exam. If you're considering canceling, check the LSAC's website to verify the most up-to-date instructions and deadlines for doing so.

Should You Cancel Your Score?

If you're wondering whether canceling is the right decision, the information in this section should be helpful. If you feel confident in your test-day performance and are not considering canceling your score, feel free to skip this section entirely.

First, let's examine the *benefits* of not canceling your LSAT score.

No matter how you "feel" about how things went, you *don't know for sure*. You may have actually done much better than you think. According to LSAC, many test takers who cancel their score and then retest would've been better off sticking with the first score. (While the examinee never finds out the cancelled score, the LSAC still computes it internally and can compare the cancelled and subsequent results.)

Additionally, if you cancel your score, you will never have access to the answers you selected during Test Day. If you take any of the LSAT exams that are released to the public and keep your score, you will receive an official score report and a copy of the test you took. This information can be extremely helpful if you do choose to take the test again, as you will be able to review and evaluate the decisions you made during an official LSAT, when everything was on the line. Allowing your score to stay in place gives you access not only to the right answers, but also to the answers *you* picked. Even weeks later, you'll be amazed as you go question by question through the sections of the exam and say, "Hmmm, now why did I find wrong answer (A) so alluring?" or "I should've stuck with my first answer there!" By canceling your score, you forfeit access to this information.

Another reason why it may not be in your best interests to cancel a score is that in recent years, more and more law schools are *not* averaging scores. In fact, law schools have been given careful guidelines from LSAC *against* averaging. That doesn't mean that every school follows this policy, though, and our recommendation from above still stands: The most preferable scenario is to take the test once and ace it. However, if your decision is between canceling and taking it again and *not* canceling and taking it again, it's likely that the latter option will be preferable. (Remember, schools can see when you cancel.) Even a so-so score followed by a much better score won't hurt you as it would have in the past, when averaging was the common practice. As a rule, law schools want to assess you fairly, and most agree that the fairest thing is to take the better of two scores, irrespective of the order in which tests were taken. So, even if you decide you want to retest at the next administration, there will be less pressure next time if you don't cancel *this time*. By having a score already on record, you won't have the anxiety of thinking that you absolutely must use the retest score.

It's also important to remember that there is a limit on how many times you may take the LSAT. As of the September 2019 administration, you are allowed to take the test 1) three times in any one testing year (June 1–May 31 of the following calendar year), 2) five times over any 5-year period, and 3) seven times in your lifetime. Even though you do not receive a score, your cancelled test counts as one of the times you took the LSAT.

So, based on the benefits of not canceling, the following situations **would NOT warrant a score cancellation:**

- There were some minor distractions during your test. Of course, it's hard to define exactly what counts as "minor" versus "major." Maybe you were able to hear a little noise from outside that you weren't expecting, but if you were able to put it out of your mind and get on with the test, that's pretty minor. It's unlikely that you'll ever have a perfectly distraction-free atmosphere!
- You didn't get to finish or forgot to click a bubble in the last few questions of a section, even though you usually finish that section when you practice. While your time management may not have been ideal, it doesn't warrant a cancellation. Yes, a few questions here or there can affect your overall score, but the material at the end of a section can be of a higher level of difficulty, so even if you had completed those questions, there is no guarantee they would have markedly affected your score. Also, there is always the possibility that a section you struggled with was the unscored, experimental section.

Now, let's talk about **when you should cancel your LSAT score:**

- If you have already taken the real test two or three (or more) times, you probably have a much better "feel" for whether or not a particular exam has truly gone well. Also, with two or three scores already on the record, a single cancellation isn't going to significantly damage your profile.
- If you had been consistently scoring in a certain range but became physically ill on test day, or if you had some other serious difficulty during the test that prevented you from staying focused to the point that you were unable to complete large sections of the exam, then you should consider canceling. This may have been due to test anxiety, lack of sleep the night before, personal stress not related to the LSAT, severe illness, etc. To be clear, the situations described would have affected *every* section; they wouldn't cause just a moment of panic during a single section.
- Remember that you can (and should) explain valid reasons for a score cancellation in an addendum to your law-school applications.

Post-LSAT Festivities

So, you've just taken the LSAT. After months of preparation and hard work, it's finally over. What to do now? First, give yourself a great big pat on the back. You've just completed (and hopefully rocked) the most important factor in law school admissions. Go celebrate and enjoy the moment—but of course, don't celebrate *too* hard. Law schools are in the business of recruiting future lawyers, which means they're typically not interested in applicants with criminal records. Don't be the person who destroys the LSAT in the morning, then acts inappropriately in the evening.

Instead, take a moment to reach out to anyone who has helped you prepare for the test—teachers, tutors, study buddies, friends, and family members who have invested in your decision to go to law school and become a lawyer. Let them know how you did and share your success with them.

After you've celebrated, and after you've taken a couple of days off from thinking about the LSAT and law school, it's time to once again start thinking about putting together the other pieces of your application. Be sure to get a good head start on your letters of recommendation, personal statement, and transcripts.

Congratulations on your journey!

APPENDIX III

Logic Games Index

The following is a list of every logic game to appear on an officially released LSAC PrepTest. You can use this list to find additional practice games of a certain type. There is a brief description of the situation described in the game's setup to help you avoid confusion, or to find a game if you remember what it was about, but not the PrepTest on which it appeared.

Note: The index lists games chronologically by the month and year in which they were administered. PrepTest numbers correspond to the order in which the tests were released to the public. In years past, the LSAC did not always release tests chronologically.

PrepTest	Section #	Game #	Q #s	Game Type	Game Name
1	2	Game 1	Qs 1–7	Sequencing—Strict (Circular)	Trade Negotiation Treaty Seating
1	2	Game 2	Qs 8–13	Matching	Computer and Printer Years
1	2	Game 3	Qs 14–18	Sequencing—Loose	Law Firm Partner Hiring
1	2	Game 4	Qs 19–24	Matching (Spatial)	Colored Railway Tickets for January/ February
2	3	Game 1	Qs 1–5	Sequencing—Loose	Mammoth Corp Hiring
2	3	Game 2	Qs 6–12	Sequencing—Strict	Five Floor Apartment Building
2	3	Game 3	Qs 13–17	Distribution	Hannah and Her Cities
2	3	Game 4	Qs 18–24	Hybrid—Matching/ Sequencing	Six Dogs at Dog Show; Breeds & Genders
3	1	Game 1	Qs 1–7	Matching	Three Couples at Dinner
3	1	Game 2	Qs 8–13	Sequencing—Strict	Seven Families in Houses
3	1	Game 3	Qs 14–19	Matching (Spatial)	Automobile Exhibition
3	1	Game 4	Qs 20–24	Distribution	Airshow Pilots & Copilots
4	3	Game 1	Qs 1–6	Sequencing—Loose	Law Firm Salaries
4	3	Game 2	Qs 7–11	Matching	Illness Symptoms

PrepTest	Section #	Game #	Q #s	Game Type	Game Name
4	3	Game 3	Qs 12–17	Sequencing—Strict	Street Cleaning Crew
4	3	Game 4	Qs 18–24	Mapping	Ski Chalet Snow Shoveled Paths
5	2	Game 1	Qs 1–6	Sequencing—Strict	Six Course Grades A-E
5	2	Game 2	Qs 7–11	Matching	Casey's Shirts
5	2	Game 3	Qs 12–17	Selection	Aquarium Fish & Plants
5	2	Game 4	Qs 18–24	Sequencing—Strict (Triple)	Town Rankings
6	4	Game 1	Qs 1–6	Distribution	Gerbils, Hamsters, Lizards, and Snakes
6	4	Game 2	Qs 7–12	Sequencing—Loose	Soft Drink Names
6	4	Game 3	Qs 13–19	Sequencing—Strict (Square)	Park Benches
6	4	Game 4	Qs 20–24	Mapping	Island Bridges
18	1	Game 1	Qs 1–6	Distribution	Students Visiting Three Canadian Cities
18	1	Game 2	Qs 7–13	Sequencing—Strict	Fall and Spring Course Folders
18	1	Game 3	Qs 14–19	Mapping	Five Subway Lines
18	1	Game 4	Qs 20–24	Process	Firm's Annual Review for Promotion
7	2	Game 1	Qs 1–7	Sequencing—Strict	Six Songs and One News Tape
7	2	Game 2	Qs 8–12	Matching (Spatial)	Dr. Yamata's Schedule
7	2	Game 3	Qs 13–18	Distribution	Judges Voting on Datalog Corp's Petition
7	2	Game 4	Qs 19–24	Hybrid—Matching/ Sequencing	Runners & Charities
8	2	Game 1	Qs 1–5	Sequencing—Strict	Gymnastics Coaching Sessions
8	2	Game 2	Qs 6–12	Selection	Square Parking Lot Lights
8	2	Game 3	Qs 13–17	Sequencing—Strict	Seven Boys/Girls in Seven Chairs
8	2	Game 4	Qs 18–24	Matching	Antibiotics and Organisms
9	3	Game 1	Qs 1–7	Matching	Corsages
9	3	Game 2	Qs 8–13	Selection	Diplomat Dinner Attendees
9	3	Game 3	Qs 14–18	Matching	Dance Recital Partnering
9	3	Game 4	Qs 19–24	Matching (Spatial)	Cities with Hospitals, Jails, and Universities
10	2	Game 1	Qs 1–5	Sequencing—Loose	Three Classes of Three Students Each

PrepTest	Section #	Game #	Q #s	Game Type	Game Name
10	2	Game 2	Qs 6–12	Distribution	Six Film Reviewers for Four Movies
10	2	Game 3	Qs 13–18	Process	Words/Sentences Game
10	2	Game 4	Qs 19–24	Hybrid - Selection/ Sequencing	Giuliani, Rodrigo, and Vivaldi Concertos
11	1	Game 1	Qs 1–6	Distribution	Camp Counselors Supervising Activities
11	1	Game 2	Qs 7–11	Hybrid—Selection/ Sequencing	Firefighter Schedules
11	1	Game 3	Qs 12–19	Selection	Housing Committee
11	1	Game 4	Qs 20–24	Process	Apprentice Re-Assignment to Projects
12	2	Game 1	Qs 1–6	Sequencing—Strict	Individual Piano Classes
12	2	Game 2	Qs 7–11	Distribution	Nine People in Three Canoes
12	2	Game 3	Qs 12–17	Matching	Street Vendor's Four Kinds of Food
12	2	Game 4	Qs 18–24	Process	Four Colored Chemical Flasks
13	1	Game 1	Qs 1–6	Distribution	Two Four-Person Consumer Groups
13	1	Game 2	Qs 7–11	Sequencing—Strict	TV Show Contestants
13	1	Game 3	Qs 12–17	Hybrid—Selection/ Sequencing	Art Class Scheduling (Lecture)
13	1	Game 4	Qs 18–24	Matching (Spatial)	Clans in Annual Harvest Ceremonies
14	1	Game 1	Qs 1–6	Distribution	President, Manager, Technician
14	1	Game 2	Qs 7–12	Sequencing—Strict	Washing Dishes
14	1	Game 3	Qs 13–18	Distribution	Exhibited and Caged Birds
14	1	Game 4	Qs 19–24	Matching	Nikki's and Otto's Seasonal Sports
15	4	Game 1	Qs 1–6	Sequencing—Strict	Student Speeches
15	4	Game 2	Qs 7–13	Mapping	Plane Zones
15	4	Game 3	Qs 14–19	Sequencing—Strict	Four-Person Car Pool over Six Days
15	4	Game 4	Qs 20–24	Hybrid—Distribution/ Selection	Experienced/Inexperienced Plumber Teams
16	1	Game 1	Qs 1–6	Distribution	Eight Students in Three Classes
16	1	Game 2	Qs 7–12	Sequencing - Strict	Lions and Tigers in Stalls
16	1	Game 3	Qs 13–18	Matching (Spatial)	Ranch, Split-Level, and Tudor Houses
16	1	Game 4	Qs 19–24	Process	Tennis Matches Based on Rankings
17	1	Game 1	Qs 1–5	Sequencing—Strict	Doctor's Seven Patients

PrepTest	Section #	Game #	Q #s	Game Type	Game Name
17	1	Game 2	Qs 6–12	Distribution	Policy, Quality, and Sales Committees
17	1	Game 3	Qs 13–17	Matching	Vladimir and Wendy's Meals
17	1	Game 4	Qs 18–24	Hybrid—Distribution/ Sequencing	Relay Race Teams
A	3	Game 1	Qs 1–5	Sequencing—Strict	Building Decks
A	3	Game 2	Qs 6–10	Hybrid—Distribution/ Matching	Sales Presentation
A	3	Game 3	Qs 11–17	Sequencing—Strict	Academic Office Assignments
A	3	Game 4	Qs 18–24	Selection	Wool/Silk and Rectangular/Oval Rugs
19	1	Game 1	Qs 1–7	Sequencing—Strict	Factory Inspections
19	1	Game 2	Qs 8–12	Sequencing—Strict	Theater Company Workshops
19	1	Game 3	Qs 13–19	Distribution	Adults and Children in Two Boats
19	1	Game 4	Qs 20–24	Distribution	Oceans, Recycling, and Wetlands Panels
20	3	Game 1	Qs 1–5	Sequencing—Strict	Nine Airplane Seats
20	3	Game 2	Qs 6–12	Selection	Library Budget Reductions
20	3	Game 3	Qs 13–18	Sequencing—Strict	String of Colored Beads
20	3	Game 4	Qs 19–24	Hybrid—Matching/ Sequencing	Evening Concert for Three Vocalists
21	1	Game 1	Qs 1–6	Distribution	Single, Double, and Triple Dormitory Rooms
21	1	Game 2	Qs 7–11	Matching	Colored Light Bulbs into Sockets
21	1	Game 3	Qs 12–17	Sequencing—Strict	Hostile and Non-Hostile Witness Interviews
21	1	Game 4	Qs 18–24	Sequencing—Strict	Product Advertisements Over Four Weeks
"Feb 1997"	4	Game 1	Qs 1–6	Sequencing—Strict	Upholsterer Jobs
"Feb 1997"	4	Game 2	Qs 7–13	Distribution	Rock-Climbing Teams and Organizer
"Feb 1997"	4	Game 3	Qs 14–18	Matching (Spatial)	Five Train Loops
"Feb 1997"	4	Game 4	Qs 19–24	Hybrid—Distribution/ Sequencing	Lectures in Library or Studio
22	3	Game 1	Qs 1–7	Distribution	Benefit Dinner

PrepTest	Section #	Game #	Q #s	Game Type	Game Name
22	3	Game 2	Qs 8–14	Hybrid—Matching/ Sequencing	Medical Training Sessions
22	3	Game 3	Qs 15–19	Matching (Spatial)	Paintings: Oil/Watercolor and 19th/20th
22	3	Game 4	Qs 20–24	Hybrid—Distribution/ Selection/Sequencing	Juggling Teams
23	1	Game 1	Qs 1–5	Sequencing—Strict	Music Recording
23	1	Game 2	Qs 6–11	Selection	Interviewing and Hiring
23	1	Game 3	Qs 12–18	Hybrid—Distribution/ Selection	Anthropologist and Linguist Teams
23	1	Game 4	Qs 19–24	Sequencing—Strict (Triple)	Mayoral Speeches
24	4	Game 1	Qs 1–5	Distribution	Recipe Contest for an Appetizer and a Main Dish
24	4	Game 2	Qs 6–10	Sequencing—Strict	Singing Competition
24	4	Game 3	Qs 11–17	Sequencing—Strict (Double)	Advanced/Introductory Textbook Evaluation
24	4	Game 4	Qs 18–23	Selection	Nine Treatments
25	3	Game 1	Qs 1–5	Hybrid—Distribution/ Selection	Planting and Trails Committee
25	3	Game 2	Qs 6–12	Hybrid—Distribution/ Matching	Guides, Tourists, and Languages
25	3	Game 3	Qs 13–18	Hybrid—Distribution/ Sequencing	Golf and Tennis Rankings
25	3	Game 4	Qs 19–24	Sequencing—Strict	Ballads and Dance Songs
26	1	Game 1	Qs 1–7	Sequencing—Strict (Two Sequences)	Laboratory Benches
26	1	Game 2	Qs 8–12	Sequencing—Strict	Messenger Delivering Packages
26	1	Game 3	Qs 13–18	Distribution	Movie, Restaurant, Soccer Game
26	1	Game 4	Qs 19–24	Selection	Lawmaker and Scientist Panel
27	2	Game 1	Qs 1–6	Sequencing—Strict	Investors Viewing a Building
27	2	Game 2	Qs 7–12	Hybrid—Distribution/ Matching/Sequencing	Snakes' and Reptiles' Zoo Habitats
27	2	Game 3	Qs 13–19	Distribution	Fellini, Hitchcock, and Kurosawa Films
27	2	Game 4	Qs 20–24	Sequencing—Strict	Orange, Purple, and Green Cars
B	2	Game 1	Qs 1–6	Sequencing—Loose	Boat Arrivals
B	2	Game 2	Qs 7–12	Selection	Trees in the Park

PrepTest	Section #	Game #	Q #s	Game Type	Game Name
B	2	Game 3	Qs 13–18	Sequencing—Strict (Circular)	Four Couples Around the Table
B	2	Game 4	Qs 19–24	Hybrid—Matching/ Selection	Zeno's Unfinished Furniture
28	2	Game 1	Qs 1–5	Sequencing—Strict	Race Horses
28	2	Game 2	Qs 6–12	Matching	Researchers and Languages
28	2	Game 3	Qs 13–18	Sequencing—Strict	Health Officer Inspecting Hotels & Restaurants
28	2	Game 4	Qs 19–23	Matching	Morrisville's Town Council Voting
29	3	Game 1	Qs 1–6	Distribution	Accountant Paying Bills over Two Days
29	3	Game 2	Qs 7–13	Matching	Mannequin Outfits
29	3	Game 3	Qs 14–19	Sequencing—Strict	Language Awards
29	3	Game 4	Qs 20–24	Sequencing—Strict	Piano Classes
30	1	Game 1	Qs 1–5	Matching	Bread Types & Sliced/Unsliced
30	1	Game 2	Qs 6–10	Hybrid—Selection/ Sequencing	Answering Machine Messages
30	1	Game 3	Qs 11–16	Hybrid—Matching/ Sequencing	Car Wash
30	1	Game 4	Qs 17–23	Sequencing—Strict	Toy Trucks
C	1	Game 1	Qs 1–5	Distribution	Boat Race and Rescue Exercise
C	1	Game 2	Qs 6–12	Sequencing—Loose	Restaurant Rankings
C	1	Game 3	Qs 13–19	Matching	Three Parks, Five Attractions
C	1	Game 4	Qs 20–24	Hybrid—Matching/ Sequencing	Dynamic Motors' Automobile Factories
31	1	Game 1	Qs 1–6	Sequencing—Strict	Lockers—Boys/Girls
31	1	Game 2	Qs 7–13	Selection	Music Store Sale—Genre & Used/ New
31	1	Game 3	Qs 14–18	Sequencing—Strict	Company Division Tours
31	1	Game 4	Qs 19–23	Hybrid—Distribution/ Selection	Installation Crew
32	3	Game 1	Qs 1–6	Hybrid—Selection/ Sequencing	Oral Reports Mon–Wed AM/PM
32	3	Game 2	Qs 7–11	Selection	Russian/French and Novels/Plays
32	3	Game 3	Qs 12–18	Sequencing—Strict	Concert Compositions

PrepTest	Section #	Game #	Q #s	Game Type	Game Name
32	3	Game 4	Qs 19–24	Sequencing—Strict (Two Sequences)	Pet Shop Puppies & Kittens
33	4	Game 1	Qs 1–5	Sequencing—Loose	Television Program Rankings
33	4	Game 2	Qs 6–12	Selection	Bird-Watchers
33	4	Game 3	Qs 13–18	Selection	Jeweler—Ruby, Sapphire, and Topaz
33	4	Game 4	Qs 19–23	Matching (Spatial)	Oak Street Colored Lights
34	4	Game 1	Qs 1–7	Sequencing—Strict	Supermarket Stock Clerks
34	4	Game 2	Qs 8–12	Matching	Philosophy Lectures
34	4	Game 3	Qs 13–18	Sequencing—Strict	Train Arrivals
34	4	Game 4	Qs 19–24	Distribution	Doctors at Two Clinics
35	3	Game 1	Qs 1–5	Selection	Astronauts—Geologists/ Radiobiologists
35	3	Game 2	Qs 6–12	Matching	Cars & Options
35	3	Game 3	Qs 13–17	Hybrid—Distribution/ Sequencing	Opera Seats & Rows for Kim Family
35	3	Game 4	Qs 18–23	Sequencing—Strict	Professor Hiring 1989-1995
36	4	Game 1	Qs 1–6	Selection	Fruit Stand
36	4	Game 2	Qs 7–13	Hybrid—Matching/ Sequencing	Radio Talk Show Calls
36	4	Game 3	Qs 14–18	Hybrid—Distribution/ Sequencing	Bus Seats and Rows
36	4	Game 4	Qs 19–23	Sequencing—Strict (Two Sequences)	Flights With One Pilot and One Co-pilot
37	3	Game 1	Qs 1–5	Matching	Dormitory Wings
37	3	Game 2	Qs 6–11	Hybrid—Matching/ Sequencing	Truck Arrivals, Green/Red
37	3	Game 3	Qs 12–18	Distribution	Bookshelves
37	3	Game 4	Qs 19–24	Sequencing—Strict	Swim Team Relay Race
38	2	Game 1	Qs 1–7	Sequencing—Loose	Clowns Getting Out of Car
38	2	Game 2	Qs 8–13	Hybrid—Matching/ Sequencing	Farm Exhibition
38	2	Game 3	Qs 14–19	Distribution	Management, Production, and Sales Positions
38	2	Game 4	Qs 20–24	Sequencing—Strict	Musical Pieces with Two Instruments Each
39	1	Game 1	Qs 1–5	Sequencing—Strict	Red, Green, and Yellow Files

PrepTest	Section #	Game #	Q #s	Game Type	Game Name
39	1	Game 2	Qs 6–11	Matching	Capital Enterprises Three-Day Conference
39	1	Game 3	Qs 12–18	Hybrid—Matching/ Sequencing	Pohl Children—Right-/Left-Handed and Birth Years
39	1	Game 4	Qs 19–23	Selection	Barbara's Aquarium Fish
40	2	Game 1	Qs 1–5	Sequencing—Strict	Charlie's Soup
40	2	Game 2	Qs 6–10	Hybrid—Selection/ Sequencing	Cold Medication Testing
40	2	Game 3	Qs 11–17	Mapping	Zephyr Airlines
40	2	Game 4	Qs 18–23	Selection	Animal Behavioral Study
41	2	Game 1	Qs 1–7	Sequencing—Strict	Dresses in Closet
41	2	Game 2	Qs 8–12	Hybrid—Matching/ Sequencing	Children's Song Festival
41	2	Game 3	Qs 13–17	Distribution	Finance & Incentives Committees
41	2	Game 4	Qs 18–24	Sequencing—Strict (Circular)	Circular Picnic Table
42	1	Game 1	Qs 1–5	Selection	Scientist Panelists
42	1	Game 2	Qs 6–12	Sequencing—Strict	Loading Dock
42	1	Game 3	Qs 13–18	Sequencing—Strict	Bakery Cookies
42	1	Game 4	Qs 19–23	Matching	Play Reviews
43	4	Game 1	Qs 1–5	Sequencing—Strict	Civic Parade
43	4	Game 2	Qs 6–12	Sequencing—Loose	Rowing Team
43	4	Game 3	Qs 13–17	Hybrid—Distribution/ Sequencing	Museum & Art Collector
43	4	Game 4	Qs 18–22	Matching	Lunch Trucks
44	3	Game 1	Qs 1–6	Sequencing—Strict	Dignitary Meetings
44	3	Game 2	Qs 7–12	Distribution	Shelter Dog Placement
44	3	Game 3	Qs 13–17	Matching	Archaeological Sites
44	3	Game 4	Qs 18–22	Hybrid—Matching/ Sequencing	Parking Lots
45	3	Game 1	Qs 1–6	Sequencing—Strict	Meetings with Clients & Gym
45	3	Game 2	Qs 7–12	Sequencing—Strict	Chess Tournament
45	3	Game 3	Qs 13–17	Selection	Photographs
45	3	Game 4	Qs 18–22	Matching	Export Alliance
46	4	Game 1	Qs 1–6	Sequencing—Strict	Animal Guideposts
46	4	Game 2	Qs 7–11	Matching (Spatial)	Cassette Tapes

PrepTest	Section #	Game #	Q #s	Game Type	Game Name
46	4	Game 3	Qs 12–16	Hybrid—Matching/ Sequencing	Town & Precipitation
46	4	Game 4	Qs 17–22	Matching	Secret Committees
47	4	Game 1	Qs 1–5	Sequencing—Strict	Product Ads
47	4	Game 2	Qs 6–11	Selection	Lighting Switches
47	4	Game 3	Qs 12–17	Matching	Record Stores
47	4	Game 4	Qs 18–22	Sequencing—Strict	Deli Staffing
48	2	Game 1	Qs 1–6	Selection	Electrical Appliances
48	2	Game 2	Qs 7–12	Sequencing—Loose	Harvesting Fields
48	2	Game 3	Qs 13–17	Matching	Technician Repairs
48	2	Game 4	Qs 18–22	Hybrid—Distribution/ Sequencing	Folk & Rock Concert
49	1	Game 1	Qs 1–7	Hybrid—Selection/ Sequencing	International Film Festival
49	1	Game 2	Qs 8–12	Distribution	Housemates & Mail
49	1	Game 3	Qs 13–17	Selection	Summer Courses
49	1	Game 4	Qs 18–22	Sequencing—Strict	Computer Chips
50	3	Game 1	Qs 1–5	Sequencing—Strict	Airline Stops
50	3	Game 2	Qs 6–11	Selection	Educational Committee
50	3	Game 3	Qs 12–17	Sequencing—Strict (Double)	Car & Graduation Dates
50	3	Game 4	Qs 18–22	Sequencing—Strict	Alphabet Soup
51	4	Game 1	Qs 1–5	Matching	Clown Costume
51	4	Game 2	Qs 6–10	Sequencing—Loose	Hotel Suites
51	4	Game 3	Qs 11–15	Hybrid—Matching/ Sequencing	Guitarist's Demo CD
51	4	Game 4	Qs 16–22	Sequencing—Loose	Courier Deliveries
"June 2007"	1	Game 1	Qs 1–5	Sequencing—Strict	Product Codes
"June 2007"	1	Game 2	Qs 6–10	Hybrid—Matching/ Sequencing	Film Club Festival
"June 2007"	1	Game 3	Qs 11–17	Sequencing—Strict	Cruise Line Voyages
"June 2007"	1	Game 4	Qs 18–23	Matching	Recycling Centers

PrepTest	Section #	Game #	Q #s	Game Type	Game Name
52	2	Game 1	Qs 1–7	Sequencing—Loose	Water Valves
52	2	Game 2	Qs 8–12	Distribution	Field Trip Chaperones
52	2	Game 3	Qs 13–17	Hybrid—Distribution/ Sequencing	Sales Conference Seminars
52	2	Game 4	Qs 18–23	Sequencing—Loose	Bread Truck Deliveries
53	2	Game 1	Qs 1–5	Distribution	Talent Agency Performers
53	2	Game 2	Qs 6–11	Sequencing—Loose	Architects' Designs
53	2	Game 3	Qs 12–17	Hybrid—Matching/ Sequencing	Burglary Suspects
53	2	Game 4	Qs 18–23	Hybrid—Distribution/ Sequencing	Debate Team Tourney
54	3	Game 1	Qs 1–5	Selection	Dancers on Stage
54	3	Game 2	Qs 6–12	Sequencing—Strict	CD Star Ratings
54	3	Game 3	Qs 13–17	Sequencing—Strict	Cake Layers
54	3	Game 4	Qs 18–23	Sequencing—Strict	Accepted Bid
55	4	Game 1	Qs 1–6	Hybrid—Distribution/ Matching	Trial Advocacy Teams
55	4	Game 2	Qs 7–12	Sequencing—Strict	E-Mail Messages
55	4	Game 3	Qs 13–18	Sequencing—Loose	Mercotek Productivity Rankings
55	4	Game 4	Qs 19–23	Sequencing—Strict (Two Sequences)	Shuttle Van Stops
56	1	Game 1	Qs 1–6	Sequencing—Strict	Saxophone Auditions
56	1	Game 2	Qs 7–11	Matching	Furniture Moving
56	1	Game 3	Qs 12–16	Matching	Parks and Trees
56	1	Game 4	Qs 17–23	Hybrid—Distribution/ Sequencing	Executives and Manufacturing Plants
57	1	Game 1	Qs 1–5	Sequencing—Strict	Student Activities
57	1	Game 2	Qs 6–11	Sequencing—Strict	Actor Auditions
57	1	Game 3	Qs 12–17	Hybrid—Matching/ Selection	Toy Dinosaurs
57	1	Game 4	Qs 18–23	Matching (Spatial)	Charitable Grants
58	3	Game 1	Qs 1–6	Sequencing—Strict	Construction of Monuments
58	3	Game 2	Qs 7–12	Selection	Day Care Volunteers
58	3	Game 3	Qs 13–17	Hybrid—Matching/ Sequencing	Flyhigh & Getaway Airlines
58	3	Game 4	Qs 18–23	Selection	Summer School Courses

PrepTest	Section #	Game #	Q #s	Game Type	Game Name
59	1	Game 1	Qs 1–5	Sequencing—Strict	Law Firm Departments
59	1	Game 2	Qs 6–10	Sequencing—Strict	Museum Photographs
59	1	Game 3	Qs 11–16	Selection	Alicia's Courses
59	1	Game 4	Qs 17–23	Sequencing—Strict	Organization Meetings
60	2	Game 1	Qs 1–6	Sequencing—Strict	Arts and Crafts Workshops
60	2	Game 2	Qs 7–12	Sequencing—Loose	Actors in Opening Credits
60	2	Game 3	Qs 13–17	Sequencing—Strict	Landscaper with Mulch and Stone
60	2	Game 4	Qs 18–23	Hybrid—Distribution/ Matching	Travel Magazine Interns
61	3	Game 1	Qs 1–5	Distribution	Business Convention
61	3	Game 2	Qs 6–11	Sequencing—Loose	Ancient Artifacts
61	3	Game 3	Qs 12–17	Hybrid—Selection/ Sequencing	Track Team
61	3	Game 4	Qs 18–23	Sequencing—Strict	Nurses
62	3	Game 1	Qs 1–6	Sequencing—Strict	Motel Service Appointments
62	3	Game 2	Qs 7–13	Matching	Stained Glass Windows
62	3	Game 3	Qs 14–18	Sequencing—Strict	Management Skills Conference
62	3	Game 4	Qs 19–23	Sequencing—Strict	Testifying Witnesses
63	2	Game 1	Qs 1–5	Distribution	Judicial Appointments to Appellate and Trial Courts
63	2	Game 2	Qs 6–10	Sequencing—Strict	Skydiving Team
63	2	Game 3	Qs 11–17	Sequencing—Strict	Vehicle Service
63	2	Game 4	Qs 18–23	Sequencing—Strict	Street Entertainer
C2	1	Game 1	Qs 1–5	Sequencing—Strict	Three Cars of a Roller Coaster
C2	1	Game 2	Qs 6–10	Sequencing—Strict	Five-Object Stack
C2	1	Game 3	Qs 11–17	Matching	Tricolored Costumes
C2	1	Game 4	Qs 18–23	Sequencing—Strict	Radio Station's Politician Interviews
64	2	Game 1	Qs 1–6	Sequencing—Strict	Employee Parking
64	2	Game 2	Qs 7–12	Hybrid—Distribution/ Selection	Ambassador Assignments
64	2	Game 3	Qs 13–18	Matching	Bicycle Testers
64	2	Game 4	Qs 19–23	Sequencing—Strict	Bookcase Shelves
65	2	Game 1	Qs 1–5	Sequencing—Loose	Piano Recital Solos
65	2	Game 2	Qs 6–11	Sequencing—Strict	Crafts Presentations
65	2	Game 3	Qs 12–16	Selection	Luncheon Foods

PrepTest	Section #	Game #	Q #s	Game Type	Game Name
65	2	Game 4	Qs 17–23	Sequencing—Strict	TV Scheduling
66	3	Game 1	Qs 1–5	Sequencing—Strict	Chemistry Class Lab Sessions
66	3	Game 2	Qs 6–11	Sequencing—Strict	Shopping Center Businesses
66	3	Game 3	Qs 12–18	Distribution	Software Company Sales Zones
66	3	Game 4	Qs 19–23	Hybrid—Matching/ Sequencing	Wayne & Zara's Piano Solos
67	3	Game 1	Qs 1–5	Matching	Student Speeches on Friendship and Liberty
67	3	Game 2	Qs 6–12	Sequencing—Strict	Literary Theory Lectures
67	3	Game 3	Qs 13–17	Sequencing—Strict	Toy Store Aisles
67	3	Game 4	Qs 18–23	Matching	Millville's Development Zones
68	4	Game 1	Qs 1–5	Sequencing—Strict	Realtor Showings
68	4	Game 2	Qs 6–10	Distribution	Three Days of Witness Testimony
68	4	Game 3	Qs 11–16	Matching	Maintenance Service Targets
68	4	Game 4	Qs 17–23	Sequencing—Strict	Article Editing
69	2	Game 1	Qs 1–5	Sequencing—Strict	Manuscript Ages
69	2	Game 2	Qs 6–11	Sequencing—Strict	Storing Petri Dishes
69	2	Game 3	Qs 12–17	Sequencing—Strict (Double)	Juice and Snack Deliveries
69	2	Game 4	Qs 18–23	Distribution	Cases for Paralegals
70	3	Game 1	Qs 1–7	Sequencing—Strict	Benefit Concert
70	3	Game 2	Qs 8–12	Selection	Corporate Research Team
70	3	Game 3	Qs 13–18	Hybrid—Distribution/ Sequencing	Repertory Theater Screenings
70	3	Game 4	Qs 19–23	Hybrid—Matching/ Sequencing	Bird Lectures
71	2	Game 1	Qs 1–5	Sequencing—Loose	Film Releases
71	2	Game 2	Qs 6–11	Distribution	Application Evaluation
71	2	Game 3	Qs 12–16	Hybrid—Matching/ Sequencing	Literature Course
71	2	Game 4	Qs 17–23	Sequencing—Strict	Paintings in a Museum
72	4	Game 1	Qs 1–6	Hybrid—Distribution/ Sequencing	Radio News Updates
72	4	Game 2	Qs 7–12	Sequencing—Strict	Realtor's Houses
72	4	Game 3	Qs 13–18	Distribution	Sunken Ship Artifacts

PrepTest	Section #	Game #	Q #s	Game Type	Game Name
72	4	Game 4	Qs 19–23	Sequencing—Strict (Quadruple)	Summit Company Workpieces
73	3	Game 1	Qs 1–7	Sequencing—Loose	Instrumental CD
73	3	Game 2	Qs 8–13	Hybrid—Distribution/ Sequencing	Symposium Speakers
73	3	Game 3	Qs 14–18	Distribution	Historic Building Owners
73	3	Game 4	Qs 19–23	Matching	Florist's Bouquets
74	2	Game 1	Qs 1–5	Sequencing—Loose	Band Solos
74	2	Game 2	Qs 6–10	Sequencing—Strict (Two Sequences)	Art Historians' Lectures
74	2	Game 3	Qs 11–16	Hybrid—Distribution/ Selection	Colored Rugs
74	2	Game 4	Qs 17–23	Hybrid—Distribution/ Selection	Graduation Photographers
75	4	Game 1	Qs 1–6	Distribution	Employee Bonuses
75	4	Game 2	Qs 7–11	Distribution	Landscaper's Trees
75	4	Game 3	Qs 12–18	Sequencing—Loose	Librarians' Desk Duty
75	4	Game 4	Qs 19–23	Matching (Spatial)	Business Newsletter
76	3	Game 1	Qs 1–6	Sequencing—Strict	Recruiting Criminal Accomplices
76	3	Game 2	Qs 7–13	Matching	Newspaper Photographs
76	3	Game 3	Qs 14–18	Sequencing—Strict	Campus Art Gallery
76	3	Game 4	Qs 19–23	Distribution	Publishing Cookbooks
77	3	Game 1	Qs 1–5	Sequencing—Strict	Community Festival Performances
77	3	Game 2	Qs 6–12	Hybrid—Selection/ Sequencing	Ceramic Bowl Display
77	3	Game 3	Qs 13–17	Hybrid—Matching/ Sequencing	Office Selection
77	3	Game 4	Qs 18–23	Matching	Community Committee Volunteers
78	2	Game 1	Qs 1–5	Selection	Special Project Workers
78	2	Game 2	Qs 6–11	Hybrid—Selection/ Sequencing	1920s History Archives Project
78	2	Game 3	Qs 12–17	Sequencing—Loose	Antique Dealer Auction
78	2	Game 4	Qs 18–23	Sequencing—Strict	Chorus Auditions
79	3	Game 1	Qs 1–5	Hybrid—Selection/ Sequencing	Bookmobile
79	3	Game 2	Qs 6–12	Distribution	National Park Rangers

PrepTest	Section #	Game #	Q #s	Game Type	Game Name
79	3	Game 3	Qs 13–17	Distribution	Economics TAs
79	3	Game 4	Qs 18–23	Sequencing—Strict	Computer Virus
80	3	Game 1	Qs 1–5	Distribution	Student Research Teams
80	3	Game 2	Qs 6–11	Sequencing—Strict	Mystery Novel Clues
80	3	Game 3	Qs 12–18	Distribution	Art Exhibition Paintings
80	3	Game 4	Qs 19–23	Process	Trading Buildings
81	4	Game 1	Qs 1–6	Hybrid—Matching/ Sequencing	Rural and Urban Photo Essays
81	4	Game 2	Qs 7–11	Sequencing—Strict	Concert Musicians
81	4	Game 3	Qs 12–16	Sequencing—Strict	Amusement Center Obstacle Course
81	4	Game 4	Qs 17–23	Matching	Managers in Manila, Sydney, and Tokyo
82	2	Game 1	Qs 1–7	Hybrid—Distribution/ Sequencing	Instructional Film Presentations
82	2	Game 2	Qs 8–12	Sequencing—Strict	Cafe Cosmopolitano Specials
82	2	Game 3	Qs 13–18	Hybrid—Matching/ Sequencing	Investigators Interviewing Witnesses
82	2	Game 4	Qs 19–23	Matching	George, Rita, and Wendy's Student Presentations
83	4	Game 1	Qs 1–5	Hybrid—Selection/ Sequencing	Travel Agent Tour of Asian Cities
83	4	Game 2	Qs 6–11	Sequencing—Loose	Student Concert Performance
83	4	Game 3	Qs 12–17	Selection	Railway System Closures
83	4	Game 4	Qs 18–23	Sequencing—Strict	Office Tower Air Quality Examinations
84	4	Game 1	Qs 1–6	Sequencing—Loose	Flower Shop Shipments
84	4	Game 2	Qs 7–11	Sequencing—Strict	Architect Project Assignments
84	4	Game 3	Qs 12–17	Hybrid—Distribution/ Selection	Municipal Election Nominations
84	4	Game 4	Qs 18–23	Matching	Matching Corporations Offering Bonds
85	4	Game 1	Qs 1–6	Sequencing—Strict	Weekly Department Store Sales
85	4	Game 2	Qs 7–13	Distribution	Antiques Fair Information Booths
85	4	Game 3	Qs 14–18	Distribution	Textbook Editors
85	4	Game 4	Qs 19–23	Sequencing—Strict (Two Sequences)	Art Exhibitions with Musical Performances

PrepTest	Section #	Game #	Q #s	Game Type	Game Name
86	2	Game 1	Qs 1–6	Hybrid—Distribution/ Matching	Lectures at a Two-Day Conference
86	2	Game 2	Qs 7–12	Sequencing—Strict	Art Auction
86	2	Game 3	Qs 13–17	Sequencing—Strict	Mining Company Engineering Team
86	2	Game 4	Qs 18–23	Sequencing—Strict	Medical Clinic Shifts
87	4	Game 1	Qs 1–5	Sequencing—Strict	Evaluation of Occupational Groups
87	4	Game 2	Qs 6–10	Sequencing—Strict	Commercial Break Ads
87	4	Game 3	Qs 11–17	Sequencing—Strict	Oil and Watercolor Showings
87	4	Game 4	Qs 18–23	Matching	Charity Booth Volunteers
88	1	Game 1	Qs 1–6	Hybrid—Selection/ Sequencing	Animal Adoption Display
88	1	Game 2	Qs 7–12	Sequencing—Strict (Circular)	Circular Artifact Display Case
88	1	Game 3	Qs 13–17	Matching	Five Four-Flower Arrangements
88	1	Game 4	Qs 18–23	Sequencing—Strict	Accountant Meetings
89	1	Game 1	Qs 1–5	Sequencing—Strict	Customer Service Training Sessions
89	1	Game 2	Qs 6–12	Hybrid—Selection / Sequencing	Vegetable Soup Recipe
89	1	Game 3	Qs 13–17	Matching	Forensic Lab Computer Examinations
89	1	Game 4	Qs 18–23	Hybrid—Sequencing / Matching	International Factory Site Visits
May 2020 LSAT-Flex	2	Game 1	Qs 1–5	Hybrid—Sequencing / Matching	Phone Call Investigations
May 2020 LSAT-Flex	2	Game 2	Qs 6–11	Distribution	Table Tennis Games
May 2020 LSAT-Flex	2	Game 3	Qs 12–17	Matching	Academic Society Meetings
May 2020 LSAT-Flex	2	Game 4	Qs 18–23	Sequencing—Strict	Theater Festival Schedule

APPENDIX IV

Logic Games Strategies

Logic Games Method

STEP 1: OVERVIEW—THE SEAL QUESTIONS

Situation—What is the real-world scenario being described? What is the deliverable information—an ordered list, a calendar, a chart showing what's matched up?

Entities—Who or what are the "moving parts," the people or things I'm distributing, selecting, sequencing, or matching?

Action—What is the specific action—distribution, selection, sequencing, matching, or a combination of those—that I'm performing on the entities?

Limitations—Does the game state parameters (e.g., select four of seven, sequence the entities one per day) that restrict how I'll set up and sketch the game?

STEP 2: SKETCH

- Create a sketch that depicts the game's action(s) and limitations.
- Aim for a sketch that is easy to read, quick to replicate, and able to account for what is certain and uncertain based on the game's rules.

STEP 3: RULES

- Whenever possible, add information directly to your Master Sketch.
- If you cannot build a rule directly into the Master Sketch, make a shorthand graphical representation of it.
- Write the rules in a way that matches the style and conventions of the Master Sketch.
- Consider both the positive and negative implications of a rule.
- Write similar rules consistently, the same way from game to game.
- When analyzing and drawing rules, always ask the following:
    - What does the rule restrict?
    - What does the rule leave undetermined?
    - Is the rule stated in affirmative or negative terms?
    - If stated affirmatively, can I learn something concrete from its negative implications (or vice versa)?
    - Can I place the rule directly into the sketch framework?
    - If not, how can I best draw the rule to account for what it does and does not restrict?

STEP 4: DEDUCTIONS

Blocks of Entities—two or more players who are always grouped together

Limited Options—rules or restrictions that limit the overall setup to one of two acceptable arrangements

Established Entities—a player locked into a specific space or group

Number Restrictions—rules or limitations that provide guidance about the number of entities assigned to a group or space

Duplications—entities that appear in two or more rules and allow the rules to be combined

STEP 5: QUESTIONS

- Be able to characterize both correct and incorrect answer choices.
- Know the different question types and how to approach each one.
- Don't hesitate to draw a new sketch in "If" questions.
- Use deductions and past work to eliminate wrong answers quickly.

Logic Game Question Types

- **Acceptability:** Use the rules to eliminate violators.
- **Partial Acceptability:** Use the rules to eliminate violators, but some rules may not apply. It may be helpful to deduce the other entities that would be in a full acceptable arrangement.
- **Must Be/Could Be:** Characterize the one right and four wrong choices. Use deductions and previous work to eliminate wrong answers. Be strategic about testing answers.
- **New-"If"s:** Take the "new rule" through Steps 3 and 4 in a new sketch, or if the Master Sketch has Limited Options, check to see which option(s) apply.
- **Complete and Accurate List:** The sketches made for other questions in the game may help to narrow the possibilities. Test the remaining possibilities.
- **Completely Determine:** Pick the one answer that establishes every entity. Nailing down a duplicated entity or a Floater can be helpful.
- **Rule Substitution:** Identify what impact the removed rule had. Find another that has the same impact.
- **Rule Change/Suspension:** Repeat Steps 3 and 4 with the new information. Some deductions may have changed.
- **Maximum and Minimum:** Most often in Selection games. Use the Master Sketch, previous work, and number deductions from the Formal Logic rules to find the minimum/maximum known so far, then keep testing one more/less if necessary.
- **Earliest and Latest:** Most often in Sequencing games. Use the Master Sketch, previous work, and deductions to find the earliest/latest known so far, then keep testing one earlier/later if necessary.
- **Supply the If:** Use the Master Sketch to see the possibilities for the entity or slot in question and then use that analysis to determine the kind of additional restriction that would guarantee the desired result.
- **How Many:** Use deductions to count the relevant entities/slots.

Sample Logic Games Sketches

Strict Sequencing

A B C D E F

1 2 3 4 5 6

Loose Sequencing

A

B C H

E G

F

D

or

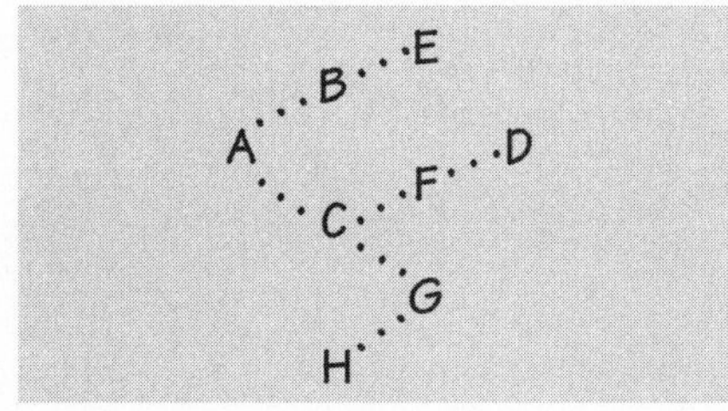

Distribution Games

All entities are used exactly one time.

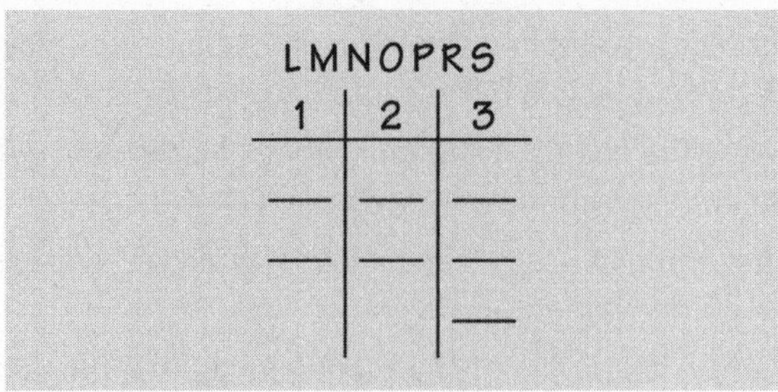

Selection Games

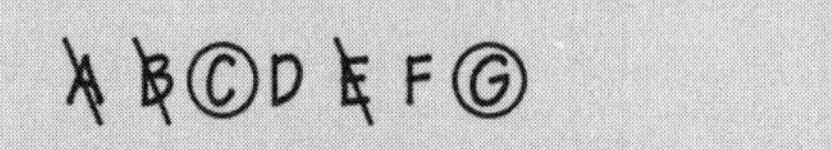

For Selection games defining a specific number of entities, some test takers prefer:

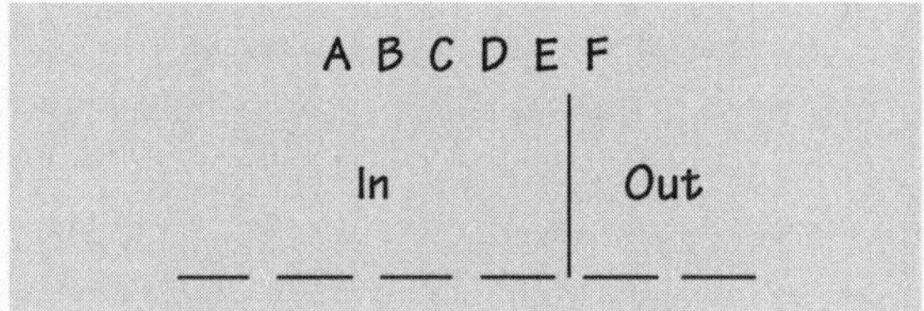

Matching Games

Entities might be used multiple times.

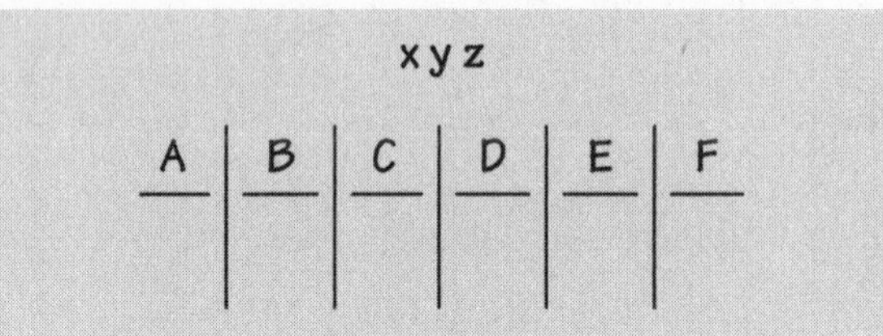

or

	A	B	C	D	E	F
x						
y						
z						

Sequencing/Matching Hybrid Games

__ __ __ __ __ __ ABCDEF

__ __ __ __ __ __ g/h

1 2 3 4 5 6

Typical Rules

Sequencing Rules

A is in a lower numbered position than B.

A...B

A gets out at some time before B.

A...B

A gets out at some time after B.

B...A

A gets out at some time before B but after C.

C...A...B

A gets out immediately after B.

BA

A gets out immediately before B.

AB

Exactly one person gets out after A but before B.

A_B

A is exactly two positions before B.

A_B

At least one person gets out after A but before B.

A_...B

Exactly one person gets out between A and B.

A/B_B/A

A is immediately next to B.

AB or BA

M got out after either V or G but not both.

V . . . M . . . G or G . . . M . . . V

or

V/G . . . M . . . G/V

(Exactly one of V or G is before M; the other comes afterward.)

P is ranked after T or before S, but not both.

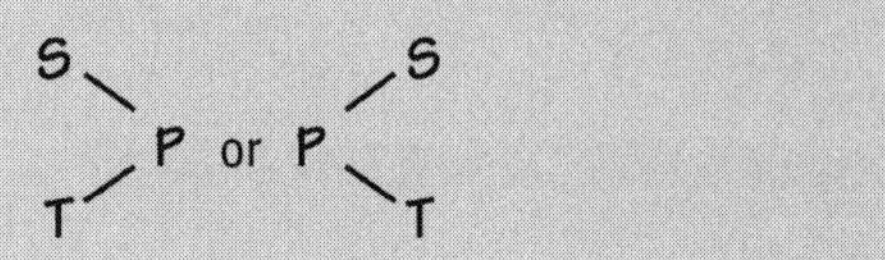

(Both S and T come before P or both S and T come after P; P can't be in the middle.)

A can come neither immediately before nor immediately after B.

~~AB~~ ~~BA~~

If A is fourth, B is seventh.

$A_4 \rightarrow B_7$

$B_{\sim 7} \rightarrow A_{\sim 4}$

If A is not seventh, A is fifth.

$A_{\sim 7} \rightarrow A_5$

$A_{\sim 5} \rightarrow A_7$

(Or. . . A is either fifth or seventh. Consider Limited Options if there are further deductions to be made.)

If A is before B, then C is before B. (in a sequence with no ties)

A . . . B → C . . . B

B . . . C → B . . . A

Selection Rules

If she selects K, she must select M.

K → M

~M → ~K

A is not selected unless B is selected.

A → B

~B → ~A

If George buys A, then he does not buy B.

A → ~B

B → ~A

(This rule says we can never have both A and B—so it is often faster/more intuitive to just write "Never AB.")

If George does not buy A, then he buys B.

~A → B

~B → A

(This rule says we must have A, or B, or both.)

If she selects G, she can select neither H nor Y.

G → ~H and ~Y

H or Y → ~G

(You can split an "and" result into two pieces—e.g., G → ~H; G → ~Y)
(You can split an "or" trigger into two pieces—e.g., H → ~G; Y → ~G)

Either A or B must be selected, but A and B cannot both be selected.

A/B

(Replace A and B with A/B in the entity list—you'll select exactly one.)

Matching/Distribution Rules

A cannot be in the same group as B.

Never AB

(Note that if there are only two groups, this means one of A and B is in the first group and the other is in the second group. This is important to help account for the numbers in each group.)

A is in a group with exactly 2 members.

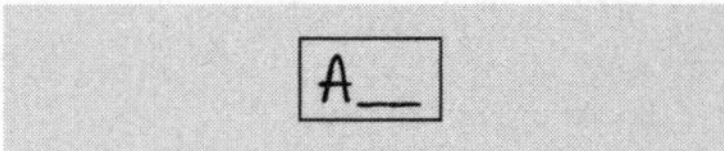

A and B are in the same group.

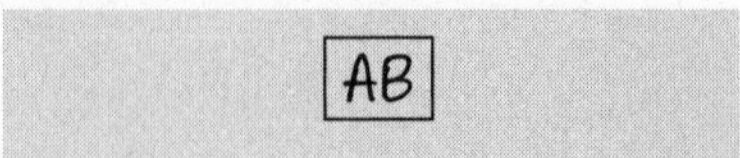

Abstract rules and considerations

J and K have at least one symptom in common. (What symptom could that be?)

L has a greater number of symptoms than K. (How many could L have? How many could K have?)

Exactly twice as many people are in group 1 as in group 2. (How many people can be in group 1? This will often lead to Limited Options.)

Exactly one entity is in every group. (Which entity could that be? Must it be? Could it not be?)

How Does the Testmaker Make a Game Harder?

- Removing the "one entity per position" limitation in Sequencing or other "natural" limitations
- Altering the definition of a week—Monday to Friday? Monday to Sunday?—or other common unit
- Incorporating multiple hybrid actions
- Including tough rules—abstract, if/then, undefined group size (Distribution)
- Creating Sequencing games with some repeating elements (four entities, seven positions)
- Using scenarios in which not all entities must be used
- Incorporating challenging/time-consuming question types (Rule Substitution, Completely Determine, Partial Acceptability, Rule Change, Supply the If, etc.)
- Writing lengthy answer choices
- Including answer choices that contain conditional statements

Variations on Games

Sequencing

Double/Triple sequencing

Sequencing over a multiple-week period, but each week has the same schedule (watch for the overlap between the end of one week and the start of the next)

Adding a characteristic to each entity—might sequence children, some of whom are boys and some of whom are girls, and have rules about boys and girls

Circular sequencing—positions might be numbered or unnumbered; could also be along the perimeter of a square

Matching

Matching entities to schedules—looks like a Sequencing game at first glance, but not every entity must be used and some will be repeated

Distribution

Distribute a group of entities that consists of smaller subgroups (e.g., distribute nine people from five children and four adults)

The exact number of entities assigned to each group is unknown

Selection

Double selection—entities selected in the first group restrict who can be selected in the second group

Select from a group of entities that consists of smaller subgroups (e.g., select four committee members from five juniors and four seniors)

Hybrid

Sequence a group of entities, then match a second characteristic to each entity

Distribute a group of entities, then within each group create a sequence (Distribution then Sequencing)

Distribute a large group into two smaller groups, which don't account for all the entities (Selection then Distribution)

APPENDIX V

Formal Logic Statements and Translations

Keywords

Sufficient:	Necessity:	Mutually Exclusive:
If	Then	No
All	Requires	Incapable
Any	Guarantees	Impossible
Every	Must	Cannot
Each	Necessary	None
When	Bound to lead to	Neither... nor
Whenever	Are destined to	Never
Wherever	Only (if)	
The only	Results in	
	Produces	
	Sure to	
	Always	
	Unless	
	Depends on	
	Without	

Translating Conditional Statements into "If"-Then Format

Formal Logic Statement	Analysis
If A, then B	If A → B
All C are D	If C → D
Every E is F	If E → F
If G, then not H	If G → ~H
No I are J	If I → ~J
Only K are L	If L → K
M only if N	If M → N
The only O are P	If O → P
No Q unless R	If Q → R
S unless T	If ~S → T
No U without V	If U → V
Without W, no X	If X → W
Y if, but only if, Z	If Y → Z If Z → Y
AA if, and only if, BB	If AA → BB If BB → AA
If CC, then neither DD nor EE	If CC → ~DD and ~EE
FF if GG	If GG → FF
HH is always II	If HH → II

Contrapositives

FORMING THE CONTRAPOSITIVE

- Reverse the sufficient and necessary terms.
- Negate each term.
- Change *and* to *or* and change *or* to *and* (whenever applicable).

Formal Logic Statement			Contrapositive		
If A	→	B or C	If ~B and ~C	→	~A
If D	→	E and F	If ~E or ~F	→	~D
If G or H	→	J	If ~J	→	~G and ~H
If K and L	→	M	If ~M	→	~K or ~L
If N and O	→	P and R	If ~P or ~R	→	~N or ~O
If S or T	→	U and V	If ~U or ~V	→	~S and ~T
If W and X	→	Y or Z	If ~Y and ~Z	→	~W or ~X
If AA or BB	→	CC or DD	If ~CC and ~DD	→	~AA and ~BB